Institutional Genes

This book explores the origins and evolution of China's institutions and communist totalitarianism in general. Contemporary China's fundamental institution is communist totalitarianism. Introducing the concept of "institutional genes," the book examines how the institutional genes of Soviet Russia merged with those of the Chinese imperial system, creating a durable totalitarian regime with Chinese characteristics – Regionally Administered Totalitarianism. Institutional Genes are fundamental institutional elements that self-replicate and guide institutional changes and are empirically identifiable. By analyzing the origins and evolution of institutional genes in communist totalitarianism from Europe and Russia, as well as those from the Chinese Empire, the Chinese Communist Revolution, the Great Leap Forward, the Cultural Revolution, and post-Mao reforms, the book elucidates the rise and progression of communist totalitarianism in China. The ascent of communist China echoes Mises' warning that efforts to halt totalitarianism have failed. Reversing this trend necessitates a thorough understanding of totalitarianism.

CHENGGANG XU is Senior Research Scholar at the Stanford Center on China's Economy and Institutions, Stanford University, a board member of the Ronald Coase Institute, and Research Fellow at the Center for Economic and Policy Research. He was the Chung Hon-Dak Professor of Economics at the University of Hong Kong, Special-Term Professor at Tsinghua University, the World-Class University Professor at Seoul National University, and Associate Professor at the London School of Economics. He also served as President of the Asian Law and Economics Association. He obtained his PhD in economics from Harvard University in 1991. Chenggang Xu was a recipient of the 2013 Sun Yefang Prize and the 2016 Chinese Economics Prize.

"Why did China become a totalitarian nation? What is the connection between Chinese communism and that in the Soviet Union, and what accounts for their differences? How might we expect the Chinese Communist Party to evolve in the future? Chenggang Xu gives fascinating answers to all these questions and many more in this bold but carefully argued book that is deeply rooted in historical and economic analysis."
Eric S. Maskin, Adams University Professor and Professor of Economics and Mathematics, Harvard University; co-recipient of the Sveriges Riksbank Prize in Economic Sciences in Memory of Alfred Nobel (2007)

"Why does democracy flourish in some countries but not others? Many people expected that China's meteoric rise would lead to the embrace of democracy, but this has not happened. Chenggang Xu's fascinating book argues that the reason is China's imperial tradition and the acceptance of limits on individual freedom and property rights, what he calls institutional genes. Engaging with the greatest thinkers, Xu applies the same idea to explain the growth of democracy in the West, but not in Russia. This is a must-read for anyone interested in arguably the most important issue of our time."
Olivier Hart, Lewis P. and Linda L. Geyser University Professor, Harvard University; co-recipient of the Sveriges Riksbank Prize in Economic Sciences in Memory of Alfred Nobel (2016)

"We hear much about China's innovativeness, its state capitalism, its market system, or its modernization. This thought-provoking book argues otherwise. It documents through historical, institutional and economic analysis that China's political and economic system is still totalitarian, despite the economic reforms initiated by Deng Xiaoping. Xu argues that communist rule changes not only institutions but many important aspects of culture in a highly persistent manner, and the Chinese system today cannot be understood without its 'totalitarian institutional genes,' which have shaped the current Chinese economy, social life and Communist Party rule. This is a must-read book for anybody interested in China and the complex world order that is emerging today."
Daron Acemoglu, Institute Professor, MIT Economics; co-recipient of the Sveriges Riksbank Prize in Economic Sciences in Memory of Alfred Nobel (2024)

"With unblinking focus, Chenggang Xu picks apart the historical and institutional genes of totalitarianism in modern China. He illuminates a new understanding of how China's governance developed from its roots in Imperial China and Russian Bolshevism. Instantly, this masterpiece of historical and political-economic analysis becomes the definitive reference to which anyone concerned with China's political system must turn. Will constitutional freedoms have a chance in China? You must read this book."
Darrell Duffie, Adams Distinguished Professor of Management and Professor of Finance, Graduate School of Business, Stanford University

"Chenggang Xu, the famous economist who, among others, wrote the classical paper on the institutions underlying China's growth miracle, now delivers what will likely be seen as the definitive analysis of the institutional roots of China's 'regionally administered totalitarianism.' Xu brilliantly analyzes China's failure to introduce constitutional rule in the 20th century, using history and the influence of the Russian revolution. China's millennial imperial system was much more autocratic than absolutist monarchies. This facilitated the import and adaptation of Bolshevik institutions, creating China's unique form of totalitarianism. A deep and extremely thoughtful analysis that is key to understanding contemporary China."
Gerard Roland, E. Morris Cox Distinguished Professor of Economics and Professor of Political Science, University of California, Berkeley

"The largest living thing in the world is not a whale but a huge and little-noticed subterranean fungus called *Armillaria ostoyae*. Similarly, the largest political organism, as Chenggang Xu shows in this startling and important book, is a communist totalitarianism whose 'institutional genes' recur at different times and places but are always determinative. Pretty words disguise merciless violence, human beings are reduced to roles, and it is the system, not its captives, that enjoys autonomy. But Xu is no starry-eyed conspiracy theorist. He comes out of the system himself, was educated at Harvard, and offers sober analyses."
Perry Link, Professor Emeritus of East Asian Studies, Princeton University

Institutional Genes
Origins of China's Institutions and Totalitarianism

CHENGGANG XU
Stanford University

Shaftesbury Road, Cambridge CB2 8EA, United Kingdom

One Liberty Plaza, 20th Floor, New York, NY 10006, USA

477 Williamstown Road, Port Melbourne, VIC 3207, Australia

314–321, 3rd Floor, Plot 3, Splendor Forum, Jasola District Centre, New Delhi – 110025, India

103 Penang Road, #05–06/07, Visioncrest Commercial, Singapore 238467

Cambridge University Press is part of Cambridge University Press & Assessment, a department of the University of Cambridge.

We share the University's mission to contribute to society through the pursuit of education, learning and research at the highest international levels of excellence.

www.cambridge.org
Information on this title: www.cambridge.org/9781108841696

DOI: 10.1017/9781108894708

© Chenggang Xu 2025

This publication is in copyright. Subject to statutory exception and to the provisions of relevant collective licensing agreements, no reproduction of any part may take place without the written permission of Cambridge University Press & Assessment.

When citing this work, please include a reference to the DOI 10.1017/9781108894708

First published 2025

Printed in the United Kingdom by Henry Ling Limited, at the Dorset Press, Dorchester, DT1 1HD

A catalogue record for this publication is available from the British Library

A Cataloging-in-Publication data record for this book is available from the Library of Congress

ISBN 978-1-108-84169-6 Hardback

Cambridge University Press & Assessment has no responsibility for the persistence or accuracy of URLs for external or third-party internet websites referred to in this publication and does not guarantee that any content on such websites is, or will remain, accurate or appropriate.

To Di Guo, my beloved wife

Contents

	List of Figures	*page* xiv
	Preface and Acknowledgments	xv
	List of Abbreviations	xxiii
1	Introduction	1
	1.1 Overview	1
	1.2 Institutional Divergence	9
	1.3 China's Institutional Evolution	14
	1.4 The Institutional Regime in Contemporary China: An Outline	16
	1.5 The Institutional Genes of Regionally Administered Totalitarianism	19
	1.6 Institutional Genes: From the Imperial System to Communist Totalitarianism	24
	1.7 Two Additional Examples of Institutional Genes	52
2	Institutions and Institutional Genes: Methodology	59
	2.1 The Primary Components of Institutions	63
	2.2 Institutional Genes in Institutional Evolution	75
3	Property Rights as a Form of Institutional Gene	91
	3.1 Ultimate Control Rights versus the Bundle of Rights: Differing Concepts of Property Rights	94
	3.2 Private Property Rights as an Institutional Gene	99
	3.3 China's Traditional Legal System: An Instrument of Dominance	105
	3.4 Property Rights and Sovereignty in the Chinese Empire	108

4 The Emergence and Evolution of the Institutional Genes of the Chinese Imperial System 122
  4.1 Fundamental Features of the Chinese Imperial System: Institutional Genes with a Trinity Structure 123
  4.2 The Genesis of Imperial Rule in China 128
  4.3 The Emergence and Evolution of the Chinese Empire 136
  4.4 The Incompatibility of China's Imperial System with Constitutionalism 159

5 The Imperial Examinations and Confucianism: The Institutional Genes for Imperial Personnel and Ideology 163
  5.1 Confucianism and the *Keju* System versus Christianity and the Church 164
  5.2 The Emergence and Evolution of Official Confucianism and the *Keju* System 177
  5.3 The Confucian *Keju* System Becomes a Mature Institutional Gene 189

6 The Institutional Genes of Totalitarian Ideology 202
  6.1 Christian Origins: The Münster Totalitarian Regime 206
  6.2 The Birth of Secular Communist Totalitarianism 213
  6.3 Origins of Babeuf's Communism: The French Enlightenment 237
  6.4 Marxist Communist Totalitarianism 253

7 Institutional Genes of Totalitarianism: The Tsarist Empire 261
  7.1 Similarities between the Imperial Systems of China and Russia 262
  7.2 The Genesis of Russia's Institutional Genes: Mongol Rule 265
  7.3 The Genesis of Russia's Institutional Genes: Eastern Orthodoxy and the Byzantine Empire 270

	7.4	The Institutional Genes of Tsarism	274
	7.5	The Product of the Tsarist Institutional Genes	299
8	The Birth of Bolshevik Totalitarianism	315
	8.1	Totalitarian Party: The Bolsheviks	316
	8.2	Institutional Conditions for the Seizure of Power by the Totalitarian Party	336
	8.3	Establishing a Full-Fledged Totalitarian System	359
9	The Failure of Constitutional Reforms and Republican Revolution	392
	9.1	Constitutionalism in Name Only: The Hundred Days' Reform	393
	9.2	Rival to Constitutionalism: Social Darwinism	403
	9.3	Failed Constitutional Reform and the Collapse of the Empire	408
	9.4	Failure of the Republican Revolution (1911–1916)	422
	9.5	Revolutionary Parties: The Institutional Genes of the "Secret Societies"	434
10	Building China's Bolshevik Party	449
	10.1	Communist "Jesuits": The Comintern's Infiltration into China	453
	10.2	The China Branch of the Comintern: The CCP	459
	10.3	Secret Societies: The Institutional Gene for Building the Party and Its Army	472
	10.4	Reign of Terror and the Emergence of a Totalitarian Leader	481
11	Building a Totalitarian Regime: From the Chinese Soviet to the People's Republic	499
	11.1	The Establishment of the Chinese Soviet Republic	501
	11.2	Mobilization and Domination: Land Reform and the Suppression of Counterrevolutionaries	512

	11.3	Emergence of Regionally Administered Totalitarianism during the Revolutionary Era	521
	11.4	Sovietization: Building a Full-Fledged Classical Totalitarian System	530
12	Regionally Administered Totalitarianism		543
	12.1	Totalitarian Rule by Instilling Fear: The Anti-Rightist Movement	544
	12.2	The Great Leap Forward: The First Wave of Establishing RADT	553
	12.3	The Cultural Revolution: Consolidating RADT	570
	12.4	The Deep-Rooted RADT System and the Shattering of Ideals	585
13	The Post-Mao Reform and Its Cessation: The Rise and Fall of Regionally Decentralized Authoritarianism		594
	13.1	Reforms for the Survival of Totalitarianism	596
	13.2	Economic Reform: Urgent Reaction to the Collapse of the USSR	614
	13.3	Towards Regionally Decentralized Authoritarianism	618
	13.4	Succession in Totalitarian Parties	626
	13.5	The Evolution of Opposing Institutional Genes during the Reform Process	630
	13.6	Totalitarian Institutional Constraints on Economic Growth	641
	13.7	Summary	653
14	Conclusion		658
	14.1	The Great Challenge: Understanding Totalitarianism	658
	14.2	Summary of Institutional Genes and Institutional Evolution	660
	14.3	An Empirical Analysis of Totalitarian Regimes	663
	14.4	Literature Overview	666

14.5 The Transformation Path in Taiwan: An Institutional
     Gene Analysis   675
14.6 Institutional Transformation of the Communist
     Bloc and the Role of Institutional Genes   688
14.7 Concluding Remarks on the Concept of Institutional
     Genes   720

References   725
Index   757

Figures

1.1	The power structure of regionally administered totalitarianism (RADT)	*page* 20
1.2	Institutional genes of the regional governance structure under RADT	21
1.3	The trinity of institutional genes comprising the governance structure of China's imperial system	22
1.4	Institutional genes of China's *junxian* bureaucracy since the era of the Sui and Tang dynasties	22
4.1	Institutional genes of China's *junxian* bureaucracy since the era of the Sui and Tang dynasties	144

Preface and Acknowledgments

This book analyzes the origins and evolution of totalitarianism from the perspective of institutional genes, focusing on Chinese institutions. Contemporary China's system is the largest and most enduring totalitarian system in human history, with a profound impact on the world. The concept of institutional genes is introduced to help overcome analytical difficulties in this multidisciplinary exploration.

It encapsulates over half a century of my research and thoughts on the totalitarian nature of communism. My inquiry into this subject began in 1967, at the height of the Cultural Revolution. This was driven by the stark contradictions I observed between the rhetoric of communist propaganda, which depicted the Communist Party/society as a paradise on Earth, and the brutal reality of the totalitarian regime and its practices. This contrast extended to the ideal of a classless society promised by communism and the actual endless, ruthless class struggles, along with the emergence of institutionalized privileged social groups in the regime. Despite approaching this subject from a Marxist perspective, my research on the communist system, which was strictly prohibited, led to over a year of imprisonment and more than five years of enforced labor on a farm. Only after the end of the Cultural Revolution was I able to resume this intellectual journey.

While earlier experiences and observations provided a foundational motivation, they alone were insufficient for a deep scientific exploration of the topics in this book. The principles and methodologies in social sciences acquired through my economics training at Harvard and subsequent professional experiences have been particularly influential. Notably, the insights from Kornai's political economy of communism, Maskin's theory of mechanism design, Hart's theory of property rights, and North's theory of path dependence have significantly shaped my perspective. These intellectual contributions are evident throughout the book.

This book reflects the profound spiritual influence of my parents, Liang-Ying Xu, a historian and philosopher of science, and Lai-Di Wang, a historian of modern China. Beyond the impact of their lifelong works, their intellectual pursuits in the last two decades are particularly relevant to this book. During this period, they embarked on a project titled "The History of Democracy" (originally "The Theory of Democracy"), which analyzed the evolution of constitutional democracy in the West and the challenges faced by China, especially in modern times. Our numerous and in-depth discussions covered a range of important concepts and historical facts, including democracy, constitutionalism, totalitarianism, the creation of the Chinese Communist Party (CCP), the challenges China has faced since the nineteenth century, and the painful yet profound reflections of some veteran CCP members on themselves and the communist regime. These conversations also delved into reform and related social issues. Despite amassing a wealth of profound thoughts and knowledge, they were unable to complete their book due to their advanced age. As such, I consider a substantial part of this book as both a continuation and a tribute to their scholarly endeavors.

My first PhD research project at Harvard involved a game theory model analyzing power structures within a totalitarian regime. I learned a lot from my co-supervisors Kornai and Andreu Mas-Colell. Although I eventually moved away from this project for my PhD due to dissatisfaction with the cooperative game-theoretical approach and the lack of predictive power in my model, my refocusing on communist totalitarianism was merely postponed.

Mechanism design theory, including theory of information and incentives, taught by Eric Maskin, was transformative for me in reconsidering how to analyze institutions and institutional changes, particularly in the context of totalitarianism. After completing my PhD, working jointly with Eric and engaging in countless discussions with him provided me with further opportunities to deepen my understanding of this aspect.

Under the guidance of Maskin and Kornai, the focus of my doctoral dissertation shifted to an analysis of the planned economy as an institutional barrier to disruptive innovation. While this work did not directly address the political power of a totalitarian system, it enhanced my understanding of the nature of a communist totalitarian system from the perspective of innovation and long-term growth.

Janos Kornai's unwavering focus on the totalitarian nature of the communist regime has been crucial in my intellectual journey. In the summer of 1989, when I was a PhD student, I had daily exchanges with him about the communist crackdown and massacres in Beijing, drawing parallels to the suppressed Hungarian Revolution from thirty years prior. Later, during my tenure at the London School of Economics (LSE) in the 1990s, Kornai invited me to lecture on China's reforms at Harvard. In his comments, he cast deep doubts on China's gradual reform, highlighting the CCP's apparent unwillingness to cede absolute power. He argued that it was impossible for the CCP to transition gradually from a one-party to a multiparty system. This perspective was reinforced a decade later. In 2009, after I presented my paper analyzing China's regionally decentralized authoritarianism at the United Nations University conference commemorating the twentieth anniversary of the fall of the Berlin Wall, Kornai responded by emphasizing the unyielding totalitarian nature of the Chinese communist regime and its potential impact on China's long-run trajectory. The version later published in the *Journal of Economic Literature* (Xu, 2011) reflects revisions made in response to his comments. So to this book.

I must express my gratitude to my long-term co-authors, Eric Maskin, Katharina Pistor, Yingyi Qian, and Gérard Roland. Some of the ideas expressed in several chapters are, to some extent, related to or inspired by our discussions during our decade-long joint work in the 1990s and the 2000s. Particularly, I would like to thank Yingyi Qian, my longest-standing collaborator. We worked together from my doctoral student days for nearly two decades. Our past discussions about Chinese institutions have influenced the formation of the ideas in parts of this book. Furthermore, some ideas discussed in Chapters 2 and 3 were inspired or stimulated by conversations with Patrick Bolton and Oliver Hart. My heartfelt thanks go out to all of them for their stimulating collaboration in the past and enduring friendship. However, the views expressed in this book are solely my own and I am the only person responsible for any potential errors or controversies.

The completion of this book is a testament to the support of many individuals and institutions. I am especially grateful to the Stanford Center on China's Economy and Institutions (SCCEI) for its generous financial backing and invaluable support in various other aspects, and to the co-directors of the SCCEI, Scott Rozelle and Hongbin Li, for their enthusiastic and long-lasting support of my work. Additionally, I wish to extend my heartfelt thanks for the 2019 Dr. Hsieh Memorial Lecture at Stanford University, the bimonthly lecture series hosted by SCCEI and many seminars organized by the Hoover Institution, during the book's development. These events provided a platform to systematically present and refine the ideas in this project and offered invaluable opportunities to share my views with multidisciplinary scholars. Feedback from insightful audiences is essential in improving the book. Moreover, I must thank Debin Ma. His invitation for me to contribute a chapter to the *Cambridge Economic History of China* provided a platform to encapsulate the core ideas of this book and an opportunity to obtain valuable feedback during the writing process.

My affiliations with the University of Hong Kong, Tsinghua University, Cheung Kong Graduate School of Business, and Stanford University have been integral to the development of this book, with parts being incorporated into some of my teachings. I am deeply thankful for the support and generous funding provided by these institutions, as well as the contributions of colleagues and students there. Additionally, my visits to Seoul National University, the

Hebrew University of Jerusalem, the Chinese University of Hong Kong, Corvinus University of Budapest, the LSE, and Imperial College London have significantly contributed to this work. The feedback and insights from colleagues and students at these institutions have been invaluable and I am immensely grateful for their support and hospitality.

Additionally, I want to thank all the participants in my presentations on related topics for their valuable feedback, comments, and critiques. These include the annual meetings of the Association for Comparative Economic Studies, the Asia Society, the Bank of Israel, University of California Berkeley, University of California San Diego, Ben-Gurion University of the Negev, Bucknell University, University of Chicago, the Chinese Economists Society, Chatham House, Corvinus University of Budapest, the Center for Strategic and International Studies, the University of Duisburg-Essen, Harvard University, the Hebrew University of Jerusalem, the University of Hong Kong, the Chinese University of Hong Kong, the Japan Association for Chinese Economic Studies annual meetings, the Japanese Institute of Development Economics, Hitotsubashi, the University of Tokyo, the Fondation Maison des sciences de l'homme, National Bureau of Economic Research, the Ronald Coase Institute (Tel Aviv and Warsaw seminars), Stanford University, Seoul National University, School of Oriental and African Studies, Tel Aviv University, Academia Sinica, National Taiwan University, Tsinghua University (Beijing), Tsinghua University (Taiwan), National Chengchi University, Utrecht University, and the World Interdisciplinary Network for Institutional Research conferences.

I must express my heartfelt gratitude to my colleagues and friends, who generously spent a considerable amount of time reading portions or all of the manuscript. Their valuable criticisms and insightful suggestions have been immensely helpful in improving this book. They are: Alexandra Benham, Lee Benham, Michael Bernstam, Patrick Bolton, Darrell Duffie, Joseph Esherick, Ge Zhaoguang, Paul Gregory, Oliver Hart, Perry Link, Michael McFaul, Eric Maskin,

Roger Myerson, Minxin Pei, Gerard Roland, Andrew Walder, Wang Yuhua, Wu Guoguang, and David Yang. Their critiques helped me correct many errors. Of course, any remaining errors in the book are my sole responsibility.

Numerous friends and colleagues have provided valuable feedback and comments in various ways. They either supported or inspired me, corrected my mistakes, or offered insights that enriched the content of this book. I want to express my sincere gratitude to all of them. While the list of those deserving acknowledgment is extensive and it is difficult to name everyone, I would like to particularly thank Daron Acemoglu, Ron Anderson, Masahiko Aoki, Ying Bai, Alexandra Benham, Lee Benham, Daniel Berkowitz, Jude Blanchette, Patrick Bolton, Xia Cai, Hsiang-Ke Chao, Tien-Chih Chen, Xiaoping Chen, Zhiwu Chen, Robert Daly, Larry Diamond, Ke Ding, David Donald, Darrell Duffie, Simon Ertz, Hanming Fang, Roger Gordon, Avner Greif, Yan Guo, Oliver Hart, Di He, Zhiguo He, Nancy Hearst, Chang-Tai Hsieh, Chao-Hsi Huang, Yasheng Huang, Ruixue Jia, János Kornai, Marton Krasznai, James Kung, Fei-fei Li, Hongbin Li, Weijia Li, Thung-Hong Lin, Yusheng Lin, Perry Link, Debin Ma, Eric Maskin, Scott MacLeod, Paul Milgrom, Kenneth Murphy, Roger Myerson, Barry Naughton, Douglass North, Minxin Pei, Yuri Pines, Shitong Qiao, Xiao Qin, Gerard Roland, Miklos Rosta, Scott Rozelle, Susan Shirk, Mary Shirley, Zheng Song, George Soros, Michael Spence, Yi-chun Tao, Glenn Tiffert, Ai-He Wang, Yijiang Wang, Barry Weingast, Roy Bin Wong, Guoguang Wu, Jinglian Wu, Yang Xie, Wei Xiong, Guoqi Xu, Yiqing Xu, David Yang, Kuo-chun Yeh, Leslie Young, Miles Yu, Li Yuan, Lun Zhang, Renzhen Zhang, Shuxin Zhang, Hang Zhou, Xueguang Zhou, Hengfu Zou, and David Zweig.

Additionally, I am indebted to many of my fellow Chinese colleagues and friends who have contributed to this book but for well-known reasons have chosen not to have their names mentioned here. Their silent support has been vital to this project.

To ensure the precise and clear expression of my ideas, reasoning, and narratives in both Chinese and English and to avoid distortions in a strict translation, this book has been written in both languages. Each version stands as an original, with neither being a direct translation of the other. In the course of my research related to this book, the majority of the original notes for the subtopics were drafted in English and others were in Chinese. In synthesizing the first draft of the entire book, the initial step involved compiling the original note fragments into Chinese. Subsequently, the Chinese draft was translated into an English draft. Based on this, the final English version was created through substantial revisions and rewriting. Then, using the English version as a reference, the final Chinese version was created by revising the initial Chinese draft. Throughout this process, my focus was on expressing ideas with clarity and accuracy, rather than achieving complete consistency in every sentence or word across the two languages. Therefore, I allowed for slight variations in expression and even in some minor details between the two language versions.

I am particularly grateful to Lei Huang and Ximing Yin for their outstanding assistance in transcribing and editing crucial parts of the initial manuscripts. I also wish to express my gratitude to Christopher MacDonald, whose excellent translation from Chinese forms the greater part of the content of this book. Following translation, the book was significantly modified and rewritten and any errors or oversights in the resulting text are mine alone. My sincere gratitude extends to Minjun Cai, Nancy Hearst, and Yingbo Shi for their editorial support. Heartfelt thanks also go to David C. Donald, Katherina Pistor, Hang Zhou, and an anonymous friend for their valuable advice and assistance with the legal aspects of this book's publishing process. Finally, I would like to express my deep appreciation to Chris Harrison and my editor, Joe Ng, for their unwavering support and expert guidance throughout this journey. The genesis of this book dates back nearly a decade, beginning with a discussion in my office at the University of Hong Kong with Chris. Joe's enthusiasm was pivotal in encouraging me to move forward with the formal publishing process. The book would not have reached its full potential without the dedication and expertise of both Chris and Joe.

This book is dedicated to my wife, Di. Her unconditional love, profound understanding, and unwavering care have been the pillars enabling me to complete this work. She is much more than my beloved companion; as a fellow scholar in the social sciences, she has been my closest colleague, my soul mate, and keenest critic of my scholarship. Throughout the decade-long journey of crafting this book, it has woven itself into the very fabric of our family life. Almost all the ideas expressed in this book were first shared with her as my initial listener and critic, often before they were committed to writing. She has been the diligent first reader and editor of every chapter, tirelessly reviewing each page in both English and Chinese. Together, we humbly hope that this book will not only enhance scholarly understanding of the totalitarian communist system but also, in time, make a modest contribution to the journey towards freedom for our fellow Chinese.

Abbreviations

AB	Anti-Bolshevik
ARM	Anti-Rightist Movement
CAC	Cyber Administration of China
CAS	Chinese Academy of Sciences
CASS	Chinese Academy of Social Sciences
CBE	Commune-Brigade Enterprise
CCP	Chinese Communist Party
CDL	China Democratic League
CEC	Central Executive Committee
CEE	Central Eastern Europe
Comintern	Communist International
CPC	Council of People's Commissars
CPPCC	Chinese People's Political Consultative Conference
CPSU	Communist Party of the Soviet Union
CR	Cultural Revolution
CRG	Cultural Revolution Group
CRP	Chinese Revolutionary Party
DPP	Democratic Progressive Party
EU	European Union
FCA	Friends of the Constitution Association
FSU-EE	Former Soviet Union and Eastern European Countries
GAC	Government Affairs Council
GDP	Gross Domestic Product
GLF	Great Leap Forward
Gosplan	State Planning Committee
GPU	State Political Directorate (Soviet)
GUGB	Main Directorate of State Security (Soviet Union)
HRE	Holy Roman Empire

IPO	Initial Public Offering
KGB	Committee for State Security (Soviet Union)
KMT	Kuomintang
KSC	Communist Party of Czechoslovakia
NEP	New Economic Policy
NGO	Nongovernmental Organization
NKVD	People's Commissariat for Internal Affairs (Soviet)
NPC	National People's Congress
NRA	National Revolutionary Army
OGPU	Joint State Political Directorate (Soviet Union)
PBOC	People's Bank of China
PLA	People's Liberation Army
PRC	People's Republic of China
PUWP	Polish United Workers' Party
RADT	Regionally Administered Totalitarianism
RCP	Russian Communist Party
RDA	Regionally Decentralized Authoritarianism
ROC	Republic of China
RPL	Railway Protection League
RPM	Railway Protection Movement
RSDLP	Russian Social Democratic Labor Party
RUC	Renmin University of China
SAMR	State Administration for Market Regulation
SASAC	State-owned Assets Supervision and Administration Commission
SBC	Soft Budget Constraint
SDP	Social Democratic Party of Germany
SEZ	Special Economic Zone
SME	Small and Medium-sized Enterprise
SOE	State-Owned Enterprise
SPQR	Senatus Populusque Romanus (The Senate and the Roman People)
SR	Socialist Revolutionary (Party)

TFP	Total Factor Productivity
TVE	Township Village Enterprise
UFWD	United Front Work Department
URW	Union of Railway Workers
USSR	Union of Soviet Socialist Republics
WTO	World Trade Organization

1 Introduction

1.1 OVERVIEW

The fundamental institution of contemporary China is communist totalitarianism with Chinese characteristics. This institution differs fundamentally from non-communist totalitarian regimes, ancient Chinese systems. It also differs in many aspects from the Soviet Union. It originated in Soviet Russia and its deep roots in China are inseparable from the foundations of ancient Chinese institutions. How does this institution dictate the behavior of the contemporary Chinese government? How have China's institutions and their basic features evolved to the shape that we observe today? In which direction will these institutions change in the future? Academic research in this area is generally weak and has many gaps. This book aims to strengthen academic research in this area and fill in those gaps. By doing so, I hope to establish a solid foundation for interpreting China's historical and contemporary context, while offering insights that may assist in predicting potential future shifts. For those who care about China's reforms, this provides the basis for recognizing where the country's fundamental problems lie and for understanding how to reform its institutions.

In this book, totalitarianism refers to an extreme type of modern autocracy characterized by total control over society through a totalitarian party, which is categorically different from any political party (further explained in Chapter 8). A totalitarian party is a modern organization that applies modern methods of control and propaganda. The descriptive definition proposed by Friedrich and Brzezinski in 1956 is still a valid summary of the system. This definition identifies six fundamental, complementary components of the system: Ideology is at the core of the totalitarian party's control of the populace; and the party monopolizes and relies on ideology, secret police, armed force, the media, and organizations (including businesses) throughout society and controls all resources through this channel (Friedrich and Brzezinski, 1956, p. 126).

The first totalitarian regime that fit the above definition emerged from the October Revolution in Russia in 1917. Since then, the world has seen totalitarian systems founded on various ideologies. However, the term "totalitarianism" was not coined until the 1920s. The value of a totalitarian ideology at the core of the system lies more in providing legitimacy, cohesion, and mobilization to the regime as a governing tool, rather than in its nominal expression, which has purposely been made misleading by the communists (see Chapters 8, 10, 11). In fact, its extreme autocratic nature determines that regardless of its nominal ideology, essential parts of its expressions will be grossly self-contradictory to the operation of that system. For example, for communist totalitarianism with a nominal ideology of Marxism, the fundamental ideology is the dictatorship of the proletariat and the party's unquestionable ruling position (Leninism). These are not only the basic principles of the specific institutional arrangements of the totalitarian regime but also the basis of its legitimacy. However, the communist ideology of absolute egalitarianism and the Marxist ideology of human freedom with humanitarian connotations are in serious contradiction with the operation of the totalitarian system. Anyone who adheres to a given nominal ideology, yet disobeys the paramount leadership, will face severe punishment under the totalitarian system, regardless of their position. They may even face physical elimination, as was the case with figures like Bukharin and Trotsky of the Soviet Union and Liu Shaoqi and Zhao Ziyang of China, among others.

While the entry of communist totalitarianism into China was initiated and strongly supported by the Soviet Communist Party, it is indisputable that the establishment of a communist totalitarian system in China, at the cost of millions of lives, was a choice made by Chinese revolutionaries, not the Soviet Red Army. The question is, the end of the Chinese imperial system (*dizhi* 帝制)[1] was brought about by a series of reforms and revolutions aimed at promoting constitutionalism,[2] but why did China ultimately choose the opposite, totalitarianism? Moreover, a recent puzzle is why China is still stuck with totalitarianism after several decades of reform and opening-up and with private enterprise already dominating its economy.[3] Why has the totalitarian system taken root in China so profoundly? A more fundamental and universal question is, why did human society give rise to a totalitarian system? Why did this system originate in Russia? What similarities exist between the institutional legacies of Russia and China? To answer these questions, this book proposes an analytical concept of institutional genes. "Institutional genes" in this book refer to those essential institutional components repeatedly present throughout history. In Chapter 2, we will discuss the definition and mechanisms of institutional genes in detail. Using this concept, we will analyze the emergence, evolution, and characteristics of contemporary China's institutions from both a transnational and historical perspective. Additionally, we will explore the genesis of totalitarianism, particularly in Russia. The concept of institutional genes and its analytical framework are significantly inspired by institutional design (mechanism design) theory[4] and the path-dependence theory of North in economics.

Between 1989 and 1992, totalitarian regimes in the Soviet Union and Central Eastern Europe collapsed. This series of historical events stimulated academic research on institutions and spurred significant developments in the field. Several scholars, such as North and Coase, received the Nobel Prize in Economics for their work related to institutions. Nonetheless, aside from Kornai's work in 1992, most renowned political economy studies have not delved into the subject of totalitarianism, nor have they analyzed the transition from totalitarian to authoritarian regimes in those countries.[5] This research gap in economics and political economics, in particular, has caused a lack of basic understanding of the regimes of China, the Soviet Union, and other former communist countries, making it difficult to anticipate or respond to political reversals in those countries. From an academic and policy perspective, this seems similar to the awkward situation economists faced in predicting and responding to the global financial crisis of 2008. However, the comprehensive consequences of a totalitarian superpower across the globe, from direct geopolitical, economic, and military impacts to the indirect influence on the institutions of other countries, far surpass the consequences of a financial crisis in terms of breadth and depth. The propositions discussed in this book, therefore, pertain to institutional evolution in general and are not limited to China, Russia, or countries experienced in totalitarian rule.

This book presents and develops the basic concept, or analytical framework, which I refer to as "institutional genes." "Institutional genes" is a term I coined in this book. It refers to essential institutional elements that serve as the foundations for other institutional elements and often appear repeatedly in history. It is a methodological approach proposed for the in-depth analysis of major issues in institutional evolution. This book applies the institutional genes framework to organize historical evidence, using historical narratives to elucidate why the constitutional revolutions in Russia and China in the late nineteenth and early twentieth centuries faltered. It also examines the paradoxical outcome of these revolutions, which, rather than fostering constitutional principles, instead gave rise to totalitarian systems that contradicted them. Further, it sheds light on the crucial institutional changes that these two countries have undergone over the past century and their lasting influence not only on their own trajectories but also on the global political economy.

There are many conceptions of institutions. In this book, the discussion of institutions focuses on three fundamental elements: human rights, property rights, and political power. In connection with this focus, the Locke–Hayek thesis on the inseparability of human rights and property rights is reinterpreted in the context of the history and reality of totalitarianism (Chapters 2 and 3). The essence is that the property rights structure of any society is inseparable from the structure of political power in that society, as can be observed from the arguably most egalitarian distributional structure of Scandinavian regimes to the most unequal structures of communist regimes. Accordingly, the concept of property rights used in this book is based on the notion of ultimate control rights – a concept employed by Locke, Marx, Mises, Hayek, and Hart (residual rights, Hart, 2017), and one that was widely accepted in academia and practice before the twentieth century. Chapter 3 explores the relationship and differences between this concept and the concept of a "bundle of rights" that has gained popularity since the twentieth century. Throughout the book, the origins of totalitarian systems are explored through historical narratives, emphasizing how the institutional genes of these regimes stemmed from a deep-rooted monopoly on property rights and power and the resulting social consensus that solidified these structures.

From the perspective of property rights and power structures, a totalitarian regime consolidates all property rights and power within society under the control of the totalitarian party, thereby subjecting all individuals' human rights entirely to the party's authority. In contrast, no dictator, government, party, or institution in any other autocratic system enjoys such comprehensive control over property rights and power. Furthermore, the nature of the totalitarian party dictates that it is not a political party in the conventional sense (as detailed in Chapter 8).

With the world currently facing the threat of the totalitarian power of the Chinese Communist Party (CCP), it is particularly important to revisit Mises' warning at the end of the Second World War – that the free world's multi-decades' efforts to contain totalitarianism have all failed. Unfortunately, this warning has long been completely forgotten. The neglect of totalitarianism in academic and policy circles has allowed the CCP to receive unchallenged assistance from the West across various domains, fueling its meteoric rise not only in economic strength but also in the expansion of its propaganda, police, and military capabilities. Even today, recognizing the totalitarian nature of the CCP remains a significant challenge in the West. Under such favorable conditions, the collapse of the Former Soviet Union and Eastern European (FSU-EE) totalitarian bloc was followed by the unfortunate expansion of the Chinese totalitarian regime into a threatening superpower – a development that could not have occurred without the support of the United States and other democratic nations. Existing academic discussions on totalitarianism, while still valid, are largely based on decades-old literature. These discussions have often been confined to philosophy, intellectual history, or the historical records of Soviet Russia, with few efforts made to systematically study the comprehensive and fundamental mechanisms of totalitarianism within the context of the century-long rise of communist totalitarian regimes. Addressing these gaps, Chapters 6 to 8 of this book explore the origins of totalitarianism as both an ideology and a system, the reasons it emerged first in Russia, and the mechanisms through which it rises and operates.

Totalitarian regimes are characterized by the complete eradication of private property and total control over society through extreme violence. Such regimes emerged from a secular political-religious movement known as the World Proletarian Revolution. This movement, driven by the pursuit of egalitarianism and a form of secular messianism, relied on so-called class struggle, which was both highly seductive and inflammatory, fueled by hatred towards the so-called class enemies. However, this secular religious movement only succeeded in societies that possessed specific institutional genes – a highly monopolized structure of property and political power, along with a corresponding social consensus (Chapter 6). The communist totalitarian movement was first established in Russia because it had the necessary institutional genes to create such a regime. These genes included the autocratic Tsarist regime, the pervasive influence of Russian Orthodoxy, and the well-developed network of sophisticated secret (terrorist) political organizations (Chapter 7).

The Bolshevik Party, the world's first communist totalitarian party, originated as a secretive political organization. Chapter 8 discusses the creation of this party and its transformation into a full-fledged totalitarian party, including the development of its operating mechanisms. The role and mechanisms of the institutional genes that facilitated the formation of the Leninist party in establishing and consolidating a totalitarian regime are analyzed. The creation of the Soviet regime involved the suppression of opposition through the dictatorship of the proletariat, the establishment of a Red Terror regime, the creation of comprehensive state ownership, and the formation of the Comintern (Communist International), the organization that spearheaded global communist totalitarian revolutions. The CCP and other communist parties around the world were established with the support of the Comintern, with their founding principles and operational mechanisms transplanted from the Communist Party of Soviet Union (CPSU). To this day, all the CCP's fundamental principles remain derived from the CPSU. Additionally, Chapter 8 systematically analyzes the basic nature and operational mechanisms of totalitarian parties and how these evolved from the institutional genes of Tsarist Russia. This analysis is essential for understanding the nature of totalitarian parties in general, making this chapter crucial even for readers primarily concerned with China.

Chapters 4, 5, and 9 analyze the origins and evolution of the institutional genes of the Chinese imperial system and the mechanisms by which these genes impeded the development of constitutionalism within it. Chapters 10–13 explore how communist totalitarianism was transplanted into China by the Comintern, how China's institutional genes facilitated the establishment of this totalitarian system, and how a Soviet-style communist regime was formed. The chapters also delve into the evolution of communist totalitarianism with Chinese characteristics – regional administered totalitarianism – during the Great Leap Forward (GLF) and the Cultural Revolution (CR) in the Mao era, and how this system supported economic development and reforms during the post-Mao era, ultimately preserving CCP rule while leading China into the trap of totalitarianism. From these discussions, it becomes clear that the so-called "middle-income trap" phenomenon observed since the late 2010s is merely a manifestation of the totalitarian trap, inherent in the nature of totalitarianism itself.

The final chapter briefly discusses the institutional transformations of the FSU-EE totalitarian bloc and Taiwan through the lens of institutional genes and explores the implications of these transformations for China's future. The key feature that distinguishes the Chinese system from the FSU-EE totalitarian regimes – Regional Administered Decentralized Totalitarianism (RADT) – was instrumental in enabling China's private enterprises to flourish under communist rule during economic reforms, becoming the primary engine of China's economic growth and thereby sustaining the Chinese Communist regime. However, the sweeping reversal since the late 2010s suggests that the CCP may not be able to fully escape the fate of the CPSU. The fundamental institutions of communist totalitarianism remain unreformable and economic reforms appear destined to fail (Chapters 13 and 14). Furthermore, the peaceful abandonment of totalitarianism by the FSU-EE communist parties was driven not only by economic stagnation but also by immense social pressure and a growing social consciousness regarding human rights and humanitarian values. These pressures and social consensus are deeply rooted in the institutional genes of the FSU-EE countries (Chapter 14). In comparison, China has a much weaker social awareness of human rights and humanitarianism. Additionally, under CCP rule, the military has long been involved in politics and the CCP has deliberately institutionalized the grooming of princelings as successors (Chapter 14). These factors suggest that even in the face of prolonged economic stagnation, it may be more difficult for the CCP leadership to peacefully renounce totalitarianism than it was for their FSU-EE counterparts.

The key to understanding Taiwan's democratic transformation lies in recognizing the pre-existing differences in institutional genes between Taiwan and mainland China, as well as the fundamental differences between authoritarian Kuomintang (KMT) rule and totalitarian CCP rule in suppressing the institutional genes necessary for constitutional democracy (Chapter 14). First, the short-lived rule of the Chinese imperial system in Taiwan ended as early as the late nineteenth century, leaving only a shallow influence of Chinese imperial institutional genes on the island. During the Taisho democracy era under Japanese rule, Taiwan began to develop the institutional genes of constitutionalism, including local elections and the assembly of political parties. Furthermore, the Comintern never reached Taiwan and the KMT was not a totalitarian party. Under KMT authoritarian rule, the institutional genes of democratic constitutionalism were suppressed but not eradicated; in fact, some were able to survive and even grow, albeit with difficulty. During the authoritarian period, when the Republic of China (ROC) Constitution was partially implemented, these institutional genes saw significant development through local elections, the rapid expansion of private enterprises, and the spread of civil society. This led to a growing social movement towards constitutional democracy. Taiwan's institutional transformation was achieved precisely because the KMT authoritarian rulers yielded to and responded to this tremendous social pressure.

1.2 INSTITUTIONAL DIVERGENCE

China, Russia, and Japan, at the turn of the nineteenth and twentieth centuries, each endeavored to promote the establishment of constitutional government. Japan succeeded while China and Russia failed. Since then, there has been an ongoing institutional divergence between these three powers that has had a major impact on the world.[6] Japan was the first non-Western country to establish a constitutional government and became the first developed nation outside of Europe and North America (a thorough discussion of Japanese institutional changes, including its period of militarism, is beyond the subject of this book). After decades of endeavors towards a constitutional monarchy and republic, which ended their imperial systems, Russia and

China, respectively, created and transplanted totalitarian institutions that ran counter to constitutionalism.

Since the end of the nineteenth century, for the first time in 2,000 years of Chinese history, the reform advocates who tried to change the Chinese institution called the traditional Chinese institution the "imperial system" (*dizhi*). This tradition has continued to this day among Chinese intellectuals who are critical of the institutions of the Chinese Empire. This book continues this tradition. The closest term in political science to *dizhi*, the Chinese imperial system, is an absolute monarchy. However, the powers in the Chinese imperial system were much more concentrated, such that there was no boundary between sovereignty and property rights and no judicial institution separate from the executives (Chapters 3 and 4 will explain further). These make the Chinese imperial system categorially different from the absolute monarchy in Western Europe. The Tsarist imperial system is more similar to the Chinese system than it is to the Western European absolute monarchy (see Chapter 7).

The study of the Chinese imperial system is highly relevant to its economic position in the international arena. This book argues that the most important reason for China's decline and the limitations imposed on its catching up is its great institutional divergence. A century and a half ago, China, or the "Great Qing Empire," had the largest economy in the world. Its economy was bigger than the sum of the second and third largest economies at that time. However, since the mid nineteenth century, China had rapidly declined. Riots, revolutions, and civil and foreign wars persisted. Concurrently, two constitutional reforms faltered, leading to the collapse of the Qing Empire and the Republican Revolution. However, the Republican Revolution also soon faltered. As a result, China became one of the world's poorest countries, mired in conflict.

In 1949, backed by the Soviet Union, the CCP established the People's Republic of China (PRC). At this point, China's per capita gross domestic product (GDP) was a mere twentieth of the United States' (calculation based on Maddison [2003]). The nation remained in severe poverty for the subsequent three decades under the new regime. It was not until the post-Mao reform that China experienced more than three decades of sustained rapid development and became the world's second largest economy. In 2018, China's nominal per capita GDP was nearly one-sixth that of the United States, or 30 percent of the US figure measured by purchasing power parity (IMF, 2019).

If China develops to follow a similar trajectory to those of Japan, South Korea, and Taiwan, its GDP per capita will reach half that of the United States within the next twenty to thirty years, by which time China's total GDP will exceed that of the United States and the European Union (EU) combined. It would be the biggest challenge not only to the global economy but also to global science, technology, politics, and even the military, similar to the expectations or fears about the rapidly developing Soviet Union during the 1960s and 1970s, even though the per capita GDP in the USSR never exceeded one-third that of the United States (Maddison, 2003). However, China's basic institutions differ significantly from those of Japan, South Korea, and Taiwan. So, will China's development trajectory follow that of Japan, South Korea, and Taiwan, or that of the Former Soviet Union or even the Qing Empire? What will happen if China cannot even maintain stability? The answer hinges on China's institutions and how they will change.

Why did China and Russia, despite initial strides towards constitutional governance mirroring Japan, eventually veer in the opposite direction? Why, after the infiltration of totalitarianism into China, did the painstaking efforts of China's intellectuals towards constitutionalism partially dissipate and partially shift the momentum in favor of totalitarianism? Why did the imported totalitarianism find a deeper foothold in China compared to that in Russia, its birthplace? Addressing these questions is essential to understanding contemporary China's institutions and to anticipating China's future trajectories.

Initiated in 1868, the Meiji Restoration represented a significant departure in institutional evolution. It laid the foundation for constitutional governance in Japan. Despite the major twists and turns of militarism, the Meiji Restoration and the subsequent constitutional democratic reforms introduced during the Taisho period laid the foundation for the final establishment of a democratic system in Japan after the Second World War. Conversely, both Tsarist Russia and Imperial China, following their respective military defeats by Meiji Japan, embarked on a series of constitutional reforms and revolutions aimed at establishing constitutional monarchies and republics. These tumultuous changes led to the collapse of both empires. However, rather than establishing constitutional rule, they rebounded to form the world's first and largest totalitarian regimes, respectively. And it was in China that the seeds of totalitarianism took the deepest root.

Russia's defeat in the Russo-Japanese War of 1905 sparked a revolution that led to the establishment of a constitutional monarchy and the State Duma, the legislative body. Despite holding several sessions between 1905 and 1917 after general elections, the constitutional monarchy remained unstable, which paved the way for the Bolshevik Revolution. The Russian efforts towards constitutionalism started in 1814, at the end of the war against Napoleon. During that year, members of the Russian military elite found themselves galvanized by the example of the French Revolution and the desire for constitutional government in Russia was first kindled. This inspiration spurred decades of tireless work by the revolutionary pioneers, culminating in the establishment of a constitutional monarchy after the 1905 revolution and a republican provisional government in 1917. Although the century-long struggle for constitutionalism was fraught with turbulence and hardship, and the Provisional Government was weak and faltering, it was not exceptional compared to the tortuous journey towards constitutionalism in most countries around the world. What made Russia profoundly influential in human history was the Bolshevik coup of 1917 (interpreted as largely a collection of coincidences by many historians), which completely ended a century of efforts towards constitutional government in Russia and created the world's first totalitarian system. Why did Russia have such difficulty achieving constitutionalism, yet later shift so easily to its opposite, totalitarianism?

By the time Soviet totalitarianism permeated China, the conditions there largely mirrored those of revolutionary Russia. Following its defeat in the Sino-Japanese War of 1895, China twice attempted to enact constitutional reforms akin to those in Japan, yet both attempts foundered. The drive for institutional reform was eventually transformed into a revolutionary call and, subsequently, the revolutionary objective pivoted from republicanism to its opposite direction, communism. After enduring several brutal setbacks, a new generation of Chinese revolutionaries embraced Bolshevik missionaries, the Comintern. They willingly adopted Soviet institutions and constructed a totalitarian system, which stood in stark contrast to the constitutional framework that their predecessors had originally aimed to establish. I refer to this significant shift as the "Great Institutional Divergence."

Since its inception in Russia in 1917, totalitarianism has spread globally at an unprecedented rate, outpacing the expansion of any other ideology or institutional model in human history. By the 1970s, the world's population under totalitarian regimes surpassed the combined membership of all Christian denominations, the world's largest religion. Moreover, without exception, all countries that voluntarily embraced totalitarianism had been autocratic states with no prior experience of constitutional government. It is evident that this phenomenon cannot be solely attributed to the ascent of a single leader or the triumph of an armed insurrection.

However, research into the patterns in the emergence and evolution of totalitarian systems remains sparse. Many scholars specializing in institutional studies, including those focusing on authoritarian regimes, tend to disregard the distinct characteristics of totalitarian systems, such as those found in China and the Soviet Union, and their influence on other nations' institutions that goes beyond geopolitics. Many China specialists tend to underestimate the Soviet Union's foundational role in shaping contemporary

China's institutions. Additionally, numerous Soviet experts often overlook totalitarianism's origins and its continuing impact on today's Russia and the world.

1.3 CHINA'S INSTITUTIONAL EVOLUTION

The downfall of the imperial system in China heralded the advent of totalitarianism. A century ago, pioneers of constitutional reform and the Republican Revolution perceived constitutionalism as an inescapable route towards China's advancement. Despite distinct approaches, both the Hundred Days' Reform (戊戌变法) and the Xinhai (辛亥) Revolution shared the common goal of instituting constitutionalism and substituting China's imperial institutions with successful models from developed countries. But these attempted institutional reforms and republican revolutions all failed.

The key question to be analyzed and discussed in this book is why China had difficulty establishing a constitutional system originating from the West (including learning from Japan) but ended up rapidly and firmly establishing a totalitarian system originating from the Soviet Union in a relatively short period. What were the institutional antecedents in China for such a development? Subsequently, China transformed Soviet totalitarianism into regionally administered totalitarianism (RADT), totalitarianism with Chinese characteristics, through the Great Leap Forward and the Great Proletarian Cultural Revolution.[7] Having been deeply rooted in society, RADT formed the institutional foundation for China's post-Mao reform and made the Chinese communist regime more adaptable and sustainable. What were the institutional origins of RADT? What is the relationship between RADT and the major challenges confronting China today?

There have been three dominant views on political reform in academic and policymaking circles about China's more than forty years of reform. The first view holds that China's national conditions or institutions are unique and that a democratic constitutional system is not suitable for China. The second holds that constitutional democracy is the ultimate objective of reform but a phase of neo-authoritarianism is needed as a transitional stage to develop the economy as a foundation for democracy.[8] The third view rejects the above two perspectives and argues that China can, should, and indeed must implement reforms leading toward constitutional democracy.

China's exceptionalism also often manifests in the form of the so-called "China model." Does China's uniqueness allow it to bypass the regularities universally observed by other nations? Can China's economy sustain stable and continuous growth in the absence of constitutional democracy? These fundamental inquiries are what this book endeavors to tackle. Each of the three perspectives above relates to a series of basic social science questions: What are the main characteristics of China's fundamental institutions? Why are these characteristics the way they are? How did they originate and evolve? Why did communist regimes emerge in Russia and China? Furthermore, what hurdles will China face as it transitions towards democracy?

Another prevalent view in academic and policy circles contends that economic development is an essential precursor to establishing constitutional democracy. This perspective argues that China requires a phase of neo-authoritarianism to address basic subsistence needs and foster a modern middle class before transitioning to constitutional democracy. However, as historical evidence abundantly demonstrates, in countries like Britain and the United States, the establishment of a constitutional democracy preceded an Industrial Revolution and economic development.

Philosopher Bertrand Russell concluded at the close of the Second World War that,

> Ever since [Rousseau's] time, those who considered themselves reformers have been divided into two groups, those who followed him and those who followed Locke. Sometimes they cooperated, and many individuals saw no incompatibility. But gradually the incompatibility has become increasingly evident. At the present time, Hitler is an outcome of Rousseau; Roosevelt and Churchill, of Locke. (Russell [1946] 1957, p. 660)

John Locke was a trailblazer in modern constitutionalism and played a vital role in drafting the documents of England's Glorious Revolution. His perspectives on human rights significantly influenced the US Constitution, the constitutions of all democracies, and the United Nation's Universal Declaration of Human Rights. A century after Locke, French philosopher Jean-Jacques Rousseau proposed that individual rights should be limited, or even nullified, for societal benefit and the so-called "general will." He also maintained that private property rights are a source of inequality. Rousseau's theory was put into practice during the French Revolution's Reign of Terror led by the Jacobins and inspired Gracchus Babeuf, who created the first communist movement with the aim of seizing power and wealth through violence to achieve absolute equality under the rule of a clandestine organization. The concepts and movements of Rousseau and Babeuf were further developed by Marx and Lenin, laying the foundation for totalitarianism.

Locke's philosophy was never popular among Chinese and Russian intellectuals. Instead, thinking derived from Rousseau and Babeuf, and later developed by Marx and Lenin, prevailed among Russian intelligentsia and Chinese revolutionaries. To understand the origins of totalitarianism, a critical question arises: Why did Russian intelligentsia and Chinese revolutionaries embrace the ideas of Rousseau, Marx, and Lenin while rejecting Locke's?

1.4 THE INSTITUTIONAL REGIME IN CONTEMPORARY CHINA: AN OUTLINE

The nature of contemporary China's fundamental institution is a subject of ongoing debate. In this book, I characterize it as Regionally Administered Totalitarianism (RADT), as previously mentioned, a concept that I expound upon in Chapters 12 and 13, along with an analysis of the regime's evolution. Essentially, it began with the total Sovietization of China in the early 1950s.

The foundation of the classic model of totalitarianism that China adopted from the Soviet Union was the Chinese Communist

Party, formerly known as China's "Bolshevik" party. This entity initially received substantial support from the Soviets. The CCP's authority was absolute, with the party maintaining comprehensive control over the executive, legislative, and judicial branches of government, the armed forces, propaganda machinery and media, all resources, as well as all state and non-state organizations and enterprises. There was no separation between the party and the government. The party directly appointed all departmental officials and regional administration leaders at every level. Regional governments lacked autonomy, let alone sovereignty, and local party-state officials were appointed by their superiors within the CCP. In these aspects, China's institutional regime mirrored the classic totalitarian model established in the Soviet Union.

In the RADT system, local party-state agencies are delegated with administrative and economic functions, as well as the bulk of resources, under the totalitarian premise of centralized appointment and political and ideological control. This institutional change from classic totalitarianism to RADT began in 1958 with the implementation of the Great Leap Forward and was solidified during the Cultural Revolution (1966–1976).

RADT was the institutional foundation of the post-Mao reform. In the initial three decades of reform, with the aim of preserving the regime, the party's societal control passively slackened as private businesses flourished in downstream manufacturing and the service industry. Simultaneously, a limited degree of pluralism began to take shape. The emergence of private property ownership, community organizations, and limited ideological diversity, along with expansion of the media, gradually diluted the party's dominance in socioeconomic matters and ideological discourse. This period witnessed a partial transition towards authoritarianism, more specifically, regionally decentralized authoritarianism (RDA),[9] albeit this shift was transitory in nature. Since the second decade of the twenty-first century, despite many of China's elites eagerly anticipating reforms towards constitutionalism, China's system has instead reverted to totalitarianism, that is to say, RADT. It is important to note, however, that history's so-called repetitions only recreate certain fundamental features in new circumstances, not every detail. Today's return of RADT in China is no exception.

Constitutionalism as an ideology made its way into China decades before the establishment of the first communist totalitarian regime in Russia. When the Russian Bolsheviks created the CCP, most of its founding members had a very limited understanding of communist ideology (as detailed in Chapter 10). But why did communist totalitarianism gain a foothold in China instead of constitutionalism? Why did totalitarianism not maintain its classic form in China, as it did in other communist countries, but rather evolved into RADT? Why has RADT become so deeply entrenched and difficult to remove in China? The answers to these questions can be found by examining the characteristics of China's institutional genes and the necessary institutional genes that underpin totalitarianism.

The institutions of Imperial China represent the most enduring and meticulously organized autocratic systems in global history. The long-term stable structure of the Chinese imperial system is directly related to its unique institutional genes. Some of the basic components of these institutional genes originated in the Warring States period before the establishment of the empire. During the early phase of the unified empire under the Qin and Han dynasties (from 221 BCE to 220 CE), imperial institutions began taking shape. In the long process of the collapse of the imperial system and subsequent reunification, the institutional genes of China's imperial system were significantly improved during the Sui, Tang, and Song dynasties (from 581 to 1279). In the following millennium, these improved institutional genes became highly stable. During the process of dynastic changes, they continuously replicated and evolved. After the Mongols and Manchus overthrew the Song and Ming dynasties, they abandoned their own ruling methods and adopted Han Chinese imperial institutions (see Chapters 4 and 5).

Institutional genes and the incentive-compatibility issue of the key players in institutional changes[10] largely determined the fate of various reforms and revolutions in modern Chinese history. The half-century-long endeavor towards democracy and constitutionalism, from constitutional reform to the Republican Revolution, ended in failure. By contrast, the process of establishing totalitarianism in China was very rapid and firm. After the collapse of the Chinese Empire, some institutional genes from the imperial period continued to self-replicate in new forms within the totalitarian system until today (see Chapters 9–12). The crux of comprehension lies in recognizing the parallels between the institutional genes of China's inherent imperial system and those of the imported totalitarian regime.

1.5 THE INSTITUTIONAL GENES OF REGIONALLY ADMINISTERED TOTALITARIANISM

The governance structure under the RADT in contemporary China constitutes an institutional trinity: a tripartite blend of fundamental institutional elements that underpin China's entire political and economic framework. Figure 1.1 delineates these institutional elements and their interconnections. The central box at the top represents the party-state bureaucracy, which lacks separation between executive and judicial functions. On the lower left, we see the party-state's control over property rights and law, manifested in state ownership of all the land, a state-dominated financial sector, and a monopoly over the economy's commanding heights. Lastly, on the lower right, we find the CCP's control over official personnel and ideology. This power structure ensures the party's absolute societal control, upholding stability by securing political, economic, and personnel support for the totalitarian system. Chapters 3–5 and 10–12 delve deeper into what makes this structure qualify as an institutional gene of contemporary China's regime and they trace its evolution.

In the RADT regime, local governments hold complete administrative and economic functions under the premise that all local party officials are appointed from above and that political and personnel

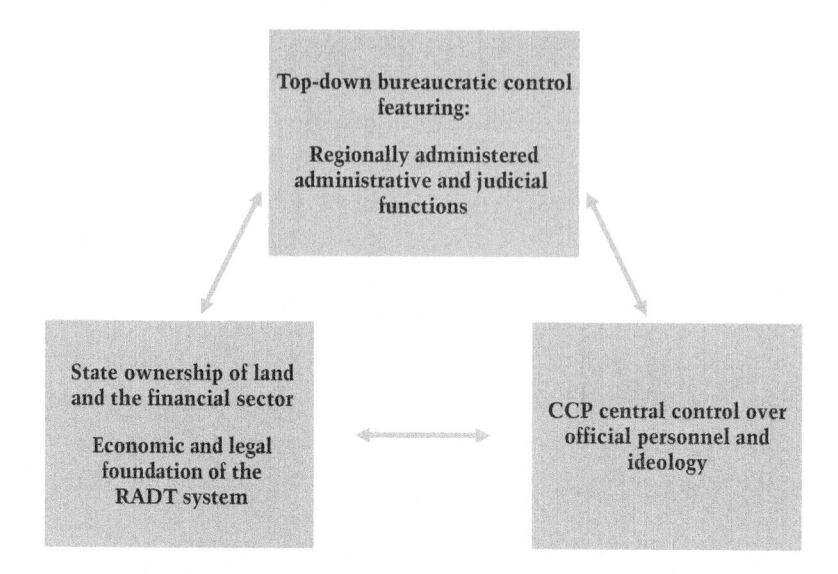

```
                    ┌─────────────────────────────┐
                    │ Top-down bureaucratic control│
                    │         featuring:          │
                    │                             │
                    │   Regionally administered   │
                    │  administrative and judicial│
                    │          functions          │
                    └─────────────────────────────┘
                       ↙                      ↘
┌──────────────────────────┐         ┌──────────────────────────┐
│ State ownership of land  │         │                          │
│ and the financial sector │         │  CCP central control over│
│                          │ ←────→  │  official personnel and  │
│  Economic and legal      │         │        ideology          │
│  foundation of the       │         │                          │
│     RADT system          │         │                          │
└──────────────────────────┘         └──────────────────────────┘
```

FIGURE 1.1 The power structure of regionally administered totalitarianism (RADT).

matters are highly centralized. The absence of specific centralized directives or planning instructions to localities in terms of specific administrative and economic management is a fundamental difference between RADT and classical totalitarianism. Figure 1.2 encapsulates the salient attributes of the central–local governance framework and power distribution under RADT. To underscore the decentralization of administrative and economic authority, Figure 1.2 only illustrates the functional arrangement at the central and county governance levels. Although similar configurations exist at intermediate levels, they are omitted for brevity. As shown in Figure 1.2, grassroots local party-state authorities possess nearly all the fundamental functions akin to those of the central authorities. Additionally, local party-state authorities take the lead in overseeing the comprehensive management of these functions. The section will delve into the pivotal role the RADT system played in China's economic reform. More importantly, Chapters 4, 5, and 9–12 will analyze the genesis, evolution, and continuity of this system throughout China's imperial period as well as during the CCP's revolutionary and governing periods.

1.5 THE INSTITUTIONAL GENES OF RADT

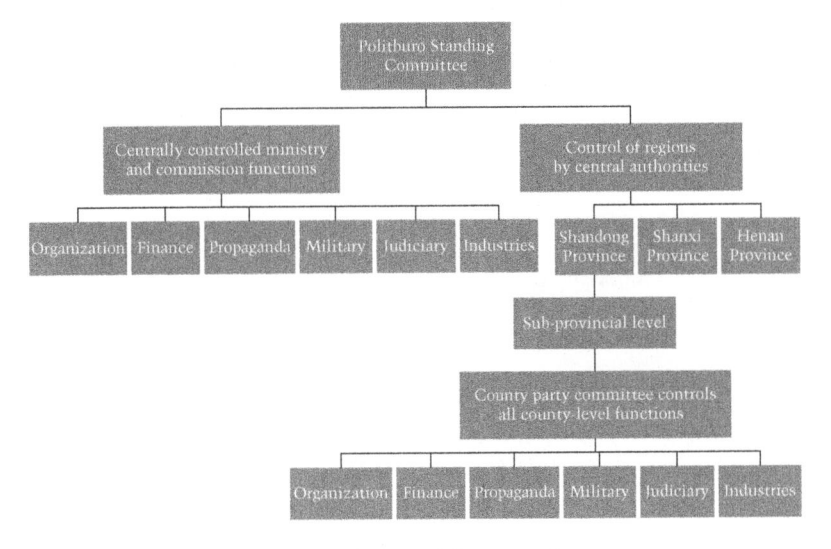

FIGURE 1.2 Institutional genes of the regional governance structure under RADT.

China's distinct RADT system came into being via the partial deconstruction of Soviet-style institutions during the Great Leap Forward and the Cultural Revolution. Chapter 12 scrutinizes why, after the comprehensive transplantation of totalitarianism from the Soviet Union, China's "continuous revolution" transformed into the RADT system.

1.5.1 Origins of the Institutional Genes of the RADT System

The institutions of contemporary China are inextricably linked to those of the former empire. To comprehend the genesis of the institutional genes underpinning China's contemporary system (as depicted in Figures 1.1 and 1.2), we need to examine the institutional genes of China's imperial system (Figures 1.3 and 1.4). A comparison of Figures 1.1 and 1.3 reveals striking resemblances between the institutional genes underpinning the power structures of both the imperial era and the present day. Subsequent chapters of this book will delve into the specific parallels between the institutional genes of ancient and

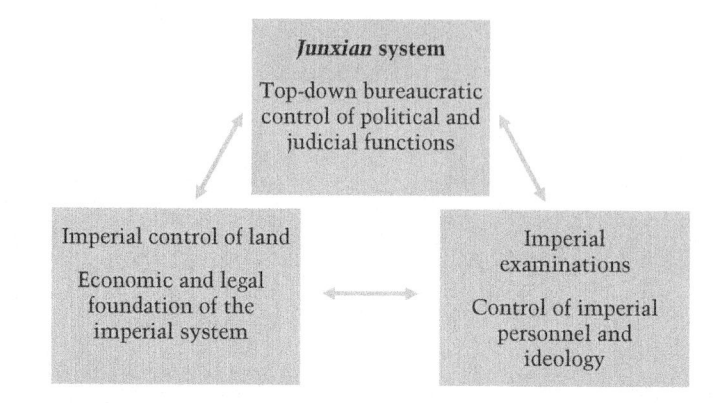

FIGURE 1.3 The trinity of institutional genes comprising the governance structure of China's imperial system.

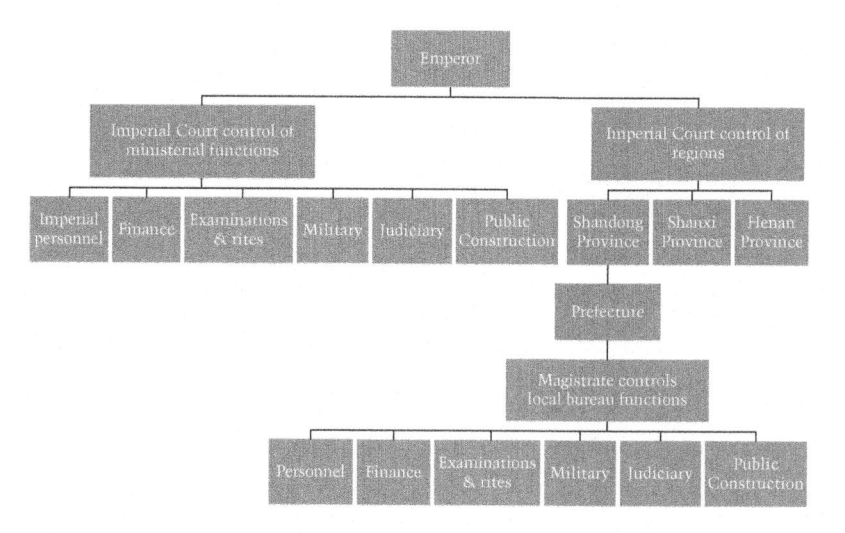

FIGURE 1.4 Institutional genes of China's *junxian* bureaucracy since the era of the Sui and Tang dynasties.

modern China, the factors contributing to these similarities, and the mechanism facilitating their transmission.

At the center part of imperial China's trinity of institutional power, as depicted in Figure 1.3, was the bureaucratic system established under the Qin dynasty (221–206 BCE), known as the *junxian* 郡县 (prefecture-county) system.[11] The judiciary was always an intrinsic part of the bureaucracy. In this top-down bureaucracy, bureaucrats appointed by the emperor replaced the aristocrats' rule over local areas during the Zhou dynasty. The judiciary was also inherently embedded within the bureaucracy. The primary threat to imperial authority was the potential rise of a new nobility from within the imperial system itself. Since the aristocracy that might arise within the imperial system was the greatest potential threat to challenge imperial power, the empire had to prevent that from happening whenever possible. The imperial land system,[12] as shown in the lower left box in Figure 1.3, instituted since the Qin dynasty, served to eradicate the aristocracy.

However, the amalgamation of imperial land control and bureaucratic systems proved insufficient to prevent the emergence of a hereditary, de facto nobility, who often intended to be independent of the emperor. The imperial examination system, formally established during the Sui and Tang dynasties (with an earlier version introduced during the Han dynasty, though it was not fully institutionalized), as shown in the bottom right box of Figure 1.3, served as a critical personnel strategy that disrupted the intergenerational transmission of power among senior officials. It was an instrument of personnel control that safeguarded the emperor's absolute authority over the bureaucracy. Simultaneously, it also served as a tool for ideological control, ensuring that all individuals entering the bureaucracy were properly indoctrinated with loyalty to the monarch. Upon the consolidation and refinement of this institutional trinity during the Song dynasty (960–1279), the emperor's and the imperial court's powers were effectively solidified. This robust institution of imperial rule remained unchallenged by any internally emerging powers for the subsequent millennium.

Establishing effective rule at the local level is a critical priority for any empire. Figure 1.4 illustrates the structure of local control within the Chinese imperial system, delineating the institutional genes of the *junxian* system. By juxtaposing Figures 1.2 and 1.4, the remarkable similarity between the *junxian* system and today's RADT becomes readily apparent. Chapter 12 examines how China's institutional genes have localized the foreign totalitarian institutional genes, which has led to the formation of China's contemporary institutional genes.

Figure 1.4 depicts the core functions of the imperial court, which were divided among Six Ministries that were responsible respectively for personnel, finance, examinations and rites, the military, judiciary (mostly penal affairs), and public construction. Each was headed by a minister appointed by the imperial court. At the local level, the expansive empire was administrated by prefectural and county authorities, or by provincial, prefectural, and county authorities, each of whom was under officials directly appointed by the imperial court. Faced with the trade-off between ensuring absolute imperial rule and the effectiveness of that rule, along with the logistical limitations in terms of communication and transportation, the empire delegated all administrative functions to officials at varying levels of local governments while maintaining strict control over the officials themselves. Each level, from the imperial court to the county, housed offices for imperial personnel, finance, examinations and rites, the military, judiciary, and public construction. These offices mirrored the functions of the Six Ministries, with a magistrate overseeing these functions at the county level. The functional structures at intermediary levels followed the same pattern, although they are not depicted in the diagram.

The institutional genes depicted in Figures 1.1 to 1.4 evolved and were refined during 2,000 years of the empire, tenaciously self-replicating at the core of the imperial system. Whether it was a dynastic change due to a peasant uprising or a dynasty ruled by invading foreign powers, these institutional genes continued to be replicated. Even after the collapse of the imperial system, these institutional genes continued to dominate the path of China's institutional evolution through the choices of reformers and revolutionary elites.

1.6 INSTITUTIONAL GENES: FROM THE IMPERIAL SYSTEM TO COMMUNIST TOTALITARIANISM

Communist totalitarianism is not native to China; it is, in fact, an imported system. Those who oppose the adoption of constitutionalism and democracy in China assert that these are foreign institutions and thus they are unsuited for China, predicting their inevitable failure. However, totalitarianism is also foreign to China. Why, then, is it deemed "suitable for China"? Furthermore, why has totalitarianism rooted itself so deeply in Chinese society? These issues are addressed in Chapters 4, 5, and 9–12.

A prevailing explanation for the revolutions in twentieth-century China centers around the country's profound nationalism. This explanation indeed captures some truth, as Chinese nationalism, whether overt or covert, played a pivotal role in the Republican Revolution and the May Fourth Movement, which laid the groundwork for the CCP. However, it is worth noting that Russia was the largest foreign occupier of Chinese territory by the end of the nineteenth century, a fact that was well known to the Chinese. Additionally, during the Russo-Japanese War, the Qing Empire supported Japan's endeavors to expel Russian forces from China. If one applies the nationalism perspective literally, the Russian-inspired revolution should have faced strong opposition from nationalist revolutionaries during the post-May Fourth nationalist upsurge. Curiously, China's radical revolutionaries, including prominent figures like Sun Yat-sen, Wang Jingwei, Liao Zhongkai, and influential participants in the May Fourth Movement like Chen Duxiu and Li Dazhao, avidly embraced the Russian Bolsheviks' revolutionary ideas immediately upon being exposed to them. Why? Regardless of the strategic choices made by individual revolutionary leaders, the revolutionary fervor of the participating, fervently nationalistic masses was not only a factor that these figures could seldom generate on their own but also one that could not be overlooked. This book delves into this inquiry by examining the institutional genes of the traditional Chinese imperial system and the totalitarian system through the lens of incentive-compatible institutional evolution.

The Hundred Days' Reform of 1898, which aimed at establishing a constitutional monarchy, was the first attempt in China's 2,000-year history to challenge the imperial system. Liang Qichao, a leading advocate of this reform, once said there had only been rebellions, not revolutions in Chinese history. By revolution, he meant replacing autocracy with constitutional government; by rebellion, he meant a change of dynasty that kept the same institutions in place. Any institutional change that curtails royal authority is inevitably incompatible with the interests of those in power. Thus, such successful changes necessitate the involvement of external forces beyond the monarchy's control. Royal authorities would never willingly endorse a peaceful transition to constitutional monarchy without significant external pressure, which is strong enough and has its own power base. However, two millennia of imperial rule in China eradicated the nobility and other significant independent sources of power, and the remaining sectors of influence outside direct royal control were kept minor and feeble.[13] The institutional genes of the imperial system, with its highly monopolized control over land rights, predetermined that a constitutional monarchy would be an institutionally incompatible change.

Indeed, the Hundred Days' Reform and subsequent Late Qing Reforms were merely expedient attempts at self-preservation by the imperial court. According to the principle of incentive-compatibility, once the threat to survival was removed, the imperial authorities would employ every resource at their disposal to resist restrictions and undermine constitutionalism. Consequently, the incentive-incompatible institutional reforms introduced to China during this period all failed in succession. Eventually, many of the reformers who had initially supported a constitutional monarchy regarded the imperial court's reforms as merely in name only, and they turned to support the revolution aimed at overthrowing the empire. The Republican Revolution of 1911 ended the longest-lasting imperial system in human history, but it failed to establish a stable constitutional alternative. The most devastating force to destabilize the Republic was Sun Yat-sen himself, the leader of the Republican Revolution. He initiated a "Second Revolution" and personally dismantled the fragile constitutional system that had just been established. Chapter 9 will delve into the pivotal role the imperial institutional genes played in many ostensibly random historical events.

A series of failed constitutional reforms and the Republican Revolution paved the way for the emergence of totalitarianism in China. Shortly after the Bolsheviks established a totalitarian regime in Russia, they created an international arm, the Comintern, which established a branch in China, the CCP. This marked the historical beginning of totalitarianism in China. When the Comintern was seeking to promote global revolution, China was considered a peripheral target. But the Comintern's efforts in all of their main target countries ultimately failed. Although the transition to constitutionalism is rarely seamless anywhere in the world, it is exceptionally uncommon for a country to willingly choose and successfully implement totalitarianism. What made China special that the CCP, with the support of the Comintern, developed so rapidly, eventually seized power, implemented the Soviet system, and further established totalitarianism with Chinese characteristics? The answer to this historical anomaly, explored in subsequent chapters, lies in the close relationship between the institutional genes of totalitarianism and those of the Chinese Empire. On the other hand, the institutional genes of the Chinese imperial system and those necessary for a constitutional system are not only far apart but also are in conflict with each other.

1.6.1 *The Genesis of Totalitarianism in Soviet Russia*

Russian Bolshevism was the world's inaugural totalitarian system. Despite Marx's assertion that a proletarian revolution could only emerge in the most developed capitalist economies, not in a backward place like Russia or China, the Bolsheviks claimed to be Marxist and labeled their revolution as proletarian. Why then was Russia the birthplace of totalitarianism? This question is directly related to an understanding of the emergence of totalitarianism in China and the future of China. The explanation in this book focuses on how the institutional genes of Tsarist Russia contributed to the creation of the Soviet totalitarian system.

Some authors describe the establishment of Soviet power by the Bolsheviks as a collection of coincidental events or the emergence of Soviet totalitarianism in Russia as the result of conspiracy, cunning, and brutal violence. Each narrative reflects important aspects of history. However, such large-scale implementation of violence requires many people to execute it voluntarily, even creatively and fanatically. The incitement, fanaticism, organization, and brutality of the Bolsheviks required a highly intense incentive mechanism.[14] So, history cannot be accounted for purely because of a gang of conspirators' atrocities. These same traits characterized the strain of Bolshevism that later arose in China with the support of the Comintern. The tragedies of China's Land Reform movement, Campaign to Suppress Counterrevolutionaries, Anti-Rightist Campaign, and Great Leap Forward, followed by the Cultural Revolution, all demonstrate the enthusiastic and active involvement of millions of zealous followers, guided and motivated by totalitarian leaders. The revolution spearheaded by the CCP generated incentives potent enough to unite the entire nation, despite Sun Yat-sen's description of the Chinese people as being as disjointed as "a sheet of loose sand." So, what incited this unity? The emotional resonance and organizational discipline of the party cannot be solely ascribed to coincidence. If it was not purely accidental, what was the underlying mechanism?

Chapters 7 and 8 analyze the emergence of three institutional genes in the Tsarist period which led to the totalitarianism of the Soviet Union: the secret political terrorist organizations of late Tsarist Russia, the Eastern Orthodox Church, and the institutions of imperial rule under the tsars. From the outset, the Bolsheviks were markedly different from other Marxist parties in their organizational principles and methods, which were inherited from the secretive terrorist political organizations prevalent in Russian society. When Lenin founded the Bolshevik wing of the Russian Social Democratic Labor Party (RSDLP) in 1903, its foundational principles closely mirrored those of the Narodnaya Volya, or People's Will, a prominent political terrorist organization of that era. Lenin's brother, who was executed following a botched assassination attempt on the Tsar, was a local leader of the Narodnaya Volya and several of the early Bolshevik leaders had strong connections with the organization. Even leading figures of the international communist movement at that time, such as Karl Kautsky and Rosa Luxembourg, criticized Lenin's Bolsheviks as a terrorist organization and asserted that the Soviet regime would bring a reign of terror.[15]

However, the totalitarian party vastly outstripped the secret political terrorist organizations in capability. The biggest difference lies in its systematic, highly appealing ideology, extremely strong incitement, and extensive, religious-like ability of mobilization that permeated society. The roots of this extraordinary mobilizing capacity can be traced back over a thousand years through the history of Christianity and the Church (see Chapter 6).

In his later years, Engels wrote about the origins of communism and socialism in early Christianity (Engels, 1895). Kautsky also explored the origins of communist thought in the Bible, pinpointing the medieval Reformation as the genesis of the earliest communist movements. Characterized by extreme zealotry and brutality, these movements – some carried out on a significant scale – were a characteristic feature of the Reformation in certain regions of Europe (Kautsky, 1897, pp. 12–17). They were evident in several towns and cities across Central and Western Europe, and sometimes in established short-lived communist societies, such as the Hussites in Bohemia and the Münster Commune in Germany. Many other aspects of Marxist thought, including the idea of historical inevitability, the downfall of the old world and the rise of a new one, belief in a savior and redemption, and martyrdom, have their roots deeply embedded in Christianity (see Chapter 6). In many ways, the international communist movement led by Marx and Engels resembled a second Reformation but with historical inevitability, communism, Marxism, and *Das Kapital* replacing God, Heaven, Jesus, and the Bible. Chapter 6, based on historical evidence from Europe, explains the Christian origins of a secular religion, that is to say, communist totalitarianism. It also explains how this institutional gene made communist totalitarianism the most influential ideology and institution at one point. This is the intellectual starting point for understanding fanatic communist movements in Russia and China.

Just as the Roman Empire's greatest contribution to Christianity was its establishment as the state religion, the Bolsheviks' primary contribution to the communist movement was the creation of a secular totalitarian caesaropapism founded on Marxist ideology. Regarding ideology and mobilization, the institutional genes for totalitarianism in Russia originated from the branch of Christianity dominant in Tsarist Russia: Russian Orthodoxy, which had permeated the population of the land long before the existence of the Russian Empire. Whether by design or inadvertently, the Bolsheviks appropriated the Orthodox Church's well-established mechanisms of propaganda, organization, and punishment to mobilize, appeal to, and govern for centuries. Through these inherited characteristics of the Orthodox Church, the Bolsheviks infiltrated and exerted control over Russian society, from ideology to organization and power structures. While it may be coincidental that Stalin received a formal education at an Orthodox seminary, the Bolsheviks' successful emulation of the Orthodox Church was more than mere happenstance. In this political religion,[16] Marxism-Leninism's classics supplanted the Bible, revolutionary martyrs displaced Christian martyrs, and communist society emerged as the new heaven. Mirroring the methods of the apostles in disseminating the news of Jesus Christ, the Bolsheviks established a cult of personality around their leader, elevating him to the status of a saint and savior. Revolutionary heroes and martyrs were canonized, their exploits commemorated, and temples erected in their honor. The religious custom of mass rituals was replicated, while penance to God was transformed into penance to the party. Liu Shaoqi coined the corresponding phrase "criticism and self-criticism" for use in China, a country devoid of a comparable religious tradition, in his 1939 book *How to Be a Good Communist*. Under Stalin's regime in the Soviet Union, classic Marxist works served as the Old

Testament, while Stalin's *History of the Communist Party of the Soviet Union (Bolsheviks): Short Course* (Stalin, 1975), supplemented by Lenin's work on Bolshevism, constituted the New Testament. Mao Zedong adopted this blueprint, converting volumes of rehashed history into China's uncontested "classics" and presenting himself as the "Great Savior of the Chinese People."

Upon seizing power, the Bolsheviks soon dominated every facet of Russian society by controlling the government and all resources. The institutional genes for totalitarianism, in terms of practical control, originated from the Tsarist Empire. These include the Tsar and his court's monopoly over political, economic, military, and judicial powers, the highly monopolized power structure of the system, control over the Church, and the social consensus (legitimacy) supporting the monopolization of power through violence. On this basis, the Bolsheviks developed a totalitarian system with a total monopoly of power and property rights that was unprecedented in human history, controlling all aspects of society wholly and comprehensively.

Marxist theory, echoing the Christian theme of salvation, posits that the international communist revolution can only triumph once everyone in the world achieves liberation.

1.6.2 The Rise of Communist Totalitarianism in China

The Comintern sent representatives to China soon after its creation but its delegates discovered that China was 500 years behind the advanced economies. According to Marxism-Leninism, such backwardness could only be peripheral to the Comintern's operations. Yet, paradoxically, China emerged as the Comintern's most significant success, if not its only success. As elucidated in Chapters 8–10, China's institutional genes bore a striking resemblance to those that engendered Bolshevism, whereas they were distinctively different from those in the West. Of the three institutional genes that gave rise to Soviet totalitarianism, two similar ones were present in China: the imperial system and a tradition of secret societies. The monopolization of power, stringent controls, and the overall institutional stability of China's imperial system were more pronounced than those of Tsarist Russia. Furthermore, China's secret societies, such as the White Lotus Sect, the Green Gang, the Heaven and Earth Society, the Triads, and the Brotherhood Society, had a more extended history and were potentially more organizationally sophisticated than their Russian counterparts. This shared lineage of institutional genes facilitated the creation of a Bolshevik system in China and the launch of incentive-compatible communist totalitarian movements there.

However, one institutional gene that was crucial in the genesis of totalitarianism was absent in China: an Eastern Orthodox tradition. The emperors had curtailed the influx of Christianity and other Western ideologies into China. There was no widespread belief or consensus regarding a monotheistic God, God's Truth, or a Savior, nor did any Church hold a national authoritative position. This absence limited the potential for generating totalitarian ideas in the vein of Marxism and Leninism and made it challenging to manifest such an ideology in the form of totalitarian institutions capable of penetrating and controlling society. Therefore, creating a totalitarian system in China necessitated direct involvement from an external force, such as the Comintern, to cultivate and support various aspects, including promoting beliefs, unifying thoughts, launching propaganda, and establishing organizations.

The largest insurrection in China's late imperial period, the Taiping Rebellion, which spanned from 1850 to 1864, borrowed elements of Christianity. Certain Christian tenets were utilized to legitimize the uprising and proved highly effective in mobilizing the masses. However, Western missionaries and Western powers refused to support the Rebellion when they discerned that it was Christian only in name. In subsequent years, both Sun Yat-sen and Mao Zedong took Hong Xiuquan, the Rebellion's leader, as a role model. Unlike the Taiping Rebellion, the Comintern directly introduced a new ideology into China, erected novel institutions, and actively endeavored to modify China's institutional genes. As Mao

Zedong declared, "The salvoes of the October Revolution brought us Marxism-Leninism."

In 1920, the Comintern dispatched representatives to establish its branch in China. From the official establishment of the CCP in 1921 until the Comintern's dissolution in 1943, the CCP functioned as a branch of the Comintern and identified itself as Bolshevik. All major decisions of the CCP had to be approved by the Comintern, which provided financial and material resources and selected the party's top leaders. In 1931, under the Comintern's guidance, the CCP founded the Chinese Soviet Republic, China's first rudimentary totalitarian regime. From 1931, when Mao Zedong joined the CCP leadership, to 1938, when he ascended to the party's highest-ranking leadership, he leaned heavily on the Comintern for recognition, direct support, and supervision. The party's Yan'an Rectification Campaign in 1942 was a Stalinist purge with Chinese characteristics, after which Mao Zedong was elevated as the unchallenged leader who had full control over the CCP. From then on, the CCP became an independent Bolshevik party with a blend of institutional genes from both Imperial China and the Soviet Union, hence constituting a new and unique Chinese institutional gene.

After the Second World War, the CCP, with assistance from the Soviet Union, emerged victorious from the Chinese Civil War and subsequently established total control over China. From 1949 onwards, with the party serving as the linchpin of the regime, Soviet totalitarianism was comprehensively transplanted into China, encompassing diverse domains such as the economy, politics, law, military, education, and scientific research, among others. Even the inaugural constitution of the PRC was formulated under pressure from Stalin and with the assistance of Soviet experts; Stalin personally reviewed the final draft.

In places where totalitarian systems have developed, they often demonstrate significant strength in their early stages. Totalitarian parties employ methods such as incitement, violence, and coercion to generate extraordinarily potent incentives that result in the formation of the "masses." These masses are manipulated into becoming formidable forces that dismantle the "old world" and construct a "new world" that paradoxically subjugates them in the end. Consequently, totalitarian parties seem to possess the capacity to establish systems that fundamentally contradict the incentives of the majority of individuals in society.

Unlike the establishment of totalitarian regimes, stable and long-term incentive-compatible systems that have emerged in human history have evolved slowly. This evolution is the process of synthesizing a large number of competitive, seemingly random short-term changes or events. In such an institutional evolutionary process, leaders and participants on all sides of the competition are mostly focused on short-term, local goals. For a conventional political party, including the early Social-Democratic parties within the communist movement, long-term objectives that were not incentive-compatible were unfeasible due to their lack of appeal for electoral support.

But a totalitarian party is an ideologically dominated, tightly controlled organization with iron discipline (internal factions are banned). The tight top-down organization and iron discipline of these parties enable them to promote highly seductive and inflammatory ideologies that conceal the truth and achieve their ultimate goal of eliminating competitors and gaining total control over society through a step-by-step plan. Ideology provides legitimacy for their totalitarian goals and step-by-step implementation is their strategy. Chapters 8 and 10–13 use historical evidence to analyze how the Bolsheviks and CCP decomposed their incentive-incompatible grand goals into multiple, often contradictory, short-term incentive-compatible goals, which were systematically and violently achieved through a divide-and-conquer approach.

Violence is an inherent component of totalitarianism. However, the resources available for violence are intimately tied to the totalitarian regime's mobilization capacity. The violent upheaval of revolution, through which totalitarian systems are forged and refined, relies upon the mass mobilization of a substantial societal elite and working class, rallying them to the revolutionary cause.[17] In China, the CCP effectively garnered mass support by leveraging China's institutional genes to transform interim objectives into revolutionary acts or campaigns that aligned with the short-term incentives of a large populace. For example, it promised democratic freedoms to the elite and made commitments to secure land and property rights for the poor rural population. However, the CCP reneged on all of these promises, backed by coercive forces, within just a few years (see Chapter 11). Furthermore, these CCP actions were like a repetition to those of the Bolsheviks (see Chapter 8).

By strategically designing a mechanism for continuous revolution, inherently incentive-incompatible objectives can be decomposed into a series of short-term, seemingly incentive-compatible stages. This was the approach adopted by the Bolsheviks and the CCP extended this strategy to its extreme, with each stage of the revolution meticulously pre-planned. Ideology, proclaimed as "theory" by the party, provided a semblance of legitimacy for frequently self-contradictory initiatives such as the Land Reform movement and agricultural collectivization. In some instances, campaigns that served the established and long-term objectives were launched in response to specific events. One such instance was the Anti-Rightist Campaign, which was initiated in response to the "episodes" of the Hungarian Revolution of 1956 and Khrushchev's secret speech to the 20th Congress of the Communist Party of the Soviet Union (CPSU). Crucially, each short-term, incentive-compatible step in the process weakened or eradicated a segment of the political or social forces resisting revolution, including those within the party itself, thereby nudging the party closer to its incentive-incompatible totalitarian objectives.

The overwhelming majority of individuals, including many within the ranks of the CCP elite and leadership circles, would likely not have opted for totalitarianism had they been aware of its true characteristics in advance. With each stride towards complete totalitarianism, the system's long-term incentive-incompatibility became more apparent to a greater number of people. The reason why a totalitarian system can still be established and solidified under such conditions is that the elimination of resistance and the establishment of totalitarian tyranny are advanced in a phased strategy. Every step along this trajectory involves the deployment of totalitarian organizations and collectives against individuals. At each stage, the party designs revolutions or movements that align with the short-term incentives to mobilize as many people as possible, aiming to gradually suppress or even eliminate dissenting individuals or groups in a piecemeal manner. At every juncture, the party harnesses sufficiently potent resources, reinforced by violence, to suppress or eradicate the targets of revolution specific to that stage. Individuals, recognizing their insignificance and helplessness in the face of this violent system, either surrender or even participate in the purging of others, thus becoming complicit in perpetuating the system. As this process repeats, the system amasses enough power to suppress any dissent towards the leader. Faced with a choice between obedience or purges under the threat of severe penalties, people generally opt for obedience, even if it entails participating in the purging of others. This forms the equilibrium of the totalitarian system under the tyrannical incentive-compatibility condition.

Although China's imperial system was, arguably, the most centralized imperial system in human history, the modern totalitarian system is still far more centralized. In a totalitarian system, all means of production are owned by the state. The party, organized and controlled from the top down, uses ideology, personnel, and the armed forces as the basic means to take complete control of the government, the nation's politics, economy, judiciary, ideology, armed forces, and every corner of society. In terms of the economy, along with thousands of Soviet experts and numerous Soviet-assisted development projects in the 1950s, the comprehensive operation of a Soviet-style totalitarian system also entered China. In this central planning system, the central ministries ruled the entire economy from the top down, a system that Mao described as a "vertically aligned dictatorship" (*tiaotiao zhuanzheng* 条条专政).

1.6.3 Institutional Genes: Regionally Administered Totalitarianism

While the personal role of Mao was important in transforming the totalitarian system in China from a classical one to one with Chinese characteristics, a much more important factor was China's institutional genes. The most direct part of that was the local power pattern in the liberated areas before the CCP seized national power. And that in itself was a sort of extension of the institutional genes of the imperial *junxian* system. Before the CCP fully controlled China, the liberated areas were governed similarly to the imperial *junxian* system. Political and personnel matters were highly centralized, yet the regions maintained substantial self-rule in the administrative and economic spheres. The process of establishing a totalitarian system was a process of transforming China's institutional genes with external totalitarian institutional genes. However, the "vertically aligned dictatorship" model of Soviet-style totalitarianism, introduced wholesale into China in 1950, proved to be significantly incentive-incompatible with the local power base of the CCP. Both the Great Leap Forward and the Cultural Revolution, launched in 1958 and 1966, respectively, were attempts to discard this Soviet model and forge a totalitarian system that delegated more authority to regional administrations. Given that the transition towards RADT involved the reinvigoration of the imperial institutional genes inherited from the imperial era, there was a certain degree of truth to Mao's self-proclamation in 1958 as a blend of Karl Marx and Qin Shi Huang, the first emperor of China.

The launch of the Great Leap Forward as a round of institutional changes first and foremost enhanced the paramount leader's political powers, while simultaneously undermining or eliminating the already weak checks and balances that existed within the party and government. The powers of the central ministries were drastically curtailed and swathes of executive functions and resources were delegated to local governments. Newly empowered local governments were motivated to compete in loyalty to the leader, with regional competition supplanting central planning. Local governments were encouraged to experiment with new systems and strategies to expedite development towards communist totalitarianism (officially referred to as the transition to communism). Official propaganda declared that China should endeavor to be the first within the international communist movement to enter communism. The People's Commune system was an invention of local governments during experimentation, while local competition was the mechanism for the rapid promotion of this system nationwide. In the process of dismantling Soviet-style totalitarianism and instituting RADT, however, the Great Leap Forward and the People's Commune movement devastated the economy and sparked a famine on an unprecedented scale.

The Cultural Revolution, inaugurated in 1966 and spanning a decade, marked Mao's second major attempt to advance the RADT system. Facilitated by a system that encouraged regional experimentation, the CR ignited a surge of Red Guards, Revolutionary Rebels, and Power-Seizing Movements nationwide. These forces, driven by personality cults and fueled by the mandate for perpetual revolution, wrought profound changes to China's political landscape. Officials deemed inadequately loyal were brought down. All powers related to politics, personnel management, and ideology were concentrated in the hands of Mao and his associates. Central ministries and commissions were largely incapacitated and several were permanently dismantled. The administrative and economic responsibilities of the central government devolved almost completely to local authorities on a scale even surpassing that observed during the Great Leap Forward. By the early 1970s, China had morphed into an RADT economy characterized by multiple self-sustaining economies at various levels. The provinces and municipalities primarily functioned through self-sufficiency. The central party-state authority had to rely on local entities to implement its directives, thus transforming the so-called central planning into a task of coordination among local economies. Mao called this a "horizontally coordinated dictatorship" (*kuaikuai zhuanzheng* 块块专政).

In 1975, the principles and guidelines of RADT were officially incorporated into the constitution. Compared to classic totalitarianism, the primary shift this prompted was in the relationship between the central and local governments. The central–local governance structure inherent in the institutional genes of RADT is illustrated in Figure 1.2. As previously noted, in terms of the central–local relationship, RADT bears a striking resemblance to the institutional genes that governed the relationship between the imperial court and local jurisdictions under the traditional imperial system, as shown in Figure 1.4. While the disasters induced by the Great Leap Forward and the CR have been extensively studied, this book seeks to illuminate how these calamities established the groundwork for the transformations in China during the post-Mao era.

1.6.4 Changed and Unchanged Institutional Genes during the Post-Mao Reform

The chaos inflicted by the CR on the CCP party-state precipitated changes in the post-Mao era, during which the party shifted its focus from class struggle and proletarian revolution to economic growth. Following in the footsteps of the Eastern bloc, where economic reforms had been in progress for over a decade, the CCP embraced market socialism and perpetuated a groundless claim that Deng Xiaoping was the originator of market socialism.

Since the late 1960s, the Eastern bloc countries commenced a series of economic reforms to counteract their stagnating economies in order to maintain communist rule. In totalitarian regimes, however, economic resources are entirely under the control of the party-state and its bureaucratic machinery. Thus, the extent, form, and agents of change are inherently tied to the interests of the party-state bureaucrats. These bureaucrats may resist reform passively through uncoordinated collective inaction or they may even actively resist if reform threatens their vested interests. Thus, addressing their incentive problems is a prerequisite for the success of any reform and economic growth. If their incentive issues are not adequately resolved, the reform program will stagnate, regardless of the theoretical soundness of the proposed blueprint. Consequently, addressing the incentive issues for bureaucrats at all levels becomes one of the most crucial tasks in implementing reform. However, this presents a formidable challenge for any reform in a totalitarian state, including China.

The economic reforms in the FSU-EE were never able to overcome the fundamental political, ideological, and institutional shackles of totalitarianism, nor did they resolve the foundational incentive issues, leading to their failure. After more than two decades of attempted reform, the entire FSU-EE system collapsed between 1989 and 1992. In contrast, China embarked on its path of reform later than the FSU-EE countries but managed to make more significant progress in preserving the regime. The most crucial difference was that private enterprises grew from scratch to become an engine of the economy in China, driving rapid development during the reform. Along with the growth of the private sector, there was a short-lived shift from a totalitarian system to a somewhat relaxed authoritarian system. However, since 2012, the basic components of totalitarianism have been reinstated, making China's successful reform temporary and preventing it from diverging from the trajectory of the Soviet and European reforms. Chapter 13 scrutinizes the evolved and unchanged parts of China's institutional genes and their roles in driving the institutional evolution.

Two primary factors account for why China's early reforms outpaced those in the FSU-EE countries. First, during the early stages of reform, China's approach to interregional competition and experimentation, based on decentralized totalitarianism, was relatively effective in addressing incentive challenges across all levels of governance. There was a gradual shift towards the market replacing central planning, mirroring the direction of reforms in Eastern Europe.

These alterations provided local officials with justification to tolerate, and even facilitate, the emergence and growth of private firms, even though technically they were not legal. Second, in order to reverse the devastating impact of the CR, the post-Mao period saw large-scale personnel changes throughout the party-state apparatus, with bureaucrats who favored economic development replacing those who favored class struggle. These sweeping changes at the top levels reduced resistance to reform and paved the way for progress across the board.

When the Cultural Revolution ended and reforms commenced, China was among the world's poorest nations and the gap with rich nations was widening further which threatened the legitimacy of CCP rule. Under these extraordinary political and economic circumstances, the CCP pivoted towards economic development in lieu of class struggle. In the top-down regional tournaments of the RADT system, the competition target was shifted to the GDP growth rate. Motivated by the robust incentive of competition and encouraged to innovate to achieve higher growth, local governments tolerated and even fostered the private sector, facilitating substantial growth from the ground up of the private economy in many regions. A wave of private enterprises subsequently engulfed the nation, significantly reinforcing the reforms and propelling economic development. Private property rights were acknowledged and safeguarded under the constitution, while non-government organizations expanded alongside the burgeoning private sector. This evolution towards limited pluralism, encompassing the emergence of private enterprises, private property rights, non-government organizations, autonomous communities, and diverse beliefs nurtured the seeds of new institutional genes in China.[18] In certain aspects, China's governing institutions gradually transitioned from decentralized totalitarianism to decentralized authoritarianism.

RADT differs from classic totalitarianism at the operational level but fundamentally, they are both totalitarian systems. If, in the process of reform, the new institutional genes formed under the

RADT (or RDA) system prove to be robust enough and if China's communist totalitarian system undergoes sustained and gradual erosion as a result, then China might embark on a relatively smooth path of institutional transformation. However, the communist totalitarian system is not only highly alert to the risks of peaceful evolution but also deeply rooted in the RADT institutional genes. Due to the CCP's strong resistance to fundamental totalitarian institutional reform, the "reform dividend" accrued in the early stages of reform quickly evaporated, barring China from becoming an anomaly among all communist totalitarian regimes. Ultimately, China will succumb to the same pattern that doomed institutional reform attempts in the FSU-EE countries.

The crucial reality is that even during periods when the CCP tolerated limited pluralism, it consciously preserved the fundamental elements of totalitarian rule. Deng Xiaoping, the paramount leader, underscored this in his Four Cardinal Principles, repeatedly stating that the CCP must remain China's unchallenged ruling party and that the dictatorship of the proletariat must be maintained.

In practice, the party's monopoly of and dependence on the secret police and armed forces have never weakened. The party consistently seeks to control every business and organization in the country, despite the fact that private enterprises have become the backbone of the Chinese economy. It maintains control over the media, even during brief periods of a loosened monopoly and fleeting spells of pluralism.

While the CCP has somewhat relaxed its grip on ideology, allowing for a degree of divergent thought as the intensity of ideology-related persecution has lessened, its domination in the ideological sphere remains unaltered. Additionally, it maintains control over all banks and the majority of the country's financial resources. The complete state ownership of land not only remains unchanged but it has become even more crucial for the party-state's local operations.

In the following chapters, we will delve deeper into the nature of the emerging institutional genes and their relationship with

1.6 INSTITUTIONAL GENES 43

China's pre-existing institutional genes. We will also examine the CCP's monopoly of power and resources and its capacity to safeguard its own interests. By maintaining absolute control over society and relying on deeply ingrained totalitarian institutional genes, the CCP is capable of reverting to a totalitarian system, even after selectively loosening its control and encouraging a degree of limited pluralism.

In the early stages of reform, when China was not yet industrialized and still extremely impoverished, the reform was able to benefit the majority of the population. During this period, the incentive mechanism of local competition provided a strong motivation for bureaucrats, propelling economic growth and reforms closely tied to this growth, as long as these reforms did not threaten the totalitarian political-property structure. As a result of this reform, private enterprises began to emerge and grow throughout China, introducing nascent institutional genes related to private property rights, civil organizations, autonomous localities, and various beliefs.

China's situation would have been quite different if the CCP had not insisted on maintaining its totalitarian rule, which, of course, would have been incentive-incompatible with the CCP's interests. Under that scenario, during the window of opportunity when the regional competition mechanism was effective, if relevant institutional reforms had been promoted, if the rule of law had been developed in the direction an independent judiciary, if the community and grassroots self-governing organizations had been allowed to develop more freely, and if state assets had been significantly reduced, it might have been possible to fundamentally transform the role of government and allow new institutional genes to take root and flourish. Such changes could have potentially paved the way for the establishment of constitutionalism in China.

However, the CCP has been vigilant in preventing the "peaceful evolution" induced by private businesses. The period of emergence and development of new institutional genes was concentrated only in the late 1990s and early twenty-first century, when the Chinese economy was facing serious challenges. After joining the World Trade

Organization (WTO) and experiencing relatively smooth economic development, the power of the old institutional genes quickly seized the opportunity to reorganize and grow significantly once again. The phenomenon of "the state advances, the private retreats" soon became overwhelming. The power of the old institutional genes overwhelmed the budding new institutional genes. As China became a middle-income country and conflicts over land resources between the government and the public intensified,[19] the negative effects of the regional competition mechanism became more pronounced, causing the window of opportunity for using this mechanism to drive reform to be completely lost.

Just as China's reform was facing a critical juncture, the global financial crisis struck. China's institutional problems were overshadowed by the financial crisis. The government took this opportunity to implement a massive fiscal stimulus, highly dependent on the mechanism of regional competition, encouraging local governments to borrow heavily and to invest in infrastructure construction. This sparked an opportunist rush to develop high-speed rail and motorway and airport projects across the land, creating an economic "miracle" on the surface, while also sowing the seeds of deep problems, for example, the uncontrollable expansion of debt of local governments and state-owned enterprises (SOEs). The biggest problem is not the high debt itself but the expansion of a soft-budget constraint-producing institution that creates unstoppable borrowing. This institution is a common cause of the failures of economic reforms in all communist totalitarian countries.

With the underlying RADT institutions and the malfunctioning mechanism of regional competition, China's politics and governance reverted to a vicious cycle of "chaos when loosened and death when tightened" that has been repeating itself for over half a century. The operating model for local government since the beginning of the reforms has been replaced by an increasingly centralized system during the Xi Jinping era. Local governments have lost their default limited power to manage administrative, social, and economic matters, including emergencies. The central authority issues orders and evaluates and monitors the performance of local governments. However, it was precisely this type of governance mechanism, along with other factors, that led to the quagmire of the FSU-EE countries. This mechanism was at the heart of the Soviet Union's inability to solve various problems of reform, particularly those related to the economy and society.

From the outset, the ultimate aim of the CCP's reform and opening-up has been to maintain, consolidate, and strengthen the party's complete rule over Chinese society. The importance of economic growth lies in its ability to provide legitimacy for party rule; everything is done for the sake of party rule, which determines the primary character of the CCP's post-Mao reform. The so-called beginning of the reform was at the same time the end of the CR, which had lasted for ten years. The devastation caused by the CR triggered a period of active political dissent more intense than any other in the history of the PRC, with participants ranging from ordinary members of the public to top CCP leaders such as Hu Yaobang. On the one hand, it provided an impetus for the cause of the reform but, on the other hand, it also challenged the totalitarian system in various aspects, including ideology and organization.

Deng Xiaoping's Four Cardinal Principles represented the reaction to these challenges even before the reform started, the crux of which emphasized the paramount necessity of upholding the unassailable leadership of the CCP.[20] To preserve the party's dominance, Deng initiated purges within the party and stringent suppression of political dissidents. These movements included the campaigns against "spiritual pollution" and "bourgeois liberalization" in 1983 and 1985, respectively, and the brutal suppression of peaceful demonstrations in and around Tiananmen Square in 1989, leading to the imprisonment and house arrest of thousands of dissidents. Since then, all discussions of political reform have been stifled, rendering the topic forbidden. After Deng, the Four Cardinal Principles, underscoring the party's supreme role in society, gained increased prominence, superseding even the law. At the CCP's 17th National

Congress in 2007, this political legacy was formally written into the CCP's constitution. Xi Jinping has taken this still further. At the CCP's 19th National Congress in 2017, Xi officially incorporated Mao Zedong's Cultural Revolution-era principle of asserting party rule over everything under the sun ("The Party exercises overall leadership over all areas of endeavor in every part of the country") into the party's constitution. Reviving the core aspects of the old institutional genes in this way is a direct response to the challenges of the new institutional genes that emerged from China's reform.

The most significant new institutional-gene components to emerge during the first three decades of the post-Mao reform were private enterprises, non-governmental entities, and limited ideological pluralism. The launch of the reform relied heavily on a comprehensive repudiation of the CR in the ideological realm. Some reformers, both within and outside of the party, conspicuously but quietly undermined the party's absolute control over ideology and the absolute dominance of Marxism-Leninism-Mao Zedong Thought in the realm of ideas, which was previously enforced by violence. As reform progressed, social science subjects that had been officially criticized and only sporadically acknowledged within Chinese academia under labels such as "Western economics" and "Western political science" gradually became acceptable as they contain necessary knowledge for operating a market economy. University courses resumed, relevant literature was published, and the media reported on them systematically. An orderly limited pluralism of ideas emerged. But the cardinal principle or the fundamental restriction has never been relaxed: no one may challenge the dominance of the CCP and its ideology. No one may establish political parties or even political organizations.

As the purpose of the CCP's post-Mao reform was to preserve and strengthen its rule, the economic development and reform had to serve this goal without undermining the party's power. The massive erosion of the role of the state sector in the economy was an inevitable unintended consequence of the reform. Following in the footsteps of the Eastern European communist parties, the CCP began reforms after the end of the CR, focusing all attention on SOEs and issues related to incorporating the market into the planned economy. Rural land reform was driven wholly by local initiatives to resolve essential matters of survival in poverty-stricken rural areas. Under the constraints of prohibiting privatization, the SOE reform experienced a series of setbacks. By the late 1990s, the entire state sector was on the verge of crisis. The privatization of massive quantities of SOE assets at the end of the 1990s and the start of the twenty-first century catalyzed wholesale improvements in business efficiency throughout China. Yet, privatization was rebranded as "restructuring" to align with the communist ideology while concealing its essence as a shift in ownership.

At the peak of privatization, the CCP's main focus was on strengthening large SOEs to preserve and reinforce party rule, a policy known as "grasping the large and letting go of the small." The State-owned Assets Supervision and Administration Commission (SASAC) was established at that time with the same purpose in mind. The CCP leadership put forward the concept that "SOEs are the foundation of party rule,"[21] in principle linking privatization with undermining party rule. Soon, even internal policy debate on privatization became a political taboo.[22] The notion that SOEs were the foundation of party rule was enshrined in CCP regulations,[23] setting political, economic, and ideological boundaries for the reform. In due course, the consequential role this played in reversing the trajectory of reform demonstrated the enduring depth and resilience of the institutional genes established in China during the 1950s.

The deeply entrenched existing institutional genes cannot be automatically supplanted by newly emergent institutional genes, nor will they allow new variants to erode the foundations of their power. The most integral component of these traditional institutional genes is the Leninist party which exerts control over all aspects of society. The foundation of any operational totalitarian system lies in the establishment, sustenance, and development of a party capable of permeating and governing the entirety of society. Without such a party, it is impossible to establish and maintain a totalitarian system.

From the inception of the Bolshevik Party, Lenin viewed the continuous recruitment of professional revolutionaries and the establishment of new branches as vital to the party's survival. This type of work, referred to as "party construction" was later termed "party-building" within the lexicon of the CCP. This principle distinguishes Leninist parties from common political parties and was a primary cause for the schism between Lenin and the Second International. Since its establishment by the Comintern, party-building has been a fundamental principle for the CCP. After a century, it has become a firmly ingrained institutional gene of the regime in China. To most CCP members and cadres, the significance of party-building is so self-evident that the vast majority erroneously consider it a Chinese characteristic, often attributing its invention to Mao Zedong.

But this basic principle, the institutional gene of party-building, is in direct contradiction with the new institutional genes that emerged from the post-Mao reform. As private firms and non-government organizations flourished during the early twenty-first century, they accounted for the bulk of China's urban employment. However, most of these companies and organizations did not have CCP cells. Meanwhile, the development of the real estate market has led to most urban residents living in private housing. These newly developed "neighborhoods" are basically devoid of party organizations. Although party branches are still nominally active in rural areas, the large-scale migration of rural residents to cities and village elections have greatly weakened the role of the township and village party branches.

As the twenty-first century began, CCP's party-building significantly declined in terms of new member recruitment and the establishment of new branches. In the private sector, where most people worked, party branches were either missing or not actively functioning. For a period of time, the party lost its capacity to penetrate and manage every corner of Chinese society. This indicates that the nature of the Chinese system had for a time evolved from totalitarianism to authoritarianism, from RADT to RDA in particular, although unintentionally. If private enterprises were allowed to flourish, new institutional genes were permitted to grow and thrive, and old institutional genes were allowed to continue to decline, then not only might totalitarianism be completely eradicated but China could also progress from a more relaxed form of authoritarianism to constitutionalism and even a democratic system.

The declining trend in party-building has the potential to fundamentally undermine CCP rule and further weaken the old institutional genes. To preserve totalitarian institutional genes, it is necessary to reverse the trend of weakening control over society and the decline in party-building. In a bid to maintain control without hampering economic development, the CCP began experimenting with methods to transform private businesses and non-governmental organizations into entities under the party's control. Utilizing a mix of party-building and direct authority, the party aimed to modify emergent institutional genes into versions more akin to the older institutional genes, in a manner more conducive to its interests.

To promote the buyout strategy on a large scale, the CCP amended its party constitution and the state constitution in 2002 and 2004, respectively. The amendments officially recognized private property rights and introduced the "Three Represents Theory." This theory aimed to attract entrepreneurs to join the CCP and to select loyal entrepreneurs as representatives of the party and the People's Congress. Entrepreneurs who aligned themselves with the party received significant benefits and protections, including access to financial and land resources, regulatory support, market access, and law enforcement. This made entrepreneurs dependent on CCP power and obedient to CCP commands.

If the CCP had successfully controlled the majority of private enterprises and non-governmental organizations, the developments of the reform period would not have led to the emergence of new institutional genes. However, buying out the entrepreneurs proved to be extremely costly and private firms proliferated throughout the country. As private enterprises became the mainstay of the national economy and non-governmental organizations increasingly dominated grassroots society, relying on a minority to buy out the majority became unsustainable and impractical.

New institutional genes were also emerging in other fields. Parallel to the development of private enterprises and NGOs, along with the development of limited ideological pluralism, the calls to promote constitutionalism and democratic institutions have been growing since the very beginning of the reform. In order to maintain total control over society, the CCP has never abandoned the use of violence and coercion to force entrepreneurs, NGOs, and political dissidents to comply. Political dissidents and non-compliant business owners have continued to be imprisoned throughout the entire reform period. Around 2006, debates about universal values (the basic values of democracy and constitutionalism) spread among intellectuals and the upper echelons of the CCP. There were activists who put their demands into action, drafting a constitutional charter and collecting signatures to promote constitutionalism. Viewing this action as a challenge to the old institutional genes, in 2009 the authorities imprisoned Liu Xiaobo for drafting and promoting Charter 08 and kept him in prison until his death (Link and Wu, 2023).

In response to the increasing call for constitutional reform in China, soon after Liu Xiaobo was awarded the Nobel Peace Prize in early 2010, the Chairman of the Standing Committee of the National People's Congress (NPC), Wu Bangguo, declared on behalf of the CCP that the ideology of constitutionalism must be banned and the CCP must remain the leader of socialist China (Wu, 2011). Furthermore, the party sought to constrain, and even eliminate, private ownership and ideological plurality. Such shifts indicated that China's earlier reform phase, characterized by a move towards authoritarianism, had reached its limit, and that party leaders were now orchestrating a comprehensive return to totalitarian rule.

The evolution toward authoritarianism has come to an end. Xi Jinping, who took office at the end of 2012, became the prime mover behind the next dramatic shift. After taking office, Xi promptly traveled to Shenzhen to deliver a secret speech in which he attributed the collapse of the Soviet system to the lack of a "real man" who could have maintained the rule of the CPSU (Buckley, 2013). This stance overturned the CCP's previous conclusion from the 1990s that attributed the collapse of the Eastern bloc to failed reforms. It also suggested that political suppression had become a more crucial tool than economic reform for the party to retain power. A few months after Xi's address, the General Office of the party's Central Committee issued an internal directive officially prohibiting debates on seven sensitive topics: universal values, press freedom, civil society, civil rights, the party's historical missteps, the privileged bourgeoisie (*quangui zichan jieji*), and judicial independence.[24] Journalists who disclosed the directive's existence were jailed. In the spring of 2015, Wang Qishan, a member of the Politburo, clearly stated to Francis Fukuyama and Masahiko Aoki, who were then visiting China, that the party must control the judiciary and that judicial independence and rule of law were untenable in China (Tatsuhito Tokuchi, 2015).

Since 2013, Xi Jinping has launched a campaign to centralize power and suppress dissent in the name of anti-corruption. His approach has evoked memories of Mao Zedong's Four Cleanups Movement (a prelude to the CR) and Stalin's Great Purge. In association with the increasing political pressures created by this campaign, all private companies, foreign companies, and NGOs are required to establish party cells. Several attempts have been made to cultivate a Mao-style cult of personality around Xi but they have all been unsuccessful. The party has also demanded direct control over businesses, universities, and research institutes, regardless of their ownership.

It is evident that after decades of private business growth and China's integration into the global economy, new institutional genes have not only emerged but also have become a fundamental part of Chinese society. People's innate motivation to protect their own interests and the enlightenment gained from an open world have given vitality to these burgeoning new institutional genes. However, the existing institutional arrangements have ensured that the institutional genes of totalitarianism are never significantly weakened. As a result, the totalitarian party always has sufficient capacity to fully reassert itself. This is precisely what has happened in reality. Moreover, the party has been deploying cyber surveillance and artificial intelligence to control society to an unprecedented degree.

China's future hinges on the interplay between the old and new types of institutional genes. Yet, under totalitarian rule, without potent exogenous shocks that could significantly weaken the totalitarian regime, it would be challenging for the new institutional genes to survive, let alone further develop. Conversely, even if the totalitarian regime were to collapse due to external forces, without sufficient development of new institutional genes supporting constitutional rule, China would still be unable to establish a constitutional democracy.

I.7 TWO ADDITIONAL EXAMPLES OF INSTITUTIONAL GENES

The concept of institutional genes proposed in this book provides an approach to analyzing the mechanisms of institutional transformation. Fundamental institutional change is based on the evolution or mutation of a system's underlying institutional genes. Without sufficient changes in these institutional genes, even well-intentioned actors' forceful revolutions, reforms, or policies aimed at improving social welfare will fail if they are incompatible with the existing institutional genes.

Taiwan's transformation into a constitutional democracy provides a good example of how institutional genes evolve and become the basis for a successful institutional transformation. Chapter 14 will use the evolution of Taiwan's institutional genes as an example to discuss the successful transformation of democratic constitutionalism. Due to the Qing dynasty's rule of Taiwan, some of Taiwan's institutional genes were similar to those of China. However, during the Japanese colonial period, Taiwan's institutional genes had already undergone some changes. After the Kuomintang took power following the Second World War, it implemented parts of the constitution of the ROC, local elections, and land reform. Taiwan gradually developed limited pluralism in property rights, ideology, and politics. This made the new institutional genes that had already emerged during the Japanese colonial period more solidified and they were able to expand. The emergence and growth of these new institutional genes laid the foundation for the institutional transformation in the late 1980s.

Conversely, Russia's institutional transformation serves as a case in point that the direction and ultimate outcome of any institutional change fundamentally hinge on the degree to which the new institutional genes can counteract the existing societal institutional genes, irrespective of how impressive that institutional change might seem, how potent the political and ideological impetus is, or how much international support it receives.

During the late 1980s, the ideological stance of the top leaders of the Soviet Union, including Mikhail Gorbachev and Boris Yeltsin, was significantly more liberal and open compared to that of their counterparts in the CCP. Gorbachev's Perestroika was a reform to liberalize and open up, a de-Stalinization reform, and a reform that fundamentally challenged the foundations of totalitarianism. In contrast, the reforms led by the CCP's main reformists in China were designed to solidify and enhance the party's control. Moreover, Perestroika built on and extended Khrushchev's reforms of the 1950s. It was a policy choice made by the elites of the CPSU, informed by lessons from numerous failed reform attempts over several decades.

The Russian pro-democracy social elite, which included the liberal wings of the CPSU and intellectuals, had a much deeper understanding of the dark side of totalitarianism and the principles of constitutionalism than their Chinese counterparts. Their standing and political influence dismantled the totalitarian regime. However, without supporting institutional genes, constitutional rule could not be established. Due to the lack of necessary institutional genes required to establish a constitutional system, Russia ultimately descended into an authoritarian regime with some form of constitutional formalities.

The prevalence of private property rights and civil society are the most important missing pro-constitutionalism institutional genes in Russia. Without these institutional genes, it is impossible that a plurality of social forces can be formed from the bottom up. A sufficiently strong bottom-up formation of pluralistic social groups representing various social interests is the basis for guaranteeing checks and balances of power and is the foundation of constitutional government. Given that China's totalitarian system came from Soviet Russia, and China and Russia share substantial parts of their institutional genes, the lesson of the Soviet failure to establish a constitutional government after the collapse of Soviet totalitarianism cannot be overlooked by anyone who cares about China's future.

NOTES

1. The term "imperial system" (*dizhi*) used in this book follows the usage by reformers and historians in China since the early twentieth century. The concept aligns closely with the notion of an absolute monarchy in political science and historiography but the latter is not accurate for our purpose. For a more detailed explanation, see Section 1.2.
2. The term "constitutionalism" (*xianzheng* in Chinese) in this book follows the traditional usage of reformers in China since the late nineteenth century. Under constitutionalism, the power of the government is restrained by laws and institutions. The authority and legitimacy of the government are contingent upon its adherence to these limitations on its power.
3. Chapter 13 will analyze why the totalitarian institutions remain in China, even after the post-Mao reform.

4. Institutional design theory emerged in the context of the great debate among Mises, Lange, and Hayek in the 1930s and the 1940s, revolving around market socialism and the contrast between socialism and capitalism. Lange proposed the concept and theory of market socialism in the 1930s, as a response to the critique of socialism by Mises published in the 1920s, demonstrating how an economy based on state ownership can be as efficient as one based on private ownership. Hayek, on the other hand, argued that in a system of state ownership, the market lacks mechanisms to solve information and incentive problems, noting that these mechanisms only exist under a market system based on private ownership. These issues are further explored in Chapter 2.
5. A defining characteristic of authoritarianism is its tolerance, to a certain extent, of relatively independent organizations, including private companies. It also allows for a degree of limited pluralist autocracy (Linz, 2000, p. 150). This is in line with the existing literature in political science. This book, however, does not delve into the subject of multiparty authoritarianism.
6. Kenneth Pomeranz's *The Great Divergence* (2000) discusses the various developmental paths taken by different regions of the world during the Ming dynasty era. However, Pomeranz does not primarily concentrate on institutions.
7. Chapters 12 and 13 will delve into the formation and mechanism of RADT. The analyses in the existing literature of these crucial events in Chinese history tend to focus on personal factors and incidental circumstances, often neglecting institutional causes. However, to comprehend how institutions evolved during the post-Mao reform process necessitates an understanding of the institutional underpinnings of both the Cultural Revolution and the Great Leap Forward.
8. In the 1980s, leaders of the CCP Central Committee such as Deng Xiaoping, Hu Yaobang, and Zhao Ziyang broached the topic of political reform, which led to the emergence of the concept of neo-authoritarianism. However, these discussions were abruptly halted. Chapter 13 will delve more deeply into this topic.
9. This term was first used when I was analyzing China's institutions in the early reform period (Xu, 2011).
10. The principle of incentive-compatibility posits that within any institution, the behavior of individuals will align with the rules of the

institution only if the incentives and constraints established by the institution are in harmony with the self-interested motivations of these individuals. This principle assures the sustainability of an institution or the success of institutional change. We refer to an institution that satisfies the principle of incentive-compatibility as an "incentive-compatible institution." Chapter 2 provides a detailed explanation of incentive-compatibility.

11. The *junxian* system, which materialized during the centuries leading up to the Qin dynasty, enabled monarchs to control territory directly through appointed bureaucrats controlling prefectures (*jun*) and counties (*xian*) rather than by sharing control with an enfeoffed nobility. It has been the basic institution of governance in China since the Qin dynasty.

12. It is important to note that the concept of property rights applied in this book is "ultimate control rights" (Chapter 3), which implies that the emperor is the ultimate landowner as long as he maintains the final say on the land, regardless of whether the rights to use, sell, or purchase, and to dispose of the land are delegated to commoners or officials (Chapter 4).

13. The imperial system in China was dependent on a large group of local gentry, who served as informal bureaucrats to carry out government functions at the grassroots level. In total, they constituted the largest societal force outside the formal bureaucratic system and had the potential to act as a check on imperial power. However, the Chinese imperial system was deliberately designed in the following way to prevent such a development. (1) The gentry were neither a hereditary aristocracy nor a stable power base. As informal bureaucrats, they did not receive a government salary, but they were still required to pass imperial examinations and assume a recognized role within the imperial system. They did not possess inherent power, nor did they have the official status needed to safeguard their interests. (2) Their influence was confined to their immediate locality and the system prohibited them from establishing alliances across different regions.

14. To this day, long after the disintegration of the Soviet Union and the murderous brutality of the totalitarian era now well understood, most people in Russia still believe that the violence of the Bolsheviks was necessary to preserve social stability (Figes, 2017, p. xv). The resilience of that public consensus, or institutional gene, which was established

under Bolshevik rule, explains Russia's preference for an authoritarian leader like Vladimir Putin and hinders the country's full transition to constitutional government.
15. Shortly after the October Revolution, Engels' successor Karl Kautsky (Kautsky, 1920), a leader of the international communist movement at the end of the nineteenth century, wrote about the Bolsheviks as a terrorist organization and terrorist regime and as the source of the terrorism that was strongly associated with the communist movement.
16. See Maier (2004) for literature on totalitarianism as political religion.
17. The discussion here refers to totalitarian regimes established chiefly by internal forces rather than imposed by a foreign invader. In the latter case, people are simply forced to obey without establishing their own totalitarian institutions.
18. These types of institutional genes, which had tentatively existed under the Chinese imperial system and experienced a brief period of growth after the collapse of imperial rule, never fully matured to effectively counteract violence-based political forces. Consequently, they were completely wiped out in the years post-1950.
19. Since the Great Leap Forward, land in China has been state-owned, thus rendering the concept of property rights in land acquisition moot for the state. However, prior to the emergence of a land market, economic growth was not associated with large-scale land seizures by the authorities. There was no incentive for the government to forcibly demolish people's homes and occupy agricultural land on a large scale for the sake of economic growth. Consequently, land did not become a significant source of conflict between the authorities and the public during that period.
20. Deng Xiaoping, "Uphold the Four Cardinal Principles," March 30, 1979. The Principles call for upholding the following: socialism, the dictatorship of the proletariat, the leadership of the CCP, and Marxism-Leninism-Mao Zedong Thought.
21. An address by the head of the Organization Department of the CCP Central Committee in 2002.
22. For instance, an article titled "Beefing Up the State-Owned Economy, Firming Up the Foundations of Party Rule," published on January 11, 2005, in the *Southern Weekly*, considered China's most liberal newspaper, depicted SOEs as the foundation of party rule, the party's

organizational basis, and the bedrock of party support among the general populace. The article further stated that consolidating the foundations of party rule was the ultimate objective of the reforms. See: http://finance.sina.com.cn/review/20050111/19161286622.shtml.

23. Several months before Xi Jinping became the CCP's top leader, he released an essay entitled "State-Owned Enterprises Are an Essential Foundation for Party Rule," available at: www.hongqi.tv/xywch/2012-04-16/270.html. In 2019, the CCP Central Committee issued the Regulations on Grass-Roots Organizational Work in CCP State-Owned Enterprises, officially stipulating that: "state-owned enterprises are an essential material and political foundation for socialism with Chinese characteristics; they are a major pillar of, and bulwark for, the party in governing and rejuvenating China."

24. The General Office of the CCP Central Committee (2013).

2 Institutions and Institutional Genes

Methodology

This chapter provides a systematic discussion of the concept of institutional genes and other related methodological concerns. For readers with an academic interest in economics, political science, and sociology, I anticipate that this new general theoretical (or analytical) framework will facilitate a deeper understanding of why the evolutionary trajectory of institutions is confined by existing institutions. It aims to open the black box of path-dependency theory by explaining how certain key mechanisms within institutions arise and re-emerge throughout their evolution and how they impact other facets of institutions. However, I have strived to ensure that most chapters remain relatively self-contained. Hence, for readers who are less interested in methodology, skipping this chapter should not impair the basic comprehension of other chapters, albeit at the cost of understanding the underlying logic.

The methodology employed in this book for analyzing institutional evolution draws inspiration from institutional design theory or mechanism design theory. This branch of economics, although often presented in a mathematical framework, emerged from the intellectual discourse in the Lange–Hayek debate of the 1930s and 1940s regarding socialist and capitalist systems. In a broader sense, the methodology utilized in this book represents a linguistic, generalized, and nonmathematical application of the principles underlying institutional design theory. By embracing the essence of this theory as an analytical framework for organizing and examining empirical evidence, I aim to delve into the origins and development of totalitarianism, with a particular focus on China. Concurrently, I also explore the institutional conditions necessary for the establishment of constitutionalism.

In this book, the concept of institution is defined with a focus on operationalization and concrete analysis rather than attempting to provide an abstract and all-encompassing definition. Specifically, institutions are defined as the fundamental and stable mechanisms of incentives and constraints that shape the behavior of key actors in major social interactions. These mechanisms or institutions encompass various aspects such as political and economic governance structures at the national and community levels, judicial systems, and mechanisms related to the protection or violation of human rights, property rights, and political decision-making power. This definition includes both tangible and intangible elements, formal and informal mechanisms of incentives and constraints, and the influence of social consensus, religions, beliefs, and ideologies that deeply impact these incentives and constraints. By adopting this definition, the book establishes an analytical framework for understanding institutional evolution, with the institutions of the past serving as the foundation for explaining subsequent institutions.

The analysis in this book emphasizes the key actors involved in major social interactions. This approach is taken to highlight the significant events and players that drive the process of institutional evolution. By focusing on the most important actors, the analysis aims to avoid the distraction of factors that play a minor role in shaping institutions. The underlying assumption is that players in various social games, including planners, organizers, and informed individuals, as well as those who may be misled or deceived, are driven by their own interests. It is the stable and fundamental incentives and constraints that influence these players, which, in turn, determine the primary conditions for major historical developments and the direction of significant institutional evolution.

Douglass North's definition of institutions as "the rules of the game" and "humanly devised constraints that structure political, economic and social interaction" is mostly acknowledged in political economy (North, 1991). Despite being humanly devised, institutions typically emerge through gradual evolution. North's definition, though comprehensive, is somewhat abstract. The operational definitions in this book are a subset of North's definition and are more conducive to concrete analysis.

This book is particularly concerned with social consensus, which is an integral part of every institution in the world, whether economic or political, peaceful or violent, democratic or authoritarian. For example, in terms of a general perception of legitimacy and justice, institutions embody a state of equilibrium or a self-sustaining balance between the contrasting ideologies of prominent social members. It is noteworthy that today's social consensus is linked to its past counterpart and often forms the basis of future social agreements. To some extent, the social consensus of today is intricately linked to that of the past and often underpins the social consensus of the future.

Institutions have been a central theme in the study of political economy since Adam Smith. David Hume, a philosopher who had a profound influence on Smith, highlighted that social norms underpin contracts, one of the most rudimentary institutions. Hume proposed that when social norms favor contract fulfillment, individuals trust others to render a service, thereby fostering an environment conducive to honoring contracts and mutual service. He drew a parallel between the interpersonal dynamics within contractual traditions and the interrelation of blocks in a stone arch, with each element supporting the other. Contemporary economics characterizes this type of contractual tradition as a self-fulfilling equilibrium (Grief, 2006; North, 1990). The contractual institution, together with the constitutional institution that protects it, forms stable and fundamental mechanisms of incentives and constraints that affect all players in the market. The social consensus on legitimacy and rationality is the core mechanism for forming, maintaining, and operating these contractual and constitutional systems.

It is worth noting that spot markets and long-term contract markets have distinct characteristics and play different roles in economic exchange. Spot markets, which facilitate immediate transactions, have existed since ancient times and can be seen as a rudimentary form of institution. On the other hand, contractual institutions, exemplified by markets for long-term contracts, are associated with economic and social progress.

History has shown that complex contractual traditions can thrive only in societies that embrace constitutionalism. Constitutionalism requires a social consensus regarding the legitimacy and fairness of constitutional provisions. In such circumstances, the executive branch of government is constrained from interfering with the judiciary or violating private property rights, and the military remains politically neutral, subordinate to civilian politicians. This consensus has effectively prevented military coups or military involvement in politics in countries such as the United Kingdom, which has lacked a written constitution since the Glorious Revolution (1688).

However, in the absence of a constitutional consensus, establishing constitutionalism can be challenging, even after the adoption of a constitution. This leaves constitutional governments vulnerable to overthrow by military forces.

Autocracies, like constitutionalist governments, also rely on social consensus for their enduring existence. Mao Zedong's well-known declaration that "political power emerges from the barrel of a gun" advocates a model of political legitimacy underpinned by violence. However, a long-lasting autocratic regime necessitates a social consensus that endows its rule with legitimacy, extending beyond mere violence.

The precariousness of a polity exclusively reliant on violence is exemplified by the downfall of the exceptionally oppressive Qin Empire (221–206 BCE). This empire, notorious for state-sanctioned repression and torture, could not survive beyond its ruling dynasty's second generation. After the Qin Empire's demise, subsequent Chinese imperial authorities cultivated a social consensus predicated on hierarchical Confucian norms, which advocated the principle that "the ruler rules, the minister ministers, the father fathers, and the son sons." This consensus, which pervaded the empire for over two millennia, ascribed everyone a place within the societal hierarchy, from family to national level, necessitating that those at lower levels yield to the directives of those above them. Any actions contradicting this consensus faced societal opposition. Attempts to fundamentally challenge this consensus (and its corresponding institutions) began in late nineteenth-century China but have yielded limited success to date. The enduring influence of the Confucian social consensus persisted for over two millennia, shaping the understanding of societal roles and limiting attempts to fundamentally transform the existing order.

2.1 THE PRIMARY COMPONENTS OF INSTITUTIONS

The institutions examined in this book primarily revolve around government, political power, and property rights. To provide a comprehensive and insightful analysis of these institutions, it is essential to outline the fundamental components that shape their nature and the intricate relationships among them. These components include human rights, property rights, and political decision-making power. Institutions that lack substantial connections to these components are not within the focus of this book's scope. By focusing on these core elements, the book aims to provide a thorough examination of the institutions that play a vital role in shaping societies and their evolution.

The first primary institutional component we examine is human rights, encompassing the natural person and the intrinsic, fundamental rights associated with the natural person, including the right to life, liberty, and property. Unless otherwise specified, all references to human rights in this book are limited to these basic rights associated with the natural person. In any society, these fundamental human rights determine the degree of control an individual possesses over their own behavior. The extent to which a society's institutions protect human rights determines the range of choices available to each individual regarding their behavior,[1] the entities responsible for resource allocation within society, and the allocation of fundamental rights and interests for all people in that society. In autocratic regimes, the vast majority of individuals, including a significant portion of the elite, are not entirely granted the rights and the power to determine their basic affairs.

John Locke is renowned for his significant contributions to the discourse on human rights within institutional frameworks. His conception of human rights served as the ideological foundation for transformative events such as the Glorious Revolution, the drafting of the United States Constitution, and the development of modern democratic constitutionalism worldwide, including the creation of *The Universal Declaration of Human Rights* of the United Nations. The fundamental consensus that all individuals have inalienable basic rights is the central pillar of constitutionalism; and constitutionalism, in turn, is the fundamental institution for protecting human rights.[2] By contrast, in regimes violating human rights to the extreme, such as slavery in ancient times and totalitarian regimes in modern times, the concept of the natural person is not recognized in principle (China only recognized the natural person and their rights in the law of 2017 but implementation of the law remains a different matter), let alone attempts to itemize the basic rights of the natural person.

The foremost fundamental human right is the right to life, encompassing specific rights such as the right to a fair trial, freedom from torture, and freedom from any form of slavery. The second fundamental right is the right to liberty, the principal aspects of which include factors such as freedom of speech, press, belief, association, and movement.

Under totalitarian rule, virtually no individual possesses basic human rights, including the political elite, except the supreme leader. Anyone, even those occupying the highest societal echelons, can be subjected to punishment or execution for speech, press, beliefs, and unauthorized associations. There is no right to private property, freedom of movement, choice of occupation, or any right to negotiate employment contracts. Even fundamental personal rights, such as reproduction and marital choice, are subject to forcible interference. Notorious instances of political elites deprived of rights include the persecution to death of China's former president Liu Shaoqi in 1969 and the execution of the former CPSU leader Nikolai Bukharin in 1938, both of whom were denied the right to defend themselves in court.

I place property rights as the second fundamental institutional component, alongside human rights. Property rights are often discussed in both human rights discourse and legal rights discourse within the fields of jurisprudence and anthropology. In the human rights discourse, Aristotle (1988), Hayek (2007), and Friedman (1962) consider property rights to be inseparable from human freedom, while Locke (1988), under the influence of Spinoza, considers property rights to be an essential component of human rights.[3] Pertaining to legal rights discourse, Hume ([1739] 1978) and Bentham ([1795] 1914) posit that property rights rely on and coexist with the provisions of the law or political power.[4] In both discourses, property rights hold paramount significance within institutions. Property rights are not only fundamental for efficiency and economic growth (as considered in economics) but are also pivotal in defining political power and social rights (as studied in political science, law, sociology, and anthropology). When the ultimate control of property rests with the government, the system manifests state ownership; conversely, when control resides in private hands, it embodies a private ownership system.

In any society, the attribution of ultimate control of most property determines the relationship between government and citizens. Property ownership determines the allocation of political and economic power in society and, therefore, the nature of the system. Extending the arguments of Aristotle and Locke, Hayek (2007) asserts that in societies which deny individual property rights, those devoid of property rights entitlements, regardless of their nominal status, are in all fundamental respects subject only to domination and effectively become slaves.[5] The essence lies in the ultimate right of control, not nominal ownership. In societies lacking the rule of law, even where private enterprises are ostensibly permitted, a totalitarian government retains ultimate control over businesses through its direct command over the owners, as exemplified by Nazi Germany.

The third fundamental institutional component is the power structure of political decision-making. In a democratic society where private property rights are protected, the decision-making process for public and community affairs is distinct from the private property-related concerns of individuals, families, private companies, and nongovernmental organizations (NGOs). In such a society, political decision-making is based on collective control, determining how decisions regarding public matters are made and who is authorized to make such decisions.

However, in societies where private property rights are not recognized or where a small group of individuals control the majority of property rights, the distinction between private and collective and between private and public becomes blurred. Individuals who lack ownership rights lose not only their property rights but also their political decision-making power. In such societies, where citizens are deprived of the right to participate in political decisions, power is concentrated solely in the hands of the ruler. This power extends into the private sphere, encompassing decisions on all significant societal matters. In the most extreme form of autocracy, such as a totalitarian regime, political power extends to complete control over every aspect of life, including property rights. The right to participate in political decisions or the power of political decision-making has therefore been a fundamental aspect of institutions in all societies throughout history.

Political power and property rights are intrinsically intertwined and highly complementary, mirrored in the legal rights discourse on property rights. Highly centralized property rights have always corresponded to highly centralized political power, while more decentralized property rights have been associated with more decentralized political power. Substantial evidence reveals that the origins of early autocratic and democratic institutions can be traced back to prehistoric practices in the form of highly concentrated and dispersed property rights, respectively. Historical facts and institutional mechanisms suggest that universal private ownership underpins democracy, while total dispossession of private ownership forms the basis of autocracy. Several scholars (Marx, Hayek, and North, for instance) argue that property rights shape political powers. However, formal recognition of property rights relies on legal provisions and political power, suggesting from another perspective that political power dictates property rights. This viewpoint is reflected in the works of Popper, Acemoglu, and Robinson (2012), among others. The extensive history of institutional evolution shows that political power and property rights have developed in parallel, in a manner reminiscent of a chicken-and-egg conundrum rather than one preceding the other. The philosopher and jurist Jeremy Bentham (1748–1832) encapsulated this notion succinctly, "Property and law are born and must die together. Before the laws, there was no property; take away the laws, all property ceases."[6] With this in mind, the central aim of this book is to dissect those institutional conditions or mechanisms that facilitate or curb the concentration of political power and property rights.

A democratic system is a structure that safeguards individuals' rights, a system where citizens collaboratively tackle matters of collective concern under the condition that individual rights are not violated in the process. The distinction between individual rights and collective decision-making power can only be drawn when individuals possess property rights and the autonomy to manage their affairs. Therefore, universal private ownership serves as the cornerstone of democracy. In a direct democracy, all citizens participate in making collective decisions on matters of public concern, such as electing leaders, determining taxation, and deciding on issues of war and peace, through direct voting. The direct democracies of ancient Greece and contemporary Switzerland, as well as referendums in modern democracies, are examples. However, most modern democracies are indirect, where citizens elect representatives (such as parliamentarians) who subsequently make collective decisions on societal matters through voting.

In contrast to democracy, in a totalitarian system political power dominates and governs every aspect of society. The foundation of this all-encompassing political power lies in the absolute control of the totalitarian party over all societal property, including direct control over state-owned assets and indirect control of private assets through controlling their nominal owners. In such a system, obedience to the party is the only option for everyone. Additionally, every facet of personal and familial life, including occupation, income, housing, and sometimes even marriage and reproduction, is subject to the authority of the party-state. This level of control by the totalitarian regime surpasses that of Imperial China. In the traditional Chinese Empire, although there was no landed aristocracy or other elite with decision-making powers independent of the royal court, social norms still maintained a boundary between the family domain and the exercise of political power.

2.1.1 Incentive-Compatible Institutional Changes

The incentive-compatibility principle is a fundamental concept in mechanism design theory and plays a crucial role in the analysis of institutions throughout this book. It states that in any given institution with specific constraints on individuals, the behavior of those individuals would align with the institution's rules only if the incentives provided by the institution are compatible with their self-interest. An institution that satisfies this principle is considered incentive-compatible.

Incentive-compatible institutions that align with the self-interest of the influential majority tend to endure, as exemplified by the establishment of constitutionalism in Britain following the Glorious Revolution. On the other hand, regimes that rely heavily on coercion and violence, like the short-lived Qin and Sui dynasties of the Chinese Empire, tend to be incentive-incompatible with the influential majority and unsustainable.

In conventional mechanism design theory, a fundamental premise is that all participation in games or relationships among the players is voluntary, reflecting the principal conditions and liberties of a free society that respects human rights. However, the institutions examined in this book are largely autocratic and totalitarian.

Under authoritarian regimes, not only do the governed individuals face violence or threats thereof but such coercive measures are often also extended to social elites. Hence, the self-interested behavior discussed in this book does not pertain solely to voluntary actions but also includes choices made under duress when individuals are deprived of their fundamental rights and live in the shadow of violence.

The concept of incentive-compatibility encompasses the decisions that individuals make based on self-interest. These choices include not just their preferred options but also those made under coercion, such as selecting the least harmful outcome when faced with torture, forced confession, or other forms of repression.

In an autocratic system, the incentive-compatibility conditions for the ruled include the coercive conditions of the use of violence by the rulers. Therefore, we need to modify the incentive-compatibility conditions in the mechanism design theory accordingly. I refer to the incentive-compatibility conditions under threats of violence as the "tyrannical incentive-compatibility" condition.

Furthermore, in any society, each person's choices and behavior are influenced by the behavior of others, the possible behavior of others, and the social consensus (which is the basis for inferring with the behavior of others). For example, being able to rule over others may bring great benefits to the ruler, while being isolated from others may subject the isolated person to severe active or passive punishment. In brief, within the analytical framework of this book, everyone in society, from the monarch to the enslaved, from the citizen to the parliamentarian, pursues strategies that serve their best interests in the circumstances they encounter.

Analyzing autocratic regimes and the constraints they face has posed a challenge for political economists and political scientists. Oversimplifying the autocratic institution into a model where a dictator solely decides everything is of little use. In reality, even the most extreme dictator depends on others for execution and the enforcers always have their vested interests. Even under the harshest regime, repressed people still have options that align with their interests, including active or passive resistance, reluctant cooperation, or opportunism. Regardless of their ruthlessness, dictators face multiple constraints linked to the incentive-compatibility conditions of their agents and the populace they govern. So they can never freely acquire everything they desire.

A dictatorship is inextricably linked to violence. The advantage of using violence is that it allows the ruler to narrow, to their benefit, the set of strategies available to those being ruled. But violence has costs, both direct and indirect, and the latter could incite a revolt, potentially leading to even higher costs. A canny dictator, therefore, cultivates conditions of tyrannical incentive-compatibility, applying violence at a level that maximizes his gains (power or material gains) while minimizing costs and avoiding provoking rebellion.

While analyzing institutional changes, we regard a particular change as incentive-compatible if it aligns with the interests of the participants and stakeholders. The institutional changes discussed in this book encompass any modification that alters an existing system, such as revolution, reform, or restoration. The key players in any institutional change are the political coalitions or alliances comprised of individuals from various societal sections. Under an autocratic regime, these alliances are often informal. The prevailing institutions themselves impose constraints on all involved while also setting the conditions for incentive-compatibility. As an institution changes, the benefits, losses, and constraints it initially imposed on those concerned change accordingly. The extent to which these changes are incentive-compatible for the main stakeholders determines whether they support or resist the reforms. Incentive-compatible institutional changes attract broad support, enabling the advocates to achieve their objectives relatively smoothly, as in the case of American independence and the Meiji Restoration in Japan, which led to the development of different constitutional systems, respectively. Conversely, incentive-*in*compatible changes often encounter widespread passive or active resistance. Therefore, even if such institutional changes succeed temporarily on the surface, they are unlikely to achieve the ultimate goals expected by the majority of the participants, as seen in the case of the Russian Revolution of 1905 and the reforms of the late Qing dynasty in China, which failed to establish a sustainable constitutional rule.

In a system wherein property rights and political decision-making powers are dispersed among the citizens, the voters collectively dictate political power through voting. In systems where these rights and powers are intensely concentrated, a select few cliques or a small class of individuals possessing property rights monopolize political decision-making. Alternatively, the cliques or classes monopolizing political decisions control property rights and govern society. Either way, the property rights and political decision-making powers left to those being governed are exceptionally weak. In a totalitarian regime, all property rights and political powers are controlled by the totalitarian political party. It is in the primary interest of the ruler and the groups the ruler relies upon for power to keep control highly centralized. Relinquishing autocratic power or limiting autocratic power would violate the incentive-compatibility conditions of all groups supporting the autocrat. Therefore, there has never been an instance in history where autocrats voluntarily and proactively ceded power in favor of constitutional governance. Instead, the autocrat always strives to maximize his interests, employing the optimal level of violence necessary to retain control over the ruled while satisfying tyrannical incentive-compatibility conditions. Throughout history, all institutional transformations that appeared to be the result of authoritarian rulers abandoning dictatorial rule in favor of constitutional democracy actually occurred under enormous and prolonged external pressure, examples of which include the Glorious Revolution and the democratic transitions in Taiwan and South Korea.

Associated with institutional changes, the conditions for incentive-compatibility tend to be highly dynamic as the perceptions and behaviors of participants and stakeholders often fluctuate under the influence of changes affecting other participants and stakeholders. Moreover, many participants and stakeholders might struggle to discern their long-term interests and may instead opt for strategies that provide immediate gains but undermine their long-term interests. Therefore, during institutional changes, incentive-compatible conditions can be classified into those offering short-term and long-term benefits, which can frequently conflict with each other, whether deliberately designed or unintentionally occurring.

Indeed, history is filled with instances where short-term incentive-compatible conditions have spurred frenzied riots, revolutions, and other drastic institutional changes that are incompatible with the long-term interests of many participants. Leaders of uprisings or revolutions are often skilled at exploiting or cultivating conditions that align with people's short-term interests to garner widespread support. This was the case with the October Revolution in Russia (including the subsequent civil war) and both the Land Reform movement and Cultural Revolution in China. These events were shaped by leaders who managed to align the short-term interests of the masses with their own, often with profound and long-lasting implications for the societies involved.

However, regardless of how tumultuous the institutional change is, the nature and sustainability of its consequences hinge on the alignment between the resultant system and the long-term interests of the participants – that is, their incentive-compatibility conditions. Individuals who recognize that the institutional change has damaged their interests are liable to harbor resentment and spark revolt and they may seek opportunities to restore an old regime.

Anticipating this, autocratic revolutionary leaders often suppress dissenters once they have solidified their power, thereby creating new tyrannical incentive-compatibility conditions and compelling people to comply. If the tyrannical repression is unsuccessful, the institutional change, being incentive-incompatible in the long term, not only fails but when it does, the regime that replaces it is often closely related to the old one.

The Hundred Days' Reform, Gengzi Reform (庚子变法), and the Xinhai Revolution are concrete examples that will be discussed in detail in Chapter 9. These episodes vividly illustrate the consequences when short-term and long-term incentive-compatibility conditions do not align and how this dissonance can lead to cycles of revolution and counterrevolution.

2.1.2 *Analysis of Incentive-Compatible Institutional Evolution*

Observation of the long historical evolution of institutions shows that of the myriad factors that influence them, the most profound and enduring come from pre-existing institutions. In any era, the institutions of the present day are a legacy of the previous institutions, which themselves are the product of institutions in a more distant past. That is, at each historical stage, the historical factors that have the most important ongoing influence on that stage are condensed in the current system.

Institutional evolution is extraordinarily complex. To make the analysis more manageable, we concentrate on first-order important causes leading to significant outcomes – namely, the factors that have had the greatest historical impact on current societies and are manifested in existing institutions. Secondary outcomes and causes, including behaviors and factors that have left no imprint on the institutional evolution, are deliberately abstracted away. This streamlined approach allows for a clearer understanding of the major forces that have shaped institutional development over time.

As previously noted, the concept of incentive-compatible institutional change introduced in this book is inspired by mechanism design theory. Although this book does not delve into mathematical analysis, the description in this subsection corresponds to a theoretical mechanism design model for analyzing institutional changes.

Institutional changes that arise in each period are the outcomes of a game played between rulers and the ruled (in autocracies) or supporters and opponents (in democracies). The players in the model are the supporters and opponents in the game of institutional change; they all benefited from or are constrained by the existing institutions. "Supporter" and "opponent" used here are neutral and can refer to either pro-government or anti-government stances. When faced with external changes or shocks (e.g., natural, technological, and other exogenous factors), the ruler or supporter (activists in democracies, revolutionaries in autocracies) maximizes their own interests through institutional change. However, they must consider the reaction of the ruled (or opponent) to such institutional changes. In fact, the response of the ruled (or opponent) constitutes the incentive-compatibility condition for institutional change. Hence, the game of institutional change manifests as the extent to which the ruler (or supporter) can alter institutions, constrained by the incentive-compatibility conditions of the ruled (or opponent). The direction and nature of institutional changes during a specific period are the outcome of this game and the institutions of each subsequent period are the result of the actions of the players in relation to the institutions of their time. "Period" here is an abstract concept, referring to any historical period in which institutional change occurred, such as a specific constitutional reform, revolution, or dynastic transition. We can assume this game to progress through an infinite number of periods, as mathematically, it is often easier to analyze a game with an infinite number of periods than a game with a finite number of periods.[7]

When all players achieve the best possible outcomes they can obtain in the game, maintaining the result of the institutional change will be in each player's self-interest. This type of result is referred to as an "equilibrium state" (or Nash equilibrium). It is crucial to emphasize that the "best outcome" or "equilibrium" here pertains to the result attained under all constraints imposed by the institution on the parties, including the conditions of tyrannical incentive-compatibility. For instance, in an autocracy, accepting forced compliance might be the optimal outcome when the punishment for disobedience is severe, such as torture.

The term "institutional change" incorporates a broad range of activities including insurrections, rebellions, revolutions, progressions, restorations, and the rise and fall of pressure groups. The costs and benefits of the institutional change brought to participants in any given period and the extent of those costs and benefits have a cascading effect on subsequent periods. In each round of the game, decision-making relies on the main results of the previous rounds, which are already implanted in the current institution.

2.2 INSTITUTIONAL GENES IN INSTITUTIONAL EVOLUTION

Although analytically inspiring, the complexity level of the mechanism-design type of theoretical model of institutional evolution is beyond the current level of economic theory. It involves numerous heterogeneous participants and a vast number of variables, with complex and highly dynamic incentive-compatibility conditions for the participants. Finding closed-form or numerical solutions for such models, including analyzing their mathematical properties, is a formidable challenge. Empirically testing this theoretical model would require a breakthrough in processing historical archives, for example using artificial intelligence approaches.

Furthermore, this type of model is based on the assumption of perfect rationality in individuals. However, institutional evolution often involves players with bounded rationality and changes frequently occur in environments with significant time constraints, intense pressure, and a lack of essential information, all of which often make improvisational decisions inevitable (*à la* Mises).

While I believe that the analytical framework of mechanism design theory maintains validity and offers substantial value for analyzing institutional evolution, even considering bounded rationality, how to model decisions concretely under bounded rationality remains an unsolved fundamental issue in social science.

To navigate these technological hurdles and make preliminary progress in the analysis of incentive-compatible institutional evolution, this book introduces a significantly simplified analytical framework or concept: institutional genes. To a certain degree, the concept of institutional genes can be considered a reduced form derived from analyzing incentive-compatible institutional change as discussed above.

In addition to its logical linkage with mechanism design theory, the concept of institutional genes also emerges from empirical observations. Upon examining long-term institutional evolutions throughout history, many historians have noticed that certain fundamental institutional components continually recur, sometimes with variations, influencing the course of institutional change. Moreover, these institutional elements, which determine the incentive-compatibility of institutional changes for the key participants, often tend to be reproduced by the participants themselves.

We refer to these foundational, self-replicating elements in long-term institutional evolution as institutional genes. This concept provides a useful lens to understand the iterative nature of institutional change and the forces that shape its trajectory over time.

This term might seem like a metaphor borrowed from biology, employing evolution and the replication and mutation of genes within organisms to illustrate the process of institutional change. While this way of understanding institutional genes is beneficial, the concept of institutional genes introduced in this book extends far beyond being merely a metaphor; it serves as a substantial analytical concept. As noted earlier, this concept emerges from systematic observation of institutional evolution and from analyzing incentive-compatible institutional changes. Hence, it is a practical and operational analytical concept. Theoretically, the concept is a reduced form derived from mechanism design theory as applied to incentive-compatible institutional change. So, the concept encapsulates key elements of highly complex institutional change in a greatly simplified fashion. This approach enables us to focus on fundamental mechanisms that repeat throughout history, playing a primary role in institutional change and being compatible with participant incentives. Empirically, institutional genes are recurring fundamental phenomena that can be observed, with many already recognized by historians. Evidently, repetition and replication, as used here, do not imply a duplication of every detail. Actually, the mutation and evolution of institutional genes form a principal aspect of our analysis.

2.2.1 Basic Characteristics of Institutional Genes

The so-called institutional genes are some of the basic institutional components that have constantly been self-replicated in determining the basic characteristics of institutions over a long period of institutional evolution. The self-replication of institutional genes is caused by their influence on the incentive-compatible conditions of the main participants in institutional evolution. In the process of institutional evolution, participants choose to reproduce the institutional components that are favorable to them out of their self-interest, resulting in "self-replication." These self-replicating institutional elements, in turn, tend to affect the incentive-compatible conditions for future institutional changes in the next round of institutional evolution. They are then replicated again under similar mechanisms and so on, repeating the cycle indefinitely.

Institutional genes have three elementary characteristics that are intrinsically complementary and indispensable to one another. They are: (1) repetitiveness, (2) incentive-compatibleness, and (3) stemness. These attributes are crucial for comprehending incentive-compatible institutional evolution and empirically identifying institutional genes.

Repetitiveness refers to the recurrence of basic institutional structures over time. It is important to note that repetitiveness here implies the reiteration of essential features rather than mechanistic replication of every detail. For instance, China's top-down bureaucratic governance, that is to say, the so-called *junxian* (郡县) system or prefecture-county system, despite undergoing significant modifications since its establishment under the Qin dynasty, has maintained its basic structure until today, even outliving the empire itself. Consequently, we identify the *junxian* system as one of the institutional genes of Chinese imperial rule (Chapter 4). Conversely, the Chancellorship system, practiced under several of China's dynasties, was not perpetuated because it was not incentive-compatible for the emperor and is thus not considered an institutional gene of China (Chapter 4).

The second fundamental characteristic of institutional genes is their incentive-compatibility; that is, the recurring structural components we identify as institutional genes must be intimately related to the incentives for participants. To a large extent, this is the mechanism for the functioning of institutional genes. The reason these recurring components are replicated is that participants choose them in pursuit of their own interests. Incentives could include opportunities for material gain, social status, and spiritual or ideological benefits.

For instance, the imperial examination system and Confucianism have not only been replicated from generation to generation for millennia but are also directly linked to the interests of the rulers and intellectuals in the Chinese Empire. Therefore, it is a fundamental institutional gene of China's institutional change which will be explored in detail in Chapter 5.

The third characteristic of institutional genes is stemness. Institutional genes are foundational for a spectrum of institutions, encompassing the basic institutional structure as well as the social consensus, such as the beliefs and ideologies that influence the consensus on the legitimacy of the authority.

For example, Russian Orthodoxy was one of the fundamental institutional genes that gave birth to Bolshevism (to be discussed in Chapters 7 and 8). Buddhism, on the other hand, despite its long history in China, does not have a foundational impact on the structure and functioning of a society's institutions in China analyzed in this book and is therefore not identified as a Chinese institutional gene.

Specific institutional genes embodying the above three attributes could encompass fundamental institutional structures directly affecting participants' status and material interests, such as basic bureaucratic structures and specific property rights arrangements, political parties, guilds, associations, clubs, NGOs, and so on. These could also include institutions of organized faith such as religion and the Church and a range of popularly held ideas, cultures, beliefs, and ideologies such as freedom, equality, justice, legitimacy, revolution, fraternity, nationalism, race, class, enemy, emperor, royalty, aristocracy, individualism, and collectivism, among others, due to their impact on social consensus.

The rationale for including social consensus as part of institutional genes is that consensus significantly influences political power structures and property rights. On the one hand, shifts in social consensus can instigate changes in power structures and property rights. On the other hand, these structures themselves impact social consensus, which could have long-term effects.

In autocracies, rulers consciously manipulate ideological control to master social consensus, aiming to maintain monopolistic structures of political power and property rights. Simultaneously, social consensus evolves with institutions, reproducing itself as it gets passed on from generation to generation.

Social consensus in a society complements the power–property structure of that society and they mutually reinforce each other. This is exemplified by the role of human rights in society. On the one hand, a consensus on human rights can only arise in institutions where a significant number of individuals already possess property rights and some political powers, that is to say, the structure of political powers and property rights are dispersed. On the other hand, the protection of human rights can only be established where there is already a consensus on the value and importance of human rights.

When a substantial portion of society has private property rights and some political powers, a consensus emerges among these people to protect their own and others' fundamental rights. Those who benefit from such an institution actively advocate for the protection of other people's human rights, thus nurturing the institutional gene of human rights in society.

As human rights become established as a social consensus, as an institutional gene, individuals with certain rights push for institutions to adopt stronger human rights protections. They aim to extend these protections to a wider range of functions (from property rights to freedoms in more areas) and to include more individuals (from rights that benefit many to universal rights). They do this in pursuit of their own self-interest, as well as in the interest of broader societal equity and justice.

The same logic applies to institutions that violate or do not recognize human rights. In absolutist regimes, such as the Chinese imperial system, all individuals, including the social elite, are subject to the rule of the emperor and his court. Everyone relies on the emperor's beneficence for their rights, survival, and well-being. The legitimacy of such a system is rooted in a social consensus that the sovereign embodies the state and that families and individuals owe their existence to the state. This implies that everyone depends on the benevolence of the sovereign and their interests align with those of the state.

This consensus breeds loyalty to the sovereign, which is transmitted as an institutional gene through the generations, preserving the supremacy of the ruler or the state. This institutional gene not only perpetuates autocratic systems but also tends to resist the emergence of new institutional components that challenge absolutism.

An awareness of human rights cannot flourish in a system where people lack fundamental rights and are powerless to instigate change. Even if the concept of human rights is introduced externally, the rulers and the absolutist institution will vehemently oppose it, employing measures such as ideological taboos because it undermines the legitimacy of autocratic rule. Moreover, under autocratic governance, the principle of human rights is often dismissed and efforts to safeguard these rights are rebuffed by the populace because the concept conflicts with the prevailing consensus on the supremacy of the ruler or state.

When the populace at large has never had any fundamental rights considered inviolable, individuals who have been intimidated and indoctrinated into accepting the supremacy of the sovereign or state are conditioned to conflate their individual rights with state interests. Consequently, they are not only likely to reject the concept of human rights but also to view the protection of human rights as a threat to the state, the sovereign, and their own interests. People in such circumstances demonstrate hostility towards actions and reforms supporting human rights. This consensus is passed down to future generations, giving rise to an institutional gene that opposes human rights. A case in point is that public opinion polls conducted in China over decades reveal that individuals whose basic rights are most violated are often the ones who most strongly resist the notion of protecting human rights.

Major institutional changes throughout human history are typically triggered by exogenous factors or forces, which are associated with significant changes or shocks in the external environment. If we concentrate solely on these exogenous shocks, history may seem like a series of incidental events. For instance, without the First World War and the clandestine return of Lenin to Russia facilitated by the German government, the Russian October Revolution, which established the Bolshevik regime, might never have occurred (see Chapter 8). Similarly, without the Xinhai Revolution initiated by Sun Yat-sen using overseas forces, the Gengzi New Deal might have led to a constitutional monarchy or even transitioned from nominal constitutionalism to more substantive constitutionalism (see Chapter 9). Furthermore, absent the Japanese invasion and the Xi'an Incident, the destiny of the Chinese Communist Party and its Red Army might have been drastically different.

However, changes spurred by external forces can set off developments in countless directions, whereas the course along which the institution ultimately evolves, grows, and sustains itself, among the myriad of possible directions, is significantly shaped by enduring domestic institutional genes. These institutional genes outline the state of the internal forces and the range of choices available to them.

The impact of multiple external forces, which could be in opposite directions, depends on the choices made by major local players based on their own interests. External forces that can be easily integrated with local institutional genes will more effectively change the local system due to these choices. In contrast, external forces that are hostile to local institutional genes tend to face resistance because they conflict with the interests of most local participants. Likewise, a specific array of external shocks can have remarkably diverse effects on different institutions, contingent upon how their institutional genes interact with these external forces. Consequently, pinpointing the pertinent institutional genes and discerning their characteristics is crucial to comprehending how an institution might react to external disruptions and to understanding the dynamics and boundaries of such changes. Hence, an understanding of institutional genes helps us explain the trajectories of past institutional change and anticipate possible trajectories of institutional change in the future.

The formation and evolution of institutional genes are not deterministic, nor are they within the domain of deliberate design or control, whether in a democracy or an autocracy. Neither voters nor dictators can exercise absolute control over the evolution of institutional genes. For instance, Christianity, which has long been a foundational institutional gene in the West, originated as a minority Jewish faith and initially faced challenges to its survival. At that point, it evolved into an institutional gene of certain societal strata. After the Roman Empire established Christianity as the state religion in the early fourth century, Christianity and the Church evolved into fundamental institutions of Western society and gradually became the institutional genes that shaped the West.

In fact, not only was the contribution of Constantine the Great, the Roman emperor at the time, limited in the establishment of these institutional genes but Constantine himself was deeply influenced by the evolving Christianity. By Constantine's time, Christianity had already amassed a substantial following and had begun to evolve from a humble grassroots faith into a popular religion with significant political, economic, and even military influence. This rise was intrinsically linked to the spontaneous spread of Christianity around the Mediterranean in the three centuries before Constantine's reign. It was this "external" factor that transformed Christianity from being persecuted by the Roman Empire to becoming the state religion of the Roman Empire under Constantine the Great.

Similarly, the imperial examination system and Confucianism as institutional genes were not created by any individual. Chapter 5 will analyze how Confucianism endured a similar transformation from being persecuted to becoming a state religion and gradually developed into an institutional gene of the Chinese imperial system.

Institutional genes are not exclusively determined by endogenous factors. While institutional genes are relatively stable, external pressures can significantly influence their evolution and prompt substantial changes over a relatively brief period. Crucially, pre-existing institutional genes deeply influence the incentive-compatibility conditions of the primary participants, thereby determining the effect of external forces as well as the pace and direction of subsequent evolution. An institution, as defined broadly in this book, encompasses all elements that profoundly affect incentives and constraints, including related factors such as religion, belief, and ideology, among others. Historically, these elements have demonstrated substantial fluidity and a transnational nature. The most prevalent systems of faith and ideology in China – excluding Confucianism and Taoism – were imported from abroad. It is even more so the case in Russia. However, not all beliefs originating from abroad will proliferate to the same extent in any given country. Endogenous institutional genes play a critical role in determining which external influences are to be assimilated and which are not. When absorbed, these external influences tend to be localized in various forms, the nature of which is intimately linked with pre-existing institutional genes.

In the subsequent chapters, we use the cases of China and Russia to analyze how external influences interact with existing institutional genes and how these can be absorbed or modified and become quasi-indigenous when they benefit the major players. Conversely, we will examine how external influences are rejected when they prove detrimental to the major players and how they are accommodated in a distorted form to meet the needs of these players when complete rejection is not feasible. This includes the fate of democratic constitutionalism and Marxism in Russia and China, respectively, along with the origins of Leninism and Maoism, which ultimately evolved into significant institutional genes in the USSR and China, respectively.

The institutional genes discussed in this book focus on fundamental structures of political power and property rights, along with the associated social consensus, which dictate the trajectory of institutional evolution in general. The types of institutions to be focused on are constitutionalism and its opposite, totalitarianism. By nature, constitutionalism employs institutional mechanisms to restrain the most potent societal elements and preclude any individual or organization from monopolizing power. Therefore, the most powerful often oppose moves towards constitutionalism. However, in societies where power and rights are already relatively dispersed, the transition to constitutionalism aligns with the incentives of individuals possessing political power and property rights. The dispersed structure of power and property rights in such a society fuels the demand for incentive-compatible institutional shifts towards constitutionalism.

This book focuses on the analysis of autocratic institutions: the first, most persistent, and pervasive institutions in human history. Despite their extensive history and diversity, autocracies share a common feature: they are headed by rulers who utilize violence – often in the name of the state or God – to maintain a monopoly over political power and property rights. In an autocracy, the prevailing social consensus often includes ideologies that advocate for the supremacy of the monarch or state. The institutional genes of autocracies invariably consist of highly monopolized political power and property rights, reinforced by social consensus.

The reason that individuals living under autocratic rule generally accept such beliefs, thereby fostering a social consensus that seems counter to their interests, lies in their exposure to generational violence and indoctrination. In societies with deep-seated autocratic institutional genes, even if the number of people pursuing constitutionalism increases due to external influences, the political and economic power of those who seek constitutional reform remains weak due to the highly concentrated power and property rights.

Promoting constitutional reform in an autocratic society invariably poses significant challenges as the forces propelling reform are often weak and there is a widespread social consensus in favor of autocratic governance. These combined factors often make peaceful constitutional reform incompatible with the incentives of autocratic rulers and their followers. Consequently, a violent uprising or revolution may seem more attractive to a large segment of the rebelling population for whom non-peaceful actions may be perceived as incentive-compatible in the short term.

However, violent revolution often results in the creation of a new system that is genetically similar to the old one. First, leaders of rebellions or revolutions find it convenient to construct autocratic institutions under the guise of revolutionary change, leveraging the existing consensus that favors autocratic rule. Second, the overwhelming monopoly on political power and property rights in society has fostered a belief that violence is the only way to bring about change, or at least the most direct way. Third, even if the revolutionary elites genuinely aspire to establish a constitutional democracy, the collective relinquishment of power after a violent takeover becomes incentive-incompatible for them because the very act of violent revolution relies on highly centralized power structures and the stakes of keeping the power are too high.

2.2.2 Institutional Genes, Path Dependence, and Institutional Design Theory

The concept and analytical approach of institutional genes and incentive-compatible institutional change developed in this book are partly influenced by Douglass North's path-dependency theory.

North's theory has had a profound impact on the analysis of institutional evolution, with more recent proponents including Acemoglu and Robinson (2012). The theory argues that past institutional choices have a deep impact on today's possible institutional choices, as the path of institutional evolution is closely tied to history. This is because institutions evolve in the direction they are already heading, driven by self-reinforcing mechanisms and increasing returns. Mechanisms that once shaped an institution also set its future course.[8] As a result, historical institutional evolution often manifests as a path of virtuous cycles and traps of vicious cycles. North's account helps explain why institutions continue to improve in some countries while spiraling down in others. However, it is less powerful at explaining delicate cases like the transformations in South Korea and Taiwan, where they seemed to have transitioned into new territories beyond their historical paths.

The most noticeable example of the virtuous circle described by North is that of the Glorious Revolution and Industrial Revolution in Britain. North sees the Glorious Revolution as the event that pushed Britain onto the path of a virtuous cycle, which was subsequently followed by the United States. While discussions of vicious circles most often refer to African and Latin American countries, there is little in-depth analysis of the systems in China, Russia, and Japan from the perspective of path dependency and virtually no discussion of totalitarian institutions.

Methodologically speaking, when discussing technological- and market-related issues like the internet, industry standards, and industrial clusters, the increasing returns hypothesis can be a useful explanation for path-dependence phenomena. However, when applied to institutional matters related to incentives, this hypothesis often becomes less relevant. In contrast, the concept of "institutional genes" in this book places greater emphasis on specific incentive mechanisms associated with institutions, which, in turn, influence institutional changes.

Using the concepts of institutional genes and incentive-compatible institutional change as analytical tools, we scrutinize the interests of participants and other stakeholders involved in institutional change. This method will explain how historical and current institutions shape the trajectory of future institutional changes, effectively opening the "black box" associated with path-dependency theory. The increasing returns of a certain institutional evolution path may occur because a certain institutional change aligns with the interests of more people within such a system. The underlying reason may be connected to existing incentive mechanisms or consensus among people within the institution, with deviations from this consensus being punished. Inherited institutional genes influence today's conditions for incentive-compatibility, leading to the reproduction of past institutional genes through today's institutional change. Current institutional genes, in turn, affect future conditions for incentive-compatible institutional change, thus influencing future institutional genes. The increasing returns mechanism in path-dependency theory may be a special case of certain institutional genes' self-replication but institutional genes do not necessarily involve increasing returns.

The concept of institutional genes and the analytical approach to incentive-compatible institutional change are intrinsically linked to mechanism design theory, which has its roots in the Lange–Hayek debate on socialism versus capitalism. Since the late 1970s, mechanism design theory has evolved into a significant branch of theoretical economics, focusing on analyzing incentives within institutions (Hurwicz, 2008; Maskin, 2008; Myerson, 2008). Furthermore, it offers a method for the empirical analysis of institutions and guides the practical design or reform of these structures. A cornerstone of institutional design theory is incentive-compatibility. This principle posits that for any effectively designed rule to be viable in practice, it must align with the incentives of those it affects. Within this theoretical paradigm, the modern theory of property rights has been expanded, elucidating why control over property – or property rights – stands as a pivotal institution in addressing paramount incentive issues (Hart, 1995; 2017). Likewise, operating within this same framework and transcending Hayek's philosophical deductions, there have been pivotal theoretical and empirical advancements concerning dynamic incentive issues in economies marked by state ownership. A prime example of such a finding is the realization that the "soft budget constraint" (SBC) syndrome is an inevitable drawback in "socialist economies" (Kornai, 1980; Dewatripont and Maskin, 1995; Kornai et al., 2003).

However, since the 1930s, debates on state versus private ownership and planned versus market economies have largely sidestepped the subjects of political power and the prerequisites for institutional transformation. Instead, they have narrowly concentrated on the resulting resource allocations from various property rights arrangements and economic coordination mechanisms. While Hayek later rightly argued that abolishing private property rights leads to serfdom, the conditions that pave the way to either serfdom or constitutionalism have not been adequately emphasized as central to this debate.

Building on a rich array of empirical observations and the latest theoretical advancements, this book aims to broaden this seminal debate that began in the 1930s. Approaching from a positive analysis standpoint, I aspire for the concept of institutional genes to enhance our comprehension of the origins and evolution of totalitarian regimes, the conditions fostering constitutional regimes, and the intricate dynamics of institutional change at large.

For instance, after the fall of communist totalitarianism in Eastern Europe and the Soviet Union, why did the transitions differ so dramatically across nations, with some moving towards constitutional democracy and others, like Russia, veering towards authoritarianism? To address this issue, in addition to the institutional genes left by communist totalitarianism, how did the institutional genes of the Russian Empire, the Ottoman Empire, and the Austro-Hungarian Empire influence the diverse transition pathways of different countries?

In another context, the United States successfully aided Japan in founding and solidifying a constitutional democracy after the Second World War. Yet it faced persistent failures in its attempts to install such a system in Iraq after the Iraq War (2003–2011). Why? Delving into the institutional genes of these countries might unlock answers to these compelling questions. What role did Japan's historical remnants of the feudal system and the Meiji Restoration play? Similarly, in Iraq's case, how did institutional genes implanted by the Ottoman Empire and those stemming from the broader Arab world and Islamic faith shape its institutional evolution?

From a normative analytical perspective, this book posits that institutional genes establish the foundational conditions impacting the success or failure of institutional or policy reforms. The inherent constraints imposed by institutional genes cannot be overlooked in the design of institutional reforms and policies. Overlooking them could result in reforms that, regardless of their impeccable logic, may either fail in execution, remain superficial, or even become a source of upheaval.

By shedding light on the significant impacts of institutional genes on existing institutions and institutional changes, I hope this book can contribute to the creation of concrete and practical policy principles for institutional and policy reforms.

NOTES

1. In economics textbooks, the range of choices for individual behavior, that is to say, the feasible set of behaviors, is often treated as exogenous. In this book, the factors that limit the range of choices for each individual in society are institutionally determined, not exogenous.
2. It is worth mentioning that human rights are rarely highlighted in the literature on economics, political economy, and even institutional economics, and that most economic theories treat the rule of law that protects human rights as a given arrangement. Human rights protections, as an external condition, are therefore excluded from the discussion. Part of the reason is that these disciplines originated primarily in the Anglo-American sphere and, from Adam Smith onwards, have focused mostly on contemporary market economies and modern history, fields in which basic human rights were already well established. The protection of human rights was therefore not a primary concern for scholars.

3. Locke was deeply influenced by Baruch Spinoza (1632–1677), so much so that Klever (1990) regards Locke's ideas as disguised Spinozism. In Spinoza's view, it is self-evident that property is a fundamental right of human beings (Matheron, 2020).
4. See "Property as a Legal Right" by Peter Garnsey, in Garnsey (2009, chapter 7).
5. The qualitative difference between the institutions of what Marx and Lenin called "socialism" and "capitalism" is defined directly on the basis of property rights. Many other important economists from the nineteenth century to the present, including Mises, Lange, Hayek, Kornai, and so on, have also defined the institutions of socialism and capitalism in this way. By this definition, all the welfare state institutions of Northern and Western Europe are capitalist, although they occasionally call themselves socialist.
6. *Principles of the Civil Code* in Bentham (1843, p. 309).
7. If we regard the institutions of each period as the state of the system, we can express institutional changes over a long historical horizon as a Markov Perfect Equilibrium model (Maskin and Tirole, 2001). In this model with an infinite number of periods, the Markov Strategy for each period includes only institutions of the previous period, along with behaviors affecting current institutions. The institutions of each period are therefore the joint product of historical institutional legacy and current behavior.
8. Besides North, another scholar who explains the path dependence of institutions based on the increasing returns perspective is the political scientist Peirson (2000).

3 Property Rights as a Form of Institutional Gene

This chapter begins the analysis of institutional genes by focusing on property rights institutions for several reasons. First, as an institutional gene, the property rights institution significantly determines the nature of the social, economic, and political systems. It essentially lays the groundwork for the functioning of societies and shapes the dynamics of their interactions. Second, the logic underpinning the evolution of institutions through changes in the property rights institution is relatively simple and clear. By focusing on property rights, we can trace a clear line of cause and effect through the development of institutions. Third, this logic is well supported by historical and archaeological evidence. Ancient Greece and Rome, for example, where private property rights were widespread, were pioneers in developing laws and institutions for safeguarding these rights. This led to them being recognized as the cradles of the rule of law, constitutional governance, and democracy as their institutional evolution was built on this foundation.

Additionally, extensive historical records show that in all countries with well-established constitutional and democratic systems, institutional development has always been supported by relatively dispersed private property rights. On the other hand, in almost all regions where property rights, especially land rights, were concentrated in the hands of a monarch or a small group of oligarchs in antiquity, there has been strong resistance to transitions towards constitutional democracy in the modern era. Ancient Iran, Egypt, and China serve as good examples of this latter trend.

The structure of property rights, be they widely distributed as private property rights or highly centralized, directly determines the foundational rights and powers of property owners. Therefore, ever since the creation of basic property rights, property owners have sought to defend and strengthen their vested interests throughout the process of institutional evolution.

In societies where extensive private property rights were established at the dawn of civilization, the collective influence of numerous such rights holders guides institutions to evolve in a manner that protects other owners like themselves. This process transforms the institution of private property rights into an institutional gene, which then persists throughout many centuries of subsequent institutional evolution.[1]

Based on archaeological evidence, this chapter discusses how widespread private property rights became the primary mechanism and driving force for the formation and development of "derivative" institutions for protecting private property rights, including the rule of law, constitutionalism, and democracy. Moreover, these derivative institutions become institutional genes self-replicating continuously because they bear on the interests of the many property owners. Thus, in countries with extensive private property rights, it is more feasible for the rule of law, constitutionalism, and democracy to become self-replicating institutional genes as the system evolves. Institutional evolution itself is, of course, a complex process that is neither seamless nor unidirectional.

Chapter 4 presents the contrasting case of China, where property rights are strictly monopolized and centralized. This situation requires the use of force to maintain. If property rights are highly centralized at the early stages of civilization, the monarch or oligarchs who control these rights will naturally aim to protect their privileges through monopolistic power backed by coercion.

Over time, rebels or conquerors who overthrow the monarch often need to establish and maintain their own monopolistic power through similarly violent means. This process turns the institution of highly centralized property rights into a self-replicating institutional gene, often sparking intense internal conflicts and warfare among monopolists. It also gives rise to institutions designed to protect monopoly powers. Some of these institutions then self-replicate and evolve into institutional genes, often at the expense of individual freedoms and rights.

Today's constitutionalism and rule of law can be traced back to the institutions and legal systems of ancient Greece and Rome. To comprehend the relationship between private property rights and constitutional governance, it is essential to understand the origins of these legal systems. The earliest corpus of law that emerged in ancient Greece and Rome, where property rights were broadly dispersed, was private law. Private law governs property and personal relationships between individuals, particularly focusing on the rights and duties of individuals. The largest part of private law deals with property rights and the issues emanating from them, such as contracts, torts, private associations, and corporations.

In ancient Greece and Rome, public power, and the public law that regulated it, was based on private law and developed after it. Public power emerged through the empowerment of individuals as agents to carry out the functions of the state. Public power, as it was called, arose through the empowerment of individuals to make them agents for carrying out the functions of the state. The most crucial component of public law is the constitution, the major purpose of which is to guarantee the fundamental rights of citizens, to protect private property rights, and to ensure implementation of the provisions of private law.

In stark contrast, since the creation of the Chinese Empire, the imperial power held ultimate control over all the lands of the empire. This fundamental principle remained in the Chinese Empire. Such a feature of the imperial system, that is to say, its institutional gene for property rights, initially served to eliminate the existing aristocracy and feudal system and subsequently prevented the emergence of a new aristocracy, ensuring the empire's unrivaled endurance. With a guaranteed monopoly on power, the empire, in its more matured later periods, was able to partially privatize land-usage rights and allow them to be traded on the open market for efficiency gains. But the supremacy of imperial power over market transactions and the interests of the people never changed under the Chinese imperial system.

The nature of land rights in the Chinese Empire has been discussed in depth by Western scholars since the eighteenth century. Up until the mid-twentieth century, these scholars commonly viewed the imperial monopoly of land rights in the empire as a fundamental feature differentiating China's imperial system from the Western system. However, in recent decades, due to shifting perceptions of property rights (although many scholars might not be necessarily aware of these changes in the legal or economics literature and, merely adhere to the prevailing understanding), some scholars have redirected their focus. Instead of concentrating on the ultimate control rights of land, which are tightly connected with political power, these scholars have singled out partially privatized land-usage rights and their market transactions. Consequently, they interpret China's imperial land system as one dominated by private land ownership. The implications of this divergent interpretation, resulting from varying conceptual understandings, are extended far beyond the realm of property rights, encompassing a fundamental understanding of China's institutions. In order to clarify these most fundamental issues, this chapter begins with a discussion of the basic concept of property rights.

3.1 ULTIMATE CONTROL RIGHTS VERSUS THE BUNDLE OF RIGHTS: DIFFERING CONCEPTS OF PROPERTY RIGHTS

The concept of property rights in this book refers to the ultimate control that an owner has over his or her property. This concept originated in ancient Greece and is the first known concept of property rights in human history. It is based on the belief that individuals have fundamental rights, including the right to control their property. This particular concept of property rights has had the most profound influence on institutional evolution. Regardless of their value judgments, whether it is Locke and Hayek, who advocated for the protection of property rights, or Marx, Lenin, and Mao, who were against it, they all agreed on one thing: property rights are about control rights over property.

However, the concept of property rights is not universally agreed upon among contemporary economists and legal scholars. In the fields of economics and law, there are three general notions of property rights: control (or residual control) rights, the bundle of rights, and possession and disposal rights. The last concept is often used in mainland China, which is why it is being mentioned here. However, it is not particularly influential in academic circles due to its rather elementary nature. It covers only a few bundles of rights and overlooks many more important ones. As such, it will not be extensively discussed in the subsequent parts of this work.

In a modern society, where contracts are well developed and multiple rights to each asset can be transferred and re-transferred separately or jointly through contracts, contemporary property rights theory contends that the major difference between property rights and other contracts lies in residual control rights. If a contract is seen as a transfer of control over an asset, then residual control refers to remaining control that is not included in the contract. For example, in the event of contingencies not covered by the contract, only the owner of the asset, that is to say, the holder of residual control rights, has the authority to determine the disposal of the asset (Hart, 1995; 2017). All rights that can be explicitly stipulated in a contract can be transferred and traded in the market; yet, regardless of how these rights are contractually ceded, residual rights not included in the contract remain with the owner as long as the ownership is not transferred. In other words, ownership defines the ultimate control over an asset. All rights other than the right of ultimate control are derived rights.

According to this concept, the attribution of ultimate control rights determines the nature of ownership. If the ultimate control rights are vested in the government, it constitutes state ownership; if they reside in private entities, it is considered private ownership. In any society, whoever ultimately owns most of the social assets largely determines the relationship between government and citizens, that is, whether the government rules the citizens or the citizens determine the government.

Modern property rights theory focusing on control rights is influenced by John Locke, who argued that private property is a fundamental right inherent in life so that people are born with the right to control their property. The power of the government is derived from citizens consciously relinquishing a segment of their own rights, thereby empowering the government to safeguard their lives and property from violation. This idea underpinned the Declaration of Rights drafted by Locke, a seminal document pivotal in establishing constitutional governance in Britain during the Glorious Revolution. The United States Bill of Rights (part of the US Constitution) and the French Revolution's Declaration of the Rights of Man and of the Citizen were both deeply influenced by Locke's thoughts on human rights and property rights.

More than 200 years after Locke, Hayek's idea that those deprived of property rights would become enslaved also originated from the concept of property control rights. Marx, in contrast to Locke, contended against private property but nevertheless concurred with Locke (and arguably sourced from Locke) the fundamental principle of property rights – that is, ownership equates to the right to control the property. Control-rights-based property rights arose several centuries BCE in ancient Greece and stemmed from social practices connected with the region's already extensive private property rights. The Stoic philosophers of the time refined these practices into fundamental concepts, holding that every individual per se is the rightful owner of their own person and private property (Long, 1997, p. 15). Stoic thinking and England's long-standing and secure private property rights together formed the foundation for Locke's ideas. In ancient Rome, the notion of the individual's fundamental right of control over their property became part of the tradition of Roman law. This concept of property rights is as essential for a market economy as air and water are for life.

However, in societies where a highly centralized system has been established since ancient times and where the ruler maintains ultimate control over all lands within the respective jurisdiction, the situation is markedly different. Land-usage rights are granted at the discretion of the ruler and can be revoked at any given moment. Therefore, in such societies, there is neither a notion of individual property rights nor an acknowledgment that a person's property rights should not be violated by either the emperor or the state. The Chinese Empire serves as a prime example of these kinds of societies.

In recent decades, the concept of the "bundle of rights" has become particularly popular in academia.[2] Under this concept, property rights are seen as a collection of rights, such as the right to possess, the right to use, the right to income, the right to dispose of (to trade, bequeath, and gift), and so on, and all rights to exercise the above rights. Compared with the traditional control-rights-based theory of property rights, this "bundle of rights" view outlines rights operationally, applying specific rights under particular conditions.

Compared with classic control-rights-based property rights theory, the bundle of rights perspective delineates rights operationally, with specific rights applied under specific conditions. This operational approach has laid the foundation for certain theoretical advances, such as defining the boundaries of property rights, which is the starting point for the Coase theorem.[3] The so-called boundaries here define the specific contents of a bundle of rights and the specific aspects of property rights that can be traded.

The concept of a bundle of rights can be helpful when the issue of control is not prominent in society. However, it is important to realize that even under constitutional government, where private property rights are adequately protected, the various rights contained in the bundle are not all equally important. The consequences arising from the enforcement or violation of different rights remain distinctive. Moreover, even in a market economy with the rule of law and order, the concept of a bundle of rights may no longer be helpful when contingencies arise beyond the provisions of the contract. In such cases, only the owner retains ultimate control of the property and has the right to decide on its disposal (Hart, 1995; 2017).

Bundled rights, other than control rights, are derived from and subordinate to control rights. Assuming that the supremacy of control rights over others in the bundle of rights is fully acknowledged, the two concepts can be viewed as complementary. Given that control rights determine other rights, the concept of a bundle of rights reflects the complex market transactions, facilitating the quantitative study of property rights and the analysis of related trade-offs. However, if the primacy of control rights is overlooked, particularly in a society lacking the rule of law, the mechanistic application of the "bundle of rights" concept can engender fundamental economic, social, and political misconceptions.[4]

In societies without the rule of law, the right to control property is typically monopolized and overrides all other rights in the bundle, including those assigned by contract. This was exemplified by the emperor of the Chinese Empire, who held ultimate control over all the land within the national territory and thus did not need to directly control the other rights associated with land ownership. Especially after the Song dynasty, the subjects of the empire were granted and allowed to trade land-use rights. No one mistook tradable land rights as their natural right or a property right in the sense of control. In principle, the emperor could exercise his control and decide on the disposal of land at any time, subject to tyrannical incentive – compatibility constraints. In practice, moreover, the emperor invoked this power to control the amount and manner in which anyone could use the land, thus preventing independent power arising from control of the land.

The control-rights-based concept of property rights is crucial for understanding the general attribution of property rights in a society, as it is related to social attributes that determine the nature of society. In contrast, the bundle-of-rights-based concept of property rights is more relevant for resource allocations and efficiency and allows for easier quantitative measurement of private property rights.

However, it is important to note that only ultimate control reflects the fundamental nature of property rights in society. In a private system, citizens ultimately control most of the property in society dispersedly. At the same time, this means that citizens, with their resources, collectively constrain the government. So universal private property rights form an institutional gene that drives society to move towards constitutionalism. In contrast, when the government monopolizes control over most property, whoever rules the regime controls the property. Autocratic rulers often attempt to consolidate and expand state ownership, resulting in its evolution into an institutional gene. Under this institutional gene of state ownership, any attempt to move towards constitutionalism is likely to encounter significant difficulties due to the government's unconstrained power.

In addition to the two main concepts of property rights described above, the protection of property rights is another popular concept. It originated from Adam Smith and was taken up and further developed by Douglass North and his followers as a measure for property rights institutions. It is common practice to measure the protection of property rights by looking at them as a bundle of rights and measuring the protection of each part of them. While useful operationally, this approach cannot replace the basic concept of control as it disregards or fails to consider the attribution of ultimate rights. Focusing on the operational aspects whilst neglecting the basic social consensus on property rights can be misleading. In Imperial China, the emperor held ultimate control rights to the land, while peasants, landowners, and high officials only held the use rights of the land granted by the emperor. For generations, people always understood the emperor's ultimate power over their land, regardless of operational details.

3.2 PRIVATE PROPERTY RIGHTS AS AN INSTITUTIONAL GENE

As previously discussed, the term "property rights" in this book refers to the ultimate right of control over property and "private property rights" is defined as the individual's ultimate right of control over their property. "Private" here encompasses family or household, as well as the individual (private ownership in antiquity was mostly a matter of household ownership). It is ownership recognized not only by the owners but also by social consensus. Archaeological discoveries confirm that private land ownership was already widespread across much of Greece from 1100 to 700 BCE (Finley [1981], Glotz [2013], and Toutain [1930], cited in Pipes [2000, p. 100]). In the norms of Greek polytheism, there were explicit rules to protect private property rights. In the early tribal system implemented in ancient Greece, religious practices stipulated that each family in the tribe had its own property rights and they were protected. On the basis of private property rights, all property owners were citizens, which gradually led to the development of Athenian citizen governance.

Archaeological findings and ancient Greek documents suggest that private land rights, which originated in ancient Greece, laid the groundwork for the world's first democracy. Owing to the unwavering determination of private owners, institutions in these societies evolved to safeguard property rights. As a result, property rights became the institutional gene that spurred the enduring institutional evolution towards constitutional democracy in such societies.

The reforms enacted by Solon in the early sixth century BCE played a pivotal role in the establishment of Athenian democracy. These reforms stipulated that a citizen's political power was determined by his property, in line with existing social practices (*Athenaion Politeia*, Aristotle [1988]). Land ownership and citizenship became intricately linked: only citizens could own land and only landowners were recognized as citizens. Later, with the reforms introduced by Cleisthenes in 509 BCE, democracy as we understand it today was established in Athens. The rights of citizens were expanded from controlling their land to collectively exercising sovereignty through voting and assembly.

Two hundred years after Athens established a sustained system of private property rights and democracy, Stoic thinkers introduced the concept of the indivisibility of fundamental human rights and private property rights, positing that private property rights form the basis of civil society. The Stoics proposed that each human individual is, by nature, the rightful owner of their property and it is inherent to human nature that individuals accumulate property rights and interact with one another as owners within a structured society. This "structured society" is the prototype for our current civil society. Locke's ideas, which form the foundation of modern democratic constitutionalism, originated from the Stoics (Long, 1997).

The question arises as to why Stoicism had such an enduring and extensive impact in societies where capitalism originated, yet faced consistent resistance and even active suppression in nations like Russia and China. My explanation is that it depends on the institutional genes in society, particularly how property rights are distributed. Civil society has taken shape in societies where private property rights are widespread and form part of the institutional genes and where the majority of the people are property owners. Stoic-Lockean ideas are compatible with the prevailing incentives of such a society. Therefore, not only will Stoic–Lockean ideas be accepted but they will also become part of the social consensus and the institutional genes.

The opposite is true in societies without private property rights or where most people are deprived of property rights. In such societies, resisting or even outlawing Stoic–Lockean ideas is compatible with the incentives of rulers who monopolize property rights. At the same time, since the vast majority of individuals did not have property rights, there was no awareness of private property rights as individuals' natural rights in society. Consequently, there was no consensus on private property rights and no motivation to protect one's own property rights.

In the Greek and Roman systems of private ownership, the concept of property rights implied absolute control of property by the owner. Correspondingly, within Stoic–Lockean thinking, private property is an inherent and inalienable natural right. Since the Declaration of the Rights of Man and of the Citizen, which emerged from the French Revolution, all constitutional democracies have described the right to property as "sacred and inviolable" in their constitutions, reflecting the absolute and fundamental nature of that right.[5] Marx labeled these "pure private property rights," free from state influence (Marx and Engels, 2012, p. 212).

Centuries before the Stoics, the Jewish Bible (known in Christianity as the Old Testament), which arose over a thousand years BCE, already clearly provides for the protection of private property rights. Among the Ten Commandments recorded in the Old Testament are prohibitions against a person coveting their neighbor's house, wife, servants, oxen, donkeys, or anything that belongs to the person's neighbor.

Moreover, the Old Testament articulates an early version of the idea of protecting property rights by constitutional rule to prevent autocratic rule. The Book of Samuel records that when the Israelites were establishing a state in the Holy Land and seeking to appoint a king, the prophet Samuel warned that a ruler could violate people's property rights and seize whatever they owned: "And he will take the best of your fields ... he will take a tenth of your sheep."

However, after Christianity was adopted as the state religion of the Roman Empire, it was exploited for imperial politics. The state Church of the empire then unprecedentedly monopolized the right to interpret the Bible and restricted the faithfuls' right to read it. It also deliberately disregarded the connection between autocracy and property infringement mentioned in the Old Testament. For several centuries before the Reformation, this hindered the dissemination of the consciousness of protecting property rights in the Bible and encouraged the autocratic infringement of private property rights by the Roman Empire and later feudal monarchies.

From the sixteenth century onwards, the Reformation revitalized the belief among the faithful in the inseparability of property rights and a person's fundamental rights. The Bible was translated into the vernacular and published for a mass readership for the first time, enabling its core ethos to become more widely understood. The role of the Reformation in this respect alone has established some of the foundations for capitalism. However, there was no Reformation of the Russian Orthodox Church and the active spread of Christianity was officially prohibited in China most of the time. Jesuit activities in China during the Ming and Qing dynasties were limited to charitable activities such as running hospitals and schools but large-scale evangelism was not allowed.

Private law, with property rights at its heart, is the foundation of judicial systems in all countries with the rule of law. Property rights law in most countries today, including China and Russia, is rooted in Roman Law.[6] China enacted its first private law in 1906 based on the principles of Roman law (through the influence of Japanese–German law, about which, see further in this section and in Chapter 9), while Russia's private law was largely transplanted from German law as part of the reforms in Tsarist Russia. However, in societies where neither property rights nor private law was part of the institutional genes in the system, transplanted private law was often little more than words on paper and it was hard for it to have much impact.

The foundations of Roman law can be traced back to the Roman Republic (509–27 BCE) with the official name of "The Senate and the Roman People" (*Senatus Populusque Romanus*, abbreviated as SPQR). To this day, "SPQR" can still be found on Rome's coat of arms, municipal facilities, and public buildings. During the Republican period, citizens voted for the Senate, which governed the Republic. As early as the beginning of the Republic, citizens with legislative powers promoted the Law of the Twelve Bronze Tables to safeguard their rights. It is the earliest written record of systematic Roman law, which was centered on private law regulating private property rights (e.g., possession and ownership of houses and land) and also included elements of related public law such as criminal law and litigation law.

Despite the Roman Republic being replaced by the Roman Empire in 27 BCE, laws safeguarding private property persisted, ensuring continued protection for citizens' property rights. Although significantly weakened, the Senate maintained certain authority, providing a degree of checks on the emperor's power. The foundation of commercial society is citizens with private property rights and of direct and immediate concern to citizens are property rights and the civil law that governs them. The government has no legitimate power to violate private property rights.

The philosophical or ideological principles regarding the essence of Roman law, with private law at its heart, can be traced back to the Stoic principle of natural law and even to the Hebrew Bible (the Old Testament), which suggests that people are born with equal rights and freedom to dispose of their property freely.[7] This spirit reflected the consensus among the ancient Greeks and the early Israelites. From ancient Greece to ancient Rome, private property rights and associated legal systems matured into institutional genes. Over the subsequent evolution of institutions spanning two millennia, while the Roman Republic has been undermined, the institutional genes of property rights have not only survived but also spread throughout Central and Western Europe, as well as to some European colonies due to the joint efforts of property owners protecting their own interests and the impact of the Roman Empire and Christianity.

From the time when law first arose in ancient Greece and Rome through to Roman Law, the Napoleonic Code, and the modern legal system, the core of which is private law (civil law), the fundamental mission of the law has been to protect private property rights from infringement. But the enforcement of private law (civil law) requires government and public authority. In jurisprudence, it is accepted that a civil code is the heart of the entire legal system (Watson, 1992, p. 191), which implies the need for other laws aside from civil law. Complementary to private law is public law, which regulates public power; central to this is the constitution, which establishes the principles of public power.

To ensure the enforcement of private law and to thwart government overreach and infringement of private rights, the basic constitutional principle (the UK has a constitutional rule without a written constitution) is to limit the power of government so that it does not infringe upon citizens' rights. Originating in the era of the Roman Republic, constitutionalism has been unwavering in its focus on preventing dictators from subverting the basic republican institution (Straumann, 2016). Constitutionalism's approach to limiting government power is rooted in the principle that the law is supreme, transcending the authority of the government, any individual, and any institution. The rule of law's primary tenet of the supremacy of law derives from the institutional gene of private property rights.

3.3 CHINA'S TRADITIONAL LEGAL SYSTEM: AN INSTRUMENT OF DOMINANCE

The so-called law in the Chinese imperial system was essentially an instrument of the emperor's rule. This represents a fundamental departure from the international concept of law, especially as conceived in Roman Law. The principles and institutions addressing legal matters in the Chinese imperial system were divided between Confucianism and Legalism (*Fajia* 法家). Confucianism prioritized ritual and propriety and supplanted codified laws with a moral code, while Legalism underscored prohibition and punishment.

In the traditional Chinese legal system, there was no distinction between civil and public law. Both legislative and judicial powers were conferred upon the executive branch at all levels of government, descending from top to bottom and culminating in the hands of the emperor, who wielded the law as a tool of governance. Administrators at all levels of government acted as agents of the emperor and were accountable to him; they did not possess rights or powers independent of the emperor.

The system commonly referred to as law in contemporary international society is fundamentally grounded in private property rights. As the English jurist and philosopher Jeremy Bentham succinctly put it, "Property and law are born together, and die together. Before laws were made, there was no property; take away laws, and property ceases" (Bentham, 1843, p. 309).

Conversely, China has never developed a legal framework based on private property rights, let alone a rule-of-law system where law is supreme and underpins constitutionalism. "Law," as understood in ancient China, originated with the Legalist doctrine of governance, which emerged during the Spring and Autumn and Warring States periods (770–221 BCE) and was fully practiced during the subsequent Qin dynasty. Legalists asserted that stringent laws were the sole means of maintaining social order and that rights existed only to satisfy the needs of the ruler (Fairbank, 2013, p. 42). From the Han dynasty (206 BCE–220 CE) onwards, elements of Confucianism, which replaced law with morality, also influenced the legal tradition. The traditional Chinese legal system was a system of rule by law, in which the law was the instrument of governance, devoid of fundamental principles or provisions relating to individual rights, freedoms, and interests. In contemporary jurisprudential terms, the ancient Chinese legal system, or ruling instrument, was centered on administrative and criminal law.

There is therefore a fundamental difference between "law" in the traditional Chinese sense and "law" as it is commonly understood internationally. Civil matters such as marriage and contracts came under public jurisdiction in an imperial system with no distinction between executive authority and the law. Until the end of the nineteenth century, China had neither concepts nor a vocabulary for private, public, and constitutional laws. Liang Qichao, a leading advocate of constitutional reform in China, wrote in 1904, "One of the most unfortunate things about our legal system is the complete absence of private law ... The law has flourished here for 3,000 years, producing countless codes, but there is virtually no provision for private law" (Liang, 1989, pp. 52–53).

Decades later, a Western-trained jurist remarked that legal terms and concepts such as "civil law" and "criminal law" were all imported to China from the West. If we follow internationally established concepts, by nature, all Chinese imperial laws dealing with civil legal matters belong to criminal law but not to civil law. Concretely, statutes covering corvée, land, housing, marriage, debt, etc. (in codes and decrees throughout the history of the empire) imposed penalties alongside the norms to be followed between individuals, using the political power of the government to ensure social order. The relationship here is still one between public authority and the people, within the realm of public law, fundamentally different from the so-called civil law ... From the Tang Code to the Great Qing Legal Code, statutory laws fall under administrative and criminal laws ... The terms public law, private law, civil law and criminal law were imported from the West and it is not an exaggeration that China had no civil law until the end of the Qing dynasty. (Wang, 1963, p. 15)

Contemporary Chinese jurists also recognize this fundamental issue: "Civil rules were periodically applied in Imperial China, historically, but they were never organized, summarized, analyzed and codified ... There was no such attribute that can be called as 'civil law' or 'private law'" (Yu, 2003, p. 11).

Not until the early twentieth century, when facing a crisis, did the Qing Empire decide to introduce civil law for the first time in Chinese history, in accordance with international practices. One of the external factors motivating the Qing Empire was the series of demands of the British, Japanese, and Americans. Their troops had previously occupied Beijing in response to the Boxer Rebellion and they pledged to relinquish their consular jurisdiction in China if China could establish laws and courts that were compatible with their own. Subsequently, the Qing government tasked Yuan Shikai and Zhang Zhidong with identifying specialists who were "proficient in both Chinese and Western law" to revise China's legal statutes. In 1902, the Bureau for the Compilation of Law was established to translate foreign laws and Shen Jiaben was appointed as the Minister for Law Compilation in 1906. However, due to the absence of an independent civil law norm or doctrine in China, Shen had no choice but to rely on Japan's codification of civil law (Zhang, 2004, p. 82).

The Draft Civil Code of the Qing dynasty was developed by Japanese advisor Yoshimasa Matsuoka and his team over seven years, drawing heavily from the Japanese Civil Code (which itself was influenced by the German Civil Code during the Meiji Restoration) and German and French civil codes. This Draft Code subsequently formed the basis of civil law in the Republic of China.

The fundamental reason for China's lack of an internationally accepted legal system, which includes the absence of private law and a constitution, is that it never developed the institutional gene of universal private property rights. Without this institutional gene, there would be no systematic private law, nor would there be a comprehensive legal system, inclusive of constitutional law or constitutionalism, with private law as its cornerstone. In the case of the unsuccessful constitutional movements of the Hundred Days' Reform and the 1911 Revolution, the reformers and revolutionaries were mainly focused on the governance structures of political power. Unfortunately, but perhaps not surprisingly, without the prerequisite institutional genes for constitutionalism, they did not pay attention to the ultimate goal of constitutionalism, which is to protect private property rights and human rights.

3.4 PROPERTY RIGHTS AND SOVEREIGNTY IN THE CHINESE EMPIRE

A fundamental institutional characteristic of China's imperial system was the emperor's supreme and comprehensive power. This included the ultimate control over all lands within the empire, implying that the emperor held the title to all land. As such, "All legislative, executive, and judicial powers belonged to him."[8] It was natural and unquestionable for the emperor, with ultimate political power and control over all lands, to possess the sovereignty of the empire. Sovereignty, as discussed in this book, concerns the social roots of a state's political power rather than international politics. The emperor's power was so evident that the concept of sovereignty did not necessitate discussion within the Chinese Empire. Indeed, "sovereignty," like the concept and vocabulary of human rights, is an import into Chinese. There are no traditional notions of these ideas in China and confusion persists about the relationship between human rights and sovereignty in China to this day.

To a large extent, the relationship between property rights and sovereignty under different systems reflects the nature of those systems. Before we delve into their relationship, it is worth noting that in societies whose institutional roots can be traced back to ancient Greece and Rome, private property and civil law regulating property rights were established first, followed by the emergence of public law to ensure the enforcement of civil law. Sovereignty was therefore established as a foundational concept of public law after the establishment of private property rights and civil law.

Before discussing how the two are related, it is worth noting that in societies drawing their institutional heritage from ancient Greece and Rome, the inception of private property and private law pertaining to property rights took precedence, with public law emerging later to ensure that private law could function. Thus, sovereignty, one of the fundamental concepts of public law, appeared after private property rights and private law.

Ulpian, a jurist of the Roman Empire, was arguably the first scholar to propose sovereignty as a jurisprudential concept. Although a jurist of the imperial period, Ulpian's thought still reflects the institutional gene of private property rights and human rights developed during the Roman Republic.[9] He claimed that the empire's sovereignty came from the people and was granted by them to the emperor (Hinsley, 1986). On the other hand, Ulpian's interpretation of sovereignty, which mirrored the political realities of his era in the Roman Empire, violated constitutional principles. He contended that the decisions of the Roman emperor constituted law by virtue of his sovereignty and the emperor was not subjected to any law.

The modern concept of sovereignty was developed by Jean Bodin (1530–1596), a French scholar of the Reformation era. He created the theory of sovereignty to bolster the French monarch.[10]

He posited that the sovereignty of an absolute monarch was a divine right, which was absolute and perpetual in nature; the monarch was accountable only to God. Bodin contended that while the monarch was not bound by laws enacted by others, he was nevertheless constrained by natural law and the constitution. Furthermore, Bodin argued that the absolute monarch's sovereignty was restricted to the realm of public authority and that the monarch could not infringe on private rights. This implies that even under an absolute monarchy, private property rights in Western European societies maintained an important position as an institutional gene.

During the English Civil War (1642–1651), before the Glorious Revolution (1688), the English philosopher Thomas Hobbes (1588–1679) proposed a doctrine of popular sovereignty based on the social contract theory, according to which the monarch's sovereignty was derived from the people. Although he opposed the constitutional separation of powers and advocated indivisible and unlimited sovereign powers to prevent violence and maintain order, Hobbes maintained that sovereignty does not entail a right to interfere in the non-violent activities of the people.[11] As for the relationship between sovereignty and property rights, Hobbes contended that, on the one hand, sovereignty defines property rights, implying that an individual cannot acquire property rights without the recognition of sovereign authority; on the other hand, certain property rights precede sovereignty and cannot be violated, otherwise, the people would be justified in revolting (Lopata, 1973, pp. 203–218). Both the latter point and the notion of popular sovereignty are reflections of the institutional genes of private property rights in England.

All modern constitutional states adhere to the constitutionalist principle of popular sovereignty. According to this principle, the inherent and inalienable natural rights of individuals are the source of a country's sovereignty. The people of a country entrust a portion of their power to the government through a social contract. This government, consisting of representatives elected by the people, uses a decentralized system of governance to protect the basic rights of individuals, including private property rights, and to maintain the public interest. This popular sovereignty principle, arguably, was first summarized by John Locke. According to Locke, private property rights, as well as other natural rights of man, predate the state and sovereignty, both of which were created to protect private property rights and the fundamental rights of man.

In summary, it is clear that from Ulpian to Locke and from ancient Rome to the Glorious Revolution, despite differences in views on the source of sovereignty and the principles of constitutional governance, there was general agreement on the relationship between private property rights and sovereignty. Western thinkers from various eras for over a thousand years have consistently viewed property rights as a natural right, largely independent of sovereignty and inviolable by sovereign power. This reflects the enduring existence of property rights as an institutional gene in societies whose systems have roots in ancient Greece and Rome. It also indirectly indicates that strong, longstanding private property rights form the institutional gene that ultimately paves the way for constitutional rule.

In Western thought, any ideas fundamentally opposing constitutionalism must represent a significant departure from the Greco-Roman system and traditional conceptions of property rights. A pioneer in this regard was Rousseau (1712–1778), who emerged before the French Revolution. While Rousseau's theory ostensibly focused on popular sovereignty based on the social contract, its essence was based on opposition to private property rights. First, Rousseau denied that property rights were natural rights predating the state and the law. He asserted that private property rights were products of violence and sources of inequality – a viewpoint that Marx later inherited and developed. Rousseau argued that property rights emerged only from collective authority, individual land rights were subordinate to the community, and the aim of the social contract was to establish equality in a society fraught with inequality rather than to protect property rights. He asserted that since the state represents the general will, its power is unlimited: "The social compact gives the body politic absolute power over all its members."[12]

Rousseau contended that law is derived from the general will of the people, signifying that legislative power, as the sovereign embodiment of that general will, cannot be alienated nor delegated. Consequently, executive and judicial powers should be integrated with law-making. Any attempt to separate these powers infringes on popular sovereignty and is thus unlawful.[13] Moreover, Rousseau considered the principle that partitions sovereignty among executive, legislative, and judicial branches to be fundamentally flawed. Accordingly, numerous theories opposing democracy, including Marxism, have drawn influence from his ideas.[14] In contemporary times, autocracies often cite Rousseau's theory of popular sovereignty and his rejection of the separation of powers as a justification for their consolidation of power.

The ideological divides mentioned above have been in existence since ancient times. Why would a given ideology have a profound effect in some societies but not in others? Why has Rousseau–Marx ideology significantly impacted social systems in Russia and China, rather than in France, Germany, and Britain, where its ideas arose? The analytical framework of institutional genes, as proposed in this book, posits that the influence of a specific ideology on a society is contingent upon its compatibility with the existing institutional genes of that society. An ideology stands a better chance of profoundly impacting a society if its incentives align with the society's institutional genes. Conversely, ideologies that do not align with these institutional genes may struggle to exert significant influence. Further, if an ideology does have a substantial effect on a society, it might become a part of the societal consensus and, subsequently, be integrated into the institutional genes of that society.

In traditional Imperial China, the systems of property rights and sovereignty differed significantly from those of their European counterparts. The most distinctive aspect of this system was the dominant power of the emperor, coupled with the lack of a tradition or concept of private property rights as inherent human rights. Marx provided a description of state power within China's imperial system, "The state is then the supreme lord. Sovereignty here consists of the ownership of land concentrated on a national scale. But, on the other hand, no private ownership of land exists, although there is both private and common possession and use of land." The state "stands over them as their landlord and simultaneously as sovereign, then rent and taxes coincide, or rather, there exists no tax which differs from this form of ground-rent" (Marx and Engels, 1993, vol. 3, chapter 47, section 2).

Marx's observations on the relationship between sovereignty and land rights in the Chinese Empire, as well as his depiction of China's imperial system, are influenced by both Western conceptions of property rights and sovereignty and Western perceptions of Eastern autocracies. As early as ancient Greece, Aristotle and Herodotus analyzed the autocratic systems and the monopolized land rights of Egypt and Persia. From the seventeenth century onwards, numerous Western scholars systematically studied the governance structures of Egypt, the Ottoman Empire, Persia, the Mughal states, and China. They coined the term "Oriental *despotis*" to collectively describe these systems (Wittfogel, 1957; Anderson, 2013).

Much like Imperial China, the Ottoman Empire lacked a hereditary aristocracy. The English philosopher and statesman Francis Bacon (1561–1626) commented on the Ottomans, stating, "A monarchy, where there is no nobility at all, is ever a pure and absolute tyranny ... For nobility tempers sovereignty."[15] The crucial point here is that, in a monarchy without an aristocracy, no one but the monarch has control rights over the land.

English political theorist James Harrington and French physician and traveler François Bernier elaborated on their understanding and observations of Eastern despotism, underscoring the disparities between Eastern autocracies and European monarchies. Both Harrington and Bernier inferred that the absence of private land ownership was a cornerstone for despotic rule.

These observations significantly influenced Montesquieu, who argued in his treatise *The Spirit of the Laws* (1748) that the lack of a traditional aristocracy constituted the foundation of Eastern despotism (Anderson, 2013, p. 464).

Fundamental ideas about institutions in any society are shaped by the characteristics of pre-existing institutions in that society. The notion of property rights as natural human rights, distinct from sovereignty, mirrors institutional genes that have been present since ancient Greece and Rome. In contrast, China did not cultivate such concepts due to the absence of these same institutional genes.

In the Chinese Empire, when all lands and political power, ranging from land control rights to state sovereignty, were vested in the emperor, the concept of sovereignty became superfluous. The authority exerted by Chinese emperors, who governed every aspect of the empire, greatly exceeded the sovereignty of European monarchs.

Before the foreign term "sovereignty" was introduced into China, there was neither a discourse on sovereignty nor a corresponding vocabulary, let alone a conceptual understanding of it. Individuals did not have natural rights; they only had those bestowed by the emperor's benevolence. As such, under the Chinese imperial tradition, there were neither concepts of property rights as natural individual rights nor notions of sovereignty. Public power and private rights were so intertwined that sovereignty and property rights could not be distinguished. This has repercussions even in contemporary China, where human rights are generally deemed subordinate to sovereignty.

The state dominion over land rights in China has roots dating back to the pre-Qin era. Concerning ultimate control, the land property rights of the nobles in the Zhou dynasty were similar to those of the current township authorities in today's China. They had nominal title to their land but, in practice, they only had rights to use and trade the land, not ultimate control over it.

According to the Royal Regulations of the *Liji* (礼记) (*Book of Rites*), the Zhou nobles were prohibited from selling arable land

3.4 PROPERTY RIGHTS AND SOVEIGNTY IN CHINESE EMPIRE 115

without the king's permission. In other words, they did not have complete disposition rights over granted lands; they only had usage rights and a partial right of disposition.

A prominent saying of the time declared, "All under the sky is the king's land, and all within the four seas are the king's subjects." For some scholars, this underscores the monarch's ownership of all the land in the empire. For others, it declares the monarch's sovereignty over the empire.[16]

However, these different interpretations are not mutually exclusive. They reflect the Zhou dynasty monarch's simultaneous control of sovereignty and land rights from different angles. They represent different facets of the unity or conflation of sovereignty and property rights.

Since the establishment of a unified imperial system under the Qin dynasty, the power of the nobility, which was derived from their fiefdoms, was effectively abolished. All power emanating from the land belonged to the emperor, which resulted in the imperial system of land power (the land state system) (Hou, 1954). Under this system, the emperor held ultimate control, primarily to thwart the potential resurgence of a landed aristocracy.

While China's imperial system maintained imperial power over land for two millennia, specific land policies varied during the dynasties. The institutional reforms of Shang Yang in the state of Qin played a pivotal role in establishing China's first unified empire. The heart of these reforms involved placing all land within the state under direct, central government control (Fairbank, 2013, p. 46). This laid the institutional groundwork for the *junxian* (郡县) system, through which the nobility was gradually weakened and ultimately eradicated.

From the perspective of modern jurisprudence and political science, the monopolization of political power by controlling land rights implies that land rights were an integral part of the emperor's sovereignty. Given that the emperor held ultimate control over the land while eradicating the nobility, individuals during the optimal periods of the Chinese Empire, such as the Song dynasty and afterwards, were granted only usage rights to the land and the ability to trade these usage rights.

Unfortunately, some scholars, unconcerned with control rights or the intricate relationship between property rights and political power, misinterpret those partial rights as private property rights. When partial property rights to land are treated as the ultimate control over land, the emperor's power to repossess or confiscate land is overlooked. More importantly, without recognizing the inseparable connection between property rights and political power, one cannot fully understand the basis and evolution of the Chinese imperial system.

To inhibit the emergence of large landlords as aristocrats, these landlords were granted only possessory rights to the land, not ownership rights. The scope of their land possession and use was stringently limited. They had to adhere to the emperor's rules, which dictated the terms of "possession" and imposed other "limitations" (Chai, 2007, pp. 53–56). Similarly, peasants solely held usage rights and the taxes they paid to the state were essentially rents (Hou, 1954).

During the Han dynasty, the share of state land swelled to 94 percent as the imperial system was cemented, leading to a gradual reduction in private usage rights. Following the Han dynasty, the Chinese Empire implemented the "equal-fields" system (*juntian* 均田), in which the emperor allocated and managed land-use rights while retaining ultimate control. This policy lasted for several centuries, spanning from 485 (Northern Wei dynasty) to the early years of the Tang dynasty in 780. Some literature misinterprets the *juntian* system as an egalitarian form of private ownership.

Particularly after the Northern Wei dynasty and under the re-established empire of the Sui dynasty (581–618), the emperor's main focus was on preserving the unity of the empire and avoiding the missteps that had led to the decline of the Eastern Han dynasty. The essence of this system was that the emperor utilized the equal distribution of the usage of "state-owned" land as a means to further restrict the gentry, control society, and secure tax revenues.

Under this system, peasants distanced themselves from their wealthy overlords and registered as state taxpayers. The system mandated that land was allocated and taxes were levied based on the labor headcount, with people prohibited from moving freely and required to cultivate the assigned land and pay taxes. Essentially, this system mirrored the state serfdom practiced in Russia hundreds of years later.

Starting from the Song dynasty (960–1279), the Chinese Empire commonly separated land ownership and land-use rights, while the emperor maintained ultimate control over the land. This partial privatization of use and disposal rights led to the blossoming of a vibrant land market, giving rise to various contractual instruments that facilitated the granting, leasing, renting, pawning, mortgaging, taxing, donating, and transferring of land.

Nevertheless, this flourishing land tenure market merely mirrored a policy decision made by the imperial authorities. At no point in any dynasty did the emperor forfeit ultimate control rights. The emperor's power superseded the results of any contract or market transaction. The emperor's approval and benevolence served as the foundational source of the rights of ordinary individuals. These realities are both historical facts and the social consensus that were established and carried forward generation after generation under the Chinese imperial system.

To forestall the emergence of a de facto landholding aristocracy and other forms of local power, emperors across all dynasties instituted restrictions on the amount of land that could be possessed by the affluent. They actively suppressed the efforts by the wealthy gentry to accumulate more land. Furthermore, they maintained the ultimate authority to reclaim and redistribute any land, even those held by high-ranking individuals such as princes and dukes.

The imperial court of the Song dynasty serves as an illustrative example of how such control was exerted, particularly in its careful regulation of a group of wealthy households known as the *xingshi hu*, or special households. This group consisted of the families of successful officials at all tiers of government as well as the leading local gentry.[17] It is documented historically that the imperial court held the authority to confiscate land from anyone.[18] As noted in the historical records, "since the Song dynasty ... it was not an uncommon occurrence for the government to confiscate or seize property from the populace" (Zhao, 2005, p. 31).

Besides political motivations, the imperial power also maintained control over land for economic reasons. During financial crises, such as the one that took place during the Southern Song dynasty (1127–1279), the government relied on its authority to reclaim and reallocate land. It sold large tracts of state land to raise funds. When the situation improved, the government obliged the wealthy to sell the land back to the state, at reduced prices.

Another illustration of the emperor's ultimate control over land is evident during dynastic transitions. New emperors often reallocated land-use rights to bureaucrats, landowners, and peasants in accordance with their political objectives. For instance, during the early years of the Yuan dynasty (1279–1368), land was primarily managed through an expansive state-run system of military cantonments. However, later, the use and partial disposal rights of most state land were privatized.

Then, when the Ming dynasty (1368–1644) took power, the emperor redistributed land to landless peasants as a way to curtail the influence of the rich and powerful. In fact, this practice was used repeatedly throughout Chinese history, becoming one of the defining characteristics of imperial rule. Each successive emperor exercised his ultimate authority over land to tailor land ownership and usage according to his political strategy.

Since ancient China, there has not been any social recognition of the right to private property or of property owners. Consequently, there was no private law that naturally emerged among property owners to manage the relations concerning their property. As the imperial power held ultimate control rights over all land, property rights and land contracts were essentially matters between the government and private individuals, belonging to public law issues as we understand them today. In fact, Chinese imperial power traditionally employed criminal law to handle these matters.

For example, disputes over property rights were treated as criminal offenses under the legal code of the Qing dynasty,[19] the fundamental principles of which were inherited from the statutes of the Sui and Tang dynasties (see Chapter 4 for a detailed discussion). This code emphasized sentencing and imposing severe punishments. For instance, unlawfully farming on state-owned land could result in a punishment ranging between 60 and 160 lashes (Pu, 2003, p. 335).

The imperial monopoly on land was the foundation of China's imperial system since the inception of the empire. Throughout the lengthy evolution of the Chinese imperial system, even though many peripheral elements underwent changes, the ultimate control of land by the imperial authority remained a constant, shaping the institutional framework surrounding land or property rights. One of its most notable features was the indistinguishability between state sovereignty and land rights.

This institutional characteristic has been crucial in shaping China into a totalitarian regime, where state ownership constitutes a central component. It has also significantly impacted China, both ideologically and institutionally, up to the present day. The reason why a series of fundamental principles of universal values – such as the primacy of human rights over sovereignty, property rights being a component of human rights, and the inalienability of private property rights – are either not accepted or are even considered heretical in contemporary China – is deeply linked to this institutional gene. Similarly, the reason why total state ownership of land cannot be challenged or discussed after years of reform and opening-up is also closely tied to this long-standing and deeply ingrained institutional gene.

NOTES

1. In any civilization, property rights, regarded as an institutional gene, emerged from the inception of civilization and exerted profound influences on other institutions and codes as they evolved. These institutions and codes, in turn, define or redefine the rules of property rights (Pistor, 2019).
2. The concept of property rights as a bundle of rights was introduced by the English jurist Henry Sumner Maine (1861). Karl Marx took extensive notes on Maine's book, Marx and Engels (1975), *Collected Work of Marx and Engels* (Chinese Edition, vol. 45) but he adopted Locke's concept of property rights in his own work.
3. The Coase Theorem argues that as long as property rights or their boundaries are well defined, property owners can always reach an optimal solution through negotiation, regardless of how the property rights are initially allocated (Coase, 1960; 1992).
4. Merrill and Smith (2001, pp. 357–398) argue that equating property rights to a bundle of rights leads to a focus on usage rights, ignoring the fact that the fundamental nature of property rights is the right of control (the decline of the conception of property as a distinctive *in rem* right).
5. Even in countries like the United Kingdom and the United States, which were among the earliest to establish modern constitutional democracies, there have been ongoing debates within academic and legal circles concerning the restrictions on and abuse of large private property rights. These debates date back to before the establishment of constitutional rule and continue to this day. While these discussions are beyond the scope of this book, they do not contradict the foundational role of universal private property rights in constitutionalism, which is the central theme of this book.
6. Islamic Law (Sharia) is the main exception. Here, the term "Roman Law" is used abstractly to highlight the origins of legal principles that protect property rights.
7. Russell ([1946] 1957, chapter 28, "Stoicism"). In attacking private ownership and "bourgeois law," Marx also clearly stated that "private ownership precedes law" and that "the essence of law is ownership." See Marx and Engels (1972, vol. 26 [1], pp. 367–369).
8. Hsieh Pao Chao, *The Government of China (1644–1911)*, quoted from Wittfogel (1957, p. 102).

9. For Ulpian's foreshadowing of the concept of human rights, see Honoré (2002).
10. Jean Bodin, *Six Books of the Commonwealth* (1583).
11. Hobbes proposed his social-contract-based theory of popular sovereignty in his treatise *Leviathan or The Matter, Forme and Power of a Commonwealth Ecclesiasticall and Civil* (1651). He argued that each individual is required to transfer power to the government by social contract so that the government can enforce the law in the public interest. The resulting sovereignty is absolute (the government must be the supreme authority) and indivisible. Hobbes, in his treatise *Leviathan*, proposed a theory of popular sovereignty grounded in the idea of a social contract. He argued that each individual willingly transfers power to the government through this social contract. The government, in turn, enforces the law in the interest of the public. The sovereignty that results from this transfer of power is absolute, meaning that the government must hold the supreme authority, and it is indivisible, meaning it cannot be shared or divided.
12. Rousseau, *The Social Contract* (translated by G. D. H. Cole), Book II, chapter IV.
13. Vile (1967) argues that Rousseau's strong opposition prevented Montesquieu's ideas from being realized in the French Revolution.
14. Pierre-Joseph Proudhon (*What is Property?* [1840]), who followed Rousseau and had a huge influence on the Paris Commune, wrote that "property is theft."
15. Bacon ([1625] 1999).
16. One common interpretation of this statement concentrates on the king's property rights, positing that all land belonged to him and all high officials were subordinate to him. Conversely, another interpretation lays emphasis on sovereignty, suggesting that all land fell within the king's dominion and all princes throughout the realm were his subjects.
17. *Xu zizhi tongjian changbian, juan yi'er* (*Sequel to Comprehensive History as a Mirror for Governance, Extension*, vol. 12), cited in Chai (2007).
18. *Jia Sidao zhuan* (Biography of Jia Sidao), in *Song shi, juan 474* (*History of Song*, vol. 474), cited in Chai (2007, p. 64).
19. Details are presented in sections of the code covering: "Land for meritorious statesmen," "Purchasing land for residential purposes," "Buying land with a mortgage," and "Cultivating land without authorization."

4 The Emergence and Evolution of the Institutional Genes of the Chinese Imperial System

> In China, since the Qin dynasty, there has been no such concept as sovereignty or state but a ruling family ... The Son of Heaven unifies the three great entities: the constitution, the state, and the monarchy.
>
> —Yan Fu (1986, p. 948)

On the eve of the Great Leap Forward, which would change the way China's totalitarian system functioned, Mao called himself, not without pride, Marx plus Qin Shi Huang (Mao, 1968a). His phrase lucidly reflects his understanding of China's ruling system. His reference to Marx represented the totalitarian system imported from the Soviet Union, with himself at the apex of this system. His reference to Qin Shi Huang symbolized the traditional Chinese imperial system, with himself as the emperor. In his view, there were abundant similarities between the totalitarian and Chinese imperial systems, thus he frequently discussed the operation of the traditional Chinese imperial system and the techniques of imperial governance, even comparing himself to Emperor Qin Shi Huang and Emperor Wu of Han.[1] In contrast, although the totalitarian system in Soviet Russia was inextricably linked to the institutional genes of Tsarist Russia, Lenin held an extreme disdain for the Tsarist emperors. Not only did he refrain from boasting about being like the Tsar but Lenin also ordered the execution of the last Tsar, Nicholas II, and his entire family.

In a sense, Mao's claim to be Qin Shi Huang seems consistent with some scholars' descriptions of the Chinese imperial system as a totalitarian one (Wittfogel, 1957; Fukuyama, 2011; Wang, 2018). China's imperial system is likely the closest antecedent of modern totalitarianism. However, the totalitarian system is a modern system with a totalitarian party at its core, making it categorically different from the traditional Chinese imperial system. This chapter delves into the Chinese imperial system, which ruled China for two millennia and its institutional genes that led China to accept totalitarianism.

The central question addressed in this chapter is about the fundamental institutional genes that exist in Chinese society, which are similar to and supportive of totalitarianism, during the transplantation and establishment of a totalitarian system in China. Chapters 10–12 further explain how these institutional genes and their evolved variations enabled Mao to transform the Soviet-type classic totalitarianism into totalitarianism with Chinese characteristics, that is to say, regionally administered totalitarianism (RADT).

4.1 FUNDAMENTAL FEATURES OF THE CHINESE IMPERIAL SYSTEM: INSTITUTIONAL GENES WITH A TRINITY STRUCTURE

Compared to the evolution of European civilization, on the surface, China's history seems to progress in reverse order. European civilization originated from the Greek and Roman republics and later degenerated into the Roman Empire, which subsequently collapsed and evolved into a feudal system. Conversely, in China, the Zhou dynasty (1046–256 BCE), contemporaneous with ancient Greece and Rome, was a feudal system which, in an abstract sense, bore resemblance to medieval Europe. Afterwards, Qin, by violence, annexed other feudal monarchies, one by one, and established a great unified empire. The feudal system of the past was replaced by the Chinese Empire, which at an abstract level, resembled the Roman Empire.

Ever since the establishment of the Qin dynasty (221–207 BCE), despite several periods of disintegration, with the longest lasting nearly four centuries, and twice succumbing to periods of foreign domination, China's imperial system, as an institution, endured until 1911. In this sense, the lifespan of the Chinese Empire is the longest since the Roman Empire. The longevity and stability of the Chinese imperial system are largely due to its unique institutional genes.

The Chinese imperial system excelled in consolidating and maintaining imperial governance. The most important component of its institutional genes was the elimination of any institutional arrangements that could potentially challenge the emperor's authority, including eradicating any political, economic, and social forces independent of the imperial power.

The most important factor that enabled the Chinese Empire to be super stable was the trinity of institutional genes that determined the imperial governance structure, that is, the prefecture-county bureaucratic system known as the *junxian* (郡县) system, which formed the core of the imperial power and operations; the imperial land control system, which established the economic and juridical basis of the empire; and the imperial examination system, known as *keju* (科举), which controlled imperial personnel and ideology. The *junxian* system and the imperial land control system took shape and were relatively well established when Emperor Qin Shi Huang first established the empire. The imperial examination system was first introduced during the Han dynasty (206 BCE–220 CE) and was officially established during the Sui–Tang period (581–907). These three highly complementary elements of institutional genes were refined during the Song dynasty (960–1279) and reached their zenith during the Ming and Qing dynasties (1368–1911).

This trinity of institutional genes not only forms the institutional foundation of the enduring rule of the Chinese Empire and the longevity of the imperial system but also profoundly shapes China's path to modernization. On the one hand, these institutional genes fundamentally conflict with constitutionalism, effectively hindering the germination and development of the institutional genes necessary for constitutional governance. On the other hand, they provide the basis for the emergence, development, and entrenchment of modern totalitarianism, becoming the foundation of totalitarian rule in China. China's contemporary totalitarian system is, in fact, the product of grafting foreign totalitarian institutional genes onto the *junxian* bureaucracy, imperial land control (state ownership of land)

and imperial examinations (bureaucratic personnel and ideological control).

This chapter focuses on the *junxian* system, preceded by an overview of the trinity of institutional genes and the origins and development of each basic component.

4.1.1 A Top-Down Bureaucracy: The Junxian System

The core of the institutional genes of the Chinese imperial system, the top-down bureaucracy, was created through centuries of evolution. Before the establishment of such a system, the foundation of governance during the Zhou dynasty, especially the Western Zhou (c. 1100–771 BCE), was a political alliance formed by the monarchs and the feudal nobility. The political alliance was derived from land ownership, which, in turn, produced economic, political, and military power. The power of the feudal nobility arose from their land ownership.

With the establishment of the Qin Empire, governance transformed into a highly centralized top-down bureaucratic system, that is, the *junxian* system. In this system, all officials, including the highest ranking officials second only to the emperor, were appointed by the emperor from top to bottom. Officials lacked an independent basis for their power and did not own land from which to derive power (except for the land used to support their families). The hierarchical bureaucratic system thereby replaced the political alliances of the feudal era.

However, limited by the technological conditions of the time, such as communication and transport, it would have been practically impossible to operate if every operational detail depended on concrete orders from the imperial court. The *junxian* system guaranteed the consolidation of political power control of imperial officials so that no individual across the empire possessed the requisite political power or resources to contest the imperial authority. Having political and personnel power fully controlled, the imperial court delegated other administrative powers to the local authorities.

The *junxian* system is characterized by a devolved administration within a centralized bureaucracy. This fundamentally differs from a truly decentralized federal system, despite occasional conflations of the two in political science and economics literature. In a federal system, chief executives at the local level are locally generated, thus possessing a local power base. However, in the *junxian* system, local leaders are centrally appointed and lack a local power base.

Federalism emerged in Central and Western Europe during the Middle Ages, evolving from the feudal system. For instance, the power base of the medieval Holy Roman Empire (HRE) was embedded in various strata of the landed aristocracy. Each tier held its own power base, making these nobles fundamentally distinct from top-down appointed bureaucrats who lacked an independent power base. Moreover, the HRE emperors were elected by the nobility at all levels and were leaders of the noble ruling coalition.

Contrarily, the Chinese imperial system, since its inception in 221 BCE, stripped the nobility of independent power and mandated the inhabitants of the land to submit unconditionally to the imperial authority. The system tirelessly endeavored to eliminate the economic and political foundations for any prospective emergence of independent power. The institutional genes of the Chinese imperial system are so deeply ingrained within society that, under traditional Chinese culture, people take this for granted. Thus, they mistakenly assume a top-down imperial bureaucracy to be part of the sole legitimate model of governance.

In essence, the *junxian* system eradicated all independent forces in society. The so-called nobles were solely nominal, with life and death hinging on the emperor's whims, a stark contrast to the independent European nobles who could amass armies for their own interests. This system guaranteed the emperor's ultimate control, free from any political provocations and threats. However, the longevity of the *junxian* system relied on other components of the trinity of institutional genes.

4.1.2 Economic and Legal Foundation of the Bureaucracy: Imperial Control of Land

The bureaucracy was the cornerstone of imperial rule. However, the bureaucracy itself required a foundation to ensure its stability and longevity. Despite the emperor's omnipotence and top-down control over the bureaucracy, it was essential to make certain that no individual ever possessed the capability to challenge imperial authority. By eliminating the aristocratic power base derived from land ownership, the imperial land control system facilitated the continuance of the *junxian* system and imperial power. This system also molded the concept of property and land rights and determined the development and evolution of China's legal system since ancient times. Therefore, the imperial system of land control is a critical component of the institutional genes of the Chinese imperial system.

The imperial *junxian* bureaucracy and the imperial land system are complementary components of the Chinese imperial institutions. The former eliminated the political basis for independent social forces within the empire and the latter eradicated the economic basis for such forces to re-emerge. Without ultimate control rights over their land, princes, nobles, leading gentry, and merchants could only rely on imperial authority to uphold their wealth and status (see Chapter 3).

4.1.3 Personnel and Ideological Foundation of the Bureaucracy: The Keju System

Historical lessons time and again show that the imperial land control system alone was insufficient to ensure the long-term stability of the *junxian* system. This is because while the empire's senior officials were devoid of land-derived powers, they could still amass and develop power through inheritance. Accumulated power, transferred from father to son to grandson, could gradually establish a de facto aristocratic power to challenge the imperial authority. Indeed, the widespread presence of such powerful de facto local vassals was the cause of the collapse of the Han dynasty. The empire had been fragmented for nearly four centuries. Taking lessons, the subsequently reunited empire, the Sui dynasty (581–618), established the *keju*, a formal imperial examination system, cutting off the path of inheriting power from senior officials to their descendants and fundamentally eliminating the emergence of de facto aristocracies. At the same time, the essential content of the examination was designed by court literati to directly interpret Confucianism for the governance of the empire and thus to determine and control its ideology.

The subject matter, budget, and operations of the imperial examination were directly controlled by the court, with the emperor presiding over the court examinations as the chief examiner. From then on, the *keju* system significantly influenced imperial politics and personnel appointments, serving as an integral part of the imperial system that complemented the *junxian* system. Particularly since the Song dynasty (960–1279), when the *keju* system was refined into a permanent fixture, the imperial institution reached its zenith of stability, despite undergoing dynastic changes and foreign invasions.

As an institutional gene, the imperial examination system (*keju*) was not only a pillar of the empire but it also profoundly influenced the mindset of the Chinese, especially intellectuals. Within the framework of the imperial system, gaining social recognition was primarily achieved through success on the *keju* examinations. This effectively eliminated the societal and intellectual foundations necessary for the emergence of independent intellectuals. The ambitions of scholars were largely confined to advancing through this particular system. Consequently, there were limited opportunities for society to produce elite intellectuals who were independent of the imperial power or who held views or perspectives divergent from Confucian orthodoxy. The intricacies of the *keju* system are further discussed in Chapter 5.

4.2 THE GENESIS OF IMPERIAL RULE IN CHINA

Reflecting on the impact of the imperial system on modern China, Mao Zedong asserted, "The Emperor [Qin Shi Huang] may be dead, but the achievements of Qin live on ... Hundreds of generations have lived by the rules of the Qin." This was Mao's explicit recognition that the Qin dynasty's system not only persisted but had been the foundational political system of China. The same poem includes, "Confucianism has an exalted reputation, but in reality, it is dross," implying that Confucian doctrines were merely a façade for the Qin regime.

There has been significant discourse in the social sciences regarding the genesis of imperial rule in China. Reflections on the origins of the Chinese imperial system, or Oriental Despotism, have been posited by thinkers such as Montesquieu, Marx, Weber, and Wittfogel, sparking a wide range of debates. A profusion of archaeological discoveries in recent decades has lent support to many of these earlier speculations, providing a sturdier foundation for related research pursuits (Chang, 1987).

Findings from excavations, such as those in Yangshao, Longshan, and Erlitou, reveal that centralized authority and highly centralized power were already in place in China during the second millennium BCE. This development coincided with the emergence of writing but preceded the formal establishment of an empire (Fairbank, 1992).

Beyond the allocation of social resources, aspects such as ancestor worship, sacred rituals, and the nascent written script had all become monopolized by the power elite, turning into tools of power in the emergent Chinese civilization. The rulers' exclusive access to the spiritual realm contributed to a comprehensive cultural unity and laid the foundation for the political unity of the state (Chang, 1983).

Archaeological evidence suggests that society at that time was clan-based and centered around a belief system focused on deities. Hence, monopolizing communication with ancestors and gods was not just a consequence of power but also served to reinforce the legitimacy of that power. The earliest Chinese script, oracle bone script, was specifically used for divination – a means for shamans to communicate with the gods. The monarch served as the chief shaman and some shamans also held courtly roles (Chang, 1983, chapter 5).

4.2.1 The Emergence and Decline of the Feudal System

As the first Chinese dynasty with a systematic written record, by the Shang dynasty (1600–1046 BCE, roughly concurrent with the drafting and compilation of the Old Testament), the term *"fengjian"* (封建), meaning "granting feudal statehood" (preface to Chang, 1987) had already appeared.

The subsequent Zhou dynasty left a more comprehensive historical record. According to these documents, the system of the Zhou dynasty, particularly during the Western Zhou period (1046–771 BCE), bore many similarities to the feudalism of medieval Europe. The "Son of Heaven" in the Western Zhou dynasty can be likened to a medieval European king, while the vassal princes of the Western Zhou mirrored Europe's dukes.

The governance structure of the Western Zhou dynasty was such that the "Son of Heaven" enfeoffed the princes, who, in turn, granted fiefdoms to their "Great Officers" (nobles at the ministerial level). Due to these similarities, the ancient Chinese term *"fengjian"* was adopted by the Japanese as a translation in the nineteenth century or earlier for the Western term "feudalism."[2]

The key difference between the Chinese feudal system, which was based on blood and clan ties (Chang, 1983), and the European feudal system lies in the distinction between the aristocracy and the ruling class. In the European system, the monarchy and vassals generally did not share blood ties. The clan-based system in China, as an institutional gene, limited the ability of the nobility to form political alliances across different bloodlines during the feudal period. This significantly impacted the way in which the Chinese landed aristocracy was eradicated during the dismantlement of the feudal system and how the evolution of the imperial monopoly on power unfolded afterwards.

From the end of the Western Zhou to the beginning of the Spring and Autumn period (770–481 BCE), the authority of the Son of Heaven steadily declined. With the collapse of the political order and the relocation of the capital, the old order of vassal obedience to the Zhou was no longer in place. They were pitted against each other in a struggle for territory and, concurrently, a primary form of the *junxian* system began to take shape. At the heart of the *junxian* system was a bureaucracy that eroded the structure of the feudal aristocracy. As the state fought over land and the old order disintegrated, a new unit of territorial administration, the *xian* (county), emerged, providing that the previous landowners – the princes and nobles – had to be replaced or eliminated. Counties were administered by appointed officials rather than the traditional nobility, allowing the new rulers to directly control the military power of the region and collect taxes (Zhou and Li, 2009). Dozens of such counties were established in the border areas of Jin and Chu around 532 BCE (Gu and Zhu, 2003). The key institutional change was that all bureaucrats were appointed by the central authority, with hereditary privileges no longer playing a role.

As warfare between the vassals intensified, the era known as the Warring States period (5th century to 221 BCE) began. Through conflict and annexation, what once were dozens of relatively small vassal states (more than a hundred existed during the Spring and Autumn period) gradually consolidated into seven large states. Concurrent with this warfare was a competition to change the system. Most notably, the already established *junxian* system evolved into a basic institutional arrangement.

The *junxian* system precipitated a decline in the power of the aristocracy, while the decrease in aristocratic power, in turn, reinforced the *junxian* system. These shifts laid the groundwork for the system that would later form a grand unified empire (Miyazaki, 1980).

The decline of the aristocracy during the Warring States period also had close ties with the development of iron technology (Bai, 2005). With the increasing use of iron tools, the adoption of oxen for ploughing, and the promotion of rice cultivation, agricultural yields improved. Under the deteriorating order of the Western Zhou dynasty, the rule prohibiting land transactions was gradually relaxed. The commonality of land sales began to erode the land-based aristocratic system (Huang, 1996).

Many states undertook reforms, bypassing the aristocracy to directly levy taxes on farmland. This not only led to a decline in the status of the aristocracy but also saw some nobles relinquishing their lands. In some traditional areas that remained untouched by war, rulers directly appointed bureaucrats to govern the region (Hou, 2005). These developments facilitated reforms that weakened the aristocracy and laid the groundwork for the emergence of the imperial system.

4.2.2 The Emergence of the Imperial Legal Principle: Legalism

In addition to the previously mentioned political, military, and economic changes during the Spring and Autumn and Warring States periods, especially the development and expansion of the *junxian* system, the emergence of so-called Legalist reforms in some states was another significant factor contributing to the creation of the institutional genes of the Chinese imperial order. Legalism (*Fajia* 法家), which emerged in the Spring and Autumn and Warring States periods (with some claims suggesting Legalist origins dating back to the Xia and Shang dynasties, although evidence is scant), advocated for the consolidation of all power into the hands of the monarch, eschewing power-sharing or checks and balances.[3] Over several centuries, Legalists played a crucial role in efforts to diminish the power of the aristocracy and to pave the way for the creation of the imperial system.

Guan Zhong (719–645 BCE), one of the founders of Legalism, advocated for the monarch to use law as a tool to suppress and reduce the aristocracy to a subservient position. He asserted that the law was created by the monarch, enforced by ministers and officials, and adhered to by the people. According to him, everyone, from the ruler and his ministers to the nobles and commoners, was subject to the law. This he referred to as Great Governance.[4] Guan's ideas were gradually implemented in the centuries following him.

It is important to note that the modern Chinese term for law, *falü* (法律), was borrowed from the ancient terms *fa* (法) and *lü* (律), which were derived from the Legalists' term in the process of translating the Western term "law." However, *fa* or *lü*, as terms in Legalism, were about a code of conduct or an executive order, coupled with some elements of criminal and administrative law. *Falü* differed significantly in terms of its definition, content, and function from the Western notion of "law." To avoid conflating Legalists' law with modern legal concepts, English literature on Chinese history and philosophy sometimes translates the Legalist law as *"fa,"* and with annotations to underscore the difference.

The first large-scale implementation of Legalism, which systematically shook the declining feudal institutions, was launched by Li Kui (455–395 BCE), the Chancellor of Wei during the Warring States period. His reforms were aimed at weakening and eliminating the nobility by abolishing the well-field (*jingtian* 井田) system,[5] which served as the institutional foundation of the Zhou aristocracy. Moreover, using Legalist methods, he systematically suppressed the nobility and other forces that could counter monarchic authority.

Li Kui gathered the achievements of Legalists from all states and compiled the *Fajing* (*The Legalist Classics*). Over the next two centuries, this work was disseminated and implemented by his followers in different states. The *Fajing* profoundly influenced the politics and legislation of the first Chinese imperial dynasty, the Qin dynasty. The essence of this book, as a component of the institutional genes, was handed down and evolved from that point forward.

It is not an exaggeration to say that the *Fajing* served as the prototype for the first laws of the Chinese imperial system. Traces of it can be found in *Qinlü* – the statutes of the Qin Empire – and in archaeological discoveries from the bamboo slips during the Qin dynasty (Yang, 1997, p. 194).

The most famous reformer of the Warring States period, and the one with the most direct impact on the creation of the Chinese imperial system, was Shang Yang (395–338 BCE) of the State of Qin, the successor to Li Kui. The essence of Shang Yang's reforms was to implement Li Kui's *Fajing*, systematically eliminating the aristocracy and fully instituting the centralized *junxian* system. Shang Yang asserted that only by fully weakening the power of the people could the goal of centralization be achieved. He posited, "A weak people means a strong state and a strong state means a weak people. Therefore, a country, which has the right way, is concerned with weakening the people."[6] The principle of finding the way to weaken the people has remained a fundamental tenet of governance in China to this day.

Shang Yang's reform greatly bolstered the *junxian* system in the state of Qin and further centralized power. Ultimately, the highly centralized state of Qin conquered all of the other six states,[7] creating the Grand Empire. Following this, Qin Shi Huang adopted the proposal of his Legalist advisor Li Si to institute "rule by the king alone under heaven." He abolished enfeoffment, eliminated the nobility, and established a centralized *junxian* system throughout the entire empire. This marked the beginning of over 2,000 years of imperial rule in China.

4.2.3 Institutional Genes of Feudal Systems: China versus Western Europe

Why did the feudal system of the Chinese Zhou evolve into a long-lasting empire with highly monopolized powers, whereas that of Western Europe produced institutional genes supporting constitutionalism?[8] A full analysis to address this question is beyond the scope of this book, yet I will highlight the most critical points. One such point is land rights and the political power derived from such rights.

A common feature among all feudal systems in Western Europe and Chinese Zhou was that the monarch and the nobility each had land as their power base. Rulership relied on alliances formed between these relatively separate powers. In contrast to the Chinese Zhou, in Western Europe the nobility's land ownership and political power derived from it were secure and evolved to become even more so over time, making it impossible for the monarch to undermine them. In contrast, in the Chinese Zhou, the evolution trajectory of these rights and the power derived from them was the opposite.

How land rights and the related political power evolved in Medieval Western Europe is closely tied to the emergence and evolution of the feudal system there. The European feudal system emerged after the collapse of the Roman Empire. Although the Roman Empire had a concentrated power structure backed by vast state-owned land, the key point is that its predecessor, the Roman Republic, was a state collectively ruled by land-owning citizens based on private land rights. The institutional genes of private property rights were deeply rooted. As the Republic expanded, the conquered land occupied by military forces became separated from the land ownership of Roman citizens, resulting in "state-owned land." As state-owned land continuously expanded and significantly surpassed the aggregate of privately owned land held by citizens, it formed the institutional bedrock for the creation of the Roman Empire. Even though political power remained highly decentralized during the imperial period, the institutional genes of private property rights, along with their corresponding legal and ideological principles, persevered. This enduring legal tradition of private property rights is exemplified by Roman law as codified in the Code of Justinian.

Furthermore, during the Roman Republic, there existed a systematic legal framework and the concept of independent justice premised on private property rights. Even though this framework was somewhat weakened during the empire, the institutional genes persisted. The tradition of a relatively independent judicial system laid the groundwork for the protection of private property rights and political power, which were relatively fragmented.

The feudal system emerged after the collapse of the Roman Empire. In this system, a ruling alliance between the monarch and the nobles was fundamental to power. The relatively dispersed private property rights and political power were underpinned by institutional genes tracing back to the ancient Greek and Roman Republic or even earlier. Under such a consensus, no lord, regardless of his military might, had legitimate power to conquer all the feudal economies and impose a centralized imperial rule.

The governance of the HRE exemplifies this point. Despite its name, the HRE was in fact a federation of many feudal states led by princes and dukes. The power of the nobles was hereditary, not derived from bureaucrats appointed by the emperor. For instance, in the HRE, the emperor was elected by the rulers of the empire's constituent polities. The relatively independent and stable power of the feudal nobility eventually resulted in mutual checks on the sovereign's power. This regional division of powers laid part of the foundation for the subsequent evolution towards constitutional government. Early forms of constitutionalism protected powers that could challenge the ruling authority through decentralization, thereby solidifying the pluralism of the political and economic landscape.

Lastly, the influence and power of Christianity and the Church weakened the king's monopoly on power and aided the nobility's counterbalancing role against the king. In contrast, in China's clan-based feudal society, the importance of family and kinship made it difficult to form a systematic, stable, political, economic, and legal system to support the relatively scattered property and political power that once existed. Against this backdrop, over the few hundred years of the Spring and Autumn and Warring States periods, the aristocracy's land ownership and political power were fundamentally eroded and eventually completely eradicated from the system.

4.3 THE EMERGENCE AND EVOLUTION OF THE CHINESE EMPIRE

Although the Qin Empire was ostensibly established through military annexation, significant wars that altered the course of history often stemmed from deeper political and economic developments.

Historical evidence demonstrates that the institutional transition from the Zhou feudal system to the creation of the Chinese imperial system was not determined solely by war or violence. The centuries from the Warring States period to the establishment of the Qin Empire witnessed a process of gradually dismantling the feudal aristocratic system and instituting a centralized system. This process ultimately led to the formation of a Grand Empire and this imperial system endured for over two millennia.

In this process of institutional change, the biggest beneficiaries were the eventual emperors and the social forces that supported the imperial system. These forces, along with the Legalist doctrine supporting the imperial system, formed the new institutional gene of the empire. The biggest losers were the entire aristocracy and the social elites associated with them. These sectors of society, together with the doctrine of Confucianism that supported *Zhou li*, constituted the old institutional genes of the feudal system of Zhou.

During the establishment of an imperial system, in which power was highly centralized and all elites except the emperor were essentially bureaucrats without hereditary power, the aristocracy and social elite, who were losing their privileges, would undoubtedly have resisted in an attempt to retain their influence. Consequently, if the shift from feudalism to imperialism had primarily benefited a select few while leaving many worse off, such an incentive-incompatible institutional change would likely have struggled to succeed. Even if it had, its persistence would have been doubtful.

Indeed, establishing and consolidating the imperial system was a long process that evolved over several centuries. At the beginning of this process, the old institutional genes supporting feudalism were continuously eroded in various aspects and this erosion was further exacerbated during the Warring States period. The institutional gene of the imperial system, the *junxian* system, gradually emerged, grew, and developed against this backdrop. The *junxian* system provided a swift pathway for social mobility for the elites who were not of noble origin, rendering the newly formed imperial system highly appealing to a large number of aspiring social elites. This expanded the pool of beneficiaries and reinforced the social forces supporting the system and contributed to the stability and longevity of the imperial system.

The indispensable role of military power in establishing the empire is evident. However, it was impossible to solidify the system solely through military means. The consolidation of the Qin system depended on the timely, thorough, and comprehensive elimination of the forces that were most likely and capable of challenging imperial power as well as the institutions that gave rise to these forces.

The most significant aspect in this respect was the eradication of remnants from the feudal era and associated institutions. The emerging imperial system was completely at odds with the vested interests of the nobility and the old institutions. The institutional elements inherited from the Zhou feudal system included not just the feudal aristocratic system but also the historical records and various doctrines that supported this system.

While it was relatively easy to eliminate the existing nobility in the short term, the task of eradicating the institutions that gave rise to and supported it, as well as eradicating their institutional genes, necessitated long-term and extensive efforts and involved a long-term and extensive effort. These tasks were complex and challenging, as they required reorganizing the social, political, and ideological structures of the society in a way that would sustain the new imperial system.

Eliminating the nobility of a conquered state simply required depriving them of their land and power, a relatively straightforward process. After conquering the other six states, the Qin emperor ordered 120,000 of their wealthiest families to relocate to the Qin capital at Xianyang. This strategic move allowed him to directly control these formerly powerful families and effectively dilute their influence and potential resistance, further solidifying the central power of the Qin

Empire.⁹ Thus, the Qin emperor weakened and eliminated the nobility, and extinguished local power (Lu, Z. and Su, R., 2005).

The difficult question that remained, however, was whether to reward Qin's meritorious officials with land and titles. In response to this fundamental institution-building issue, Qin Shi Huang adopted Chancellor Li Si's proposal. The feudal enfeoffment was completely abolished and the *junxian* system was fully imposed. Li Si argued that the Zhou feudal system had led to conflicts among feudal lords and that the establishment of feudal territories would create military rivals within the empire. In contrast, under the *junxian* system, all territories of the empire were governed by a unified bureaucratic system, in which no one retained inherent power apart from what was delegated by imperial authority. All taxes went to the imperial court, effectively eliminating independent economic or military forces at the local level. As such, the nobility lost their power base and were essentially left in name only as state offices and aristocratic titles were separated.

However, even physically eradicating the old system completely does not guarantee the elimination of the old institutional genes, nor does it mean that the old system will not be revived. Institutional genes could be in people's minds. The founding heroes who had risked their lives for Qin Shi Huang, driven by self-interest, hoped to be ennobled through the feudal system. They pushed scholars to advocate for the necessity of enfeoffment, using the arguments found in the ancient texts, particularly Confucianism.

In 213 BCE, an imperial court official responsible for the historical archives, Chunyu Yue, proposed to Qin Shi Huang that the feudal system should be restored, arguing that it was through ennobling their outstanding ministers that the Zhou rulers achieved a millennium of greatness (i.e., by implicitly recognizing the nobility). He stated, "Who would help the emperor at a time of crisis when the meritorious officials were only commoners (meaning bureaucrats without noble power) while the king of Qin had taken control of the world? ... Those who do not learn from the past cannot achieve lasting success ... To take the fruits of victory alone after victory is treachery" (Sima Qian [2010], *Shi ji* [史记] [*Record of the Grand Historian*], vol. 1, p. 555).

Chancellor Li Si refuted Chunyu, asserting that Confucianists "who study the past and do not learn from the present, oppose the times and confuse the masses ... if not prohibited, the authority of the ruler will decline from above, and factions will form from below." He further suggested that if this was not halted, the unified imperial system could be disrupted. Therefore, he proposed to Qin Shi Huang that all classical books be burned. This would effectively erase information about the institutional arrangements and underlying principles of the Zhou feudal system, thus eliminating the relevant institutional genes. Qin Shi Huang took his advice to heart and issued an order to destroy all classical literature that predated the Qin dynasty, except the *Qin ji* (*Annals of Qin*) and works on medicine, divination, agriculture, and general philosophy. Apart from one set preserved in the imperial library, everything else was turned to ashes within thirty days.[10]

But eliminating existing institutional genes can never be accomplished in one stroke. Moreover, by merely destroying the institutional genes of the old system without replacing them with new ones, the aristocracy could reemerge in a new form and new forces that could challenge imperial power would appear. A preliminary solution to this challenge was proposed by the scholar-official Dong Zhongshu during the Han dynasty.

Dong collected the Confucian classics that had escaped the conflagration and edited them into a new form to defend the imperial system. He developed the concept of the "Mandate of Heaven" which held that the mandate to rule was granted by Heaven and could be lost through poor governance. This idea conveyed an ideology that legitimized imperial rule and supported its accompanying social order. Concurrently, he proposed establishing the Confucian classics as the basis for the exams to select and assess officials. The rise of Confucianism as the sole ideological foundation of the Chinese

Empire, catalyzed by Dong Zhongshu, evolved over the centuries into a comprehensive examination system. This system became an integral part of the institutional genes of the imperial system. Chapter 5 will further discuss this subject.

4.3.1 Growing Institutional Genes of the Chinese Empire: The Qin and Han Dynasties

The governance of the Zhou dynasty was inherently confederation-like by nature. In size and structure, its closest counterpart in European history was probably the Holy Roman Empire of medieval Europe – a loose confederation of polities, famously characterized by Voltaire as neither holy, nor Roman, nor an empire. However, these resemblances are superficial. Critical distinctions between the Zhou dynasty and the HRE shaped their divergent trajectories in institutional evolution.

In the HRE, the relative decentralization of property rights and political power limited the authority of the ruler's family or clan. Substantive power was relatively dispersed, with any concentration of power necessitating alliances among the feudal aristocrats of each constituent state. Even within these states, rulers relied on alliances with local nobility for governance. Some kings were elected by local nobility and did not inherit their positions. This was particularly true at the top level of the HRE, where the emperors were elected by participant states, similar to the EU today. Indeed, today's EU recognizes Charlemagne, who laid the foundation for the creation of the HRE, as a precursor.

The landed aristocracy and the ecclesiastical authority deeply embedded within European society – frequently superseding secular power – both thwarted the establishment of a highly centralized authority within the HRE. From the perspective of institutional evolution, the relative decentralization of property rights and political power formed the institutional genes that ultimately facilitated Europe's transition towards a constitutional system.

In contrast, the Zhou dynasty's feudal system was clan-based. In the Zhou dynasty, the family of the Son of Heaven (i.e., the king of kings) ruled over the "whole world," which consisted of numerous states, each governed by its own royal family. The affairs of the royal family and the affairs of the state were one and the same. This clan system, which prevented the formation of political alliances across bloodlines, allowed the most powerful clans to gradually eliminate all other clans, one by one. Thus, a clan-based ruling arrangement was a fundamental institutional gene that gave rise to the later highly centralized, grand unified imperial system.

After establishing the empire, Qin abolished the feudal system. The power of the various kingdoms and royal households, rooted in their own clans, was gradually eliminated as a political force and their ruling positions were successively lost. However, the principle of clan-based rule endured. The federation of multiple household-kingdoms was transformed into a grand unified household-empire, where power was concentrated within one empire and one royal household. The institutional gene of clan-based rule evolved from a system governed by multiple clans to one where all power was controlled by a single clan. In this ultra-centralized system, only the emperorship was hereditary and the emperor's household held ultimate political power. No other clan was permitted to challenge the bureaucracy ruled by the emperor. All other political power outside the imperial household depended on the bureaucratic status conferred by appointment. This system laid the foundation for the centralization of power over the next 2,000 years.

The Han dynasty also laid the foundation for the administrative system of the Chinese Empire. Since then, there were only incremental changes in the administrative aspect of the empire until its collapse in 1911. During this period, the Chancellor was the highest administrator, assisted by several ministers each of whom was responsible for a specific bureaucratic area. The Chancellor, the Grand Commandant, and the Imperial Secretary, collectively known as the Three Councilors (*san gong*), represented the most prestigious state offices. The central government was administered by Nine Ministers (*jiu qing*), a term originating from the royal household stewards who managed various

4.3 THE EMERGENCE AND EVOLUTION OF THE CHINESE EMPIRE 143

domestic affairs within the royal household.[11] The managerial and executive authority of each councilor and minister, including that of the Chancellor, rested on appointment by the emperor. No individual in the high office had an independent power base.

The prototype of a centralized administrative bureaucracy, which laid the foundation for establishing a complete *junxian* system for an entire empire, was fully established in the Han dynasty. Later the central bureaucratic system evolved into the Three Departments (*san sheng* 三省) and Six Ministries (*liu bu* 六部) structure. The so-called Three Departments referred to the *Zhongshu sheng* (Palace Secretariat), the *Menxia sheng* (Chancellery), and the *Shangshu sheng* (Department of State). The Palace Secretariat, originating during the Han dynasty, managed palace affairs. The Chancellery, arising from the office of palace attendants during the Qin and Han periods, functioned as the emperor's advisory or staff department. This office developed into the Chancellery during the Sui–Tang period. In certain dynasties, there were multiple Chancellors, leading the Chancellery to become the office of one of the Chancellors. The Six Ministries were each assigned specific functions, which included managing bureaucratic personnel (Ministry of Personnel), overseeing taxation and finance (Ministry of Revenue), conducting imperial examinations (Ministry of Rites), administering military affairs (Ministry of War), handling judicial affairs (Ministry of Penalties), and supervising construction and manufacturing projects (Ministry of Works). These are summarized in Figure 4.1. The bureaucratic framework that emanated from the system of the Three Departments and Six Ministries was a fundamental institutional element of the imperial administrative system, with its direct influence enduring up until the final days of the empire. The underlying principles and traditions established by this system continue to impact China today.

The most critical element of the *junxian* system was to maintain control at the local level. The tug-of-war between central and local authorities within the bureaucracy in contemporary China

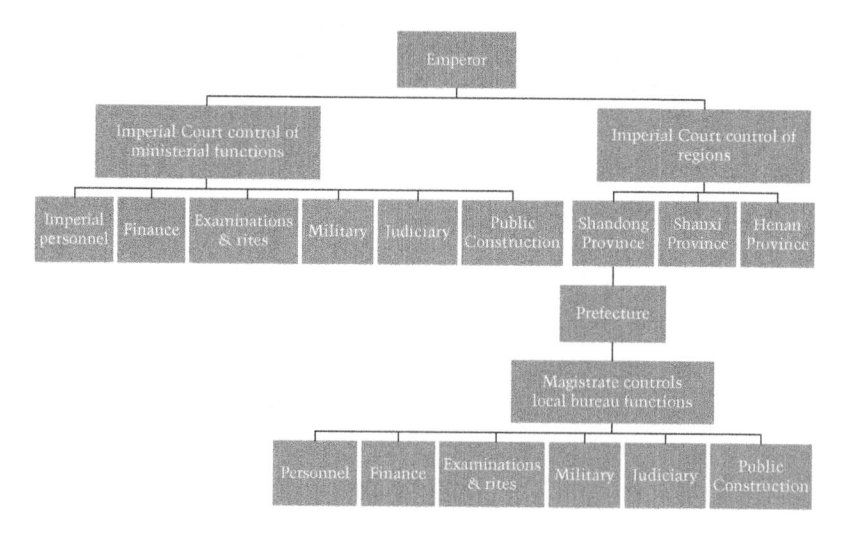

FIGURE 4.1 Institutional genes of China's *junxian* bureaucracy since the era of the Sui and Tang dynasties.

has been a significant issue since the Han dynasty. Although local officials were appointed by the emperor and nominally accountable to him, implementation faced serious incentive problems due to a high degree of information asymmetry. To prevent local bureaucrats from deceiving the imperial court, the Han dynasty implemented a systematic inspection and auditing system, requiring local authorities to submit their financial and statistical records to the central government annually. To prevent data fabrication, the central government deployed inspectors to regularly patrol the country, which was divided into thirteen investigative districts. Despite their low official ranking, these inspectors, as the eyes and ears of the government, held significant power.

4.3.2 The Imperial Institutional Genes: Disintegration verses Unification

The institutional genes of old systems rarely vanish immediately following the collapse of the old system. This was certainly true for the Zhou feudal system. It was not until the tenth century, with the establishment of the Song dynasty, that the remaining feudal institutions potentially leading to the formation of local vassals (including de facto vassals) were completely eradicated. Thus, from that point forward, the institutional genes of the Zhou feudal system were entirely eliminated.

Shortly after the death of Qin Shi Huang, the Qin dynasty was overthrown by power struggles and armed rebellions. The subsequent Han dynasty largely inherited the imperial system of the Qin dynasty, while partially restoring the pre-Qin aristocratic feudal system. This restoration was compelled by incentive reasons which dictated the survival of the regime. The emperor of Han directly controlled the most important parts of the country through the *junxian* system, while also granting kingdoms and princedoms to meritorious officials who founded the empire. It was a measure adopted to stabilize rule when the old institutional genes were still strong. In order to prevent local vassals from accumulating power and challenging imperial authority, the central government of the Han dynasty always limited the power of these feudal kings and princes, especially their hereditary power. As a result, most feudal rulers lost their domains after three or four generations (Twitchett and Loewe, 1986).

Nevertheless, the institutional genes of the feudal system remained prevalent. In the late Eastern Han dynasty (25–220 CE), de facto vassal kings re-emerged. As rebellions spread across the country and power struggles within the central government proliferated, the Han Empire eventually collapsed and split into competing kingdoms. China then went through a lengthy period of fragmentation and strife, often referred to as the Period of Disunity or the Six Dynasties period, which lasted for nearly four centuries. This era was characterized by a series of rival dynasties vying for control.

The transition from the Zhou's feudal federation to the imperial regime of the Qin and Han dynasties resulted in an extremely centralized Grand Empire. This sharply contrasts with post-Roman medieval Western and Central Europe, where power was dispersed and interregional and interstate competition was the norm. Even though the collapse of the Qin and Han dynasties was attributed to the emergence of de facto vassals within the imperial system and the imperial system was dismantled, the feudal system seemed to have been restored in some countries at various times in the Central Plains region and the success or failure of the imperial and feudal systems depended on which institutional genes prevailed.

If the feudal institutional genes gained dominance, the nobility could collectively resist an imperial system that infringed on their foundational powers. A feudal governance structure, based on an alliance between the monarch and the nobility, would have prevented the creation of a grand empire. Conversely, if the imperial institutional genes proved dominant, the centralized and absolutist nature of the system would result in any ambitious individual eventually being ruled, dominated, or killed. The same logic applies to interstate relations. The empire had to expand until it either conquered or destroyed all rivals within its reach or it was conquered by them.

The reinforced imperial institutional genes and the weakened feudal institutional genes dictated that greater social forces supporting violent expansion through plundering of the land and self-proclaimed kingship were dominant. Therefore, throughout history, ambitious aggressors repeatedly chose to risk their lives in pursuit of a grand empire as their equilibrium point in the game.

Although the Qin and Han dynasties ceased to exist and their Grand Empire disintegrated, the imperial institutional genes they passed down persisted. The Jin dynasty (265–420) and the subsequent dynasties all inherited the critical institutional gene from the Qin and Han, the *junxian* bureaucracy. The Jin also inherited a significant portion of the Han dynasty's test-based meritocratic recommendation system. Similar to the Han era, these systems constantly produced de facto nobility due to the remaining feudal institutional genes. However, the inherited institutions from Qin and Han dictated that the de facto nobility did not have the legitimacy to establish a stable ruling alliance and restore the feudal system. The constant creation of de facto nobility in such a flawed imperial system destabilized the Jin dynasty.

Subsequent kingdoms and dynasties suffered similar short-lived existences for identical reasons. The same deficiencies in the institutional genes of the imperial system repeated across centuries of history.

The Northern Wei (386–534), which had a significant direct influence on the subsequent imperial system, carried out reforms to centralize powers in the later part of its reign under Emperor Xiaowen. In many respects, these reforms echoed those implemented by Shang Yang during the Warring States period. Besides the inherited *junxian* system, the Northern Wei undertook additional steps to undermine, and even eradicate, the nobility. For instance, in order to weaken the nobility, the Northern Wei introduced the equal fields system, under which farming households were spun off from their wealthy overlords and registered as national taxpayers.

As discussed in Chapter 3, this measure further weakened the nobles in economic and personnel terms. The Western Wei dynasty (535–556), which followed the Northern Wei, was the direct precursor of the Sui dynasty; it fully inherited the *junxian* system of the late Eastern Han dynasty. In 556, on the eve of the creation of the Sui dynasty, it was announced that the old laws of the Qin and Han dynasties would be restored, with the central government holding full power over local officials' appointments. Concerning the economic system, the Western Wei not only inherited the equal fields system of the Northern Wei but also expanded the extent of military cantonments, which fell under the purview of the imperial court.

The fact that the Northern Wei and Western Wei dynasties perpetuated the Qin-Han imperial system is not coincidental. Although the emergence of de facto vassals under the imperial system precipitated the empire's disintegration at the end of the Eastern Han dynasty, subsequent dynasties essentially upheld the institutions of the Qin-Han period. Granting lands and titles proved to be an effective strategy for motivating military commanders as kingdoms and regimes grappled with one another. But as long as the regime was relatively stable, even if it was not a unified empire, the states defaulted to the centralized structure of the *junxian* bureaucracy and imperial control of the land to diminish the role of the nobility. That is, the institutional genes of the Qin and Han were transmitted across generations for several centuries, even in the absence of a grand empire.

The coexistence of the institutional genes of the imperial and feudal systems in Chinese history ensured that the nobility did not have secure power in the states that were at war with each other. Therefore, a balance of power, which would arise only from a pluralistic power structure, could not occur. The equilibrium structure of the power struggle was an ultra-centralized one, in which the ruler overwhelmed all others and deprived them of their power. In this structure, contenders for the throne had to compete fiercely until a winner emerged and all rivals were vanquished. The power structure, created by this institutional gene, also made it difficult to form alliances between states and eventually reach a balanced equilibrium. Consequently, a strong state would eventually annex all others and form a unified empire.

In contrast, even within the most autocratic and absolutist monarchies of Europe, nobles retained substantial power, as did the Church. Absolute monarchs still needed a coronation by the Church and they partially relied on fraught alliances with the nobility. Therefore, alliances formed between the plurality of forces were the basis there for achieving a balanced power structure, both domestically and between states. The difference in institutional genes that developed in Chinese and Western history not only determined the difference in domestic power structures but also determined two different equilibrium states: China's imperial monopoly structure, which overlaps with the institutional features of totalitarianism, and Europe's coexistence of multiple competing forces, powers, and states.

4.3.3 Imperial Institutional Genes Reached Their Peak: Sui–Tang and Afterwards

Just as the Qin unified their world, the Sui dynasty (581–619) brought an end to nearly four centuries of division, reinstating China's Grand Empire. Drawing from the disintegration of the empire in the past, the Sui introduced a series of reforms to bolster and refine the Qin system, fundamentally fortifying the imperial order. The refined institutional genes, which prevented the empire from undergoing any sustained fragmentation later, have been transmitted to successive dynasties up to the present day.

The Qin Empire laid the foundations for two fundamental parts of the Chinese imperial institutional genes' trinity, meaning, the *junxian* bureaucracy and imperial control of land. The Han Empire solidified and improved these institutional genes and fostered the imperial examination system which evolved into the *keju* system. This *keju* system became a fundamental component of the institutional genes of the Chinese imperial system from the Sui dynasty onwards. Consequently, the complete trinity of imperial institutional genes took shape during the Sui and Tang dynasties.

The key to maintaining the longevity of the imperial system was to prevent internal challenges to imperial authority, ensuring the bureaucracy did not degenerate into an institution of aristocratic rule while still functioning effectively. One of the critical factors here was the selection and control of bureaucrats. In the centuries since the Han dynasty, it was clear that as long as there was no well-established personnel system in place, bureaucrats originally appointed by the court, with power and resources under their control, developed and accumulated over generations, often evolving into de facto nobles or vassals. Once conditions were favorable, these emergent vassals would challenge imperial authority, destabilize the imperial system, and eventually fragment the empire.

To address personnel issues in the bureaucracy, the Western Jin dynasty (265–316) introduced the nine-grade system of ranks. Over the several hundred years of the Wei, Jin, Northern, and Southern dynasties, this system was continuously replicated and evolved, becoming an integral part of the institutional genes of the imperial system. The principle of the system was to select and promote officials based on merit and family background. While it initially worked well in the early years of a new dynasty, it gradually became dysfunctional over time, giving rise to new nobility and shaking the imperial system.

When the Sui dynasty re-established the Grand Empire after nearly four centuries of disintegration, it wished to prolong imperial rule and address lessons learned over centuries due to the recurrent rise of internal aristocrats challenging imperial power. To this end, the Sui instituted a comprehensive formal imperial examination system, the *keju*, supplanting the existing nine-grade system. Anyone aspiring to hold a position in the imperial bureaucracy had to pass the *keju* test. This eliminated the pathway for the offspring of high-ranking officials to automatically secure positions within the upper echelons of government. By making the *keju* the primary determinant of bureaucratic staffing, this system effectively eradicated the production of de facto nobility. Thus, it became a fundamental part of imperial politics and a pillar for the consolidation and longevity of the imperial system. Later, once the system was more established, the emperor acted as the examiner, personally overseeing examinations at the palace. Those who passed the palace examinations were automatically classified as students of the emperor.

Further improved by the Tang and Song dynasties, the *keju* system was fully institutionalized from the Song dynasty onwards, simultaneously forming a complete bureaucratic system based on merit. From the Song dynasty to the collapse of the Chinese Empire, the system never again experienced disintegration due to the emergence of nobility. Chapter 5 delves into the *keju* system.

The Sui dynasty also refined the institutional genes of the *junxian* bureaucracy in many ways, primarily by optimizing the administrative system and establishing comprehensive administrative and criminal laws. It formally instituted the broad-reaching system of Five Departments and Six Ministries at the central level, replacing the central bureaucratic structures that had been in place since the Qin and Han dynasties. Moreover, it substituted the Han's province-prefecture-county structure of regional control with a prefecture-county system, further consolidating control by the central government and diminishing the power of local authorities.

From the Sui dynasty, the Department of State, the highest central executive body, had six subordinate ministries, as shown in Figure 4.1. From then on, this governance structure remained largely unaltered for more than a thousand years, through dynastic changes including two periods of foreign domination, until the fall of the Qing dynasty. In a sense, today's State Council in China is roughly equivalent to the Department of State of that era. In a highly centralized system, even though the Department of State was the highest executive body, its function was primarily to execute assigned tasks and implement policies; it had limited authority to interfere with the most crucial decisions.

Of the Six Ministries under the Department of State, the Ministry of Personnel, responsible for bureaucracy personnel matters, was the most important. This is a pattern common to all highly centralized systems. In contemporary China, the Organization Department under the direct control of the CCP Central Committee, holds a position of comparable importance. Yet, even more important, perhaps, is the arrangement of bureaucratic administrative functions at both the central and local levels in the *junxian* system. Within the central institutions of the imperial court, the Court Supervisor Office (*dutang*) was bordered on the left by the offices of the Ministries of Personnel, Revenue, and Rites, and on the right by the offices of the Ministries of War, Justice, and Works. This arrangement was mirrored in the administrative units at all levels of local government, from the capital city to the prefecture and county governments.

Although each local government had all the functional offices, these local functions were not directly accountable to those of the ministries, as the real executive power was vested in the local governors. At each level down to the county, the final decision on administrative matters rested in the hands of the local chief executives. A county magistrate oversaw all administrative matters within his county and a minister of the imperial court would not intervene in the county's affairs without going through the magistrate. This governance structure persisted until the collapse of the Chinese Empire in the early twentieth century. Moreover, the RADT system, established during the GLF, institutionally revived this governance structure (see Chapters 12 and 13).

With the refinement of the imperial system and the evolution of the bureaucratic system towards centralizing power, the unification of administrative regulations became paramount. In response to this need, the Sui dynasty emerged as the pioneer in Chinese imperial history in formulating comprehensive administrative and criminal laws. In 583, Emperor Wen of Sui (r. 581–604) promulgated the Kaihuang Code (开皇律), drawing on regulations, customs, and criminal laws developed over centuries and tracing back as far as the Qin and Han dynasties. This Code profoundly influenced the evolution of the imperial system. It comprised twelve sections, encompassing administrative statutes and criminal law. The first section addressed general criminal law; the second focused on safeguarding the emperor's personal safety, sovereignty, and borders; the third concerned the establishment, appointment, and duties of officials, along with punitive measures for infringements. The fourth section centered on household registration and land management, intrinsically linked to land and taxes. The fifth section regulated state-owned livestock, while the sixth section focused on military matters. The remaining sections primarily dealt with criminal law.

In 653, based on the foundational Kaihuang Code, the Tang Code was promulgated. This legal document had an enormous influence on subsequent dynasties and various East Asian countries. After its establishment, the structure of imperial governance remained largely stable with relatively few significant changes. The legal codes of the Song, Yuan, Ming, and Qing dynasties were, to a great extent, derived from and heavily influenced by the Tang Code.

The significance and influence of the Kaihuang Code in the Chinese imperial system are largely equivalent to that of the Justinian

Code (promulgated under the Byzantine Empire in 529) in Roman Law. Both were systematic collections of laws accumulated over several centuries. The Tang Code had an influence beyond the empire itself, somewhat akin to the Napoleonic Code (a subsequent variant of Roman law). Until Western influence entered East Asia, the Tang Code profoundly impacted the legal codes of East Asian countries. For instance, Japan's Taihō Code of 701, Korea's Goryeo Law of 958 (Zhang, 2016), and Vietnam's 1483 Hồng Đức Legal Code all originated and were localized from the Tang Code.

However, it is important to note that the Chinese imperial legal code primarily constituted a collection of administrative regulations and criminal laws. It never culminated in a modern conception of private law based on private property rights, nor its counterpart public law within which constitutional law resides. Therefore, any comparison with Roman legal codes is only superficial, limited to a comparison of historical influences and regional impacts. While the Roman legal tradition has shaped the legal frameworks of Western countries, contributing to concepts of property rights, contracts, and civil law, the Chinese legal tradition primarily focused on maintaining imperial control, regulating administrative functions, and prescribing criminal penalties.

In a system characterized by the high centralization of property and political power, rulers naturally aspire to further concentrate power as a means to maintain their authority. Their already consolidated power base allows them to persistently strive to increase the centralization of power. In such a system, the law exists primarily to serve the emperor's interests. Thus, when an emperor perceives that the existing institutions and codes hinder his power, he possesses the discretion to override institutional regulations and laws as he sees fit.

Starting with the Sui dynasty and continuing through subsequent dynasties, there was a constant process of power centralization in the hands of the emperor. By the later periods of the Ming and Qing dynasties, emperors began to circumvent the bureaucratic system, instead governing directly through their immediate circles. This practice resulted in an unprecedented concentration of power.

The practice of governing the empire through court eunuchs during the Ming or via the Military-Political-Affairs Office (*Junji chu* 军机处) during the Qing illustrates this point. Once the emperor's power was sufficiently consolidated within a centralized system, he had the authority to revoke those laws and regulations that had served his predecessors for generations.

A key initial step in centralizing power during the Song dynasty involved weakening the authority of the Chancellor (*zaixiang* 宰相). In the preceding Tang dynasty, edicts were promulgated by the Chancellor with the emperor's approval. In contrast, during the Song dynasty, not only was the Chancellor deprived of this power to issue decrees but the control of fiscal matters was also transferred to three special departments and the control over personnel was reverted back to the emperor. Essentially, the Chancellor was reduced to merely following orders. After the Song dynasty was overthrown by the Yuan dynasty, the Mongols preserved the main institutions of the Song for almost a century of rule, with the Chancellor assuming the role of the director of the Palace Secretariat.

At the beginning of the Ming dynasty, the Chancellor was still the Secretariat director. However, in a significant shift, Emperor Hongwu abolished the Chancellorship in 1380. From this point onwards, the position of Chancellor was permanently discarded from the annals of Chinese imperial history, signifying an irreversible trend towards power centralization. As Emperor Hongwu endeavored to dismantle ministerial offices with the aim of centralizing power, court eunuchs rose to become auxiliary forces for the emperor. This shift resulted in the marginalization of the once expansive imperial bureaucracy.

After conquering the Ming dynasty, the Manchu-led Qing dynasty inherited the highly centralized system, carrying forward the institutional genes of the Chinese imperial system much like the Mongol Yuan dynasty did from the Song dynasty. Building on the pre-existing centralization within the Chinese imperial system, the Manchu emperors intensified power centralization further. The Qing dynasty did not have Chancellors; power was concentrated to the greatest possible extent within the purview of the emperor, who personally attended to matters of all magnitudes, making every critical decision himself, which further diminished the roles of senior officers within the Six Ministries. However, in reality, the Manchu emperors were no more equipped to manage all affairs themselves than their Ming predecessors. During Emperor Yongzheng's reign (r. 1722–1735), the *Junji chu* (Military-Political-Affairs Office) was established. Similar to the Ming court eunuchs, it assisted the emperor in issuing the most important decrees. As direct servants to the emperor, the Military-Political-Affairs Office could issue orders in the emperor's name to the ministers of the Six Ministries and to the military and civil governors of the provinces.

The highest echelons of the CCP, in their quest for ever-greater centralization of power, have paralleled the actions of the late Ming and Qing emperors by undermining established institutions and statutory norms. The Central Leading Groups (*lingdao xiaozu*) established by Mao Zedong during the periods of the Great Leap Forward and the Cultural Revolution, and later by Xi Jinping from 2013 onwards, bear functional similarities to the Military-Political-Affairs Office of the Qing dynasty. These groups exercise powers that traditionally fell within the purview of the party-state bureaucracy, thereby enabling the supreme leader to bypass the bureaucracy and its procedures to directly implement decisions. This striking similarity between the imperial and communist regimes underscores the enduring influence of the institutional genes of the Chinese imperial system within modern-day totalitarian China.

4.3.4 *The Institutional Genes of Unconstrained Power*

A fundamental attribute of the Chinese imperial system was the lack of a mechanism for checks and balances of power. Nevertheless, some scholars argue that during the Tang dynasty, there were mechanisms for balancing power, particularly between the sovereign and the Chancellor (e.g., Qian, 2010). Some even label it as constitutionalism "with Chinese characteristics" and assert that the Tang dynasty's *Zhengshi tang* (政事堂) (Hall of Government Affairs) functioned as a Chinese form of parliament. However, other scholars, based on historical evidence, contend that these claims fundamentally misunderstand the essence of checks and balances and constitutionalism. They argue that in reality, there was no genuine counterbalance to power at the top echelons of the Chinese imperial system (Wu, 1984, pp. 556–562).

The historical reality at the core of this discussion is as follows: In the Tang dynasty, the emperor appointed three high-ranking bureaucrats to serve as Chancellors. These individuals respectively headed the Palace Secretariat (*Zhongshu* 中书), the Chancellery (*Menxia* 门下), and the Department of State Affairs (*Shangshu* 尚书). As holders of the highest offices in the empire, their primary role was to assist and support the emperor, not to act as a check on his power. The Palace Secretariat's main task was to draft imperial edicts on behalf of the emperor. The Chancellery, in turn, reviewed these draft edicts. The Hall of Government Affairs served as a meeting place where the Chancellery and the Palace Secretariat convened joint sessions, which were attended by all three Chancellors. Orders passed during these meetings in the Hall of Government Affairs were sealed by both the Palace Secretariat and Chancellery, ratified by the emperor, and finally dispatched to the Department of State Affairs for execution.

It is an undisputed fact that all three Chancellors attending the Hall of Government Affairs were bureaucrats appointed by the emperor. Their task was to serve the emperor, not oversee him. As such, to claim that this system was a mechanism for checks and balances, a prototype constitutional mechanism, or even a parliament, is deeply misleading.

The term "checks and balances" refers to a system where multiple independent powers constrain each other. This prevents one side from monopolizing and encroaching upon the interests of others when conflicts of interest arise. The term "constitutionalism" refers to a governance system with institutionalized checks and balances, the core component of which is the existence of multiple independent powers.

The parliament, an independent legislative body, operates separately from the executive power, serving as one of the main checks on the executive power. In contrast, the Hall of Government Affairs and the offices of the Three Chancellors were all bureaucratic organizations established by the emperor. Their function was to assist him in formulating and implementing policies.

Their power originated exclusively from the emperor and, therefore, they were obliged to represent the emperor's interests and authority. Any debates among them were limited to strategies for preserving and serving the emperor's power. They could help the emperor achieve self-restraint for the long-term interests of imperial power.

However, if the imperial power infringed upon the interests of any social group or individual, these Chancellors were duty-bound to help devise and implement specific infringing policies. Appointed by the imperial court, they neither had the motive nor the power to restrain the emperor's powers.

Another subject that confuses many is the admonishment system (*jian-guan zhi* 谏官制) of the Tang and Song dynasties. Some scholars interpret this system as a check on the emperor's powers. In this system, the appointed admonishers (*jian-guan*) were assigned the role of admonition, with their primary duty being to criticize the emperor's decisions and policies if they believed they were incorrect or harmful, regardless of whether this was favorable or unfavorable to the emperor. However, their role was merely to advise or guide the emperor from the perspective of the emperor's and the court's interests and the emperor had full discretion as to whether or not to heed their advice. As relatively low-ranking bureaucrats, admonishers had neither the intention nor the power to restrict the emperor.

Historical accounts record instances of brave admonishers risking their lives to provide advice to emperors. However, without exception, all such advice served the interests of imperial power, if not solely for the personal enjoyment of the emperor himself.

In contrast, the systems that existed at that time in Europe, and today in all democracies, to check and balance monarchical powers are inextricably linked to mutually independent social forces. Only external forces can constrain a monarch. The existence of mutually independent powers within a society is the only way to form a system of mutual checks and balances. However, all institutional arrangements established by Chinese emperors were intended to serve imperial power. Therefore, they could not function as a constraint on imperial authority. Nor could they be transformed into credible institutions for self-restraint because any emperor unwilling to exercise self-restraint possessed all the power needed to break any rule, whether established by himself or his predecessors. Consequently, the effect of any self-restraint mechanism could be, at best, fleeting.

A classic anecdote about Empress Wu Zetian (r. 690–704) illustrates the impracticality of self-restraint for those on the throne. Chancellor Liu Weizhi implored Wu to adhere to the established procedures of the Tang dynasty, questioning, "How can it be an edict if it has not been passed before the Palace Secretariat and the Chancellery?" Despite acting in the interest of the empire and strictly following the rules, Liu was ordered to commit suicide.

Similarly, Emperor Zhongzong (r. 705–710) openly disregarded the rule that official posts should only be assigned following review by the two aforementioned departments. He purposely signed the official appointments in black rather than red and sealed the envelopes diagonally. This sent a clear message to all bureaucrats that he intended to break the rules, not out of negligence but deliberately, and he expected all bureaucrats to disregard the rule accordingly.

By the time of the Song dynasty, the superficial rules for the emperor's self-restraint had completely disappeared and would not reappear, indicating that self-restraint rules incompatible with incentives not only break easily but also cannot endure in the long term.

In fact, the general evolutionary trend of the Chinese imperial system was one of continuous centralization of power. During the Han dynasty, a single Chancellor, who also headed the Censorate (*Yushi tai* 御史台), was responsible for monitoring and inspecting the conduct of state officials at both the central and local levels. To weaken the Chancellorship's power, Tang emperors established a separate Censorate, creating a tri-Chancellor system, thus making it easier for the emperor to control and diminish the power of the Chancellors. This runs contrary to the claim that the Chancellor's power was set up to constrain the sovereign's power. Any connection between self-restraint on the emperor's part and mutual restraint among the Chancellors had dissipated by the end of the Song dynasty. In the subsequent Ming and Qing dynasties, the convention of self-restraint became totally obsolete due to its incompatibility with the power incentives, leading to the permanent disappearance of the Chancellorship from the system.

After Emperor Hongwu of the Ming dynasty abolished the Chancellorship in 1380, the practice of ruling without a Chancellor was adopted by subsequent rulers, including the Manchu. That is to say, the office of the Chancellor completely disappeared from the Chinese imperial system for centuries to come. This demonstrates that the evolution of the imperial system was a process of continuous centralization of power by the emperor, with the aim of eliminating any potential alternative sources of power. Ultimately, even the Chancellorship, a role originally created to assist the emperor, had to be eradicated.

4.4 THE INCOMPATIBILITY OF CHINA'S IMPERIAL SYSTEM WITH CONSTITUTIONALISM

The Chinese imperial system is fundamentally incompatible with constitutionalism. This conclusion is drawn not only from historical facts but also from the inherently conflicting mechanisms of the two systems. The evolution of the Chinese imperial system can be outlined in several major trends. The first stage was the abolition of the power of the aristocracy. This was followed by the eradication of the foundations of the aristocratic system, which included the removal of the institutional basis of all independent social forces and the elimination of all potential threats to imperial power. The third stage was to diminish the actual power of all high-ranking officials, with the weakening of the power of the highest official, the Chancellor, forming part of this general trend. Finally, during the Ming and Qing dynasties, imperial power reached its pinnacle of centralization following the complete elimination of the Chancellorship.

The deeply ingrained and evolved institutional genealogy of the Chinese imperial system constituted a fundamental barrier to transitioning towards a constitutional system. This is a universal mechanism observed across all absolutist institutions. For instance, the Russian Empire, formed under the influence of both the Mongol and Byzantine empires, not only obstructed Russia's constitutional revolution in 1905 but also laid the institutional groundwork for the emergence of the Bolsheviks (refer to Chapter 7). The institutional genes of the absolutist imperial system in China have developed longer and more comprehensively than anywhere else in the world, making the introduction of constitutional reform particularly challenging in this country.

Within the two-millennia history of the Chinese imperial system, every reform (*bianfa*) was fundamentally aimed at consolidating imperial power and extending imperial rule. Even the Republican Revolution of 1911, which overthrew the Qing dynasty, was driven more by the desire to dethrone the Manchus – a similar sentiment to the ousting of the Mongols in the late Yuan dynasty – rather than the pursuit of constitutionalism or republicanism. Despite the outward call for a constitutional republic, the protection of citizens' fundamental rights was neither the driving force nor the objective of the revolution. This stands in sharp contrast to countries that established constitutional systems, including Taiwan (see Chapter 14). However, this is not surprising considering the historical context and institutional genes of China. Given these circumstances, individuals in China generally lacked basic rights and, consequently, they neither had the awareness nor the power necessary to advocate for a revolution or reform aimed at safeguarding their rights.

NOTES

1. A prominent example is found in Mao Zedong's self-revelatory poem titled "Snow" ("Qinyuan chun").
2. From 1930 onwards, some scholars, mechanically applying Marx's historical materialist account of development stages, categorized the Zhou dynasty as a slave system and ascribed feudalism to the Qin system, marking the onset of the imperial system. This interpretation was later adopted in the official histories of the PRC and incorporated into textbooks from primary school to university.
3. These are fully conveyed in *Han Feizi*, a compilation of legalist theories penned by Han Fei in the late Warring States period. For related literature, see Fu (1996), Tamura (1997), and Chen (1975).
4. "The one who generates law is the ruler; those who uphold law are the ministers; those who are regulated by law are the people. Rulers and ministers, superiors and inferiors, nobility and commoners; all are subject to law. This is the Great Governance" (*Guanzi: Renfa* [Guanzi: Reliance on Law]).
5. The well-field system was a Chinese feudal land-redistribution regime that existed from the ninth century BCE to around 260 BCE. Under this system, lands were controlled by the aristocracy but peasants were granted equal-sized land-use rights.
6. From the *Book of Lord Shang* (trans. Y. Pines, 2017, p. 143).
7. Joy Chen (2024) uses data from the Warring States period to demonstrate that it was advantageous for the attacking sides to have a centralized *junxian* system rather than a feudal system.
8. Zhao Dingxin (2015) posits that the shift towards centralized power during the Warring States period and the emergence of the bureaucratic state resulted from protracted warfare. While this logic may suit the history of the Warring States period, it seems inadequate for Western European history. Warfare evidently cannot explain Western Europe's evolution from medieval feudalism to modern constitutional democracy. In the centuries, if not millennia, of escalating large-scale

wars in Western Europe, not only was there no overriding trend for feudalism to be overtaken by centralized power but France, where power was relatively more centralized and bureaucratic, repeatedly lost its wars with England.

9. "[The empire] transferred 120,000 households from across the realm to Xianyang," from *Shi ji: Qin Shi Huang benji* (*Records of the Grand Historian: Records of the First Qin Emperor*) by Sima Qian (2010).
10. Sima Qian (2010), *Shi ji* (*Records of the Grand Historian*).
11. Post-Zhou dynasties maintained the roles of the Three Councilors and Nine Ministers. In the pre-Qin era, these positions were held by nobles. From the Qin and Han dynasties onwards, they constituted the empire's highest offices of the state.

5 The Imperial Examinations and Confucianism

The Institutional Genes for Imperial Personnel and Ideology

The *keju* (科舉) system, or the imperial examination system, was one of the crucial institutional genes of the entire Chinese imperial institution. It ensured the imperial institution remained unchallenged ideologically and prevented the rise of de facto nobles or local lords through its control of the personnel system. The *keju* system incorporated the ideological principles of "Confucianism,"[1] and also regulated the selection and placement of bureaucrats through the imperial examination system. This institutional gene instilled a deep-rooted concept of hierarchy in people's minds, fostered a population that obeyed authority unconditionally, and suppressed aspiration to pursue individual rights. It aligns closely with the institutional genes required to establish a totalitarian system. Conversely, it is diametrically opposed to the institutional genes necessary for forming a constitutional system.

Keju, which began in 124 BCE and ended in 1905, "lasted for two thousand years, concurrent with the dynastic empire itself" (Yu, 2005). As the content of the *keju*,

> Confucianism in China ... has a notable feature, that is, the high degree of integration between politics and religion – they are inseparable and unified. The emperor also serves as the pope, or vice versa. Divine authority and political power are intertwined. The doctrines of Confucianism are delivered in the form of governmental decrees. The imperial "imperial edict" is a sacred decree, equivalent to the papal bull. In medieval Europe, a king's coronation required the Pope's anointing, which was considered as receiving God's approval. In contrast, when a

Chinese emperor ascended to the throne, all he needed to do was to issue a proclamation to the world. The proclamation always began with, "By the Mandate of Heaven, the Emperor decrees," making the emperor's decree carry the authority of a papal directive. (Ren, 1999, p. 5)

In contrast, the Church is a comparably crucial institutional gene in Western countries (including Russia), encompassing both Christianity as a religion and ideology and the Church as a social organization of a government-like structure. From the time Christianity became the state religion of the Roman Empire until the nineteenth century, the Church and secular power in Europe (including the area of modern Russia) were closely intertwined. However, they never completely merged into one. The Church and secular power maintained their status as separate entities.

This chapter discusses the *keju* system and the Church as institutional genes, considering their basic characteristics, origins, evolution, and their impacts on institutional evolution as social organizations and governments. It is important to clarify that from a social science analytical perspective, we focus on the *keju* system as an institutional gene of the Chinese imperial system, not on Confucianism per se, or its authenticity, specific schools, philosophy, or religious aspects. From an institutional research viewpoint, we are interested in aspects that have played significant roles in shaping institutions and history.

5.1 CONFUCIANISM AND THE *KEJU* SYSTEM VERSUS CHRISTIANITY AND THE CHURCH

5.1.1 *Confucianism and the* Keju *as an Institutional Gene of the Chinese Imperial System*

The *keju* system was initially established to support imperial rule by altering personnel selections of the imperial bureaucracy and reinforcing legitimacy through the propagation of Confucianism. However, through centuries of evolution, it became an integral component of the Chinese imperial system and evolved into institutional genes. During the reign of Emperor Wudi of Han (r. 141–187 BCE), less than a century after Emperor Qin Shi Huang first established the empire, the prototype of the imperial examination system, directly operated by the emperor and the court, was created to consolidate imperial rule. Nearly 400 years later, by the end of the Eastern Han dynasty, Confucianism evolved into a structured system under the emperor's direct cultivation. The main purpose of implementing an imperial examination system and using Confucianism as an ideology was to legitimize imperial rule and to weaken the political power base of the social elite by making it difficult for the descendants of high officials and nobility to hold office without passing an examination.

However, the partially institutionalized *keju* system could not prevent the disintegration of the empire at the end of the Han dynasty. It took nearly 360 years before the empire was reunified under the Sui dynasty (581–618). Learning from the collapse of the empire at the end of the Han dynasty, the rulers of the Sui dynasty formalized the examination system, ending the hereditary posts of the nobility and systematically limiting the opportunities for the offspring of prominent families to attain prestigious positions. In this way, they curtailed the potential challenges these families could pose to imperial power.

The *keju* system, once it reached maturity, became the basis of the imperial personnel system, dictating the entry and often the future career trajectory of the majority of imperial bureaucrats. This system, formally initiated during the Sui dynasty and later refined during the Song dynasty, guided China in developing a comprehensive, merit-based bureaucratic structure. This structure effectively suppressed the emergence of an aristocracy, thus ensuring that the empire remained unchallenged and undivided from within until the dawn of the twentieth century.

The cornerstone of Confucianism, the content of the *keju* examination, was loyalty – towards the emperor, imperial authority, and the empire itself. The Confucian classics that were used for the *keju* exams were carefully collected and interpreted by imperial scholars and then approved by the emperor. Candidates, who were prospective bureaucrats, had to memorize these classics and only after passing the exams could they secure positions in the imperial bureaucracy. For the highest tier of these exams, the palace examination, the emperor himself acted as the chief examiner. He personally presided over the examination held in the palace and successful candidates were automatically considered his disciples. Moreover, from its organizational methods to its budget support, the *keju* system was a fundamental part of the empire's politics and finances.

For two millennia, the Chinese Empire channeled intellectuals into the examination system, effectively indoctrinating unwavering loyalty towards both the emperor and the empire. The allure of the imperial examinations, combined with the stringent prohibition of any organized intellectual pursuits outside the exam's scope, effectively nullified the existence of organized, independent intellectual entities capable of challenging imperial dominion. Consequently, the examination system evolved into an institutional gene that solidified and perpetuated the imperial order in China, persisting for two millennia. Individuals with different beliefs or ideologies were forced to adapt in order to conform to official Confucianism. Even Jesuits sent by the Vatican had to disguise themselves as Confucian scholars to maintain their presence in China and any visible signs of missionary activity were threatened with prohibition or expulsion.

In stark contrast, despite significant bureaucratic institutions of the West, particularly those pertaining to civil service examinations which were imported from China by the Jesuits during the seventeenth and eighteenth centuries (Landry-Deron, [1735] 2002), there was no direct link between the Church and the secular processes for civil appointments. Moreover, the contents of the civil service examination in the West focused more on intellectual merit and less on brainwashing.

5.1.2 Separation of Church and State as an Institutional Gene of Western Europe

Christianity, the state religion of Europe's feudal monarchies (except in regions under Ottoman rule), saw its monarchs crowned by the

Pope. Some monarchs successfully exerted control over the Church within their borders, yet the demand for separation of Church and state persisted. Conventionally, the Church and the state bureaucracy maintained their distinct identities and any attempt to subordinate the former under the king's control would have contravened this norm. The independent coexistence of these two institutions developed into a fundamental, albeit contentious, institution within feudal Europe. The monarch's inability to control the Church is completely inconceivable from the perspective of the Chinese imperial system. However, the question is how this institutional gene, which separates religious and secular authorities, came into existence.

From the very beginning, even before the formal establishment of the Christian Church, Christian communities were independent of secular power. Christianity faced brutal oppression by the Roman Empire in its early years. The Gospels express a notable aversion to autocracy and even direct opposition to the Roman Empire. For example, Paul the Apostle, who perished in prison in the Roman Empire in 64 CE, portrayed the reign of Christ as antagonistic to the prevailing authorities of an evil age (Yang, 2010). He characterized the rulers and authorities of the Roman Empire of his day as the embodiment of that evil age, manifested as a "fallen" form of power. As recorded later in Galatians of the New Testament, Paul urged resistance to the Roman Empire. Rulers, he said, oppressed the people out of fear, and their reliance on violence only further emphasized this fear. Plenty of such content in the Bible formed an important part of the institutional genes that later led to the Reformation. Even before Martin Luther, Erasmus posed a theological challenge to Roman Catholic doctrine based on his reinterpretation of St. Paul's writings.

Only when the Christian Church had matured as an institutional gene and Christianity had become an irresistible force did the Roman Empire recognize its legitimacy. The escalating influence of the Church eventually led the emperor to establish Christianity as the state religion. Given that the Bible had been widely disseminated and the Church had emerged as a well-established formidable entity with extensive congregations, the independence of Christianity and its Church was hardly shaken by Roman or any other secular authorities. Unlike the Qin Empire, facing the institutional gene of Christianity, the Roman Empire lacked the ability to execute a mass book-burning, nor could it instigate a new religion like the Han dynasty, let alone rewrite the Bible.

For centuries, this institutional gene, promoting the separation of Church and state, found fertile ground in Europe throughout various pivotal eras such as the Renaissance, the Reformation, and the Enlightenment, and in England from the Magna Carta to the Glorious Revolution. Figures like Martin Luther embedded this separation at the core of the Reformation. His "Two Kingdoms" doctrine, also known as the "Doctrine of the Two Governments," posed a direct challenge to the Pope's interference in secular affairs.

In contrast, Confucianism, which originated from the so-called Five Teachings associated with the ancient saintly kings of China, although worshipped as a theological system (to be elaborated upon in the later part of this chapter), was simply a creation of monarchs. Subsequent monarchs followed the practices of King Wen and King Wu of the Zhou dynasty for the sake of their rule. Confucius extended those courtly practices of the Zhou to a wider society and his teachings were further refined by his followers through the generations into what is known as the Five Classics of Confucianism. Confucianism has the Son of Heaven (i.e., the emperor) as its religious leader, Confucius as its forefather, and the *Yijing* (*Book of Changes*) as its source of divine wisdom. In essence, the Confucian imperial examination system constituted an entirely artificial system of beliefs and institutions created by secular authorities to support imperial rule and to serve the emperor. Everything about Confucianism, from the classics to the rituals, was under the complete control of the emperor to strengthen his power.

After becoming the state religion, Christianity received financial and military support from the Roman Empire. The state Church gradually monopolized the spiritual discourse and its teachings became orthodox, stifling other interpretations of Christianity, with no mention of other beliefs. At the time, illiteracy was widespread among the commoners, so the Bible was mainly accessed by the clergy, who represented the papacy, while the faithful relied on their interpretations. As the state religion of the Roman Empire under the patronage of the emperor, the Church tended to interpret the parts of the Bible that were most favorable or compatible with the imperial rule, which gradually became dogma.

The Church used orthodoxy to indoctrinate Europeans in a manner similar to the way the Chinese Empire used Confucianism to brainwash Chinese. But the difference is that the Roman emperor could not directly dictate the Church's teachings or its interpretation of the Bible. The Church was an independent bureaucracy, led by the Pope, with its operations determined by the clergy themselves. Neither the Roman emperors nor the medieval monarchs had the power to alter the Bible, dictate how it should be interpreted, or directly manipulate the Church's operations. Yet, the close relationship between imperial institutions and the Orthodox Church in the Byzantine Empire sets it apart from the institutional genes of the Roman Catholic regions. We will delve into the crucial role of the Orthodox Church and the Byzantine Empire in the origins of Tsarism in Chapter 7.

Because of the relative institutional independence of the Christian Church and the secular polity, both the Roman Empire and the medieval monarchies were subject to certain constraints imposed by the Christian Church. Even in cases where religious authority and secular rule were intertwined, with one dominating the other, they still maintained separate identities and a degree of mutual restraint existed. This stands in contrast to the consolidated imperial system in China.

The medieval Catholic Church, with its ideology, provided the fundamental legitimacy for secular power and its highly organized bureaucracy surpassed that of the secular kingdoms. As a result, it was challenging for national monarchs to exert control or manipulate the Church. Secular incursions into ecclesiastical power primarily concerned the appointment of bishops, while in the reverse direction, the Church frequently infringed upon royal authority. In either instance, breaching the sanctified separation of Church and state invariably elicited fervent resistance. The Investiture Controversy, a protracted conflict between the Pope and the Holy Roman Emperor over the appointment of bishops in the eleventh and twelfth centuries, exemplifies the extent to which Europe's spiritual and secular authorities were held in mutual check.

On the basis of the originally established institutional genealogy which ensured mutual restraint between theocracy and secular power, the Reformation emerged, creating numerous Protestant sects and challenging the Catholic monopoly on theocracy. This movement further spurred the separation of Church and state, solidifying it into a more robust institutional gene. Initially, Protestants were labeled heretical by the Catholic Church and faced persecution and execution in many countries. This hostility and animosity between the Catholic and Protestant Churches ignited decades of religious warfare. To safeguard freedom of belief and expression, the separation of Church and state was institutionalized during the Glorious Revolution and became a pivotal factor in establishing constitutional government in England.

In contrast, the *keju* Confucianism system was an inseparable part of secular authority from its inception. There was never a separation of *keju* and state in Chinese history, nor any demand for such a separation. The sole function of the *keju* system was to serve and uphold imperial authority. Notably, even for prominent pro-constitution reformers of the Late Qing period, such issues were never up for debate or deliberation.

Finally, let me conclude this section by emphasizing that even where the Church fell under royal influence, it preserved its separate identity. This distinction is clear because the divine right of kings had to be ratified by the Church. When the Church ordained a monarch, it communicated to its subjects that it was acting as the executor of God's will and judgment. This stands in contrast with the Chinese model, where the emperor was inherently divine and regarded as the Son of Heaven. Confucianism and the *keju* system formed a conglomerate of beliefs and institutions, carefully crafted by imperial scholars to reinforce imperial rule. Everything linked with Confucianism, from religious doctrine to rituals, fell under the emperor's control.

5.1.3 Independent Scholarship: The Church versus the Keju System

Under the tradition of relative separation of Church and state, a prominent characteristic of higher education and scientific research systems in medieval Europe was the relative autonomy of Church-run educational and academic institutions from secular governments. Given that Christianity was the state religion, secular authorities had to acknowledge that God reigned over both government and monarchy, thus they could not exercise full control over how the clergy and their congregations explored God and the Bible. Consequently, believers could pursue an understanding of the Creator's wisdom independently of the secular regime and were allowed to assemble, publish, and preach within the boundaries sanctioned by the papacy. As history turns out, the independent scholarship facilitated by the separation of Church and state is fundamental to the nurturing of constitutionalist thought and pivotal for scientific progress.

While the medieval monarchy was autocratic, the Church, being relatively independent of royal authority, was able to systematically and institutionally cultivate intellectuals who dedicated their entire lives to understanding God and His created world. Such an understanding could indirectly challenge secular authority. This is because when the divine right of kings is invoked, any suggestion that the king is misguided about God presents a fundamental challenge to the secular order. Consequently, it was not just the Church but also the medieval monarchies that were highly stringent about banning and suppressing heretics. A divergent interpretation of God could fundamentally undermine the foundations of secular power and its perceived "legitimacy."

These independent explorations in theology and social issues drove the Reformation, catalyzed the Enlightenment, and systematically laid the groundwork for concepts of human rights. These thinkers postulated that, since God is superior to the monarch, any monarch or man-made institution must defer to the will of the Creator. Consequently, all humans, being creations of God, should inherently possess inalienable basic rights. In this respect, our modern understanding of human rights, the rule of law, and the institutional and ideological constraints imposed on monarchs are all intrinsically linked to the fundamental concepts of Christianity. This forms the origin of the foundational ideas regarding human rights and equality as articulated by Locke prior to the Glorious Revolution.

Another crucial aspect pertains to the incentives offered by the contrasting institutions. In Europe, the separation of secular and divine power meant that the Church, barring corruption, had no secular or material incentives. Clergy and believers focused solely on God, viewing the promise of reward in the afterlife as the only incentive rather than seeking power and wealth in their earthly lives. The doctrine of original sin stipulated that anyone seeking entry into heaven had to atone for their sins during their lifetime. As this atonement could not be quantified, the promised reward was of a spiritual, not worldly, nature.

However, Christianity (along with its precursor, Judaism and the deist and pantheist beliefs which evolved from Christianity following the Enlightenment) offered powerful spiritual incentives to believers. Redemption, coupled with the curiosity and passion to comprehend God's world, inspired selfless pursuits among the faithful, including a deep quest for spiritual and scientific truth, sometimes extending to the brink of martyrdom.

This spiritual incentive was in stark contrast to the one provided by the *keju* system, where participants were primarily driven by the goal of securing governmental positions. Pursuing an understanding of God and the principles of Creation, scholars affiliated with the Church committed themselves to meticulous reasoning and the systematic observation of the cosmos and the living world. They postulated that since all things were created by God and adhered to God's laws, the only way to truly know God was to understand the natural world and the rules it followed. Consequently, contrary to the Chinese *keju* system, which functioned as an extension of state power, the Christian Church established and nurtured educational institutions independent of secular authority. This, in turn, facilitated the emergence of an educated class that was independent of the government.

Conversely, within the Chinese Empire, advanced education and the *keju* system were simply extensions of the imperial court. Alongside the development of a nascent examination system, the Han dynasty established the Grand Academy (*taixue* 太学) in the capital, Chang'an. This academy was tasked with serving the empire and it was supported by affiliated academies at all local levels throughout the country. From this point forward, the empire's education system evolved in lockstep with the examination system. During the Sui-Tang period, the Grand Academy was renamed the Imperial University (*guozi jian* 国子监), a designation it retained until the *keju* was abolished in the late Qing dynasty.

As the cultivation of court personnel was the raison d'être of China's educational institutions, learning and politics were invariably intertwined. Therefore, in Chinese history there never was a system of learning independent of the imperial court, nor were there ever any calls for such a system. Even during vigorous scholars' movements, when reformists debated on how to reform the empire, the notion of independent scholarship was never brought to the forefront.

Confucianism, the cornerstone of the *keju* system, espouses the hierarchical principles of obedience to bureaucracy, with the sovereign at the apex, analogous to the obedience of a son to his father. The Grand Academy was tasked with training students with the express purpose of serving the emperor, the Son of Heaven, fostering in them unwavering loyalty to his rule and instilling in them the principle of never challenging the imperial court on matters concerning the rights of the people. The boldest Confucian scholars documented in Chinese history only ever broached policy issues intending to promote the longevity of the empire and enhance the merits of the emperor. Moreover, a typical Confucian scholar in Imperial China displayed little to no interest in natural phenomena or technology and, consequently, would neither engage in independent academic pursuits nor express a desire for academic autonomy.

Institutionally speaking, as the backbone of the empire's personnel and education systems and the primary promoter of Confucianism, the *keju* system offered potent, tangible material incentives to scholars across society. Within the imperial system and its educational structure, the singular opportunity for a scholar's personal advancement was to secure a government position, the only pathway to which lay through the examinations. Anyone who succeeded in these examinations had the chance to rise above their station in society. This was encapsulated in a common saying: "A farm lad at dawn; a court official by dusk." A scholar's accomplishments, social status, and rewards were all determined by his exam results.

The following report vividly illustrates the intense motivation among Chinese students to participate in the *keju* system towards the end of the nineteenth century. After the failure of the Hundred Days' Reform, there was a period when modern educational institutions and the traditional imperial examinations coexisted in certain regions. Yet, students attending modern institutions, even those who were chosen for study abroad programs, were eager to participate in the *keju* examinations at any given opportunity, even to the point of risking expulsion from their schools. "The allure of the *keju* exams was irresistible for school pupils, resulting in many lacking the motivation to further pursue their studies [after the abolition of the *keju* system]" (Guan, 2017, p. 132).

Faith and science are unrelated to the *keju* exams. They were neither tested nor encouraged. The emperor, regarded as the Son of

5.1 CONFUCIANISM & KEJU SYSTEM VS. CHRISTIANITY & CHURCH

Heaven, was believed to be the only legitimate interpreter of Heaven's will. Confucian temples were not equivalent to "churches"; they held no authority in interpreting Confucianism, which was the central content of the exams. The examination system was purely a tool for the emperor to maintain control over the state personnel and ideology. The elements of Confucianism to be tested on the *keju* exam were compiled and revised by imperial scholars.

For the majority of candidates, delving beyond the content of the *keju* exam to seek deeper insights into Confucianism or to contemplate what constitutes credible historical evidence was unnecessary, as their primary concern was meeting the examiners' expectations. For them, not only was there no deity superior to the emperor but there was also no ambition beyond securing an official position in the imperial bureaucracy. Their world was confined within the parameters set by the emperor and the *keju* system reinforced this mindset, leaving little room for free intellectual exploration and it fostered a culture that largely ignored faith and science.

Motivated by the prospect of attaining an official position, generations of talented scholars throughout Chinese history devoted themselves to the pursuit of government careers, fixating on the imperial court and bureaucracy as they secured roles and engaged in power struggles. Generally, these individuals exhibited no interest in exploring the world beyond their official duties. They did not typically seek spiritual fulfillment and had even less curiosity about the natural world or science. The potent incentives provided by the combination of examinations and official evaluations left China with a weak foundation for the development of faith and science. By "science," in this context, I refer to the pursuit of truth, akin to faith in its own right, rather than merely a collection of techniques or skills.

The *keju* examinations of the Tang and Song dynasties once included mathematics, astronomy, and calendrics, which were of great value for observing celestial phenomena, compiling almanacs, and guiding agriculture. But for nearly 700 years, from the restoration of the *keju* in the Yuan (1315) to its abolition (1905), mathematics and science were completely excluded from the imperial examination. This was because if the proliferation of skills in these disciplines led to predictions and the compilation of almanacs from unofficial sources that contradicted those of the state astronomy offices, it would have undermined the legitimacy of the imperial court. Thus, generations of scholars who devoted themselves to the imperial examinations after the Yuan dynasty did not study mathematics and science. Even traditional Chinese medicine, providing significant practical value for the emperor and the court, never featured as a topic on the examinations. Those who studied Chinese medicine were often scholars who had failed the examinations. For example, the eminent doctor Li Shizhen was forced to study Chinese medicine after failing the advanced *keju* examinations several times, although he passed the bottom-level examination.

The *keju* had a profound impact on morality in China. Generally, the essence of morality consists of the principles or beliefs that individuals adhere to for self-discipline in situations that cannot be assessed or monitored. However, moral instruction in the *keju* version of Confucianism was designed to legitimize and maintain the ruling order and it was constructed with testing in mind. Generations of scholars, enticed by the prospect of success on the examinations and securing an official position, prioritized the version of Confucian morality that was being tested in exchange for official roles and material incentives. As a result, the focus of the social elite was shifted towards material gain, leaving faith and morality in the shadows. The notion that "all things are inferior; only learning is superior" has influenced Chinese society for generations, whereas in this context, "learning" refers to excelling on examinations and climbing the rungs of the imperial bureaucracy.

Dai Zhen of the Qing dynasty sharply criticized Zhu Xi's hypocrisy (later in this chapter I will explain Zhu Xi's contribution to Confucianism) in his moral teachings – "Cultivate the principles of Heaven, extinguish the desires of Man," noting that "Cruel officials kill by laws while Neo-Confucians kill by their preaching." Lu Xun of the early twentieth century was more direct, saying that although "every page of Chinese history has the words 'benevolence, righteousness, and morality' written on it," the actual meaning was "cannibalism" (*Diary of a Madman*). In line with the criticisms levied by Dai Zhen and Lu Xun, there exists an old Chinese adage lamenting hypocrites who "bear virtue and morality on their tongues but harbor greed and lust in their bellies."

5.2 THE EMERGENCE AND EVOLUTION OF OFFICIAL CONFUCIANISM AND THE *KEJU* SYSTEM

Confucianism and the *keju* in China, along with Christianity and the Christian Church in the West, have had profound impacts on Chinese and Western societies from both institutional and cultural perspectives throughout two millennia. They serve as the "institutional genes" that guide institutional evolution in both East and West. In this section, I will investigate and compare the emergence and evolution of these two systems. I will begin by examining the topics of religious and institutional monism and pluralism in both China and the West.

Religious monism and pluralism arose in significantly different historical contexts in China and the West. Christianity was predominantly monolithic prior to the Reformation. The Church was intolerant not only of other religions but also of heterodox interpretations of the Bible and God by various Christian sects. The Reformation ignited a protracted series of wars between Catholics and Protestants. Only after the Western countries gradually established constitutional governments, which safeguarded freedom of belief and expression, did religious pluralism become the standard norm.

In contrast, under China's imperial rule, where everything was tailored to serve the secular power, the empire was relatively tolerant towards religions and ideologies, as long as they obeyed the authority, notwithstanding fluctuations over time. On the religious side, there was a degree of tolerance and pluralism at certain times in the empire's history, provided they pledged to obey the emperor's orders. Consequently, the official version of the Confucian classics was adjusted to include elements of Taoism, Buddhism, and other beliefs. However, on the secular front, there was never any tolerance for pluralistic ideas that challenged the imperial authority, and religions were compelled to submit to imperial rule.

Contrary to the coexistence of divine and secular dual institutions in Europe, the Chinese imperial system was a monopolistic institution. No other system was permitted to exist outside the control of the imperial power and the *keju* system served as the backbone of this monolithic imperial order. Functionally and by design, it was an exclusive system, allowing no room for competition. As for the apparent "inclusiveness" of the official interpretation of Confucianism, such assimilation was entirely intended to serve the monarchical rule of the emperor.

All imperial systems shared a common characteristic: the utilization of violence to suppress and eradicate any ideology or religion that threatened their dominance (for the concept of a imperial system, see Section 1.2). This is evident in both the nascent unified Chinese Empire, which witnessed book-burning and live burials of Confucian scholars, and the Roman Empire, which fiercely suppressed the emerging Christianity. Strikingly, these same empires, in later years, would elevate the ideologies they once sought to extinguish, promoting them to the status of a state religion or the guiding philosophy of state institutions.

After consolidating his empire, Qin Shi Huang took dramatic measures to dismantle the residual aristocratic power of the Zhou dynasty's feudal system. He abolished the enfeoffment of nobles and converted their ancestral lands into possessions of the emperor. The so-called *junxian* system (referenced in Chapter 4), which was widely established at the time, ensured that each region within this vast unified empire was governed by officials appointed by the central government. There were no hereditary noblemen with local power; only the emperor held hereditary authority.

Legalist governance (also detailed in Chapter 4) was particularly rigorous with its system of punishments and rewards, reinforcing the principle that, "those who obeyed would prosper and those who disobeyed would perish." Despite these measures and the establishment of a unified imperial system, the empire continually faced challenges from remnants of the feudal aristocracy, Confucian scholars, and their affiliated literature.

5.2.1 Emergence of the Examination System and the Creation of the Confucian Classics

Institutions are inextricably linked to public consensus. The Qin Empire established two institutional genes of China's imperial system: the *junxian* system and the imperial land system. However, tyranny, established solely on the basis of violence and expropriation, confronted serious challenges to its legitimacy of rule.

Qin Shi Huang's transition from feudalism to the imperial *junxian* system disrupted noble interests and sparked fierce opposition. In 213 BCE, the official, Chunyu Yue, demanded a return to the practice of feudalism, citing the Confucian classics and arguing that ignoring historical practices would lead to administrative failure. On the contrary, Chancellor Li Si, a Legalist, criticized Confucians for dwelling on the past at the expense of the present and proposed banning Confucianism. Qin Shi Huang adopted Li's advice, burned all the Confucian classics, including the *Book of Songs* and the *Collection of Ancient Texts*, and executed those found discussing those works by burying them alive.

Using the Legalist approach of book-burning and live burials of Confucian scholars, without an ideology to lend legitimacy to its rule, the Qin Empire was short-lived. The succeeding Han Empire sought to legitimize its reign by endorsing the official version of Confucianism as the sole ideology and suppressing all other schools of thought. Simultaneously, it introduced an early form of the imperial examination system to select government officials, thereby strengthening the imperial bureaucracy.

From the Han dynasty's endorsement of official Confucianism to the establishment of the formal *keju* system in the Sui dynasty and its subsequent refinement throughout the Song dynasty and beyond, the official Confucianism, which formed the essence of the *keju*, consistently evolved in tandem with the evolution of the imperial system. The reason I use the term official "Confucianism" is to remind readers that much of what is recognized as a Confucian classic was not actually written by the founding sages Confucius and Mencius. As Kang Youwei discovered through textual research, *The Ancient Classics*, which had been the core of the imperial examinations since the Eastern Han, were in fact forged by Liu Xin at the end of the Western Han dynasty (206 BCE to 24 CE). According to Liang Qichao, this work by Kang "has shaken the very foundation of the orthodox school of Qing Confucian learning, and all ancient books must be re-examined and revalued."[2]

Once Confucianism was securely entrenched as the "state religion," the book-burning and live burial of scholars became taboo in the Chinese imperial tradition, reviled and cursed by officials and literati throughout the ages. Yet, the burning-burial atrocities lingered in the institutional genes of the imperial system, intrinsically linked to autocracy, and the legacy eventually manifested itself in the form of totalitarianism. Mao Zedong, the CCP chairman, proudly portrayed the campaigns against counterrevolutionaries and "rightists" and the Cultural Revolution as a continuation of Qin's burnings and burials (Chapters 11 and 12). On May 8, 1958, at the 2nd Session of the CCP's 8th National Congress, Mao depicted Qin Shi Huang as a master strategist, who prioritized the present over the past, and he declared:

> Qin Shi Huang? He's nothing. He merely buried 460 Confucian scholars; we've buried 46,000! In our campaign against counterrevolutionaries, haven't we exterminated some counterrevolutionary intellectuals? I've debated with democrats. You label us as Qin Shi Huang, but no, we surpass him a hundredfold. You berate us as dictators, likening us to Qin Shi Huang, and we admit to all of it. The pity is you don't say it enough, and often we have to add to it. (Mao, [1956] 1968a, p. 72)

The Han Empire, succeeding the brief rule of the Qin, inherited the latter's institutions. Its four-century-long reign and substantial territorial expansion were inextricably linked to its efforts to complement the exercise of violence with the establishment of legitimacy. The Han Empire molded the Confucian teachings into state-sanctioned classics to legitimize the ruling order and the emperor's authority, which it promoted extensively. Gradually, the Chinese imperial system evolved into a comprehensive control mechanism that combined Confucianism with the severity of Legalism. The official interpretation of Confucianism emphasized the emperor as the Son of Heaven and the sole legitimate ruler. Only officials appointed by the emperor held legitimacy, thus excluding the hereditary landed aristocrats from the system. This underlying logic paralleled the Roman Empire's decision to accept Christianity, which it had once persecuted, as the state religion.

After its violent establishment, the Han Empire sought to offer incentives to significant figures within the emperor's alliance. Emperor Han Gao Zu ennobled over a hundred of his political and military allies, leading to a hybrid system of centrally governed districts and enfeoffed principalities. This action partially relinquished the *junxian* system and reintroduced a form of feudal order. Throughout the empire, lands were granted to the emperor's siblings and most accomplished ministers, while areas surrounding the capital remained under direct imperial rule.

This arrangement bore resemblances to the Warring States period (475–221 BCE), when rulers of self-governing royal houses aimed to attract "roving advisors" – the most intellectually distinguished individuals – to their service. "In the early years of the Han, feudal lords and princes managed their own people and sought wise counsel. The Prince of Wu, for instance, recruited roving advisors from all directions."[3]

Institutional genes inherited from the old Zhou regime were further reinstated following the death of Emperor Han Gao Zu. As regional lords began vying for power and defying the central imperial authority, Emperors Wen and Jing sought to regain control, leading to the Rebellion of the Seven States in 154 BCE. In response to rising feudal powers, Emperor Wu (r. 141–87 BCE) issued the renowned "Grace Decree" (*Tui-en Ling* 推恩令).

The decree allowed vassal descendants to inherit fiefs, alleviating resentment. However, it also mandated the division of fiefs among all sons of the vassals, thereby systematically diluting and limiting their power. This ruling, while aimed at curbing and eventually eliminating the influence of the vassals, cleverly aligned with the self-interest of most vassal descendants.

From that point on, all Chinese imperial rulers adopted this strategy, which proved conducive to their objectives. Consequently, the primogeniture system was officially abolished in the Chinese Empire, making the rejection of primogeniture an integral element in the institutional genes of the imperial land system. This shift fundamentally weakened the power of the local lords and eradicated the base of the landed aristocracy.

Nevertheless, local lords continued to resist integration into the unified empire's territory, recruiting scholars to aid their cause.[4] In competition with these vassals, to draw these advisors towards serving the unified imperial governance, Emperor Wu of Han established the Grand Academy system in 136 BCE. Located in the capital, this Academy was pivotal in training government officials. Meanwhile, provincial and prefectural authorities were tasked with assessing and nominating suitable candidates, subject to quotas, for government positions (Yu, 2005).

In a bid to legitimize the unified imperial system that centralized power and aligned the itinerant advisors with a shared ideology, Emperor Wu adopted scholar-official Dong Zhongshu's proposal to, "Dismiss other schools of thought and revere only the Six Confucian Classics."[5] Dong's Confucian teachings, like the "mutual correspondence between Heaven and man" and the "Grand Unity" of the universal empire, were adopted as the official doctrine. Consequently, Confucianism became the dominant philosophy in the Han Empire,[6] and an examination system was established to select intellectuals who conformed to Confucianism as candidates for the imperial bureaucracy.[7]

5.2 OFFICIAL CONFUCIANISM AND THE *KEJU* SYSTEM

By the second half of the first century BCE, the Grand Academy enrolled up to 3,000 students and approximately 100 individuals passed the official examinations each year, earning positions in various government departments. This marked the early form of the *keju* system. As a result, the Confucian principles regarding protocol and rituals were officially codified into law. However, it is worth noting that the official version of Confucianism deviated from and even contradicted certain aspects of the original Confucian teachings.

The book-burnings during the Qin dynasty resulted in a scarcity of resources for Confucian scholars during the early Western Han (the Western Han was the first part of the Han dynasty) period. This scarcity, coupled with the significance of Confucian texts, created an opportunity for fabrication. Towards the end of the Western Han period and during the short-lived Xin dynasty (9–23) that followed, the scholar-official Liu Xin (刘歆) claimed to have discovered a vast collection of pre-Qin Confucian texts, which had a transformative impact on Confucianism. Due to his close relationship with the throne, particularly with the Xin dynasty's founder Wang Mang (seen as a temporary usurper from the Han perspective), Liu Xin's "old texts" became the new classics of Confucianism. These texts subsequently became the central material for the imperial examinations and continued to hold that position until the abolition of the *keju* system in the twentieth century. However, since Sima Guang in the eleventh century, many scholars have argued, providing evidence, that Liu Xin falsified these classics to gain favor with the emperor.

During the later part of the Han Empire, the Eastern Han dynasty, Confucianism underwent extensive standardization, promoted by several generations of emperors and imperial courts. Emperor Zhang of the Eastern Han dynasty convened the Bai Hu Tang Meeting in 79 CE, building upon earlier imperial symposia on Confucianism. The discussions and outcomes of this meeting were compiled into a document known as the *Baihu tongyi* (白虎通义) (Comprehensive Understandings from White Tiger Hall). This document outlined the core principles and regulations of Confucianism and served as a governance code during the Eastern Han period (Li, 1999, vol. 1, p. 506).

The *Baihu tongyi* systematically transformed the official Confucian teachings into official Confucianism, asserting that the sovereign possesses divine status. Simultaneously, it reaffirmed the doctrine of the Three Principles and Five Virtues (*Sangang Wuchang*), the foremost principle of which stipulates that "ministers are subject to the orders of the Sovereign" (*jun wei chen gang*). In Confucianism, the Son of Heaven serves as both the head of state and the ultimate religious authority. Hence the statement: "To no one but the Son of Heaven does it belong to order ceremonies, to fix the measures, and to determine the written characters."[8]

In this context, "ceremonies" refer to religious protocol and rituals. "Measures" denote the bureaucratic system, other political and economic systems, and the system of weights and measures. "Written characters" symbolize a unified written script, a consistent system for textual verification, and a unified national ideology based on a singular collection of writings.

In summary, official Confucianism was shaped by the emperors and their advisors, who deliberately assembled and selected from the corpus of the Confucian classics. The deities and canon of Confucianism were forged through official processes, even though they were presented as ancient classics to bolster their authority when needed. This differs significantly from the evolution of Christianity, where the divinity of Christ and the establishment of the Bible as the Christian canon were firmly in place long before Christianity became the state religion of the Roman Empire. Furthermore, Christianity evolved from Judaism, an already mature religion, providing it with a well-established theological foundation.

But even among the Confucian scholars who had to adhere to the prescribed norms, some early doubters questioned the authenticity of the official Confucian scriptures. Song dynasty scholars such as Sima Guang and Hong Mai expressed skepticism about the Confucian classic *Zhou li* (*Rites of the Zhou*), suggesting it was a forgery by Liu Xin (Yu, 1991). More detailed scrutiny was undertaken by Qing scholars, including Liu Fenglu, Gong Zizhen, Wei Yuan, Shao Yichen, and Liao Ping in the eighteenth and nineteenth centuries. Their work confirmed that Liu Xin had fabricated and misconstrued the ancient scriptures.

Building on the research of Liao Ping and others, Kang Youwei published his magnum opus, *Xinxue weijing kao* （新学伪经考）(*A Study of Forged Classics from the Xin* Dynasty), in 1891. This work played a pivotal role in advocating for the Hundred Days' Reform movement, of which Kang was a key proponent.

In his summary of the evidence from prior studies, Kang concluded that several so-called "ancient" classics such as the *Zhou li*, *Yi li* (逸礼) (*Etiquette and Rites*), *Guwen shangshu* (*Old-Text Book of Documents*), *Zuo zhuan* (*Zuo's Commentary*), and *Mao shi* (毛诗) (*Book of Songs, Mao Version*) were in reality "pseudo-classics" fabricated by Liu Xin during the late Western Han dynasty to assist Wang Mang in usurping power.

Kang opined, "Liu Xin falsified the classics, distorting the teachings of the sages; and Zheng Xuan propagated the forgeries, leading Confucian learning astray." Kang further pointed out that the forged classics used in the *keju* exams were designed to aid the emperor and reinforce the existing imperial order.

Historian Qian Mu challenged the claims of Liao Ping and Kang Youwei. However, independent research by scholars such as Qian Xuantong, Gu Jiegang, Guo Moruo, and others confirmed that Liu Xin's "discovery" of the ancient texts was indeed fraudulent. For instance, Feng Youlan argued that Liu Xin had fabricated the *Zuo zhuan* by extracting content from the *Guoyu* (*Discourses of the States*) (Feng, 1985).

Because of the resistance of the old institutional genes, for the new institutional genes to emerge and attain dominance, it often requires many iterations. Although the Han dynasty created Confucianism and the imperial exam system, this nascent system failed to be universally implemented. In the late Eastern Han dynasty, leading lineage families dominated politics, creating a de facto aristocracy that rendered the imperial government impotent. The Grand Academy and the *keju* examination system went into decline and the dynasty eventually dissolved.

5.2.2 The Establishment of a Full-Fledged Keju System

For over 360 years following the Han dynasty, the unified empire ceased to exist, except for a brief period of unification during part of the Western Jin dynasty (265–316 CE). This period constituted the longest stretch of disunity in the more than two-thousand-year history of Imperial China. In 581 CE, Emperor Wen of Sui reunified the empire by force.

Learning from the experience of the Han dynasty, the Sui emperors institutionalized the imperial examinations to solidify the unified imperial system and prevent the accumulation of power within the nobility. In terms of its contribution to the creation of a long-lasting imperial system, the establishment of the *keju* system in the Sui dynasty was as pivotal as the establishment of the *junxian* system (prefecture and county system), and the imperial land system in the Qin dynasty.

Emperor Wen's initial move was to abolish the inherited nine-grade ranking system in the bureaucracy, thereby ending the appointment of officials based on lineage ranking. At the central level, the government was restructured into Five Departments and Six Ministries. Local authorities were reorganized into prefectures and counties. To weaken the power of the nobility, Emperor Wen emphasized that regional governors must be appointed by the imperial court and could not be representatives from the local clans.

Addressing the fundamental issue of identifying capable bureaucrats and managing ideology, the emperor expanded the institutions inherited from the preceding dynasty, the Grand Academy and the National University (*guozi xue*), which was the predecessor of the Imperial University (*guozi jian*) under Emperor Yang, promoted Confucianism, encouraged the practice of rituals, and elevated

Confucianism to the status of an indispensable part of governing the empire.[9] He also mandated localities to select and recommend candidates regularly to the central government, where their suitability for official positions would be determined through examinations on Confucianism. Consequently, schools proliferated across the regions, leading to a flourishing of Confucianism.[10]

The second emperor of the Sui dynasty was the official creator of the *keju* system. Upon his ascension to the throne in 604, an imperial edict was issued to establish Confucianism as the sole doctrine, excluding all other teachings. At the same time, the Imperial University and the Grand Academy were re-established and prefecture-and-county-level colleges were created.

In the second year of his reign, he instituted the *jinshi* degree, which was directly assessed by the imperial court, thereby laying the foundation for the *keju* system. Two years later, the emperor issued further edicts concerning various aspects of the examination system, including the introduction of ten examination subjects (Du, 1988). From then on, the *keju* system became the foundational system for controlling state personnel and ideology in the empire.

The initial *keju* system was divided into the *xiucai* (秀才) and *jinshi* (进士) sections. The relatively junior *xiucai* section was responsible for selecting official support staff, while the more senior *jinshi* section was in charge of selecting officials. The Ministry of Rites was tasked with assessing both the students of the Imperial University and those recommended by local authorities. The *jinshi* examination eventually became the principal gateway to a career in officialdom. Candidates who were successful on the *jinshi* examinations would then sit for a special examination conducted by the Ministry of Personnel before they were assigned official posts.

In the early years of the *keju* system, senior officials still maintained the privilege of bypassing the examinations to place their sons and protégés into government posts. However, this privilege was eventually eliminated. Initially, students from the Imperial University were primarily descendants of the nobility, as only the wealthy could afford to study and take examinations over several years. Most of the sages recommended by the local authorities also came from privileged backgrounds. However, these advantages diminished over time, systematically reducing the opportunities for the elites to form forces that could challenge imperial power.

Building on the foundations of the Sui, the *keju* was further stabilized and institutionalized during the Tang dynasty (618–907). Emperor Taizong of the Tang (r. 626–649) expanded access to education, enlarging schools and increasing student numbers. Empress Wu Zetian (r. 690–705) initiated what became the palace examinations when she began personally assessing nominees on policy and administration in the imperial palace. During the reign of Emperor Xuanzong (r. 713–756), eight court examinations were conducted by specially appointed senior officials, a practice that became standard. From Empress Wu onwards, the *keju* system included examinations in literacy and martial arts but never in science or technology – a situation that continued until the abolition of the *keju* in the early twentieth century.

Despite the *keju* system being consolidated and expanded during the Tang dynasty, it was still not sufficiently institutionalized. The enduring influence of traditionally powerful families facilitated some local high officials to evolve into de facto aristocrats, becoming local warlords whose power could be passed down through generations. Consequently, feudal warlords re-emerged in some regions during the mid-to-late Tang period.

In this context, General An Lushan leveraged his high-ranking righteous father and ultimately instigated the rebellion known as the An-Shi Rebellion, which precipitated the terminal decline of the Tang dynasty. In the process of suppressing the rebellion, the Tang court was compelled to bestow territories on rebel generals to secure their support, further fortifying the power of these lineages. In turn, these same families made efforts to undermine Confucianism and the *keju* system, seeking to maintain their dominance and challenge the imperial authority.

After the An-Shi Rebellion, some Confucian scholars sought to convince the emperor to re-establish the *keju* system and restore Confucianism in order to save the empire from further decline. They claimed that the root cause of the societal unrest was the decline of and general disregard for Confucianism. They emphasized that the essential Confucian principles of reverence for family and political hierarchy, along with loyalty to a wise sovereign, could have prevented the An-Shi Rebellion and halted the disconnection of local governors from central authority (Li, 2000, vol. 2, p. 9).

Nonetheless, the nobility had grown powerful by then and resistance against the *keju* was robust. After the Huang Chao Uprising (878–884), more territories fell under the control of local warlords and the regional nobility emerged stronger than ever before. The Tang Empire collapsed under the pressures exerted by this rising aristocracy, leading to the disintegration of the united empire once again.

5.3 THE CONFUCIAN *KEJU* SYSTEM BECOMES A MATURE INSTITUTIONAL GENE

The Confucian *keju* system, established by the imperial court since the Han, Sui, and Tang dynasties, was aimed at creating an ideological framework that legitimized imperial rule and at strengthening the imperial bureaucracy that weakened, and even aimed to eradicate, the nobility. But the Confucian *keju* system was not fully institutionalized in that period. It suffered a decline towards the end of the Han and Tang dynasties, paving the way for the emergence of a de facto aristocracy, territorial fragmentation, and the eventual collapse of the unified empire.

Nevertheless, the Confucian *keju* system, which had been evolving for centuries, emerged as an institutional gene, although it was far from mature at the end of the Tang dynasty. Adhering to the institutional heritage of the Tang, the monarchs of the Five Dynasties and Ten Kingdoms, the rulers of the fragmented Chinese Empire, each incorporated Confucianism to lend legitimacy to their rule and utilized the *keju* system to maintain a hold on their bureaucracies.

The behavior of the founder of the short-lived Liang dynasty (907–923) illustrates this point. Despite his notoriety for being untrustworthy, he claimed that his regime was divinely ordained. Throughout his reign, he venerated Confucius and revived and expanded the *keju* system.[11] It is noteworthy that during this period, in conjunction with the expansion of the *keju* system, the Confucian classics were first produced using woodblock printing (Li, 2000, vol. 2, pp. 86–107), a development that occurred more than four centuries before the Bible was printed.

Upon re-establishing a unified empire and with the institutional genes of the Confucian *keju* system substantially developed, the Song dynasty fully institutionalized the Confucian *keju* system. This resulted in a stable and unified structure of the imperial system in China from the Song dynasty onwards. Subsequently, no aristocratic force capable of challenging the imperial power ever surfaced again.

Emperor Taizu of the Song dynasty (960–1279), who ascended to the throne by a military coup, was aware of the lessons of the decline of Confucianism in the late Han and Tang dynasties and of the urgent need to establish the legitimacy of his rule. At the beginning of his reign, he began to restore and construct Confucian temples, build new schools, and facilitate the mass printing of the Confucian classics for circulation. Thereafter, throughout the Song dynasty, expanding Confucianism and improving the *keju* system remained a priority for the court, further enhancing this integral part of the institutional genes of the Chinese imperial system.

During the Song dynasty, two major reforms to the Confucian *keju* system were undertaken, each leaving a profound imprint on the functioning of the system in subsequent dynasties. The first was initiated by Wang Anshi, who sought to restore the original interpretations of the Confucian classics and update the examination topics accordingly. Wang contended that the original teachings of Confucianism had been lost in the wake of the Qin dynasty's book-burnings and live burials, resulting in the proliferation of heterodox teachings facilitated by fabricated content in the classics that had been handed down ever since.[12] In 1072, Emperor Shenzong (r. 1067–1085) gave his approval to Wang Anshi's proposal and appointed him to lead a new bureau tasked with reinterpreting the classical texts of Confucianism. Wang Anshi's reinterpreted versions of these classics became the foundation for the *keju* exams. Editions of these reinterpreted classics were distributed to the imperial family, the Grand Academy, and prefectural colleges all across the country.

Wang Anshi utilized reinterpreting the classics as a theoretical instrument for advocating his reforms. While on the surface he appeared to be reviving the Confucian canon, in reality, he was extrapolating from these texts his own perspectives on contemporary governance. This approach was known in antiquity as "invoking ancient precedents to promote reform." In essence, he tried to influence and unify the thinking of all *keju* candidates by abridging, interpreting, and annotating classical sources, and thereby to justify and promote reform. As a result, the Neo-Confucianism of the Song dynasty replaced the classicist Confucianism of the Han and Tang dynasties, both on the *keju* and in society at large. Nine centuries later, Wang Anshi's strategy was replicated by Kang Youwei, whose critiques of the Confucian content of the *keju* examinations sparked the Hundred Days' Reform movement.

An important part of Wang's *keju* reform was to establish his work, *The Three Classics*, as a classic in its own right and alter the form and content of the *keju*. Old rules for recruiting officials, based on poetry and prose skills, familiarity with excerpts from the classics, and textual exegesis, were discarded. A new *jinshi* examination was introduced, with standard answers drawn from the *Three Classics*.

Subsequently, generations of Chinese scholars studied this version of the ancient classic in preparation for the *keju* exams. The *Three Classics* had a profound influence on Neo-Confucianism during the Song dynasty, prompting a shift from the dissemination of exegesis of Han and Tang Confucianism to a pursuit of righteousness. The key point here is that although Confucian schools and the content of the imperial examinations could differ, their ultimate goals were all the same. They were designed for the sake of secular emperorship, not for divine authority. Essentially, what Wang Anshi did for Emperor Shenzong mirrored what Liu Xin had undertaken for Emperor Wang Mang of the Xin dynasty – interpreting the classics to facilitate political rule.

The philosopher Zhu Xi (1130–1200), from the late Southern Song dynasty, had an even greater influence on the development of the Confucian classics and the *keju* system than Wang Anshi. Zhu Xi served the court under four Song emperors, moving up and down the ranks of the bureaucracy. Having a thorough knowledge of the classics and court politics, he was acutely aware of what was most useful for the *keju* exams and knew how to adapt the Confucian classics to serve political needs.

Zhu Xi's method of standardizing and popularizing the Confucian classics held immense value for the empire, hence his work was canonized by emperors succeeding the Song dynasty. His most enduring legacy was the distillation of the essence of Confucianism into a framework of the Three Principles and Five Virtues (*Sangang Wuchang* 三纲五常), which provided moral guidance for individuals and also served as the ideological foundation for the imperial societal order. The first principle emphasized that the ruled, as subjects of the sovereign, were obligated to obey and could not challenge the emperor in any manner. This framework, he claimed, constituted the universal principle of imperial rule, which would endure regardless of which dynasty was in power or who was the ruler. He declared:

> There is only one principle in the universe. The heavens obtain it and become the heavens, the earth obtains it and becomes the earth, and all living beings born between heaven and earth obtain it and follow their nature. Its extension is manifested in the Three Principles, and its order is established in the Five Virtues. This principle flows everywhere, there is nowhere it does not reach.[13]

Zhu selected what became the Four Classic Books from the Confucian classics, in order to unify the concepts of the Three

Principles and Five Virtues. The Three Principles stated that: "When a subject serves his ruler, a child serves his father, and a wife serves her husband, the three relationships are in harmony, and the world is in order. If the three relationships are contrary, the world is in chaos."[14] Zhu's distillation of these notions was so effectively instilled into society that everyone was brainwashed even before they could read.

In addition to the Confucian classics, Zhu Xi promoted the ancestral shrine system to further extend Confucianism to every corner of society in an institutionalized manner, far beyond the scope of the imperial examinations. In the time of Confucius and Mencius, during the Zhou dynasty, rulers worshipped their ancestors in local clan temples. After Qin established the unified empire, local bureaucrats replaced regional princes and nobles. Even the most influential officials were deprived of their land-based powers and were not allowed to build clan temples in the areas they were sent to. These imperialist practices undermined the foundations of Confucianism. The Confucian texts destroyed by the burning of books could be recreated by collecting the old and fabricating the new. But after the destruction of the social tradition on which Confucianism rested, Confucianism would find it difficult to become the state religion in society, if there were no corresponding new traditions being created in society. It is from this aspect Zhu Xi's contribution was profound. He proposed that leading clans should construct ancestral shrines in their hometowns. The ancestors of the outgoing officials had family members to worship in their hometowns. According to the classics, only Grand Masters and above could maintain an ancestral shrine, but the practice gradually spread through society. During the Ming and Qing dynasties, it became common for ordinary families to construct their own clan temples. This widespread ancestral worship reinforced a Confucian mindset, which emphasized the emulation of ancestral models, contributing to the empire's social stability. Additionally, ancestral shrines served a secular function by preserving a moral framework built upon clan rules. Thus, while politics and religion merged within the structures of Confucianism at the imperial level, a similar union occurred within the Confucian micro-kingdoms of the ancestral shrines at the community level (Li, 2000, vol. 2, pp. 590–592).

In terms of the *keju* system, the Song *keju* started by following the Tang tradition. However, it later underwent several far-reaching reforms. Most notably, Emperor Taizu instituted the palace examination. All who passed the palace examination were designated as "disciples of the Son of Heaven," effectively students of the emperor, which furthered the imperial control of ideology and personnel.

Additionally, the Song dynasty also introduced a three-tier system of examinations, comprising prefectural, provincial, and palace examinations. Successful candidates from the prefectural examination were sent to the imperial capital as *juren* for the provincial examination, which lasted for three days. The final examination, the palace examination, took place in the imperial palace. The emperor himself presided and decided on the final ranking of the successful candidates. From the time of Emperor Taizu onwards, those who acquired a *jinshi* degree on the palace examination were directly appointed as officials, bypassing the need for further evaluation by the Personnel Ministry. The three-tier examination system was maintained in this way for over a millennium.

The Song dynasty raised the quota for award of the degree of *jinshi* to 70 or 80 per examination cycle, up from 20 or 30 in the Tang dynasty. The best graduates were divided into three grades: *jinshi* with distinction (first class), *jinshi* with merit (second class), and associate *jinshi* (third class). During the 320 years of the Northern and Southern Song era, the imperial examinations were held 118 times and over 20,000 graduates were accepted as officials.

The Southern Song was conquered by the Mongol-ruled Yuan Empire (1271–1368) shortly after Zhu Xi's time. The Mongol emperors recognized the importance of the Confucian *keju* system for asserting ruling legitimacy and establishing a bureaucracy. So, they swiftly adopted the corresponding institutional elements. Even before assuming the throne, the Yuan founder, Kublai Khan, engaged Liu Bingzhong and other Confucian scholars to devise a governance plan based on Confucian principles.[15] Kublai not only embraced the title "Great Master of Confucianism" (Rossabi, 1994) but also, on Liu Bingzhong's advice, named the empire Great Yuan (meaning "primordial force"), drawing this term from the Confucian classic, the *Yijing*.

The Mongol emperor, Renzong (仁宗) of the Yuan dynasty revived the *keju* in the second year after he acceded to the throne after the complete annihilation of the Southern Song dynasty (1313 CE). He decreed that scholar-officials would hereafter be assessed based on Zhu Xi's work, marking the first time in history that Zhu Xi's work had been elevated to such a stature. Renzong utilized Confucianism as a tool for governance, compelling Mongols and others of Central Asian ethnicity within the empire to study *Zhenguan zhengyao* (*The Essentials of Governance of Emperor Taizong's Reign*), *Zizhi tongjian* (*Comprehensive Mirror in Aid of Governance*), *Daxue yanyi* (*Expanded Interpretation of the Great Learning*), and related works. He mandated that candidates for official posts be examined based on Zhu Xi's *Sishi jizhu* (*Collected Commentaries on the Four Books*), instituting Zhu's Neo-Confucianist teachings as the basic syllabus for the *keju* examinations. During the Yuan dynasty, there were over 400 academies of classical learning and the number of prefectural and county schools reached a peak of over 24,400. What is even more significant is that the examination system remained in its form from 1313 until 1905, when the *keju* system was abolished.

In 1370, shortly after establishing the Ming dynasty, Emperor Taizu declared: "All Chinese and foreign civil servants must be selected by the *keju*, and no one would be allowed to obtain an official position without passing the examination." Moreover, examinations would be grounded in the classic commentaries of Zhu Xi and his fellow thinkers. Emperor Chengzu (also known as Emperor Yongle) later officially made the *keju* the state's main channel for recruiting officials, thus opening the route for landlords and even commoners to enter the official-gentry class (Guo, 2017, p. 2). Interestingly, despite Taizu's violent seizure of power and his brutal suppression of challengers to the regime, he strived for stability. He bestowed vassal kingships of various regions to his twenty-five sons but he also explicitly maintained the emperor's power to curtail these regional rulers (Wang and Gao, 2017, pp. 20–45). He actively promoted the *keju* as the decisive system for state appointments. Ultimately, it was the *keju* system that secured the stability and unity of the Ming dynasty.

Ever since the Han emperors fostered Confucianism and established the *keju*, rulers of every dynasty have sustained and enhanced these in order to retain power. History not only perpetuates systems that work but also tends to repeat many of the specific operations involved, such as manipulating the Confucian classics for the purpose of ruling. In addition to the abridgements and amendments of the Confucian classics by the imperial scholars in the Eastern Han period, the Ming emperors also tampered with the Confucian classics to meet their needs. By comparing the Ming and pre-Ming editions of the Confucian classic *Mencius*, contemporary scholars discovered nearly a hundred deletions. Numerous passages dealing with the ruler's self-constraint and respect for the people should allow people to criticize the ruler and oppose harsh taxes, the due benevolence of the ruler and the responsibility of the monarch for any social decay have been removed (Shao, 2007; Rong, 1947).

After the mid-Ming dynasty, almost all important posts within the imperial bureaucracy were occupied by *keju* graduates with a *jinshi* (進士) degree, as reflected by the saying, "No one could join the Hanlin Academy without a *jinshi* degree, and no one could join the cabinet unless he was a Hanlin."[16] Furthermore, rankings in the imperial bureaucracy aligned closely with examination grades. A Ming minister Wang Lun praised his government's exemplary management of the *keju* system, extolling its "orderly selection procedure and graded appointment system" (Guo, 2017, p. 9).

Based on that under the Song and Yuan, the *keju* under the Ming became more mature and more universal and institutionalized. It made admission to a school a prerequisite to participate in the *keju*. Excellent students selected from prefectural and county schools would be permitted to enroll directly at the Imperial University.

Provincial school officials held two levels of examinations and the candidates were divided into six classes according to their performance. Those ranked first and second class progressed to the provincial examination and were classed as *xiucai*.

The Ming dynasty *keju* was organized into three tiers: provincial, metropolitan, and palace examinations (乡试、会试、殿试). Provincial examinations were held every three years in each provincial capital. Candidates who passed the provincial examinations earned a *juren* (举人) degree. The metropolitan examination, in turn, was a national examination conducted by the Ministry of Rites in the year following the provincial examinations. *Juren* from across the nation would journey to the national capital for the metropolitan examination, administered by a chief imperial examiner. Candidates who succeeded on the metropolitan examination were called *gongshi* (贡士) and subsequently progressed to the palace examination, held later that same year. The palace examination was presided over by the emperor, who personally determined the final ranking of the examinees. No candidate was eliminated at this level, with the top three examinees gaining "first class" status and the top candidate being granted the title of *Zhuangyuan* (状元), a distinction which often precipitated rapid promotion.

In the Ming dynasty, the "eight-legged" essay, known as the *baguwen* (八股文), was the first assessment in the provincial and metropolitan examinations, a format carried over to the examinations of the Qing dynasty. The *baguwen*, a distinctive writing style, evolved from the Song dynasty's interpretations of the classics, primarily based on the annotations of Zhu Xi. Passages from the Four Books and Five Classics were chosen as examination topics in the *baguwen*. Candidates were mandated to use words representing the teachings of the sages, to adhere to a specific essay structure, to limit the number of words, and to maintain paired syntax. Over time, this mechanistic writing style became increasingly rigid. The late Ming reformist, Gu Yanwu, suggested that the emphasis on the *baguwen* led examiners to overlook the essence of the Confucian classics. He criticized that "while the *baguwen* flourished, the canonical texts of Confucianism were neglected; while the 18 offices [of examiners] thrived, the histories were forgotten," adding, in his view, that, "the harm done by the *baguwen* is worse than the burning of books [by Qin Shi Huang]."

What repressed the scholars more than the *baguwen* was the prohibition on freedom of speech. From the outset of large-scale education in the Ming dynasty, explicit decrees banned students from expressing opinions on political, social, and judicial matters. During the reign of Emperor Taizu of the Ming dynasty, all schools were required to house a slab stele in their study hall, engraved with this prohibition.[17] Violators faced severe punishment. This restriction on freedom of speech was entirely inherited by the Qing dynasty. Shunzhi, the first Qing emperor, implemented the scholar-official examination system, simultaneously mandating the text to be inscribed on Confucian study hall steles throughout the country, prohibiting scholars from expressing heretical views.

In the first year after the Manchus overthrew the Ming Empire (1644) and established the Qing dynasty, the first Qing emperor, while violently suppressing the Han revolt, issued an edict stating that the Confucian *keju* would be continued in order to enlist and stabilize the people. In the following year, the Qing court promulgated the *Keju* Provisions, which followed the procedures and contents of the Ming system. Provincial examinations were held in six provinces that year. From then on, large numbers of scholars were lured to take the examinations and in essence defected to the Manchu. Using a combination of soft power and military force, the Qing successfully subjugated the Ming Empire.

For 200 years, the Qing dynasty essentially maintained the *keju* system similar to that of the Ming dynasty, although some operational changes were made. These included expanding the examination disciplines, thereby providing more opportunities for entrance into officialdom. The metropolitan examinations adopted a selection process on a province-by-province basis, ensuring a certain level of regional equality in the intake of officials. A budgeting system for the examination was also institutionalized. As a fundamental part of the bureaucratic system, like in the Ming dynasty, the *keju* was the primary pathway to officialdom in the Qing dynasty. Those who gained entry into officialdom through other routes were not only fewer in number but also held less prestige and had fewer promotion opportunities compared to those who went through the *keju* (Hu and Li, 2017, pp. 1–3).

Over centuries of evolution, the Confucian *keju* system, since the Song dynasty, became an indispensable institutional gene for maintaining a high degree of stability within the imperial system. This was further refined in the Ming and Qing dynasties. By creating official Confucianism, the long-standing empire established a uniform ideology that supported imperial rule and social order. Almost all imperial officials ascended through the ranks by passing the *keju* examination, becoming deeply versed in standardized Confucian content encompassing ethics, morality, loyalty, filial piety, and etiquette. The *keju* system, with its high-powered incentives to study and ascend into officialdom, held formidable allure. The purpose of studying was not rooted in faith, curiosity, or the pursuit of truth but in realizing the dream of transitioning from "a farm lad at daybreak to a court official by dusk." This was how the system enticed scholars to remain loyal to the regime, warning people never to challenge the legitimacy or authority of the rule. However, by the end of the imperial era, the Confucian *keju* system confronted unprecedented challenges. Despite both the imperial system and the *keju* officially ceasing to exist after 1911, the institutional genes they left behind continue to influence society significantly, manifesting in various transformed forms.

NOTES

1. From a historical and scholarly perspective, scholars, including Liao Ping, Kang Youwei, Liang Qichao, Joseph Levenson, Du Weiming, Li Zehou, and Ren Jiyu, consider Confucianism to be a form of religion. Conversely, other researchers, such as Feng Youlan, Zhang Dainian, Chen Yongming, and Zhou Youguang, downplay the religious element

in Confucian doctrine and philosophy. This book focuses on the official ideology of the dynasties and the associated systems of rule, deliberately avoiding academic disagreements not directly related to the imperial examination system.

2. Liang Qichao, *Qing dai xueshu gailun* (Introduction to Qing Scholarship), in Liang (2006).
3. *Han Shu: Zou Yang zhuan* (*History of Han: Biography of Zou Yang*).
4. "The kings of Huainan and Hengshan ... once recruited advisors from every direction. The Confucian and Mohist scholars of Shandong all gathered between the Yangtze and Huai Rivers, holding discussions, writing essays, and publishing dozens of books. But, they ultimately rebelled, plotted treason, and were executed along with their clans" (*Yan Tie Lun: Chao Cuo* [*Discussions on Iron and Salt: Chao Cuo*]).
5. Dong Zhongshu, *Ju xianliang duice* (*Recommendations for Raising Up the Worthy and Wise*).
6. The proposal attributed to Dong Zhongshu, "Dismiss all other philosophical schools, Confucianism alone is honored," originates from Sima Guang's *Zizhi tongjian*, a text from the Song dynasty, but is notably absent from the *Shiji* (*Records of Grand Historian*) of the Han dynasty. Since the Qing dynasty, many historiographers have suggested that Sima Guang may have invented this passage to highlight Dong's significance. However, despite these disputes, it is undeniable that the policy of prioritizing Confucianism had taken root during the Han dynasty around the first century BCE.
7. *Hanshu: Rulin zhuan* (*History of Han: Biographies of Confucian Scholars*).
8. *Liji: Zhongyong* (*Book of Rites: Doctrine of the Mean*), translated by James Legge.
9. Emperor Yang of Sui once proclaimed: The emperor serves under the Mandate of Heaven, with fortunes and calamities ensuing in its natural order. If one behaves with propriety, auspicious omens are certain to descend; without it, disasters and anomalies emerge. Humans, while possessing the five constant virtues, have distinct spirits; with propriety, *yin* and *yang* harmonized in virtue, but without it, their hearts revert to a beast-like state. In governing the country and establishing oneself, nothing is achievable without propriety. (*Sui shu: juan 47: liezhuan 12: liu ji* [*Book of the Sui: vol. 47: Biographies 12: Liu Ji*])

10. *Sui Shu: juan 75: liezhuan 40: rulin (Book of the Sui: vol. 75: Biographies 40: Confucian Scholars).*
11. *Jiu wudai: Liang shu: Taizu ji (Old History of the Five Dynasties: Book of the Liang: Annals of Taizu).*
12. In Wang Anshi's own words: "I posit that only by selecting talent based on classical knowledge can a nation truly prosper, whereas misleading the populace with erroneous doctrines leads to a country's decline" (*Xiechu zuopuye biao. [Memorial by the* xiechu zuopuye]).
13. *Zhu wengong wenji, juan shiqi: Du da ji (Collected Works of Zhu Wengong, vol. 17: Reading the Great Chronicle).*
14. *Hanfeizi: Zhongxiao (Master Han Fei: Loyalty and Filial Piety).*
15. *Yuan shi: Shizu ji (History of the Yuan: Chronicles of Shizu)* and *Yuan shi: Liu bingzhong zhuan (History of the Yuan: Biography of Liu Bingzhong)* in Li (1999, vol. 2, p. 541).
16. (Zhang, 1974, vol. 70, p. 1702).
17. *Ming shi: Xuanju zhi yi (History of the Ming: Selection and Appointment of Officials 1).*

6 The Institutional Genes of Totalitarian Ideology

A totalitarian system employs levels of violence unprecedented in human history to exert total control over all aspects of society. Marx termed the violence inherent in communist totalitarianism as "the dictatorship of the proletariat." However, violence must be implemented by individuals. A regime as exhaustive in its control as totalitarianism, which detrimentally impacts nearly everyone – including those who execute the purges – cannot sustain itself on violence alone. An underlying ideology is essential. Thus, totalitarian ideology forms the system's crux. It is this pivotal element that breeds, expands, and sustains totalitarianism.

The first fully realized totalitarian system in the world – the Bolshevik system – was built upon the communist ideology of Marxism-Leninism. From the October Revolution in Russia in 1917 through the 1970s, this ideology spread globally and with it, the principles of totalitarianism.[1] The communist movement gained significant traction, especially in developing countries, leading to the emergence of China as the world's largest communist nation. Despite years of reform and opening-up, the communist totalitarian regime remains deeply rooted there. Even in modern developed and democratic societies, elements of communist thought continue to appeal strongly to certain segments of the population, including intellectuals. But where did communist thought originate and how did it form the basis for totalitarian regimes? Why has this ideology demonstrated such resilience? This chapter will explore the institutional genes that gave rise to communist ideology.

Communism, as a concept, belief, or ideology, originates from Christianity, or even Judaism. Early communist ideas are methodically presented in the Bible (both the Old and New Testaments), the most influential tome of its kind in the history of civilization. The entire New Testament, for example, recounts how Jesus and the Apostles advocated and practiced equality of all before God (including equality of income and wealth). By voluntarily renouncing their property in favor of communal ownership (referring to the community of the faithful), they effectively made themselves proletarians. They demanded that all who spread the faith do the same, creating a form of proletarian equality within the early Christian community. This example was emulated by missionaries and followers throughout much of the religion's ensuing history.

Egalitarianism has remained the primary source of the enduring appeal of communist ideas over the centuries. However, communism, both as a term and as it was understood, was first created in the late eighteenth century during the French Revolution for the movement led by François-Noël Babeuf (1760–1797).[2] It was not until 1842 that Engels learned about the term and concept of communism from John Goodwin Barmby (1820–1881), a British Utopian minister. It was only then that Engels discovered the communist movement that had been flourishing in France for decades.[3] Engels and Barmby jointly established the London Communist Propaganda Society (Busky, D.F., 2002). Several years later, Karl Marx learned about communism and the communist movement through Engels.

The Bolshevik system, while based on the ideology of communism, has pushed its principles of organization, mobilization, and centralization to their limits. The development was exceedingly rapid. It took just 120 years from the birth of Marxism to sweep the globe and rule a third of the world's population. Or rather, it took only half a century from the creation of the Bolshevik totalitarian regime for such a system to dominate a third of the world's population. In contrast, Christianity, the most influential religion in human history, took over a thousand years to grow to encompass a third of humanity. Some attribute the enormous systemic changes brought about by totalitarianism to Marx, the founder of the modern communist ideology and the spiritual leader of the communist movement. Others attribute it to Lenin, who created the totalitarian regime, because without him, the communist movement would have remained an ideology and not become a governing system. Some credit it to Stalin, who turned the newly born, precarious totalitarian regime ruling Russia into a powerful international bloc that, at its peak, covered a third of the world's population. Others emphasize Mao Zedong's contribution, as he not only established a totalitarian regime in China, the most populous country in the world, but also his totalitarian regime continues to evolve even after the collapse of the Soviet Union and the Eastern bloc. Although none of these different opinions is entirely without merit, each is far from the whole truth. Moreover, even if all of these views were combined, they still would not explain why these few individuals were able to create history.

Totalitarian ideology bears many similarities to religion in various aspects. Many scholars refer to this type of ideology as a political or secular religion or political messianism (e.g., Maier, 2004, vols. 1–3; Talmon, 1952). This quasi-religious nature endows totalitarianism with a strong capability to incite fanaticism and appeal. Meanwhile, similar to the development of all religions, the ideology and system of totalitarianism were not created *ex nihilo* by its founders Marx and Lenin. The institutional genes that spawned the communist ideology and totalitarianism existed hundreds of years before Marx and Lenin. It was through harnessing and mobilizing the institutional genes rooted in Christianity and the Christian Church as well as autocratic systems that the totalitarian ideology and system of Marxism-Leninism achieved such power.

At the heart of communist totalitarian ideology is absolute egalitarianism and the abolition of private property. And the system upon which the complete achievement of these highly inflammatory ideological goals rested is a totalitarian one. As this chapter explains, the ideology of Marxism directly originates from the thought of Rousseau on the eve of the French Revolution and the thought of Babeuf during the French Revolution. The logic of

Rousseau–Babeuf–Marxist ideology is that inequality arises from private property (Rousseau); to achieve permanent and complete equality, private property must be abolished (Babeuf); the society established after the abolition of private property can only be ruled through a dictatorship (Babeuf).[4] The dictatorship of the proletariat, as proposed by Marx eighty years after Babeuf, is a totalitarian system aimed at achieving total equality in theory (but in reality has never been implemented by any totalitarian regime). This system is designed around a party-state with a core communist ideology (which was developed and actualized by Lenin three decades after Marx's proposal). Within this system, the party-state monopolizes all aspects of power and property rights in society.

It is worth mentioning that in the socialist movement of the nineteenth century, Fabianism and other socialist movements disagreed significantly with the communist movement led by Marx and Engels. One of these disagreements revolved around the issue of private property. In contrast to the communist movement, socialist movements did not oppose the existence of private property rights.

Eliminating private property rights was the goal of communist movements and the ideological and social basis of totalitarianism. However, throughout world history from the Middle Ages to the present, in any society where everyone has lost property rights, people have not only failed to achieve economic equality but have instead become what Hayek refers to as serfs in all respects. Locke made it clear in the seventeenth century that human rights and property rights are inseparable. Any infringement on an individual's property rights inevitably violates their human rights. In a society where the general public is aware of these rights as articulated by Locke and Hayek, movements advocating the abolition of private property would lack appeal, and the establishment of a totalitarian system would be much more difficult.

The desire for equality is a fundamental part of benevolent human nature. Traces of egalitarianism or communism can be found in almost all ancient civilizations, including ancient China, demonstrating the universal allure of the communist ideology. Egalitarianism is not only attractive to those in extreme poverty but it also holds a strong appeal for many conscientious individuals, including the affluent and the educated. The appeal of egalitarianism to the masses often transcends any other reasoning. The Christianity of those intentional proletarians had enormous power to inspire the struggle for equality. Over hundreds of years, its reach transcended cultures and regions, making it the religion with the most followers in human history. Given that Christian communism and Christian socialism have long been a part of the Christian tradition, it is not difficult for a communist totalitarian movement to arise under the guise of these long-standing ideologies. This makes it easy for innocent individuals to be incited and drawn into supporting these movements, unaware of the potential danger of totalitarianism.

6.1 CHRISTIAN ORIGINS: THE MÜNSTER TOTALITARIAN REGIME

Both proponents and opponents of communism, among scholars and well-informed revolutionaries, are in agreement that action-oriented communist thought has its roots in Christianity. However, when considering the pure intellectual underpinnings of communism though devoid of action, one can trace its origins back to Plato. In his later years, Engels wrote "A Contribution to the History of Primitive Christianity," discussing the Christian origins of communism. Critics of socialism/communism like Ludwig von Mises, along with many others who worked on the history of thought and Christianity, also discussed the Christian roots of communism (Mises, 1981, p. 424; "Early Christian Communism," in Guthrie, 1992, p. 46; Ellicott and Plumptre, 1910). Kautsky, Engels' successor and a leader of the international communist movement at the end of the nineteenth century, wrote *Communism in Central Europe in the Time of the Reformation* (Kautsky, 1897), which records the communist creed in the Bible and the Acts of the Apostles and explains how these formed the source of communist thought. Indeed, the New Testament Book of Acts records the following:

> Now the whole group of those who believed were of one heart and soul, and no one claimed private ownership of any possessions, but everything they owned was held in common.... There was not a needy person among them, for as many as owned lands or houses sold them and brought the proceeds of what was sold. They laid it at the apostles' feet, and it was distributed to each as any had need. (Acts 4:32–35 [Metzger, 1989] [NRSV, Bible])

The communist philosophies of "from each according to his ability" and "to each according to his needs" are presented in Acts 11:29 ("The disciples determined that according to their ability, each would send relief to the believers living in Judea") and Acts 4:35 ("and it was distributed to each as any had need"), respectively. Much archaeological evidence proves that the content mentioned above indeed reflected the practices of early Christian communities, despite being regarded as missionary propaganda later. These practices, based on Jewish and Christian theology, were widespread in different Christian communities in the Roman world, persisting until at least the second century (Montero, 2017, p. 5).

Communist ideology has a powerful appeal to many people who believe that equality is the best and ultimate purpose of humanity. The initial establishment of compulsory communist systems in a city-state can be traced back to the Reformation period in medieval Europe. However, communism that is entirely aligned with the Christian spirit can only be established voluntarily. This voluntary principle dictates that this type of communism can only exist within a relatively small community.

As chronicled in the New Testament, early Christians, in the nascent stages of the faith, emulated Jesus and the apostles by relinquishing property rights and willingly embracing a life without private possessions. They contributed to the community in accordance with their ability, trusting people within the community could take according to their needs. This spirit was extended in Sir Thomas More's *Utopia* in the early sixteenth century, inheriting the essence of Christianity and Platonic idealism. In this fictional utopia, More systematically described his envisioned communist system, where private ownership was abolished, property was collectively owned, citizens were equal, and everyone worked.

The later experiments of Saint-Simon in France and Owen's cooperative farm-factory communities in Britain and America in the eighteenth and nineteenth centuries represent influential utopian experiments based on voluntarism. But all of those experiments are limited to a small scale and lasted for a relatively short period. Arguably, the most prolonged experiment in voluntary socialism has been the Israeli kibbutz, or collective farm. Since the early twentieth century, the kibbutz movement, influenced heavily by Jewish tradition and imbued with strong utopian overtones, has represented a large-scale experiment in this kind of communal living and shared resources. However, despite their decades-long success, a century later, they have been transitioning towards privatization.

It is noteworthy that throughout history all voluntary forms of communism, whether successful or not, have been confined to isolated farms, factories, or communities because of the voluntary principle. Voluntarily established communist communities are commonly limited in size and run autonomously by those within them. As such communities are formed out of individual choice, they are often harmonious and pleasant environments, at least when they are successful.

In contrast, all compulsorily established communist city-states or states, without exception, were established and ruled by violence and were totalitarian in nature. It is implausible to expect all residents of an entire city or nation to voluntarily relinquish their property. Therefore, any historical attempt to establish large-scale communism throughout a city or country invariably resorts to the use of violence of a totalitarian nature, regardless of how the rulers depict their regime. Above all, overcoming the resistance of property owners requires agitation and violence. More importantly, totalitarianism is the inevitable consequence when complete, centralized control of property rights is enforced coercively across society.

All the coercive communist regimes that have emerged in human history from the Reformation to the present have used violence to maintain total control over society and embody totalitarianism. To be precise, the history of the establishment of communist systems from the sixteenth century to the present represents the evolution of totalitarian regimes from their infancy to their maturity. In the following chapters of this book, all discussions of communism refer to coercive communism unless otherwise noted.

The first communist regime in history was established during the Reformation by the Anabaptists. Anabaptism demanded its followers to adopt the most devout and earnest attitudes towards the original doctrines of Jesus and the apostles as recorded in the Bible. They advocated for re-baptism for adults and believed that only true believers were Christians and that only adults could determine their own faith. Absolute equality among all believers was part of their belief. To a significant extent, Marxism as a secular communist movement has inherited the revolutionary spirit of Christian communism from the era of the Reformation.

Kautsky, a leader of the communist movement, contended that original Christianity encapsulated the spirit of communism. However, since Christianity became the state religion of the Roman Empire, the Church underwent a transformation. It morphed into a supreme power entity, intertwining itself with the establishment and becoming a fundamental part of authority (Kautsky, 1897). The Church, representing the wealthy and powerful, manipulated the communal principles of early Christianity for its own advantage and the benefit of the secular power class. It often labeled the egalitarian tenets of Christianity as paganistic. During the Reformation, radical revolutionaries among the Anabaptists utilized the spirit of early Christianity as a tool in their efforts to strip the Church of its wealth. They aimed to control communities and society by bringing the Church under their dominance. These revolutionaries sought to return to the roots of the faith, with its emphasis on communal living and equality, as a means of challenging the established order (Kautsky, 1897, pp. 13–15).

The first violent communist revolution in human history was part of the German Peasants' War (1524–1525) during the period of the Reformation (1517–1648). This uprising was planned and initiated by Thomas Müntzer (1489–1525), a co-founder of the radical Anabaptist sect and a figure on the extreme end of the Lutheran spectrum. His significant role has been discussed by Marx, Engels, and Kautsky.[5] This war was the most extensive popular uprising in Europe before the French Revolution. The revolt was characterized by bloodshed and violence towards those of differing ideologies. It ended in the brutal suppression by the Catholic and Lutheran Churches.

Thomas Müntzer was an exceptionally charismatic agitator and revolutionary leader. He asserted that he had received divine revelation, prophesying that the Apocalypse was imminent and that the old world, which oppressed the poor, would be replaced by a new one. Presenting himself as the Messiah, Müntzer condemned wealth as sinful and rallied the impoverished peasants (the proletariat) to join in the fight to obliterate the old world, follow the Messiah, and establish a new one. According to his rebellion plan, "church property was to be confiscated and made public. The unified Holy Roman Empire was to be transformed into a unified, indivisible republic."[6]

In 1525, Müntzer led the rebel army to seize control of Mühlhausen, where he established a communist city-state. Implementing a regime of compulsory communal ownership, he instated a totalitarian communist theocracy, having forcibly expropriated private property. In Mühlhausen, people invoked Christ's name to demand food or clothing from the affluent. If these were not given willingly, they were seized by force. This institutionalized expropriation was justified by Christ's commandment that everything should be shared with the less fortunate (Shafarevich, 1980, p. 57). This theocratic government lasted for over a year (the literature varies on this) before being suppressed, with Müntzer being executed (Johann Becherer [1601], *Newe Thuringische Chronica*, cited in Kautsky, [1897, p. 183]).

After the suppression of the Müntzer-led revolt, the communist theocratic ideals of the Radical Anabaptists were not extinguished. On the contrary, these ideals manifested in the establishment of a caesaropapist communist theocratic city-state in the German city of Münster during 1534–1535. If Mühlhausen is considered the first temporary communist base, then Münster represents the establishment of the first fully fledged totalitarian regime.

During the sixteenth century, the western part of the Holy Roman Empire, which was predominantly Germanic, was divided into several ecclesiastical principalities, also known as dioceses. The local aristocrat-ecclesiasts elected a prince-bishop from among themselves to represent and rule over them. These prince-bishops were usually secular dukes. The capitals of each diocese, often controlled by local oligarchic guilds, enjoyed a considerable degree of autonomy. Münster was the capital of the largest Catholic bishopric in northwestern Germany.

During the period of the Peasants' War, Anabaptist uprisings were commonplace in these ecclesiastical kingdoms, with Münster being one of them. In 1532, with the support of the citizenry, the primarily Lutheran guild pressured the bishop into recognizing Münster as a Lutheran city. Subsequently, a significant number of Anabaptist believers surged into Münster. Some Lutherans, even those in leadership roles, converted to Anabaptism.

The Anabaptist movement in Münster propagated a return to the original communism of the early Christian Church. In this society, the properties of all clergy and the wealthy were to be confiscated. Each person would receive what they needed from society. Under the allure of this communism, thousands poured into Münster, comprised not only of devout Anabaptists but also of many who were materially motivated, destitute, and hopeless debtors. Incomers to the city included many from the Netherlands and others from various far-flung places.

The Anabaptists further proclaimed the imminent end of an unequal world, predicting that the world would be destroyed within a month or two and that only the communist Münster would be preserved, becoming the new Jerusalem. Violent Anabaptists soon seized complete control of Münster, launching a large-scale experiment in communism.

The first step of this experiment was the confiscation of the property of those who were expelled. The impoverished were encouraged to take the confiscated wealth. Those who resisted the plunder were labeled as non-believers and publicly executed. The public was told that these executions were for their own benefit, and they were encouraged to sing hymns praising their own slaughter.

Their next propaganda campaign declared private ownership as anti-Christian, insisting that all wealth should be communal. Thus, all money had to be handed over to the ruling group. Those attempting to conceal wealth were arrested and punished. After two months of Christian propaganda advocating the abolition of private property, combined with threats and intimidation, Münster abolished private property altogether. All money was confiscated by the government, which it used to buy goods and services from other cities.

The theocratic government became the sole employer of all people in Münster, paying wages in kind. A rationing system was implemented citywide. People dined in public dining halls while reading passages from the Old Testament. It was a communal society without private households and where the closing of doors was illegal. Any outsider could take up residence in Münster and all private homes were opened to accommodate an influx of immigrants. This coercive communism was realized under a rule of terror, all in the name of the community and Christian "love."

The Münster Rebellion was ultimately suppressed in 1535 and its leader, Jan van Leiden, was tortured to death in the following year. With the collapse of the first communist-totalitarian regime, the Radical Anabaptists were significantly weakened and they never regained substantial influence. The decline of Christian communism in German land demonstrated that the institutional genes there were not conducive to the survival of this ideology, let alone to its expansion. However, secular communist totalitarianism, cloaked in the mantle of equality, emerged systematically two centuries later in regions where the institutional genes were more receptive to it.

6.2 THE BIRTH OF SECULAR COMMUNIST TOTALITARIANISM

Contrasting with the theocratic communist totalitarian regimes established by the Anabaptists in the sixteenth century, modern communist totalitarianism presents as a secular ideology-movement regime. Its foundational legacies can be traced back to the Jacobin Reign of Terror (1794–1795) during the French Revolution, Babeuf's Conspiracy of the Equals (1796) in its aftermath, as well as the influence of Blanquism in the Paris Commune (1871).

6.2.1 *Jacobin Dictatorship and Bauerian Communism*

Marxist communism was constructed directly on the foundations laid by Babeuf, who invented it during the period of the Jacobin dictatorship (Israel, 2015, p. 678). If one were to judge Marx's writings on communism/socialism using academic norms, they might find that Marx's ideas closely resemble those of Babeuf, bordering on plagiarism. Guided by Babeuf's ideologies, his followers conspired to seize power by armed force, abolish private property, and establish communism. After the plot failed, they persevered with his ideas and inaugurated the world's first authentic "communist" movement in France. Auguste Blanqui, a contemporary of Marx and subsequent leader of the communist movement, explicitly stated that the communist movement represented a war between the proletariat and the bourgeoisie (Spitzer, 1957, p. 6, 101). Many historians agree that the concept of class consciousness among the proletariat originated during the French Revolution and was specifically attributable to Babeuf's "Conspiracy of Equals" (Rose, 1978, p. 341).

Babeuf can indeed be considered the true progenitor of communist totalitarianism. He originated the concept of communism and advocated for the use of violent class struggle to dismantle the existing world and realize communism.[7] Marxism, as a systematic theory, was developed from Babeuf's communist ideologies. Marx's major contribution was to "scientifically" substantiate Babeuf's postulation that the downfall of the old capitalist world and the ascendancy of the new communist world were inevitable.

Moreover, Marx's theory of proletarian dictatorship was also constructed on Babeuf's ideas of seizing power and property rights through force and maintaining the communist regime via coercive governance. However, Marx was arguably shrewder than Babeuf, as Marxism is a messianic faith deliberately modeled after Christianity. As Engels, the co-founder of Marxism, articulated, Marx's doctrines serve as the Bible of the proletarian communist revolution.

The contributions of the French pioneers of communist totalitarianism extend beyond theory. They provided practical models for organizing totalitarian movements and implementing totalitarian governance. Lenin's models for the formation of the Bolsheviks were inspired by the Jacobin Club and its leader, Robespierre, as well as by Blanqui, who carried forward Babeuf's legacy.

Indeed, Marx, Engels, Lenin, and Mao all referenced the French Revolution extensively, especially the Paris Commune, as a precursor to violent communism. In China, the People's Communes were established in the 1950s and 1960s and the revolutionary committees of the Cultural Revolution were direct imitations of the Paris Commune. These examples illustrate how ideas from the French Revolution influenced and shaped modern communist movements and regimes.

Well-informed readers might notice that my discussion about the origins of Marxism omits many well-known figures and their theories, such as Hegel, Feuerbach, Smith, and Ricardo, among others. This is deliberate. My intention is to understand communist totalitarianism as a social phenomenon, focusing on those who had significant direct social impacts rather than mere philosophies or pure theories.

The history of civilization has produced a plethora of ideas, spanning from the extreme left to the extreme right. However, the vast majority of these ideas, often encapsulated within philosophies and pure theories, self-perpetuate with minimal societal impact. Only a few ideas are embraced by society, evolving into societal ideologies and even forming part of the institutional genes, exerting a lasting and significant influence on society. The ideas that have the most substantial impact are often those in high demand at a particular historical moment. Which idea will become prevalent in society? Will the prevalent ideology change the society? And if it changes, how does it do so? To a large extent, the existing institutional genes of a society are one of the key determinants in answering these questions.

The French Revolution serves as an illustrative example. Medieval France and England were very similar and closely related (including warfare). However, at the end of the eighteenth century, attempts to promote constitutional reform in France faced enormous challenges. These efforts sparked a "revolution" that drove the movement in the opposite direction and ultimately led to the restoration of an absolute monarchy. The immediate outcome of the failure of the constitutional movement was the Jacobin dictatorship and Babeuf's communist movement. Over the following century, communist totalitarian ideologies and organizations such as the Jacobins, Robespierre, Babeuf, Blanqui, and so on, proliferated. Why was this the case? What were the institutional genes in that society that gave rise to communist totalitarianism? Alternatively, why did France give rise to modern communist totalitarian ideology and initial regimes in the eighteenth and nineteenth centuries? These are intriguing questions worth exploring further.

A detailed analysis of France's institutional genes is beyond the scope of this work. However, we will summarize the institutional evolutions in France in the two centuries or so between the Reformation and the end of the eighteenth century, which laid the foundations for the emergence of early communist totalitarianism. First, one of the most prominent features of totalitarianism is highly centralized power that is omnipresent and entirely unchecked. Thus, one of the most significant factors in the evolution of the old regime in pre-Revolutionary France was the formation of an absolute monarchy, the control of society by a central bureaucracy, and the prevalence of the doctrine of sovereignty supremacism (which was clearly opposed to the separation of powers). These factors laid the foundations for the development of totalitarianism in terms of power structure and ideology.

Second, any society capable of producing totalitarianism must eradicate all social forces capable of limiting the power of government. In medieval France, there were originally checks and balances between the monarch, the Church, and the nobility. However, as France transitioned into an absolute monarchy, the French aristocracy was hollowed out by the bureaucracy and their power was greatly diminished. All efforts by the aristocracy to maintain and regain power were suppressed and undermined by the monarchy (Tocqueville, 1856). By the time of the Revolution, the French aristocracy had lost its ability to constrain royal power. In an era when the bourgeoisie was not strong enough, the decline of the aristocracy meant that efforts to promote a constitutional monarchy remained at the level of discourse and text, with no substantial backing. In a society where all social forces other than the monarchy were weak, the failure of constitutional reform was inevitable. The more serious problem, however, was that overthrowing the old system without establishing constitutionalism created a power vacuum, thus setting the stage for the emergence of nascent totalitarianism.

Third, compared to the decline of the nobility, the disintegration of ecclesiastical authority not only undermined the balance of power but also facilitated the emergence of a communist totalitarian ideology. With the establishment of an absolute monarchy,

6.2 THE BIRTH OF SECULAR COMMUNIST TOTALITARIANISM

ecclesiastical power was increasingly weakened and controlled by the monarchy. Before the Revolution, the Church was the largest landowner and the wealthiest institution in France. On the surface, its power seemed much stronger than that of the nobility. However, the bloody Wars of Religion that came with the Reformation and the Enlightenment's fierce attack on ecclesiastical power meant that, by the time of the Revolution, the Church's reputation had greatly declined and it was even loathed by many. During the Revolution, priests were massacred en masse. But the centuries-old Christian faith of the French people would not automatically disappear due to their hatred of the Church. This specific social condition created an opportunity for the emergence of secular messianism and for it to replace Christianity as the popular belief. Consequently, Christian communism transformed into secular communism. Revolutionary leaders replaced Jesus Christ, and the revolutionary party replaced the Church, instructing the revolutionary masses (believers) that the sinful old world was doomed and a beautiful new communist world was destined to be born. Their violence was necessary to realize all of this.

Fourth, the emergence of totalitarianism cannot be separated from the fervent belief and action of the masses. Establishing a totalitarian regime is a violent process while violence cannot take place without a "revolutionary mass" seduced by a totalitarian ideology. The emergence of a totalitarian ideology in a society is one thing, it is quite another for large numbers of people to embrace it and actively contribute to its violent manifestation. The French Revolution gave birth to both.

More accurately, Babeuvism was not solely the product of Babeuf's imagination or that of a few thinkers. It was also borne out of the fanatical and radical mass violence of the Revolution, coupled with the social conditions and certain ideologies that took root before the Revolution. In Marxist terms, Babeuvism represents the theory of the proletariat. Without the "proletariat" or the presence of mass violence, Babeufism would not exist. The emergence of the proletariat or fervent masses forms the social basis for the creation of Babeuvism.

Under the medieval feudal system, each nobleman was responsible for his own domain and administered the people within it, including providing assistance and relief for the poor within it. But the absolute monarchy changed all that. The nobility lost its rights and duties within its territory and the monarchy and bureaucracy had neither the interest nor the ability to help and relieve the poor. The growing awareness of their position and the demand for direct access to power by those at the bottom of society formed the basis for the transformation of popular sovereignty into social consciousness during the Revolution. At the same time, this metamorphosis created the social conditions necessary for the lower classes to engage in widespread violence in the name of popular sovereignty.

6.2.2 Absolute Monarchy and Supreme Sovereignty

The doctrine of sovereign supremacy has played a uniquely significant role in the development of totalitarianism. This ideology originated in medieval France, which gave rise to a powerful absolute monarchy. Unlike England or France in the past, royal power in France since Louis XIV exerted a high degree of control over society, with the aristocracy losing much of its ability to check royal power.

Since ancient times, monarchs worldwide have striven to centralize power for their own interests. However, the extent to which a monarch can centralize power depends on the forces that inhibit such centralization. Under the feudal system, the greatest force restraining the monarch was typically the nobility.

Since the Middle Ages, the evolution of French institutions resulted in a powerful absolute monarchy where the king's power was highly concentrated in society and the nobility gradually lost its ability to check the royal power. The power of the French crown became increasingly centralized from the fourteenth century onwards. The territorial expansion following France's victory over England in the Hundred Years' War in the late fifteenth century provided further opportunities for centralizing power and the absolute monarchy was established from the sixteenth century onwards (Baumgartner, 1995). From then on, the institutional genes of the absolute monarchy, from ideology to governance structures and social foundation, developed greatly in France.

In stark contrast, the thirteenth-century Magna Carta movement, launched by the English nobility, charted a distinct course for England. The Magna Carta was a collective action by the nobility aiming to limit royal power. Over the subsequent centuries of this royal power limitation movement, the real power of the nobility within the Parliament became increasingly entrenched. This not only prevented the English monarchy from becoming an absolute monarchy but also gradually weakened it. After a long period of development, full of twists and turns, the monarch became increasingly restricted by the collective nobility. By the end of the seventeenth century, this ultimately transformed England's monarchy into a constitutional one. This divergence had substantial impacts and played a crucial role in sparking the French Revolution.

In the sixteenth century, when the absolute monarchy was established in France, Jean Bodin (1530–1596) developed the concept of monarchical sovereignty. By his definition, sovereignty is an absolute right, which is exclusive, indivisible, and not subject to legal arbitration. In his theory, sovereignty is supreme and the state is the entity of sovereignty; the owner of the sovereignty of the state is called the "sovereign" and the sovereign is the king, who derives his power from God. The basic characteristic of sovereignty is that the sovereign legislates by his own will. Bodin's concept of sovereignty, on the grounds that sovereignty is indivisible, explicitly opposes the separation of powers. At a time when religious wars had just ended, Bodin put forward his absolute monarchy and sovereignty theory and explicitly opposed democracy. The rationale was that democracy undermines social stability and leads to rule by the ignorant (Durant and Durant, 1961, pp. 630–632).

For Bodin, the ultimate aim was social stability. However, the reality starkly contradicted Bodin's contention. Over time, it was absolute power – supported and further reinforced by the theory of sovereignty – and the ideas and institutional arrangements antagonistic to democracy that obstructed the constitutional development of France and undermined its social stability. France's social instability persisted until constitutionalism took the place of sovereign supremacy and autocracy was supplanted by democracy.

It is noteworthy that Bodin's concept of sovereignty includes legislative power but not property rights. This implies that a monarch with exclusive legislative power cannot infringe upon property rights. Such an inference is grounded in the sixteenth-century reality when the absolute monarchy was formed; the nobility still retained significant power. Therefore, abolishing the property rights of the nobility would undermine the foundations of the feudal monarchy and thus obstruct the establishment of sovereignty. However, in an absolute monarchy where sovereignty took precedence over human rights, the monarch ultimately obtained the ability to use sovereignty to limit property rights, including those of the nobility.

The principle of the supremacy of sovereignty was further reinforced during the Enlightenment era with an important twist. The intellectual greats of the French Enlightenment, notably Rousseau, were more concerned with who should hold sovereignty rather than the relationship between sovereignty and human rights. Inheriting Bodin's idea of supreme sovereignty, Rousseau redirected the locus of sovereignty from the monarch towards the "people." In his work, *The Social Contract*, Rousseau emphasized that popular sovereignty supersedes all else. Moreover, he argued that popular sovereignty gives rise to the right to demand individual compliance in the name of the so-called general will. This means that supreme popular sovereignty can infringe upon human rights.

Rousseau's concept of popular sovereignty gradually pervaded French society, obstructing constitutional reform. Moreover, it created fertile ground for the establishment of totalitarian practices. This shift in ideology was a crucial turning point in the subsequent emergence of totalitarianism. Figures such as Robespierre and Babeuf, both self-proclaimed disciples of Rousseau, adopted the doctrine of supreme sovereignty during the French Revolution. The Jacobin regime, although characterized by violence, referred to its leading figures as representatives of the people and Babeuf proposed the abolition of private ownership, asserting the principle that sovereignty determined property rights, thus laying the groundwork for a nascent form of totalitarianism. During the Revolution, the Jacobin dictatorship was the first regime to systematically violate human rights under the guise of popular sovereignty.

6.2.3 Decline of the Aristocracy and the Rise of the Absolute Monarchy

The ideology of absolute monarchical sovereignty alone was not enough to completely suppress the resistance of the nobility, as they still held significant land and power. In order to consolidate their authority, absolute monarchies implemented administrative reforms that marginalized the nobility. A top-down bureaucracy was established to centralize power and reduce the influence of the aristocracy. This dismantling of the nobility's power structures further strengthened the authority of the monarchy.

In the two centuries preceding the Revolution, the aristocracy was weakened to a nominal position with no real power (Tocqueville, 1856, pp. 51–54). The French nobility had fewer powers compared to their counterparts in England since the early Middle Ages. They lacked a parliament of their own and had no legislative authority. In the Estates-General, the national assembly of that time, the nobility held the second rank among the three estates. The first estate consisted of clerics and the third estate encompassed commoners, including representatives of the bourgeoisie, peasantry, and lower classes. Each estate held one vote in the assembly, enabling any proposal from one estate to be vetoed by the other two.

Furthermore, the Estates-General was limited to an advisory role in its communication with the sovereign and did not function as an independent legislative body. The summoning of the

Estates-General was solely at the discretion of the king, as there were no established rules or regular intervals for its convening. In fact, the Estates-General did not meet from 1614 until the brink of the Revolution. The weakened status of the French aristocracy within the Estates-General, coupled with its lack of legislative power, contributed to its nominal role and diminishing influence.

Another significant development was the increasing number of nobles selling their land to peasants. By the eighteenth century, on the eve of the French Revolution, over half of France's land had been transferred from the nobility to the peasantry, leading to the erosion of the former's power base. Although the nobles were initially content with maintaining their power, their attempts to regain power were suppressed by the monarchy. As a result of these developments, France diverged significantly from the pattern of institutional evolution seen in Britain before the Glorious Revolution (Tocqueville, 1856).

As the power of the nobility weakened, they sought to assert their interests and regain their lost influence in the face of an increasingly absolutist monarchy. The Fronde rebellion in the mid-seventeenth century marked the last major effort of the French nobility to challenge the monarchy before the Revolution. However, its failure dealt a significant blow to the nobility and effectively prevented them from collectively limiting the power of the monarch.

The Fronde rebellion (1648–1653) originated from the endeavors of reformist nobles in the *Parlement*,[8] who wanted to establish a constitutional government with the objective of limiting monarchical power. The rebellion took place when the Thirty Years War between Protestants and Catholics came to an end and the nobility was overburdened with heavy taxes.

Inspired by the successful armed resistance of the English nobility against King Charles I, the French nobility were keen to emulate them. In 1648, the nobles of the *Parlement* of Paris opposed the tax plan of the then prime minister and demanded systematic reforms. They proposed twenty-seven reforms, including the abolition of governors appointed by the central government to restore the power of the nobility in the provinces, the requirement that all new taxes be approved by the *Parlement*, and the prohibition of arbitrary arrests by the monarch.

As tensions escalated and a peaceful resolution became unattainable, an armed rebellion erupted in Paris, causing the young King Louis XIV to flee the city. The rebellion earned its name, the Fronde, from the rebels' frequent use of slingshots, or "frondes."

Subsequently, Louis XIV mobilized the military to suppress the rebellion and later used the army once more to quell a resurgence of the uprising in Paris. Given the significant decline in the French nobility's independence by the seventeenth century, the king managed to divide them, securing sufficient aristocratic support to extinguish the rebellion on both occasions. This contrasted sharply with the unity of English nobility against the royal family.

After the rebellion, Louis XIV consolidated his rule by shifting his base away from Paris, the stronghold of aristocratic power, and by building the Palace of Versailles, which became his new residence. He took steps to further divide and weaken the aristocracy by enticing prominent nobles to live in his newly built palace, while simultaneously outlawing their private armies.

As a result, the traditionally militant nobility, which had previously wielded great power, transformed into a class of powerless courtiers: opulent, yet devoid of any real power. The French nobility ceased resorting to armed resistance to defend their rights. The practical operational power, which was once held by the nobility, gradually shifted to the bureaucracy. Additionally, the now powerless nobility, stripped of their lands, increasingly moved to Paris to enjoy tax exemptions and seek the favor of the king.

6.2.4 Replacing the Church by Secular Messianism

The joint rule of divine authority, represented by the Catholic Church, and monarchical authority was the system of the medieval European nations. The two powers were both aligned and conflicting. This determined their mutually restraining relationship. France was one of the countries where the Catholic Church wielded great power. The Crusades were largely drawn from France and for a large part of the fourteenth century, the Pope lived in Avignon, a situation which led to a schism in the Church.

Nevertheless, the Catholic Church experienced a decline in authority in France after the Reformation. The threat of Protestantism and the ensuing protracted religious wars fractured spiritual and emotional loyalties, while discontent brewed among the clergy. In addition, with the establishment of an absolute monarchy, the king's control over the Church gradually increased. One mechanism of royal control was to secure the support of the Church through tax exemptions. As a result, the Church progressively facilitated the dictatorial rule of the monarch, thus becoming the richest institution and largest landowner in France.[9]

The Church's divine authority was weakened as it colluded with the monarchy and amassed wealth as a major landlord, provoking resentment among the French populace. This resentment was echoed and amplified during the Enlightenment in France, with eminent intellectuals like Voltaire and Rousseau leveling harsh criticism against Christianity and the Catholic Church, leading to its profound discrediting.

For the impoverished, perhaps the most anger-inducing, even revolting, aspects were the close ties between the Catholic Church and the monarch, coupled with the tax exemptions and substantial wealth enjoyed by the clergy. The anger boiled over during the Revolution, when churches were looted and demolished and clergymen were slaughtered en masse.

As the Church's image as a theocratic agent collapsed, the traditions of Christianity, entrenched in the minds of the French people for over a millennium, nonetheless persisted. The institutional legacy of Christianity suggested that the people needed a form of religion that did not involve Jesus Christ or the Pope. Deism, which emerged during the early Enlightenment, served as a substitute for Christianity among the intellectual elite.

However, Father Jean Meslier secretly formulated and advocated for atheistic communism (a topic to be explored later in this chapter), and under his influence, Rousseau promoted what is now known as "civil religion." These ideologies were ambitious attempts to establish alternatives to Christianity, aimed at dismantling the established order and creating an egalitarian paradise for the broader populace. Historically, this form of communist belief, which eventually supplanted Christianity and garnered mass support in some countries, essentially constituted a messianic secular religion bearing significant resemblances to Christianity in key aspects.

Christian believers anticipate the return of their savior, Jesus Christ, whom they believe will deliver them from a world full of tribulations. Upon his return, it is believed that he will destroy the old world of suffering and create a new world where all individuals are equal, similar to a heavenly paradise.

In secular messianism, which lacks a figure like Jesus Christ, revolutionary theory replaces Christian doctrine and revolutionary leaders stand in for the role of Christ. The scientific revolutionary theory prophesies that the masses, under the leadership of revolutionary figures, will inevitably overthrow the old world of inequality using their own strength, replacing it with an equal, communist new world.

In this worldview, secular faith and the revolutionary party substitute for Christian faith and the Church, allowing religion's traditional strengths to manifest in a secular movement. This provides immense power to beguile, enthrall, incite, organize, and dismantle. The theory and movement of communist totalitarianism were, in fact, created jointly by Meslier, Rousseau, Robespierre, Babeuf, radical intellectuals, and the proletariat of France during the French Enlightenment and Revolution era. Marx, Lenin, Stalin, Mao, Deng, and Xi are their followers.

6.2.5 *Failure of Constitutional Reform*

The French Revolution is, in fact, a term encompassing a series of significant historical events that unfolded in the wake of failed constitutional reform efforts in France at the end of the eighteenth century. While some historians argue that this failure led to the Revolution, others contend the opposite. While this debate over causality is important, the crucial point of this book is that the failure of constitutional reform set the stage for the birth of totalitarianism. This pattern echoed in the historical narratives of Russia and China, where similar failures of reform paved the way for totalitarian regimes.

The first important point to clarify is that the constitutional reform in France during that period was initiated in response to a financial crisis, rather than as a result of a premeditated, organized effort. France's continued involvement in foreign warfare, especially the Anglo-French War of 1778–1783 (including the support for the American War of Independence of 1775–1783), had led to a severe financial crisis in the country and made it impossible for France to meet its obligations.

The fiscal difficulties facing France were largely a reflection of the inherent weaknesses of the absolute monarchy, which permitted the monarch to declare war and incur expenditures without checks or balances. Furthermore, the absolute monarchy compromised the legitimacy and credibility of the French government, preventing it from borrowing its way out of trouble and necessitating heavy reliance on taxation.

To address the financial crisis, Jacques Necker, who was appointed Controller-General of Finances in 1777, proposed a tax reform plan. This included the abolition of tax exemptions for the nobility and clergy, along with an increase in borrowing. However, this proposal faced opposition from ministers and provincial nobility.

Caught in a dilemma, Louis XVI convened the Assembly of Notables in 1787. The participants called for a session of the Estates-General, hoping to initiate constitutional reforms akin to those of England's Glorious Revolution, with the aim of establishing a constitutional monarchy (Tocqueville, 2001).

In 1789, nationwide general elections produced representatives for the Estates-General. It was the first meeting of the Estates in over a century.[10] Due to conflicts between the Third Estate and the other

6.2 THE BIRTH OF SECULAR COMMUNIST TOTALITARIANISM 227

Estates, a separate National Assembly, claiming to represent the people, was formed a month later. Representatives from the other two Estates were also invited to join. The Assembly later changed its name to the National Constituent Assembly.

Confronted with the National Constituent Assembly's push for a constitutional monarchy, Louis XVI wavered between making concessions, resisting the push, or preparing for repression. His dismissal of the reformist Controller-General Necker for the second time triggered a massive revolt among Parisians, with the support of portions of the French Guard.

On July 14, the rebels seized the Bastille, looted weapons and ammunition, and carried out brutal massacres of high-ranking officials, including those who had voluntarily cooperated. They established the Paris Commune, which became the governing body of Paris, marking a turning point in which the peaceful reform effort devolved into an uncontrollable violent revolution.

The Paris Commune became the dominant authority during the French Revolution, adopting increasingly radical revolutionary goals and brutal methods. It was from this tumultuous process that the embryonic communist movement emerged. However, the turbulence was eventually brought to an end by Napoleon's armed coup, leading to the restoration of the absolute monarchy.

Faced with the imminent threat of more riots, the king relented. Necker was reinstated and the Marquis de Lafayette, a renowned aristocratic general with a track record of victories during the American War of Independence and a supporter of the Third Estate, was appointed Commander of the French National Guard.

On August 26, 1789, the National Constituent Assembly issued the Declaration of the Rights of Man and of the Citizen. This seminal document, jointly drafted by Lafayette and Sieyès, a representative of the Third Estate, asserted liberty, property, security, and resistance to oppression as inalienable human rights. Furthermore, it articulated the principle of the separation of powers between the judiciary, executive, and legislature, and affirmed the equality of all before the law.

The declaration drew on a range of influences, including the different ideas of Montesquieu and Rousseau, as well as the United States Declaration of Independence and the individual state Bill of Rights. Notably, it also benefited significantly from the input of Thomas Jefferson, who was serving as the United States Ambassador to France at the time.

In 1791, France enacted its first constitution, effectively establishing the country as a constitutional monarchy. The Declaration of the Rights of Man and of the Citizen was integral to this constitution, which aimed to safeguard human rights and balance the power of the monarch with that of an elected assembly. If this constitutional arrangement had been successful, France might have evolved into a constitutional monarchy similar to Britain. However, the constitution faced opposition not only from the monarch but also, more significantly, from radical factions and the inflamed, violent masses. Frequent violations of the constitution reduced the constitutional monarchy to a largely nominal status.

With the encouragement of the Jacobins and the Paris Commune, the populace grew increasingly radicalized. Riots and armed uprisings were common, with widespread resentment targeted towards the monarchy, clergy, and nobility. Thousands of clergy members and nobles were slaughtered (Shusterman, 2013). As a result, not only was the constitutional monarchy effectively non-existent in practice but the physical safety of the monarch himself was also at risk. In June 1791, Louis XVI was arrested following a failed escape attempt. In 1792, the National Convention, elected via universal suffrage, declared the abolition of the monarchy and the establishment of a republic. This power shift put the primary advocates for the republic, the Girondins, into power.

6.2.6 The Jacobin Dictatorship: A Prototype of Totalitarianism

The Girondins held a stance far more radical than that of those advocating for a constitutional monarchy. They abolished the constitutional monarchy and established a republic. However, the impoverished masses, who frequently resorted to street violence, were significantly more radical. In September 1792, under the banner of "Justice," radical factions among the poor slaughtered about 2,700 individuals, including priests and nuns, who had been imprisoned since the Revolution began. The Girondin-led National Convention tried to halt these acts of violence by centralizing judicial power in the hands of the government. This move, however, incited the anger of the impoverished masses who, in 1793, staged an armed uprising that overthrew the Girondin regime. This rebellion paved the way for the establishment of a Jacobin dictatorship under Robespierre, which then took control of the French Republic (Linton, 2006, p. 23).

The Jacobin dictatorship was the first prototype of modern totalitarianism, which emerged largely due to the dominance of the impoverished population during the Revolution coupled with a strategic alliance between the Jacobin elite and these masses. On one side, the Jacobin elites found themselves having to pander to the radical demands of the masses, resulting in a significant influence exerted by the latter. Without their staunch support and active involvement, the Jacobins may not have gained control, and their radical rhetoric could have remained just words. Conversely, without the Jacobin dictatorship, the poor rebels would have been a disorganized mob and there would have been no systematic and institutionalized reign of terror, and the French Revolution as we know it would not have happened.

As an early prototype of a totalitarian regime, the Jacobin government established the Reign of Terror, the core of which was the Committee of Public Safety and the Revolutionary Tribunal. Terroristic violence was an official policy of the Jacobin regime and was executed efficiently from the top down (Linton, 2006, p. 23). Following this precedent, all modern totalitarian regimes, including those of the Bolsheviks and Chinese communists, systematically emulated this approach. They saw the use of violence as an essential means to eliminate political opposition and to establish and uphold their own regimes. As Robespierre said, "The springs of popular government in revolution are at once virtue and terror.... Terror is nothing other than justice" (Halsall, 1997). The Girondins, with their dissenting political views, were the primary targets of the Jacobins' terror. Most Girondin representatives in the National Convention, including revolutionary aristocrat Louis Philippe d'Orléans, the leading advocate for the French Republican Revolution, Madame Roland, and Antoine-Laurent de Lavoisier, the father of modern chemistry, were all guillotined. Marquis de Condorcet,[11] one of the leading figures of the Enlightenment, a political scientist, mathematician, and leading author of the Girondin constitution, was imprisoned on charges of conspiracy and subsequently persecuted to death. Even Jacobin leaders who disagreed with Robespierre were imprisoned and executed.

During the Reign of Terror, 25,000 individuals were executed nationwide (Greer, 1935); 16,594 of them were guillotined, 2,639 in Paris alone (Linton, 2004). The Jacobin dictatorship, under the guise of pursuing equality and revolution, surpassed even the darkest periods of the absolute monarchy in terms of its comprehensive and ruthless infringement on human rights. The impact of the Jacobin dictatorship extended far beyond France. In addition to becoming the origin of totalitarianism, it also shook the confidence of other countries in republicanism. For instance, terrified by the horrors of the Jacobin type of rule, the Dutch rejected the draft of the republican constitution in their referendum of 1797 (Israel, 2015, p. 675).

Since the storming of the Bastille, the primary participants in the riots and atrocities of the Revolution were the *sans-culottes* – the social underclass of the poor. They were impoverished workers and urban poor, the majority of the initiators and executors of the street violence and the mainstay of the revolutionary military forces. Politically, they advocated direct elections. They also embraced the use of violence to eliminate those who stood in the way of their goals, including the moderate reformists.

Given the significant role of the lower classes in the French Revolution, the literature often refers to them by a specific term, *sans-culottes*, meaning "men without knee-breeches." As the French

Revolution is not the main focus of this book, I will use the term "the poor" to denote the *sans-culottes* of the Revolution in an effort to minimize the use of specialized terminology. In the works of Marx, Engels, Kautsky, and some authoritative historians of the French Revolution, the *sans-culottes* are referred to as the proletariat and their acts of violence are seen as an embryonic form of proletarian revolution.[12]

Although labeling them as the proletariat may not be entirely accurate in terms of conceptual definition, it is an undeniable historical fact that there was a significant concentration of poor and disgruntled individuals in France, particularly in Paris, both before and during the Revolution. Lacking assets, these individuals served as the kindling and explosive force of the Revolution. The self-proclaimed revolutionary consciousness, resentment, and propensity for violence of the poor Parisian rebels are well-documented.[13]

The rise of the disgruntled poor masses was a product of the social evolution that had taken place under the old regime prior to the French Revolution. While stark social inequality was a significant factor, even more impactful were the transformations brought about by the absolute monarchy.

Under the medieval feudal order, the poor were governed by local nobles. These nobles had a duty to assist the poor in their domains, a responsibility they accepted as part of the price for power and support within their territories. The nobles' efforts to maintain their power often made it difficult for the poor in their respective jurisdictions to develop what is known as "class consciousness."

However, the advent of the absolute monarchy disrupted the medieval feudal order. Nobles, stripped of their lands, rights, and obligations, abandoned their territories and moved to Paris, thereby ending their aid to the poor.[14] The centralized bureaucracy that ruled the entire country had neither the capacity nor the motivation to assist or alleviate the condition of the poor.

Furthermore, heavy taxes were imposed on the vast numbers of the poor, while the wealthy Church and aristocracy were exempt from taxation. This disparity exacerbated the resentment of the poor towards the monarchy, the Church, and the aristocracy.

Through multiple riots, the impoverished masses became the de facto primary force of the Revolution. Their violence was aimed not only at the nobility but also at any moderate revolutionaries who hindered their establishment of an "egalitarian republic" (Soboul, 1972, p. 158). They sought to curtail private property rights, directly challenging the principles of the Declaration of the Rights of Man and of the Citizen. Under their violent onslaught throughout society, the human rights declarations and constitutions promulgated on several occasions during the Revolution were reduced to mere words (Soboul, 1975, pp. 332–334).

Their leading theorist, Babeuf, explicitly advocated for the abolition of private property and the establishment of communism. Before Napoleon's coup, the sheer numbers, fanaticism, and violence of these impoverished masses had, to a considerable extent, shaped the trajectory of the Revolution.

But one key distinction between the Jacobins during the French Revolution and the Bolsheviks lies in the way they engaged with the poor. The acts of violence and riots perpetrated by the poor during the French Revolution were neither orchestrated nor led by the Jacobins. Instead, Robespierre found it necessary to actively appeal to the poor, meet their demands, and draw their support.

In contrast, having learned from the French Revolution, subsequent totalitarian parties such as the Bolsheviks and the Chinese Communist Party deliberately incited, nurtured, and organized the poor, transforming them into mobs. Both the Bolsheviks and the Chinese Communist Party heavily relied on inciting violence and atrocities to mobilize the masses of workers, peasants, and soldiers in their armed seizures of power and in their "continued revolutions" to consolidate power, which are detailed in Chapters 8 and 10–12.

6.2.7 *Babeuvian Communism*

The trajectories leading from the Jacobin dictatorship to the Bolshevik Revolution in Russia and then to the Communist Revolution in China all followed a similar pattern. Each of these movements originated from a revolution aimed at establishing constitutionalism. However, in each case, while the old order was dismantled, the revolutionaries ended up establishing a totalitarian regime that was even more dictatorial than the one it overthrew.

Babeuf is considered the prophet of communist totalitarian movements. During the time of the Jacobin dictatorship, Babeuf developed his vision of communism and pioneered the idea of using a violent conspiracy to seize power and implement communism. After the Jacobin dictatorship was overthrown, Babeuf and his revolutionary comrades became extremely dissatisfied with the direction the Revolution was taking. They were particularly resentful of the Directory (governing body), which had staged a coup to overthrow the Jacobins. In response, they conspired to create a new society characterized by complete equality, one that would eliminate private property rights and all forms of privilege, including those enjoyed by the revolutionary government.

After his unsuccessful attempt to stage an armed coup in 1796, Babeuf was executed the following year. Subsequently, his followers disseminated his ideas throughout France, giving rise to the earliest communist movement. John Goodwin Barmby (1820–1881), a British utopian missionary, learned about the communist movement from one of Babeuf's disciples during a visit to Paris in 1840. From the French word *communisme*, he created the English term "communism." Barmby later introduced Engels, who had recently arrived in England, to communism both as an ideology and as a movement. Marx learned about the communist movement through Engels. Thus, Babeuf is rightfully considered the first communist revolutionary (Rose, 1978).

If we use Christianity and the Church as metaphors for communism and the communist church,[15] then Babeuf, as the founder and martyr, resembles Jesus Christ, while Barmby, Engels, and Marx, as disseminators and perfectors of doctrine and founders of the Church, can be likened to Saint John, Saint Paul, and Saint Peter, respectively. Lenin, as the architect and founder of the totalitarian system, transcended all in the history of Christianity and the Church, even though the basic elements of communist totalitarianism were already present in the theories of Marx and Engels.

Babeuf was a theorist for the revolutionary poor. Drawing from Rousseau, he emphasized that a legitimate government must express the general will. The "general will" he advocated for was the elimination of private property, which he believed would result in happiness for all and the eradication of crime. He and his comrades (who were tried and executed with him) contended that not only was the equality outlined in the Declaration of the Rights of Man and of the Citizen necessary but also was absolute equality, for which all other rights could be sacrificed (Israel, 2015, pp. 676–677). As such, they planned to seize political power through secretive armed plots in order to realize communism.

The overly violent Babeuvism made him unacceptable even to the Jacobins. Therefore, Babeuf was never a key member of the Jacobin Club (Phillips, 1911, pp. 93–94). To a large extent, the violent proletarian revolution promoted under Marxist ideology later sought to actualize Babeuf's ideals from theory to practice but on a larger and more systematic scale. The secret proletarian Bolshevik Party founded by Lenin was directly modeled on the Conspiracy of the Equals organized by Babeuf. However, by inheriting the institutional genes of Russian secret terrorist organizations, the Bolsheviks were more meticulously planned and more rigidly organized.

The Reign of Terror under the Jacobins saw not only the mass execution of priests, nobles, and anyone accused of treason across society but also the imprisonment and execution of dissenters among the revolutionaries themselves. In the summer of 1794, moderate revolutionaries, seeking to escape the pervasive fear they were subjected to, overthrew the Jacobin regime and executed the Jacobin leaders, including Robespierre, in a coup d'état. In 1795, they established the Directory. More radical than most Jacobins, Babeuf and his comrades viewed the Directory as exploiting the revolution for its own privileges and argued that the revolution was not complete enough. They advocated for the total abolition of private property in order to achieve absolute equality.

The Conspiracy of the Equals (Conjuration des Égaux) was subsequently established to violently overthrow the Directory and implement the first constitution of the French Republic, enacted in 1793 but never put into effect. Babeuf proclaimed the aim of the revolution was to "abolish private ownership" and "establish public administration to oversee the distribution of these products, while strictly observing the principle of equality." Because private ownership inevitably resulted in inequality, its abolition was the only way to achieve "true equality" (Babeuf cited in Soboul, 1983). The plot intended to confiscate private land and the means of production after seizing political power, aiming to attain "complete equality" and "common happiness."

The Manifesto of Equals, issued by the Conspiracy of the Equals in 1796, declared:

> We need not only that equality of rights written into the *Declaration of the Rights of Man and Citizen*; we want it in our midst, under the roofs of our houses. [...] Let it at last end, this great scandal that our descendants will never believe existed! Disappear at last, revolting distinctions between rich and poor, great and small, masters and servants, rulers and ruled. [...] The moment has come to found the REPUBLIC OF EQUALS, the great home open to all men. [...] The organization of real equality, the only one that responds to all needs, without causing any victims, without costing any sacrifice, will not at first please everyone. The selfish, the ambitious, will tremble with rage. (Maréchal, 1796)

The total forced elimination of private property rights, the annihilation of the old world, and the violent establishment of a new communist world are the fundamental characteristics of communist totalitarianism, a theory and a movement pioneered by Babeuf. In his 1795 *Le manifeste des plébéiens* (*Manifesto of the Common People*),

Babeuf issued a revolutionary call for secular salvation, advocating for the replacement of the dying old world with an egalitarian new one. His eloquent call to create chaos in the world, to destroy the old world and create a new one, made even Mao seem to pale in comparison 200 years later (see Chapter 12 for details). Babeuf said,

> People! Awaken to hope! ... Rejoice in the coming of a happy future! ... all calamities have come to a head; they can no longer get worse. They can only be destroyed by a complete overhaul! Let everything be destroyed! Scramble all spontaneous forces together, let them mix and clash! Let there be chaos, and from chaos a new and rebuilt world! (Quoted from Soboul, 1983)

Babeuf's attempt to implement a communist totalitarian system in practice laid the groundwork for the Blanquists of the Second Paris Commune and the Bolsheviks in the early twentieth century. Babeuf established a top-down conspiratorial organization with a "strong leadership." At the core of this conspiracy was a leadership group led by Babeuf, known as the Secret Directory. This leadership relied on a small number of "revolutionary representatives," who had been tested and who operated underground. These representatives served as liaisons between the revolutionaries and the patriots, conducting propaganda, organizing activities, and attracting the masses. However, the patriots and democrats were not privy to the secrets and "specific objectives" of the Conspiracy. Babeuf's revolutionary comrade, Philippe Buonarroti, described the Conspiracy's plan as follows, "After an armed insurrection to overthrow the old state, the Secret Directory was to establish a revolutionary regime, with itself at the core, in order to transform society and establish a new system. The Secret Directory was also to keep watch on the Assembly."[16]

Marx inherited and expanded upon Babeuf's communist theory and tactics, opposing constitutionalism and advocating for dictatorship from an early stage.[17] Later in his life, he explicitly stated that his greatest contribution was the invention of the concept of proletarian dictatorship. He argued that establishing a proletarian dictatorship was a prerequisite for abolishing private property and establishing public ownership. He clearly stated:

> In destroying the existing conditions of oppression by transferring all the means of labor to the productive laborers, and thereby compelling every able-bodied individual to work for a living, the only base for class rule and oppression would be removed. But before such a change could be effected a proletarian dictature would become necessary, and the first condition of that was a proletarian army. The working classes would have to conquer the right to emancipate themselves on the battlefield. (Marx and Engels, 2010, vol. 22, p. 634)

6.3 ORIGINS OF BABEUF'S COMMUNISM: THE FRENCH ENLIGHTENMENT

Babeuf's communist theory drew heavily from the French Enlightenment, including the communist ideas of Abbé de Mably and Étienne-Gabriel Morelly, who advocated for the abolition of private property, and Rousseau's concepts of general will and popular sovereignty (Talmon, 1952). The Conspiracy of the Equals, whose participants were members of the Jacobin Club, emerged as a more radical movement under Jacobin rule. The ideas of the Jacobin Club, Robespierre, and Babeuf originated from the French Enlightenment and further developed during the Revolution.

The Enlightenment since the seventeenth century, as a prelude to the French Revolution, had produced a variety of ideas, many of which were mutually contradictory. Among the most famous of these thinkers were Locke and Montesquieu, who advocated for constitutional democracy with an emphasis on human rights and property rights. Others, such as Meslier, Mably, and Morelly, championed the elimination of private property and the establishment of communism (Mably explicitly opposed Montesquieu); Rousseau stressed mandatory popular sovereignty; and Meslier and Voltaire were fierce critics of religious authority. Both the English Glorious Revolution and the French Revolution were deeply influenced by the Enlightenment. The French Revolution initially sought to establish a constitutional monarchy, mirroring the English Glorious Revolution. However, the question arises: Why were constitutionalist ideas abandoned by the French radical revolutionaries during the Revolution? Why did they gravitate towards authoritarianism and, in the case of the most radical, even spawn a communist totalitarian movement?

The Declaration of the Rights of Man and of the Citizen, issued at the outset of the Revolution, contained fundamental principles of inviolable rights and the separation of powers, influenced by Locke and Montesquieu. However, within months of its proclamation, these principles were completely eclipsed by the bloody tide of the Revolution. The ensuing years were characterized by terror, carnage, and systematic human rights violations, leading to a drastic surge in the violation of human rights in France compared to the pre-revolutionary era.

Montesquieu's theories, based on a century of British constitutional practice, had a considerable impact on the American Constitution. And, in turn, the early constitutionalism of the French Revolution drew explicitly from the American experience. However, rather than Montesquieu's principles, it was Rousseau's autocratic principle of the indivisibility of sovereignty – which stands in direct opposition to constitutional principles – that prevailed in the regime established by the Revolution. The principle of the separation of powers was, at best, nothing more than empty rhetoric in the constitution.

The notion of equality, rather than constitutionalism, appears to be most prevalent during the French Revolution. Almost all French Enlightenment thinkers, including Montesquieu, Voltaire, and Rousseau, advocated for equality. However, their conceptions of equality not only significantly differed from one another but were even in conflict. Social reform or revolution based on different principles of equality led to completely opposite outcomes. Montesquieu emphasized the equality of basic rights, particularly in terms of human rights and property rights. In contrast, Meslier, Mably, and Morelly championed absolute equality to the point of completely abolishing private property and even the family. Rousseau also emphasized absolute equality and asserted that private property is the source of inequality, which later influenced Marx. However, he stopped short of explicitly calling for the abolition of private property. During the French Revolution, the most radical revolutionaries, particularly the impoverished rebels, viewed absolute equality as their overriding demand or creed. For the most radical among them, everything could be sacrificed for such a sacred goal, including the physical elimination of anyone who stood in their way (Soboul, 1972, pp. 158–161).

The ideas that revolutionaries and rioters accept and resist are their own choices, determined by their self-interests and the ideologies they espouse, that is, the existing institutional genes. Rousseau's concept of popular sovereignty was prevalent and further developed during the Revolution because the supremacy of sovereignty and its indivisibility were both an old tradition of French absolute monarchy and directly beneficial to any political group eager to seize power, whether they called themselves revolutionaries or royalists. Indeed, Rousseau's doctrine of popular sovereignty and the principle of the "indivisibility of sovereignty" were taken as the theoretical basis for the Jacobin dictatorship during the Revolution (Talmon, 1952). In the name of popular sovereignty, the Jacobin regime arrested and executed thousands of people, including their revolutionary comrades. Its despotism and brutality were a continuation but it far surpassed the system overthrown by the French Revolution. The mechanism behind this irony is the evolution of the same kind of institutional genes under different names.

In contrast, many great ideas originating from the French Enlightenment had no influence during the Revolution or were selectively discarded. For instance, while Voltaire was sharply critical of the monarchy, the aristocracy, and the Church, he also emphasized tolerance. Radical revolutionaries adored his criticism of the old regime, which they amplified to the point that Voltaire's voice on tolerance was completely drowned out. The violent revolution conducted by means of terror not only contradicted Voltaire's call for tolerance in practice but some radical revolutionaries even claimed that executing all dissidents was a condition for the success of the revolution (Soboul, 1972, pp. 158–161).

The brutal persecution of the Marquis de Condorcet exemplifies how the radical revolutionaries in the name of justice and equality abandoned all ideas of democratic constitutionalism during the Revolution. As a leading figure of the French Enlightenment, Condorcet and his theory of democracy remain influential today. In the 1970s and 1980s, the Nobel Prize in Economics was awarded twice to theoretical studies that were developed based on Condorcet's work. Besides his theoretical contributions, Condorcet had an active role in the French Revolution and was a key architect of the Girondin Constitution project of 1793. Nevertheless, his theories were disregarded and the constitution he drafted was scorned by the Jacobins who usurped power in that same year. Condorcet was subsequently arrested, imprisoned, and persecuted to death, becoming one of the pioneering revolutionaries to die in that way under the first totalitarian regime. Over a century later, similar tragedies unfolded in Russia, China, and other places under totalitarian rule.

6.3.1 From Christian Communism/Messianism to Secular Communism/Messianism

The element of a communist utopia is inherently embedded in the Christian spirit, as previously discussed.[18] According to the New Testament, Jesus Christ and his followers practiced the principles of communism from the inception of their faith, emphasizing voluntariness and self-sacrifice. The Reformation revitalized this early Christian ethos but it also gave rise to the first instance of coercive communism, although the latter was ignored by most scholars as it was small in scale and did not last long. The Anabaptists, a radical group, established short-lived communist city-states in the sixteenth century, which represented the first generation of enforced communist regimes and nascent totalitarian regimes in human history.

During the Enlightenment movement, which sought to replace religion with secular reasoning, several utopianists, such as Gabriel Bonnot de Mably and Étienne-Gabriel Morelly, explored and designed their ideal communist societies from theoretical and institutional perspectives. However, the one who had the most profound influence was Father Jean Meslier, who clandestinely transformed Christian communism into a comprehensive philosophy of atheist communism, laying the theoretical groundwork for transforming the Christian communist ideal into a secular communist movement in the future.[19]

On the one hand, any form of communism that aims to eradicate private ownership inherently necessitates widespread violence. Any discourse about such communism becomes hollow without substantial popular support. Conversely, the ideas that gain influence are invariably those that large numbers of people need and are willing to adopt. In a society marked by acute inequality, there is a pervasive demand for greater equality. Thus, with a radical call for absolute equality, communism becomes appealing to both elites and radicals from the lower classes.

The upheaval during the Reformation period underscored the potential of Christian messianism as a catalyst for violent popular revolution. Therefore, proponents of secular communism were always mindful of retaining this messianic element as communism transitioned from a Christian to a secular ideal.

As a revolutionary theorist who advocated for the poor during the French Revolution, Babeuf was among the pioneers in transforming communism from its Christian origins towards the secular realm through agitation and action. Secular messianism, a derivative of Christian messianism, believed that the old, unequal world was on the verge of perishing and being replaced by a new world of equality (Babeuf's *Le Manifeste des Plébéiens*, 1795).[20] The immediate impact of secular messianism during the French Revolution can be largely attributed to its underlying ideals, which were drawn directly from Christianity by "communist clergy," ensuring its compatibility with the deep-rooted tradition – referred to here as the "institutional gene" – of Christian messianism in France. An additional factor was the repeated implementation of violent revolution during the early stages of the French Revolution. Even before the establishment of the Jacobin dictatorship, the revolutionary fervor had already dismantled the monarchy and the Church of the old regime. Subsequently, France's first republic was overthrown by the poor through violence, enabling the Jacobins to form a nascent totalitarian regime under the banner of popular sovereignty. Each revolution drew its justification from the enduring messianic spirit: the old world was coming to an end and a new one was about to be born.

The Revolution began by violently abolishing the old system of monarchy and theocracy. Then the Jacobins used violence to dismantle the newly established "old system" known as the French Republic. Ultimately, according to Babeuf, what had to be destroyed was private ownership, which has existed since the dawn of human civilization. This captivating messianic ideology sounded the call to mobilize the population for a revolutionary purge. However, in the transformation of Christian messianism into a secular belief, Christianity itself became the target of a "violent revolution."

The Catholic Church had been a cornerstone of French society since the early Middle Ages and its demise destabilized society. Faith in Christianity began to waver amidst the interdenominational rivalries and the brutal religious wars that followed in the wake of the Reformation. In the seventeenth century, Christianity was further weakened by the breakthroughs of empirical science and the emergence of a growing spirit of rational inquiry. Deism,[21] which developed under the influence of empirical science, directly challenged the inerrancy of Christian doctrine. Among some intellectuals, deism replaced Christianity as the dominant faith. During the Enlightenment, it greatly influenced philosophy and science, with early proponents including Descartes, Locke, Newton, and Adam

Smith. Many prominent figures of the French Enlightenment, including Descartes, Voltaire, Montesquieu, Rousseau, and the Jacobin leader Robespierre, followed deism. In contrast, Babeuf rejected all forms of religion. If Meslier was the first to theorize secular communism, albeit secretly, then Babeuf was the first to attempt a secular communist revolution. However, the followers of Babeuf's movement in France never amassed sufficient numbers to launch a significant, violent revolution.

The intellectual elites who played a leading role in both the Glorious Revolution in Britain and the French Revolution shared a common belief in deism and largely held skeptical attitudes towards Christianity. However, their attitudes towards religion and the Church were markedly different. The British elite tended to be more tolerant towards the Church.[22] After the signing of the Bill of Rights, there was never any large-scale violence against the Church in Britain and religious freedom and tolerance were largely exercised. In contrast, Voltaire assailed Christianity and the Church with violent language and the revolutionary poor and the Jacobin government directly targeted the Church and clergy with brutal violence during the French Revolution.

One of the relatively straightforward reasons for the differences between the two revolutions is that the Glorious Revolution emerged in the late Reformation, while the French Revolution started when the Enlightenment, which had already proceeded for a century, challenged the monarchy and the Church, promoted human rights, democracy, constitutionalism, questioned religious dogmatism and control, and advocated tolerance. However, when it came to societal transformation and the creation of new philosophical ideas, the French Enlightenment tended to be overly radical, even exhibiting an autocratic tendency (Berlin, 2013).

At the time of the Glorious Revolution in Britain, the Enlightenment was just beginning and had not yet posed a severe challenge to Christianity. The main religious issue facing English society was the dispute between Catholicism and Protestantism.

The unique historical circumstances of England at the time of the Reformation meant that revolutionaries and reformers, from radical to moderate, generally advocated religious tolerance. By the time the Enlightenment posed a radical challenge to Christianity, the English constitutional system had already been consolidated and stabilized. In contrast, the French Revolution broke out a century after the Glorious Revolution, when the Enlightenment's critique of Christianity, the Church, and theocracy had disseminated from the leading intellectuals to the French masses.

Voltaire played a pivotal role in criticizing Christianity and the Catholic Church and in mobilizing French intellectuals against the theocracy. Because of his attacks on the theocracy and the aristocracy, he was forced into exile in England. During his nearly three years in exile, he became greatly interested in Locke's political ideas, Newtonian physics, and deism. He went on to become a strong advocate of deism during the French Enlightenment.

Unlike his English "teachers" Locke and Newton, who approached Christianity with reason and tolerance, Voltaire harbored a deep animosity towards Christianity and the Church. His criticism of Christianity was so sharp that it bordered on denunciation and even incited hatred. In a letter to Frederick II, King of Prussia in 1767, Voltaire wrote:

> [Christianity] is assuredly the most ridiculous, the most absurd and the most bloody religion which has ever infected this world. Your Majesty will do the human race an eternal service by extirpating this infamous superstition, I do not say among the rabble, who are not worthy of being enlightened and who are apt for every yoke; I say among honest people, among men who think, among those who wish to think. (Mathews, 2009, p. 16)

Jean Meslier, the Catholic priest who influenced both Voltaire and Rousseau, systematically discussed his lifelong concealed atheist, materialist, and communist beliefs and theories in his magnum opus *Testament* (Meslier, 2009). He loathed monarchs. A contemporary of

Louis XIV, he criticized the king as a thief, murderer, and exploiter, responsible for massacres, wars, and famine (Onfray, 2006). Meslier did not believe in the existence of God and he vehemently opposed everything about Christianity and the Church, including the Bible. He put forth a vision of a communist society in which private property and the family had been eradicated. Meslier prophesied that a violent revolution would be necessary to achieve communism and he even claimed that it would be worth killing a few kings to reach this goal (Durant and Durant, 1967, p. 80).

Voltaire published an abridged version of Meslier's manuscript, which was widely disseminated. However, he altered Meslier's atheism into deism and misrepresented his theory of communism (Wade, 1933, pp. 381–398).

In the end, through the communist movements led by Babeuf, Marx, and Engels, Meslier was recognized as a precursor of modern communist thought. Indeed, the Bolsheviks praised Meslier as having a significance in the revolutionary communist enlightenment akin to the role Descartes played in the development of the Western Enlightenment and modernity (Onfray, 2006).

Voltaire's hatred for Christianity and the Church was initially limited to antagonism against papalism and theocracy. Influenced by Meslier, this later transformed into an attack on the Bible, Church dogmas, and eventually even Jesus Christ, whom he portrayed as a fallen man (Daniel-Rops, 1964, p. 47). In *La Bible enfin expliquée* (*The Bible Finally Explained*), Voltaire wrote:

> It is characteristic of fanatics who read the holy scriptures to tell themselves: God killed, so I must kill; Abraham lied, Jacob deceived, Rachel stole: so I must steal, deceive, lie. But, wretch, you are neither Rachel, nor Jacob, nor Abraham, nor God; you are just a mad fool, and the popes who forbade the reading of the Bible were extremely wise. (Cronk, 2009, p. 199)

Alexis de Tocqueville (1805–1859), famous for his works *Democracy in America* and *The Old Regime and the Revolution*, pointed out that Voltaire was more inclined to attack and destroy the old regime than to build a new one. He wrote:

> The old edifice of government had long been insecure; it shook, though no man struck it. Voltaire was hardly thinking of it. Three years' residence in England had enabled him to understand that country without falling in love with it.... He was not struck with their political laws, which he rather criticized than praised. His letters on England ... hardly contain any allusion to Parliament: he envies the English their literary liberty, but cares little for their political liberty, as though the one could exist for any length of time without the other.[23]

In contrast, Montesquieu clearly pointed out the systemic problems in France. For example, he wrote that the reason for low output from the land in France compared with that in England was that, "The yield of land depends less on its fertility than on the freedom of its occupants" (quoted in Tocqueville, 1856, chapter 12).

As our purpose is to analyze social phenomena rather than merely discuss theory, it is important to note that in any society, the emergence of thought or theory is one thing, while the acceptance or rejection by the populace is entirely another. The former is the creation of thinkers within the society in which they live, reflecting both the conditions of that society and personal factors. The latter depends on the demands by different interest groups within that society.

Voltaire's opposition to the theocracy resonated strongly with the French populace because such a voice was needed in French society. Given the high level of discontent with the Church, particularly among the lower classes, the incitement of hatred against Christianity and the Church by intellectual leaders like Voltaire had a substantial impact. On the other hand, the theories of Montesquieu were not received by radical revolutionaries and the poor as they were considered too moderate. In fact, Voltaire had foreseen the Revolution before it happened. In a letter from 1764, he predicted that the revolution in France would be as powerful as a landslide (Durant, 1933,

p. 187). After being imprisoned by the mob, Louis XVI lamented that Rousseau and Voltaire had destroyed France (Durant, 1933, p. 261). Sadly, he not only discovered the influence of Rousseau and Voltaire too late but probably never realized that, in his great-grandfather's time, Meslier had already sown the seeds of undermining the theocracy, the pillar of the French Empire.

6.3.2 General Will, Popular Sovereignty, and Absolute Equality

The French Enlightenment movement encompassed a variety of ideas, with some advocating for constitutionalism while others opposed it. What then, determined the direction of social change? Montesquieu's theory of the separation of political powers stood in clear contradiction to Rousseau's notion of absolute rule by the general will and the absolute nature of sovereignty. It is worth noting that Rousseau was not the one who invented this term. For example, long before him, Spinoza discussed this concept with a viewpoint opposite to Rousseau's (Israel, 2020). This book only focuses on Rousseau's notion of general will. However, revolutionary leaders like Robespierre and revolutionary groups like the Jacobins abandoned Montesquieu in favor of Rousseau. They pushed Rousseau's discourse towards outright autocracy, violence, and terror. A question arises, why, in an era when constitutionalism was clearly disseminated and demonstrable models such as Britain and America existed, did the French populace choose to follow extreme autocracy, masked under the guise of attractive reasoning? To a large extent, this can be explained by the institutional genes left by the old regime and the revolutionaries who were shaped by these genes.

One of the foundational theories supporting the Jacobin dictatorship established during the French Revolution was Rousseau's concept of popular sovereignty. As expounded in *The Social Contract*, this theory opposes the constitutional principle of the separation of powers. Although certain aspects of Rousseau's social contract and popular sovereignty were influenced by Locke, the essence of his concepts stands in opposition to those of Locke. The decision of the revolutionary poor and the Jacobin elite in France to embrace Rousseau's ideas over those of Montesquieu reflects the needs of French society during the French Revolution. Ultimately, these societal needs determined the role of different thinkers during the Revolution.

The primary distinction between the philosophical positions of Locke and Montesquieu, as opposed to those of Rousseau, pertains to human rights and property rights. In Locke's view, human rights and property rights are inextricably linked; human rights are superior to sovereignty and sovereignty exists to protect human rights. Under no circumstances should sovereignty be allowed to infringe upon human rights. Locke argued that the government's sole purpose is to safeguard human rights and, to achieve this objective, it must abide by the principles of constitutionalism, which involve the separation of powers and thereby ensure the restriction of governmental power.

Conversely, Rousseau believed that popular sovereignty, as a manifestation of the general will, held precedence over all individuals and entities, and could exert coercive power over the populace. He emphasized the indivisibility of sovereignty and stood against the separation of powers (Rousseau, 1923), rejecting the principles of constitutionalism. Notably, in *Discourse on the Origin and the Foundations of Inequality Among Men*, Rousseau asserted that private property rights were the root cause of inequality, fundamentally contradicting Locke's thought (Rousseau, 1997). Moreover, in *The Social Contract*, he advocated absolute equality, although he did not employ this exact phrase.

While the concepts of equality and wealth distribution are ingrained in Christianity, they are framed as matters of faith. In Christian belief, there is no inherent conflict between equality and private property, nor is there any suggestion of coercion. In fact, the Bible has always upheld the principle of protecting private property rights, dating back to the Old Testament. However, in times of severe societal inequality, radical revolutionaries exploited the profound antipathy towards inequality felt by the poor. Drawing on Rousseau's theory, they incited the masses to dismantle the social order that protected private property rights, all in the pursuit of absolute egalitarianism.

In a revolution characterized by a hatred of inequality and a desire for absolute equality, the disdain for private property evolved and transformed into a revolution committed to the complete abolition of private property rights. This constituted the foundational logic of Babeuvian communism that emerged during the Jacobin dictatorship, with Babeuf drawing his theory from the works of Rousseau and Meslier. Marxism, which emerged several decades later, and Leninism are both continuations and evolutions of Babeuvian communism.

Rousseau's concepts of the general will, the social contract, sovereignty, and freedom encapsulate the conflict between the tradition of absolute monarchy in mid-to-late-eighteenth-century France and the Enlightenment spirit of liberty. In his formulation, the social contract forms a "moral community" in which each individual places his individuality and powers under the supreme leadership of the "general will." The collective expression of this general will becomes a "public figure" into which each individual is incorporated. Rousseau referred to this "public figure" in different contexts as the republic, the state, the sovereign, the people, and the citizen. He asserted that each individual, guided by the general will, should be compelled to accept the general will and become part of the public figure. Furthermore, sovereignty is the expression of the general will. The social contract grants the "body politic" absolute power over its members, and it is this power to express the general will that bestows the name of sovereignty. To ensure expression of the general will, there must be no "partial society" within the state. In Rousseau's ideal world, there would be a "real democracy" never seen before, "equality would be everywhere, ... as in rules and wealth" (*The Social Contract*, Rousseau, 1923, Book IV, chapter 3).

Central to Rousseau's philosophy is the concept of the general will.[24] In *The Social Contract*, he argued, the general will is the will of the sovereign. "Sovereignty ... is the exercise of the general will" (Rousseau, 1923, Book II, chapter 1), and the sovereign must oversee and control the government because the general will expressed and implemented by the government is a particular will, relative to the sovereign. Under this conception, he delineated two types of liberty: natural liberty and civil liberty, asserting that natural liberty is "bounded only by the strength of the individual," while civil liberty is "limited by the general will" (Rousseau, 1923, Book I, chapter 8). He underscored that these limitations encompass coercion, positing:

> In order then that the social compact may not be an empty formula, it tacitly includes the undertaking, which alone can give force to the rest, that whoever refuses to obey the general will shall be compelled to do so by the whole body. This means nothing less than that he will be forced to be free; for this is the condition which, by giving each citizen to his country, secures him against all personal dependence. (Rousseau, 1923, Book I, chapter 7)

In his argument against the separation of powers on the grounds of the indivisibility of sovereignty, Rousseau echoed the same reasoning Jean Bodin utilized in his defense of absolute monarchy as part of his doctrine of sovereignty. Rousseau also resisted indirect democracy, a stance that would later be used to justify many of the atrocities perpetrated by revolutionary groups of the poor. He wrote:

> Sovereignty, for the same reason as makes it inalienable, cannot be represented; it lies essentially in the general will, and will does not admit of representation: it is either the same, or other; there is no intermediate possibility. (Rousseau, 1923, Book III, chapter 15)

Rousseau's views on English democracy starkly contrasted with those of Montesquieu and Voltaire, as he contemptuously asserted:

> The people of England ... is free only during the election of members of parliament. As soon as they are elected, slavery

6.3 ORIGINS OF BABEUF'S COMMUNISM

overtakes it, and it is nothing. The use it makes of the short moments of liberty it enjoys shows indeed that it deserves to lose them. (Rousseau, 1923, Book III, chapter 15)

Rousseau consistently underscored the notion that the general will and sovereignty necessitated coercive power over citizens. He wrote:

It is therefore essential, if the general will is to be able to express itself, that there should be no partial society within the State, and that each citizen should think only his own thoughts. (Rousseau, 1923, Book II, chapter 3)

As nature gives each man absolute power over all his members, the social compact gives the body politic absolute power over all its members also; and it is this power which, under the direction of the general will, bears ... the name of Sovereignty. (Rousseau, 1923, Book II, chapter 4)

The Sovereign can only be considered collectively and as a body; but each member, as being a subject, is regarded as an individual.... the larger the State, the less the liberty. (Rousseau, 1923, Book III, chapter 1)

Rousseau's series of concepts regarding the general will, sovereignty, coercion, and citizen freedom have drawn criticism from numerous scholars. Hegel opined that Rousseau's general will would lead to a reign of terror (Hegel, 1991), while Russell deemed it to be anti-democratic (Russell, [1946] 1957). Talmon contended that Rousseau's argument for the general will was a crucial precipitant towards totalitarian democracy (Talmon, 1952).

However, Rousseau's more direct contribution to the emergence of communist totalitarianism lies in his opposition to the principles of constitutionalism and the separation of powers, his endorsement of caesaropapist rule, and his advocacy for sovereign control over property rights and opposition to private property. In the second volume of *The Social Contract*, Rousseau devoted a chapter to *The Indivisibility of Sovereignty*, presenting arguments that are in direct conflict with constitutionalist theory. Engels highly praised Rousseau, considering the conflict between Rousseau and Montesquieu as important as Luther–Calvin's Protestantism against Catholicism (Marx and Engels, 2012, vol. 4, p. 643). Going further than the doctrine of indivisible sovereignty, Rousseau explicitly advocated secular, caesaropapist rule, considering the government and the Church as manifestations of secular and divine sovereignty, thus they cannot be separated. He argued that secular and divine power should be directed into "political unity, without which no State or government will ever be rightly constituted" (Rousseau, 1923, Book IV, chapter 8). He advocated for the establishment of a theocratic secular regime and civil religion "of which the Sovereign should fix the articles.... While it [the sovereign] can compel no one to believe them, it can banish from the State whoever does not believe them" (Rousseau, 1923, Book IV, chapter 8).

Rousseau advocated for absolute equality, asserting that, "In a real democracy, equality would be everywhere, in morals and talents as in rules and wealth" (Rousseau, 1923, Book IV, chapter 3). He believed that private property was the root of inequality. Thus, Rousseau argued for sovereign control over property rights as a means of achieving such absolute equality.

But even under European absolute monarchy, sovereignty did not have full power to control the property rights of the nobility and the power of the Church. The key step towards communist totalitarianism is to break the boundary between sovereignty and property rights, allowing sovereignty to legally control property rights. Rousseau made a significant contribution in promoting this change. In Rousseau's conception, sovereignty represents the general will and is superior to the individual. So there is no clear boundary between sovereignty and property rights. He said that, for the sake of equality,

> Each member of the community gives himself to it, at the moment of its foundation, just as he is, with all the resources at

his command, including the goods he possesses.... The State, in relation to its members, is master of all their goods. (Rousseau, 1923, Book I, chapter 9)

What man loses by the social contract is his natural liberty ...; what he gains is civil liberty and the proprietorship of all he possesses. (Rousseau, 1923, Book I, chapter 8)

6.4 MARXIST COMMUNIST TOTALITARIANISM

It took only a century from the advent of Marxism for communist totalitarianism to sweep the globe and rule one-third of the world population. For comparison, Christianity took over a millennium to become the world's largest religion, covering a quarter of the world's population and Islam took thirteen centuries to become the second largest, covering a fifth. The swift expansion of communist totalitarianism in the modern era is inextricably linked to large-scale violent revolutions. Yet, violence itself is an insufficient explanation as it would not have been possible without the allure and incitement of revolutionary ideologies among the masses. An ideology that can incite millions to sacrifice their lives for revolution must have a potent appeal, rooted in elements already deeply ingrained in people's minds. Therefore, the decisive factor in creating an unprecedented scale of a communist totalitarian movement within a century must involve more than just theories invented by geniuses or methods of incitement and organization created by revolutionary leaders. This chapter illustrates the institutional genes of the communist totalitarian ideology – institutional elements long-existing within Christianity and deeply rooted in people's minds. These institutional genes persisted when the ideology transitioned from Christianity to secularity. The novelty of communist totalitarianism was primarily centered on the communist messianism labeled as "science." This ideology made the construction and realization of a system of total dictatorship and absolute violence possible.

The central ideas of the communist totalitarian ideology, as established by Marx, are as follows: (1) A proletarian revolution should be initiated to abolish private property and establish a society of absolute equality. (2) The establishment of a proletarian dictatorship should be prioritized. (3) Capitalism, due to its inherent self-destructive forces – including its creation of the proletariat – will inevitably perish. (4) The global proletarian revolution will invariably lead to the establishment of worldwide communism.

The first component above is the primary factor that attracts intellectuals and the general public to embrace communist totalitarianism. It relies on the proletarian violent revolution to thoroughly eliminate private property and establish an absolutely equal society in which everyone equally loses property rights (*The Communist Manifesto*, Marx and Engels, [1848] 1998). The pursuit of absolute equality and the necessity of using violence to achieve it have existed throughout history. When Meslier and Babeuf transformed Christian communism into secular communism, the principles they espoused were essentially aligned with this goal. However, from Meslier to Babeuf, the role of violence became increasingly significant. Marx's contribution was the theorization of violence, rendering the violence of the proletarian revolution as an indispensable "science" that is more systematic, concrete, and essential for the revolution.

The concept of the dictatorship of the proletariat, a theoretical blueprint designed for modern totalitarianism, was the invention that Marx considered to be the greatest contribution of his life. He asserted that to enter communism, as the first step an entirely new state, which will be a system of violence under the dictatorship of the proletariat, must be created. This state rules over everything and controls all property in society. It is a system in which sovereignty and property are united and politics and religion are united. In this state, political power decides everything (*Critique of the Gotha Program*, Marx, 1938). As a concept, the dictatorship of the proletariat was actually not so much Marx's invention as it was in fact his summary of coercive communism encompassing the Reformation, the French Revolution, and his contemporary event, the second Paris Commune. All previous experiments in coercive communism exhibited highly autocratic systems where sovereignty and property were unified, as were politics and religion. Each had the essential characteristics of a totalitarian system.

However, a "scientific theory" of proletarian revolution and the dictatorship of the proletariat alone were not sufficient to persuade, tempt, and incite social elites and the masses to participate fanatically in the communist revolution at the cost of their own lives and those of others. In addition to "science," communist totalitarian ideological agitation relied on communist messianism. In fact, in the unprecedented rapid development of communist totalitarianism, communist messianism is indispensable. The core of communist messianism is the so-called "inexorable law" of social development (Marxism), similar to Christian messianism in spirit. Christianity claims that the Savior is about to arrive, that the catastrophic old world will perish, and a beautiful new world is about to be born. Marxism asserts that the old world of inequality based on private property will inevitably collapse and that proletarian revolutions throughout the world will inevitably break out in full force, burying the old world of human exploitation and eventually engendering the wonderful world of communism.[25]

In Marx's era, the communist revolution had not yet occurred. Theoretically, the savior is the proletariat itself, as stated in the *Communist Manifesto* and the *Internationale* (the song of the international communist movement). It is the theoretical sublimation of the Jacobin-Babeuf revolution. But in practice, in all communist revolutions and under all communist totalitarian regimes, their Great Leaders were sanctified as saviors. In the official language of the CCP, Mao was the "Great Savior" who liberated the Chinese people and guided the people of the world.

The ideology of communist totalitarianism serves as an essential foundation for constructing a totalitarian system. However, the regions where this ideology exerts the most influence are not necessarily its places of origin, and this influence relies on various conditions. This ideology indeed first emerged in Germany, France, and

Britain, but despite this, it did not gain widespread acceptance or prevalence in these countries from the late nineteenth century onwards. In stark contrast, the Russians and the Chinese, especially the latter, enthusiastically embraced it. Notably, most Chinese, including their leaders, did not have a thorough understanding of the theory and origins of this ideology. Yet, they emerged as the world's leading proponents of communist totalitarianism. The acceptance of an ideology within a society is heavily influenced by the society's institutional genes. Chapters 7 and 8 that follow elucidate why the first modern communist totalitarian system sprang up in Russia, considering the perspective of institutional genes. The subsequent chapters delve into why the communist totalitarian system, freshly established in Soviet Russia, was swiftly accepted in China and deeply ingrained itself there.

NOTES

1. In this book, the term "totalitarianism" is used as a concept within political science, referring to a specific type of political institution. However, its original usage was associated with the regimes of Italian Fascists and German Nazis from the 1920s to the 1940s, which combined extreme nationalism with socialism. In fact, the term "totalitarianism," first coined to describe Italian Fascism (Pipes, 1995a), came into existence several years after the Soviet system was established. A critical work that employed and expanded on this term and concept was *The Doctrine of Fascism*, co-authored by Mussolini and the fascist philosopher Giovanni Gentile in 1932 (Mussolini, 2015). Before founding the National Fascist Party, Mussolini was a member of the Italian Socialist Party and had associations with Lenin. He considered Marx the most prominent theorist of socialism and identified himself as a Marxist (Smith, 1983). Mussolini both aspired to emulate the Bolsheviks' rise to power and explicitly echoed the language of Lenin's New Economic Policy. Gentile was also significantly influenced by Marxism. The Nazi Party – officially called the National Socialist German Workers' Party (NSDAP) – was a nationalist socialist party, exhibiting similarities to the National Fascist Party.

2. Babeuf, also known as Gracchus Babeuf, was a French revolutionary philosopher and leader during the French Revolution. He organized the Conspiracy of the Equals, advocating for violent revolution to abolish private property. After his execution for his role in the conspiracy, his followers initiated the communist movement in Europe, making him a pioneer in the communist movement.
3. During his visit to Paris in 1840, Barmby was introduced to the French communist movement by Babeuf's followers and he derived "communism" from the French term *communisme*. Engels explicitly linked communism with Christian beliefs in his "Letter to the Editor on Communism in France" (Engels, 1844).
4. These statements by Babeuf underpin the Marxist theory of communism. Marx and Engels did not consistently adhere to academic conventions when citing the sources that had most directly informed their thought. This is particularly the case with the works of Rousseau and Babeuf, although the influence of these scholars on Marxism has been thoroughly discussed by historians. Engels once noted the similarities between Rousseau's *The Social Contract* and *Discourse on Inequality* and Marx's *Das Kapital*, writing: "We already see in Rousseau not only the exact same process of thought present in Marx's *Das Kapital*, but also, in his detailed account, the exact same series of dialectical arguments as used by Marx" (Marx and Engels, 2012, vol. 3, p. 519).
5. In *Anti-Dühring*, Engels delineates historical movements headed by proletarian pioneers, the first of whom was Müntzer (Engels, 2010).
6. "In Thomas Müntzer's programme, the division of the church estates was transformed into confiscation in favor of common property, and the unified German *empire*, into the unified and undivided republic" (Engels, 1926).
7. In *The Communist Manifesto*, Marx referred to Babeuf's works as the documents of modern proletarian revolution. Several of Babeuf's associates contributed to the development of communist thought (Israel, 2015). Without going into details here, Babeuf is used to summarize the contributions of all those individuals.
8. The high court (*Parlement*) of medieval France was a pivotal component of the *ancien régime*. Its members were nobles who operated independently from the king. The *Parlement* served as a court of appeal and was responsible for registering royal edicts. It also had the "right of remonstrance," which allowed it to oppose edicts that did not align

with customary or national law. However, it held no real power. Royal edicts were registered as laws, provided the king was personally present. The *Parlement* of Paris, established in the fourteenth century, was the first and largest court of its kind in France and gave rise to the English word "parliament." The parliamentary system was later transferred from England to France, which in turn adopted relevant parliamentary terminology from England (Shennan, 1998).

9. Some state that the Catholic Church in France held a quarter of the national wealth during the seventeenth century and was considerably richer than the king, though conservative estimates put the Church and the king on an equal footing at the time (McManners, 1998, p. 95). By the early eighteenth century, however, the Church owned a third of the national wealth (McManners, 1998, p. 97).

10. Of 1,201 deputies to the Estates-General, 303 were from the First Estate, representing 100,000 clergy (who held 10 percent of the land); 291 were from the Second Estate, representing 400,000 aristocrats (who owned 25 percent of the land); and 610 were from the Third Estate, representing 95 percent of the French population (Doyle, 1989).

11. Ken Arrow and Amartya Sen were awarded Nobel Prizes in Economics in 1972 and 1998, respectively, for their further development of Condorcet's seminal theory of voting.

12. Kautsky (1920, pp. 20–24). Moreover, Albert Soble, an authority on the French Revolution, also called them the proletariat. Some historians disagree with the invocation of the concept of class in this context while acknowledging that *sans-culottes* belonged to the lower strata of society.

13. In order to maintain order, the revolutionary government arrested some of the more radical leaders of the militant poor in Paris. The testimonies these individuals provided during the subsequent investigations constitute a portion of the valuable historical documentation.

14. Tocqueville systematically records how, in the traditional feudal societies of Western Europe, the nobles were obliged to help and relieve the poorest families on their own estates. The Church had a similar obligation to the poor of every parish. With the establishment of the absolute monarchy in France, however, "lords were deprived of ancient powers, and thus of ancient obligations too" (Tocqueville, 2001, p. 82).

15. Barmby founded the Communist Church in 1843 and later the Communitarian Church. He also invented communitarianism, which highlighted communal voluntary communism as distinct from violently imposed communism and it remains influential today. Although the communist movement of Marx and Engels never used the term "church" and even criticized religion and the Church, the propaganda and agitation of the communist movement, from its language to its organization, had a great deal of biblical and ecclesiastical overtones.
16. From Buonarroti's *Histoire de la Conspiration pour l'Égalité dite de Babeuf* (*History of the Conspiracy for Equality Named after Babeuf*) cited in Soboul (1983).
17. Marx called the constitutional theory of the separation of powers decadent Montesquieu-de Lolme doctrine (Marx and Engels, 2001, vol. 5, p. 474) and stressed that a "dictatorship – a strong one at that – is needed in any temporary political situation after a revolution.... to crush and remove vestiges of the old regime" (Marx and Engels, 2012, vol. 1, p. 437).
18. Karl Popper (*The Open Society and Its Enemies*, 1945) traces the philosophical roots of totalitarianism back to Plato, followed by Hegel and Marx. His discussion on totalitarianism primarily focused on epistemological issues within philosophy, rather than on operating totalitarian regimes as social phenomena, such as the communist totalitarian system. Therefore, he regarded Marx as a philosopher, rather than as the revolutionary leader of the communist movement advocating for the dictatorship of the proletariat. He also did not pay attention to the fundamental role of Christianity in the emergence of totalitarianism as a phenomenon and the unique position of the concept of "equality" within totalitarianism.
19. Excerpts from Meslier's work, which had previously been circulated only privately, were compiled by Voltaire into a renowned book titled *Extraits des sentiments de Jean Meslier* (*Excerpts from the Thoughts of Jean Meslier*), which was published in 1762. However, it watered down the most resolute and significant aspects of Meslier's argument (Wade, 1933).
20. Babeuf's *Le Manifeste des Plébéiens* ([1795] 2010).
21. Deism rejects the fundamental doctrines of Christianity, including the Trinity of the Father, the Son, and the Holy Spirit. It does not recognize

the "miracles" claimed in Christianity and believes that after the creation of the world, God ceased to intervene in its affairs.
22. Even the dictator Oliver Cromwell advocated for tolerance of different religious beliefs. The reason the Glorious Revolution was able to establish a stable constitutional government was that, by the late seventeenth century in British society, nobles, merchants, and the middle class had gradually accumulated relatively secure property rights and collective political power. This condition enabled the principal actors within British society to adopt a generally conservative and rational stance. This mindset, in turn, boosted their capacity to collectively establish a constitutional government to safeguard their interests and tackle emerging issues.
23. Tocqueville (1856, chapter 15). In line with Tocqueville's observation, in the preface to Voltaire's book, *Letters Concerning the English Nation* (Voltaire, 2009, p. 6), the editors of the correspondence specifically explained to the reader why Voltaire had reservations about constitutionalism in England, although in some letters, Voltaire describes the separation of powers in the English parliamentary system as better than the ancient Roman parliament because of the checks and balances on the monarch and the eventual dissolution of slavery (pp. 34–35).
24. The concept of the general will originated from late medieval France, where it was understood as the general will of God. In Rousseau's time, the concept was transformed into the general will of the secular age (Riley, 1986).
25. The old world of exploitation, based on private property, is destined to perish, according to Marx in *Capital* (Marx and Engels, 1993). The salvation of this world inevitably lies in communism, which abolishes private property (and the market) and the family. The proletariat can only liberate themselves (achieve communism) by liberating all of humanity (abolishing private property globally). And this will inevitably occur (*The Communist Manifesto*, Marx and Engels, 1998).

7 Institutional Genes of Totalitarianism

The Tsarist Empire

The communist totalitarian system, established in Russia in 1917, was entirely unprecedented in human history. As discussed in Chapter 6, during the Reformation period, some regions in Europe had set up city-scale communist totalitarian systems. Moreover, between the end of the eighteenth and the beginning of the nineteenth centuries, France also experimented with ephemeral communist totalitarian regimes. However, these attempts proved neither stable nor enduring.

The emergence of a new system is intricately linked to the institutional genes inherited from its predecessor. A new system can only develop stably when its prerequisite institutional genes are compatible with those of the existing system. Communist totalitarian regimes are no exception. The short-lived totalitarian regimes in medieval Europe and nineteenth-century France represented mutations that lacked sufficient support of the necessary institutional genes. As such, each of these systems was transient, a flash in the pan.

When a substantial portion of society resists totalitarian control in its own interest, and when the political, economic, and military forces opposing totalitarianism outweigh its power – as observed in Reformation Europe and nineteenth-century France – the institutional mutation of totalitarianism is contained or even eradicated by the existing institutional genes incompatible with the mutation.

A crucial factor enabling the Bolsheviks to establish a communist totalitarian regime in Russia lay in the pre-existing institutional genes in the Tsarist system that fundamentally supported the Bolshevik regime. These institutional genes included: (1) the imperial system of Tsarist Russia; (2) the Russian Orthodox Church and its faith; and (3) active secret political organizations, often known as political terrorist organizations, within Russian society.

The totalitarian regime established after the October Revolution became one of the most significant political systems in human history. It expanded globally, ruling over one-third of the world's population at one point. Of these, China was the largest within this totalitarian camp. The reason why China was shaped by the institutional genes transplanted from Soviet Russia and why the communist totalitarian system took deeper roots and developed more robustly in China than in its country of origin, Russia, was that the institutional genes of communist totalitarianism strongly resembled those of China's traditional imperial system. More importantly, the institutional genes of the traditional Chinese imperial system provided a more suitable environment for the institutional genes of communist totalitarianism to thrive.

However, without the communist totalitarianism imported from Soviet Russia, China's own institutional genes would not have been sufficient to produce such a system. Understanding the institutional genes that gave rise to totalitarianism in Russia and the evolution of these institutional genes themselves is therefore pivotal for comprehending communist totalitarianism and gaining insights into contemporary China. These are the key topics discussed in this and the subsequent chapters.

7.1 SIMILARITIES BETWEEN THE IMPERIAL SYSTEMS OF CHINA AND RUSSIA

The Tsarist regime and the traditional Chinese imperial system share many commonalities, especially when contrasted with Western Europe and Japan. In particular, both imperial systems had eliminated any independent political, economic, and social forces within their empires that could potentially challenge the imperial authority. China, compared to Russia, eradicated these independent forces much earlier and more comprehensively, hence resulting in a much more enduring imperial rule.

With the suppression of independent political and economic forces within their societies, both Tsarist Russia and Imperial China lacked the inherent social forces necessary to pursue and uphold constitutionalism. Neither society possessed a substantial social group that recognized their own rights and interests, sought their protection, and had the capability to do so. The absence of organized social forces to propel systemic change made the advancement towards constitutionalism extraordinarily challenging in these societies.

In the premodern or early modern world, every country that successfully achieved a constitutional transformation was primarily driven by the aristocrats, merchants, and their representatives, who had the power to politically, economically, and even militarily challenge the imperial power. Constitutionalism can only be realized on the basis of checks and balances among various forces with differing interests and it was in the absence of these conditions that the reforms intended to promote constitutional monarchy in China and Russia failed in 1898 and 1905, respectively. The reform in China was propelled by radical Confucianists in alliance with Emperor Guangxu, while in Russia, it was initiated by the radical intelligentsia (to be elaborated later).

The Chinese Empire commenced its formal drive to establish an elected parliament in 1906 but it never achieved substantial checks and balances on power. The Xinhai Revolution, a few years later, put an end to 2,000 years of imperial rule but also ended the peaceful transition to a constitutional monarchy. In Russia, under the newly established constitutional monarchy system, the parliamentary system operated for twelve years and the State Duma was convened four times but it never succeeded in checking the Tsar's power. Ultimately, the Russian imperial system collapsed during the February Revolution in 1917. It is vital to understand that, although constitutional reform did not begin until 1905, Russia had already undertaken several related institutional reforms towards liberalization since the late nineteenth century, decades before China. Moreover, compared with China's radical Confucianists, the Russian radical intelligentsia were much more powerful in society and had a much deeper and broader understanding of the principles of constitutionalism and the arguments for and against it. All of these factors played a significant role in the emergence of communist totalitarianism in Russia, which we will discuss further in this and the next chapters.

One commonality between the failed constitutional monarchic reforms in Russia and China is that they both inadvertently paved the way for the establishment of totalitarian regimes. To a certain extent, they also share similarities with the French Revolution, though the French totalitarian regime was short-lived. A substantial portion of the endogenous forces driving (or supporting) the constitutional revolution in Russia and China consisted of radical intellectuals. Simultaneously, even more radical anti-constitutional forces arose among these intellectuals in both countries. They bear part of the blame for the failure of the constitutional reform (revolution) in their respective countries. Concurrently, the failure of constitutional reform bred more anti-constitutional radical intellectuals, akin to the Jacobins and Babeuvists during the French Revolution. These radical intellectual groups ultimately incited and led the anti-constitutional communist revolution, establishing communist totalitarian parties and the new communist totalitarian system in both China and Russia.

In Russia, the February Revolution of 1917 led to the virtual collapse of the Tsarist Empire. A multiparty coalition established a republican provisional government with a promise to hold national elections and a Constituent Assembly in November, creating the Russian Republic. But the Bolshevik's coup d'état, known as the October Revolution, ended the constitutional process, overthrew the provisional government, and suppressed all other parties, including all left-wing parties that had been allied with the Bolsheviks. From then on, the first totalitarian regime in human history was created.

In China, Sun Yat-sen led the Republican Revolution in 1911, putting an end to the empire that was in the process of constitutional reform and establishing the Republic of China. However, he initiated a "Second Revolution" in 1913, attempting to overthrow the very republic that he had established just two years prior. Upon facing defeat, he turned to Lenin and the Communist International (Comintern) for aid, inviting them to reorganize the Kuomintang along the lines of the Bolsheviks. He was fully agreeable to the suggestion from the Comintern to cooperate with the newly established Chinese branch of the Comintern, the Chinese Communist Party. This laid the groundwork for the CCP's growth and development.

This and the following chapter will analyze the origins and evolution of the institutional genes that gave rise to totalitarianism in Russia. It lays the analytical foundation for comparing China's institutional genes with those of Soviet totalitarianism and accounting for the emergence of totalitarianism in China.

7.2 THE GENESIS OF RUSSIA'S INSTITUTIONAL GENES: MONGOL RULE

Compared with China and Western Europe, Russia has a shorter history as a civilization and as a nation. Russia's history as an empire, however, is almost as long as Russia's history as a nation. Hence, a popular assertion among Russian intellectuals is that Russia has been an empire since its creation.

Until the sixth and seventh centuries, the vast expanse that would later become Tsarist Russia, stretching across the trans-Eurasian continent, was largely uncivilized and sparsely populated, characterized by barren woodlands, swamps, and tundra. The Slavs, relying on subsistence farming for their livelihood, inhabited the basins of rivers such as the Dnieper, Oder, Vistula, and Bug. Their primitive method of slash-and-burn agriculture necessitated constant migration as they had to abandon depleted lands and reclaim new ones. Such a lifestyle could only support a low-density population, delaying the formation of large-scale settlements in Russia. Thus, the emergence of rudimentary social and political structures in Russia lagged behind that in Western Europe and Central Asia by centuries, if not millennia. It was not until the tenth century that records of Russia, referred to as the Rus' or Kievan Rus', started appearing in Byzantine, Western European, and Arabic texts. These accounts spanned from Kiev in the south to Novgorod in the north. Even later still was the development of a written language indigenous to Russia.

According to the *Primary Chronicle* of Kievan Rus' from the ninth to the twelfth century, the Slavic tribes in the Novgorod region invited Rurik, the leader of the more organized Varangians, to become their Grand Duke in the ninth century. However, some historians speculate that it was the Varangians, with their advanced military capabilities, who first captured and ruled the Novgorod region, rather than being invited to do so. This event marked the establishment of the first Russian dynasty, the Rurik dynasty, which lasted until the end of the sixteenth century. During these centuries, the hereditary system continued to evolve and mature. The families of the subsequent Grand Princes of Muscovy and Tsars all traced their lineage to Rurik.

The Varangians ruled the territory from Kiev to Novgorod, a collection of competing principalities rather than a unified kingdom or empire. Contemporary documentary sources, as well as a wealth of archaeological evidence, confirm that the rulers of Kievan Rus' were Nordic, with Slavs making up the majority of the population. As a result, some historians believe that Kievan Rus' was a Nordic colony, although this claim remains controversial. Over time, the Rus' and Slavic peoples mixed together to produce what is known as Russia today. In fact, the word "Russia" is derived from "Rus.'"

By the time the Mongol Empire subjugated Kievan Rus', the region had only recently adopted its writing system and was in a nascent stage of political, social, and economic organization. Thereafter, the Mongols ruled the region for 200 years, fundamentally transforming nearly everything.[1] What remained largely unchanged were the predominantly Slavic population, the Slavic languages, and the Orthodox Church, which had entered the region prior to Mongol rule.

Batu, the grandson of Genghis Khan, took control of the Caspian Sea region in the first half of the thirteenth century. The Mongols subsequently invaded south-central Kievan Rus', advancing directly towards Poland and Hungary. They established their capital at Sarai on the Lower Volga and founded a new khanate of the Mongol Empire (out of the four khanates that the Mongol Empire comprised, the Yuan dynasty was one). This khanate was known as the Golden Horde, which ruled over the majority of the territory that later became known as Russia (except for Eastern Siberia).

The Mongols adopted a distinct strategy in managing the relatively underprivileged region of Kievan Rus', as opposed to their direct occupation and rule in China and Persia. The Golden Horde sought to utilize the pre-existing political structure, incorporating as many local princes as possible, to exercise control over the vast majority of Kievan Rus'. They applied direct rule only in the wealthiest areas, maximizing the returns – taxes and corvée – at the least cost. Princes who openly pledged their loyalty to the Mongols were essentially made puppet rulers of the empire, maintaining their positions of power on the condition that they acknowledged the status bestowed upon them by the Great Khan. As vassals, they ensured that their respective territories submitted taxes and supplied manpower to the Golden Horde.

Although they were separate entities, the four khanates of the Mongol Empire collaborated and assisted each other in matters of governance. The Golden Horde recruited experts from China's Yuan dynasty to impose a style of governance that resembled the traditional Chinese imperial system. This system, which was more mature and efficient at the time than anything in the Russian territories, brought the institutional genes of the Chinese imperial system to these lands. The system was grounded on a population census managed bureaucratically.

In the Rus' lands, a system of grassroots rule based on households and a system of taxation and corvée were introduced for the first time. The direct administration of the census and tax collection by imperial officials in the vassal states meant a greater extent of Mongol rule and diminished power for the vassal princes. Some vassal princes instigated rebellions but others who were loyal colluded with the Mongol overlords to weaken or eradicate their rivals – all of whom were also descendants of the Ruriks – and expand their own power. With the military backing of the Mongols, these loyalists managed to suppress any opposition to Mongol rule among their fellow Rus' princes.

The Golden Horde exercised its power through proxies, using their internal conflicts to weaken and control those proxies. Disputes between princes were common during the two centuries of the Golden Horde's rule. The most important was the strife between the principalities of Muscovy and Tver, which led to the creation of a united Russia and determined the future rulers of the Tsarist Empire. This critical juncture arrived in the early fourteenth century when tax resistors in Tver assassinated a senior Mongolian tax official. At the behest of the Golden Horde, Ivan, the Grand Prince of Muscovy, marched his troops into Tver, successfully suppressing the resistance. Consequently, he secured the trust of the Mongol Empire and was permanently installed as the Grand Prince of Vladimir. Additionally, he was entrusted with the power to collect tribute from all parts of Rus' on behalf of the Golden Horde. By synchronizing the taxation of the principalities and bringing them under Moscow's control, Ivan brought about the initial unification of Russia, laying the foundation for his successor to establish the Tsarist Empire.

In the early days of Russia's foundation, during the Kievan Rus' period, the property rights of the boyars (nobility) were notably precarious. A Western European-style feudal system never fully developed there (Pipes, 1995a). Following the Mongol invasion, the rights and powers of the nobility were further undermined. Regions valued by the Mongol Empire were entirely governed by imperial bureaucrats. Russians were permitted to serve as officials in these areas but most of them did not possess any hereditary power, essentially relegating them to the role of bureaucrats and representatives of the Mongols. This considerably further weakened and even effectively eliminated the local nobility in those regions to a great extent.

Simultaneously, the Rus' princes learned how to govern a centralized empire. Although the princes retained their aristocratic titles while serving the Golden Horde, they were managed and directed by imperial officials, including those from the Chinese Yuan dynasty. Whenever they were bestowed titles, they had to abide by protocols set by the Mongol imperial administration in Sarai, the regional capital of the empire.

As the Mongol Empire began to decline towards the end of the fifteenth century, Ivan III, the Grand Prince of Muscovy, managed to consolidate many Rus' principalities and reduce the remaining ones to vassal states. Consequently, the entire region of Rus' came under the jurisdiction of Moscow. At the onset of the sixteenth century, Muscovy ceased its tax contributions to the Golden Horde, bringing about not only the unification but also the independence of Russia. By conquering a huge area of land through a series of wars, Ivan III claimed the title "Ivan the Great" and became the first Russian ruler to adopt the title of "Tsar," meaning "Caesar," a term previously used by Mongol rulers, to signify his rule over all of Rus'. Ivan III's grandson, Ivan IV, expanded his territory further and founded the extensive Tsarist Empire, formally adopting the title "Tsar," or emperor.

The united Russia that emerged due to the violence of the Mongols and Ivan the Great came at the cost of the power of the nobility, which was further curtailed as regional consolidation continued. Notably, the distinction between sovereignty and property rights was ambiguous under the hereditary political rule established during the Kievan Rus' period. Consequently, the aristocratic tradition in the Rus' principalities was weak, striking a stark contrast with the feudalism in Western Europe. Meanwhile, as an institution, the ancient Greek and Roman traditions inherited by Western Europe were irrelevant to the Rus' principalities and only a very few Russians knew about it. The violation of the right to property in the name of sovereignty was an institutional gene of the Russian state from the very beginning, due to the existence of a powerful monarch and a weak nobility, and it grew stronger as the Tsarist Empire began to take shape. As observed by Montesquieu in the eighteenth century and Weber (2002) at the outset of the twentieth century, the political and property rights institutions of the Tsarist Empire bore a closer resemblance to those of the Chinese Empire than to Western Europe. From the perspective of institutional genes, those observations remain valid today as far as the underlying mechanisms of state governance are concerned, despite much controversy over the specifics.

7.3 THE GENESIS OF RUSSIA'S INSTITUTIONAL GENES: EASTERN ORTHODOXY AND THE BYZANTINE EMPIRE

During more than 200 years, from being ruled by the Mongol Empire to the formation of a unified Russia, the country took shape for the first time under the rule of the Golden Horde and with the assistance of the Mongols' political and military power. In this period, the nobility and bureaucrats of unified Russia consistently implemented the system of the Mongol Empire, absorbing elements of its bureaucratic governance system, including components transplanted from the Yuan dynasty, into the Russian system. The Tsarist Empire, established later, partly developed its system based on these institutional influences, creating visible similarities between the imperial systems of Tsarist Russia and Imperial China.

However, despite these resemblances, substantial differences existed in terms of culture, religion, and religious institutions. A defining feature that set the Russian Empire apart from China was the introduction of Eastern Orthodoxy and the Orthodox Church from Byzantium. In its early stages, the Rus' region was geopolitically influenced by the Byzantine Empire, an influence that was instrumental in shaping the institutional roots of Kievan Rus' and the Grand Principality of Muscovy.

The Byzantine or Eastern Roman Empire was the largest empire on earth in the early sixth century (when the Chinese Empire had disintegrated). It had effectively assimilated the Mediterranean as an internal sea. Politically, the empire was highly centralized, with officials appointed from the top, bearing similarities to the Chinese

Empire in this and several other aspects. However, later Byzantium was severely weakened by Muslim conquests and the Crusades and, by the early eleventh century, its Turkish and Greek territories constituted the last remnants of its once expansive realm.

The period of rapid decline of Byzantium coincided with the emergence and expansion of Rus'. In the tenth century, Christianity was introduced into the Rus' region from Byzantium, which officially separated from the Roman Church in the middle of the eleventh century to form the Eastern Orthodox Church. However, other religions, including polytheism, persisted in the lands of Rus'.

In order to reinforce his legitimacy and form an alliance with the Byzantine Empire, Vladimir I, the Grand Prince of Kiev, adopted Christianity as the state religion and married a Byzantine princess. He enforced Christianity in his domains through mass baptisms and other means and outlawed polytheism. Christianity did not grow by its inherent appeal or power of faith among the Rus'. Rather, it was used as an instrument for rule, for power, and for politics. This was one of the important aspects that distinguished the Christianity that entered Russia in a top-down manner from the Christianity that spread in Western Europe in a bottom-up fashion.

Since then, Old Church Slavonic, a script invented by the Byzantine priests for preaching and translating the Bible, was adopted in the Rus' region, replacing the Old Slavonic script that had fallen into obscurity. Old Church Slavonic laid the foundations for the modern Russian language and its subsequent evolution was further influenced by Peter the Great's script reform and the linguistic changes introduced by Pushkin.

From the ninth to the fifteenth century, Byzantium claimed the Russian principalities as a part of the Byzantine commonwealth (Obolensky, 1970). The commonwealth was a loose alliance of polities over which the empire exerted no direct rule, neither appointing officials nor maintaining military garrisons. The Byzantine Empire had been shrinking with the expansion and encroachment of the emerging Ottoman Empire. However, in the Golden Horde, the Mongol rulers allowed the Orthodox Church to grow as long as it submitted to Mongol rule. The Orthodox Church was not required to pay taxes and as its congregation expanded, it grew into a formidable force.

Towards the end of Mongol rule, upon the initial unification of the Rus' region, Ivan I relocated Patriarch Vladimir to Moscow and commissioned the construction of the Dormition Cathedral in the Kremlin. In doing so, he demonstrated his command over both religious and political power and his legitimacy to unite Russia. Henceforth, this cathedral served as the site where generations of elites from various regions have sworn allegiance to the Russian monarch.

By the late fourteenth century, the Patriarch of Constantinople, Anthony IV, wrote to the Grand Prince of Muscovy, recognizing the Byzantine emperor as the emperor of the Russian principalities.[2] In 1452, the year before the fall of Constantinople, the Grand Prince of Muscovy acknowledged the suzerainty of Byzantine Emperor Constantine XI.[3] On the verge of the collapse of the Byzantine Empire, the Roman pontiff facilitated the marriage of the Byzantine emperor's niece, Princess Sophia Palaiologina, to Ivan III, and transferred the Orthodox base from Constantinople to Moscow. Subsequently, Moscow became the "Third Rome," providing a foundation for Ivan III's claim to the throne. After the dissolution of the Byzantine Empire, the emergent Tsarist Russia, home to the Orthodox base, became the successor to the Byzantine Empire.

Princess Sophia brought a considerable number of books to Russia, including a complete collection of religious classics. As a result, Muscovy inherited some of the best religious and classical literature of the time. Of particular institutional significance, Sophia transformed the royal court to Byzantine standards, setting a precedent for extravagance at the court in Moscow. Meanwhile, the coat of arms of the Byzantine Empire was adopted as that of Russia. Since then, the protocols and etiquette of the Russian court have blended the traditions of Kievan Rus', the Golden Horde, and the Byzantine Empire.

As the successor to Byzantium, Russia was most significantly influenced by Eastern Orthodoxy and the system of caesaropapist rule, both of which had already taken root in the Rus' region before the Mongols arrived. In this system, on the one hand, the emperor was considered divinely ordained, with his rule granted by God; on the other hand, the emperor also ruled the Church and used it to serve secular power. This system stood in sharp contrast to that of Western Europe, where monarchs needed recognition from the papacy and were subject to its constraints.

Russia not only inherited Byzantium's system of caesaropapism but also, from the very beginning of its adoption of Christianity, lacked a large congregation of believers truly founded in faith. This condition was even more pronounced after the reign of Peter the Great (1682–1725), as the Tsar then gained almost complete control over the Church.

However, regarding other institutional areas, the influence of Byzantium on Russia was fairly limited if at all. For instance, in terms of law, Russian legal codes were derived from the customary laws of various Rus' principalities rather than from secular Byzantine law, that is, Roman law, which did not have a significant influence on Rus'. Russia, as the nominal heir of the Byzantine Empire, never adopted a legal code aligned with the Roman code. In fact, the Byzantine Code of Justinian was translated into Russian centuries later.

The development of any effective legal system is a process that requires institutional evolution over time. Indeed, the Code of Justinian was not directly created by the Roman Emperor Justinian; instead, it was compiled during his reign, based on existing codes, with the aim of unifying various laws through the institutional evolution of the Roman Empire.

In terms of ownership institutions, political systems, and law, Russia was fundamentally different from the Roman Empire and Western Europe from its very beginning. It thus carried a distinct set of institutional genes. The written law in Rus' emerged in the eleventh century under the Grand Prince of Kiev and spread throughout the Rus' region from the twelfth century onwards. Russia's highly centralized autocratic system came into being and developed during the Kievan Rus' and Golden Horde periods and was heavily influenced by the Mongols who once ruled the Rus' region. The *Sudebnik* of 1497, the first legal code of the Tsarist Empire, was compiled based on the existing laws of various Rus' principalities, which had no connection with Roman Law. The Tsarist system, lacking checks and balances, complemented the caesaropapist Orthodox Church, forming unique institutional genes that laid the foundation for impeding Russian constitutional reform in the nineteenth century and establishing totalitarian rule in the twentieth century. We will analyze these institutional genes of Tsarist Russia in more detail in what follows.

7.4 THE INSTITUTIONAL GENES OF TSARISM

7.4.1 *Tsarism*

As previously stated, Russia quickly proclaimed itself an empire shortly after becoming unified. The Tsar's control over the empire's political and economic power then became the most notable feature of the Tsarist system. Overall, society lacked a system of checks and balances.

Just as Qin Shi Huang "united" China, Ivan III created a united Russia by conquering smaller states through military means. This empire stretched across Europe and Asia, with a territory six times larger than Moscovy. Ivan III began dispossessing the nobility on the one hand, and institutionalizing serfdom, which had been practiced since the mid-fourteenth century on the other (Vernadsky, 1939, p. 315).

Ivan III's ability to deprive the nobility of power was due to the long-standing weakness of the nobles, an institutional gene inherited since the Rus' era. The boyars of Rus' had traditionally held land, power, and military might and the grand princes needed support from boyar nobility, which may seem similar to the feudal system of Western Europe. The difference, however, was that Rus' boyars did not have a contractual relationship with their princes, unlike the nobles and monarchs of Western Europe. Hence, they were able to move and switch allegiance. In the traditional Rus' system, the grand princes were most concerned with maximizing their land, so the boundary between sovereignty and property rights had long been ambiguous in the Rus' principalities. The empire's expansion was essentially a process of squeezing the aristocracy (Pipes, 1995a).

In the early stages of Russian expansion, when the Boyar nobility still held significant military power, Ivan III took measures to secure their approval and support for major decisions, such as his marriage to a Byzantine princess. However, once all the principalities were conquered, steps were taken to curb the hereditary powers of the nobility. On the one hand, the Boyar Duma was downsized; on the other hand, access to the Boyar Duma became increasingly dependent on merit and service to the grand prince (Alef, 1967, pp. 76–123). By the end of the sixteenth century, the boyars had largely lost their power base and had become regional commissioners under the authority of the grand prince.

Striking historical similarities can occur in countries with similar systems, even when they are culturally and geographically distant. In order to establish a highly centralized imperial system, both Ivan IV (1530–1584) and Qin Shi Huang were ruthless in their efforts to weaken and eliminate the powers of the nobility through institutional and material means. Ivan IV was crowned in 1547 when China was under the reign of Emperor Shi Zong of the Ming. He completely deprived the Boyar Duma of its political rights and functions and abolished the limited autonomy originally enjoyed by the hereditary princes, turning the leaders of historical principalities into boyars in the service of the Grand Prince (Vernadsky, 1939, p. 318). He confiscated many boyars' lands and brought the Tsarist Empire into a new phase, for which he became an idol worshipped by both Peter the Great and Stalin.

As an important part of perfecting the Tsarist imperial system, Ivan IV established the first secret police system in Russian history in the 1560s, the infamous institution of the Oprichnina (special police force). The Oprichnina enabled him to extensively quash opposition from the boyars, arresting and executing the leading figures on charges of alleged treason. This secret police system continued to develop and mature, becoming an important institutional gene of Tsarism. Ivan IV killed approximately 4,000 high-ranking nobles between 1565 and 1572, diminishing the power of the top echelon of the nobility by bolstering the power of minor nobles and citizens and capitalizing on the tension between these two groups and the high nobility. Consequently, Russia was left with a minor nobility ill-equipped to challenge the Tsar.

Following the death of Ivan IV, serfdom was fully and officially institutionalized throughout the Tsarist Empire. From 1592 to 1593, land and household registration was introduced; peasants registered under a landlord's name were classified as serfs, and landlords were given the right to pursue runaways. The Code of Law of 1649 further cemented serfdom, making landlords fully responsible for their serfs and granting them the authority to sentence, flog, and torture serfs on their estates.

By the end of the seventeenth century, Peter the Great ascended to the throne and further centralized what was already Europe's most centralized empire, thereby heightening Russia's absolute monarchy. He replaced the Boyar Duma with the Governing Senate, all of whose members were appointed by him. Although the boyars had essentially functioned more as elite bureaucrats than as nobles since the reign of Ivan IV (Kliuchevskii, 1960), Peter's formal dissolution of the Duma further undermined the power and status of the boyars. Historically, the Boyar Duma lacked legislative powers and plenary sessions were only irregularly convened by the Tsar. However, it had remained a loose institution where the nobility could at least converse, voice grievances, and network. With its official dissolution, the nobility was stripped of a legitimate forum for meetings and discussion. The institutional genes thus formed laid the foundation to inhibit the emergence of constitutionalism in Russia.

In contrast to Russia, the nobility and other influential social groups in Western Europe participated in parliamentary assemblies. Their roles in these assemblies and the alliances they formed constrained the power of the monarchs, paving the way for constitutional governance. Nevertheless, in a comparison between Tsarist Russia and Imperial China, the Russian aristocracy was in a significantly better position. While Tsarist monarchs sought to weaken the nobility over a few centuries, the Chinese Empire had been undermining and even eradicating its nobility for over a millennium. In fact, there was nothing in the Chinese Empire that resembled the Boyar Duma of Tsarist Russia. For most of its history, the Chinese Empire's nobility was merely nominal. When it did exist, it was merely local power, kept firmly under control by the imperial court, which did not allow it to cooperate or even consider setting up a parliament. Even after the dissolution of the Duma by Peter the Great, the residual power of the nobility in Tsarist Russia still far exceeded that of the nominal nobility of the Ming and Qing dynasties.

In order to bolster caesaropapism, Peter the Great annulled the Patriarchate, supplanting it with the Holy Synod, which was a council of bishops functioning as an instrument of his regime and under his control. He restructured the administrative divisions of the state, nullified the hereditary order of precedence, and instituted a meritocratic system of appointment. The residual powers of the aristocracy were further diminished, transforming hereditary nobles into bureaucrats subservient to the Tsar's rule. All officials, regardless of their familial lineage, commenced at the lowest level in the bureaucracy, with promotions contingent on merit.

Through a large-scale importation of Western technology and centralization of power, Peter significantly augmented efficiency across Russia, consolidated his power, and fortified the

Tsarist institution. In 1721, after defeating Sweden, then the largest empire in Northern Europe, Peter officially renamed his country the "Russian Empire."

Since the eighteenth century, the Tsars, relying on their monopoly of political power and economic resources, further eroded the rights of individuals and groups and monopolized public information in Russian society. This process transformed the institutions of the Russian Empire, which started with a greater concentration of power than the most extreme Western European absolute monarchies, into a type of system that this book refers to as an imperial system. The defining characteristics of Tsarism include the omnipresence and unquestionable sovereignty of the monarch and the primacy of sovereignty over property rights.

The French Enlightenment of the late eighteenth century sparked considerable interest among Russian intellectuals and the societal upper class. In the following period, Russia underwent decades of reforms. The control of the Tsarist regime over private property rights and certain political rights was somewhat relaxed. Discussions about constitutionalism became widespread among intellectuals and the upper echelons of society, even exerting societal pressure on the Tsarist autocracy. However, the Tsar and his followers staunchly believed in the Tsar's unlimited legislative and executive powers. All laws had to originate from the Tsar. These followers included not only the elites but also a large mass of monarchists, particularly the Russian peasants who had just been "liberated" from serfdom by the Tsar by the Emancipation Reform of 1861. Lacking basic knowledge of their individual or political rights, these followers firmly believed that the Tsarist government must be strong and that the people must obey the Tsar unconditionally. For them, any restriction on government power or permission to challenge it was intolerable. On the other hand, the establishment elites argued that the development of parliamentary politics was unrealistic given the vast size and complexity of Russia and the low level of education of the populace. They contended that Russia should focus on administrative efficiency and reform (Pipes, 1991, pp. 54–57).

Peter the Great regarded the learning of technology and management from the West as crucial for his reign. He hoped that the introduction of science, technology, and management from Western Europe would improve Russian science and technology, increase the efficiency of Russian administration and business, and serve him in strengthening centralized power. On the other hand, he feared that the inspiration of constitutional ideas gained by the young Russian nobles studying in the West would shake up his autocratic rule. Hence, Peter the Great issued a policy restricting the aristocracy's freedom to study in the West.

It was not until the beginning of the nineteenth century that American independence and the French Revolution inspired the Russian aristocracy to push for social reforms in the pursuit of their rights. The Russian nobility staged a coup d'état in 1801, leading to the accession of Alexander I to the throne. Under pressure from the nobility, Alexander restored some basic rights to nobles, including allowing them to study in the West, which was instrumental in the later Russian Enlightenment and the propagation of constitutional ideas. To augment governmental efficiency, Alexander introduced a ministerial system in 1802, with ministers appointed directly by the emperor. Ministries were highly specialized, with interministerial coordination prohibited, transforming the government into a strictly compartmentalized, vertically managed system. This development deprived ministers of independence and amplified the Tsar's control over the empire. Simultaneously, it hindered the capacity of ministers to collaborate and formulate an organically integrated national economic policy (Pipes, 1995a, p. 66).

The highly specialized, vertically managed ministerial system established by Alexander evolved into a Tsarist institutional gene that later was inherited directly by the Soviet central planning system and subsequent planned economies of all communist totalitarian regimes, until the demise of those regimes. In contrast, another type of institutional gene of bureaucracy, inherited in China since 200 BCE, which was characterized by the maintenance of the integrity of functions of each locality, has also influenced the governance of China to this day (see discussions in Chapters 12 and 13 on regionally administered totalitarianism).

The most prominent institutional feature of the imperial system, which this book emphasizes and which distinctly separates it from an absolute monarchy, is that the imperial bureaucracy constitutes the very foundation of governance. In this respect, the characteristics of the Tsarist bureaucracy bear more resemblance to those of China than of Western Europe. Within the Chinese imperial system, the royal family and the state were synonymous. Similarly, Russia never developed a governance system based on a stable alliance between the monarch and the nobility throughout its state formation history. The sovereignty of the Rus' princes largely depended on their property claims and their clans' support. There was no distinction between the royal clans' households and the principalities. With the formation of a unified empire, the roles of Ivan III's chamberlains transformed into elements of the imperial bureaucracy (Pipes, 1995a). Hence, the Tsar's household was the empire itself. The imperial bureaucracy primarily served the Tsar and its senior officers were the Tsar's servants (Pipes, 1991, p. 61). There was no system or notion of a clear separation of the state bureaucracy from the house of the royals.

Finally, it is crucial to note that Kang Youwei, the leading proponent of the first constitutional reform in China, erroneously regarded what Peter the Great did as a model for constitutional reform in China. As the spiritual leader of the reform, his grave misunderstanding of Russia illustrated the superficial understanding of Chinese intellectual leaders regarding China's constitutional reforms (more details in Chapter 9). When advocating for the Hundred Days' Reform, he presented his book, *Chronicle of Peter the Great's Governmental Reforms*, to the emperor as a blueprint for reform. However, Kang failed to recognize that Peter the Great's centralization of political power necessitated the elimination of checks and balances, and the dissolution of the already weakened Duma.

7.4.2 The Institutional Genes of Russian Orthodoxy and the Russian Orthodox Church

Chapter 6 discussed the Christian origins of communist ideology. However, modern constitutionalism, which stands in opposition to communist totalitarianism, was intimately related to the foundation laid by the Reformation in Western Europe. Superficially, Orthodoxy and Catholicism are distinguished by the use of Greek and Latin scripts, respectively, and their geographical locations in the East and West. However, the Reformation occurred only in Central and Western Europe, as did modern constitutionalism, while communist totalitarianism emerged in regions associated with Russian Orthodoxy. Why did the Reformation not take place in the Eastern Orthodox regions? What was the relationship between the Bolshevik Revolution and Russian Orthodoxy, along with its Church?

First, the timing and general context of the introduction of Orthodoxy in Russia had already dictated that the differences between Orthodoxy, which was set to influence Russia, and Catholicism went far beyond language and geography. By then, Orthodoxy had been the state religion of the Byzantine Empire for centuries. It had become highly bureaucratic and had long lost the inherently challenging connotations of Christianity. In stark contrast to the Catholic regions where the Reformation was taking place, Orthodoxy and its Church were teetering on the brink. On the eve of a catastrophic crisis in Constantinople, the base of Orthodoxy was forced to move from the soon-to-be Ottoman-conquered Byzantine capital to Moscow. Hecker, an expert on Russian Orthodoxy, noted, "being imposed upon the people by order of a despotic ruler ... was simply grafted upon the existing paganism, much of which has survived to this day in the religious cult and customs of the common people" (Hecker, 1933, chapter 2). Even today, traces of these primitive religions can still be seen in religious worship and civilian customs in Russia.

Moreover, the overall literacy level in Russia was exceptionally low. Meanwhile, there was no Bible in the Russian language and barely any clergy could read the Bible in Greek. In this context, the Church in Russia indigenized and Russified Orthodoxy by simplifying its teachings. Moreover, it was the principality rulers who decided to adopt Christianity and establish it as the state religion, imposing it on the populace by decree and collective baptism. Given that the faithful were largely illiterate and lacked religious education, a considerable amount of pagan fetishism became interwoven into Russian Orthodoxy. Consequently, many believers and some clerics regarded the cross, icons, and Bible as magical amulets (Hecker, 1927, chapter 3).

Furthermore, there were deeper and more intricate aspects of the issue. The Reformation refers to the religious movements that spanned England, Bohemia, the Netherlands, Germany, France, and the rest of Western Europe in the fifteenth and sixteenth centuries, alongside the emergence of theological theories. This phenomenon could not have materialized without Latin as the common language of Catholicism. Through centuries of communication facilitated by this shared linguistic medium, Catholicism attracted numerous intellectual luminaries, fostering the development of advanced theological theories. It laid the groundwork for the intellectual challenges that were to surface later, which included not only Luther's reformist manifesto in Germany, Calvin' religious, political, and social vision in France, Erasmus' philosophical conjectures in the Netherlands but also the utopian aspirations of Thomas More in England. Any noteworthy or challenging idea from one region could quickly permeate all Catholic regions through Latin, energizing the faithful.

In addition to language, another fundamental difference between Orthodoxy and Catholicism concerned the organizational structure of the Church. One of the key demands of the Reformation was regional autonomy, prompted by resistance to the over-centralization of the Catholic Church. In other words, the high degree of centralization within the Catholic Church ignited the spark to revolt against it, intensifying the depth, scale, and intensity of the rebellion. In contrast, in an effort to facilitate dissemination, the Orthodox Church had endeavored to develop local scripts and translate the Bible into local languages in different countries from the very beginning. As a result, not only did the Orthodox Church lack a highly centralized structure but it also did not possess a common Orthodox language script. Over the centuries, this led Orthodoxy to evolve into a collection of Orthodox churches using different languages, which obstructed communication among clerics from different regions and limited the potential for theological advancements. This, in turn, rendered the Orthodox Church increasingly conservative.

The Catholic Church, due to its high degree of centralization, had substantial ecclesiastical power. Thus, the Catholic Church constantly clashed with secular authorities in Western Europe. In contrast, the Orthodox Church was relatively fragmented, resulting in less ecclesiastical power. The Russian Orthodox Church and the Russian monarchy had a highly integrated relationship between church and state. Historically, the establishment of Christianity as the state religion of the Roman Empire and the relocation of the empire's capital to Byzantium happened concurrently. The emperors of the empire supported the state religion while also endeavoring to control it. Therefore, ever since Byzantium (Constantinople) became the capital of the Roman Empire, the Greek Orthodox Church had been under significant control by the secular powers. The Byzantine Church prided itself on its harmonious relationship with the Roman Empire.

The relocation of the Roman Empire's capital created a power vacuum in Rome, providing an immense opportunity for the growth of the Latin Roman Christian Church. It not only gained high independence in ecclesiastical power but the powerful Roman ecclesiastical authority was often also eager to intervene in secular matters. The Roman Church's influence thrived even more after the fall of the Western Roman Empire. Coronation by the Roman Church became a prerequisite for the legitimacy of all Western European monarchs.

In stark contrast to the powerful Catholic Church, the Greek-speaking Christian Church had been under secular control since the Roman Emperor moved to Byzantium. Coupled with the lack of a unified language and a centralized Church in Orthodoxy, the Orthodox Churches in various countries have generally been controlled by local secular powers over centuries of evolution. These characteristics of Orthodoxy made it more localized and more submissive to local secular powers. Orthodox clergy, protected by secular power, when becoming wealthier and more influential, were ironically more dependent on secular power. Under the patronage of secular power, the Orthodox clergy grew richer and more influential and became further dependent on secular power (Pipes, 1995a, pp. 224–225).

The absence of a common language also curtailed theological developments within Orthodoxy, making substantive theological challenges unlikely. As a result, Orthodoxy did not produce theological luminaries like Aquinas, nor theological challengers or reformers like Erasmus and Luther.

Orthodoxy had been the state religion of Russia since the formation of Kievan Rus', Russia had been the seat of Orthodoxy since the fifteenth century, Russia's grand princes and tsars had regarded Orthodoxy and the Church highly, and both Orthodoxy and the Church had deeply influenced the population and culture. Despite all of these factors, there was an astonishing dearth of substantive exploration of the Christian canon and Greek classics in Russia. Russian Orthodoxy placed formality and ritual above theory and understanding and was not concerned with preaching the Bible or teaching theology. Its clergy generally lacked both the knowledge and motivation to educate the faithful and priests in rural areas were often illiterate (Hecker, 1927, pp. 10–11). The first complete translation of the Bible into Russian was not available until the 1870s, underscoring the superficiality of Russian Orthodoxy among its followers. Worse still, even in many seminaries, clergy members were not taught Latin or Greek. The pervasive level of ignorance within the Russian Orthodox Church was indeed shocking (Pipes, 1995a, pp. 225–227). On the other hand, deep yet superficial belief is a key element in fostering fanatical masses, which can fuel a totalitarian movement.

The Renaissance, Reformation, and Enlightenment in Western Europe, along with the emergence of empirical science and modern thought, including the establishment of modern constitutionalism, were all inextricably linked to the Church and its associated universities, which were independent of secular power. However, the Russian Orthodox Church was not only lacking in independence but it also rarely delved into systematic and in-depth exploration of theological texts, let alone presented any challenges to theological theories. Russia did not undergo a renaissance or a reformation and the Enlightenment that it experienced was largely detached from the Church, having more roots in European influence. These phenomena are all associated with the Russian Orthodox Church's lack of independence and its overall superficial nature. No school within the Russian Orthodox Church evolved into an institution that made contributions outside of theology. The major universities in Russia were all established by the Tsarist government, beginning in the eighteenth century. As a result, empirical science and modern thought in Russia were largely reliant on imports from Western Europe.

Nevertheless, the Russian Orthodox Church had a profound influence on Russian society. Superficial and fanatical religions tend to foster blind religious zeal among ignorant believers. In the late 1670s, rumors of the imminent end of the world were rife among the Russian Orthodox faithful. Many fanatics went to extremes such as nailing themselves into coffins and more than 20,000 people self-immolated. Some even went as far as threatening to burn Russia to the ground (Pipes, 1995a, p. 236).

From the sixteenth century onwards, Russia developed an entire set of ideologies concerning the relationship between the Orthodox Church and secular power. Moscow was hailed as the Third Rome, not only as the successor of the Roman Empire but also as the ruling center of the Orthodox world, and even the entire

Christian world. Russian priests claimed that the Russian Church was purer and more sacred than the Byzantine Church, the reason being that the Byzantine Church had abandoned its principles and merged with the Roman Church at the Council of Florence in 1439 and this position was reversed only when Moscow replaced Byzantium as the center of Orthodoxy. In Russia's distinctive theory of divine mandate, the power of the crown came from God, yet also overrode the divine. Therefore, the monarch governed the Church. In practice, the monarch decided the appointment of the Patriarch, determined the list of attendees for the Holy Synod, and interfered in religious courts. The Church was content with such arrangements. Aside from the tradition of the Orthodox Church being controlled by imperial power for centuries, the Church eradicated heresies by relying on the absolute monarchy (Pipes, 1995a, pp. 232–234).

In the early days when the Orthodox Church was introduced from Byzantium to Russia, despite enduring secular intervention, it was still independent or semi-independent of secular power. Byzantium referred to the relationship between the Church and secular power as a harmonious one. The golden age of the great development of Orthodoxy in Russia was the period of Mongol rule. Under Genghis Khan's charter for the protection of Orthodoxy, the Orthodox Church was granted privileges such as tax exemptions. Meanwhile, under Mongol rule, the grand princes were merely vassals of the Mongols and had no power to interfere with the Church.

As Russia gained independence from the Mongols and eventually became an empire, the Church formed a relatively independent Patriarchate. However, the Tsars sought to directly control the Church and put it in the service of the state. After decades of effort, Peter the Great finally abolished the Patriarchate (Hecker, 1933). He eliminated the secular judicial immunity enjoyed by the Church, confiscated its revenues, and transformed the Church into an administrative branch of the government (this was continued and completed under Catherine II). Moreover, he mandated the clergy to report to the authorities any content detrimental to the monarch and the government that they heard during confessions (Pipes, 1995a, pp. 239–241).

But unlike Confucianism in the Chinese Empire (see Chapter 5), the Tsar and the Russian imperial court did not significantly interfere with the doctrine and religious rituals of the Orthodox Church. This was mainly because these had been inherited from Byzantium before the rise of the Tsar and had already taken root in Russia. In addition, following the tradition of the Byzantine Empire, the Orthodox Church had always served secular power during the formation of the Russian Empire. Russian Orthodoxy controlled Russian society through faith and ideology, fully instilling in the Russian people a religious interpretation legitimizing the Tsar's rule. It was one of the core components of the Tsarist system. Over the centuries, it portrayed the Tsar as God's agent on earth and declared that disobedience to the Tsar was a sin. As an effective tool, the Church helped to prolong the autocratic rule of the Russian Tsars (Hecker, 1933, p. 23). Nobel laureate for Literature Aleksandr Solzhenitsyn once commented, "If the [Russian] church had not surrendered its independence and had continued to make its voice heard among the people as [the Catholic Church] does, for example, in Poland," then Russian history might have been "incomparably more humane and harmonious in the last few centuries" (*New York Times*, March 23, 1972, p. 7).

Since the emergence of the Russian language, Orthodoxy had been an inseparable component of Russian culture. It played a vital role in popularizing education in Russia. The vast majority of Russians learned to read and write through the education provided by the Orthodox Church (Pipes, 1991, pp. 87–89). The Russian Orthodox Church was exclusivist, disallowing changes in faith. Its canonical law explicitly stated that all Orthodox believers must raise their children in the Orthodox faith (Leroy-Beaulieu, 1896, pp. 512–513). All the most important Russian revolutionaries, whether Social Revolutionaries or Bolsheviks, even those who proclaimed themselves atheists or anti-Orthodox, could not escape the profound influence of Russian Orthodoxy, which was reflected in their revolutionary theories and the revolutionary spirit they revered.

Nikolay Chernyshevsky, the founder of Russian socialism and populism, was representative in this respect. Born into an Orthodox priest's family and graduated from a seminary, he was the spiritual leader of several generations of Russian intelligentsia, including all the founders of the Russian Social Democratic Party and the Bolsheviks. He claimed to be an atheist but his works were replete with deep Christian influences, many of which were secular expressions of Christianity. His famous novel *What Is to Be Done?* portrayed the revolutionary Rakhmetov, who was in fact a secular reinterpretation of many Christian martyrs. The anarchist leader Kropotkin claimed that this book had a greater influence on Russian youth than Turgenev, Tolstoy, or any other writer, saying, "it was a kind of banner for Russian youth" (Kropotkin, 1915). Lenin read the book numerous times during his life – the book and the character of Rakhmetov had a great impact on his revolutionary drive.

As discussed in Chapter 6, communist ideology has its roots in Christianity and the first communist organization was founded by Engels in collaboration with a Christian priest. Moreover, both Marx and Engels, consciously or otherwise, shaped the ideologies and movements they initiated to be highly similar to Christianity in many ways, making them all the more enticing. The communist movement in Russia was no exception to this.

Pavel Axelrod, one of the founders of the Russian Marxist movement, stated that his dedication to the cause of socialist revolution originated from religious faith. He anticipated the inclusion of a God-building program within the socialist movement. Pioneers of Russian Marxists like him disseminated Marxism and established Marxist organizations not because they were fully convinced after studying Marxism but because they, as revolutionaries, found Marxism to be more useful. This group of Russian revolutionaries did not passively adhere to the Marxist theory of historical stages;

instead, they sought to realize their ideal of a revolution of religious nature (Rowley, 2017, pp. 3–4). Such ideals were common to the Land and Liberty society and its successors, including the Socialist Revolutionary Party (SR Party), the Mensheviks, and the Bolsheviks. More precisely, the Bolsheviks inherited such aspirations from the Land and Liberty.

The influence of Orthodoxy on the Bolshevik leaders was profound and extensive. It affected their revolutionary ideals, the formation and design of the communist totalitarian system, and their methods of propaganda and governance. Stalin, along with Lunacharsky, the first Bolshevik responsible for culture and education, Dzerzhinsky, the head of the Cheka,[4] and several other leading figures from the first generation of Bolsheviks, all came from a formal Orthodox educational background.

Gorky and Lunacharsky saw Marxism as a religion that offered salvation in advance and advocated for a God-Building Project. Bolshevik propagandist Aleksandr Voronsky claimed that some revolutionary terrorists were guided by the Christian Bible in their attempts to overthrow the Tsarist regime (Slezkine, 2017, p. 23).

Some historians have referred to the Marxist-Leninist religion in Russia as "Millenarian Bolshevism," alluding to the fact that the Bolsheviks used Christian millennialism to disseminate their ideology and attract people (Rowley, 2017). The Millennium prophecy predicted that Christ would return to Earth to punish sinners through the Last Judgment and put an end to the corrupt old world, thus saving mankind, who would enter a paradise under Christ's reign.

The Bolsheviks made promises highly similar to this Millenarian prophecy. Marx's prophecy that the old world (the sinful class society) would be buried by violent revolution and that humanity would enter a communist paradise resonated with those who had been indoctrinated into Christianity, making it easier for them to believe in Marxism. Radicals could become revolutionary martyrs.

Moreover, many people confused the two. Indeed, in the late nineteenth and early twentieth centuries, many Russian revolutionaries believed that revolutionary socialism was a form of Christianity. Likewise, many considered Christianity to be a form of revolutionary socialism.

7.4.3 The Institutional Genes of Secret Political Organizations

Similar to the Chinese imperial system, in the Russian imperial system, the Tsar monopolized all power. This resulted in the absence of any independent force in society that could negotiate with it. The situation stemmed from the historical formation of the Russian Empire, which was marked by the weakening and eventual elimination of various independent social forces. Under a series of Western influences, including the French Revolution and the establishment of a constitutional republic in the United States, a generation of social classes, known as the "intelligentsia," emerged in Russia, eager to transform society radically. It was a group of intellectuals who pursued political power and were fascinated by revolution.

The term intelligentsia lacks a universally accepted definition. This group differed from the broadly defined intellectuals. While some of this group were highly educated, many others were not. They had a strong sense of social responsibility and political radicalism and were passionate about revolution. Some were exceptional revolutionary writers, philosophers, leaders, and so on, while others could barely read. The major disagreements among them concerned their visions for a new world and strategies for disrupting the old one. Some aimed to dismantle the old world through plots, violence, and even acts of terror while others advocated for disseminating education and waiting for a favorable moment for revolution. Some were eager to establish constitutional governance and a republic, without realizing that constitutionalism is inseparable from compromise. Some were keen to establish socialism, while others were passionate about the dictatorship of the proletariat ("The Intelligencia," in Pipes, 1991).

The emergence of the intelligentsia was a particularly crucial phenomenon in Russia, having its roots in Europe. The phenomenon and terminology of the intelligentsia evolved in France and Germany before being transmitted to Russia. This development occurred in conjunction with social movements and transformations such as constitutionalism, socialism, and Marxism. In France, severe repression of reform-minded intellectuals by the absolute monarchy, which denied them the opportunity for peaceful change as seen in England, led to a collective radicalization of this group, forming the intelligentsia (Tocqueville, 1856). However, by the end of the nineteenth century, the establishment of a constitutional government in France enabled reformist intellectuals to operate effectively, leading to the gradual receding of the intelligentsia class.

The Tsarist regime in Russia was even more oppressive towards reformist intellectuals than the French absolute monarchy. In Tsarist Russia, the conditions for the existence of open social organizations were absent, as was a foundation for rational discourse. Moreover, the Russian Orthodox tradition had evolved into an empty shell devoid of religious substance, fostering theoretical superficiality, emotional euphoria, and self-sacrificing fanaticism among Russian intellectuals. These conditions catalyzed the evolution of the Russian intelligentsia. The French intelligentsia was the central force behind the formation of the Jacobin dictatorship, while the Russian intelligentsia laid the foundation for Bolshevism and played a vital role in establishing the totalitarian regime.

Since the nineteenth century, the intelligentsia had been at the forefront of social change in Russia. The majority were secular. Yet, even those self-professed atheists were deeply influenced by Russian Orthodoxy. The Decembrists, an early radical group who attempted an armed coup (while it is debatable whether they were part of the intelligentsia, their influence on it henceforth is undeniable), had a profound and far-reaching influence. The Bolsheviks inherited some traditions of the Decembrists, particularly in conspiring armed coups to seize power.

The ideas of constitutionalism that impacted Russian society came from the French Revolution, especially its early stages. Following the Napoleonic Wars, Tsar Alexander I initiated tentative reforms, including drafting a constitution and partial emancipation of the serfs. However, some radical young aristocratic officers, including those who had participated in the war and had been in France as part of the victorious troops, believed that the Tsar was merely stalling on reform. Confronted with the Tsar's autocratic rule and inspired by the French Revolution, they were convinced that constitutionalism could only be achieved by forcefully abolishing the Tsarist autocracy. As a result, they established several secret revolutionary societies, the earliest being the Union of Salvation, which advocated for a constitutional monarchy, and the Union of Prosperity, which called for the establishment of a republic.

In 1825, Alexander I died. Various secret societies conspired to stage an armed uprising on the eve of Nicholas I's accession to the throne. They drafted a republican constitution and planned to convene a Constituent Assembly immediately after overthrowing the Tsarist government and declaring the abolition of serfdom. The uprising was scheduled for December of the Russian calendar, hence the name of the participants, the Decemberists.

After the suppression of the Decembrist uprising, Nicholas I pushed the Tsarist Empire, already one of the most authoritarian in Europe, one step further towards totalitarianism to prevent further armed insurrections. He aimed to establish a police state that integrated ideology and autocratic rule based on the Russian Orthodox Church. Nicholas I enhanced the secret police system, including the network of informants, and proposed the trinity of fundamental principles for governing Russia: Orthodoxy, autocracy, and nationality (Riasanovsky and Steinberg, 2011).

This trinity directly contradicted democratic constitutionalism. It declared to the public that the Orthodox faith was the foundation of Russia and that all beings were created by God and were subject to His will. The populace was warned not to entertain thoughts of changing Russia's autocratic system. The Tsar's absolute authority was depicted as a sacred power bestowed by God, inviolable and similar to a father's authority over his family. Building upon this foundation of Orthodoxy and autocracy, the concept of nationality referred to the unique characteristics of the Russian people and their deep loyalty and affection for the Tsar.

This trinity of principles, as summarized and proposed by Nicholas I, persisted into the twentieth century and even continued after the establishment of a constitutional monarchy in 1905. The ideology of the Tsarist Empire, along with the caesaropapist rule and the rigorous secret police system, evolved into institutional genes that were inherited by the totalitarian regime.

At the same time as Tsarist rule became increasingly autocratic, the tide of striving for democratic constitutionalism and advocating socialism was rising in Europe. These two factors further strengthened the Russian intelligentsia. The spirit of the Decemberists, with their secret societies and conspiratorial violence, became a model for generations of Russian intelligentsia with strong religious messianic sentiments. Like secular religious believers, they saw themselves as having a sacred duty to save Russia and the world, including through intrigue and violence, when necessary,

An important successor to the spirit of the Decemberists was Alexander Herzen. Together with his follower Chernyshevsky, he was one of the most influential revolutionary leaders among Russia's intelligentsia. As a young man, Herzen was influenced by Jacobinism and inspired by the Decemberists to stand firm against private property. He founded the ideology of Russian socialism, arguing that the peasant communes (*Obshchina*) prevalent in the Russian countryside were socialist in nature and that the peasants were a revolutionary class. He believed that by mobilizing the peasants to overthrow the Tsar, Russia could bypass capitalism and make an immediate transition to socialism. To attract the intelligentsia committed to the ideal of agrarian socialism, he launched the Populist movement, or Narodniks, participants of which proclaimed themselves to be the "essence of the people" and were known as Populists. Before it was suppressed by the Bolsheviks in 1918, the Populist movement was not only the most impactful initiative of the Russian intelligentsia but also the one with the strongest support from the Russian public. Ironically, it was also the cradle of the Bolsheviks, linking them to the Decemberists.

Populist socialism, like Marx's communism, originated from the utopianism of Christianity. Both advocated the violent overthrow of the old world through class struggle to realize a utopia. The key divergence between the two was that Marxists believed that social development proceeds through inevitable stages, adhering to the immutable laws of historical materialism. As such, Russia had to first pass through the capitalist stage before entering socialism. Populists, however, believed that Russia could bypass capitalism and directly enter socialism through violent revolution, with the momentum of revolutionaries acting as the transformative force in society. The so-called Leninism, which advocated that Russia could lead the world communist revolution, fundamentally departed from the orthodox Marxist theory of historical stages, effectively originating from Herzen and populist theories. Beyond ideology and theory, the Bolsheviks inherited the Populists' method of organizing secret societies, embraced their revolutionary spirit, and utilized their broad influence among the intelligentsia.

In 1861, a few years after Russia's defeat in the Crimean War, Tsar Alexander II abolished serfdom. The Tsarist government attributed their defeat to the serfdom system. Although the aims of this decision were to strengthen the military, enhance national power, promote the prosperity of the empire, and had nothing to do with the emerging socialist ideology advocating the emancipation of the serfs, Russian peasants hailed Alexander II as the "Liberator" for abolishing serfdom. However, in reality, the majority of peasants, unable to afford to buy land, remained financially dependent on the nobility and resentful of them. Thus, the abolition of serfdom further weakened the Russian nobility while enhancing support for the Tsar.

The Populists saw the abolition of serfdom as a reform towards capitalism and feared that it would destroy the existing communal system and transform the Russian peasantry from serfs into a proletariat exploited by the bourgeoisie. Chernyshevsky even considered the abolition of serfdom a deception and thought it necessary to immediately incite a peasant uprising to overthrow Tsarist rule. Consequently, Herzen and Chernyshevsky founded the secret organization Land and Freedom in the early 1860s. They planned to organize an armed coup by the peasants against the Tsar's rule in order to realize autonomy for rural communes and establish Russian socialism (a concept invented by Herzen, as opposed to Marxism). They propagated the idea that history was made by outstanding leaders and it was the intelligentsia's responsibility to instigate a peasant revolution, overthrow Tsarist rule, and establish socialism. The more radical members believed that immediate assassination attempts must be made to overthrow Tsarist rule.

Land and Liberty brought together a variety of beliefs and political forces in Russia opposing Tsarist rule, with the most popular being the left and extreme left. Notably influential members included anarchist leaders Bakunin and Kropotkin, who advocated instigating a comprehensive peasant uprising, and also included the socialist revolutionaries, who argued for the radical intelligentsia to seize power through conspiratorial methods like assassination. The founders of the Russian Marxist movement were originally Populists. By the late nineteenth to early twentieth centuries, the Populists reorganized and their mainstream established the SR. After the Bolsheviks' October Revolution, prior to its suppression by the Bolsheviks in 1918, it was the party that gained the most votes in the general elections of Russia in 1917.

The mainstream of the Populists advocated for a peasant revolution to overthrow Tsarist rule and transition towards socialism based on Russian rural communes. They went to the countryside to propagate their ideas in order to arouse class consciousness among the peasants. They incited revolution, agitated for the overthrow of

Tsarist rule, and called for land redistribution. However, most peasants held more faith in the Tsar and the Church than in the propaganda disseminated by the intelligentsia. The failure of these revolutionary activities led some intelligentsia to realize that perhaps Marxism was closer to the truth that Russia could not bypass the capitalist stage. In this sense, the Land and Liberty, directly or indirectly, nurtured the first generation of Russian Marxist leaders, including Plekhanov and the founder of the Bolsheviks, Lenin.

Plekhanov joined the Land and Liberty Party in 1875. Then he went into exile abroad after being imprisoned for organizing a demonstration. From there, he was introduced to Marxism, becoming the first revolutionary to systematically introduce Marxism to Russia. He also established a personal relationship with Engels. In 1883, Plekhanov and Pavel Axelrod, who originally introduced Plekhanov to the Land and Liberty Party, as well as Vera Zasulich, established the first Marxist party in Russia, Emancipation of Labor. In 1898, this party was reorganized into the Russian Social Democratic Labor Party (RSDLP), from which the Bolsheviks split in 1903. All the leaders of the Russian communist movement, including Lenin, had once been members of the Emancipation of Labor (Baron, 1995). However, Plekhanov was an adherent of Orthodox Marxism in the sense of historical stages, thus fundamentally disagreeing with Lenin. Once he recognized the nature of the Bolsheviks, he strongly opposed the party's tendencies towards terrorism and dictatorship. He explicitly opposed the violent revolution later. After the October Revolution, to escape persecution by the Bolsheviks, he fled to Finland.

It is worth mentioning that on the eve of the creation of the Emancipation of Labor, Vera Zasulich wrote to Marx to inquire about the feasibility of a populist socialist revolution, which aimed at the regeneration of Russian society based on the Russian rural commune. Marx pondered repeatedly and revised his draft four times. Although theoretically ambiguous, he affirmed that the commune would be the fulcrum for social regeneration in Russia. However, harmful influences needed to be eliminated to achieve this (Shanin,

1983). Zasulich later became a leader of the Mensheviks and resolutely opposed the Bolsheviks' October Revolution (Bergman, 1983).

Whether Marxism can gain traction in a country crucially hinges on whether there are enough people who need Marxism (regardless of their understanding of the theory itself), or whether the revolutionary ideals of Marxism are compatible with the incentives of a substantial number of people. This compatibility largely depends on the society's institutional genes. Furthermore, those in Russia who needed Marxism had diverse objectives. Many Russians who subscribed to Marxism also adhered to other ideologies. Since the Decembrist uprising, political terrorism and various philosophies, strategies, and tactics closely related to it had gained popularity among the Russian intelligentsia. It was this aspect of political terrorism that set Lenin apart from Plekhanov and, likewise, distinguished the Bolsheviks from the German Social Democratic Party (which was the largest and most crucial party in the international communist movement at that time). Moreover, the aspect of political terrorism within the Bolsheviks laid the groundwork for the split between Russian Marxist groups and the international communist movement, catalyzing the development of the Bolsheviks and the subsequent purges within the Bolshevik Party.

The political terrorism of the Bolsheviks was not a creation of their own but stemmed from Russia's institutional genes. The seeds of terrorism sown by the Decembrists rapidly grew among the radical intelligentsia in Russia under the extremely autocratic Tsarist regime. After repeated failures, many revolutionaries in the Land and Liberty became more radicalized, believing that their revolutionary goals could only be achieved through terrorist activities. In 1879, some of its core members secretly established the People's Will Party (Narodnaya Volya), a political terrorist organization that later served as a model for other such organizations. Upon establishing the People's Will, they declared a death sentence for Tsar Alexander II (Pipes, 1991, p. 142).

The People's Will claimed that its aim was to overthrow the Tsarist regime through terrorist means and ultimately to establish a national parliament. It was a highly centralized organization and all members were required to be ready to sacrifice everything for the revolution and unconditionally obey the decisions of the Executive Committee. These organizational principles later became the foundational principles of Leninist party-building.

The advent of the People's Will ushered the Russian Revolution into a new phase. Although Rousseau had long argued that sovereignty represented the general will of the people and could compel obedience, and the Jacobins had practiced dictatorship in the name of the general will, it was not until the establishment of the People's Will that Russian revolutionaries began to self-proclaim as representatives of the people, claiming to embody the will of the people and make decisions on their behalf. They systematically legitimized violent terrorism as a primary political tool, under the guise of the people's will.

On March 1, 1881, the People's Will successfully assassinated Tsar Alexander II, a move that greatly encouraged violent revolutionary and terrorist activities in Russia, Europe, and even worldwide. Determined to overthrow the Tsarist regime, they also planned to assassinate Tsar Alexander III. Lenin's older brother was executed for his involvement in this plot, a circumstance that not only propelled Lenin's later commitment to violent revolution but also greatly shaped his values and revolutionary strategy. Lenin stated that Chernyshevsky's *What Is to Be Done?* had molded both him and his brother into revolutionaries and, from his youth, he had aspired to become the revolutionary hero Rakhmetov, as portrayed by Chernyshevsky (Sebestyen, 2017).

A widely held belief among the Russian intelligentsia was that revolution could not be disentangled from violence and conspiracy and that secretive organizations were necessary. In this respect, the various radical groups were in sync. They prepared themselves as secular crusaders and propagandists, ready for martyrdom, and accumulated decades of experience in secretive organizations and terrorist activities. For instance, the SR Party, a rival to the Bolsheviks and a consistent victor in elections, had always maintained several clandestine branches involved in political assassinations. The Bolsheviks' highly centralized and secretive organizational principles for party-building were derived from the institutional genes of secret political organizations originating in Tsarist Russia. These principles evolved based on these institutional genes and were not entirely Lenin's invention. The following chapters (Chapters 8–10) will further analyze the specific role that the institutional genes of secret terrorist organizations played in the construction of the Bolshevik Party and the Chinese Communist Party, respectively.

7.5 THE PRODUCT OF THE TSARIST INSTITUTIONAL GENES

The efforts and imaginations of a few great revolutionary leaders/thinkers alone can never lead to the emergence of communist totalitarianism. Both in Russia and China, the birth of communist totalitarianism was a direct consequence of the failure of constitutional reforms. The 1905 constitutional revolution in Russia nominally transformed the country into a constitutional monarchy. If this constitutional monarchy had been successful and Russia had followed a path similar to that of Britain or the Netherlands, the foundation for establishing a totalitarian regime would have been eradicated. The reality is the opposite. It was the failure of the constitutional revolution that paved the way for the emergence of totalitarianism. This book attempts to explain, from the perspective of institutional genes under the Tsarist regime, the failure of Russia's constitutional reforms (in this chapter) and the subsequent emergence of communist totalitarianism (in Chapter 8).

7.5.1 *Constitutional Plight and the Birth of the Soviets*

The inception and centuries-long evolution of the Russian Empire did not foster the development of institutional genes necessary for constitutionalism, such as secured and dispersed private property rights and freedom of association. The Tsarist system and Eastern Orthodoxy drove a wide and profound chasm between Russia and Western Europe in terms of institutions and ideologies, a divide that only widened and deepened after the Renaissance and Reformation. Tsar Peter the Great studied in Western Europe and, recognizing Russia's backwardness (a consensus among Russian intellectuals for centuries), was determined to Westernize its arts and technology. However, he not only insisted on retaining but also on strengthening and centralizing Russia's autocratic system. He aimed to consolidate the autocratic system through the acquisition of Western scientific and technological knowledge. As a result, while fortifying a centrally controlled autocratic system, he built many Western-style factories, attracted numerous Western experts to Russia, and sent intellectuals to study in the West. He also established Russia's first Western-style university, paving the way for economic and cultural exchanges with the West and marking the onset of Russia's enlightenment.

Inheriting Peter the Great's legacy, Catherine the Great (r. 1762–1796) further propelled Westernization in Russia across various fields. Born into Prussian nobility, she ascended to the throne through a coup d'état supported by the nobility. Her reign coincided with the flourishing Enlightenment movement in Western Europe. Catherine was particularly interested in the liberal ideas prevalent during the Enlightenment. She maintained extensive private correspondence with intellectual leaders of the French Enlightenment, such as Voltaire, and was a generous patron to Denis Diderot, who urged her to transform Russia into a utopia and proposed specific implementation strategies (Durant and Durant, 1967). While promoting liberalization in culture, she firmly upheld imperial power. She only permitted discussion of ideas of constitutionalism but not its practice, nor the formation of any significant social force that could potentially challenge the imperial power.

Since the Enlightenment in the eighteenth century, Russia found itself in a predicament where liberal ideas were widespread but could not be implemented. The variance over time was merely the extent of control by the Tsarist government. During more lenient periods, people could openly advocate for liberalization and constitutionalism. In stricter periods, dissidents were banished to Siberia or expelled from the country. However, when some intellectuals were prepared to die for freedom, the deterrent effect of punishments became limited. Consequently, liberal ideologies such as human rights, democracy, freedom, and constitutionalism spread rapidly and gained popularity in Russia from the late eighteenth century onward. This early phase of Enlightenment, which Russia had undergone, served as another distinguishing factor from China, apart from Orthodoxy.

Russian intellectuals and aristocrats, having not experienced the Renaissance or the Reformation, were abruptly exposed to liberalizing ideas from the West and became enthusiastic about actualizing these new ideals. However, within the Russian system, even moderate constitutionalist goals were a utopia that could only be dreamed of but not realized. Shortly after the beginning of the French Revolution, Catherine realized that liberalization could lead to revolution, endangering the imperial rule. Subsequently, Russian monarchs deliberately resisted the idea of a constitutional monarchy, striving to maintain the autocratic system.

Among Catherine's successors, Alexander II went the furthest in terms of liberalization. The most significant of his reforms was the emancipation of the serfs, although this was intended to strengthen the country's military and economy. He also initiated top-down reforms on local administration and established autonomous zemstvo assemblies at the local level. Although the members of these assemblies were elected, they did not possess legislative power and only managed local administration. His judicial reforms, which fully implemented jury trials, public hearings, and a counsel system, abolished noble privileges in legal proceedings, seeming to take a step towards institutional justice. However, he stipulated that the Tsar was not subject to judicial constraints, thereby weakening the nobility compared to their status before the reforms. Nevertheless, these reforms did lead to the creation of numerous lawyers and related intellectuals. Similarly, the establishment and development of district and regional assemblies cultivated a desire for local autonomy among elected officials and led to the formation of legally recognized local organizations. Universities also saw significant development, becoming the primary breeding grounds for the intelligentsia. All of this laid the groundwork for the subsequent creation of generations of intellectuals and social change in Russia.

However, Alexander II was assassinated. On the day of the assassination, he had just signed the document for constitutional reform (Montefiore, 2017, pp. 446-449). The substantial content of this reform involved inviting various sectors of society to consult on national policies, relaxing restrictions on freedom of speech, and expanding local election rights. However, it had nothing to do with any social force that could counterbalance the Tsar, nor was it related to constitutionalism in any conceptual sense. In fact, Alexander II made it clear that the power bestowed upon him by God could not possibly be shared with any so-called elected representatives, let alone be constrained by them (Montefiore, 2017, pp. 429-446). Count Loris-Melikov, who drafted the reform document on behalf of the Tsar, was a general with numerous military honors and a record of successfully suppressing political terrorists and was one of Alexander II's most trusted loyalists.

After Alexander II was assassinated, his successor Alexander III completely reversed all reforms with liberal tendencies. Through the establishment of a more stringent secret police system and harsher repression, Alexander III further solidified the Russian system, pushing one more step closer to totalitarianism. This bred more radical actions that violently resisted the Russian government, further nurturing the growth of the intelligentsia and their radicalism.

Towards the end of Alexander III's reign, another crucial social event in Russia shook the foundation of imperial rule – a devastating famine with massive casualties. Faced with a disaster that was beyond its control, the Tsarist government reluctantly issued a decree calling for voluntary relief, eliciting an enormous response from all sectors of society. Tolstoy led tens of thousands of volunteers, raised funds, and opened hundreds of soup kitchens in the affected areas. Almost everyone, from zemstvo assemblies to universities, intellectuals, and political groups ranging from conservatives to liberals and even the most radical factions, participated in the relief efforts. This fostered the widespread development of radical ideologies, political parties, and terrorist organizations within Russian society. The severe crisis brought on by the famine was transformed into an opportunity to stimulate and politically mobilize Russian society (Figes, 2017, pp. 157–164).

This devastating famine marked a turning point in the fate of Marxism and thus communist totalitarianism in Russia. During this period, many radical populists who had previously disdained Marxism came to realize that Marxist historical materialism was more insightful and persuasive and the global proletarian revolution proposed by Marx was more appealing. Both Lenin and Martov, who later became the leader of the Mensheviks, transformed into Marxists during this time and joined the Labor Emancipation League. Simultaneously, many populist ideas, such as the collective definition of workers and peasants as "the working people" (Figes, 2017, pp. 151–152), were incorporated into Bolshevism through Lenin. This concept was the theoretical launching pad from which the Bolsheviks initiated the communist totalitarian revolution in Russia. However, it contradicted the Marxist theory about the proletariat and proletarian revolution, thus violating the logic of Marx's theory. Nonetheless, from the perspective of the communist totalitarian revolution, theories that can incite the people are most valuable, even if their logic is flawed. Decades later, the term "working people" was passed on to China, becoming a fundamental concept of the Communist revolution there and to communist revolutions worldwide.

The remarkable growth of civil society organizations throughout the country in the process of voluntary relief posed a threat to the Tsarist government. Once the severity of the disaster slightly abated, suppression was reinstated. In an attempt to suppress the spread of radical organizations and radical ideas, the Russian government's persecution of university students became blatant. This sparked a full-scale revolt on university campuses, with thousands of students joining the Social Revolutionary Party, the Social Democratic Party, and the Union for Liberation, the latter of which, unlike the first two left-wing parties, aimed to achieve constitutional reform. Alexander Kerensky, who later became prime minister of the Provisional Government, joined the Social Revolutionary Party during this period.

At the same time, the government also persecuted intellectuals, zemstvo members (the assemblies were monarchist but also reformist), social celebrities, and aristocrats. In 1899, after the Tsarist government closed down all zemstvo assemblies, the originally moderate conservative members and nobles established a constitutional reform organization known as the Forum (Beseda), which became the main force for constitutional reform (Figes, 2017, pp. 164–165).

However, the attempts to promote constitutionalism were weak and far from capable of carrying out constitutional reform. What eventually forced the Tsarist government into constitutional reform was a combination of internal and external pressures. The Tsar did not promise constitutional reform or the establishment of a State Duma until the disastrous defeat in the Russo-Japanese War. A month after the defeat, Russia signed an armistice with Japan as the defeated party.

The Russo-Japanese War was a war fought on Chinese territory and in Sino-Japanese waters due to Tsarist Russia's encroachment on Chinese land, which infringed on Japanese interests in China. By bribing high-ranking officials of the Qing Empire in the final years of the nineteenth century, the Tsarist government obtained China's consent to build a railway across Manchuria. In 1896, under the pretext of attending the coronation of Nicholas II, Li Hongzhang, the Qing Minister, visited Russia and signed a secret treaty, forming a Sino-Russian alliance to jointly respond to Japan's aggression. However, two years later, the Tsar deployed troops to capture Port Arthur (Lüshun) on the Liaoning Peninsula of China. Sergius Witte, one of the Russian signatories, mentioned in his memoir that the Chinese side greatly treasured this secret treaty with Russia. After the Japanese Army helped the Russians to invade Beijing during the Eight-Nation Alliance, the Russians found the original copy of this secret treaty signed by Witte, surprisingly stored in a safe in the Empress Dowager's bedroom. Witte commented with a hint of regret that had Russia adhered to the Sino-Russian secret treaty, the disastrous Russo-Japanese War could have been avoided (Witte, 2016, pp. 68–79). Contrary to Witte's wishes, in 1903, Nicholas II decided to fully annex Manchuria, posing a threat to Japan. After a series of protests, Japan launched an unexpected attack on the Russian forces in Manchuria in 1904 (Pipes, 1991, p. 13). Thus, the Russo-Japanese War began.

The Russo-Japanese War stirred a nationalistic frenzy in Russia, completely overwhelming all divisions on other issues. Almost all political parties, including the majority of radicals, fervently sided with the government. Japan was portrayed as the Yellow Peril, as Mongols, and even as spiders and monkeys. This event seemed to present the Tsar with an excellent opportunity to resolve domestic issues. However, the Russian military quickly fell into disarray and defeat. What initially appeared as potential nationalistic fervor that could have been beneficial for the Tsarist government quickly turned into a comprehensive denouncement of the government's incompetence. The defeat became a catalyst for the destruction of the absolute monarchy and caused deep panic within the Tsarist government, and in May 1905, the news that the Russian fleet had been wiped out in the Battle of Tsushima triggered an immediate internal reaction from Nicholas II: a call was made for the urgent deployment of a maximum police force to suppress any anti-government reaction at home (Pipes, 1991, p. 31).

In the face of both internal and external threats, the Tsar was more concerned about the internal ones. At the height of the Russo-Japanese War, when Russia's defeat became evident, the Tsar's favorite, the chief of police Vyacheslav von Plehve, was assassinated by the Terrorist Brigade of the SR. The turning point in Russian history came with the Bloody Sunday events in early January 1905, sparking a constitutional revolution and giving birth to the first Soviets.

The events of Bloody Sunday began with a non-political petition organized by a semi-official, semi-religious union, the Assembly of Russian Factory and Plant Workers. The Assembly was initially orchestrated by the police head Plehve to counter the autonomous trade unions. Its members were typically devout Orthodox Christians who considered themselves loyal to the Tsar. The main purpose of the petition was to call for better working conditions for workers. The Assembly had discussed coordination and mutual support with the zemstvo (which was pro-tsar but favored constitutional monarchy) representatives prior to the petition and it also had support from the Union of Liberation. However, the government not only banned this non-political petition but threatened violent repression if it went ahead. This angered the workers who had hitherto been loyal to the Tsar. On January 9, over 100,000 enraged workers marched to the Winter Palace to petition the Tsar about the welfare of the workers. Pre-arranged military police opened fire on the demonstrating crowd, causing hundreds of casualties. The tragedy, known in history as Bloody Sunday, pushed Russia to the brink of chaos and fueled the emergence of totalitarianism. In response to the threat from the Tsarist government, a month later, nearly 150,000 workers in Petersburg elected the Petersburg Soviet of Workers' Deputies through anonymous voting (Pipes, 1991, pp. 21–27). It was the first elected, region-wide workers' organization in Russian history. However, groups composed of individuals without property rights do not primarily aim to limit governmental power in order to protect property rights. Therefore, even if they are elected, they cannot become the main driving force for constitutionalism. Indeed, the Bolsheviks later used the Soviets, which initially had no connection with them, as a tool to seize power and rule, making them a part of the totalitarian system. This led to the Soviets becoming the official name of the first communist totalitarian regime in history.

In the months following the Bloody Sunday events, the near total destruction of the Russian fleet in the Tsushima Strait fully exposed the weaknesses of the Tsarist government and military, greatly shocking Russian society. Half a century earlier, people attributed the great defeat of the Russian Army in Crimea to serfdom. This time, the incompetence of the Russian military was generally attributed directly to the Tsarist autocracy. National radical organizations were actively operating and collectively established a general national alliance, the Union of Unions. The primary goal of most parties within this Union was to establish constitutional governance, with the ultimate aspiration of transforming Russia into a democratic republic. To exert pressure on the Tsar, they planned to organize general strikes across the country. The mobilization was concentrated on university campuses. Radical students from various factions within the Union of Unions turned these campuses into bases for propaganda, organization, and incitement of workers. In this way, the Union transformed spontaneous workers' movements, originally organized for welfare purposes by individual factories, into large-scale political strikes.

Menshevik and SR university students ventured beyond their campuses to assist in the large-scale establishment of workers' councils, or Soviets. These young communist/socialist revolutionaries mobilized the power of workers, positioning the Soviets as institutions competing for power with the soon-to-be-established parliament. On October 13, the day when a large-scale strike paralyzed the national railway, the Saint Petersburg Soviet convened its first plenary meeting, with the SR Party, Mensheviks, and Bolsheviks each taking a third of the seats. However, the Mensheviks exerted the most influence over the Soviets, with Trotsky as their key leader. Ironically, the Bolsheviks at the time scorned, mistrusted, and even antagonized the Soviets, as they were solely concerned with the conspiratorial activities (Figes, 2017, p. 190). They even once boycotted the Soviets, citing the proletariat's yet unrealized seizure of power as the reason (Pipes, 1991, p. 41).

Under the impetus of the SR Party and the Mensheviks, Soviets were established in more than fifty cities across the country, organizing larger-scale strikes. Peasant riots and even armed uprisings took place in more than a fifth of the country's counties. The Tsarist government's repression proved ineffective. Prime Minister Witte and other ministers strongly advised the Tsar to accept moderate demands for constitutional reform in order to avert the escalating revolution. Under immense pressure from internal and external threats, on October 17, Nicholas II felt he had no choice but to sign a decree, announcing the initiation of constitutional reforms. This document, known as the October Manifesto, pledged allegiance to the Tsar and announced the pursuit of reforms in three major areas: recognizing basic citizen rights, holding elections for the State Duma, and legislating by the State Duma (Witte, 2016, p. 174). The October Manifesto was drafted by Prime Minister Witte on his own initiative and he painstakingly persuaded the Tsar to sign, under the long-term pressure of the Union of Liberation and the zemstvo and pressure from the Union of Unions and ongoing national strikes. Subsequently, in response to the demands for voting rights from the striking workers, the Tsarist government promulgated a new State Duma Election Law on December 11.

However, constitutional governance cannot be established solely through laws or edicts. For the establishment of such governance, it is essential to address and resolve numerous deep-rooted societal issues. Paramount among these is the necessity for a force to exist within a society that can balance imperial authority, a precondition for making constitutional governance viable. Indeed, the Tsar's signing of the October Edict served merely as an expedient last resort. In addition, various factions opposed to constitutional governance became more active within Russian society, particularly the Bolsheviks. As such, from its very inception, Russia's constitutional reform was pervaded by the risk of failure.

7.5.2 *A Failing Constitutional Reform*

Constitutionalism is a system of rules designed to limit and govern powers, ensuring mutual restraints between competing forces. These rules regulate the interplays of interest groups, facilitating their mutual compromise and keeping them in check. Many striving for constitutionalism often concentrate on the formulation of these rules. However, the history of the global quest for constitutional democracy over the past two centuries proves that the existence of mutual checks and balances in society is a prerequisite for establishing constitutionalist institutions. Written constitutional rules alone, when formulated in the absence of evenly balanced power blocs, often fail to function in practice.

The evolution of the Tsarist imperial system represents a process of suppressing and dispossessing the nobility. The Tsars explicitly made autocracy the fundamental principle of governance, systematically employing violence and the secret police to annihilate any competition. The intelligentsia that surfaced in response to this autocracy aspired to institute a constitutional system in Russia akin to those found in Western European nations. However, Russia fell short of the necessary social forces capable of counterbalancing the imposing imperial autocracy. As a result, tensions soared between the Tsar's pursuit of self-preservation – which mandated further autocracy – and the intelligentsia's endeavors to champion constitutionalism by challenging the status quo. This fraught climate of constitutional reform and mounting discord presented ripe opportunities for the Bolsheviks not only to undermine the constitutional reforms but also to kindle a communist totalitarian movement.

Following the issuance of the October Manifesto, the Tsar soon regretted the concessions. He maintained that he had no alternative at the time but he strongly believed that royal authority should remain unrestricted, viewing this as an inviolable principle. To avoid implications of power checks and balances in the constitution, Nicholas deliberately titled the officially promulgated 1906 charter as the "Fundamental Laws," rather than the constitution. He stated, "I did not create the Duma to direct me, but to advise me." He further affirmed his prerogative to both grant and revoke the power of the Duma and the Fundamental Laws. Prime Minister Pyotr Stolypin made it abundantly clear that the 1906 Fundamental Laws were a grace bestowed by the Tsar, not an agreement reached through negotiation between the ruler and the ruled. Thus, Russia had no real constitution at all (Pipes, 1991, p. 154).

Despite Nicholas sanctioning of the Fundamental Laws with the intent of preserving the Tsar's autocratic dominance, the Laws did pave the way for the establishment of the Duma, catalyzing the first general elections in Russian history. More notably, the Duma, born from these elections, held a modicum of legislative power and control over a segment of the state budget, marking a small stride toward a constitutional monarchy. However, the Fundamental Laws unequivocally declared the Tsar as a despot, firmly grasping the reins of fundamental authority including administration, armaments, foreign relations, the right to declare peace or war, and oversight of the imperial courts. The Tsar also retained the prerogative to dissolve the Duma. In a move to further dilute the power of the elected Duma, the Fundamental Laws restructured the State Council, an entity dating back to the reign of Alexander I, into the Duma's upper house. This upper house was heavily influenced by the Tsar, with half of its representatives being nobility appointed by him.

When Prime Minister Witte initially endeavored to convince the Tsar to approve the October Manifesto he had composed, his efforts were propelled not solely by the imperative to reconcile with the constitutionalists but also by his sanguine expectations about the electoral outcomes. The government, under the assumption that the peasants – comprising over 80 percent of the Russian populace – would rally behind the Tsar and pro-monarchist right-wing faction, severely miscalculated public sentiment. The electoral results painted a starkly different picture: right-wing parties only managed to secure 45 out of 497 seats. In contrast, the centrist-left Constitutional Democratic Party, a vigorous advocate for constitutionalism, clinched 184 seats, making it the majority party. The left-leaning factions gained 124 seats and a significant number of the largely centrist-left independents captured 112 seats (Riasanovsky and Steinberg, 2011, pp. 406–408).

Immediately upon the Duma's establishment, stark internal divisions began to emerge. After heated debates, the Duma passed a political reform program on May 5, 1906. A mere few days later, Chairman of the Council of Ministers, Goremykin, speaking on behalf of the government, contended that the Duma had overstepped its jurisdiction with its reform demands, thereby rejecting the Duma's program. Countering this, Nabokov, representing the Constitutional Democratic Party, sharply retorted, "The executive power must be subordinate to the legislative power." Consequently, the Duma passed a resolution demanding the immediate resignation of the current cabinet. In a swift act of retaliation, the Tsar promptly disbanded the first State Duma.

The second State Duma convened at the dawn of 1907, with the Social Democratic Party, encompassing both the Bolsheviks and Mensheviks, capturing approximately 10 percent of the seats. However, on June 3, 1907, the Tsar, not for the first time, issued a decree to dissolve the Duma. He rationalized his decision by alleging that "a significant proportion of the members of the second State Duma were insincere," and in a subsequent move, he subjected the Bolshevik and Menshevik representatives to judicial trials, grueling labor, or life-long banishment. By twice dissolving the nationally elected Duma immediately after the inception of the constitutional system, the Tsar clearly conveyed to the electorate the profound failure of the constitutional monarchy. Furthermore, by sentencing Bolshevik leaders to punitive measures, he inadvertently transformed them into martyrs of the revolutionary cause.

In the aftermath of dissolving the Duma, the Tsar unilaterally modified the electoral law without the involvement of the legislative body, which violated the Fundamental Laws. Under the newly instituted electoral law, landowners were slated to occupy half of the Duma's seats. Nicholas II justified this change by claiming that his divine autocratic authority as the Tsar entitled him to rescind past promises. The new electoral law led to a shift in the Duma's composition, with the Octobrist Party, a centrist faction favoring a constitutional monarchy, becoming the largest party and the Constitutional Democratic Party emerging as the main opposition. Although the Octobrists aimed to advance moderate conservative constitutional reforms, they found themselves increasingly marginalized by the Tsar's government. Their representation diminished from 154 seats in the third term to a mere 95 in the fourth.

The ten years of the third and fourth Dumas were characterized by extreme left- and right-wing terrorist organizations undertaking rampant assassinations of government officials and Duma deputies, as well as the government's frantic suppression of opposition. Collectively, these forces pushed Russia towards the brink of collapse, laying the groundwork for the birth of the more violent Bolshevik totalitarian regime. In just two years from 1906 to 1907, the SR Party assassinated 3,400 people. The far-right assassinated several Duma representatives of the Constitutional Democratic Party. In response to these terrorist activities, Stolypin's government greatly enhanced the already rigorous secret police system, including the informant system. This sophisticated and rigorous system, perfected by him, would subsequently morph into a critical component of future totalitarian regimes. Ironically, Stolypin himself was assassinated in 1911 by police agents with revolutionary ties (Figes, 2018, pp. 230–231).

From the onset, the Bolsheviks, as a Marxist-Leninist party, were fundamentally opposed to constitutionalism, viewing it as their primary target for revolutionary action. Their goal was to seize power through armed struggle to establish a proletarian dictatorship. Therefore, during the inaugural Duma elections, they initiated a nationwide strike to boycott what they termed "bourgeois Duma elections," all under the banner of advocating for universal suffrage. This move, however, resulted in a significant setback. Years later, Lenin acknowledged the Bolsheviks' boycott of the Duma elections in 1906 as a strategic miscalculation. Consequently, the Bolsheviks began to perceive the Duma as a battleground for undermining its constitutional reforms. Although the Bolsheviks were relatively weak at this time, and their strategies for derailing constitutionalism did not significantly affect society, the pervasive institutional genes resisting constitutionalism in Russian society were strong enough to help the Bolsheviks.

Indeed, from the first Duma onwards, the majority of elected deputies were from the left, reflecting the fundamental situation in Russia at the time. Because all the far-left parties like the SR Party, Bolsheviks, and Mensheviks boycotted the Duma and refused to participate in elections, the center-left forces dominated the first Duma. The Constitutional Democratic Party, which held the largest number of seats, nominally aimed to pursue democratic constitutionalism with all its might. If they had taken the Fundamental Laws as a starting point to promote constitutionalism gradually, seeking opportunities for compromise and steadying each small step in the process, and if the government, too, had compromised under pressure, there might have been a chance for constitutional democracy in Russia to develop. However, the Constitutional Democratic Party almost repeated the practice of the constitutionalists in the Estates-General on the eve of the French Revolution. This similarity was not coincidental. Russian constitutionalists were intentionally learning from the French Revolution. They believed that with voters' support, they could pressure the Tsar to surrender sovereignty to the Duma. Therefore, not only did they refuse to compromise with the government on any issue but they also declared that they did not recognize the Fundamental Laws and demanded the immediate convening of a constitutional assembly to formulate a constitution. They further demanded the resignation of the whole government and the Duma to legislate for land reform to equally distribute land (Figes, 2017, p. 217).

In the end, the ultimate failure of the constitutional revolution resulted in a power vacuum upon the collapse of the imperial regime. This provided the Bolsheviks with an opportune moment to seize power through military force. The institutional genes of Russia facilitated the Bolsheviks, post-coup, to establish an even more despotic totalitarian regime. In the ensuing chapter, we will substantiate, through historical evidence, the reasons why the failure of the constitutional revolution in Russia was inevitable, even in the absence of Bolshevik sabotage. We will then delve into how Russia's institutional genes, including aspects such as the Russian Orthodox Church, the Tsarist imperial system, and the tradition of covert political organizations, laid the groundwork for the creation and evolution of the Bolshevik totalitarian regime in varied ways.

NOTES

1. Ostrowski (1998) provides extensive evidence and convincing discussion on the profound influence of the Mongols on the Rus' land.
2. *Acta Patriarchatus Constantinopolitani*, II, 188–192; cf. *Russkaya Istoricheskaya Biblioteka*, VI, appendix 40, cols. 265–276 (Miklosich and Müller, 1860). Some historians note that the Grand Prince of Muscovy at the time did not recognize the patriarch's claim.
3. Archaeological Committee (1880), Russkaya Istoricheskaya Biblioteka, VI, 577.
4. Cheka is the first Soviet secret police agency and a predecessor to the KGB.

8 The Birth of Bolshevik Totalitarianism

Communist totalitarianism, born in Russia after the October Revolution of 1917, once reigned over a third of the world's population. It stands as one of the most significant and foundational institutions in human history. What is more, this system continues to evolve in China, presently the world's second-largest economy and potentially soon to be the first. As such, comprehending this institution is paramount for understanding China. Furthermore, given the profound impact of such an institution, coupled with the relative scarcity of research in this domain, investigating this institution presents one of the most challenging tasks in both academic research and policy-making. This chapter delves into the origins of the first enduring communist totalitarian system in human history and its institutional foundations.

Every totalitarian regime, from its earliest iterations, has been predicated upon seizing power through force and implementing rule by coercion. As discussed in Chapter 6, this includes short-lived, nascent totalitarian regimes throughout history, such as the theocratic totalitarianism of Münster during the Reformation and the Jacobin totalitarianism of the French Revolution. Ultimately, the stable development of a system hinges on its alignment with the interests and ideologies of the societal majority. In Western European contexts, when the majority of society opposes totalitarianism for its own interests and when the social forces resisting totalitarianism outweigh those that support it, any drift towards totalitarian institutional genes will eventually be eliminated by forces aligned with the prevailing institutional genes. As a result, pre-twentieth-century totalitarian regimes in Western Europe were invariably isolated and ephemeral. However, the scenario that unfolded in Russia was markedly different. To elucidate the mechanisms underpinning the emergence and development of totalitarianism in Russia, this chapter scrutinizes how Russia's institutional genes allowed communist totalitarianism to plant its roots and flourish amidst the ruins of the Tsarist Empire.

The reason Bolsheviks were able to create an enduring communist totalitarian system in Russia can be ascribed to the compatibility between the institutional genes of Tsarist Russia and the foundational principles of the Bolshevik system. The key institutional genes that bolstered this alignment included the far-reaching societal control exercised by the Tsarist imperial system, the crucial role and influence of Orthodoxy and the Orthodox Church in Russian society, and a tradition of clandestine political organizations dating back to the early nineteenth century.

These three potent institutional genes posed significant barriers to constitutional reform. Even more critically, they provided the groundwork upon which the communist totalitarian system could be erected. Although the failure of constitutional reforms is a common historical phenomenon in many regions globally, the modern totalitarian system stands as a uniquely Russian contribution to history. In this chapter, we will delve into how the institutional characteristics of Tsarist Russia shaped the trajectory of constitutional reform and how they paved the way for a totalitarian party to seize power and establish a communist totalitarian regime.

8.1 TOTALITARIAN PARTY: THE BOLSHEVIKS

Totalitarianism is a modern institution. Its primary distinguishing feature from contemporary dictatorships and those of the Middle Ages and antiquity lies at the heart of the system: the modern totalitarian party. The formation of a totalitarian party, in this case, the Bolsheviks, represents the first and most pivotal step in establishing a totalitarian system. While the Bolsheviks were incapable of causing the collapse of the Tsarist regime or the failure of Russia's constitutional reform, these developments nonetheless set the stage for the Bolsheviks' rise. After a lengthy period of scheming and preparation, they seized the power vacuum left in the wake of the Tsarist system's collapse, violently overthrew the provisional government, and installed a one-party totalitarian regime. Without the Bolsheviks, communist totalitarianism would not have come into existence. Consequently, understanding the birth of the totalitarian party is an indispensable prerequisite to discussing the establishment of the totalitarian system.

The totalitarian party sprouted from the context of a modern multiparty system, yet its fundamental nature deviates markedly from that of political parties functioning within a constitutional framework and indeed from all other modern political parties. This entity is explicitly antagonistic towards any multiparty system, its primary objective being the forceful elimination of all competing parties, irrespective of their ideological leanings. As a modern institution and phenomenon, the totalitarian party is deeply interwoven with modernization processes in countries such as Russia and China. One strand of modernization theory asserts that economic growth fosters democracy (Lipset, 1959). This perspective, however, overlooks the significant variations in human rights, property rights, and political decision-making power within different systems, as well as their profoundly divergent roles in driving long-term societal development. According to this line of thinking, if economic growth is feasible under totalitarianism, it might suggest that totalitarianism represents a viable path towards modernization and that economic growth could eventually trigger a democratic transformation within a totalitarian society. But as abundant historical evidence testifies, economic growth under a totalitarian system is entirely irreconcilable with democratic values. A thorough comprehension of totalitarianism necessitates a clear-sighted examination of the totalitarian party's character and mechanics.

8.1.1 The Nature of Totalitarian Parties

In modern society, political parties serve as the vehicles for political competition. Max Weber's definitive description of a political party is, "By definition a party can exist only within an organization, in order to influence its policy or gain control of it" (Weber, 1978, p. 285). Weber's definition presumes a degree of competition among parties but this definition or fundamental assumption is completely contravened by totalitarian parties. The Bolshevik Party, crafted by Lenin, was a political monopoly that did not tolerate political competition. Instead of merely participating within an organized system, it dominated every organization, infiltrated every societal sector, and dictated all significant decisions. It wielded control over all organizations and presided over all aspects of society. Most critically, the Bolsheviks disallowed the existence of any organization that functioned independently of the party within society – even non-political organizations were mandated to secure its approval and fell under its supervision.

Weber also defined a political party as an association that recruits members freely, a principle that Leninist parties categorically contradict. Indeed, the Bolsheviks' split from the RSDLP in 1903 was primarily due to their opposition to the principle of free membership recruitment.

Every totalitarian party, modeled on Leninist principles and established anywhere globally, adheres to the Bolsheviks' basic principles. Namely, these are not organizations that freely recruit members but rather they operate as secret associations of political elites under autocratic control. Leninist parties explicitly stipulate the dictatorship of the proletariat as the fundamental system in their party charters and constitutions.

These parties are the only political entities, exercising an almost complete monopoly over society's numerous facets, encompassing politics, economy, military, media, and more. Totalitarian parties that have not yet seized power aim to do so through armed force, striving to establish a one-party dictatorship. Those who opt to join the governing totalitarian party willingly acquiesce to autocratic rule, seeking to ascend to the ranks of political elites via this pathway.

Modern political parties, as organizations vying for power openly, draw their institutional genes from earlier parliamentary caucuses and social organizations that represent diverse interests. These types of parliaments and organizations have existed for several centuries and, in some places, for two millennia in Europe.

By comparison, apart from the alien Marxist theory of the proletarian dictatorship, the institutional genes that gave rise to the Bolshevik Party were the absence of the parliamentary tradition and the secret political organization or the political terrorist organization that already existed in Russia. The nature of terrorist activities ensures that these organizations are hierarchical, autocratic, and clandestine.

To summarize, there are two fundamental differences between totalitarian parties and modern political parties. First, totalitarian parties are organizations that seek to monopolize power, not to compete for it. They are resolute in their intention to dismantle any organization that might compete with them, using violence or other means if necessary.

Second, members of totalitarian parties are selected to join a secretive organization that imposes strict, and sometimes lethal, discipline on them. This is in stark contrast to open organizations that permit free recruitment, exit, and debate.

8.1.2 Emergence of the Bolsheviks as a Secret Political Organization

The Bolsheviks evolved directly from the Russian Social Democratic Labor Party, which itself spun off from the Land and Liberty movement and adopted the title and ideology of the Social Democratic Party of Germany (SDP), a Marxist entity. The original ideology of Land and Liberty was Russian socialism proposed by Alexander Herzen and Nikolay Chernyshevsky. This particular ideology advocated for the transformation of ownership through dispossession to create a fully egalitarian society, culminating in the transfer of land to rural communes and factories to workers.

Within the ranks of the Land and Liberty revolutionaries, there was a considerable divergence in revolutionary strategies. While some foresaw the establishment of a highly centralized utopian socialism, others leaned towards anarchy, pushing for autonomy in rural communities and factories. However, apart from their shared socialist aim of abolishing private property, they typically upheld Russia's tradition of violent revolution, championing the use of covert and violent means through either armed uprising or assassination.

What is of paramount significance is the broad and profound influence that Land and Liberty exerted in Russia. In the first All-Russian Constituent Assembly at the end of 1917 (two months after the October Revolution), parties that were either directly or indirectly linked to Land and Liberty won nearly 70 percent of the total votes. Parties advocating for various forms of dispossession of private property held a clear majority in the elections. This inherently suggests that even in the absence of the armed Bolshevik coup to overthrow the Provisional Government, or without the establishment of a totalitarian system, it would have been challenging for Russia to establish solid property rights and institute constitutionalism.

Despite sharing a common goal with these parties – to abolish private property rights – the Bolsheviks, following their armed seizure of power, moved swiftly and forcibly to suppress all these parties. They focused particularly on the largest party in Russia at the time, the Socialist Revolutionary Party, and the Mensheviks, another faction of the Marxist movement.

Understanding the Bolsheviks requires an appreciation of the institutional genes they inherited from Land and Liberty. Founded by Alexander Herzen (the progenitor of Russian socialism) and Nikolay Chernyshevsky (a leading figure of Russian socialism), Land and Liberty was a secret organization. The group belonged to the broader school of thought known historically as the Populists. Most secret organizations at that time adhered to Chernyshevsky's teachings, forming radical factions intent on violently dispossessing private property.

These entities were not political parties as defined by Weber. Instead, they were covert, violent groups that engaged in revolutionary propaganda, incited armed insurrection, and plotted assassinations.

Taking a leaf from the Russian Decemberists' playbook, they sought to instigate a violent coup d'état. In reality, since the mid-nineteenth century, most groups opposing the Tsarist regime in Russia had inherited the legacy of the Decemberists, transforming themselves into secret violent organizations. Of these, Land and Liberty was the largest and most enduring.

The People's Party, a faction of Land and Liberty, declared in its political platform that its task was:

> To achieve the goal that supreme ownership belongs to the entire people ... through popular uprising.... At the moment of popular uprising, the Party should organize a provisional government capable of leading the revolutionary struggle.[1]

During the late nineteenth century, two crucial organizations arose from the radical wing of Land and Liberty, setting the stage for the emergence of the Bolsheviks. The first was the Emancipation of Labor, founded in 1883, which served as a precursor to the RSDLP and, by extension, the direct predecessor of the Bolsheviks. The second was the People's Will (Narodnaya Volya), a terrorist organization established in 1879. While the Bolsheviks adopted influences from both organizations, their legacy from the People's Will directly precipitated their split from the rest of the RSDLP, particularly the Mensheviks.

From the Program of the Executive Committee of the People's Will, we are able to find key principles that were adopted later by the Bolsheviks. This Program stipulated that the People's Will should:

> organize various secret groups and unify them around a center. Organizing small secret groups for various revolutionary tasks ... is essential for performing the Party's multifaceted duties ... It is necessary to unify around a central institution ... The primary task of the Party among the people is to educate the people to promote change ... to maintain the prestige of the Party among the people and defend the Party's ideas and goals.[2]

The Program of the Terrorist Faction of the People's Will, written from prison by Lenin's brother, stated: "We are the terrorist faction of the Party ... we undertake the task of waging a terror struggle against the government ... Terrorist actions ... force the government to make concessions ... arouse the people's revolutionary spirit, ... act as a powerful propaganda for the masses."[3]

The founders of the RSDLP, including Lenin, underwent a transformation of their ideology from Russian socialism to Marxism. Simultaneously, they inherited the tradition of secrecy and violence from the terrorist organizations within the Land and Freedom Society. One influential source of this transformation was Lenin's elder brother, Aleksandr Ulyanov, who was executed for his involvement in a failed attempt to assassinate the Tsar. Lenin closely followed in his brother's footsteps, diligently studying the theories of Land and Liberty and the People's Will, absorbing their spirit. He also delved into Aleksandr's favorite books, with Chernyshevsky's writings being the most influential among them. Lenin said that before coming into contact with Marxism, Chernyshevsky's thoughts had "deeply ploughed" his mind (Offord, 1986, pp. 150–151).

During this period, a series of radical revolutionaries emerged from Land and Liberty, all of whom regarded Rakhmetov, a character depicted in Chernyshevsky's novel *What Is to Be Done?* as a revolutionary figurehead. Lenin stated that he repeatedly read this novel throughout his life, considering Rakhmetov as his role model. Guided by this spirit, Lenin dedicated his life to violent revolution, with the objective of overthrowing the Tsarist regime and ultimately establishing a classless society.

Even after becoming a Marxist, Lenin deliberately distanced himself from the pioneer of Russian Marxism, Nikolai Fedoseyev, in order to uphold the deep-rooted tradition of the People's Will that resonated within his heart (Trotsky, 1972). However, Lenin recognized that the People's Will alone could not achieve its goals through individual assassinations. Influenced by the radical revolutionaries

Sergey Nechayev and Pyotr Tkachev from Land and Liberty, Lenin concluded that effective leadership capable of orchestrating comprehensive, large-scale terror was necessary to overthrow the government and seize power.

Nechayev and Tkachev were instrumental figures who actively worked on centralizing authority within secret violent revolutionary groups, planning large-scale terrorist activities, and inciting revolution. Their profound influence extended to both the People's Will and the Bolsheviks. Many of the key elements that distinguish Leninism from Marxism in terms of party-building theory and revolutionary strategy can be attributed to Nechayev and Tkachev. Lenin regarded Nechayev as a revolutionary titan and required all communist revolutionaries to study his works (Mayer, 1993, pp. 249–263).

Lenin held Nechayev in high esteem for his exceptional organizational talent, his ability to devise new conspiratorial methods, and his remarkable skills in articulation (Parry, 2006, pp. 135–136). During his student years, Nechayev drew inspiration from the Decemberists and actively participated in the radical revolutionary activities of Bakunin's anarchist wing, at one point maintaining a close association with Bakunin himself. He also emulated the practices of Rakhmetov, the ascetic revolutionary character created by Chernyshevsky. Nechayev had a profound admiration for the Jacobins and Blanqui, which greatly influenced his ideology. He advocated for an uncompromising and ruthless strategy to achieve revolutionary goals, which ultimately became the spiritual foundation of Leninism, Bolshevism, and communism.

Nechayev possessed exceptional skills as an agitator and was adept at propagating the radical revolutionary ideas of the Jacobins, Blanqui, and Chernyshevsky with precision and power. Lenin deliberately learned these capabilities from him. Nechayev advocated that violent revolution was of paramount importance, considering humanity and morality as dispensable in the pursuit of revolution. He believed that revolution could and must employ any means necessary. All of these ideas had a significant influence on Lenin and, through him, on the fundamental spirit of the Bolsheviks.

In terms of shaping the party-building ideas of the Bolsheviks, Tkachev played a particularly significant role through his skilled methods and practices in establishing terrorist or conspiracy revolutionary organizations. Tkachev emphasized the pivotal role of leaders in shaping history and argued that major historical change could only be achieved through a radical shift from one historical order to another. To accomplish this shift, leaders were essential in motivating people to strive for excellence. Tkachev believed that a genuine revolution must commence with the seizure of power under the guidance of leaders. Subsequently, through the education of the masses and the implementation of a series of economic, political, and legal reforms, the revolutionary goals could be realized.

In preparing for a coup to seize power, revolutionaries had to establish strict discipline. Success could only be attained if they built an organization as tightly knit, solid, and disciplined as an army, characterized by high centralization. Tkachev's principles of revolutionary organization, in a sense, synthesized Nechayev's concept of conspiratorial organization. Furthermore, Tkachev drew inspiration from Jacobinism and Blanquism, recognizing the necessity of coercion within the revolutionary organization to pursue top-down centralization (Offord, 1986, pp. 13–16).

8.1.3 The Early Period of the Totalitarian Party: The Bolsheviks

The Chernyshevsky–Nechayev–Tkachev trio exerted significant influence on socialist revolutionaries in Russia during the late nineteenth and early twentieth centuries, providing the ideological foundation for the emerging Bolshevik group. Nechayev's works, including the *Catechism of a Revolutionary*, directly influenced Lenin's theory of party-building and revolutionary strategy. It is worth noting that while Lenin is often credited with the principles of party-building for the Chinese Communist Party, which succeeded the Bolsheviks, the true origin can be traced back to this source.

Lenin introduced his principles for party-building at the Second Congress of the RSDLP in 1903. He emphasized the necessity of a highly centralized and disciplined party, comprising professional revolutionaries who were subservient to the party leader. However, there were opponents to Lenin's proposals, including Martov, Trotsky, and Axelrod, who expressed concerns that his ultra-centralized structure would transform the party into a dictatorial organization led by an elite group of professional conspirators. They also objected to Lenin's strategy of using ruthless internal coercion to establish party leadership and were apprehensive about the unethical attacks on dissenters within the party carried out by his followers (Getzler, 1967, p. 16).

In summary, Lenin's party-building principles were not a personal invention from scratch but rooted in pre-existing institutional genes. The creation of a coercive totalitarian party depended on the presence of a group of fanatical revolutionaries who willingly obeyed the coercive rules, rather than solely relying on the imagination of a powerful individual. In fact, Georgy Plekhanov had proposed similar party-building principles eighteen years earlier, based on the same institutional genes (Le Blanc, 2015, p. 54), and his support for Lenin's principles at the 1903 Congress was instrumental in forming Lenin's Bolshevik faction (Bolshevik means "the majority") within the RSDLP.

However, once the totalitarian party was established, the threats posed by its dictatorial rules became evident. In such a party, coercion takes precedence over revolutionary voluntariness and willingness. Georgy Plekhanov, one of the prominent Russian communist revolutionary leaders, had not anticipated these consequences when discussing the principles in an abstract manner. Nevertheless, he soon shifted his support to the Mensheviks, who were critical of the Bolsheviks' approach. A decade later, Plekhanov firmly opposed the Bolsheviks' October Revolution and eventually fled to Finland in order to escape the threat of violent repression.

In fact, Lenin published a pamphlet titled *What Is to Be Done?* one year before the birth of the Bolsheviks in 1903. This pamphlet brought together previously scattered principles and laid the foundation for the model of a totalitarian party, which paved the way for the practice of communist totalitarianism (Meyer, 1957, p. 19). At the core of this model was the deliberately misleading principle known as democratic centralism, which enabled the totalitarian leader to exert complete control over the party.

The essence of democratic centralism lies in its emphasis on centralism. It ensures that there are no checks and balances within the party structure. Obedience is the fundamental principle: subordinates obey superiors, the entire party obeys its central committee, and the central committee obeys the party leader. The term "democratic" is used misleadingly to introduce totalitarianism in a misguided manner. It was officially interpreted as a process of consultation and discussion before making decisions.

It is crucial to note that the concept of democratic centralism has created significant confusion in understanding democracy in China. Misguided by communist propaganda, a majority of the Chinese today still mistake "democratic centralism" for democracy, particularly with Chinese characteristics. However, it is important to recognize that all communist parties that have followed the Bolsheviks since its inception have lacked freedom of expression within the party and personal safety has been at great risk.

The Marxist leaders of the Second International, despite advocating the dictatorship of the proletariat, did not comprehend that the Leninist principles would be the only practical means to achieve such a total form of dictatorship. Ironically, they were the first to voice concerns about the dangers of the Leninist party. They observed that the extreme centralization within the Bolsheviks signaled the autocracy of the Central Committee and the dictatorship of its leader. Rosa Luxemburg criticized Lenin for reiterating the Jacobinism of the French Revolution and the Blanquism of the Paris Commune period (Luxemburg, 2006). Karl Kautsky pointed out that while the

Bolsheviks may have had noble intentions, their dictatorial autocracy, which granted unlimited power to their supreme leadership, would inevitably transform them into a terrorist institution (Kautsky, 1920). Kautsky depicted the Bolsheviks as a clandestine organization seeking power through a coup d'état and fostering a society dominated by bureaucracy, constructed on principles that enslaved and sacrificed people's self-esteem (Kautsky, 1946). However, they failed to realize that the one-party dictatorship and the internal dictatorship within Leninist parties were essentially the same as the dictatorship of the proletariat.

Indeed, when the RSDLP divided into Bolsheviks and Mensheviks over principles of party-building, Martov, the leader of the Mensheviks, labeled Lenin's principles as dictatorial. Lenin accepted this charge, asserting that dictatorship was the sole option during a revolution (Sebestyen, 2017, p. 149). It is important to note that, while Lenin played a significant role in establishing and developing the Bolsheviks, this could not have occurred without the enthusiasm of many fanatical "revolutionaries" for organizing violent revolutions through secret societies and for a dictatorial system, and their readiness to voluntarily submit to the rule of the dictator. Without these zealots, it would have been impossible for anyone to create something like a Bolshevik Party under his total dictatorial control.

By prohibiting other independent parties and organizations, a totalitarian party distinguishes itself from a conventional political party. In line with this principle, a totalitarian party strictly prohibits factions within its ranks. In essence, if the prohibition of outside parties is a fundamental proposition of totalitarianism, the prohibition of factions within the party is a corollary derived from that proposition. This proposition and corollary are crucial for understanding any communist party or movements launched by the party, as well as any communist totalitarian regime, including all major events in communist China in the past and present.

During the French Revolution, the Jacobins had already put this proposition and corollary into violent practice, resulting in the execution of numerous dissidents within their own ranks. However, it was with the Bolsheviks that the first fully institutionalized totalitarian party emerged. The formal ban on party factions was officially established at the Tenth Congress of the Russian Communist Party (RCP) in 1921. (The Bolsheviks had changed their name to the Russian Communist Party in 1918 and later to the All-Union Communist Party at the end of 1925.) At that time, several factions existed within the party, including the joint faction of Trotsky and Bukharin, which advocated for greater independence and a more prominent role for trade unions; the Workers' Opposition, which opposed bureaucratic tendencies; and the Democratic Centralists, who sought increased autonomy for the Soviets. Concurrently, the party leadership was divided between Leninists and Trotskyists.

After securing majority support, Lenin called for a complete prohibition on factions within the party. The Party Congress swiftly passed a resolution banning factions and stipulating expulsion from the party for anyone who organized or joined a faction. However, despite the official ban, factions within the party did not automatically disappear due to their own interests. Factions associated with workers' organizations, such as Workers' Truth and the Workers' Group, continued to fight against the bureaucratization of the RCP and staged frequent strikes. Trotsky (1975) believed that the lack of internal democracy was at the root of the problem. Nevertheless, these factions were eventually suppressed. In the end, the totalitarian party leader had the power to suppress factions in the name of the dictatorship of the proletariat. The winner takes all and prohibits all factions, which also determined the intensity of the factional fights, as for them it was a matter of life and death.

Stalin's Great Purge was an application and refinement of the Leninist system. Leninist totalitarian parties, wherever they exist, have consistently relied on purges to suppress internal factions. The fundamental mechanisms and requirements of totalitarian systems shape the history and reality of totalitarianism. The principles outlined in Lenin's blueprint for the totalitarian party met the demands of totalitarianism and made it feasible.

8.1.4 Characteristics of the Totalitarian Party: Personality Cult and Red Terror

Once established, totalitarian parties' own institutional genes are developed through mutation and evolution based on their inherited institutional genes, giving them a life of their own and the ability to adapt to their needs. One such gene is the personality cult surrounding the leader, which encompasses culture, ideology, and institutions and is driven by the self-interest of those who promote it.

The personality cult is not unique to totalitarian parties; it has its roots in the institutional genes of the Christian Church. For centuries, the Church has promoted personality cults centered around Jesus Christ and Christian saints as a fundamental aspect of its development. The Protestant challenge to the Catholic Church, for example, criticized its institutionalization of personality cults through practices like canonization.

In Russia, the cult of personality around the Tsar was one of the pillars of imperial rule, fostered by the Orthodox Church, which had been under the control of the Tsar for centuries. This influence was so deep that Tsar Nicholas II genuinely believed in his divinely granted powers and was revered by the Russian people. Consequently, he vehemently opposed constitutionalism and disregarded domestic crises, opting instead for reckless mobilization for war.

After seizing power, the Bolsheviks began creating a personality cult around their supreme leaders. This was driven partly by the need to suppress opposition and control the population and partly by the desire to consolidate power within the party and triumph in leadership struggles. The inherited institutional genes of the Russian Orthodox Church played a significant role in the Bolsheviks' ability to accomplish this.

Lenin, the founder of the first totalitarian political party, was known for his autocratic tendencies but relied on personal charisma, persuasive argumentation, and skillful agitation to suppress opposition and establish his own personality cult. While Lenin recognized the significance of a personality cult for maintaining his power, he also understood that those advocating for a religious-style personality cult were primarily motivated by their own pursuit of power. Consequently, when he had the authority to make important decisions, he imposed limitations on the development of religious-style personality cults within the party.

However, during a period of temporary incapacitation following an assassination attempt, the Bolsheviks began promoting an extensive religious-style personality cult around Lenin, disregarding his rejection of many of those practices upon his recovery (Sebestyen, 2017, pp. 419–420). This demonstrates that within a totalitarian regime, the cult of personality is often incentive-compatible with those seeking to consolidate power and control the party and the populace.

During Lenin's later years, the leadership of the RCP, with Stalin at the helm, began to cultivate a personality cult around the party leader, adopting techniques reminiscent of the practices employed by the Russian Orthodox Church in promoting the Tsar and canonizing saints. This cult of personality reached an unprecedented level during Stalin's rule, with the leader being elevated to a deified status, beyond question or criticism. The leader's words were transformed into doctrine, immune to contradiction. Dissent was systematically eliminated, as the leader stood above the system itself. The personality cult created the conditions for the leader to exercise total control over the party and, in turn, for the party to exert total control over society. Stalin's extreme personality cult, drawing upon the traditions of the Russian Orthodox Church, set a precedent for totalitarian parties worldwide.

On the third day after Lenin's assassination attempt, Grigory Zinoviev used language reminiscent of the Orthodox Church to praise Lenin, referring to him as the "Jesus Christ" of the Communist cause. Zinoviev portrayed Lenin as a divine gift to the Russian revolution and hailed him as "the greatest leader mankind has never had before" (Sebestyen, 2017, pp. 419–420).

After Lenin's death, the Central Committee of the Party, under Stalin's control, established an Immortalization Commission with the aim of preserving Lenin's body, thereby elevating the personality cult to its peak. Simultaneously, there was an effort to suppress Lenin's last testament, which potentially contained unfavorable remarks towards Stalin. Stalin, who had received Orthodox training, and Dzerzhinsky, a former Catholic priest, ardently advocated for the permanent preservation of Lenin's body, drawing comparisons to the veneration of religious saints. However, Trotsky opposed this practice, considering it a reflection of medieval religious worship.

Lenin's widow published an article in *Pravda* opposing the permanent preservation of his body and the growth of the personality cult. Instead, she called for the circulation of Lenin's last testament within the party. In response, she faced threats and suppression from Stalin's regime (Sebestyen, 2017, pp. 503–509).

At the 13th Congress of the RCP after Lenin's death, the primary slogans were: "Lenin's banner, Lenin's teachings, the direction guided by Lenin, the unity on the basis of Leninism." A significant event during this time was the organization of thousands of Youth Pioneers who pledged loyalty to Lenin and his cause at Lenin's tomb. Additionally, the city of Petrograd was renamed Leningrad in honor of Lenin.

During this period, Lenin was essentially canonized and Leninism became the orthodox doctrine and the foundation of legitimacy. Opposition to Lenin or anti-Leninism was considered the most severe crime, and Stalin's clique utilized accusations of anti-Leninism to defeat their opponents in power struggles, including figures like Trotsky, Bukharin, Zinoviev, and other opponents in power struggles (Gill, 2010, pp. 180–197).

Personality cults and ruthless purges are two integral aspects of any ruling totalitarian party. This pattern is primarily determined by the inherent mechanisms of a totalitarian party, with party leaders also playing certain personal roles. During Lenin's time, Trotskyists, despite being criticized as anti-Leninist, were still able to express their opinions. However, after Stalin came to power, he pushed the party to new extremes of totalitarianism, systematically eliminating communist dissidents and using terror to silence opposition within the party. The initial targets of Stalin's crackdown were veteran members of the party who refused to submit unconditionally. Faced with Stalin's repression, Lenin's old friends, such as Kamenev and Zinoviev, along with Trotsky, formed the United Opposition. They called for freedom of expression within the party, limitations on bureaucratism, and an end to the New Economic Policy (NEP). They also criticized Stalin's policy of promoting cooperation between the KMT and the CCP, arguing that it undermined the CCP.

Due to their significant influence among party members, workers, and the army, confronting these veteran party figures posed challenges. Stalin employed the Soviet secret police (the State Political Directorate, GPU) to conduct surveillance, create divisions, weaken their positions, and exert pressure on them. Eventually, the United Opposition was crushed, and its leading figures were expelled from the party. Trotsky was deported from the Soviet Union in 1929 and later assassinated by NKVD (People's Commissariat for Internal Affairs, predecessor of the KGB) agents at his home in Mexico in 1940 (Rubenstein, 2011). As a Soviet statesman, Trotsky enjoyed support and had numerous sympathizers and followers within the party and the global communist movement. However, during the Great Purge of the late 1930s, the vast majority of these individuals, whether they were Russians or Chinese operating in Russia or China, were almost invariably purged and a significant number of them were executed. The purge of Trotskyists in China lasted until the Cultural Revolution.

Totalitarian regimes have consistently relied on both terror and the personality cult of their revered leaders. Not only were counterrevolutionary movements brutally suppressed but dissenting comrades within the revolutionary ranks were also ruthlessly targeted. Invariably, where terror was present, a cult of personality would emerge. The personality cult surrounding Lenin, coupled with the established principles of Leninism, laid the groundwork for the further development of the personality cult within the Soviet Communist Party. With each wave of purges, the cult of personality grew stronger. In the late 1920s, during the purge of Trotsky, an extensive campaign was launched to promote the personality cult of Stalin. Stalin was depicted as the sole successor to Lenin, embodying the principles of Leninism and representing the will of the proletariat. Opposing Stalin was equated with opposing Lenin and the party itself. As an example of this cult, the city of Tsaritsyn, where Stalin had played a significant role during the Russian Civil War (1917–1922), was renamed Stalingrad in his honor, although he feigned ignorance about the decision.[4] Stalin's personality cult reached a fever pitch at the 16th and 17th congresses of the party, with delegates to the 17th Congress chanting "Long Live Comrade Stalin!" and singing songs praying for him to enjoy a long life (Gill, 2010, pp. 242–246).

Trotsky concluded that the bloodshed of the Stalinist era distinguished Stalin from Lenin. Stalinism was established on the foundation of the Great Purge, a sweeping campaign against virtually all the veterans of the party. The catalyst for the Great Purge was the so-called Sergei Kirov affair. On December 1, 1934, Sergei Kirov, a member of the Politburo and first secretary of the party's Leningrad Regional Committee, was assassinated. A few months earlier, at the Central Committee elections, Kirov had shown significantly higher standing within the party than Stalin. Both Khrushchev (Khrushchev, 2005, vol. 1, p. 60) and many historians suspected that Stalin orchestrated Kirov's assassination, though direct evidence remains elusive to this day. Stalin promptly attributed the murder to the Trotsky-led opposition and arrested most of the party's veterans.

Seizing the opportunity, Stalin swiftly eliminated his main rivals within the party. In the three Moscow Trials held between 1936 and 1938, prominent figures who had been close to Lenin and veterans of the party, including Zinoviev, Kamenev, Bukharin, and others, were subjected to torture to extract public confessions before being executed. The scale of the purge was immense, with 78 percent of Central Committee members being arrested and executed and 56 percent of the delegates who participated in the 1934 Central Committee elections facing charges of counterrevolution. By 1934, 81 percent of the party's elite had joined the party before 1921 but, after the Great Purge, this figure dropped to 19 percent by 1939.

The Great Purge extended beyond the political sphere to the military. More senior officers of the Red Army were executed during this period than were killed in the Second World War. Among the five marshals of the Red Army, three were executed and a majority of senior and middle-ranking officers also faced the same fate. According to the KGB archives, by the end of the 1930s, over 3.59 million people had been arrested by the NKVD and approximately 1.36 million of them were held in concentration camps. Throughout the 1930s, it is estimated that between 10 and 11 million people were executed or died due to starvation as a result of the purge (Suny, 2010, pp. 282–289).

During the late 1930s, alongside the height of terror, the cult of personality surrounding Stalin reached its peak. He was depicted as not only the successor to Lenin but as someone who had surpassed him. Anastas Mikoyan famously proclaimed, "Lenin was a gifted man, but Stalin is a genius." The party press and party congresses propagated the image of Stalin as the greatest leader, teacher, genius, and thinker in human development, even going as far as referring to him as the "golden sun" that "illuminated the entire world" (Gill, 2010, pp. 291–293). Many of these practices and expressions were later adopted by Chinese communist leaders, who had been trained in Russia, to create a personality cult around Mao during China's Cultural Revolution three decades later.

The key to creating a personality cult is to manufacture miracles and to deify the leader. This was achieved by creating mythology as well as by revising and fabricating the histories of the October Revolution and the RCP. Unlike the miracles of Christian saints, which were compiled and adjudicated posthumously, the "miracles" of the RCP and Stalin were all personally orchestrated by Stalin himself. *The History of the Communist Party of the Soviet Union (Bolsheviks): Short Course* written under Stalin's direction was published in 1938 (Stalin, 1975). This work, considered as the most significant text disseminated by the Soviet Communist Party and the Comintern, was dubbed the "Communist Bible." The book set a precedent for the construction of totalitarian parties, instructing them on how to create a cult of personality by manufacturing terror and miracles, thereby controlling both the party and society.

Mao and his followers closely studied and learned from Stalin in these practices. Mao personally directed that Stalin's *Short Course* should be the central textbook during the Yan'an Rectification Campaign (Chapter 10). He stated: "it is the best synthesis and summary of the worldwide communist movement in the past hundred years; a model of the integration of theory and practice, and so far the only comprehensive model in the whole world" (Mao, 1965).

The essence of totalitarianism lies within the unique nature of the totalitarian party. This type of party is designed to establish and maintain a dictatorship, whether it is called the dictatorship of the proletariat or the people's democratic dictatorship. Its organizational structure follows a strict top-down dictatorial system, where subordinates unquestioningly submit to their superiors, the entire party submits to its central committee, and the central committee submits to the party leader without question. Any dissent or disagreement, even among senior party leaders, is met with severe punishment or even elimination, as seen with figures like Trotsky, Bukharin, Liu Shaoqi, Peng Dehuai, Hu Yaobang, and Zhao Ziyang, to be discussed in Chapters 12 and 13.

The totalitarian party serves as the core for seizing and holding onto power, as well as the creator, disseminator, and regulator of ideology. During the revolutionary period in Russia, when the first totalitarian party was formed, Leninism argued for the necessity of such a party to achieve victory in the revolution. Many of the founding revolutionary figures had strong religious undertones and were willing to sacrifice themselves as martyrs in pursuit of their utopian ideals. Those who embraced Leninism willingly gave up their personal freedoms and unconditionally submitted to the party, its superiors, and its leader. It was through their sacrifice of personal freedom that the institutional genes of the totalitarian party were established. Once these institutional genes took root, the powers of dictatorship, privilege, and propaganda became the mechanisms driving the party's development and expansion, rendering voluntary martyrdom unnecessary.

Not all societies have the capacity to produce totalitarian parties and even in those that do, they may not thrive or exert significant influence. The emergence, growth, and development of a totalitarian party in any society, as well as its ability to influence that society, depend on the existing institutional genes present in that society. In the case of Russia, the institutional genes embedded in the ruling Tsarist imperial system, Russian Orthodoxy, and the traditions of secret societies laid the foundation for the creation of a totalitarian party.

Specifically, through the analysis of historical narratives, we have observed the evolution of the Russian Marxist movement and the Labor Emancipation League (later known as the Russian Social Democratic Labor Party, the RSDLP), which originated from the Land and Liberty organization. Furthermore, we have seen how the Bolsheviks emerged from the RSDLP, heavily influenced by the People's Will party. Conversely, when applying the same line of reasoning, one can understand why Leninism had relatively few followers in countries such as Britain, the United States, Germany, and France.

8.2 INSTITUTIONAL CONDITIONS FOR THE SEIZURE OF POWER BY THE TOTALITARIAN PARTY

The collapse of the Tsarist imperial system and the subsequent power vacuum in Russia created opportunities for the Bolsheviks to seize power and establish a communist totalitarian regime. If the preliminary constitutional system established in 1905 had functioned steadily for several decades, the institutional factors that favored totalitarianism could have been significantly weakened, allowing Russia to potentially transition towards constitutionalism. However, the strong resistance to constitutionalism embedded in the institutional genes of Tsarism prevented this development. Indeed, these institutional genes continued to influence Russia long after the imperial system ended.

8.2.1 A Provisional Government with No Constitutional Foundation

An important historical fact to note is that not only the pro-Tsarist conservative forces but also all the Russian left-wing parties resisted constitutional reform. With the exception of Trotsky, the leader of the Mensheviks who played a critical role in organizing strikes and establishing Soviets that disrupted the functioning of the constitutional parliament, most of the leaders of the Russian left-wing parties, including the Bolsheviks, Mensheviks, and the left-wing of the SR, were abroad when the constitutional revolution broke out in 1905. Furthermore, they boycotted the first Duma election and resisted the newly established constitutional rule. Even when they later participated in the Duma elections, their primary objective was to use the Duma as a platform to fight against constitutional rule and they had limited seats and minimal impact on society and the Duma. The influence of the Bolsheviks was particularly weak during this time, as their leaders were either exiled abroad or to Siberia. They even did not have much influence in the Soviets, which were organized by the Mensheviks.

Since the third Duma in 1907, each subsequent Duma managed to complete a term of five years. Russia's constitutional monarchy appeared to be on track and the economy experienced rapid growth. Many historians and politicians of the time believed that if Russia had continued along that path peacefully for about a decade, the Russian constitutional monarchy might have succeeded. One prominent figure of that era, Prime Minister Pyotr Stolypin, was assassinated by an anti-Tsarist terrorist group in 1911. Before his death, he left a testament stating that given twenty years, Russia would catch up with the developed countries of Western Europe. He further advised the Tsar to allow Russia a chance for peaceful transformation and to avoid starting a war (McMeekin, 2017).

However, due to the absence of a counterbalancing power in the Tsarist imperial system, the Tsar had both the motivation and the ability to obstruct constitutional rule, which was intended to limit his power. This set the stage for significant historical events to unfold. In 1907, the Tsar made changes to the electoral law, resulting in the loss of the representativeness of the Duma, as it became more symbolic of the right-wing and center-right social elites. Despite this compromised situation, if the Constitutional Democratic Party, the Octobrists, and the Zemstvo Congress had been able to find common ground with the Tsar's representatives on important social issues and reforms, an imperfect constitutional system could have gradually evolved and improved. Even relatively weak checks and balances could have helped prevent many of the major mistakes made by the Tsarist government.

The deeper problem lies in the fact that checks and balances and constitutional reforms are never achieved through a dictator's rational reasoning or benevolence. They can only be achieved through substantial forces within society that are capable of checking and balancing power for their own interests. Rulers, driven by self-interest, will always resist any attempts to restrain or limit their power, as it is seen as a matter of life and death for the dictator and his followers.

The establishment of the world's first constitutional monarchy, such as the one achieved through the Magna Carta, required four centuries of negotiations and the gradual erosion of the monarch's power, along with the emergence of institutional genes conducive to constitutionalism. Even with such solid social foundations, the success of the Glorious Revolution was ultimately achieved by forcing King James II, who refused compromise, into exile, allowing for the creation of a new king who could accept a constitutional settlement.

In the case of the Tsarist imperial system in Russia, the absence of countervailing forces and the preservation of the Tsar's unconstrained power prevented the development of checks and balances and the possibility of a constitutional settlement. The main body of the Constitutional Democrats and the Octobrists consisted of intellectuals, lacking significant social influence. Additionally, the newly formed Zemstvo Congress had not developed substantial power and the Tsarist government intended to keep it that way. Without a countervailing force, the Tsar had no need to compromise with any party or coalition in the Duma. Since the promulgation of the October Manifesto and Fundamental Laws, the Tsar consistently undermined the role of the Duma as a check on power, including dissolving it and placing various obstacles in its path. As the Tsar repeatedly emphasized, he had the right to convene and dissolve the Duma. The institutional genes of the Tsarist system supported the Tsar's resistance to any attempts to limit his power, ultimately extinguishing the chance for the monarchy to survive and evolve in Russia.

Several tsars, particularly Catherine the Great, held a deep admiration for French traditions. However, the institutional genes in France proved to be detrimental to constitutional reform. The opposition to constitutional rule from both radical revolutionaries and King Louis XVI ignited a turbulent revolution. Under the strain of an entrenched absolute monarchy, the revolution eventually culminated in Napoleon's coup d'état, which restored the monarchy.

In comparison to France, the institutional genes of Tsarist Russia presented an even greater obstacle to constitutional reform. Tsar Nicholas II firmly believed in the concept of the divine autocrat, considering himself immune to any form of restriction. In the absence of compelling countervailing forces, Nicholas remained unconvinced about accepting constraints from a parliament that held no real power. He regretted signing the October Manifesto, a preliminary constitution drafted by his prime minister, Sergei Witte. He also regretted establishing the Duma, which he had initially intended as a temporary measure.

Nevertheless, at the dawn of the twentieth century, when almost all states in Western Europe were under constitutional rule, Russia's political elite widely believed that the prevailing trend in Europe was towards constitutionalism. In order to avoid a republic, it was in their vested interest to preserve the monarchy in any feasible form. Even staunch royalists advocated for a constitutional monarchy as the best means of ensuring the monarchy's survival. However, the subsequent implementation of the constitution rendered the Duma ineffective in terms of both checks and balances and policy formulation. Essentially, Tsarist Russia failed to transition into a constitutional monarchy. Nicholas II retained his extensive power but became increasingly isolated, assuming the role of a solitary figure. His isolation, coupled with the rising tide of nationalism, led him to make a series of fatal misguided decisions.

Eager to enhance Russia's prestige in the Balkans as the pan-Slavic savior, Nicholas acted contrary to the advice in Stolypin's will, initiating national war mobilization. This decision significantly contributed to the outbreak of the Great War and Russia's full-fledged involvement in the conflict. Voluntarily joining the war exacerbated the empire's existing challenges, pushing it further into a comprehensive sociopolitical-economic crisis. The Tsar's series of "mistakes" ultimately sealed the fate of the Tsarist regime, paving the way for the Bolsheviks to seize power, much to the regret of historians.[5]

At the onset of the Great War, nationalism surged within Russia, with the Duma and the public overwhelmingly supporting the war mobilization. The anti-war sentiment propagated by Lenin's Bolsheviks was not only insignificant but was also vehemently opposed by nearly all left-wing parties. With public opinion and the Tsar aligning closely on the war issue, the Tsar could have used this chance to leverage the Duma as a conduit between the Tsarist government and society, aiding national mobilization and social stabilization. However, the Tsar misinterpreted the public's support for the war as proof of the Tsar's greatness and the grandeur of the empire,

8.2 INSTITUTIONAL CONDITIONS FOR THE SEIZURE OF POWER 341

which further spurred him to reject the involvement of the Duma and the public in major imperial decisions.

Subsequently, as the war situation deteriorated, the country faced severe problems with food, fuel, and so on. Using the war as a pretext, the Tsar poured all national resources into the conflict, plunging an already fraught society into crisis. Society quickly became unstable. Under these circumstances, the Tsar ignored the advice of his most loyal nobles and even disregarded a secret police report at the end of 1916, which revealed widespread public hatred for the government.

As the possibility of urban riots loomed and the Tsar failed to respond to a situation on the brink of chaos, all social elites and factions, regardless of political affiliation, blamed the Tsar and his government for the problems.

With the Tsar's inaction in response to the chaotic situation caused by potential urban riots, all social elites and factions began to view the Tsar and his government as the root of the problems. Fearing the outbreak of a revolution and the loss of public support, even the conservative Constitutional Democratic Party, which held dominant force within the Duma and traditionally emphasized law and order, adopted a radical policy. They directly engaged with the masses and promoted general elections. Moreover, they publicly accused the incumbent prime minister, Boris Stürmer, of treason, despite lacking evidence. Supported by the Tsar, Stürmer remained unfazed and threatened to dissolve the Duma, the source of these groundless allegations.

However, recognizing the gravity of the crisis facing Russian society and the significance of the Duma, the United Nobility, a right-wing group that had long been a staunch supporter of the Tsar, publicly endorsed the Duma's proposal to dismiss Stürmer and reorganize the government. The United Nobility had been one of the key pillars in the defense of Tsarist autocracy since the establishment of the constitution in 1905. Their stance compelled the Tsar to sacrifice Stürmer, who was innocent, and accept the Duma's demand for a cabinet reshuffling. As a result, the Tsar lost support from all parties (Pipes, 1991, pp. 250–258).

Calls for the Tsar's abdication grew louder. The left wing insisted that the Tsar must be overthrown and the Tsarist system must be dismantled before socialism could be established. Amidst the crises, loyal royalists, the upper echelons of the Tsarist bureaucracy, and right-wing forces all were particularly averse to the Tsar's continued reliance on Orthodox priest Grigori Rasputin. They believed that both the Tsar and the Empress had fallen under his wicked influence. Therefore, they concluded that the only way to save the monarchy was to force Nicholas to abdicate. They began plotting a palace coup at the end of 1916, planning to force Nicholas II to abdicate and transfer power to his brother, Grand Duke Michael Alexandrovich. The plot was well organized; the only issue was finding the right time to execute it.

Arguably, the workers' organizations in Petrograd and Moscow were the primary driving force that directly triggered the collapse of the Russian Empire. One key organization, the Petrograd Central Workers' Group (predecessor of the Petrograd Soviet),[6] was established in 1915 by the Mensheviks. This civilian organization played a crucial role in maintaining social order in Petrograd and emerged as a rival to the Duma at the time. While initially holding a nationalistic stance and supporting the government and military during the Great War, it also advocated for the immediate abolition of the monarchy and the establishment of a democratic interim government.

In January 1917, the Petrograd Central Workers' Group announced a plan to mobilize thousands of workers for a general strike during the Duma congress scheduled for February 1917. Their intention was to hold demonstrations in front of the venue of the Duma congress to advance their demands. However, the day after the announcement was published, all leaders of this group were arrested by the secret police. Simultaneously, the Tsar ordered the dissolution of the Duma, declaring that new Duma elections would be held in December 1917.

Despite the cancellation of the general strike on February 14 due to government pressure, 90,000 people spontaneously staged a peaceful demonstration on that day (Pipes, 1991, pp. 259–271). A few days later, on International Women's Day (February 23 in the old Russian calendar), even more Petrograd workers took to the streets to protest for bread and fuel. What began as a peaceful demonstration soon turned into anti-war and anti-autocratic protests that quickly escalated. On February 24, the number of protestors reached 200,000, with demands for the Tsar's abdication. Almost all factories were closed the next day (Curtiss, 1957, pp. 1, 30). Nicholas issued a telegraph order demanding that the army firmly suppress the protestors. After dozens of demonstrators were shot and killed by the army on February 26, a mass mutiny occurred the next day. The rebelling soldiers joined the demonstrations, along with workers and citizens, attacking armories and seizing a large amount of ammunition. This left the Tsarist government in the capital with no military power and a complete loss of control (Figes, 2017, pp. 307–323).

As the bulk of the forces loyal to the Tsar were on the front lines of the Great War, the mutinies in Petrograd and Moscow meant that the situation there was completely uncontrollable. Under these circumstances, despite the Tsar's order dissolving the Duma just a few days prior, the Duma convened on February 27, establishing the Provisional Committee of the State Duma. The Committee announced the establishment of the Provisional Government, whose members were predominantly center-leftists. The most important cabinet members included the leader of the Constitutional Democratic Party, Pavel Milyukov, the leader of the October Party, Alexander Guchkov, and an SR member, Alexander Kerensky. The prime minister was Prince Geogii Lvov, president of the Zemgor, a union of zemstvos and municipal councils (a zemstvo was an elected local government institution established by Alexander II).

A few days after the establishment of the Provisional Government, the Tsar, left with no other options, appointed Lvov as prime minister. At this point, the monarchists began to execute the long-planned "palace coup" and under their pressure, the Tsar announced his abdication, giving way to his brother, Grand Duke Mikhail. However, recognizing that the legitimacy of succession to the throne could be challenged, the Grand Duke decided to renounce the throne. He stated that he would only accept the throne under conditions where an elected Constituent Assembly deemed him monarch (Browder and Kerensky, 1961, vol. 1, p. 116). He urged the Russian people to obey the leadership of the Provisional Government, reiterating that he might consider becoming a constitutional monarch if a Constituent Assembly decided on a constitutional monarchy (Pipes, 1991, pp. 319–320). From then on, executive power was transferred to the Provisional Government. This major event in Russian history is known as the February Revolution (modeled after the Glorious Revolution in England). However, the opposition of most left-wing parties and their Soviets, which dominated the streets and social order, made it impossible for the Provisional Government to establish a constitutional order. Most notably, the Bolsheviks and other left-wing parties aimed to overthrow the Provisional Government through armed means.

The Provisional Government, being a temporary organization, lacked full legitimacy and control over the cities, countryside, and even the army. In reality, the Soviets exerted control over the cities and some segments of the military. Consequently, the Provisional Government was eager to negotiate with the Soviets in order to stabilize the situation. The interests of the Soviets and those represented by the Provisional Government were starkly different. Moreover, dominated by the SR and the Mensheviks, the Soviets were opposed to many basic constitutional principles, such as private property rights. However, they reached a consensus to quickly convene a Constituent Assembly and hold a nationwide general election to elect the political leaders and legislators representing the voters and to decide Russia's political system.

However, to prevent any progress towards constitutionalism before the Constituent Assembly could be convened, the Bolsheviks urgently launched an armed coup in the name of the Soviets, that is, the October Revolution. This further led to the outlawing of all other parties and organizations. As a result, the century-long effort towards constitutionalism in Russia was completely reversed. The Tsarist system, which was based on autocracy, transformed into a totalitarian system based on the dictatorship of the proletariat. The core of this modern system is the communist totalitarian party.

8.2.2 Seizing Power in the Name of the Soviets

Only by seizing power could the Bolsheviks establish a totalitarian system with total control over all aspects of ideology, politics, the economy, and society, and could turn themselves into a true totalitarian party. Otherwise, they would have remained only a secret political organization of totalitarian ideology. Since the establishment of the Bolsheviks, Lenin's objective was to establish one-party rule through an armed coup. Constitutionalism was always his biggest enemy throughout, by definition and by practice. During the Great War, he urged the proletarian parties in the belligerent countries to oppose their governments and seize power, turning the Great War into civil wars in those countries. His position was in direct conflict with the nationalism that prevailed during the war and he was isolated from the international communist movement because of this. However, he was always looking for opportunities to seize power through armed force.

The sudden outbreak of the February Revolution opened Lenin's eyes to the arrival of a major opportunity. Lenin had been in Zurich since the start of the Great War and was not very familiar with developments in Russian society. He misjudged almost all the major international and domestic events that took place during the war (Sebestyen, 2017). Thus, the sudden collapse of the Tsarist government, the sudden rise to power of the Provisional Government, and the latter's announcement of convening a national Constituent Assembly were all shocks to Lenin. Trotsky once described the then Lenin as a cornered beast, eager to return to Russia and seize power.

Largely unaware of Russia's internal situation, Lenin sent a telegram to the Petrograd Bolsheviks on March 19, 1917, demanding that the Bolsheviks must not trust the Provisional Government, especially not Kerensky. He demanded the arming of the proletariat, the immediate election of the Petrograd Duma (surprisingly, even then, he still did not realize that the Soviets could be a tool to be used), and never to cooperate with any other party. But after a long exile, Lenin's leadership within the Bolsheviks was precarious. His urgent instructions from abroad had no effect on the Bolsheviks at home.

Before Lenin issued his directives, the Petrograd Committee of the Bolshevik Party (the largest committee) had already decided to cooperate with the SR and the Mensheviks in support of a Russian victory in the Great War. Stalin played a key role in this. Upon receiving Lenin's telegram, the Petrograd Committee ignored it and instead announced an intention to merge with the Mensheviks to seize power. Subsequently, the All-Russian Bolshevik Congress, held in Petrograd, approved Stalin's motion to unite with other progressive forces (i.e., the Mensheviks and the SR), control the Provisional Government, and prepare to seize power (Pipes, 1991, pp. 386–389).

From its inception, the Provisional Government found allies in Britain, France, and America, who viewed it as an institution of constitutional democracy and promptly recognized and supported it. Conversely, the German government suspected that the Provisional Government was the result of a coup orchestrated by British agents in Russia. Seeking to destabilize Russia, the German government saw value in Lenin's opposition to the Russian government and the potentially disruptive role that the Bolsheviks could play from within. They entered into a secret agreement with Lenin, offering substantial financial support to him and the Bolsheviks, with the condition that they would destabilize the Provisional Government and hinder its mobilization for war. A special train was arranged to secretly transport Lenin and several dozen revolutionary cadres back to Russia (Pipes, 1991, pp. 390–392). According to German archives, the German government provided Lenin with a total of 50 million gold marks, equivalent to over 1 billion US dollars today (McMeekin, 2017, p. 134).

On the last day of the All-Russian Bolshevik Congress, Lenin arrived in Petrograd and immediately gave a speech against the war and called for a revolution to seize power. He advocated for the overthrow of the bourgeois Provisional Government, transferring all power to the Soviets, an immediate ceasefire, the launch of a socialist revolution, nationalization of land, and more. But the party resisted these calls, which Lenin then released as his *April Theses*. The newly established Central Committee of the Bolshevik Party immediately passed a resolution opposing Lenin's *April Theses*. The party newspaper, *Pravda*, initially refused to publish the *April Theses* and when it had to yield under pressure from Lenin, it included an editorial comment stating that the *April Theses* were unrelated to the party's stance. Yet, a German spy promptly reported to Berlin that "Lenin has successfully entered Russia. He is working exactly as we hoped" (Pipes, 1991, p. 394).

Although the Provisional Government had assumed control of Russia, the country remained a constitutional monarchy in name only. Without a national parliamentary election and parliamentary approval for the reorganization of the government, there was neither a legitimate monarch nor a legitimate government. In contrast, the Soviets, the largest civil organizations in Russian cities, held real power. The public, which had previously challenged the Tsarist regime, now had the ability to equally challenge the Provisional Government. The directives of the Provisional Government could only be effectively implemented with the assistance of the Soviets among the workers, soldiers, and citizens. This led to de facto joint rule by the Provisional Government and the Soviets. However, at that time, there was no all-Russian Soviet. The only group that realistically had the ability to influence the national situation was the Executive Committee of the Petrograd Soviet (Ispolkom), which represented the capital's million workers and soldiers.

When the establishment of the Provisional Government was being deliberated in the Duma, Kerensky, leader of the SR, proposed liaison with the Petrograd Soviet to secure practical control over society. His proposal was rejected by other Duma members, leaving the Provisional Government without formal communication channels with the protesters and the Soviets. Nonetheless, a few days after the establishment of the Provisional Government, every city in the country followed the example of the Petrograd Soviet and established their own Soviets. These local Soviets explicitly demanded that the directives issued by the Provisional Government meet the Soviets' demands, otherwise they would resist. Importantly, the defected soldiers and lower-level officers also organized or joined the Soviets. The main body of the Ispolkom, the Petrograd Soviet Executive Committee, was composed of Mensheviks and SR members. The only one capable of bridging the gap between the Provisional Government and the Soviets was Kerensky, the leader of the SR Party, who soon became the prime minister of the Provisional Government (Pipes, 1991, pp. 286–307).

Given the influence of the Soviets in Russian society, whoever controlled the Soviets controlled Russian society. At that time, the Soviets were primarily led by the SR and the Mensheviks. The first All-Russian Soviet Congress was convened in Petrograd in June. The SR was the largest party in the Soviet and had 285 representatives; the Mensheviks had 245 representatives; and the Bolsheviks had only 105 representatives (Riasanovsky and Steinberg, 2011, p. 468).

The primary reason the Bolsheviks lagged behind other left-wing parties in the Soviet was their revolutionary elite ideology. Their approach centered around the elite seizing ruling power, imposing the dictatorship of the proletariat on the population. Lenin's strategy, as outlined in his *April Theses*, aimed to incite the public and create chaos as a means to create favorable conditions for seizing power. However, this approach faced resistance from the leadership of other radical left-wing parties, including the Socialist Revolutionaries and the Mensheviks. Lenin's ideas held little appeal among intellectuals and the Soviet leadership, positioning him on the losing side in terms of inciting a revolution.

Nevertheless, the radical revolution that Lenin advocated for had a strong allure for the masses of workers, soldiers, and peasants. Also, the Bolsheviks were greatly aided by secret funding from the German government, which facilitated their ability to produce and distribute propaganda materials.[7] In July alone, the Bolsheviks printed 320,000 newspaper publications and 350,000 pamphlets, with a significant portion specifically targeting military personnel (Pipes, 1991, p. 410). This military-focused propaganda played a crucial role in laying the groundwork for future mutinies. By controlling the propaganda narrative and actively inciting the masses, Lenin not only successfully influenced the population but also regained the leadership of the Bolsheviks.

The propaganda war led and orchestrated by Lenin had the explicit goal of inciting widespread violence and chaos. It focused on fueling class hatred and revolutionary fervor, employing grandiose promises without providing concrete actions or specific guidance. The Bolsheviks carefully crafted their radical propaganda agitations and slogans, deliberately borrowing popular slogans from the Constitutional Revolution of 1905 and the February Revolution of 1917, such as "fight for freedom," "fight for democracy," "fight for land," and more. These slogans had already been ingrained in the masses by the radical left-wing parties, particularly the influential SR Party, and proved highly effective in propaganda and agitation. As a result, the Bolsheviks rapidly gained popularity among the masses.

Furthermore, during the war, especially after the establishment of the Provisional Government, most left-wing parties shifted towards nationalism, prioritizing the fight for national interests over revolution, making them indistinguishable from the Provisional Government, at least in terms of the war efforts. This left the Bolsheviks as the sole party advocating for revolution during wartime. In a period marked by growing war weariness and social instability, this granted the Bolsheviks a distinct advantage. On the one hand, they continued to employ the familiar slogans of democracy, freedom, land, and socialism to stir up basic emotions among the masses. On the other hand, they introduced new slogans criticizing the war and the Provisional Government, calling for "All Power to the Soviets," directly inciting the masses to initiate "spontaneous" revolutions and fueling social chaos.

Bolshevik propaganda and agitation had a widespread and significant impact on soldiers and workers. They successfully incited several large-scale "spontaneous" demonstrations against the Provisional Government in cities like Petrograd and Moscow, which involved armed conflicts and resulted in significant bloodshed. Witnessing the bloody demonstrations instigated by the Bolsheviks, Lenin's old friend Maxim Gorky expressed concern, stating: "Lenin will soon lead us all into civil war. He is a completely isolated man. But he is very popular among the uneducated workers and some soldiers" (Figes, 2017, p. 404). Gorky's concerns became a reality within a few weeks.

As Russian society descended into chaos under the Provisional Government, the French government intercepted and deciphered some of Lenin's secret telegrams to the German government, which it shared with the Provisional Government. Independently, the Provisional Government also gathered intelligence revealing that Lenin was receiving ongoing funding from the German government and that the Bolsheviks had infiltrated parts of the military. In response, the Provisional Government issued orders for the arrest and prosecution of Bolshevik leaders on charges of treason. It also disbanded the First Machine Gun Regiment, which had fallen under Bolshevik control. Learning of these developments, most Bolshevik leaders, including Lenin, fled to Finland.

Meanwhile, Trotsky, who was then leading the Mensheviks, swiftly established a Provisional Revolutionary Committee on behalf of the Bolsheviks and secretly convened meetings with the leaders of the Machine Gun Regiment. Additional units joined their mutiny plan. On July 3, 1917, a large-scale mutiny erupted in Petrograd, with thousands of soldiers and workers taking to the streets. Numerous witnesses documented the brutal acts committed by the armed mob during the unrest. The following day, in the face of the armed masses, Trotsky declared, "The representatives of the workers' and soldiers' Soviets have already seized power." Under these circumstances, Lenin secretly returned to Russia, preparing for the next step in his takeover (McMeekin, 2017, pp. 166–172).

When the armed coup seemed to be successful, the Provisional Government publicized evidence of Lenin's collusion with Germany. It called back troops from the front lines to suppress the mutiny, citing the need to combat treason. In response, Lenin fled abroad once again and hundreds of Bolshevik leaders were arrested. This marked the failure of the first armed coup staged by the Bolsheviks, known in history as the July Days. Some historians speculate that if the Provisional Government had continued to prosecute and try the Bolsheviks for treason, they might have been completely eradicated.

However, the subsequent Kornilov Affair introduced a dramatic twist to the historical narrative. Duke Lvov resigned as prime minister of the Provisional Government shortly after the July Days. Kerensky, the leader of the SR Party, took over as prime minister. He appointed General Lavr Kornilov, a former Tsarist general, as the Commander-in-Chief of the Provisional Government's armed forces. However, Kerensky soon became suspicious of Kornilov's intentions and believed that he aimed to become a military dictator. Coincidentally, based on false intelligence, Kornilov mobilized troops towards Petrograd at the end of August, under the belief that a Bolshevik uprising was imminent. When the troops discovered the misinformation and did not enter the city, Kerensky accused Kornilov of rebellion and had him dismissed and imprisoned.

The Mensheviks and other left-wing parties used the Kornilov rebellion as a pretext to pass a motion in the Duma, calling for the creation of a "Committee for the People's Struggle Against Counterrevolution." In alliance with the Bolsheviks, they proposed arming the masses. Seeing Kornilov as their most significant threat,

Kerensky reversed the charges against the Bolsheviks, issuing a pardon to all who had been arrested following the July Days coup (McMeekin, 2017, pp. 182–191).

As a result of the Kornilov Affair, the Provisional Government lost the trust of the army and of its ability to mobilize troops effectively. This created a crucial condition for the success of the next Bolshevik coup. In the aftermath of the July Days, generals with Tsarist military backgrounds became increasingly concerned about the possibility of a Bolshevik mutiny. To prevent such a mutiny, they initiated a widespread purge of the Bolsheviks within the military. However, this cleansing process faced significant challenges due to the deep infiltration by various extreme leftist factions, beyond just the Bolsheviks, into the military over an extended period.

Unexpectedly, Kerensky abruptly reversed the charges against the Bolsheviks, thereby assisting them in regaining strength and accelerating their infiltration into the military. In military units like the Fifth Army, the Bolsheviks had already gained control over communication and command departments at the military level. By the time the German army was approaching Petrograd, the Bolsheviks had virtually completed their infiltration of the military in the Baltic region. German spies monitoring the Russian military forces excitedly reported back to Berlin that the Russian army in that region was entirely pro-German (McMeekin, 2017, pp. 193–196).

What Kerensky did was not a random mistake but rather driven by his SR stance, which regarded the Bolsheviks as their revolutionary comrades while viewing Tsarist generals like General Kornilov as untrustworthy. Therefore, the Kornilov Affair was a reflection of overall Russian society at that time, with the socialist parties exerting overwhelming influence in the Provisional Government and society. In line with this perspective, in September Kerensky released not only Trotsky but also other Bolsheviks and disbanded the intelligence agency investigating Bolshevik treason. Additionally, on September 12, the Petrograd Soviet Executive Committee issued a resolution demanding protection for Lenin and Zinoviev.

At this critical moment, the Provisional Government's Counterintelligence Department discovered significant new evidence of a planned Bolshevik mutiny. However, considering the Bolsheviks as the only force he could rely on, Kerensky disbanded the Department and authorized the re-arming of the Bolsheviks, who acquired over 40,000 firearms from the arsenal (McMeekin, 2017, pp. 197–198). The Kornilov Affair not only enabled the Bolsheviks to further infiltrate and control the military but also broadly enhanced the Bolsheviks' prestige, helping them to gain control of the Soviets in some cities. On September 19, the Bolsheviks obtained a majority of seats for the first time in the Moscow Soviet. On September 25, they gained a majority in the Ispolkom in Petrograd, and Trotsky, now Bolshevik leader, was elected chairman. The Bolshevik Military Organization also claimed to be authorized by the Petrograd Soviet Military Committee (Milrevkom). In the past, when the Soviets were controlled by the Mensheviks, calls for revolution were only abstract. With Trotsky as the Chairman of the Ispolkom representing the Bolsheviks, they could take concrete actions and promote the slogan "All Power to the Soviets" to prepare for the Bolsheviks to seize power. On October 3, during the Ispolkom meeting, Trotsky proposed the arrest of not only Kornilov's supporters but also of members of the Provisional Government (McMeekin, 2017, pp. 199–202).

On September 1, Kerensky and the Minister of Justice jointly declared that Russia's political system would be a republic and the state would be called the Russian Republic. However, the State Duma Committee and the Petrograd Soviet had previously stipulated that the Provisional Government could not unilaterally decide the political system of Russia before the convening of the Constituent Assembly. Under this constraint, the Provisional Government announced that the formal confirmation of changing Russia to a republic would be left to the decision of the Constituent Assembly in November (Browder and Kerensky, 1961, pp. 1657–1658).

This announcement sparked a strong reaction from Lenin, who was in exile in Finland at the time. He wrote to the Bolshevik Central

Committee, stating that waiting for the Constituent Assembly would be detrimental to the Bolsheviks. He argued that the recent Bolshevik victories in the Petrograd and Moscow Soviets indicated that an uprising in the cities could succeed immediately. Lenin emphasized the urgency, stating: "We must not be deceived by the voting numbers; elections do not prove anything ... If we cannot seize political power now, history will not forgive us" (Figes, 2017, p. 469).

Soon after he had secretly returned to Russia, Lenin declared that "the decisive moment is fast approaching" and urged for an immediate armed uprising during a meeting of the Bolshevik Central Committee on October 10. During the same meeting, Kamenev and Zinoviev expressed concerns that an uprising before the all-Russian Constituent Assembly election, scheduled for November by the Duma and the Provisional Government, would harm the popularity of the Bolsheviks. Lenin countered their objections by arguing that as long as the peasants had the right to vote, the Bolsheviks could never win national elections, thus necessitating the immediate seizure of power. Faced with the practical challenge of insufficient strength and a limited popular base, Trotsky proposed using the Soviets as a façade to gain popular support, while actual power would be monopolized by the Bolsheviks. Eventually, the Bolshevik Central Committee approved Trotsky's concrete plan: on October 25, during the Second All-Russian Congress of Soviets, an uprising would be launched under the slogan "All Power to the Soviets," with the aim of seizing power from the Provisional Government and establishing a Bolshevik regime under the guise of the Soviets (McMeekin, 2017, p. 203).

The armed uprising of the Bolsheviks commenced on the morning of October 25. By noon on that day, Kerensky, aided by the US embassy, fled Petrograd, hoping to replicate the events of July by amassing heavy troops and easily suppressing the Bolsheviks upon his return. However, his recent arrest of Kornilov and other generals had shattered their trust, leading to a complete loss of support. The inability to mobilize the army paralyzed the Provisional Government, rendering its efforts to quell the rebellion utterly futile.

The unpreparedness of the Provisional Government, coupled with its inability to deploy troops to Petrograd, facilitated the swift capture of the city. During the evening assault on the Winter Palace, the cruiser Aurora fired only blanks, resulting in minimal casualties. The overall casualties during the entire uprising numbered fewer than ten, fewer even than those incurred during the subsequent filming of the attack on the Winter Palace by the Soviet Communist Party (Pipes, 1991, p. 496).

In the early morning of the uprising, Lenin, acting on behalf of the Military Revolutionary Committee, impatiently announced that the Provisional Government had been overthrown. The Military Revolutionary Committee assumed power on behalf of the Petrograd proletariat and garrison, ushering in the era of a totalitarian system.

8.2.3 *A Regime in the Name of the Soviets*

Marx, in *Critique of the Gotha Program*, and Lenin, in *State and Revolution*, among others, had long-designed plans for a communist totalitarian utopia under the dictatorship of the proletariat. Just as the construction of a totalitarian regime in practice began with the overthrow of the Provisional Government by the Bolsheviks in the name of the Soviets, the establishment of totalitarian rule was again in the name of the Soviets.

The blueprint for a communist totalitarian system had been meticulously prepared, with the main challenge lying in its realization. In reality, the Bolsheviks held limited influence over the entire Russian army, and their capacity to mobilize troops for a mutiny was quite small. Despite this, Lenin relentlessly advocated for an immediate Bolshevik coup as early as September 1917. However, lacking the necessary strength and popular support, the Bolsheviks faced significant obstacles in successfully carrying out an armed uprising on their own.

Even if they managed to seize control of Petrograd and Moscow by capitalizing on the absence of the main Russian forces at the front lines during the war, their control over the entire nation would still be far from certain. Russia's wartime allies – Britain, France, and the United States – all had troops present in Russia and strongly opposed the Bolsheviks, offering unwavering support to the Provisional Government. It seemed, therefore, that overthrowing the regime established by the Bolshevik coup would not be a relatively easy task and the Bolsheviks appeared destined for failure.

However, the Bolsheviks employed a combination of violent suppression against opposition forces and propaganda tactics to sow divisions among their adversaries. While the Provisional Government, anti-Bolshevik factions, and foreign governments appeared formidable, their underestimation of the seemingly vulnerable Bolsheviks led to a grave misjudgment of the overall situation.

The Bolsheviks faced their own set of challenges. Without sufficient support, launching an armed uprising would be impossible. As a clandestine organization, they lacked substantial public backing, even among the working class. To address this issue, Trotsky proposed seizing power under the guise of the Soviets, with the aim of attracting workers, citizens, and soldiers and encouraging their spontaneous participation. However, the Bolsheviks did not have control over the Soviets themselves. In order to conceal their true intentions, Trotsky orchestrated the inclusion of two representatives from the SR Party (alongside three Bolshevik representatives) in the top management of the Military Revolutionary Committee (MRC), the revolutionary command organ. Trotsky later explained that this move was crucial in presenting the Bolsheviks' seizure of power as a Soviet endeavor (Figes, 2017, p. 480).

As planned by the Bolsheviks, the uprising was scheduled to coincide with the Second All-Russian Soviet Congress. On the evening of October 25, the Congress convened at the Smolny Palace in Petrograd, marking a pivotal moment in the Bolshevik seizure of power under the guise of the Soviets. The Bolsheviks made special preparations to ensure a maximum number of Bolshevik delegates in attendance, while many other political parties and organizations refused to participate. Among the delegates from other parties, the majority consisted of SRs and Mensheviks. There was widespread support among the delegates for the slogan "All Power to the Soviets" and the establishment of a Soviet government. Consequently, the primary objective for all the delegates was the formation of a Soviet government. Menshevik leader Martov proposed the formation of a democratic coalition government based on the existing distribution of seats among the Soviet parties and his proposal passed through a secret ballot. If implemented, this arrangement would have prevented the Bolsheviks from monopolizing the government (Figes, 2017, pp. 489–490).

The Congress then moved on to debate the Bolsheviks' armed coup carried out under the name of the Soviets. The Menshevik and SR delegates strongly criticized the Bolsheviks' actions, denouncing the coup as a "criminal venture" that would lead to civil war. The Mensheviks issued a formal statement accusing the Bolsheviks of launching an armed coup in the name of the Soviets without the consent of other parties, thereby sabotaging the Soviets. In response, the Bolshevik delegates vehemently countered their arguments. Eventually, delegates from the other parties decided to withdraw from the Congress in protest and to distance themselves from the Bolsheviks (Figes, 2017, pp. 489–490). This was precisely what the Bolsheviks desired, as it allowed them to gain control over the Soviets and operate under their name. Trotsky disparaged the departing delegates as pitiful creatures destined for history's dustbin, whilst other Bolshevik delegates encouraged the departure of other delegates with jeers (Pipes, 1991, p. 498).

Following the other parties' delegates' withdrawal, Lenin arrived the next day at the Bolshevik-dominated All-Russian Congress of Soviets. The Congress established a new Provisional Government known as the Council of People's Commissars (CPC or Sovnarkom). All the significant positions in this Bolshevik-organized Sovnarkom were controlled by the Bolsheviks: Lenin was Chairman, Trotsky was Minister of Foreign Affairs, Stalin was Commissar for Nationalities, and Lunacharsky oversaw propaganda, amongst other things (Pipes, 1991, pp. 499–501).

Furthermore, the Congress approved Lenin's "Decree on Peace," which called for an immediate end to the war, and the "Decree on Land," endorsing the SR's land policy of protecting private land rights of small farmers and expropriating large landholdings without compensation. Notably, considering the imminent national Constituent Assembly elections, the Bolsheviks delayed their plans for comprehensive nationalization of land to secure the votes of the peasantry. Similarly, until 1918, the Bolsheviks continued to promise that they would adhere to the results of a popular vote in the Constituent Assembly. However, both were merely stopgap measures.

Only through a successful armed seizure of power could the totalitarian party establish itself as the core of a totalitarian system. This section of the narrative explains how the institutional genes inherited from the Tsarist imperial system not only hindered the progress of constitutional reform in Russia but also created favorable conditions for the Bolsheviks' armed takeover. Some scholars argue that the October Revolution was a historical accident dependent on specific circumstances. For example, had the Provisional Government managed to establish a stable republic, the Bolsheviks would not have had an opportunity to establish a totalitarian regime. Similarly, if Lenin had been assassinated on his way to the Smolny Palace for the Soviet Congress following the October Revolution, the Bolsheviks may have lost their chance to control the Soviets. History is replete with contingencies, and no theory of historical determinism can precisely predict the individuals, timing, or locations involved in successful revolutions. However, a robust theory can identify the conditions conducive to successful reforms or revolutions, with institutional genes, which are relatively stable, playing a crucial role. Recognizing the presence of institutional genes within a society and understanding their relationship with the relevant events can offer insights into the overall trajectory of history.

The institutional genes of Tsarist imperial Russia were the most fundamental factor that determined the failure of the constitutional reforms. As institutional genes cannot change rapidly, the

Provisional Government had neither the social foundation for establishing a constitutional government nor any real power to control or influence society. Instead, under the influence of the inherited institutional genes of the Tsarist imperial system, the Orthodox Church, and secret political organizations, it was the Soviets of workers and citizens that had real influence on Russian society at that time. Based on these institutional genes, all the parties that influenced the Soviets, composed of a social class with no property, including the SRs and the Mensheviks, opposed private property rights. Therefore, regardless of how historical contingencies unfolded, even if the Soviets had not been hijacked by the Bolsheviks as tools for their seizure and consolidation of power, they still represented the basic social force undermining constitutional rule. Indeed, it was the characteristics of the Soviets, rooted in the institutional genes of Russian society, that provided the opportunity for the Bolsheviks.

Lastly, it must be noted that the October Revolution was not led by a single leader, Lenin, but by a group of Bolshevik leaders who, under the guise of "All Power to the Soviets," orchestrated a coup to seize power from the Provisional Government. Thus, with or without Lenin, the specific policies of the totalitarian party might have been somewhat different but the fundamental nature would have remained the same. Trotsky and Stalin's totalitarianism could have differed from Lenin's in detail but they all represented proletarian dictatorships and their underlying nature was the same.

8.3 ESTABLISHING A FULL-FLEDGED TOTALITARIAN SYSTEM

> Power is not a means; it is an end. One does not establish a dictatorship in order to safeguard a revolution; one makes the revolution in order to establish the dictatorship.... The object of power is power.
>
> —George Orwell (2013, p. 252)

In a communist totalitarian system, everyone seems equal as no one has private property. However, it is the opposite of egalitarianism as individuals are all ranked and everything, including resource allocations, is determined by power. Thus, power is the end, which is derived from the nature of the totalitarian institution. This applies to all individuals within the institution, including sincere revolutionaries whose genuine aim is egalitarianism and universal liberty.

The Soviet government, along with its CPC, led by the Bolsheviks and established on November 8, 1917 (October 26 in the old Russian calendar), governed Russia for seventy-four years until the dissolution of the Soviet Union in 1991. It stands as the first enduring totalitarian regime in human history, distinct from the short-lived Jacobin regime of the French Revolution and the temporary theocratic totalitarian system established in Münster during the Reformation. The defining characteristic of this regime was its total rule by a single party that allowed only one ideology. This ideology functioned as a secular religion, with the party acting as the almighty church of this secular faith. All other political parties were forcibly dissolved and alternative ideologies were purged as heresy. The sole party exerted comprehensive control over administration, legislation, law enforcement, means of production, armed forces, media, education, research, and all social organizations. By its very nature, it was a totalitarian party.

8.3.1 *The Proletarian Dictatorship: Suppressing Opposition*

After the Bolsheviks established the first proletarian dictatorship regime, they further developed it into a totalitarian system whereby the party had control over every aspect of society. In theory, Marx claimed that his most significant contribution was the concept of the dictatorship of the proletariat for achieving socialism.[8] Therefore, adherence to the idea of the proletarian dictatorship is the fundamental principle that distinguishes Marxist parties from other socialist parties. However, the reality is that the dictatorship of the proletariat has remained merely a nominal concept. In practice, a party that claims to be a dictatorship must exercise dictatorial power, both internally and externally. The actual dictatorship that

8.3 ESTABLISHING A FULL-FLEDGED TOTALITARIAN SYSTEM

exists in a one-party system is, in essence, the dictatorship of the party's leader, including control over other leaders within the party who may not be submissive. Therefore, the distribution of power and power struggles become crucial aspects of a communist totalitarian system. Although the concept of the dictatorship of the proletariat does not accurately represent historical reality, it is used for ease of explanation in the following discussions.

Seizing power through a coup in the name of the Soviets may have been achieved by luck but consolidating their power posed significant challenges for the Bolsheviks. First, the idea of determining a political system through popular vote and adhering to constitutional principles had been the shared goal of all non-Bolshevik parties in Russia for decades. While the Bolsheviks were a relatively young offshoot of the RSDLP with a history of just over a dozen years, parties like the SR had deep roots dating back several decades. Despite the Bolsheviks' use of violence to seize power, they held far less influence in Russia compared to the SR and Mensheviks.

The Soviets were originally self-governing councils promoted by and founded with the help of the SR and the Mensheviks. Not only were the Bolsheviks not the founder but they also did not hold general leadership in the Soviets. "All Power to the Soviets" was merely a pretext for the Bolsheviks to launch the October Revolution. Subsequently, taking advantage of other parties' absence, the Bolsheviks monopolized the Soviets, thus monopolizing power. However, these actions were not able to establish legitimacy neither nationally nor within the Soviets. The Bolsheviks failed to sufficiently convince workers, peasants, and soldiers to follow them, let alone to silence other parties. After the seizure of power, the evasion of the restrictions and promises made by Lenin as a "revolutionary strategy," which would have weakened the power of the Bolsheviks, was key to the establishment of the world's first one-party dictatorship. Since power was seized through violence, it was also possible to repudiate any provisions or promises recently announced by Lenin through violence.

To make their incentive-incompatible totalitarian goals executable, the Bolsheviks employed a strategy of breaking them down into short-term, incentive-compatible pieces or deceptions. In practice, they used deception as a means to buy time and seize opportunities to consolidate their power.

When the CPC was established on November 8, 1917, the Bolsheviks issued a decree declaring it as a provisional government. They stated that the final political system and legitimate government would be determined by representatives elected in a national election at the Constitutional Assembly, scheduled to take place a month later. However, this posed a challenge for the Bolsheviks as they were a minority at that time. How could they gain a mandate through elections when they lacked broad support?

Furthermore, in order to gain approval from the Soviet Congress, the resolution of the Second All-Russian Soviet Congress, which was drafted by Lenin himself, stipulated that the CPC would be accountable to and under the control of the Congress and its Central Executive Committee (CEC). However, the CPC was fully controlled by the Bolsheviks. How could they possibly gain recognition from the Soviets in such a situation?

Fearing a Bolshevik monopoly on Soviet power, the first to resist the Bolsheviks was the Union of Railway Workers (URE). On November 11, the URE formally demanded that all socialist parties must be included in the CEC and threatened to launch a national strike to paralyze all railway transport if their demands were not met. Over the past decade, nationwide URE strikes had played a major role in several major political changes in Russia. At that time, with Kerensky rallying forces to suppress the Bolshevik coup, the Bolsheviks desperately needed the unimpeded operation of the railways. Therefore, the Bolshevik Central Committee accepted the Union's demand, agreeing to share power with other parties. The Union then canceled the strike.

Later, as the threat of civil war lessened, the Bolsheviks learned their lesson and changed their strategy. They abandoned their blatant immediate monopoly on power and promised to share it with all socialist parties. However, this so-called "sharing" essentially meant sharing with the controllable Left SR, a strategy similar to what they did with the Military Revolutionary Committee prior to the coup. Even so, the fully Bolshevik-controlled CPC continued to bypass the CEC to issue decrees. Moreover, after the Bolsheviks had consolidated their power, they openly labeled parties opposed to their orders as counterrevolutionary and restricted the freedom of expression of all political parties.

In order to overcome challenges from the Soviet Congress and CEC, the Bolsheviks took steps to establish the legislative authority of the CPC, effectively limiting the power of the CEC to repeal existing laws. However, this move faced opposition from the Left SRs and even some Bolsheviks within the CEC itself. They demanded explanations from Lenin and Trotsky regarding this initiative. Despite their responses, the majority of the CEC remained unconvinced.

To sway the decision of the CEC, Lenin and Trotsky, who were not members of the CEC, insisted on participating in the vote. With their two votes, Lenin's proposal was eventually adopted by the CEC. As a result, the legislative functions of the CEC and the Soviet Congress were diminished, relegating them to advisory roles, while the CPC became the primary legislative body. This significant change allowed the Bolsheviks' decrees to hold sway over the Soviets and Russia, marking a new era (Pipes, 1991, pp. 516–525).

Simon Liberman, a former member of the CPC, recalled that in practice, everything was under the control of the Bolsheviks. Even within the Council, decisions were not subject to discussion; the focus was solely on implementing the decrees signed by Lenin (Liberman, 1945, p. 13).

Despite the Bolsheviks' efforts and the institutional genes of the old regime, it was not straightforward to establish a one-party totalitarian regime as Russia had already spent decades striving for a constitutional government to replace the Tsarist regime. All parties, as well as the Soviets and non-governmental organizations, believed that the issuer of commands needed social recognition for them to be implemented at the grassroots level. The legitimacy issue of the Bolsheviks could not be solved by simply amending the charter through deception and autocracy.

Indeed, from the very outset, the Bolsheviks were prepared to address these challenges through the use of force. On the next day of the October Revolution, the Military Revolutionary Committee took action by shutting down several newspapers under the pretext of countering counterrevolutionary activities. The CPC also passed a decree on censorship in publishing (Lenin, 1972a, pp. 283–284).

However, various parties in the Duma, including the Mensheviks and the SRs, jointly established the Committee to Save the Homeland and the Revolution (Komitet Spaseniia Rodiny i Revoliutsii). Their aim was to resist the Bolsheviks' seizure of power in the October Revolution. Teaming up with the Union of Government Employees, they initiated a large-scale strike, demanding that the Bolsheviks relinquish their power. This strike gained momentum when, a week later, the All-Russian Union of Postal and Telegraph Employees joined. Moreover, various organizations such as the state banks, the Ministry of Finance, and the Ministry of Foreign Affairs refused to acknowledge the authority of the Bolsheviks and joined the strike, creating significant challenges for the Bolsheviks.

In response, the CPC issued an order requiring banks to cooperate and accept government cheques, warning that bank managers would face arrest if they failed to comply. When this approach proved insufficient, soldiers were dispatched to banks to forcibly obtain money. Similar situations unfolded in various government departments. When Trotsky, serving as the new minister, attempted to assume control of the Ministry of Foreign Affairs, he faced ridicule from the staff. In mid-November, Lenin ordered troops to enter all government departments to enforce compliance (Pipes, 1991, pp. 526–533).

However, the greatest challenge to the establishment of a one-party dictatorship was the promise made by the Bolsheviks to hold an All-Russian Constituent Assembly on November 25. The Bolsheviks had previously vowed to respect the decisions of the Provisional

Government and the Duma, as universal suffrage and constitutional governance were long-standing aspirations of the people, shaped by decades of constitutional movements. The Soviets themselves had emerged from this background. The All-Russian Constituent Assembly represented the first truly representative constitutional assembly in Russian history and was eagerly anticipated by all political parties.

Before the October Revolution, in their quest for legitimacy to seize power, the Bolsheviks strongly criticized the Provisional Government for deliberately delaying the convening of the Constituent Assembly. They argued that only the Soviets could ensure the timely elections for the Constituent Assembly. After seizing power in the name of the Soviets, when they desperately needed popular support, Lenin presented a document to the Second Congress of Soviets, declaring that the Soviet government would "guarantee the timely convening of the Constituent Assembly." He emphasized that only the national Constituent Assembly could resolve the land issue and the newly established Provisional Workers' and Peasants' Government would only manage the state until the Constituent Assembly was convened (Lenin, 2017, vol. 33, pp. 5, 18, 22). He vowed that if the Bolsheviks failed in the Constituent Assembly elections, they would abide by the choice of the masses (Schapiro, 1987, p. 80).

The challenge faced by the Bolsheviks was that the Constituent Assembly elections implied multiparty competition, which contradicted their goal of establishing a one-party totalitarian rule. Additionally, the Bolsheviks were not the largest party in Russia and had no chance of winning a majority in the general elections. However, if the Bolsheviks canceled the Constituent Assembly elections, their coup d'état in the name of the Soviets would lose all legitimacy and they would face intense resistance from all parties and the people of Russia, including the Soviets.

Therefore, the general elections for the Constituent Assembly proceeded as planned. At the beginning of the election, when the Bolsheviks were doing well in Petrograd, Lenin not only acknowledged the results of the ballot count but also stated that the Constituent

Assembly was the most perfect way to express public opinion (Lenin, 1965). However, in the end, the SR defeated the Bolsheviks with over 40 percent of the votes. The socialist parties shared nearly 69 percent of the total votes, fully reflecting Russia's highly left-leaning public sentiment at that time (Pipes, 1991, p. 542).

Given the unfavorable outcome of the Constituent Assembly elections, the CPC, in order to maintain the Bolsheviks' monopoly on political power, made the decision to indefinitely postpone the opening of the Constituent Assembly. Simultaneously, it instructed local Soviets to rerun the elections citing irregularities in the previous ballot, while mobilizing armed sailors supportive of the Bolsheviks to Petrograd, and prepared for potential violent suppression. The Council, aiming to replace the Constituent Assembly, scheduled the Third All-Russian Soviet Congress for January. However, all socialist parties strongly opposed the decision to delay the Constituent Assembly. They formed an interparty coalition to defend the Constituent Assembly and organized a large demonstration in Petersburg under the slogan "All Power to the Constituent Assembly." Unfortunately, the demonstration was forcefully suppressed by soldiers armed with live ammunition.

The Bolsheviks adopted a piecemeal approach to suppress other parties. They reassured the socialist parties, which held significant influence in the Soviets while suppressing the non-socialist Constitutional Democratic Party by labeling it an enemy of the people and arresting its leaders.[9] Lenin declared that the slogan "All Power to the Constituent Assembly" was counterrevolutionary. He said that if the Constituent Assembly runs counter to the Soviet regime, it is destined to perish politically (Yao, 2009, p. 200). Lenin described the Soviets as a higher form of democracy, as the elected deputies of the Constituent Assembly did not genuinely represent public opinion.[10]

In this context, the remaining legitimate left-wing political parties, including the SR, made the decision to organize a large-scale peaceful demonstration on January 5, 1918, in an attempt to salvage the Constituent Assembly and establish a coalition government of socialist parties. They rallied behind the slogan "All Power to the Constituent Assembly." To ensure a peaceful demonstration, they insisted that all participating military personnel be unarmed. However, the Bolsheviks, citing the need to counter a supposed counterrevolutionary plot by Kerensky, deployed troops a few days prior and declared a state of emergency in Petrograd. During the demonstration on January 5, the troops mobilized by the Bolsheviks opened fire. Following the crackdown, the Constituent Assembly convened under the military control of the Bolsheviks (Smirnov, 1997). Despite this, the deputies of the Constituent Assembly rejected the proposal to recognize the Soviet government through a majority vote and the leader of the SR was elected as the chairman of the Assembly by a significant margin. The following day, the Bolsheviks announced the permanent dissolution of the Constituent Assembly and used military force to seal off the Tauride Palace, where the Assembly was located. Lenin's old friend Gorky was deeply shocked by the brutality of the Bolshevik troops firing on the demonstrators, stating that it was no different from the Tsarist government's suppression of constitutionalist demonstrations in previous years (Gorky, 1918).

Three days after the Bolsheviks dissolved the Constituent Assembly, they convened the Third Soviet Congress and established the country's official name. They abandoned all the temporary terms used a few months prior and officially designated the country as the Federation of Soviet Republics. Thus, the Soviet Union was born and the Congress of Soviets formally became its legislative body (Pipes, 1991, pp. 550–555).

Despite the relentless and violent repression by the Bolsheviks, the socialist parties, trade unions, and various civil organizations still held out fanciful hopes and still saw the Bolsheviks as socialist comrades with dissenting views. They urged workers and soldiers not to adopt the methods used against the Tsar in previous years, that is to say, no strikes and demonstrations and no large-scale public confrontations with the authorities. This gave the Bolsheviks an opportunity to undermine, divide, subvert, suppress, and eventually destroy all these parties and associations one by one.

Facing the dissolution of the Constituent Assembly, the Bolshevik monopoly of power, scarcity of food and fuel, as well as the Bolshevik's humiliating armistice agreement with Germany, an increasing number of workers in major cities like Petrograd became increasingly discontented with the Bolsheviks. This dissatisfaction was particularly strong among workers who had initially voted for other parties and those who had been elected as deputies to the Constituent Assembly. To protect their rights, these workers established the Council of Workers' Plenipotentiaries in Petrograd in May, aiming to organize large-scale worker movements in the capital, Moscow, and other cities. All these efforts were subject to the scrutiny and suppression of the Cheka (officially called the Extraordinary Commission for Fighting Counterrevolution and Sabotage), the core institution of the dictatorship of the proletariat. The Cheka arrested sixty-six leaders involved in the plenipotentiary movement and confiscated their printed materials. Meanwhile, the Bolsheviks urgently announced the convening of the Fifth Soviet Congress two weeks later, with delegate elections restricted to the Bolsheviks and the Left SRs. From then on, the Mensheviks, the SR, and other parties officially lost their right to run independently in elections. On the day the election results for the Fifth Soviet Congress were announced, the Council of Workers' Plenipotentiaries organized a general strike. However, the remaining Mensheviks and the SRs still dissuaded the workers from striking, stating that their differences with the Bolsheviks were mere disagreements among socialist comrades. Shortly thereafter, the Cheka sealed off the Council of Workers' Plenipotentiaries and arrested anyone daring to take the lead (Pipes, 1991, pp. 558–565). From that point, the independent Russian workers' movement ceased to exist, and the Soviets became entirely a tool of Bolshevik one-party rule.

8.3.2 *The Proletarian Dictatorship: Red Terror*

Marx argued that the key to socialism was the dictatorship of the proletariat, the theory of which demanded the complete physical and intellectual annihilation of the bourgeoisie as a prerequisite for establishing socialism (Marx, 1964; 1938; Lenin, 2021). Both Marx and Lenin asserted that violent means such as war and terror were necessary to eliminate the bourgeoisie. Marx, Lenin, and their followers all characterized constitutional democracy as a bourgeois constitutional system, branding parties and individuals advocating constitutional democracy as bourgeois. Both in theory and in practice, totalitarian regimes are built upon institutionalized terror.

In practice, the Bolsheviks established a system of Red Terror from the very first day they seized power by force, with the Cheka playing a central role. They arrested and assassinated leaders of the constitutional democratic parties. As the Bolsheviks' power grew and they faced increasing resistance, their rule became increasingly reliant on terror. They disbanded the Constituent Assembly and employed violence against protesting citizens. Whenever the Bolsheviks faced opposition in Soviet elections, they deployed the Red Army and the Red Guards to suppress it. The concept and tactics of Red Terror were originally used by the Jacobin regime during the French Revolution but it was the Bolsheviks who institutionalized the Red Terror as a permanent system and spread it globally. Lenin and Trotsky often referred to the French Revolution as a model for institutionalizing the Red Terror and employing terror as a strategy. They were also influenced by Marx's belief that the failure of the Paris Commune was due to its lack of decisive implementation of the Red Terror and delay in establishing the dictatorship of the proletariat. The scale of the Red Terror carried out by the Bolsheviks far exceeded that of the Jacobin regime, thanks in part to the institutional genes inherited from Tsarist Russia, which laid the foundations for the Bolsheviks' implementation of the Red Terror. Whether it was the Jacobin elite of the French Revolution, the founding elites of the Bolshevik revolution, or the elites behind communist revolutions in China and elsewhere, they all firmly believed that their goals could only be achieved through the ruthless suppression of a few enemies.

But once the system of tyranny and terror is established, it takes on a powerful life of its own. It possesses a relentless drive to expand and overpower all forms of reason, following its own twisted logic that can be turned against anyone. Those who hold power in a dictatorship can wield terror as a weapon against anyone they choose, including their own dissident comrades. Dictatorship and terror know no boundaries; they transcend borders and infiltrate every aspect of society. The concept of a proletarian dictatorship is, in reality, the dictatorship of a totalitarian party. In its most extreme form, totalitarianism becomes the dictatorship of the party leaders themselves. The totalitarian system and its dictatorial terror are inseparable, relying on one another for mutual support.

Dictatorship and terror have been present throughout human history, but it is in totalitarian systems where dictatorial terror reaches its most horrifying heights. In such systems, every aspect of society is under complete control, making it impossible for anyone to escape the reach of terror. The scale of terror and the depths of cruelty witnessed in totalitarian regimes are unparalleled in human history. The very nature of these regimes, with their omnipotent and invincible weapons of dictatorship, drives them to expand and intensify their tyranny without limit. The extreme forms of dictatorship seen in totalitarianism have surpassed the visions of Marx and the imaginations of intellectuals who debated the concepts of the dictatorship of the proletariat and communism. Whether it be the sixteenth-century Münster, the twentieth-century Soviet Union, Red China, Red Khmer, or the twenty-first-century North Korea, the totalitarian regimes experienced by a significant portion of the world's population across numerous countries have all shared a similar logic of Red Terror. This underscores the intrinsic connection between totalitarian governance and the reign of terror.

The Constitution (Basic Law) of the Russian Soviet Federative Socialist Republic, passed at the Fifth Soviet Congress on July 10, 1918, marked a milestone in the creation of a totalitarian regime. It was a deliberately crafted law that used a constitutional vocabulary to undermine the principles of constitutionalism. This constitution served as the starting point for all subsequent totalitarian constitutions. The 1936 Soviet Constitution, which was modeled after it, became the blueprint for the constitutions of socialist countries worldwide.

The first part of the 1918 Constitution was the "Declaration of the Rights of the Working and Exploited People," drafted by Lenin, which disguisedly mimicked the "Bill of Rights" in the US Constitution. While the "Bill of Rights" aims to protect the inherent and inalienable fundamental rights of all individuals, the aim of this Declaration was to codify the dictatorship of the proletariat. It categorized people into classes and stipulated the deprivation of human rights for those labeled as exploiters, as arbitrarily defined by the party.

It was the first constitution in the world that comprehensively denied private property rights in the form of a constitution, blatantly deprived part of the population of their fundamental rights, and constitutionally mandated a dictatorship (called the dictatorship of the proletariat). It also stipulated that Russia was a Soviet Republic, represented by workers, soldiers, and peasants, with all power vested in the Soviets, and that practiced the dictatorship of the proletariat, which was diametrically opposed to the constitutional principle of checks and balances. Of course, the Soviets were entirely controlled by the Bolsheviks, so "All power to the Soviets" was actually a smokescreen for "All Power to the Bolsheviks." This fact became explicit only in later Soviet Constitutions.

One-party dictatorship and full nationalization are the foundations of the totalitarian system. Full nationalization eliminated private property rights, meaning that the property rights of any person or institution other than the Bolshevik-controlled Soviet were deprived. And one-party rule meant that no other organ of power was allowed to exist, let alone checks and balances of power. Under the dictatorship of the proletariat, where there are no checks and balances and no private property, anyone can be classified as a member of the exploiting class and be stripped of their basic rights. The rights and freedoms stipulated by the Soviet Constitution, such as the rights and freedoms of workers to belief, speech, assembly, association, and free education, all contradict the principles of the dictatorship of the proletariat. In the history of totalitarianism, some of the top leaders of the dictatorial parties, including Trotsky, Bukharin, and Zinoviev of the Bolsheviks, Liu Shaoqi, Hu Yaobang, and Zhao Ziyang of the CCP, were purged for their dissident political views.

The KGB was arguably the most notorious agency of Soviet dictatorial rule, tracing its direct origins to the Cheka, whose institutional genes came from the Tsarist secret police system. The Cheka, an institution foundational to the one-party dictatorship, established by the CPC, was initially led by Felix Dzerzhinsky. The power and responsibilities of the Cheka were kept secret from the public and even from the majority of senior Bolsheviks until the relevant documents were declassified in 1958 (Pipes, 1991, p. 800). In its early days, the Cheka's primary target was resistance from the white-collar class. However, it quickly expanded to target all dissenters. Lenin explicitly instructed, "All able-bodied men and women in the bourgeoisie should be enlisted in labor corps and put to work. Resistors should be shot on the spot, and all the other enemies of the Soviet government, such as speculators, saboteurs, and counterrevolutionary agitators, should be summarily executed" (Lenin, 1972d). The Cheka was the executor of Lenin's principles and thus held the power to arrest and even execute without trial. By the time of Stalin, the Cheka had become a weapon for purging dissent among high-ranking Bolsheviks.

The forced dissolution of the Constituent Assembly by the Bolsheviks in early 1918 led to widespread resistance from all parties in Russian society. Right-wing parties organized so-called White Army armed uprisings in various regions. Some left-wing SRs resumed their past assassination tactics used against the Tsarist authorities, including collective actions planned by the Combat Group of the SR Party and individual assassinations. Lenin was targeted in an SR assassination attempt on August 30, 1918. Following his injury, Lenin instructed, "We must prepare ourselves to carry out a mass terror against them" (Lenin, 1972d; Andrew and Mitrokhin, 2000).

Amidst widespread Bolshevik propaganda promoting terror, the CEC issued the "Red Terror" decree on September 5. The decree advocated creating a climate of Red Terror through mass arrests and executions, claiming this was an extreme necessity to ensure the stability of the home front. The Cheka, inheriting the complex secret police system established during the Tsarist era, became the key enforcer of the Red Terror. However, the scale of its operations was much larger, and its methods of suppression were more brutal. Within weeks of the decree, the number of people executed by the Cheka exceeded two to three times the total number executed by the Tsarist regime over nearly a century.

Simultaneously with the Red Terror Decree, the Decree on Hostages was released, mandating public mass executions to instill an atmosphere of terror. It demanded the arrest of all right-wing SRs and any suspects using pseudonyms. It allowed for mass arrests of hostages and, if Bolshevik personnel or activities were attacked, for mass executions to create an atmosphere of terror in society. It also stipulated that those who hesitated to enforce this decree were considered counterrevolutionaries. The decree stated, "When using large-scale terror tactics, there must be not the slightest hesitation, not the slightest indecision." Additionally, the Cheka was granted greater powers of arrest and execution. Cheka Order No. 47 stipulated, "In matters of search, arrest, and execution, the Cheka is a fully independent agency accountable to the Council of People's Commissars and the Central Executive Committee" (Pipes, 1991, pp. 817–821).

Dzerzhinsky argued that enemies lurk in almost every institution. Therefore, they must employ entirely different methods of struggle. On these grounds, the Cheka was granted the authority to independently arrest anyone suspected of counterrevolutionary activities, speculation, or other crimes. It had the power to enter any government and public offices, enterprises, schools, hospitals, residences, theaters, and transportation stations. By 1920, the Cheka oversaw all party and governmental institutions, from dissenters to businesses, becoming a super-institution overseeing everything from politics to daily life. It decided on the life and death of all people, including party and government officials (Pipes, 1991, pp. 829–831).

From 1917 to 1922, the number of individuals executed by the Soviet totalitarian regime was thousands of times that of the Jacobin regime. The executed encompassed individuals from all social strata, including the nobility and the entire family of former Tsar Nicholas II. The information on the execution of the Tsar's family remained classified until the dissolution of the Soviet Union. The era of Red Terror also led to the establishment of the concentration camp system. Within a few years, by 1923, there were 315 concentration camps detaining over 70,000 people (Pipes, 1991, p. 836).

Due to the arbitrary nature of punishments during the Red Terror, it was difficult to accurately record statistics, leading to debates among historians regarding the number of victims. Declassified archives have suggested estimates of around 120,000 deaths resulting from the Red Terror between 1918 and 1922 (Leggett, 1987, p. 359), while others have put the figure in the hundreds of thousands (Gellately, 2007, p. 72). Additionally, another estimate places the number of people who died directly as a result of the Red Terror between 1917 and 1922 at 750,000 (Rummel, 1990, p. 47).

The sheer scale of the fatalities inflicted by the Red Terror shocked many moderate Marxist revolutionary leaders. Karl Kautsky, a leader of the Second International, described Lenin's rule as a reign of terror (Kautsky, 1919). Georgi Plekhanov, a founder of the RSDLP, branded Lenin a new Robespierre after the progenitor of the first Red Terror.

The dictatorship of the proletariat theory proposed by Marx and his commentary on the failure of the Paris Commune underscored violence and terror as indispensable elements of socialism. When Lenin was planning to seize and consolidate power, he frequently used the phrases "shoot dead" and "execute." He even casually suggested execution when discussing basic administrative efficiency issues (Sebestyen, 2017). The Bolsheviks, with their ruthless and unscrupulous tactics in seizing power, inevitably resorted to brutal methods to maintain it. Dzerzhinsky claimed that the Cheka saved the revolution (Pipes, 1991, p. 838). More accurately, the Red Terror and the Cheka went far beyond saving the revolution, beyond consolidating the totalitarian regime, it became a fundamental pillar of the regime itself. Furthermore, it was expanded to be an indispensable instrument in internal power struggles as well.

A regime founded on violence can only be sustained through further violence, often becoming increasingly reliant on such means. The NKVD, which originated from the Cheka and later transformed into the KGB, served as the central apparatus for controlling the party and society. Notably, in both Russia and China, those who held positions of power within these institutions often found themselves becoming targets of purges orchestrated by the very machinery they once commanded. These purges and their implications will be explored further in this chapter, as well as in Chapters 10–13. Targets of purges ranged from other parties to dissenting party members, intellectuals, rich peasants (*kulaks*), and clergy. The number of executions during Stalin's purges from 1930 to 1953 was 1,600 times the total number of death sentences during the most brutal thirty years of the Tsarist era.

During Stalin's Great Purge, almost all academic leaders were labeled "smugglers of hostile thoughts." The director of the Leningrad Agricultural Institute and the heads of research institutions in cotton, animal husbandry, agricultural chemistry, and plant protection were successively executed. Twenty percent of astronomers were arrested. Almost all researchers at the Central Institute of Gas and Fluid Mechanics of the USSR and all academic backbones of aviation science were imprisoned. The Ministry of Internal Affairs established special prisons to ensure the continuity of warplane research and development during the purges.

Statistics based on extensive historical records reveal that forced agricultural collectivization from 1929 to 1933 resulted in the deaths of 11.44 million individuals; the Great Purge from 1936 to 1938 directly killed 4.34 million; and repression from 1945 to 1953 of the late Stalin era claimed over 15 million lives (Rummel, 1990, p. v). The establishment of the Red Terror and the implementation of purges are not isolated occurrences attributed solely to the personalities of individual leaders such as Lenin and Stalin, nor are they limited to specific circumstances within Soviet Russia. Rather, they are intrinsic elements of totalitarian regimes. Countries that adopted communist totalitarian systems have invariably established their own variations of the Cheka as a means of governance. For instance, China's Campaign to Suppress Counterrevolutionaries in the early 1950s and the CR in the 1960s were large-scale political purges that were no less brutal than Stalin's purges. The Khmer Rouge, heavily influenced by the Chinese Communist Party during the CR, perpetrated a Red Terror that resulted in the mass slaughter of a quarter of Cambodia's population. The communist regimes in Central and Eastern Europe were likewise marked by such practices, underscoring the pervasiveness of these methods across different contexts. Those executed included Traicho Kostov, General Secretary of the Bulgarian Communist Party, Imre Nagy, Minister of Foreign Affairs of Hungary, and Rudolf Slánský, General Secretary of the Czechoslovak Communist Party. Others, such as Władysław Gomułka, First Secretary of the Polish United Workers' Party (PUWP), and János Kádár, First Secretary of the Hungarian Socialist Workers' Party, were arrested and detained. The Mongolian People's Republic also carried out large-scale political purges within the country.

8.3.3 Total State Ownership: The Foundation of Totalitarianism

The primary aim of the communist revolution is to establish comprehensive state ownership by confiscating private properties and replacing private ownership with state ownership (Marx, 1938). Comprehensive state ownership is a pillar of a totalitarian regime as it fundamentally eradicates citizens' rights and their power to protect their rights, thereby disrupting the balance of power within society. The Marxist theory of the dictatorship of the proletariat is essentially a blueprint for totalitarianism, which establishes and maintains state ownership. A totalitarian system is not fully established until the party has gained complete control over all properties. However, the total expropriation of private property directly conflicts with the interests of the property owners, thus violence is inevitable. As previously mentioned, all left-wing parties in Russia opposed capitalism and generally advocated for the abolition of private ownership. Similarly, socialist parties of the Second International also aimed to eliminate private property rights and establish communism. However, it was only the Bolsheviks who put these ideas into practice. Through violent seizure of power, the establishment of a dictatorship, and the use of dictatorial methods to eliminate private property rights, a fully state-owned economy was established.

In the process of establishing the first totalitarian regime in the world, the Soviet Union underwent the Cultural Revolution (in the late 1920s), the Great Purges, the "great leap forward" (without emphasizing this term), and the NEP. China later mimicked all of them. Particularly, China's "Reform and Opening" policy was essentially a duplication of the Leninist NEP (see Chapter 13). Comparing China's institution-building processes with those of the Soviet Union, it is evident that almost every principal element in China's decades-long construction of a totalitarian system was invented by the RCP. While there were variations in specific details and timing, the fundamental principles of the two were almost identical.

The basic principles for establishing a complete communist totalitarian system were designed by Lenin even before the founding of the Bolsheviks. However, many of the specific decisions regarding practical implementation were determined by specific conditions or opportunities. Some were driven by necessity, while others were originally intended as temporary measures. But once put into practice, the majority of these decisions became institutionalized.

To ensure full control of the economy, the Bolsheviks established the Supreme Board of the National Economy in 1917, right after seizing power. Bolshevik statesman Alexei Rykov first headed it, but after his promotion to Prime Minister, the head of the Cheka (which was then renamed the Joint State Political Directorate, known as the OGPU), Dzerzhinsky, took over in a part-time capacity. Ironically, under the totalitarian system, the secret police were in charge of the national economy, creating the conditions for recruiting economic experts, as otherwise, no one else would dare consult those experts. This resolved the problem of the survival of the Bolshevik regime at a time when it was in its infancy and particularly vulnerable (Liberman, 1945, pp. 194–196).

After seizing power, one of the fundamental tasks in building a functioning communist totalitarian regime is to establish a planned economy with comprehensive state ownership. In 1920, the All-Russian Communist Party established key institutions for a centrally planned economy: the Council of Labor and Defense and its subordinate, the State Planning Committee (known as Gosplan). The objective was to create a system where planning and the market could coexist, enabling the regime to leverage Western technology in building the economic foundation. It was during this period that Lenin proposed his famous slogan, "Communism is Soviet power plus the electrification of the whole country." To achieve this goal, the State Commission for Electrification of Russia was established.

But the attempts to create a centrally planned economy faced significant challenges as the Bolsheviks encountered widespread resistance from peasants due to their mass expropriation of private land and deprivation of property rights. Given that 80 percent of Russia's population resided in rural areas at the time, armed uprisings erupted in certain regions, posing a threat to the survival of the fledgling Soviet regime. In the face of this formidable challenge, Lenin made a major concession in March 1921 by introducing the NEP. The NEP aimed to tighten political control while temporarily loosening economic restrictions. Politically, the Bolsheviks strengthened their control by banning all other parties and prohibiting factionalism within the party. Economically, limited private enterprise was permitted, including private retailing, with prices determined by the market. Efforts were made to attract foreign capital and direct foreign investments, leading to significant investments from figures such as Armand Hammer and Averell Harriman (Suny, 2010, pp. 153–155). This shrewd Leninist policy was emulated by the Chinese communists six decades later. During the early stages of China's reform, Deng Xiaoping explicitly stated that the direction of reform and opening-up drew inspiration from Lenin's NEP. Deng's discussions on this matter have been widely documented.[11]

The establishment of the central planning apparatus was a result of brutal internal power struggles, followed by widespread coercive actions against the population. After Lenin's death, Trotsky strongly advocated for ending the NEP and initiating the construction of a socialist economy. However, Stalin, in alliance with Bukharin, who supported the continuation of the NEP, managed to overthrow Trotsky. Soon after defeating Trotsky within the party, Stalin adopted a similar party line and fully abandoned the NEP, instead embracing radical nationalization and collectivization. The First Five-Year Plan, implemented from 1928 to 1932, marked the beginning of the movement towards nationalization, industrialization, and large-scale agricultural collectivization, establishing the world's first planned economy based on state ownership. During this period, the 16th Party Congress was held in 1930, when the party declared it a congress of "socialism ... eliminating the Kulak class and achieving comprehensive collectivization." The so-called "elimination of the Kulak class" involved the physical extermination of millions of Kulaks. Thus, the tripartite totalitarian system consisting of a planned economy, state ownership, and the dictatorship of the proletariat was fully established.

The cornerstone of a planned economy is complete state ownership of the means of production, which is under the absolute control of the party. The implementation of complete state ownership involves not only violent and forced expropriation but also the suppression of dissent. While some economists may argue that the choice of property rights and the choice between central planning and market mechanisms are purely economic matters unrelated to politics, the deprivation of property rights cannot be separated from the deprivation of other fundamental rights. Nikolai Bukharin, a Bolshevik leader who opposed the elimination of the Kulaks and the collectivization of agriculture, which led to a devastating famine, was executed as a traitor. The communist totalitarian institutions have repeatedly resulted in similar outcomes throughout history in different nations. Several decades later, China's Marshal Peng Dehuai suffered a similar fate to that of Bukharin, being purged resulting in his death.

The process of establishing a planned economy in the Soviet Union began in 1927 when the state assumed control over price determination, thus replacing the market. However, this action precipitated grain shortages as farmers were hesitant to sell their crops at the state's low set prices. Stalin attributed this crisis to the Kulaks' sabotage and their grain hoarding. In December 1927, he advocated for the establishment of "collective farms" while simultaneously aiming for the "elimination of the Kulaks," associated with the confiscation of Kulak properties and their subsequent expulsion from their land.

Despite increasing pressure, peasants remained unwilling to join collective farms, with only 1.7 percent of households having joined by the end of 1928. It became evident that more drastic measures were needed for the success of collectivization. Stalin then declared that those who resisted collectivization were enemies of the people, socialism, and allies of the kulaks and other exploiters (Stalin, 1954b, vol. 7, pp. 135–154).

Subsequently, the 16th Party Congress decided to forcefully promote collectivization. Under harsh conditions, farmers were coerced into joining the collectives through threats and intimidation. During this process, approximately 6–8 percent of all peasants were classified as Kulaks and subjected to various punishments, including direct execution, labor camp imprisonment, and exile to Siberia. Many of them perished due to extreme cold and hunger.

Through these harsh coercive measures, by the end of 1933, the majority of households had been forcibly integrated into collective farms, effectively achieving the official goal of agricultural collectivization. However, the success of collectivization came at a devastating human cost, a pattern initiated by Soviet Russia. Grain output in 1932 dropped to less than 81 percent of the 1913 levels, totaling only 69.6 million metric tons. It was not until 1937 that it rebounded to 97.4 million metric tons. This substantial decline in agriculture was largely because collectivization violated the basic interests of the peasants. Many of them responded by slaughtering livestock, burning grain, and damaging tools before they could be dispossessed.

In 1933, the total number of livestock in the Soviet Union had decreased by nearly 50 percent (Moss, 2010). Between 1932 and 1934, the total agricultural output declined by 23 percent (Engerman, 2000), leading to a severe famine in which tens of millions perished. Approximately 6 to 10 million people were affected in regions including Ukraine, the North Caucasus, the Volga region, Kazakhstan, and Siberia. The Great Famine in Ukraine was particularly severe, affecting 2.5 to 5 million people (Engerman, 2000). Amidst these brutal conditions, the government reinstated serf-like regulations reminiscent of the Tsarist era, prohibiting peasants from residing in towns (Mathias and Pollard, 1989). In addition, rural uprisings were suppressed by military force (Shen, 1994).

Through the implementation of the First Five-Year Plan, the first central planning strategy in human history, a comprehensive totalitarian system was initially established. This represented a significant step in accelerating the Soviet Union's economic development and industrialization, securing both the survival of the communist regime and its legitimacy to rule. As Stalin emphasized, "those who lag behind get beaten." This sentiment was later echoed by Mao Zedong and Deng Xiaoping, each in his own way, seemingly presenting the idea as his own. However, the origin of this sentiment can be traced back to Lenin.

In 1931, during the early stages of the First Five-Year Plan, Stalin stated, "On the eve of the October Revolution, Lenin said: 'Either perish or catch up and surpass all advanced capitalist countries.' We are fifty or a hundred years behind the advanced countries. We must make good this distance in ten years. Either we do it, or we shall be crushed" (Stalin, 1945, p. 356). Stalin's ambition to cover a century's gap in just ten years and to catch up with developed countries as rapidly as possible significantly influenced Soviet economic development.

This ideology also shaped China's Great Leap Forward decades later, which aimed to catch up with the UK within fifteen years and the US within fifty years. Despite the different contexts and timelines, these efforts yielded similar outcomes, largely due to the shared institution and ideology that underpinned them.

The Soviet Union, through the forceful execution of the First Five-Year Plan, became the progenitor of the first command economy in human history. Within this system, industry was given top priority and adhered strictly to planning directives issued by the party-state. Meanwhile, agriculture was collectivized to facilitate compulsory government acquisition, effectively raising agricultural taxes and providing funding for early industrialization. This model was later replicated by China and other communist totalitarian regimes.

The focus of the Soviet Union's Second Five-Year Plan was the large-scale development of heavy industry. In the first ten years of implementing the plan, the GDP grew at an average annual rate of 18 percent. The Third Five-Year Plan prioritized development of the military industry, culminating in the Soviet Union becoming a heavy industry and military powerhouse by the conclusion of the Third Five-Year Plan in 1941.

At the core of a fully nationalized economy is the party's total control over the economic landscape. This is one of the fundamental cornerstones of a communist totalitarian system. Establishing such a system necessitates the deprivation of private property rights and transferring them to the complete control of the party. Once the party seizes control over all the means of production in society, the foundations for independent social forces and potential bases for their emergence are eradicated.

Before long, such total control over property rights by the party-state evolves into the institutional genes of totalitarianism.

Masquerading as the representative of the entire working class, the party-state controls all property and resources in society. As a result, by controlling the party-state, the party leader essentially controls the resources, rights, capacities, and freedoms of all people and institutions within society. This, in turn, further strengthens the leader's control over the party and the party's control over society. This vicious cycle forms the mechanism of the institutional genes of the totalitarian system.

As long as the comprehensive deprivation of individual rights, including property rights, freedom of speech, and freedom of association, is implemented – no matter how lofty the justifications, be they communism, socialism, social equality, or human freedom – the outcome will invariably stand in stark contrast to these lofty ideals. It was these utopian promises, incited by demagoguery, that fueled the violent communist revolution and subsequently gave birth to communist totalitarianism.

8.3.4 The Comintern: The Missionary Organization

> The proletarians have nothing to lose but their chains. They have a world to win. Workers of the world, unite!
>
> —*The Communist Manifesto* (1848)

The key to totalitarianism is the entirety and total control, not only over every aspect of a single nation's society but also over the entire world. In this respect, it functions like a secular religion. However, rather than advocating for peaceful evangelism, it pursues violent revolutions across the globe. The famous slogan of the communist movement, "Workers of the World, Unite!" encompasses both an ideology and a revolutionary movement with global coverage. Communist totalitarian ideology is an ideology about the whole world. And it is to be a universal value through propaganda and domination by force. In order to gain control over the entire world, the communist totalitarian party must establish branches of that party in every corner of the globe.

The relationship among the early Marxist parties is reminiscent of that of the Christian churches before the establishment of Christianity as the state religion in the Roman Empire, when all Christian churches were loosely connected by both alliances and rivalries. *The Communist Manifesto* (Marx and Engels, 1998) was initially drafted by Marx for the clandestine Communist League. The basic principle of the communist movement, largely inherited from Babeuf (Chapter 6), posits that only when the proletarian revolution has gained power globally can communism be established and victory achieved.

From the inception of Marxism to the Bolshevik seizure of power, the focus of the communist movement's debate over several decades centered around strategies for seizing global power and identifying which country should be the first to establish a communist system. In 1914, when the Russian Revolution was yet to emerge, Lenin had already begun planning a new international communist organization to replace the Second International. The ultimate goal was to launch a global revolution and seize power comprehensively in every country.

Compared to the loose alliances of past communist movements, the Leninist totalitarian party is more akin to the Catholic Church, with Moscow as its Rome. Indeed, Moscow's rise to prominence as a great city in history began when it was referred to as the "Third Rome" during the Middle Ages. Historical coincidences aside, what matters are the institutional genes.

According to his historical materialist theory, Marx predicted that the proletarian revolution should first take place in Germany, leading to a comprehensive victory for the proletariat globally. Lenin, partly drawing from Russian Socialist ideas, on the other hand, hoped that the Russian Revolution would spark a German revolution, realizing Marx's dream. Thus, to those who followed Marx and Lenin at that time, Germany was the crux of the world revolution.

At the end of the First World War in late 1918, having been defeated, Germany and Austria collapsed. A mutiny occurred in Germany, riots broke out in cities like Berlin, and the power vacuum signified the advent of a revolutionary opportunity. However, the Social Democratic Party of Germany, the largest Marxist party in the world during Marx's era, had abandoned the principle of violent seizure of power since 1914. A revolution similar to Russia's February Revolution occurred in Germany, leading to the establishment of a German Soviet but not under Communist control. Within this Soviet, the SDP (similar to the Mensheviks but even more moderate) was likely to become the largest party and take power.

In a bid to seize power there, Lenin urgently dispatched Karl Radek, accompanied by Nikolai Bukharin, to Germany to control the newly established German Communist Party and attempt to reverse the situation. They aimed to adopt the methods used by the Bolsheviks in the Russian October Revolution, targeting an armed seizure of power on the eve of a national vote. Unlike the Mensheviks in Russia, the SDP invited military intervention and quelled the German communist uprising. Radek was arrested. Subsequently, the SDP won 38 percent of the votes, becoming the largest party in the National Assembly. It formed a coalition government with other parties. However, Lenin persisted in spreading communism there, dispatching envoys to instigate armed uprisings in several German cities. The goal was to seize banks and land and incite the public to join the uprising. However, reverence for private property rights was strong in Germany. Support for such a revolution was weak and all the uprisings failed (Pipes, 1995b, pp. 167–170). Although the fate of the violent revolution in Germany was sealed, the mission of the global revolution of communist totalitarianism had just officially begun, marking the starting point of the communist totalitarian revolution in China.

In March 1919, the Communist International (Comintern, also known as the Third International), was established in Moscow, and its first congress was convened. It proclaimed this to be the "greatest event in world history." Two years later, Grigory Zinoviev, then head of the Comintern, declared that communism would triumph worldwide (Pipes, 1995b, pp. 174–175). The aim of the Comintern was to create Leninist parties all over the world under the command of Moscow to promote a Bolshevik-style world revolution. It was to be the center of command, propaganda, general staff, and logistics of the world revolution. A year later, Lenin announced the Twenty-One Conditions for Comintern membership, among which the most important was to be a Leninist party. Any Marxist, communist, or socialist party that did not comply with the Leninist principles of party organization not only could not join the Comintern but also had to clearly distinguish itself from it. National branches that joined the Comintern at its inception were essentially members of the Second International (officially named the Socialist International). Having witnessed the victory of the proletarian party (the Bolsheviks) seizing power for the first time in human history, many international delegates were eager to follow the same path (Suny, 2010).

The Comintern was designed to be a unified global communist totalitarian party, and totalitarian rule had to be first applied to all party branches in every nation. Lenin made these points clear at the Second Congress of the Comintern. First, a Communist Party had to be established in all countries as soon as possible. At the same time, the Second International had to be dismantled completely, from its organization to its principles. The Communist Party had to submit to iron discipline and obey Moscow unconditionally. Second, the Communist International was a unified party with only one center, not an alliance of parties. Parties of each country had to obey the Executive Committee of the Comintern (Comintern Executive), which was a department of the Central Committee of the All-Russian Communist Party. The necessary condition for joining the Comintern was obedience to Moscow, and anyone who did not obey would be expelled. The immediate task of the communist parties in each country was to infiltrate workers' organizations and other progressive organizations and seize control of them. Based on this, they prepared to establish a Soviet Republic led by Moscow worldwide (Pipes, 1995b, pp. 183–185).

Upon its establishment, the Comintern, under the actual leadership of Lenin and Trotsky (the official leader was Zinoviev during the period from 1919 to 1926), immediately promoted violent seizure of power or instigated civil war in various countries. Béla Kun, who served in the Red Army of Russia, returned to his homeland and established the Communist Party of Hungary. A few months later, he established the Hungarian Socialist Republic by allying with the Hungarian Social Democratic Party and seized power. Under Lenin's guidance, by purging the Social Democratic Party, the Communist Party monopolized power. During the first few months after the establishment of this regime, the Hungarian Communists replicated all the practices of the Bolsheviks: purging the Social Democratic Party and dissenters, confiscating private property, and establishing collective farms. All of these led most of the public, including workers and peasants, to oppose the Hungarian Communist Party (Pipes, 1995b, pp. 170–172). After the fall of the Hungarian Socialist Republic, Kun fled to Moscow. But eventually, he fell victim to the communist Red Terror and was executed during the Great Purge after being accused of being a Trotskyist (Borsanyi, 1993).

Lenin harbored high expectations that the Comintern could swiftly orchestrate successful international communist revolutions. In a 1920 telegram to Stalin, Lenin conveyed that he, along with Zinoviev and Bukharin, believed that with the Comintern's support imminent revolutions in Italy, Hungary, Czechoslovakia, and Romania would be victorious, thus hastening the establishment of Soviet systems (Pipes, 1995b, p. 177). The Comintern also saw substantial developments in the UK, Germany, France, Bulgaria, and Poland, yet all these endeavors ultimately failed (Pipes, 1995b, pp. 194–197).

In 1921, the Comintern dispatched Béla Kun, who had fled Hungary to Moscow, to Germany to incite an armed uprising known as the March Action, but it was unsuccessful. Again in 1923, the Comintern organized armed riots in various locations, with the Soviet Union's Red Army even prepared to dispatch troops to Germany. However, all these uprisings failed (Broue, 2006). The Comintern also exerted efforts in numerous European countries, such as Italy, the UK, and Estonia (Courtois et al., 1999).

Despite all the failed attempts to seize power in Europe, the Comintern achieved significant success in China by establishing the

Chinese Communist Party. This triumph contradicted the Marxist theory of historical stages, given China's socioeconomic status was even more backward than Russia's, which startled communist revolutionaries. To adapt to China's circumstances, the Comintern primarily propagated Lenin's theories of anti-imperialism and anti-colonialism, thus becoming an essential part of the CCP's ideology from the outset. Influenced by John Hobson's theory of imperialism (Hobson, 1902), Lenin asserted that imperialism was the highest stage of capitalism and that colonies were the lifeline of capitalism. By integrating the national liberation movement of colonial countries into the world proletarian revolution, although contradicting the logic of Marxist theory, Leninism and the Comintern substantially expanded the scope of the communist movement.

Just as Western missionaries introduced Christianity and the Church to China, the Comintern brought communist ideologies and the framework of the Communist Party to China. In the same vein that the Chinese Catholic Church operated as a branch of the Roman Church, the Chinese Communist Party functioned as an extension of the Comintern. It was not until the dissolution of the Comintern during the Second World War that the CCP became fully independent. Beyond establishing the CCP, the Comintern also forged a close alliance with Sun Yat-sen and restructured the Nationalist Party (the Kuomintang, or KMT) to mirror a Bolshevik-style revolutionary party. This will be explored further in Chapters 9 and 10. Interestingly, Sun Yat-sen demonstrated his enthusiasm to participate in the international socialist movement as early as 1905. He even visited the Second International headquarters in Brussels, proposing that his Revive China Society become a part of it (Duan, 2009, p. 257).

The death of Lenin in 1924 marked the beginning of a significant period: the complete defeat of the Comintern in Europe, the ascendancy of Stalin, and a shift in revolutionary internationalism. Stalin reinterpreted this concept to focus on defending the Soviet Union, as he considered it the foundation of the world revolution (Stalin, 1954a). Consequently, the Comintern shifted its strategy to command various countries' communist parties to protect the Soviet Union. Understanding this aspect is crucial when evaluating the Comintern's directives to China.

Post the purges of Zinoviev and Bukharin within the Comintern, a large-scale purge of Trotskyists occurred globally, including in China. The Yan'an Rectification Movement within the CCP practically mirrored Stalin's Great Purge, serving as a continuation of the purge against Trotskyists (see Chapter 10). From the early 1930s until its dissolution during the Second World War, the Comintern was under the leadership of Georgi Dimitrov.

Creating a full-fledged totalitarian system is a continuous process of seizing power across all domains. After overthrowing the Provisional Government and taking state power, the Bolsheviks suppressed other parties, which eventually resulted in the formation of a one-party ruling system. Eliminating other parties and organizations was not only an end in itself for totalitarianism but was also necessary to ensure its illegitimate rule went unchallenged. However, potential challenges to totalitarianism were ubiquitous, stemming from public dissatisfaction and differing opinions within the party. The Red Terror and purges, which were initially required for the survival of the totalitarian regime, evolved into the regime's basic institutions. While the abstract concept of the dictatorship of the proletariat comes from Marx's theory, the practice of the Red Terror was inherited from the People's Will and the Jacobins.

The socioeconomic foundation of totalitarianism was initially established through the nationalization and collectivization imposed by the violent dictatorship of the proletariat. All resources were controlled through power and power, in turn, was reinforced by control over society's resources, culminating in a totalitarian system that was comprehensive and holistic. The totality of totalitarian ideology is not restricted to total control over a single country but rather extends to total control over the entire world.

Indeed, the proletarian revolution (a term used by the Bolsheviks, despite questions from many scholars, including devout

Marxists like Kautsky and Luxemburg, as to whether Leninist despotism was a proletarian revolution) triumphed in Russia, which was just the starting point of the communist movement. As Marx and Engels claimed, "the proletariat cannot attain its emancipation ... [without] emancipating society at large" (Marx and Engels, 1998).

According to Marxist-Leninist theory, achieving a comprehensive victory worldwide is not just the goal of the proletarian revolution but also a necessary condition for a single country's proletarian revolution to survive and evolve. Therefore, following the victory of the October Revolution, the Bolsheviks immediately established the Comintern, a missionary institution to export revolution to all the world's countries. It was from the Comintern that the Chinese communist revolution stemmed.

Once totalitarianism is born, it generates its own institutional genes and consequently follows its unique evolutionary path. In this system, no institution or individual can survive without the party's endorsement. In this system, there is no economy separate from politics, nor is politics separate from the economy. The Marxist theory of the dictatorship of the proletariat posits that dictatorship is a requisite means for transitioning to communism. However, this theory mistakenly presumes that institutions can be arbitrarily created as tools without comprehending the inherent regularities of the institutions. Any sustainable institutionalized system, including the dictatorship of the proletariat, once established, generates a potent incentive mechanism and possesses its own expansive vitality and power. When the unchecked power granted by dictatorship allows a dictator to decide everything of significance, including the life and death of all, power itself becomes the end goal. Those in power seek to maintain it, while those aspiring to power strive to seize it. During the Cultural Revolution, Lin Biao, Vice-Chairman of the CCP, candidly expressed the understanding of power by the leaders of totalitarian political parties. He stated, "Political power is the power to repress ... With political power, ... you have everything. Without political power, you lose everything" (Lin, B., 1966).

NOTES

1. Compilation and Translation Bureau of the CCP Central Committee (1983, pp. 550–551).
2. Compilation and Translation Bureau of the CCP Central Committee (1983, pp. 522–523).
3. Compilation and Translation Bureau of the CCP Central Committee (1983, pp. 1014–1015).
4. Stalin, "I did not request to change Tsaritsyn to Stalingrad," in Stalin (2016, p. 176).
5. Pipes, McMeekin, Slezkine, Figes, and Riasanovsky and Steinberg, among others.
6. The name of the Russian capital was Russified to "Petrograd," following the declaration of war against Germany, because "Petersburg" sounded too German.
7. Operating under severe financial constraints, the Bolsheviks were substantially assisted by a generous grant from the German government. This aid allowed Lenin to reestablish control over the party, especially in relation to propaganda where the effects of limited funding were acutely felt. Propaganda, in turn, played a crucial role in enabling the Bolsheviks to extend their influence and ultimately solidify their control within the Soviet Union (McMeekin, 2017). On December 3, 1917, the German foreign minister reported to the Kaiser, asserting that the financial support rendered by the German government was solely responsible for the success of *Pravda*, the Bolsheviks' potent propaganda tool, in broadening its influence among the Bolsheviks (von Kühlmann, Minister of Foreign Affairs, to the Kaiser, December 3, 1917, cited in Carr [1985]). A wealth of evidence from declassified archives lends credibility to this claim (McMeekin, 2017).
8. Marx and Engels (1973, vol. 28). Marx's letter to Joseph Weydemeyer in 1852.
9. Lenin (1972b, [Decree on the arrest of ...], p. 351).
10. Lenin (1972c, [Theses on the Constituent Assembly ...], pp. 379–383).
11. A Google search with the keywords "邓小平 列宁 新经济政策" returned over 5.84 million results on May 10, 2021.

9 The Failure of Constitutional Reforms and Republican Revolution

Communist totalitarianism, transplanted to China from Soviet Russia, has taken deep roots in China, deeper than anywhere else in the world. After the collapse of the Soviet Union and the Eastern European Communist Bloc, Communist China not only survived but further expanded, becoming the world's second-largest economy. This development gives communist totalitarianism further opportunities to exert profound influence on the world in the future. Such a significant phenomenon could not have occurred merely by chance. At its core, the institutional genes of the Chinese imperial system rejected Western constitutional democracy, leading to the failure of decades-long efforts towards constitutionalism. Furthermore, China's traditional institutional genes were highly compatible with those of the communist totalitarianism introduced by the Comintern. This compatibility facilitated their amalgamation, enabling the imported totalitarianism to thrive in China.

Ever since the establishment of the unified Qin Empire and the formation of the institutional genes of the Chinese imperial system, throughout the long history of the Chinese Empire, all major institutional evolutions have aimed at perfecting these imperial genes. The most monumental reforms in Chinese history, from Emperor Xiaowen's institutional adjustments during the Northern Wei dynasty to Wang Anshi's measures in the Northern Song dynasty and Zhang Juzheng's in the Ming dynasty, were all, without exception, efforts to enhance and improve imperial governance. As a result, the institutional genes of the Chinese imperial system became increasingly entrenched and sophisticated, remaining unaltered even when foreign invaders conquered and ruled the empire without attempting to challenge it.

From the end of the nineteenth century onwards, impacted by powerful external forces, there was an attempt to change the imperial system into a constitutional monarchy for the first time in the history of the Chinese Empire. However, the concept of constitutional rule was completely foreign to the Chinese. More significantly, the establishment of constitutional rule anywhere in the world results from a compromise among competing powers. It is an arrangement based on checks and balances of power. It is premised on the fact that the opposition party already has substantial power. To protect its rights and interests, it challenges the party in power based on the power it possesses.

However, the Chinese imperial system had long been institutionalized in such a way that, outside of the emperor's rule, from the highest echelons of governance down to the county level, no independent political, economic, or cultural groups possessed substantial power to challenge the emperor's authority. As such, the constitutional reforms of the late Qing dynasty did not arise from a challenge to the emperor's power in defense of independent interests. Instead, they emerged as a state-driven initiative to improve and modernize the imperial system. The reformers viewed constitutional monarchy as a necessary modernization of the imperial system and a means to keep pace with global trends. Thus, early reformers, from those disseminating the ideology to those implementing the reforms, were invariably loyal supporters of the Crown, if not directly associated with it.

9.1 CONSTITUTIONALISM IN NAME ONLY: THE HUNDRED DAYS' REFORM

For most of its history, the Chinese Empire remained largely isolated from the Western world due to geographical, linguistic, and institutional barriers. Even the most learned Chinese scholars had little knowledge about the world beyond China, including its diverse systems and religions. Similarly, Europe's understanding of China was predominantly superficial and cursory.

It was not until the late Ming and early Qing dynasties that Jesuit missionaries managed to enter China. However, strict restrictions imposed by the court on their activities rendered their survival uncertain. These missionaries had to exercise self-censorship, selectively transmitting scientific and technical knowledge to China. Their propagation of Christianity was heavily curtailed, let alone their capability to disseminate knowledge on Western institutions, such as the parliamentary, judicial, and property rights systems, as well as the relationship between Europe's secular and ecclesiastical institutions.

As late as the mid-nineteenth century, even the most knowledgeable Chinese scholars and officials remained uninformed about European academic literature on institutions. They were largely oblivious to the Renaissance, the Reformation, or the Enlightenment. The concept of the British constitutional monarchy was alien to them, let alone the Industrial Revolution and the emergence of the first industrialized nation, the British Empire.

The understanding and prevalence of the spirit of constitutionalism in a society depends not only on the dissemination of knowledge but, more importantly, on the institutional genes of that society. At its core, constitutionalism is a system established to protect individual rights and property rights. In societies with a strong demand for these protections, the spirit of constitutionalism will eventually emerge. However, in societies where individuals lack property rights and are unaware of their rights, even if the concept of constitutionalism is introduced externally, it remains an elusive concept circulating among only a few scholars or advocates, resulting in little societal demand for it. This was the case in Tsarist Russia and, even more so, in Imperial China.

Russian intellectual elites began to grasp a rudimentary understanding of constitutionalism in the late eighteenth century, influenced by the European Enlightenment. After participating in the Napoleonic Wars, the Russian intelligentsia began to strongly advocate for the establishment of a constitutional system from the early nineteenth century onwards. By the mid-to-late nineteenth century, a sizable group of intelligentsia with a partial understanding of constitutionalism, the Populists, emerged, who were ready to fight for it. However, the Russian intelligentsia, actively promoted a version of constitutionalism that advocated the abolition of private property.

On the surface, their ideas seemed to stem from Rousseau's theory against private property. Yet, the reason the Russian intelligentsia preferred Rousseau over Locke and Montesquieu was deeply rooted in the institutional genes of Tsarist Russia: the general absence of individual and private property rights. It was such institutional genes that made Rousseau's theories particularly appealing among Russian intelligentsia, so much so that some were even willing to make significant personal sacrifices as martyrs. Driven by secular religious fervor, Russian intelligentsia sought to create a utopia, a fertile ground upon which communist totalitarianism later emerged.

Similar to the situation in Russia but nearly a century later, the understanding of constitutionalism was brought to China primarily by intellectuals returning from abroad when Japan transitioned to a constitutional monarchy and constitutionalism was becoming the general trend in Western Europe. These radical intellectuals took the initiative to organize and promote constitutional reforms and the Republican Revolution at the end of the nineteenth century. Only after the Russo-Japanese War in 1905, however, did substantial interest arise among intellectuals and officials, leading to more active engagement with constitutionalism. But the concept of constitutionalism remained nebulous in China and there was limited knowledge about Europe's history, culture, and contemporary conditions. Even leading reformers, such as Liang Qichao, had a superficial and somewhat misguided understanding of constitutionalism.

Since the Ming dynasty, the Chinese Empire had been closed off for centuries. The imperial court monopolized foreign trade and hindered intellectual exchanges. The Chinese people knew virtually nothing about the Western world. It was not until the eve of the

First Opium War that a handful of Chinese officials and intellectuals became aware of the existence of a constitutional system.

From the eighteenth century, Britain expanded its trade globally, including with China. China's isolationist economy, coupled with the court's imposition of high import tariffs, resulted in a significant trade deficit for Britain. The high demand for opium among the Chinese people led to opium smuggling becoming a means for British companies to reverse the trade deficit. Large-scale opium smuggling caused the Qing dynasty to shift from a trade surplus to a deficit, with a severe outflow of silver. In 1838, the Qing government appointed Lin Zexu, the Viceroy of Huguang, as the Imperial Commissioner to ban opium in Guangdong (Guo, 1979).

In the long-isolated empire, from the emperor to bureaucrats and scholars, all considered China as the center of the world and were completely oblivious to the sudden expansion of trade in the world, the establishment of constitutionalism in Britain, and the ensuing profound changes. To solve the opium issue and understand Britain, Lin Zexu organized the translation of foreign literature, which became the first written materials systematically introducing Western political institutions in China's modern history.

The most influential work, *Sizhou zhi* (*Records of the Four Continents*), was an abridged translation of Hugh Murray's *An Encyclopaedia of Geography* (1834). It was the first time that the Chinese became aware of the British Parliament, which was described as a system where significant state affairs "must be approved by the Parliament. If the king errs, the person responsible is penalized in Parliament." Wei Yuan, a staff member of the Viceroy of the Liangjiang region, compiled *Haiguo tuzhi* (*Illustrated Treatise on the Maritime Nations*) based on *Sizhou zhi*. Published in 1842, it further described the power and operation of the parliamentary system in Europe and America and the limitations on the powers of the monarch and government. In 1848, Xu Jiyu, the Viceroy of the Min-Zhe region, published *Yinghuan zhilüe* (*A Short Account of the Maritime Circuit*), providing a clearer explanation of the constitutional systems in Britain,

America, and Europe than *Sizhou zhi* and *Haiguo tuzhi*. He implicitly pointed out that the West's superiority over China was due to its institutions, not merely its weapons and technology. However, Xu Jiyu was soon dismissed from his post for his political views and his book was banned (Drake, 1990, pp. 3, 151). The deeper problem for China at the time was that there was no societal appetite for knowledge about constitutionalism and the volumes mentioned above did not have a significant impact until thirty or forty years later. In Japan, by contrast, the *Sizhou zhi* and *Yinghuan zhilüe* played a significant role in promoting the Meiji Restoration (Xu and Wang, 2015, pp. 183–188).

The spread of constitutional ideas in China only began after Chinese society developed a need to engage with Western civilization. As the Chinese Empire controlled ideology and cultural exchange within society, changes in policies and knowledge exchange could only occur when there was an official demand. The primary interests of the imperial court were military technology, followed by engineering and science. It was not until much later that a handful of Chinese officials and intellectuals began to become aware of the institutions that underpinned these sciences and technologies.

As the Taiping Rebellion (1850–1864) came to an end, the insurgents were defeated by the superior Western weaponry and way of organizing the military. Recognizing the need for modernization, prominent figures such as Zeng Guofan, Li Hongzhang, and Zhang Zhidong championed the Self-Strengthening Movement (*Yangwu yundong*). This campaign aimed to systematically acquire Western technologies, especially those related to naval vessels and artillery, marking China's first "opening-up" to the outside world after centuries of seclusion.

In 1866, the Qing Grand Council (Zongli Yamen) sent its first delegation to Europe and, by 1868, diplomatic missions had been established in Europe and America. From 1872 onwards, students were officially sponsored to study in the United States. These measures took place concurrently with similar initiatives by Japan's Meiji government.

However, while the objective of the Meiji Restoration was to understand and assimilate Western institutions, the goal of China's Western Affairs (Self-Strengthening) Movement was, as already noted, to assimilate Western technology while preserving China's existing institutional framework.

Although the Qing authorities prohibited any discourse about institutions, asserting the official doctrine of "Chinese learning for essence, Western learning for application," the boundaries of knowledge have always been challenging to define. The Self-Strengthening Movement employed numerous foreigners and set up various translation agencies. The *Wanguo Gongbao (The Globe Magazine)*, established in 1868 originally called *Jiaohui Xinbao (Church News)* and renamed in 1874 under the editorship of the American missionary Young J. Allen, devoted substantial efforts to introducing Western constitutional governance and Japan's constitutional reforms. This periodical became the most influential publication in China at the turn of the nineteenth and twentieth centuries. When Kang Youwei established the Wanmu Caotang (The Thatched Hall of Ten Thousand Trees) in 1891 to propagate reformist ideas, he used the *Wanguo gongbao* as self-study material for his students (Xu and Wang, 2015, p. 190).

However, due to China's institutional genes, virtually no attention was given to checks and balances on power or to the protection of human and property rights. On the rare occasions that these issues were raised, such voices were swiftly silenced. Thus, until the mid-twentieth century, the majority of China's intellectual elite lacked a comprehensive understanding of the essence of constitutionalism. Whether it was the Hundred Days' Reform, the late Qing reforms or the Revolution of 1911, although the nominal objective was to establish some form of constitutional system, the actual impetus was towards strengthening the nation. Even the radical reformers and revolutionaries did not have constitutionalism or the protection of civil rights as their goal.

Arguably, the first Chinese who recognized the severe institutional problems confronting the Chinese Empire was Guo Songtao, the first Qing ambassador to the United Kingdom. Over twenty years before the Hundred Days' Reform, he pointed out that "the reason for the West's enduring prosperity is that the sovereign and the people are joint masters of national government" (Zhong, 1993, p. 179), whereas "China has been doing the opposite for more than two thousand years since the Qin-Han period" (Guo, 1982, p. 373). He observed that "in establishing a nation, the West has a root and a branch. Their roots are in the governance of the state and the Church, and the branch lies in commerce and trade." And he advocated "following the practice of Western governance" (Zhong, 1993, p. 212). In a letter to Li Hongzhang about establishing a shipyard, Guo Songtao remarked, "The benefits of steamships are universally acknowledged.... Whereas the obstruction came from the gentry ten years ago, the obstruction since then has come from the officialdom ... did not allow the common people to invest and [to build shipyards]."[1]

If Guo's advocacy had been adopted by the Chinese authorities or accepted by Chinese society, China could have established constitutional rule around the same time as Japan. However, such political views were considered hostile and not tolerated by the Qing authorities. As a result, Guo was swiftly ordered to resign. His written work on constitutional systems, *Shixi jicheng* (*Compilation of Timely Learning*) was banned (Zhong, 1993, pp. 196–197). Thus, his influence was limited only to those with whom he had direct contact, the most important of whom was Yan Fu.

During Yan's studies in England, he was in close communication with Guo. Discussing the vast disparity between Chinese and Western systems in terms of private property and individual rights, Yan Fu stated that in the West, "the people govern their own affairs essentially by themselves, without interference from the authorities" and that "there is a great difference between the East and the West in the basis on which the state and its citizens are governed ... Chinese people do not have the slightest control over the state, nor the slightest rights that cannot be deprived."[2]

Moreover, the leading advocates for reform during the same period as Guo Songtao were all focused on self-strengthening rather than addressing issues caused by the unchecked power inherent in the Chinese imperial system. For instance, Wang Tao, once highly regarded and influential to both Li Hongzhang and Sun Yat-sen, was one of the earliest proponents of constitutional monarchy. The constitutional monarchy he advocated was designed to foster "communication between the monarch and the people" and was seen as a means to achieve "wealth and power."[3] His work is aptly titled *Reform and Self-Strengthening (Bianfa ziqiang)*. Similarly, Zheng Guanying, another influential advocate for constitutionalism, believed that constitutionalism was a tool for self-strengthening and winning the hearts of the people.[4] These lines of thought, which stem from the institutional genes of the Chinese imperial system, found much wider acceptance and attracted much more followers in China.

The leading advocates and intellectual figures of the Hundred Days' Reform movement, Kang Youwei and Liang Qichao, branded the reform as a movement towards constitutional monarchy. However, from the very beginning, it was merely a label, as the movement did not genuinely strive towards establishing constitutional rule. *An Investigation into the Reforms of Confucius (Kongzi gaizhi kao)*, published by Kang a year before the reform, encapsulates his philosophical outlook and reform agenda. His theory is a blend of Confucianism, Buddhism,[5] and what was then recognized as Western learning. Kang, not literate in any Western languages, referred to "Western learning" as including translated texts such as those previously mentioned, *Haiguo tuzhi*, *Yinghuan zhilüe*, and *Wanguo gongbao* and works by leading Chinese scholars who had returned from the West, such as Yan Fu, Wang Tao, and Zheng Guanying.

In his work, *An Investigation into the Reforms of Confucius*, Kang introduced his so-called "Three Ages" theory, claiming that human history must pass through three stages. He named the first stage the "Age of Disorder," when monarchist rule is most appropriate. The second stage is the "Age of Transition," in which a constitutional monarchy is most suitable. Kang believed that China was at this stage during his time. Ultimately, human history will reach the "Age of Great Harmony," when a republican system should govern. Kang's so-called "Great Harmony" refers to a global unification, an expansion of the concept of unified rule under the Chinese imperial system. He believed that achieving wealth and power were the primary political goals for China and reform was a means to reach those goals (Chang, 2016).

The factors that triggered the Hundred Days' Reform had nothing to do with any attempts to constrain imperial power. Moreover, during the Reform, there was no motive or social force advocating for the protection of individuals' rights from imperial encroachment. On the contrary, the Reform was initiated to strengthen the empire.

In April 1895, the year following China's defeat in the First Sino-Japanese War, when China and Japan were on the verge of signing the Treaty of Shimonoseki, Kang Youwei and Liang Qichao, along with over 1,300 imperial examination candidates from eighteen provinces, signed the Petition to the Throne (drafted by Kang), also known as the *Gongche shangshu*. This petition opposed the Treaty of Shimonoseki, proposed institutional reforms, and called for the establishment of a parliament through elections. Although this *Petition to the Throne* failed to be presented to the emperor, it was widely circulated among the examination candidates and literati.

A month later, another petition, The Memorial to the Emperor by Weng Dingxiang, again drafted by Kang Youwei, was presented to Emperor Guangxu. The emperor praised the petition and forwarded it to the provincial governors. This became the prelude to the Hundred Days' Reform.

The campaign for institutional reform was initiated by Confucian scholars who had gathered for the imperial examinations (*keju*). These scholars, who were candidates in the millennium-old *keju* system, had been trained to think from the perspective of the imperial court and aspired to serve in it. They were encouraged to devote themselves to eradicating misgovernance and strive to improve imperial rule, at all costs, even their lives. However, notions of "individual rights" or "civil rights" were never part of their concerns, or even part of their consciousness.

In fact, the enthusiasm to petition for institutional reforms was sparked by China's defeat in the First Sino-Japanese War and the consequent humiliation of the imperial court. The initiative was taken ultimately for the sake of the empire and the "nation." The idea of constitutionalism was perceived as a tool for strengthening the empire rather than for safeguarding individual rights and constraining government power.

The plan and reality of the Hundred Days' Reform aimed to restore the power of Emperor Guangxu and enable him to implement reforms. Although this de facto palace coup was under the guise of a constitutional monarchy, modeled on Japan's Meiji Restoration, the essence was not to establish constitutional rule. The litany of proposed reforms submitted by Kang to the emperor through a series of petitions, beginning with the *Gongche shangshu*, did not at all involve limiting the power of the monarch, protecting human and property rights, or ensuring the rule of law. In reality, all the reform decrees issued during the Hundred Days' Reform were confined to administrative reforms, with no mention of a constitutional monarchy or shared rule by the monarch and a parliament (Xu and Wang, 2015, pp. 201–209).

In essence, the Hundred Days' Reform was merely a power struggle. The conflicts between the so-called conservative and reform factions were intrinsically political factions and power struggles within the court and did not reflect fundamental societal interests. Without any independent social forces outside the court propelling the reform, even if Emperor Guangxu had triumphed in the power struggle and all the reform decrees issued during the Hundred Days' Reform were implemented, it would not have been associated with the establishment of constitutional rule. Moreover, the self-interest of the emperor and the court would have dictated that in the future, they would neither voluntarily limit their own power nor actively establish a parliament that would curtail their authority. Thus, as a failed palace coup, the Hundred Days' Reform was far less significant to China than the Constitutional Revolution of 1905 was to Russia.

9.2 RIVAL TO CONSTITUTIONALISM: SOCIAL DARWINISM

Inspired by the Japanese Meiji Restoration and jolted by China's defeat in the Sino-Japanese War, many Chinese intellectuals attempted to advocate for reform following the Japanese model of a constitutional monarchy, while others called for a Republican Revolution to establish constitutional rule. However, the fundamental principles and spirit of constitutionalism failed to gain a foothold in China due to the country's lack of relevant institutional genes. This lack of grounding in the foundational principles of constitutionalism made it difficult for these reforms to truly take root and led to widespread criticism. Moreover, many competing ideas also arrived in China and many were better received by the Chinese populace. Together, the prevalence of these ideas and the resistance to constitutionalism from those ideas led to the abandonment of constitutionalism.

One of the leading competing ideas was Social Darwinism, a theory of social evolution. This idea was introduced to China almost at the same time as constitutionalism and immediately became a rival of constitutionalism, although many of its believers did not realize the conflicts between the two. Social Darwinism was highly compatible with a significant part of China's institutional genes and social tradition. Thus, it was immediately endorsed enthusiastically by China's intellectuals across the political spectrum without needing evidence or further elaboration. Many of China's foremost constitutionalists, from the early Yan Fu and Liang Qichao to the later Hu Shih, failed to distinguish the fundamental differences between these different theories from the West and often were confused. They promoted both constitutionalism and social evolution, with the latter becoming far more popular and more deeply rooted in China than the former.

Principles such as historical determinism and the historical stage theory, as well as the ideology of survival of the fittest in Marxism, are so consistent with Social Darwinism that one could argue that Marxism essentially derived from Social Darwinism. Consequently, Marxism and Bolshevism, which came to China following Social Darwinism, found fertile ground among intellectuals already influenced by the theory of social evolution. The contrasting fortunes of constitutionalism and Social Darwinism in China were intimately linked to the subsequent rise of communist totalitarianism in the country.

From the outset, the "Western Learning" literature compiled by Chinese intellectuals at the end of the nineteenth century aimed to identify ways to strengthen and prosper the nation. Constitutionalism was viewed as one of the several means to achieve national prosperity, rather than to protect civil rights. As such, there was little interest in understanding the original driving forces and mechanisms of Western constitutionalism. Concurrent with the emergence of early literature introducing constitutionalism to the Chinese, such as the works of Wang Tao and Zheng Guanying, a series of periodical articles on Social Darwinism, *Tianyan lun* (天演论) *(The Evolution of Nature)* by Yan Fu, were published. These articles quickly exerted a significant influence on Chinese intellectuals, including constitutional reform leaders Kang Youwei and Liang Qichao. Moreover, the publication of these articles coincided with Kang's drafting of his *Kongzi gaizhi kao* (孔子改制考) *(An Investigation into the Reforms of Confucius)* before he launched his reform efforts, thus directly influencing the formulation of his reform proposals.

Yan Fu's *Tianyan lun* ostensibly was a Chinese translation of Thomas Huxley's *Evolution and Ethics* (1893) but, in fact, it was partly Yan's original work as it incorporated the views of Herbert Spencer, Huxley, and Yan Fu himself. Long before translating *Evolution and Ethics*, Yan was already familiar with the theory of social evolution, or Social Darwinism, established by Herbert Spencer. To promote Spencer's theory, Yan chose Huxley's *Evolution and Ethics* as the basis. Yan combined a translation of the first half of Huxley's work with his own commentary and writing to present his thoughts on social evolutionism through critiquing Huxley.[6] Whether or not Yan's book is an accurate representation of Spencer's theory is not our focus here, the point is its profound impact on Chinese understanding of constitutionalism and on the later communist revolution in China.

The widespread acceptance of Darwinism in China laid the groundwork for the eventual embrace of the subsequently arriving communist totalitarian ideology. The founders and leaders of the CCP, such as Li Dazhao, Chen Duxiu, Cai Hesen, and Mao Zedong, were all deeply influenced by *Tianyan lun* before embracing Marxism (Wang, 2010, pp. 206–227). The variant of Marxism that many of them came to believe in was, in fact, heavily informed by Social Darwinism. This connection is not surprising, considering that Marx himself was influenced by Darwinism, including the theories of Huxley.[7]

It is no exaggeration to say that Yan Fu played a pivotal role in the widespread dissemination of both constitutionalist and social evolutionary theories in China. He was the most influential translator of constitutionalist works in early twentieth-century China. Notably, his translation of Montesquieu's *The Spirit of Laws*, entitled *Fayi lun*, was among his most important works on constitutionalism. However, Yan firmly regarded constitutionalism as a tool of social evolution and a system for strengthening a nation. He neither believed in revolution nor the anti-constitutionalist ideas of Marxism. Yan devoted the latter part of his life to promoting constitutionalism. He played a crucial role in drafting the 1914 constitution, also known as the Law of the Republic of China (*Zhonghua Minguo Yuefa*), and supported Yuan Shikai's constitutional monarchy. Yet, Yan's work on constitutionalism was far less popular than his *Tianyan lun*, which gained him overnight fame in China.

Then the questions arise: Why has *Tianyan lun* retained its influence across nearly all political spectrums in China for over a century? Conversely, why has the notion of constitutionalism faced numerous obstacles in China? These phenomena depend both on the substantive content of the theories of social evolution and constitutionalism and on the institutional genes that determine the demand for these divergent ideologies among the Chinese populace.

The basis of social evolutionism, or Social Darwinism, was a philosophical concept created by Herbert Spencer during Darwin's era, though it was not directly related to Darwin himself or the theory of evolution. The term "Social Darwinism" did not emerge until shortly before Darwin's death. Inspired by Darwin's *On the Origin of Species* (1859), Spencer invented the principle of "survival of the fittest" in an attempt to explain universal phenomena. In terms of society, Spencer considered the survival of the fittest, or the law of the jungle, as the fundamental cause and principle behind history. His theory, which failed to withstand scrutiny in the realm of natural science, quickly lost its academic influence. However, the part of his theory used to explain social phenomena gained popularity in the West during the late nineteenth century, also extending to Marx. The social evolution theory contains elements of strong racialism, which, though proven unscientific, once served as the theoretical basis for Fascism and Nazism. Conrad Bornhak, for example, whose views on social evolution were once celebrated by Liang Qichao, later drafted the content of the constitution for the Italian Fascists.[8]

The drive towards self-strengthening and national prosperity among Chinese scholars and officials in the late nineteenth and early twentieth centuries essentially stemmed from a wave of nationalism, partially inspired by Europe when nationalism was popular there. Anti-Manchu sentiment, which later became widespread, contained stronger elements of nationalism. Anti-Manchu sentiment was actually the most powerful propaganda agitation of the Revolution of 1911. In this context, the social evolution theory, with a racist interpretation of nationalism, had a significant impact upon its introduction to China. Although the majority of Chinese were unaware of terms like "Social evolution" and "Social Darwinism," or even Yan Fu and

Tianyan lun, the spirit of social evolution had been deeply ingrained in the minds of the Chinese people since the late Qing dynasty and most advocates of revolution agitated the masses by using Social Darwinist logic that would win strong reactions. Thus, Social Darwinism grew increasingly intense with each revolution.[9]

The spiritual leaders of Chinese constitutional reform were all enthusiastic followers of Social Darwinism. Kang Youwei hailed *Tianyan lun* as "foremost among works of Western learning in China" (Wang, 1982). Liang Qichao played an even more critical role in promoting Social Darwinism. John Fairbank, a leading China expert, recognized Liang's crucial role in spreading Social Darwinism in China, describing Liang's influence as akin to Saint Paul's role in spreading Christianity in Europe (Pusey, 2008, p. 84). Liang wrote, "competition for survival is the natural order of things. With competition, the superior will win, and the inferior will inevitably lose. This is an unavoidable rule since the beginning of life" (Liang Qichao, 1899). Hu Shih, one of the most influential liberals of the Republican era, not only studied *Tianyan lun* diligently from his early school years but even renamed himself "Shih," meaning "fitness" in Chinese, in alignment with the principle of survival of the fittest. Upon maturing academically, Hu Shih regarded Yan Fu as "the first [in China] to introduce modern thought" (Wang, 1982, p. 41).

The intellectuals represented by Yan Fu, Liang Qichao, and Hu Shih did not regard constitutionalism as a means to protect the basic rights of individuals. Instead, they saw constitutionalism as a tool necessary for the survival and evolution of the nation to the next stage. Consequently, even for them, constitutional theory held less importance than Social Darwinism expressed by *Tianyan lun*.

But what made Social Darwinism truly important in China is that it paved the way for the introduction of the Bolshevik revolutionary theory into China. Every founder of the CCP, without exception, was deeply influenced by *Tianyan lun* before learning Bolshevism from the Comintern. The most important among them, Chen Duxiu, had read the freshly published *Tianyan lun* since his high school years. He believed that biological evolutionism, human rights, and socialism were the three major characteristics of modern civilization. He saw everything within the trajectory of social evolution as a struggle for survival. Similarly, Li Dazhao regarded evolution as a universal principle and saw Marx's "history of class struggle" as merely one stage of social evolution. Cai Hesen's *Shehui jinhua shi* (*History of Social Evolution*) integrated Social Darwinism with Marxism. Cai's good friend, Mao Zedong, was also deeply influenced by *Tianyan lun* (Wang, 2010, pp. 206–212).

9.3 FAILED CONSTITUTIONAL REFORM AND THE COLLAPSE OF THE EMPIRE

The Hundred Days' Reform was technically the first constitutional reform in Chinese history, yet only nominally so. The genuine inaugural attempt to establish a constitutional monarchy and assemble a parliament in China was embodied in the Xinzheng reforms (Late Qing New Policies). Like the Hundred Days' Reform, which was instigated by the defeat in the Sino-Japanese War rather than by domestic challenges to the monopolistic power of the imperial system, the Xinzheng reforms were also spurred by significant external threats. Concurrently, violent revolutionary groups intent on overthrowing the imperial government were emerging. Despite many of these groups self-identifying as "constitutional republicans," the majority possessed little understanding of, or interest in, constitutionalism.

9.3.1 *A Top-Down Endeavor without Social Support*

The decision to establish constitutionalism under the Late Qing New Policies came after Russia's constitutional revolution of 1905. Both countries' constitutional reforms ultimately failed. Russia's constitutional monarchy endured for twelve years, while the Qing's stint with constitutionalism was significantly shorter. Meanwhile, the Russian republican provisional government, established following the February Revolution of 1917, lasted only a few months. On the other hand, the Republic of China, established after the Xinhai

Revolution, maintained a presence for over thirty years on the mainland. However, both fledgling republics were ultimately overthrown by Communist forces.

The cornerstone of any constitutional rule lies in the spontaneous organization of the people. Constitutionalism aims to constrain the power of the monarch or government, relying on the independent and spontaneous forces that already exist within society. When such forces are already in play, citizens can further leverage them to push for the establishment of a parliamentary system and the creation of constitutional rule. This will serve to limit government power and protect their interests through the election of representatives from these forces. Conversely, if these independent forces do not pre-exist, merely establishing a parliament cannot conjure these forces into being.

The failure of constitutional monarchy in China and Russia was largely due to the extreme concentration of power in their imperial systems, which far surpassed that of the absolute monarchies in Europe. Over centuries of autocratic rule in China and Russia, independent social, economic, and political forces that could challenge imperial power were obliterated. One of the main reasons why Russia's constitutional reforms were relatively more successful than those of the late Qing dynasty is that Tsarist rule did not eliminate independent forces within society as comprehensively as the Chinese imperial system did.

The direct impetus for the New Policies was to rescue the faltering Qing Empire, which found itself on the brink of collapse when foreign armies from the Eight-Nation Alliance seized Beijing in August 1900. This military intervention was the collective reaction of these nations to the Boxer Rebellion, during which the Qing government had incited the Boxers to massacre their diplomats and missionaries. Fleeing from Beijing, Empress Dowager Cixi and Emperor Guangxu took refuge in Xi'an. In an attempt to salvage the Qing regime, while concurrently negotiating an armistice treaty, they searched for a final recourse to manage their disintegrating empire. In early 1901, Empress Dowager Cixi, in the name of Emperor Guangxu, issued an imperial edict to solicit reform proposals from ministers and established a dedicated office to manage related affairs. This marked the inception of the New Policies, which endured for ten years until the Qing dynasty's downfall. Initially, the New Policies, akin to the Hundred Days' Reform, had no intention of establishing a constitutional government. Instead, they were confined to education (abolishing the *keju* and promoting Western-style teaching), the military (building Western-style armies and military schools), and administrative reforms. The imperial decree declared that the reform was merely to learn foreign languages and literature, rather than "the source of Western governance."[10]

In preparation for specific reform measures in 1902, trade issues were given priority. The goal was to simplify transactions between China and other nations by revising existing laws and regulations. Shen Jiaben and Wu Tingfang were tasked with examining the laws of other nations and proposing necessary changes.[11] In April, the office for overseeing administrative affairs, led by Prince Qing, was established to coordinate reform matters. Subsequently, Li Hongzhang, Ronglu, and others were appointed as the minister-level secretaries of that office, with Liu Kunyi and Zhang Zhidong as associate secretaries, and Yuan Shikai as a later addition. From 1901 to 1905, a series of New Policies decrees covering education, military, commerce, and other aspects were issued. But none of these were related to constitutional reform.

When the Qing Empire was struggling for its very survival, a devastating blow was dealt. Russia's crushing defeat in the Russo-Japanese War of 1904 shattered any remaining illusions the Chinese public held about the long-term viability of their empire under the existing two millennia-old governance structure. The Chinese public perceived the war as a conflict not merely between Japan and Russia but between two contrasting systems of government: constitutional and autocratic. They believed that the political system essentially determined the outcome of the war (Gao, 2012, p. 79). The outcome of the war was widely seen as a triumph of Japan's constitutional government over Russia's Tsarist autocracy. Scholars posited that the lack of a constitutional system was to blame for China's recurrent defeats at the hands of the major powers. Hence, both the public and the government concurred that it was impossible to motivate the people and strengthen the nation without adopting constitutionalism (Zhang, 2007, p. 5). Although the general populace was largely unaware of the specifics of what constitutionalism entailed, their demand for it was growing. In response to the mounting pressure, the Qing government dispatched five senior ministers in late 1905 to study the political systems of Japan, Britain, the United States, Germany, and France and to assess the feasibility of implementing constitutionalism in China. Following their journey, all five ministers recommended the adoption of a constitutional system. Similarly, Qing ambassadors stationed overseas submitted memoranda asserting that adopting constitutionalism was in the monarchy's best interest.

The confidential memoranda of Duanfang and Zai'ze were particularly influential among the reports of the ministers who traveled overseas. In his memorandum on national security, Duanfang commented that the Western Affairs (Self-Strengthening) Movement had inverted cause and effect, resulting in minimal effect as it had "aped the periphery while ignoring the core." By "core," he was referring to institutions. He wrote, "An autocratic state is governed by man, not by law; thus, it is easily destabilized; a constitutional nation is governed by law not man, hence it is secure." He further elaborated, "Based on our investigations, it is evident that the progressive strength of countries, both in the East and West, is due to their adoption of the constitutional political system." Citing the Russo-Japanese War as an example, he concluded, "There is no other way for China to prosper and increase its military power but to adopt a constitutional system." Duanfang proposed six stages for establishing a constitutional government and urged the emperor to "proclaim these six matters to all by a decree" (Gao, 2012, pp. 111–113).

Zai'ze, in his memorandum, emphasized that constitutionalism would only benefit, not weaken, the rule of imperial power. He claimed to have learned from Ito Hirobumi and other veterans of the Meiji Restoration that after the establishment of a constitutional system in Japan, seventeen critical powers and responsibilities, including legislation, law enforcement, convening and dissolving parliament, appointing and dismissing officials, commanding the military, and revising and promulgating the constitution, were vested in the emperor. Therefore, a constitutional monarchy would make the "imperial position eternally secure" and eliminate internal unrest, including revolutions (Gao, 2012, pp. 114–115).

In July 1906, a decree kickstarting constitutional reform was announced. Emperor Guangxu issued the Imperial Edict on Emulating the Constitutional System (Qing Dynasty Record Bureau, 1986), declaring, "By emulating the constitutional model, the ruling authority will reside at the imperial court, and government affairs will be made public, laying the foundations for ten thousand years of virtuous governance."

The edict prescribed:

> All sections of the bureaucratic system are to be examined and enhanced, laws must be meticulously revised, education is to be widely promoted, finances are to be audited, national defense is to be reorganized, and security patrols are to be implemented across the realm. Both the gentry and commoners should be apprised of government policies to prepare the ground for a constitutional government.

This imperial edict ordered senior officials to ready themselves for a suite of reforms targeting the establishment of constitutionalism.

In 1908, the bylaws and electoral statutes of the Provincial Advisory Councils (*Ziyi Ju*) were established. In August, the first constitution in Chinese history, "The Outline of the Constitution Compiled by the Imperial Order" (hereafter referred to as the Constitutional Outline), was promulgated. It declared that a National Assembly would be convened nine years later and a constitutional government system would be fully operational by then.

9.3 FAILED CONSTITUTIONAL REFORM & COLLAPSE OF EMPIRE 413

In the subsequent year, the bylaws and election rules for the National Assembly (Zizheng yuan), the preparatory body for the National Assembly, were established, and the Provincial Advisory Councils were convened. The next year, the National Assembly was inaugurated, a new criminal law was enacted, and the launch date for the constitutional system was moved up to 1913.

However, the Xinhai Revolution, also known as the 1911 Revolution, erupted in 1911, leading to the abdication of the Qing emperor. The efforts to establish a constitutional monarchy ultimately failed (Zhang, 2007, p. 6).

The top-down constitutional reforms launched at the end of the Qing dynasty were driven by a desire to preserve the imperial order against both foreign aggression and domestic revolution. None of the leading advocates for constitutionalism represented the interests and power of civil rights. Outside the court, the most influential figures pushing for constitutionalism, such as Liang Qichao and Zhang Jian, were primarily motivated by national salvation. They believed that only through constitutionalism could the country be saved, a sentiment that was in harmony with the court's self-preserving reaction.

Viewed from this perspective, the constitutional reform in the late Qing period was more distanced from true constitutionalism than the concurrent constitutional reform in Tsarist Russia. Compared to Russia, China had even weaker civil organizations willing and capable of counterbalancing the government's power. In fact, there were hardly any substantive debates among the reformists on these topics. This suggests that the constitutionality aimed for in the late Qing dynasty was merely an instrument for political survival.

From its inception, the Qing court took significant measures to ensure no power would be ceded to the forthcoming National Assembly. Official documents reveal that the National Assembly, intended as a preparatory body for the National Assembly, had no role in balancing or checking the government's power. Moreover, the government was under no obligation to implement its resolutions. On a provincial level, governors-general retained the authority to dismiss resolutions from the Provincial Advisory Councils. A similar state of affairs existed at the prefecture and county levels. Essentially, these preparatory bodies at all levels lacked legislative power and served only as consultative and advisory entities.

The Constitutional Outline, while ostensibly modeled on the Meiji Constitution of Japan, notably omitted any content that restrained the sovereign's power, even though the Meiji Constitution itself was not comprehensive in the modern sense. The Outline comprised fourteen articles that primarily served to consolidate the power of the sovereign, fundamentally asserting that the assembly should not interfere with the monarch's authority. As proposed by Zai'ze, the Outline established that the emperor held the power to dissolve the assembly; that the assembly lacked any authority to influence cabinet personnel; that judicial power resided with the emperor (articulated as "the sovereign wields the power of justice"); and that the emperor retained full control over the army, including the right to declare martial law, thus constraining the freedoms of his subjects (Fairbank, 1985, part 2, pp. 388–393).

On the other hand, the Outline ostensibly referred to a separation of powers, with provision for checks and balances among the legislature, executive, and judiciary authorities. It also granted certain basic rights to the people, including freedom of speech, press, assembly, and association, the right to own private property, vote, and be elected, and so on. Restrictions on newspapers and political parties were also relaxed.

However, it is crucial to note that the essence of constitutionalism lies in the checks and balances on power. Without independent social forces capable of keeping the sovereign power in check, the provisions on paper are merely ornamental, particularly when the Outline was designed based on the principle that the assembly should not interfere with the emperor's power. Without clearly defined and institutionalized boundaries between the powers of the parliament and the sovereign, constitutionalism in its true sense does not exist.

The pre-existing institutional genes of a society determine to a large degree the feasibility of establishing constitutional rules within it. All countries that have successfully established constitutionalism had the institutional genes conducive to constitutionalism in place before the constitutional reform began. Specifically, they already had a large number of citizens with private property rights and organizations within civil society that protected these citizens' property rights and other liberties. Constitutional reform, thus, arises from organized efforts by citizens, acting in their own interest, to protect their personal and property rights. In other words, constitutional democracy can only evolve based on the presence of existing pro-constitutionalism institutional building blocks.

Conversely, China's institutional genes were shaped by two millennia of imperial rule. Both the wealthy and the poor realized that they had only two choices in the face of this imperial authority: obedience or rebellion. However, obedience did not automatically imply adherence to the will of the imperial court. If they chose not to rebel, they predominantly adopted a passive approach towards the governing authority as a form of self-protection across generations. As a result, during the final years of the Qing dynasty when the government initiated its New Policies, most of the wealthy were more preoccupied with the potential harm that this reform might inflict upon them rather than actively celebrating or participating in it.

Faced with a top-down constitutional reform that seemed detached from their interests, most property owners chose not to support or participate in China's first elections, opting instead to stay away to protect their own interests. All upper-chamber representatives in the National Assembly were imperial appointees, unconnected to the electoral process, while lower-chamber representatives came only from the elected Provincial Advisory Councils. The election regulations for Provincial Advisory Councils stipulated that only educated males or those owning a business or property valued at a minimum of 5,000 yuan were eligible to vote.

The requirement of assets for voting rights was a characteristic of early constitutional governments, as the champions of constitutionalism sought to protect their own interests, reflecting the driving force behind the establishment of a constitutional government. However, the late Qing constitutionalism was not related to the protection of property rights and the stipulation of asset requirements was merely an imitation of foreign precedents.

Fearing that participation in elections would expose their wealth and make them targets for government exploitation, property owners generally sought to avoid them, leading to an extremely low voter turnout. It was reported that "those possessing businesses or property of 5,000 yuan or more feigned ignorance. They even turned a deaf ear to repeated advice about their voting rights ... Some, despite their eligibility, hesitated for fear of disclosure of their wealth and subsequent taxation." Less than 0.4 percent of the population were registered voters, with only a small fraction participating in elections. For instance, in Guangzhou, one of China's most advanced and open regions, a mere 1,600 voters were registered and only 399 cast their votes (Zhang, 2008, pp. 51–56).

However, local administrations were under orders from the court to hold elections and produce results. Thus, where necessary, local authorities appointed candidates for the Provincial Advisory Council. The US ambassador to China commented on the election that, "only a minuscule percentage of eligible voters cast their vote. The authorities' influence on the election of deputies was so substantial that in certain provinces, it resembled an appointment process." In domestic records, the election was characterized as a "popular election in name, an official appointment in practice" (Zhang, 2007, pp. 17–18).

9.3.2 *The Collapse of the Empire: The Xinhai Revolution*

A half-hearted constitutional reform, while incapable of establishing constitutional rule, can function as a catalyst to hasten the collapse of the imperial regime. On the one hand, the imperial court sought to avoid the reality of constitutionalism and the associated loss of power, while the public lacked both the substantive power and awareness necessary to advocate for true constitutionalism. This made it challenging to execute constitutional reforms in a society devoid of pro-constitutionalism institutional genes.

On the other hand, the instigation of a new system involving elections (albeit with a remarkably low turnout) and a parliament composed of elected deputies (even a parliament devoid of legislative power) had already marked a departure from autocratic rule. If such an institution was allowed to develop into a tradition and become part of people's general aspirations for society, new institutional genes could evolve from it.

Once the elected members had the right to meet openly to represent public opinion and speak out publicly, people could leverage existing rights to protect their interests and fight for more rights. For the first time in Chinese history, parliamentarians were elected, and Provincial Advisory Councils and the National Assembly were established. This not only allowed constitutionalists to advocate for reforms openly and put pressure on the court to expedite the process but also provided political parties with a platform to mobilize the public and defend their property rights.

In the name of preserving the empire and spurred by a shared spirit of nationalism, members of both local and central assemblies, including some of the appointed members, initiated three large-scale petition campaigns in December 1909, January 1910, and June 1910. These campaigns sought to accelerate the timetable for implementing a constitutional monarchy. The movement was spearheaded by the Speaker of the Jiangsu Advisory Council. On the cusp of the Advisory Council's inauguration in 1909, he invited elected representatives from all provinces to discuss the necessity of pressuring the government to convene the National Assembly as soon as possible.

The rationale was that while domestically combating revolutionaries, China was at risk of partition by foreign powers. Should these foreign powers act, China would instantly collapse. Furthermore, if a revolution were to break out, these same powers would take advantage of the resulting chaos. The only way to prevent both scenarios was to expedite the convening of the National Assembly. This would demonstrate unity to the world and secure popular support domestically. Thus, the formal launch of the Advisory Councils provided a platform for deputies from different provinces to unite.

The deputies collectively cited the following reasons in their petitions for an expedited establishment of the National Assembly: (1) the preliminary work for the constitutional system had proven ineffective and needed oversight from the National Assembly; (2) China was grappling with significant internal and external disturbances and was on the brink of financial collapse, a situation only the National Assembly could rectify; and (3) the existing government was ineffectual and a competent replacement could only emerge under the supervision of the National Assembly.

Despite being endorsed by 200,000 and 300,000 people, respectively, the first two petitions were disregarded by the Qing court. However, the third petition, which involved ten groups and amassed 25 million signatures, forced the court to decree the early establishment of a constitutional system. Simultaneously, in an attempt to eradicate this organized challenge, the court ordered the dissolution of the organizations involved in the petitioning initiative. This move backfired, incensing the constitutionalists. Some constitutionalists deduced that a revolution was necessary to overthrow the regime. Even Liang Qichao, who had consistently been opposed to revolution, expressed his sympathy for this sentiment (Zhang, 2007, pp. 84–90).

The Qing court's order to dissolve the petitioning organizations was entirely in line with the autocratic system of the Chinese Empire, which had consistently prohibited the formation of independent groups. However, the formal establishment of Advisory Councils, as an essential part of the Qing court's New Policies, contradicted this ban and provided constitutionalists with the opportunity to form parties publicly. In May 1911, taking advantage of the second session of the Advisory Councils' convocation, constitutionalists established the first national political party in Chinese history – the Friends of the Constitution Association (FCA), in Beijing.

With Liang Qichao as its intellectual figurehead, the FCA clearly outlined in its manifesto that its aim was to "develop civil rights and implement constitutional governance." The party endorsed a "constitutional monarchy." Importantly, the party's provincial leaders were the speakers and deputy speakers of their respective Provincial Advisory Councils (Zhang, 2007, pp. 91–94).

In retrospect, it can be argued that the FCA played a more pivotal role in the downfall of the Chinese Empire than the revolutionaries of the Xinhai Revolution, which erupted merely few months after the FCA's inception. This is primarily because the FCA collectively held sway over the fate of most provinces – the very foundation upon which the collapse of the Qing Empire was precipitated (Zhang, 2007, p. 102).

The FCA had consistently championed the peaceful transition to constitutional monarchy governance and had resisted violent revolution. However, ironically, it was the FCA-led Railway Protection Movement (RPM) in Sichuan that unintentionally ignited the violent Xinhai Revolution. The RPM was not only a trigger for the overthrow of the Qing Empire but was also one of the most significant fundamental driving forces behind the Revolution.

In Sichuan, the constitutionalists, spearheaded by Pu Dianjun, Luo Lun, and Xiao Xiang, who were the speaker and deputy speakers of the Sichuan Provincial Advisory Council, had initiated significant local development projects, including the construction of a railway line from Sichuan to Hankou by the Sichuan Railway Company.

In May 1911, while Pu, Luo, and Xiao were attending the inaugural meeting of the FCA in Beijing, Minister Sheng Xuanhuai, representing the Qing court, announced the nationalization of the Sichuan Railway Company. Sheng's blatant and comprehensive infringement of property rights during the constitutional reform had its legal foundation in the recently adopted "Constitutional Outline." This document, primarily concerned with safeguarding imperial power, imposed no restrictions on imperial authorities infringing upon property rights. Thus, not only did it justify the authorities' discretionary disposal of property rights but it also expected such actions to meet with no resistance.

After Sheng Xuanhuai's nationalization plan refused to offer a cash refund to more than 20 million Sichuan investors, Pu, Luo, and Xiao proposed remedies. When all of their proposals were rejected, they returned to Sichuan out of desperation and established The Railway Protection League (RPL). To the 20 million furious investors, nationalization was tantamount to the expropriation of their property. Many swore to resist the scheme even at the cost of their lives. The RPL effectively mobilized a large-scale peaceful movement consisting of strikes and demonstrations. However, this peaceful movement was violently suppressed. Nine leaders, including Pu Dianjun, were arrested and on September 7, the Qing court killed dozens of demonstrators, creating a bloodbath in Chengdu and thereby transforming the RPM into a province-wide armed uprising (Zhang, 2007, pp. 105–114).

The RPM, organized by the FCA, provided an opportunity for the revolutionaries led by the Tongmenghui (United League), a secret society and the precursor to the Kuomintang, founded by Sun Yat-sen. They quickly joined the movement with the intention of transforming this once peaceful protest into an armed rebellion. One month before the bloody crackdown in Chengdu, in preparation for armed insurrection, the Tongmenghui and the Brotherhood Society formed the Comrades' Army for Railway Protection. They assigned the Brotherhood's leadership to armed insurrections in eastern, southern, and northwestern Sichuan. Following the massacre in Chengdu, the Tongmenghui–Brotherhood alliance immediately initiated uprisings in several places (Shao, 2010, p. 70). In September, the Comrades' Army, under the leadership of Wu Yuzhang, a Tongmenghui member who later became a founding member of the CCP, declared independence for Rong County in Sichuan. It was the inaugural political administration established by the Tongmenghui during the revolution.

In an effort to quell the uprising, the Qing authorities dispatched a significant number of New Army troops from Hubei to Sichuan, leaving Wuchang vulnerable. The Tongmenghui capitalized on this situation and incited a mutiny within the New Army, leading to the Wuchang Uprising on October 10. Following the capture of the three towns of Wuhan, the mutineers declared Hubei independent and proclaimed the establishment of the ROC, with its first central government being the Military Administration of the Hubei Army of the ROC. Li Yuanhong, a Qing general who had led the New Army there, was appointed military governor, despite having no connection with the Tongmenghui.

Similar uprisings broke out spontaneously throughout the country and by November 2, thirteen of the eighteen provinces had declared their independence from the Qing Empire, with most of them led by the FCA. The Qing government effectively lost control of the empire. By the end of November, all provinces had recognized the ROC government in Hubei. Subsequently, the revolutionary forces established a provisional coalition government in Nanjing in December. On January 1, 1912, the ROC was officially established, with Sun Yat-sen, the leader of the Tongmenghui, serving as the provisional president of the republic. This marked the end of the Qing dynasty.

The history spanning from the Taiping Rebellion (to be discussed later in this chapter) to the Xinhai Revolution demonstrates that the collapse of the Qing Empire was largely self-inflicted. During the last unstable decade of the Qing Empire, its rulers and officials, as well as literati loyal to the imperial system (including the reformist leader Kang Youwei), struggled to save the empire by implementing reforms. The emperor and the court only reluctantly accepted the constitutional reform when they realized that their system was on the brink of collapse.

However, such top-down reform was rooted in a key principle: the absolute rule of imperial power must persist indefinitely and any elected parliament must be subordinate to imperial authority. Therefore, on the one hand, the imperial court and bureaucrats – including those involved in the Western Affairs (Self-Strengthening) Movement – continued to believe it was natural for imperial authority to deprive the people of their rights and for the populace to submit to overwhelming imperial power.

On the other hand, even though its representation was limited and it lacked legislative power, an elected parliament took on a life of its own once established. When imperial power directly infringed upon and deprived tens of millions of people of their rights, the otherwise weak parliament played a leading role in initiating and coordinating the defense of people's rights.

The Tongmenghui, which originally was not in a position to trigger, let alone lead, a colossal upheaval only able to successfully incite the armed uprisings and riots known as the Xinhai Revolution in a few provinces due to the backing of the RPM by parliamentary bodies. In most of the provinces that declared independence, their opposition to imperial rule was primarily led by the FCA, or by parliamentary bodies, rather than by the Tongmenghui.

The emergence of elected parliaments, after two millennia of imperial rule, represents a new mutation or potential new institutional genes. But while new military and political forces, including the Beiyang Army and the emerging Tongmenghui-KMT (to be discussed in the next section), were making their presence felt across the country, new versions of the old institutional genes prevailed, fighting off and suppressing this new mutation.

The age-old, ever-evolving genes of imperial rule were able to survive the fall of the empire by changing their appearance and using new methods to strangle the emerging new institutional genes. This created significant challenges for the development of a constitutional system.

9.4 FAILURE OF THE REPUBLICAN REVOLUTION (1911–1916)

Faced with the Xinhai Revolution and the proclamation of independence from most provinces, the Qing government appointed Yuan Shikai as the Imperial Envoy to lead the Beiyang New Army to quell the revolution. Hoping to temper anti-Manchu sentiments within the revolutionary forces, the National Assembly elected Yuan as the Prime Minister, directing him to form a cabinet primarily composed of Han Chinese.

While the Beiyang Army was significantly stronger than the Revolutionary Army on a military level, Yuan Shikai was not genuinely loyal to the Qing court. Leveraging his battlefield victories, Yuan pressured the revolutionaries to negotiate with him. Support for the Republic was widespread among the governors and many provincial parliamentarians viewed Yuan Shikai as the true powerholder and a crucial figure in the reforms. They were not only eager to negotiate with him but also hoped he could persuade the emperor to abdicate and even become the President of the ROC. Furthermore, Yuan also received backing from the foreign powers that supported the Republic (Hsu, 2001, p. 476).

On the other hand, despite most provinces having declared independence, the Revolutionary Army of the Tongmenghui remained too weak to overthrow the Qing court by force. Even worse, the military forces of most of these independent provinces had no affiliation with the Tongmenghui. Furthermore, the majority of the pro-republican political and military forces in most provinces preferred Yuan Shikai for the position of President. In light of this, on January 22, 1912, Sun Yat-sen, who had recently been elected provisional president, publicly declared that he would consent to Yuan Shikai's presidency if Yuan supported the Republic and could persuade the Qing emperor to abdicate.

As most provinces had already broken away from the Qing, and the Qing court's primary military power rested in the hands of Yuan Shikai, the court had no choice but to acquiesce to Yuan's negotiation terms. On February 12, the court issued the abdication edict of Emperor Xuantong, effectively bringing the Chinese Empire to an end. On March 10, Yuan Shikai was inaugurated as the second provisional president of the ROC (a formal presidency would await official elections) and the provisional government relocated from Nanjing to

Beijing, which had been the capital of the Qing Empire and also the power base of Yuan. However, the establishment of a new institutional framework depends on the presence of corresponding institutional genes within the society.

Whether a constitutional republic could arise in China following the demise of imperial rule was contingent on the existence and strength of pro-constitutionalist institutional genes in the country. However, the institutional genes dominant in the revolutionary party were not predominantly pro-constitutionalism. Most of the Tongmenghui's members came from China's secret societies, which followed traditional secretive rules and aimed at restoring the Han Chinese–dominated Ming dynasty rather than implementing a constitutional government. Only a handful of intellectuals within the party held a genuine interest in constitutionalism. Furthermore, the driving forces behind the provinces' declarations of independence and the subsequent control of these provinces were primarily the New Army commanders-in-chief and Provincial Advisory Council deputies. In reality, the commanders-in-chief, who held actual power – military power – often used their influence to manipulate politics to their advantage, thereby making it difficult to establish a constitutional government. Although many parliamentarians were in favor of a constitutional system, they neither held nor represented the necessary power to bring such a system into existence.

The reason a system of self-restraint of power often fails is that it fundamentally contradicts the self-interests of those in power. In other words, it is incentive-incompatible with the power holders. For this reason, constitutional rule, which essentially represents a contract among various interest groups to limit each other's power for mutual benefit, is more reliable. The more significant the power – such as that of the ruling party or government – the greater the need for checks and balances. Constitutionalism, therefore, can only be established through compromises among various groups, each wielding a degree of power, and by instituting a system of mutual checks and balances.

However, when revolutionaries from a secret organization seize power through violent means and declare their goal to be a republic, a question arises: Can such revolutionaries, even if they are sincere constitutionalists, establish constitutional rule by voluntarily restraining and relinquishing some of their hard-won power? Are they willing to negotiate a mutually binding agreement with diverse interest groups and power holders, thereby endorsing a system that curbs their own privileges? Logically, the answer is most likely no, as relinquishing their power is incentive-incompatible with their interests. Historical facts confirm this "theoretical prediction."

At the outset of the ROC, the small minority genuinely advocating for constitutional government believed that constitutional rule could be realized merely through a written constitution devised by the social elite. However, this is merely a constitutional utopia, as a system that genuinely curbs governmental power can only materialize through compromises reached among powerful groups that represent diverse social interests during the constitution-making process. This is the only way to maintain checks on the political power of different groups and confine their conflicts within the constitutional framework.

Communist utopia leads to totalitarianism and constitutional utopia, while not as extreme, may also run counter to its promises. Having assumed power through force under the banner of establishing a constitutional republic, the Xinhai revolutionaries started to draft a constitution. However, this was primarily a monopolized nominal exercise, largely disconnected from the goal of instituting substantive constitutional rule.

The first two constitutions of the ROC, the Organizational Outline for the Provisional Government adopted on December 3, 1911, and the Provisional Constitution of the ROC adopted on March 8, 1912, were both products of the KMT-led Joint Conference of Representatives of the Southern Provincial Governorates and the Provisional Senate, respectively. In both cases, the essence was to consolidate and strengthen the KMT's power within the new regime.

The Organizational Outline was a rushed job, hastily drafted and approved in just a few days. With Sun Yat-sen's provisional presidency already secured, the provisional constitution was designed without providing for checks and balances on the presidential or national assembly powers. Echoing this, Sun made no mention of democratic government or checks on power when he was inaugurated, announcing instead that the five guiding principles for his administration were to be national, territorial, military, domestic political, and financial unity.

In today's world, almost every nation has a constitution. However, only a few of these constitutions truly serve to balance government power and political forces. Whether a constitution functions in such a role depends primarily on how it was crafted. Only when the major societal forces engage in constitution-making, where the ensuing compromises transform into a contract, that is to say, a constitution, can the process succeed. Conversely, the constitution-making process at the start of the ROC was characterized by the exact opposite, as the KMT made no effort to involve major societal forces in the negotiations. By dominating the constitutional process, the KMT aimed to monopolize power and use the constitution as its own tool. Rival political forces, power groups, or interest groups were wholly excluded from the process. This exclusion was exemplified by the KMT's treatment of the Beiyang military and political forces represented by Yuan Shikai. The revolutionaries sought Yuan's help to peacefully end the imperial system while simultaneously excluding him from the constitution-making process. Consequently, the negotiations between Sun Yat-sen, Huang Xing, Li Yuanhong, and Yuan Shikai were nothing more than exchanges of political deals on relatively minor issues following the collapse of the Qing dynasty, rather than substantive negotiations on the nation's constitutional framework. Their actions resembled spot trading on the market rather than negotiating a long-term contract among the parties.

The KMT's exploitation of the constitution-making process to strengthen the party's power is best illustrated by how it altered the first two provisional constitutions. The Organizational Outline, the first provisional constitution enacted before Sun's assumption of the provisional presidency, established an American-style presidential system that maximized the powers of the president. However, a mere three months later, it was revised just before the promised transfer of the presidency to Yuan Shikai, who had succeeded in persuading the Qing Emperor to abdicate. On March 8, the Provisional Senate replaced the Organizational Outline with the Provisional Constitution of the ROC, marking a shift to a French-style cabinet system designed to limit presidential powers.

The divisions within the KMT regarding the principles of constitution-making are noteworthy. A faction represented by Sun Yat-sen, had initially advocated for an American-style presidential system, while another faction, represented by Song Jiaoren, favored a European-style cabinet system. Although Sun's faction initially prevailed, Song made it clear that the political motivation behind the constitutional amendment was to resist Yuan Shikai. It was for this reason that the provisional constitution was revised. Not surprisingly, when a constitution is crafted by a single political party, it tends to become a tool for that party and it is disconnected from true constitutionalism.

Without establishing firm constitutional rule, the nascent constitutional government of China eventually collapsed due to a series of devastating blows. The first came from the so-called "Second Revolution" launched by the very initiators of constitutional government in China, the KMT. This was followed by Yuan Shikai's unsuccessful attempt to restore imperial rule. Lastly, the Northern Expedition, a military campaign conducted by the KMT and the CCP, with planning and support from Soviet generals and military aid, dealt the final blow.

Sun's "Second Revolution" was deeply rooted in the absence of a belief in constitutional principles among the republican revolutionary leaders and most of the other key participants in the new regime, despite superficially appearing to be triggered by various incidents. In March 1913, the KMT won a significant victory in the National

Assembly elections. Song Jiaoren, the party's leader, was expected to form a cabinet and become the ROC's first premier, but he was assassinated before he could be inaugurated. Convinced that Yuan Shikai was involved in the assassination, despite a lack of evidence, Sun Yat-sen was determined to stage an armed coup to overthrow the fledgling republic. However, Huang Xing and other KMT leaders believed that the assassination of Song should be addressed through the Republic's judicial system rather than through an armed uprising.

The KMT-dominated National Assembly believed that Yuan, grappling with fiscal challenges, had infringed upon the constitution by directly borrowing from a consortium of foreign banks, bypassing consultation with the Assembly. The KMT faction opposing a "Second Revolution" contended that the party, given its dominance in the Assembly, should confront Yuan through parliamentary means. In contrast, Sun's faction argued that the president's unconstitutional foreign borrowing was in itself a legitimate justification for a "Second Revolution."

Persisting with practices he had adopted before the Xinhai Revolution, Sun, since the commencement of the "Second Revolution," was dedicated to liaising with secret societies, forming an underground political party, and instigating armed uprisings to topple the ROC. In 1914, he established the Chinese Revolutionary Party (CRP), which was patterned after traditional Chinese secret societies. Each individual who joined the party had to make a vow to "willingly sacrifice life and freedom to obey Mr. Sun, and readily accept death as the penalty for disloyalty" (Zou, 2011, p. 159). A key figure in the KMT, Huang Xing, who had been an ally of Sun since the Tongmenghui era, strongly disagreed with Sun. He argued that clandestine organizations founded on personal loyalty sharply contradicted the basic principles of the Republican Revolution. However, Sun contended, "There is no mentor of the revolution other than me ... Many of you have limited knowledge and experience, so you should obey me unconditionally" (Ju, 1954, pp. 81–82).

In addition to the "Second Revolution," the founding principles of Sun's new party, the CRP, further revealed Sun's beliefs. The CRP was organized much like a traditional secret society, and its objectives resembled those of a typical peasant rebellion: to seize power and rule the nation. The party's charter declared that non-members would not be citizens until a "constitution" was ratified. Meanwhile, its members were categorized into three tiers according to the sequence in which they joined the revolution. Founding Citizens, in the first tier, had the privilege of participating in politics. Associate members, known as Meritorious Citizens, were part of the second tier and had the right to vote and run for elections. The third tier consisted of ordinary party members who only had the right to vote. Non-party members were not allowed to vote.

Even though the impact of the CRP was limited, it encapsulated the institutional genes of rebel factions under the Chinese imperial regime. These were strikingly similar to some of the institutional genes of the Bolsheviks. This similarity laid the foundation for the subsequent reorganization of the KMT along Bolshevik lines and the success of the Comintern in establishing the CCP.

China's institutional genes rendered the establishment of a constitutional government in China difficult, even following the demise of the imperial system and the ostensible creation of a republic, parliament, and constitution. Observers at the time, especially from the United States, commented that a wholesale transplantation of the American system to China would be untenable, "[Establishing] in China in 1911 an imitation of the American republic ... was a fiasco because it had no roots in Chinese history, traditions, political experience, institutions, instincts, beliefs, attitudes, or habits" (Peffer, 1958).

Both constitutional advisors to the ROC and Yuan Shikai, Professor Frank Goodnow (1859–1939) at Columbia University and Japanese jurist Nagao Ariga (1860–1921), noted significant challenges that China faced in its attempt to establish a constitutional government. They observed that China's elites lacked a fundamental understanding of law and, more importantly, the principles of constitutionalism. Consequently, they were highly skeptical about the prospects for a constitutional republic in China.

According to Ariga, "The ROC was founded not purely due to the public will but came into existence because the Qing emperor ceded the right to rule ... as it was initiated first by the Wuhan uprising and only became fully established once the former Qing emperor had ceded power." The national law of the ROC was, therefore, different from the law in a republic established out of the public will (Nagao, 2019, pp. 79–81). Ariga published "Gonghe xianfa chijiu ce" ("Sustainable Policy on the Constitution of the Republic") in the newspaper *Shun pao*, on October 30 and 31, 1913, opposing the cabinet-system constitution, which had been drafted by the KMT-dominated National Assembly. Instead, he advocated for a constitutional establishment of a centralized presidential system (Shang, 2013).

Goodnow held a view similar to Ariga regarding the ROC's presidential system. However, both failed to fully recognize the brutal, autocratic aspect of the imperial legacy that post-empire China had inherited. By the end of 1913, Yuan Shikai had declared the KMT illegal and banned it, alleging that it had initiated a "Second Revolution" and conspired to launch a military coup. While declaring the KMT illegal arguably might have been legitimate given the allegations, Yuan's subsequent actions made it clear that he was trying to dismantle all restrictions on his power that had been imposed by the newly established constitutional rules.

In 1914, he dissolved assemblies at all levels and legally imposed press censorship. The government then took control of the Chambers of Commerce, the post office, the railways, and so on, and suppressed dissidents with impunity. The Western press of the time reported that Yuan's reckless dictatorial actions had decimated popular support for him (Fairbank and Feuerwerker, 1994, part 1, chapter 4).

Around that time, the reformed Senate adopted a "Constitutional Compact" to replace the Provisional Constitution that had been previously instituted by the KMT-dominated National Assembly. Several articles regarding the centralization of presidential powers were drafted by Goodnow. Later, Goodnow wrote to the president

9.4 FAILURE OF THE REPUBLICAN REVOLUTION (1911–1916) 431

of Columbia University, Nicholas Butler, acknowledging that this constitution afforded Yuan too much power. However, he conceded that in the end, the Chinese would do no better than the constitution they had adopted because constitutionalism was not their tradition and they had neither a concept of the rule of law nor an organizational body worthy of being called a court (Kroncke, 2012).

Goodnow, as revealed by his defending words years later, was perhaps confused between his academic research and his role as an advisor, and was also confused between taking Yuan as an object of research and Yuan as the provisional president of the ROC with an ambition of becoming an emperor. Without comprehending the danger of fueling political chaos by revealing the truth to the wrong person, in a memorandum written to Yuan Shikai in 1915, Goodnow stated that China was not ready for a republican system and that a monarchy was more suitable. He wrote,

> The intelligence of the great mass of its people is not high.... The change from an autocratic to a republican government at once was too sudden a move to expect good results.... China is bound to be in trouble in the future with the presidential succession ... [and] if the disorders were not immediately extinguished, it might seriously imperil the independence of the country.... undoubtedly, it would be better for China to have a monarchy than a republic. (Goodnow, 1924)

Goodnow went on to argue that the Republican Revolution in China had already failed. Ariga had similar views, albeit not as systematically articulated. One year before Goodnow, Yan Fu had published similar views. In his criticism of the republican system, Yan Fu also conflated Locke and Rousseau and criticized them (Wang, 1976, pp. 92–93).

Indeed, Yuan and his followers quickly exploited Goodnow's position for dismantling the constitutional rules. Yang Du,[12] a promonarchy advocate who claimed to be Yuan's imperial mentor, used Goodnow's memorandum to advocate for the restoration of the monarchy, even though Goodnow insisted that his memorandum was merely a discussion of principles and was not intended to alter the political system (Kroncke, 2012).

Only a few days after Goodnow's memorandum was published, Yang Du sought out Yan Fu. On the surface, the meeting was to discuss Goodnow's views on republicanism but Yang's real motive was to seek Yan Fu's support for his monarchist initiative.[13] Yang said, "I am establishing a society with my comrades, to be named the Chouan hui (Society for Peace), devoted to exploring whether our country is more suited to being a monarchy than a republic. Goodnow has made a start, and we will strive to take up the task" (Schwartz, 2010, p. 153).

Yuan Shikai and his followers might not have been sufficiently powerful to bring about the changes they desired. However, both the KMT and the constitutionalists unintentionally aided Yuan. The KMT's "Second Revolution" was largely seen by constitutionalists as a threat to the newly established republic. Notable figures, including Liang Qichao, Cai E, and Tang Jiyao, not only strongly endorsed the suppression of the "Second Revolution" but, in response, they also supported centralization in the name of the republic. Cai E and Tang Jiyao even participated directly in the military suppression of the revolution.

The constitutionalists' support for centralization provided Yuan with an excellent opportunity to weaken the emerging institutional genes of constitutionalism. Yuan ruthlessly suppressed dissent and forced Premier Xiong Xiling, the honorary director of the Progressive Party (which had been co-founded by Liang Qichao), to resign.

The institutional genes of the old regime laid the foundation for a new wave of anti-constitutionalism under the ROC. Power-holders in the provinces declared themselves subordinate to the central authority. This, combined with the publication of Goodnow's memorandum, led to a public outcry supporting the idea that constitutionalism was unsuitable for China. Under these conditions, the vigorous push by the Chouan hui to restore the monarchy proved effective.

On October 6, 1915, the Senate received eighty-three petitions from provincial delegates advocating a shift to a constitutional monarchy. Later, on December 11, under a new law drafted by the Senate, nearly 2,000 elected deputies unanimously agreed to change the state system to a constitutional monarchy and to rename the country the Empire of China.

While constitutionalism did not take deep roots in China, it is clear that a significant portion of Chinese elites had a desire to abandon the imperial system. The move to restore a monarchy, particularly with Yuan Shikai at the helm, was widely regarded as illegitimate. Yuan Shikai's proclamation to change the national designation immediately sparked fierce opposition and armed resistance from constitutionalists such as Liang Qichao, Cai E, and Tang Jiyao. Yunnan Province declared independence from the empire and the National Protection Army was established,[14] triggering armed uprisings in multiple provinces.

Yuan's restoration also encountered covert resistance from his long-time loyalists. Notably, Feng Guozhang, the general who played a key role in quelling the "Second Revolution" and who became the new Chief of Staff after Yuan's self-coronation, secretly reached out to generals from four provinces in 1916. Together, they issued a clandestine telegram to all provincial generals, soliciting opinions on the possibility of revoking the monarchy (Tian, 1999, p. 123).

Foreign powers such as Japan, Britain, and the United States also refused to recognize the restored empire. Under intensified domestic and international pressure, Yuan was compelled to abolish the monarchy and reinstate the republic. However, the ROC was in a state of turmoil. The country was fragmented into several separate military-controlled regions: the south controlled by the Yunnan army, the lower reaches of the Yangtze under Feng Guozhang, the northern areas controlled by the Beiyang government, and the northeast under Zhang Zuolin (Fairbank and Feuerwerker, 1994, part 1, chapter 4). Thereafter, the ROC was in fact ruled by a coalition of regional warlords and the constitutional rules were only partially implemented. But this was soon swept away by the KMT's Northern Expedition, which was planned and supported by Soviet forces (to be described in detail in Chapter 10).

9.5 REVOLUTIONARY PARTIES: THE INSTITUTIONAL GENES OF THE "SECRET SOCIETIES"

No new system, constitutional or totalitarian, can be instituted without the support of the relevant institutional genes already in that society, regardless of how much effort the advocates expend. Only when the gap between the existing institutional genes of a society and the desirable institutional genes of the system to be established is not too wide can it yield the results anticipated by the reformers or revolutionaries.

Indeed, one of the institutional genes that led to the rise of the Bolsheviks was the tradition of secret political organizations that were prevalent in Tsarist Russia. Correspondingly, a similar institutional gene existed in the Chinese imperial system in the form of secret societies. It was this particular institutional gene that played a significant role in the birth of the Tongmenghui-KMT. Most importantly, this gene was one of the key factors that facilitated the Comintern to create the CCP, enabling it to establish a foothold and subsequently thrive in China.[15]

Under the Chinese imperial system, clandestine organizations were the only bodies left that were conducting organized activities, since no open, organized, independent social forces were permitted.[16] Even clan groups could face prohibition if they grew too large or spread across regions, especially if they posed a threat to the authorities. This strict control made clandestine organizations essential for maintaining parts of the societal structure and channeling certain social forces in China.

Secret societies with political and power ambitions had been part of Chinese history since at least the Song dynasty (920–1279).[17] Among these, the White Lotus Society (Bailian jiao) is particularly noteworthy. It emerged towards the end of the Yuan dynasty, a period during which the Rus' region (the predecessor to Russia) was still under the control of the Mongol Empire's Golden Horde. More than a religious body, the White Lotus Society was a secret political organization, although its religious background can be traced back to the White Lotus sects (Bailian she) and other Buddhist religious sects, such as Maitreya, established as early as the early fifth century (Yang, 2004; Haar, 1992; and Qin and Tan, 2002, vol. 2, pp. 43–46). Seen as heretical by the court, these sects were driven underground, eventually becoming the forerunners to other covert sects that surfaced during the Ming and Qing dynasties (Qin and Tan, 2002, vol. 1, pp. 14–27). It was the Red Turban rebellion, primarily led by the White Lotus, that ultimately precipitated the downfall of the Yuan dynasty and the ascendance of the Ming dynasty.

Zhu Yuanzhang, who ascended to become the first emperor of the Ming dynasty, was propelled into power by the Red Turban Rebellion (Qin and Tan, 2002, vol. 2, pp. 56–69). Having first-hand knowledge of the potential threat such societies posed to the regime, the Ming dynasty outlawed the White Lotus, among other groups, deeming them heretical. According to Ming laws, participation in those organizations was punishable by death, irrespective of one's social status. The early Ming period witnessed a particularly brutal suppression of the White Lotus, with Emperor Yongle's reign (r. 1402–1424) seeing tens of thousands of nuns across multiple provinces arrested and many killed to capture a single female leader of the White Lotus (Qin and Tan, 2002, vol. 2, pp. 81–82).

During the Qing dynasty, there was a rapid proliferation of secret societies. In addition to traditional Confucian, Taoist, and Buddhist sects, covert Christian groups like the Society of God Worshippers began to appear. The Qianlong period (1735–1796) saw a surge in the development of secret societies across the country. Archival records suggest that the majority of these societies' members were without property and unemployed. Although these societies often presented themselves under the guise of religion, most, including their leaders, possessed little religious knowledge or beliefs.

In the absence of religious grounding, secret societies often forged connections through sworn brotherhood, solidified by blood rituals and oaths of mutual allegiance. The act of making and upholding such oaths effectively bound members into a familial network. For instance, all members of the Tiandihui (Heaven and Earth Society) adopted the surname Hong, referring to each other as "Hong family brothers." The rule was "no withdrawal after joining," with severe punishments, including torture, for any breach of this stipulation.[18]

The evolution of secret societies in China led to the establishment of relatively stable traditions, both organizationally and ideologically. These traditions subsequently laid the groundwork for the Comintern to found a Communist totalitarian party in China, effectively becoming part of its institutional genes. Many of these secret societies championed causes like the abolition of private land ownership and the promotion of absolute egalitarianism. For example, the Longhua Sect in Zhejiang Province adhered to the principle that "land should be communal property ... so that everyone can live in peace and have enough to eat" (Hirayama, 2017).

Many of these societies were essentially semi-permanent bandit gangs and armies, primarily engaged in banditry and smuggling. The Jintian district of Guangxi, for instance, was already "riddled with thieves" by the mid-nineteenth century. They pledged loyalty to clan chapters, with some chapters comprising "as many as three to four thousand members, totaling more than ten thousand ... dedicated to pillage, ransom, and extortion."

In the 1840s, Zhang Jiaxiang's Yiyi tang (Joyous Righteousness Gang) in Guangxi became known for "killing officials and sparing the people, robbing the rich and aiding the poor," attracting thousands of followers. These conditions set the stage for the Taiping Rebellion, which resulted in over 70 million fatalities within just a decade, making it the deadliest civil war in human history.

The Taiping Rebellion severely rattled the Qing Empire across its social, economic, and military sectors, marking the beginning of the end for China's longest-standing empire. Beyond the immense destruction and loss of life, the Taiping Rebellion had a profound historical impact.

First, the Taiping army substantially challenged the traditional Qing forces by extensively utilizing foreign weapons. As a result, Qing commanders such as Li Hongzhang increasingly relied on these foreign arms to suppress the rebellion. This shift directly prompted the Western Affairs Movement (or the Self-Strengthening Movement), the first significant reform of the late Qing era, which lasted for several decades. Many historians see the Taiping Rebellion as marking the beginning of modern Chinese history (Fairbank, 1985, part 1, p. 257).

Second, and perhaps more significantly, the Taiping Rebellion laid the groundwork for the violent revolution that eventually toppled the Qing Empire. Hong Xiuquan, the leader of the Taiping Rebellion, later became a revolutionary icon for Sun Yat-sen, Mao Zedong, and other leaders of the Chinese Communist Party.

The Taiping Rebellion, with its reliance on Christianity to stir up revolt and provide legitimacy, hinted at the nascent signs of what would later become the Chinese Communist movement. Hong Xiuquan was originally a Confucian scholar. Like many of his contemporaries, he initially dedicated himself to his studies and aspired to attain official status. However, after failing his third provincial examination, Hong found solace in a pamphlet narrating the story of Christ. Consequently, he claimed to have converted to Christianity and to have received a divine calling. He even referred to himself as the son of God Jehovah and the brother of Jesus.

Several years later, he studied the Bible with an American Baptist missionary named Issachar Roberts. However, Roberts did not endorse Hong's interpretation of biblical scripture, let alone acknowledge his self-proclaimed divine status, and therefore refused to baptize him (Fairbank, 1985, part 1, pp. 260–264). Roberts later worked for a time in the Taiping government and, based on his experience, believed that Hong Xiuquan's version of Christianity was not true Christianity.

Hong claimed to have been granted a divine mission to instigate both spiritual and secular revolutions and convert all Chinese to Christianity. He joined forces with Feng Yunshan, a masterful organizer, to establish a militarized sect named the "God-Worshipping Society" in the Hakka areas of Guangxi, where militia groups were well developed. The version of Christianity propagated by this clandestine organization, known as Hong Xiuquan's Christianity, introduced unprecedented new ideologies to the locals. Yet, its organizational structure bore a striking resemblance to that of the Triad Society, one of the largest secret societies in China. In 1851, Hong established the Taiping Heavenly Kingdom in Jintian, Guangxi Province. During its expansionary campaigns, the Taiping army integrated many Triad groups into its ranks (Fairbank, 1985, part 1, pp. 263–267).

After conquering the southern part of the empire, in 1853 Taiping rebels established their capital in a major southern city, Nanjing (renamed as Heavenly Capital). Thereafter, the Taiping Heavenly Kingdom developed a comprehensive military bureaucracy. Parts of this bureaucratic hierarchy and functional structure were derived from *Zhou li* (*Rites of Zhou*). As the head of state, Hong styled himself as the Heavenly King, naming four others as kings of the North, South, East, and West. The most influential figure under Hong was Yang Xiuqing, the King of the East, who also served as the supreme commander of the army. Key strategic orders were often given by Yang in the form of séances to convey God's intentions. The Taiping Heavenly Kingdom issued a series of proclamations declaring its intention to establish a heavenly kingdom on earth, with some elements drawn from the Bible. Hong Xiuquan was portrayed as a dynastic founder chosen by divine mandate, while the Manchus were depicted as incarnations of the devil. The ideological basis for the Taipings was a mixture of Christianity, traditional Confucianism, Taoism, Buddhism, and anti-Manchu nationalism (Fairbank, 1985, part 1, pp. 268–269).

Hong's doctrine was rooted in Christian terminology, interwoven with phrases and passages from *Liji* (*Book of Rites*) about

"Great harmonization" and "commonwealth of the whole world." He claimed that once everyone followed God, "the world will be one, and there will be peace for all" (Fairbank, 1985, part 1, p. 270). Although viewed as heretical from both Catholic and Protestant perspectives, Hong, like Thomas Müntzer who instigated the German Peasants' War in the name of Protestantism, and the Anabaptist Communist regime of Münster (see Chapter 6), drew on the most enticing common ideals and incendiary components of Christianity. These convinced the destitute masses to commit violent acts in the pursuit of a communal heavenly kingdom and to behave recklessly in their quest for absolute equality.

However, violence is never compatible with democracy or equality. Utopian regimes established through violence always depend on an extraordinary concentration of political, military, and economic power. The highly centralized structures determine that those being ruled lose not only control over public affairs but also their basic rights, including the most basic economic rights. Thus, even if the original intention of the initial unleashing of violence to achieve utopia is to achieve equality, its actual operation is strictly hierarchical. Such strict hierarchy naturally contravenes the concept of equality. This pattern was evident in the Münster regime in the Middle Ages, the Jacobin regime at the beginning of the nineteenth century, and the Soviet regime at the start of the twentieth century. The Taiping Heavenly Kingdom was no exception.

The Taiping Rebellion, serving as a precursor to later communist revolutions, demonstrated that the institutional genes of China's old regime bore a striking resemblance to the institutional genes necessary for fostering communist totalitarian institutions. Under the highly appealing principle of great harmonization, the "Land Ownership System of the Heavenly Kingdom" instituted state ownership of land and state control of labor and deemed the produce of the land as state property. Farmland was allocated to all based on absolute egalitarian principles. All consumption was limited to basic survival needs in an absolutely equal manner, with all excess surrendered to the state treasury. For a time, gender segregation was enforced and even married couples were not allowed to have sexual relations to eliminate family units (Fairbank, 1985, part 1, p. 271). However, the leaders themselves were ennobled and enjoyed luxuries beyond those of emperors, demonstrating that from the leaders' perspective, absolute equality served more as a slogan for driving revolution, rather than a real concern in practice.

The Taiping Heavenly Kingdom not only inherited the institutional genes of secret societies such as the Triads but also those of imperial rule. Before his assassination, Yang Xiuqing, King of the East, who effectively governed the Taiping, organized his government in the traditional imperial administrative structure of Six Ministries. The Taiping Heavenly Kingdom also introduced a *keju* system that largely mimicked practices from past dynasties, with the main difference being the addition of Christian content.

In the name of pursuing equality, the Taiping Rebellion, which evolved from secret societies and drew heavily on Christianity, implemented a state-controlled land system that ensured absolute egalitarianism, a variant of Christian communism. This secular, caesaropapist regime was extraordinarily brutal, sharing many similarities with the Christian communist regime of Münster in the Middle Ages. It was thereby a totalitarian regime in embryonic form. Its rule was strictly enforced, with draconian punishments for any violations of the "Heavenly Laws" (the laws of the Taiping Heavenly Kingdom).

In the name of equality, the regime denied human and property rights more than the traditional imperial system did. As such, power was more concentrated. Under near-totalitarian rule without checks and balances, everyone's fate was determined by those wielding supreme authority. Moreover, senior officials like Yang Xiuqing well understood Hong Xiuquan's legitimacy stemmed from his self-proclaimed divine right, which led to a relentless power struggle among the top leaders. Having taken over half of the Qing Empire, the top echelons of the Taiping had become embroiled in power infighting, slaughtering thousands of their own brothers and eventually crumbling under both internal and external pressure. Historian Cao Shuji estimated that the Taiping Rebellion resulted in as many as 73.3 million deaths in the seven provinces of the central war zone alone (Cao, 2001, vol. 5, p. 553). This bloodiest rebellion inspired Chinese revolutionary leaders, Sun and Mao, in the twentieth century.

Sun Yat-sen's revolution, while ostensibly a Republican Revolution, was more akin to the Taiping Rebellion in its early stages. It was a nationalist uprising under the slogan "Expel the Tartars, revive China." Besides nationalism, Sun advocated for state and communal ownership of land (Sun, 1981, vol. 6, p. 56). Indeed, Sun regarded a "glorious history of our national revolution" (Sun, 1981, vol. 1, p. 217) and claimed himself to be the second Hong Xiuquan (Sun, 1981, vol 1, p. 583). Also similar to the Taiping Rebellion, the revolutionary organization they established and the armed uprising they launched in the name of the Republican Revolution were based on and intimately related to secret societies. These secret societies, many of which comprised bandits, had nothing to do with constitutionalism. Most of their members were the proletariat, more interested in seizing land from wealthy landlords than in protecting private property. Therefore, from the outset, even if Tongmenghui's so-called Republican Revolution had settled into a stable regime, it was not destined to produce a constitutional system protecting human and property rights.

Founded in Tokyo in 1905, Tongmenghui was a union of various secret societies that advocated for the violent overthrow of the Manchu Qing government, including Sun Yat-sen's Xingzhonghui (Revive China Society), Huang Xing's Huaxinghui (Chinese Revival Society), and Cai Yuanpei and Tao Chengzhang's Guangfuhui (Restoration Society). Each of these covert organizations was deeply connected to larger secret societies within China, with many local branches even being founded on the structures of long-standing secret societies. The Xingzhonghui had close ties with the Gelaohui (Brotherhood Society) and the Sanhehui (Triad Society) and the Huaxinghui was linked with the Gelaohui and the Hongjiang Society, while the majority of the Guangfuhui were secret societies from Jiangsu and Zhejiang provinces.

The Republican Revolution in China was, to a large degree, grounded in China's prevalent secret societies. These societies had expanded in both size and influence towards the end of the nineteenth century, developing increasingly rigid organizational structures and complex codes of conduct. Tao Chengzhang, co-founder of the Guangfuhui, thus also a co-founder of the Tongmenghui and the KMT, devoted most of his revolutionary efforts to liaising with these secret societies, becoming an expert in this field.[19]

Tao asserted that, "China has two major clandestine groups, strong enough to influence the nation ... One is the White Lotus, or the Red Turbans. The other is the *Tiandihui*, or the Hong Fraternity ... the Triad Society, the Brotherhood Society and various other societies are all spinoffs of *Tiandihui*" (Tao, [1928] 2020).

There was no clear boundary between the religious sects and secular secret societies. For instance, the Dadaohui (Big Swords Society), which ignited the Boxer Rebellion, was an offshoot of the White Lotus. Both the Taiping Rebellion and the Boxer Rebellion emerged from existing secret societies (Chesneaux, 1972; Shao et al., 1993) and the impact of these rebellions, in turn, reinforced the tradition of secret societies. This tradition formed the social foundation for the establishment of the Tongmenghui and served as an institutional gene for the emergence of the CCP.

Sun Yat-sen's views on a revolutionary party bear similarities to those of Lenin. This resemblance illustrates more than just personal beliefs; it showcases shared institutional genetics. Both figures clearly distinguished between revolutionary parties and political parties, emphasizing the secret society characteristics of the former. Sun contended that "it is necessary to take risks, shed blood and sacrifice lives and property to achieve the success of the revolution. This is the mission of a revolutionary party" (Sun, 1981, vol. 3, p. 35).

Sun saw a revolutionary party as an instrument to overthrow the government using violence, whereas a political party was a tool of governance. He stated, "The purpose of a political party is to consolidate the country, that is, to represent the people's wishes, to solidify the country and bring about social peace" (Sun, 1981, vol. 2, p. 469). Consequently, he intended to establish a political party after the formation of the Republic (Sun, 1981, vol. 3, p. 4).

To harness the power of the secret societies, Sun personally joined the Zhigongtang of the Hong Fraternity and was conferred the high-ranking title of Hong Baton. Upon the establishment of the Xingzhonghui in Honolulu, a substantial number of its founders were either members or affiliated with secret societies. In its headquarters in Hong Kong, approximately 30 percent of its members came from secret societies.

In order to make the Tongmenghui a unified front against the Qing, its charter specified, "All societies with similar objectives and willing to ally with the Tongmenghui should be recognized as members of the Tongmenghui." The handful of uprisings that the Tongmenghui provoked between 1907 and 1908 were largely led by secret societies (Xiao and Tan, 2007).

The Xinhai Revolution of 1911, while seemingly organized under the guise of a republic, primarily conveyed its objectives through nationalist slogans such as "expel the Tartars." Given that members of secret societies formed the backbone of the revolution, and these societies were committed to "opposing the Qing and restoring the Ming dynasty," the primary objective of the key forces within the Tongmenghui was to return imperial power to the Han Chinese, about which they knew almost nothing.

The Second Guangzhou Uprising, which occurred in April 1911, offers a particularly illuminating example of the primary revolutionary force within the Tongmenghui. The original plan was to rely on support from the New Army. However, when this proved impractical, the decision was made to lean on the core strength of the Tongmenghui. The uprising ultimately failed and of the 72 individuals killed in action, 68 were members of the Hong Fraternity. This reflects the significant role the Hong Fraternity, a traditional secret society, played within the Tongmenghui.

Sun Yat-sen harnessed the influence of secret societies in establishing both the Xingzhonghui and the Tongmenghui and his original vision for the revolution was to "start by advancing the secret societies" (Xiao and Tan, 2007). Indeed, at that time, all groups that advocated violent revolution were reliant on secret societies. Inheriting the institutional gene of secret societies, these revolutionary organizations operated in ways that were characteristic of secret societies, which fundamentally contradicted constitutional principles.

The assassination of Tao Chengzhang, a founding leader of the Tongmenghui, by Chiang Kai-shek, serves as a quintessential example of the behavior of the Tongmenghui-KMT. Tao founded the Guangfuhui in 1904 with the aim of "restoring the Han nation and recovering the homeland." The society was spearheaded by Cai Yuanpei, who served as chairman, alongside Zhang Taiyan, Xu Xilin, Qiu Jin, and Tao, all famous revolutionary figures in Chinese history. One of Tao's primary duties was to liaise with secret societies in the Jiangsu–Zhejiang region to prepare for the overthrow of the Manchu regime. After the Tongmenghui-KMT was established, the Guangfuhui was integrated into it as one of its founding organizations.

In 1907, a disagreement over funding within the Tongmenghui triggered a split between Tao and Sun Yat-sen. As a result, Tao restructured the Guangfuhui. In collaboration with the Hong Fraternity and other secret societies in the five southeastern provinces, Tao established the secretive Revolutionary Alliance. The alliance sought to overthrow the Qing dynasty through assassination and rebellion and aimed to establish an empire as magnificent as the Ming and Tang dynasties, under the principle of equal land rights.

Subsequently, Tao accused Sun Yat-sen of misappropriating public funds and called for his dismissal as premier. Tao's close collaboration with secret societies across various provinces on military and social control matters, as well as his reputation in Zhejiang, made Sun and his supporters view Tao as a significant threat to their authority within the revolutionary forces.

After the Wuchang uprising in 1911 and the liberation of Hangzhou, Tao was elected president of the Interim Senate in Zhejiang, a stronghold of republican revolutionary forces. In 1912, Chen Qimei, one of Sun's allies, instructed his subordinate Chiang Kai-shek to assassinate Tao. In his diary entry on July 26, 1943, Chiang noted that the assassination of Tao "was the responsibility of me alone" and that "this matter was never mentioned between me and the premier" (Yang, 2017). Chiang later stated that it was from the assassination of Tao that he earned the trust of Sun (Chiang, 2016).

Drawing upon the institutional genes of secret societies, the Tongmenghui-KMT ostensibly launched a Republican Revolution. Nevertheless, the predominant ethos throughout the organization, from top to bottom, favored violence and a desire for a monopoly on power, with constitutionalism resonating only among a minority.

Whenever the KMT's authority was significantly threatened, an armed uprising seemed almost inevitable, irrespective of whether incidents such as the assassination of Song Jiaoren had occurred. It was therefore no accident that the KMT launched a "Second Revolution." However, the "Second Revolution" bolstered Yuan Shikai with strong support from constitutionalists, allowing him to centralize power and prepare for the restoration of the imperial system. This dealt a fatal blow to the ideal of realizing a constitutional republic in China.

Only advanced for a few years, the constitutional reform of the Qing Empire was overtaken by a Republican Revolution led by the Tongmenghui-KMT amidst popular protests triggered by the full-scale encroachment of imperial power on civil rights. The new Republic, in turn, was soon largely buried by the KMT and Yuan Shikai with the "Second Revolution," restoration of the imperial system, and the KMT Northern Expedition.

These unfortunate developments, and the institutional genes behind them, paved the way for communist totalitarianism to influence China, take its roots, and proliferate in the country.

NOTES

1. Guo Songtao: *Guo Songtao shiwenji* (*Collected Poetry and Prose of Kuo Sung-tao*), cited in Yuan (2001).
2. Yan Fu: notes on *Shehui tongquan* (*General Commentary on Society*), in Yan (1986), Vol. 4, pp. 928–929.
3. In a system where a sovereign reigns at the apex and democracy forms the foundation, a robust connection is facilitated between the governing bodies and the governed populace. This profound connection fosters stability and resilience, making it unlikely for either internal unrest or external invasions to prevail. The firm bedrock of such a nation would remain steadfast. The extensive reach and influence of this system would inevitably pave the way for national prosperity and the ascendancy of its power. (Wang Tao: *Tao Yuan wenlu waipian* (*Further Records of the Statements of Tao Yuan*), cited in Xiao (2003)).
4. "To augment the power of the state, no strategy surpasses winning the hearts of the people; to win the hearts of the people, no method surpasses resonating with the public sentiment; to resonate with the public sentiment, no approach surpasses the establishment of an Assembly" for public deliberation on political matters. Efforts to ensure "internal security and repel external aggression ... must initiate with the establishment of an Assembly" (Zheng Guangying, *Shengshi weiyan* [*The Perils of a Golden Age*], cited in Xu and Wang (2015, p. 199)).
5. Kang Youwei's seminal work on reform from a Confucian perspective was *Xinxue weijing kao* (*Examination of the Forged Classics of the New* Text), penned in 1891. It began to significantly impact society a few years after its publication. The treatise argued that the Confucianism at the heart of the imperial examination system was a counterfeit version, based on corrupted interpretations of the classics from the late Western Han period. During this era, Liu Xin had manipulated the Confucian canon to legitimize the usurper Wang Mang (see Chapter 5). The critique had enormous implications and impact on both Confucianism and the imperial examination system, a magnitude similar to the transformative influence of Martin Luther during the onset of the Reformation. Indeed, Kang's disciple, Liang Qichao, referred to him as the "Martin Luther of Confucianism" (Liang Qichao, *Yinbingshi wenji* (Ice-Drinker Studio Collected Works), cited in Pusey (2008)). Kang's masterwork, the *Datong shu* (Book of the Great Unity),

mostly completed in 1895, amalgamated elements of his Confucian and Buddhist philosophies.
6. Yan Fu never fully translated Spencer's major works on social evolution, which were much harder to translate. Instead, Huxley's succinct and methodical critique of Spencer was easier to comprehend. Furthermore, critiquing Huxley allowed Yan Fu an avenue to fully express his own viewpoints (Schwartz, 2010).
7. Institut marksizma-leninizma (Moscow, Russia) (1956, p. 106); and Marx and Engels (1975).
8. Despite the fact that racist theorizing has been largely dismissed in the West since the downfall of the Nazi regime and Social Darwinism has substantially lost its appeal, such ideologies or philosophies continue to wield significant influence in China.
9. As Ge (2018) documented, what is China? Is it a national state or an empire? What is the nationality of Chinese? These are intriguing questions that incited generations of Chinese intellectuals and revolutionaries since the late nineteenth century.
10. *Daqing dezong shilu* (*Veritable Records of the Guangxu Emperor*), cited in Fairbank (1985, part 2, p. 369).
11. *Guangxu chao donghua lu* (*Guangxu Reign Records*), cited in (Yuan, 2001).
12. Through his close connection with Du Yuesheng, Yang Du rendered significant intelligence and other services to the CCP. In 1929, he was covertly inducted into the party by Zhou Enlai, upon the introduction by Pan Hannian. Among the critical tasks he performed for the CCP was providing protection for Mao Zedong's sons (Zuo, 2013). Yang's covert affiliation with the CCP remained undisclosed until shortly before Zhou's death. Zhou stated that Yang "joined the party in his later years and was under my leadership until his death" (Wang, 1978).
13. Yan Fu's political convictions saw some changes over time. Initially, he was an advocate for a constitutional monarchy and expressed opposition to the idea of a republic. However, after the establishment of the Republic, he stood firmly against attempts to restore the imperial system. He challenged the legitimacy of Yuan Shikai's claim to the throne specifically. Despite this, due to Yang Du's manipulative influences and the persistent pressure from Yuan Shikai, Yan eventually agreed to co-sponsor the Society for Peace (Wang, 1976, pp. 87–95).

14. Later, the National Protection Army merged with Sun Yat-sen's Constitutional Protection Movement, becoming the driving force behind the Northern Expedition. Founding generals of the communist army, including Zhu De, began their revolutionary careers within the National Protection Army.
15. China experts have observed that secret societies exist globally but the degree of their intensive and extensive influence on Chinese history is quite unique (Perry in Haar, 1992).
16. This discussion pertains to national, regional, or trade sector formations that involve a large number of people, rather than community clan groups or solitary temple societies.
17. Extensive archival research has been conducted both in China and abroad to uncover the long and complex history of Chinese secret societies. According to some scholars, the origin of these societies and sects in China can be traced back to the end of the Han dynasty in the third century (Chesneaux, 1972).
18. Cai (1987, pp. 10–14). For a systematic documentation of Tiandihui, including its origin, organization, and ideology, see Haar (1998).
19. Tao Chengzhang, a revolutionary figure who forged connections with secret societies and pursued studies in Japan, was the pioneer in conducting extensive research into Chinese secret societies in the modern era. Tao's ties to these secret societies were pivotal to the evolution of the Guangfuhui and similar associations were equally significant for the other entities that amalgamated to form the Tongmenghui. In 1908, following a disagreement with Sun Yat-sen, Tao allied with branches of the Hong Fraternity across five southeastern provinces to establish the Revolutionary Association. This separate clandestine organization adhered to the rules of the Hong Fraternity and emerged as the revolutionary military force for these provinces.

10 Building China's Bolshevik Party

The establishment of the Chinese Communist Party as the cornerstone of a communist totalitarian system in China could not have been accomplished without the missionary activities, financial support, and direct recruitment and organizational efforts of the Comintern in China. The Chinese were unaware of Marxist-Leninist ideology until the October Revolution, let alone capable of organizing a Leninist party independently. Comintern agents infiltrated China during a time of intensifying nationalism and a surge in anti-Western and anti-Japanese sentiment, which were stoked by the May Fourth Movement. The immediate catalyst for this movement was the Versailles Treaty at the end of the First World War in April 1919. This treaty ceded sovereignty over Shandong, a Chinese province, from Germany (a defeated nation in the war) to Japan (a victorious nation), even though China had also been on the winning side.

The anti-West frenzy in China provided an excellent opportunity for the Comintern. In 1920, it established its China branch, the CCP, which recruited fifty members nationwide in its first year, thereby sowing the seeds of totalitarianism in China. This was the Comintern's most significant accomplishment in its global communist revolution endeavors. Just over a decade later, by 1931, the CCP had rapidly grown, leading to the establishment of the Chinese Soviet Republic. By 1949, the CCP took control of the whole country after defeating all forces advocating or sympathizing with constitutionalism.

As discussed in Chapter 9, there was a significant gap between China's institutional genes and those required to establish constitutionalism, resulting in the failure of both the constitutional reforms of the late Qing era and the subsequent Republican Revolution. But communism, like constitutionalism, was an imported concept and was even less understood by the Chinese until the 1950s. Why, then, had Bolshevism's fate in China been diametrically opposed to that of constitutionalism? This chapter explains why and how Bolshevism was able to take root in China by analyzing its institutional genes.

The communist totalitarian system established by the Bolsheviks was based upon three basic institutional genes from Tsarist Russia: Tsarist autocracy, secret political organizations, and the Orthodox Church. While communist ideology originates from Christianity, several distinguishing aspects of communist totalitarianism – first realized by Bolshevism – are rooted in Russian Orthodoxy. These include its penetration into all corners of society, the use of propaganda, traditions of confession and a personality cult, a spirit of martyrdom, and a secular governance system of caesaropapism.

Without Russian Orthodoxy as a critical institutional gene, it would have been impossible for China to develop an indigenous communist ideology or a communist totalitarian system centered around this ideology. Indeed, Marxism was only introduced to China in the early twentieth century by a handful of students studying in Japan. Their understanding of Marxism was at best superficial and had much less influence among intellectuals than anarchism did (Xu and Wang, 2015). This small group of Chinese who had a superficial understanding of a few Marxist-Leninist pamphlets could not have made a significant impact on society, let alone established a party like the Bolsheviks. Therefore, the work of the Comintern was indispensable in setting up a totalitarian party in China.

However, simply attributing the success of the CCP in China to the Comintern does not provide a fully convincing explanation, as the Comintern's efforts to export revolution largely failed elsewhere in the world. For instance, in Germany, it was unable to persuade the Social Democratic Party (SDP) or other significant revolutionary leaders to adopt their stance. It also encountered substantial hurdles in other countries. Why was the Comintern able to make a significant impact in China? There must have been other elements, beyond the efforts of the Comintern alone, that facilitated the eventual triumph of communist totalitarianism in China. The most crucial of these factors is the similarity between certain institutional genes in China, primarily those associated with imperial rule and secret societies, and those of Bolshevism.

Compared to Tsarism, China's imperial system was more centralized, sophisticated, and deeply rooted in history. In both China and Russia, the imperial tradition served as one of the foundational institutional genes for establishing a modern totalitarian system. Public support for imperial autocracy was even stronger and more widespread in China than in Russia. For the majority of Chinese, particularly intellectuals, the imperial order was the only structure they recognize. Their support for autocratic rule of an imperial nature was often a subconscious response. This remains somewhat true even in today's China.

Additionally, another institutional gene essential for a totalitarian party is the history of secret insurgent groups in China, a tradition that dates back to the Song dynasty. This parallels the custom of clandestine political organizations in Tsarist Russia. As previously discussed in Chapter 9, the Tongmenghui-KMT was inextricably linked with traditional secret societies like the Hong Fraternity from the early days of the Republican Revolution. Intriguingly, the institutional gene of secret political organizations was indeed an essential and basic ingredient in the establishment and development of the CCP. More interestingly, the CCP deliberately used secret political organizations in the revolution under direct instructions from the Comintern.

To comprehend why Soviet Russia and the Comintern had such a special appeal to some radical Chinese intellectuals, one should consider their positions and demands. As shown in Chapter 9, the great majority of constitutionalist intellectuals (including their leaders and whether they championed a constitutional monarchy or a republican revolution), were primarily concerned with national salvation rather than the basic rights of the people or limiting the power of the monarch or government. Of all the ideologies introduced to China from the West and Japan, Social Darwinism had the most significant influence as it aligned with the ethos of Chinese scholars who believed in the principle that, "Every man bears responsibility for the nation's rise and fall" (guojia xingwang, pifu youze). This ethos is referred to as "nationalism" in this book for simplicity, though space constraints prevent elaboration of whether this spirit is precisely nationalistic.

After the failure of the "Second Revolution" and Yuan Shikai's claim to the throne, the government of the ROC in Beijing, known as the Beiyang government, not only controlled merely a portion of China's territory but also became the target of radical intellectuals. The radicalism of those intellectuals was not rooted in constitutionalism but rather in passionate nationalism, criticizing the government for "selling out the country." Even moderates were interested in what was known as the New Culture Movement rather than constitutionalism.

In early 1919, China, as a victor of the First World War, participated in the Paris Peace Conference. By the end of April, the world's major powers voted to transfer the rights and interests of defeated Germany in Shandong Province to victorious Japan. This decision led to the outbreak of the May Fourth Movement, spreading from Beijing to major cities across the country. Ultimately, the government conceded, refusing to sign the Treaty of Versailles. The significance of this movement lies in its profound influence on students and intellectuals. Nominally, the slogans of the Movement included "Mr. Democracy" and "Mr. Science." Yet the substance of democracy was largely absent from publications of the time; the inseparable connection between democracy and constitutionalism was not recognized; there were only abstract slogans that were open to interpretation (Xu and Wang, 2015, chapter 5). Among the Chinese people, intellectuals in particular, the greatest impact of the May Fourth Movement was a surge in nationalistic and anti-imperialist sentiment.

Lenin astutely seized the momentum of rising nationalism and anti-imperial sentiment in China, making Bolshevism highly appealing to Chinese radical intellectuals. Resistance to imperialism and advocacy for nationalism became the primary conduits for Bolshevism to infiltrate China. The First Soviet Declaration on China (The Karakhan Manifesto), issued in July 1919, proclaimed the unconditional restoration of all rights and interests previously seized from China by the Tsarist regime. It denounced imperialism and exploitation and advocated for a classless society led by the proletariat. Such a strategy rapidly attracted Chinese intellectuals and politicians, already stirred by nationalistic fervor following the May Fourth Movement, towards the Bolsheviks. As stated in the Documents of the First National Congress of the Chinese Socialist Youth in 1922, "Marxism in China ... has been present for only about three years ... It was the international capitalist oppression and the Russian proletarian revolution that facilitated its spread" (CASS, 1980, vol. 1, pp. 26–45).

10.1 COMMUNIST "JESUITS": THE COMINTERN'S INFILTRATION INTO CHINA

Prior to the Comintern's arrival, the Chinese imperial system deliberately obstructed the systematic dissemination of any Western ideologies, including Christianity, in China. Although Christianity reached China as early as the Tang dynasty, without a concerted missionary effort, Christian doctrine and Western culture largely remained unknown in China until the Ming dynasty. The Jesuits were the first to attempt a systematic propagation of Western religion and the Church in China. However, from Matteo Ricci's arrival in China in 1583 to the expulsion of the Jesuits by the Communist Party in 1952, Christianity's impact in China remained limited. While both the Comintern and the Jesuits were missionary organizations, the former's accomplishments were incomparable to those of the latter.

Similar to Christianity's early days in China, only a few Chinese knew of Marxism as one of several varieties of socialism through

Japanese literature before the October Revolution. Anarchism was by far the most popular among Chinese radicals at that time. In the initial stages of the October Revolution, the press and public opinion in China were highly skeptical of the Bolsheviks, seeing them as "greedy and aggressive" with a bloodthirsty appetite for power. Therefore, ways had to be found to "guard against" the Bolsheviks in China (quoted from Shen et al., 2016a, p. 5). After the October Revolution, a few Chinese intellectuals were exposed to the rudiments of Bolshevism in Japanese literature. Li Dazhao was among the earliest to hail the victory of Bolshevism at the end of 1918. However, what he cheered for was less the ideology of Bolshevism itself but rather its religious appeal. He observed that Bolshevism in Russia had "a sort of religious authority and became a mass movement. Not only Russia of today but the world of the twentieth century may not escape being dominated by this religious authority and swept up by this mass movement" (Li, 1979, vol. 1, pp. 163–165).

At that time, Chinese radical intellectuals embraced various forms of anarchism and socialism, including both Marxist and anti-Marxist ideologies. For instance, Chen Duxiu, one of the founders of the CCP, still believed in anarchism until the end of 1919 (Tang, 2013, chapter 4). Xu Xingzhi, another founder of the CCP, recollected that he, like many others post the May Fourth Movement, was heavily influenced by anarchism until 1922 when he encountered the pamphlet *Historical Materialism* translated by Li Da.[1]

As such, Li Dazhao was very much an exception even within the radical left. This peculiarity is part of the reason why Li was the first person the Comintern contacted to organize activities in China. Not surprisingly, Li Dazhao's understanding of Bolshevism and influence on his fellow radical intellectuals were rather limited. Even his most accomplished follower, Zhang Guotao, recalled that before the Comintern's delegates arrived in China, the Chinese had virtually no knowledge of Bolshevism, only a few knew about socialism – primarily anarchistic socialism (Zhang, 1991, pp. 40–41).

The rapid spread of Bolshevism in China was largely attributable to the entry of the Bolshevik "Jesuits" – the Comintern. More proactive than Jesuit or other Christian missionaries, the Comintern went beyond simply promoting ideology. It took direct political and military actions, financed the establishment of a Leninist Revolutionary Party in China, and coordinated with Li Dazhao and Chen Duxiu. The strategy that proved to be most effective was not promoting Marxism or even communism but rather exploiting the inflating nationalistic sentiment in China.

Following Soviet Russia's Karakhan Manifesto, which announced that Tsarist-era agreements with China would be nullified and all property that Tsarist Russia had looted from China would be returned, it issued the Second Declaration in 1920. This promised to return the Chinese Eastern Railway and all leased mines and gold mines without compensation, renounced the Boxer Indemnity, and gave up all Russian privileges in China.[2]

This strategy of Soviet Russia resonated perfectly with the surge in nationalist sentiment that had been sweeping China since the May Fourth Movement. The press praised this Russian initiative as an "unprecedented step towards the betterment of all mankind in world history" and the KMT generally favored Soviet Russia (Shen et al., 2016a, p. 9).

It was not until then that Chen Duxiu, the first leader of the CCP, began to embrace Bolshevism. In the New Year's issue of *Xin qingnian* (*La Jeunesse*) in 1920, Chen hailed the "progressive Leninist government, declaring its intention to assist China." Chen and Li Dazhao secretly met with Comintern representatives in February and Chen began to systematically promote Leninism after that. Subsequently, with the financial support of the Comintern, *La Jeunesse* translated and published theories on the dictatorship of the proletariat, causing his colleague Hu Shih to complain that *La Jeunesse* had become a journal for the translation of Soviet literature (Tang, 2013, chapter 4).

However, the Bolsheviks, presenting themselves as anti-imperialist allies of China, received widespread acclaim from the

Chinese press. Almost all Chinese intellectuals held an uncritical admiration for Soviet Russia. One minor incident illustrates this point clearly. The British philosopher, Bertrand Russell, visited China in 1920. When he shared his recent observations about Soviet Russia and his criticisms of the Bolshevik revolution, he was met with hostility from leading Chinese intellectuals who had previously admired him. Russell's "anti-Soviet" stance was criticized by prominent intellectuals across the political spectrum, including Hu Shih, Lu Xun, Li Dazhao, Chen Duxiu, Li Da, Chen Wangdao, Shao Lizi, and Cai Hesen, among others. The man who played the largest role in China's Russell Fever was Zhang Shengfu, a co-founder of the CCP. He introduced Zhou Enlai, Zhu De, and Zhang Guotao to the party and was Mao's boss in the Peking University library. Realizing the reactions to his speech, Russell stated in a letter to Zhang, "[I] was persuaded you hated me on account of my criticism of Bolshevism" (Schwarcz, 1992, p. 134).

In line with the propaganda efforts of the Karakhan Manifesto, Soviet Russia assigned a secret envoy, M. Popov, to investigate China in 1919 (Chapman, 1928), and secret contacts were held between N. G. Burtman, a covert member of the RCP, and future CCP founders Li Dazhao, Deng Zhongxia, and others between 1919 and 1920. In early 1920, with news of the Karakhan Manifesto reaching China, the RCP dispatched Grigori Voitinsky and two assistants to carry out systematic propaganda, agitation, and organizational work in China based on the efforts of Popov, Burtman, and others, causing a great stir in political and intellectual circles (Ishikawa, 2006, p. 40). In fact, even before Voitinsky arrived in China, Li Dazhao and Chen Duxiu had met secretly with another Soviet emissary in Tianjin in February (Zhang et al., 1984, p. 98).

Voitinsky's arrival laid the foundations for the establishment of the CCP in terms of ideology, organization, and funding. He subsequently became the Comintern representative in China (Ishikawa, 2006, p. 84). Among all of Voitinsky's efforts, arguably, the most important was setting up the first Marxist study association, the first foundational organization of the CCP, in Li Dazhao's office, as Zhang Guotao recalled (Zhang, 1991, pp. 86–88). At Li's recommendation, Voitinsky moved to Shanghai and made it the seat of the East Asian Bureau of the Comintern (Ishikawa, 2006, pp. 93–96). In early 1920, Chen Duxiu and Li Dazhao founded the Socialist League in Beijing, a reading group composed of people with various forms of socialist ideas, mainly anarchists (Ishikawa, 2006, p. 157).

The first discussion about establishing a communist group or party in China took place during a talk between Voitinsky and Chen in Shanghai in early July 1920. The head of the East Asian Bureau of the Comintern, V. D. Vilensky, then made a special trip to Beijing in August to convene the first congress of the RCP members in China (Tang, 2013, chapter 4). The most important topics at the congress were the establishment of the Chinese Communist Party, the convocation of a congress of Chinese communist organizations, and specific measures for propagating communism in China.[3] The East Asia Bureau then convened a conference of Far Eastern Socialists in Shanghai, which Chen Duxiu attended as China's delegate. The conference emphasized the task of establishing communist parties in countries such as China, Japan, and Korea.

In mid-August 1920, Voitinsky reported to the East Asian Bureau, the precursor of the Comintern Far Eastern Bureau, that he had established a Shanghai Revolutionary Bureau with Chen Duxiu, among others. He detailed his achievements in China, stating:

> We have established a Revolutionary Bureau in Shanghai comprising five people (four Chinese revolutionaries and myself), with three departments, namely Press, Propaganda, and Organization.... Our Organization Department will establish a Central Bureau of Trade Unions.... I have drafted resolutions that were discussed and adopted by the Shanghai Revolutionary Bureau.... Our Press Department will launch the inaugural issue of a Chinese language newspaper *Workers' Voice* ... to be printed by our printing house. Our task now is to establish organizations

like this in various industrial cities of China.... and it is hoped that a General Socialist Youth League can be established within this month.

Voitinsky acted as the Comintern representative to the Revolutionary Bureau, with Chen Duxiu as Secretary, Wang Yuanfang as the head of the Press Department, Li Da as the head of the Propaganda Department, and Zhang Guotao as the head of the Organization Department.[4]

Under Voitinsky's direct guidance, from the mid-1920s onwards, communist groups were established throughout China under various names and various publications were launched to propagate Leninism and the "orthodox" Bolshevik Marxism and communism. In August, Chen Duxiu and Voitinsky established a preparatory group for the founding of the communist party. In November, the monthly magazine *Gongchandang* (*The Communist Party*) was launched.

In just a few years, under the leadership of the Comintern, communist groups across China effectively replaced various socialist ideas from Japan and the United States with Bolshevist ideologies. Notable among these groups was the Hunan New People's Society, an organization of anarchists directed mainly by Mao Zedong (Tang, 2013, chapter 4). Mao, who had initially leaned towards Hu Shih in the debate between Li Dazhao and Hu (Tang, 2013, chapter 4), claimed that from the summer of 1920, he was influenced by Chen Duxiu and he had converted from an anarchist to a Marxist by reading Bolshevik literature translated by Chen's organization (Snow, 1979, p. 127). Historical documents record that Mao did not participate in the preparatory work to establish the party in 1920 (Tang, 2013, chapter 4). At the 1921 New Year's meeting of the Hunan New People's Society entitled "Transforming China and the World," the participants voted on five policies proposed by Mao, which included Leninism and anarchism, with the majority favoring Leninism (the violent dictatorship of the proletariat).[5]

It is important to note that while the Comintern's primary objective was to instigate a Bolshevik revolution, with Bolshevik ideology forming an integral part of this goal, China's radical intellectuals had been more focused on "national salvation" since the late nineteenth century. And they were primarily concerned with theories or ideologies that served this particular purpose. As such, Social Darwinism was the first to gain popularity. Recognizing this, the Comintern strategically integrated China's quest for national salvation into the broader goal of a world communist revolution. Through this approach, the Comintern persuaded and guided Chinese radical intellectuals to look to Soviet Russia as a model, adopting Bolshevism, forming a Communist Party under the Comintern's leadership, seizing power through violent means, and establishing the dictatorship of the proletariat.

Bao Huiseng, who attended the CCP's first congress, recalled, "Most of our comrades became Communists before they studied Marxism-Leninism." Liu Renjing recollected that when the CCP was established, people generally only knew about the terminology or dogma. Liu, referred to as a nerd by Zhang Guotao, was one of the very few people in the party who had read Marx's *Critique of the Gotha Program* at that time (Ishikawa, 2006, p. 276).

10.2 THE CHINA BRANCH OF THE COMINTERN: THE CCP

It took only two years from the Comintern's initial infiltration into China in 1919, when the Chinese population knew almost nothing about Bolshevism, to the official founding of the CCP in 1921. The inception of the CCP was designed, decided upon, engineered, and implemented by the Comintern. Zhang Tailei, as the first delegate of the CCP to the Comintern, claimed in his report to the Third Congress of the Comintern in Moscow that the first communist groups in China had emerged in May 1920. Additionally, in his report of June 1921, he stated that "The work we have done is still preparatory," implying that the CCP was still in its formation stage.[6]

Indeed, under the drive of the Comintern, the CCP had already begun to establish some foundational preparatory organizations by this time and these organizations clearly indicated their associations with the Russian Revolution and the Comintern. For instance, a section of the CCP's Manifesto, released by the end of 1920, was dedicated to discussing Russia's proletarian dictatorship, portraying it as the inaugural victory of the global revolution. Moreover, the First Resolution of the CCP in 1921 specified in its concluding section that "the Central Committee of the party is obligated to submit monthly reports to the Third International" (the term Third International refers to the Comintern).[7]

In addition to organization, the fledgling CCP was heavily reliant on the Comintern for its financial needs. This dependence was so acute that even a short interruption could have severe repercussions. After Voitinsky's departure, there was a temporary lapse in Comintern representation in China and as a result, "the financial support for the interim central was interrupted, causing a disruption in all tasks and leading to the suspension of the monthly publication of *The Communist Party* for several months" (Ishikawa, 2006, p. 110). Later, the Socialist Youth League was also forced to disband. The problem was not resolved until June 1921 when the Comintern sent Voitinsky's successor to Shanghai (Ishikawa, 2006, p. 245).

The preparations for the formal establishment of the CCP began in early 1921, initiated by the Comintern's Far Eastern Bureau. In March, the Bureau reported to its Executive Committee in Moscow that it was preparing an outline for the commencement of work in China, which would be deliberated "at the congress of Chinese communists in Shanghai in May under our guidance." The representatives dispatched by the Far Eastern Bureau to this inaugural CCP congress were V. A. Neiman-Nikolsky and Maring (whose actual name was Henk Sneevliet). Neiman-Nikolsky represented the Comintern leadership, claiming that he must be a part of all the CCP's leading body meetings. He was also entrusted with the task of funding the party. Neiman-Nikolsky's assistant, Maring, who succeeded him as the Comintern's representative in China after the former's return to Russia, became a more influential figure later (Ishikawa, 2006, pp. 246–247). The Dutch, British, and Austrian governments had long been concerned about Maring. In the six months before his arrival in China, embassies and courts of those governments had been sharing intelligence about his travels and sending notifications to the Chinese government.[8]

Orders and financial support from the Comintern directly dictated the operational matters for the first CCP congress. The Comintern provided each delegate with around 1,000 yuan for travel expenses, equivalent to the monthly salary of 100 workers in China at the time (Ishikawa, 2006, p. 254). As Chen Duxiu was in Guangzhou by then, execution of the Comintern's instructions fell to Li Da, the temporary leader of the Shanghai Communist Party. Li later recalled, "In June, the Third International sent Maring and Neiman-Nikolsky to Shanghai. They instructed me to immediately convene a party congress, announcing the official establishment of the CCP. At that time, the party had seven local units. I sent out seven letters requiring them to select and send representatives to Shanghai" (Ishikawa, 2006, p. 251). Mao Zedong was one of the representatives from outside Shanghai who received the letter from Li and attended the First Congress. Maring was the de facto chairman and main speaker at the First Congress.[9]

The decision by the Comintern to hastily establish the CCP in Shanghai in the summer of 1921 was not wholly welcomed by the first CCP leader, Chen Duxiu. Maring reported to the Comintern that Chen was reluctant to accept the Comintern's "guardianship" over the CCP.[10] Maring emphasized to Chen and all CCP leaders that "from its inception, the CCP has been part of the Third International, and it is a branch of the International," thus subject to the leadership and financial assistance of the Comintern. Accordingly, "whether you acknowledge this or not is unimportant" (Bao, 1983, p. 370). However, Chen insisted that "we must take responsibility for the Chinese revolution" (Zhang, 1991, p. 159) and that "we should not ask for money from the Third International" (Bao, 1983, p. 7). Maring complained to Zhang Guotao that Chen's comments were "simply not those of a communist" and he could not "shoulder the responsibility of a secretary." He urged Zhang to replace Chen as the leader of the CCP (Zhang, 1991, p. 161). The disagreements between Maring and Chen were resolved later and then Chen announced that the CCP Central Committee embraced the Comintern and fully accepted its financial aid (Tang, 2013, chapter 5). Under the direction and funding of the Comintern, the newly established CCP had to model itself after the Bolsheviks in Russia and its members were obliged to become Leninist revolutionaries. When Bao Huiseng, a founding member of the CCP, was sent to Wuhan as branch secretary there, he was told by Chen Duxiu that his "living expenses would be paid by the Secretariat of the Labor Association," thus implying that he had become a Leninist "professional revolutionary" (Bao, 1983, p. 8).

All substantive activities of the CCP, including the establishment of various communist groups, the cultivation of elites, organization, propaganda, personnel, strategies, and so on, transpired after the Comintern's arrival in China, particularly following the convening of the First Congress of the CCP. After the First Congress, Chen Duxiu regularly reported to the Comintern details about the CCP's execution of the Comintern's orders. In his report to the Comintern on June 30, 1922, Chen noted that the number of CCP members had grown from just over 50 at the time of the First Congress to 195. Funding was primarily provided by the Comintern; they had received 16,655 yuan from the International, whilst only 1,000 yuan was raised by the CCP itself. The political propaganda carried out with the support of the Comintern was predominantly the printing of Lenin's works and Russian communist propaganda. Reports were detailed down to the name and printing number of each propaganda item, the specifics of each local strike, and the creation of each workers' school and club. Concerning the party's development plan, the report stipulated "rigorous centralization is to be practiced."[11]

In July 1922, the Second Congress of the CCP declared in its Resolution on the Admission of the Chinese Communist Party to the Third International that "the Chinese Communist Party is the Chinese branch of the International Communist Party." The annex to the resolution, titled "Conditions of Admission," stipulated that:

> All parties of the International Communist Party must be built upon the principle of democratic centralism ... must fully support the Soviet Republic in its fight against counterrevolution ... must be named the Communist Party of a certain country – a branch of the Third International Communist Party ... The central organs of the Communist Parties of various countries must publish all important official documents of the Executive Committee of the International Communist Party.[12]

Additionally, Article 3 of the CCP Constitution passed by the Second Congress stipulated that, "members of the Communist Parties of various countries recognized by the Third International can become members of this party."[13] The Comintern's leadership role was fully evident in the Comintern's instructions given to China and in its Resolution of the Fourth Congress of the Communist International on "Tasks of the Chinese Communist Party."[14]

10.2.1 The Comintern and the KMT

The Comintern sowed the seeds of Bolshevism in China by establishing its branch there. However, nurturing the growth of these seeds and strategizing how to seize power in China necessitated further tactical planning. One pivotal measure the Comintern adopted was the reorganization of the KMT. Historically, this move also aimed at dismantling the remaining constitutional structure of the Republic of China. Notably, this reorganization was largely conducted at the invitation of Sun Yat-sen. This fact alone underscores the critical role that China's own institutional genes played in the transplantation of Bolshevism.

The Comintern's purpose in reorganizing the KMT was to make it more closely resemble the Bolsheviks, or at the very least, to transform it into a type of Russian left-wing SR party, and to establish a united front with it. The initial instructions from the Comintern to the CCP followed its strategy of inciting revolutions around the globe, with a particular focus on exporting the Bolshevik model of revolution. This included spreading Leninism and initiating workers' movements. The Leninist approach, which prioritized anti-imperialism as the spearhead of the international communist revolution, dovetailed perfectly with the surge of nationalism in China.

According to the Comintern's evaluation, the KMT was the largest nationalist party in China and thus became the focal point of their work since the CCP was too feeble. In 1922, the Comintern's representative in China reported back to the Far Eastern Bureau, stating that the CCP, along with the associated communist groups, was "insignificant in number ... disconnected from the masses ... with poor operational ability." Moreover, they "had no connection with the Chinese national revolutionary movement ... and were hardly capable of engaging in practical revolutionary work."[15] Therefore, the Comintern was striving hard to win over the KMT. In early 1920, A. S. Potapov, a senior Bolshevik intelligence officer, established contact with KMT leaders, including Sun Yat-sen, Chen Jiongming, and Dai Jitao. Potapov even forwarded a letter to Lenin on behalf of Chen Jiongming (Ishikawa, 2006, pp. 73–79).

As previously mentioned, ever since the Karakhan Manifesto was issued by Russia, Bolshevism exerted a significant influence on KMT elites across the political spectrum. Some founding members of the KMT, such as Dai Jitao, were also among the founding members of the CCP. In this context, Chiang Kai-shek, who was then an unimportant figure, wrote in his diary as early as 1919, "I plan to learn Russian in preparation for an investigation trip to Russia." In early 1920, he petitioned Sun Yat-sen, requesting to "take the Soviet ... as a model" (Yang, 2008, pp. 114–116). Sun had been communicating with Soviet Foreign Minister Georgy Chicherin as early as 1921.

Following the First Congress of the CCP, Maring, with Zhang Tailei, immediately contacted Sun Yat-sen and other KMT leaders in Guangdong. In early 1922, the Comintern held the Far East Laborer's Delegates' Conference in Moscow. Not only did Lenin meet with the CCP delegate Zhang Guotao but he also met with KMT delegates such as Zhang Qiubai. During the event, Lenin's sole meeting with the CCP representative was intended to promote cooperation between the KMT and the CCP. Both parties' delegates expressed their willingness to accept his advice (Zhang, 1991, p. 198). Sun Yat-sen and Chen Duxiu respectively supported Lenin's suggestion in principle.[16]

After Maring's meeting with Sun, Adolf Joffe, the Russian plenipotentiary in China (known as Yue Fei in Chinese documents), arrived in China in August 1922. Joffe corresponded extensively with Sun and sent representatives to meet with him. Sun requested that Joffe convey his thoughts to Lenin and Trotsky.[17] Then, on January 26, 1923, the Sun-Joffe Manifesto was issued, announcing the alliance between the Soviet Union and the KMT and the reorganization of the KMT (Kurdyukov, 1959, pp. 64–65). Thereafter, the Politburo of the Central Committee of the RCP officially decided to provide the KMT with economic and military aid, establishing a committee headed by Trotsky to specifically guide Joffe's correspondence with Sun and requesting that Sun centralize the leadership of the KMT as much as possible. Joffe informed Sun that the Soviet Union was to provide large-scale military aid to Sun in northern and western China. In late-July of 1923, Stalin, on behalf of the Politburo of the Central Committee of the RCP, appointed Mikhail Borodin as Sun's advisor (Kurdyukov, 1959, pp. 173–175). Since then, Borodin became the most important representative of the RCP and the Comintern in China. Stalin requested that he "submit a work report to Moscow on a regular basis, if possible, once a month" (Kurdyukov, 1959, p. 266).

In September 1923, Sun sent General Chiang Kai-shek, then the Chief of Staff of the army, to lead a delegation to visit Moscow. The delegation included CCP members who had joined the KMT, including Shen Dingyi and Zhang Tailei. During the nearly three-month visit, they met with top RCP leaders such as Trotsky, Zinoviev, and Lunacharsky. Chiang Kai-shek told the Secretary of the RCP Central Committee Secretariat that "the KMT is very close to the RCP in spirit" and he agreed to send a permanent KMT representative to Moscow.

In a meeting with the Red Army Commander-in-Chief Kamenev, a detailed plan was agreed upon for the Soviet Union to reorganize and train the KMT army modeled on the Red Army, including the troop size, funding, operational bases, and more. Chiang was dissatisfied that the RCP was unable to provide full support for Sun's request for large-scale military aid because the RCP and the Comintern were primarily focused on Germany rather than China due to significant changes in Germany at that time.

However, upon receiving a telegram from Sun informing him that Borodin had arrived in Guangzhou, Chiang was extremely grateful, stating, "It is now very clear who are our friends and who are our enemies." In his communication with the RCP, he proposed that "some influential comrades" from the Comintern should be sent to China to "lead us." At the Executive Committee meeting of the Comintern, Chiang reported on the KMT's "vision of world revolution," stating that "the main base of world revolution is in Russia." Upon the victory of the revolution in Germany and China, an alliance of these three countries would be formed, after which "we could overthrow the capitalist system worldwide." Finally, the Comintern entrusted Chiang with delivering its Executive Committee's resolution regarding the KMT to Sun (Kurdyukov, 1959, pp. 271–280). Two months later, all the basic elements in this resolution became the fundamental principles of the KMT.

In late January 1924, under significant influence from the Comintern, the KMT held its First National Congress, marking the beginning of a comprehensive reorganization. Sun Yat-sen announced at the meeting that the KMT would be restructured along the lines of the Bolshevik Party and that China's revolution would "learn from the Russian model." However, unbeknownst to the KMT, the Comintern's long-term goal was for the KMT to lay the groundwork for the CCP's development and, when opportune, to facilitate the CCP's full seizure of power. Apart from Sun Yat-sen, every key leader within the KMT, including Chiang Kai-shek, Liao Zhongkai, and Chiang Ching-kuo, had visited or received extended training in Russia. The structure, protocols, and rules of the inaugural congress were modeled on those of the RCP, with the general stipulations of the party constitution being almost identical to those of the RCP counterpart. Furthermore, the manifesto approved at the congress interpreted Sun's "Three Principles of the People" in a manner practically identical to Comintern resolutions. RCP representatives were astonished by the KMT's official interpretation of the Three Principles, which was clearly "based on the resolutions of the Comintern" (Yang, 2008, pp. 34–35).

In accordance with the Comintern's directives, during the reorganization of the KMT, CCP members joined the KMT en masse. However, some elites within the KMT expressed skepticism about the inclusion of communists. They suggested that CCP members should renounce their communist affiliation to demonstrate their loyalty to the KMT and the Three Principles of the People. The CCP leader Li Dazhao responded by declaring that the CCP was an extension of the Comintern rather than an independent Chinese organization, making its dissolution implausible (Yang, 2008, p. 37). CCP members came to occupy significant roles within the KMT. Mao Zedong became the Secretary of the Organization Department, while Yun Daiying became the Secretary of the Propaganda Department (Yang, 2008, p. 40). An influx of CCP members into the KMT Central Committee resulted in traditional KMT elites, such as Chiang Kai-shek, being marginalized (Yang, 2008, p. 120).

As momentous as the KMT's reorganization was the establishment of the Whampoa Military Academy in Guangzhou in mid-1924, supported by the Comintern in every aspect. The academy was marked by its Soviet-style systems, staffing structures, and curricula. Military instructors were primarily Soviet Russians, and it had a party department reminiscent of that of the Soviet army. The academy's commandant, Chiang Kai-shek, declared that: "what we want to emulate is the Soviet Russian revolutionary party." The Comintern not only demanded the incorporation of a political department and party representation but also the strategic placement of CCP members within the academy, thereby tipping the balance of power in the CCP's favor. Only two of the five executive and supervisory members of the first party committee were from the KMT (Chiang being one), while the remainder were from the CCP. In the second term, Chiang was the sole KMT member alongside six Communists (Yang, 2008, p. 124). Following the abrupt death of Sun Yat-sen in late 1925, Wang Jingwei and Chiang emerged as the most influential leaders of the KMT, owing to Borodin's endorsement and a series of calculated political maneuvers. Chiang acknowledged, "Without the reorganization of our party and the guidance of Soviet comrades ... the National Revolutionary Army (NRA) would not have been formed by now. What we have achieved today is largely attributed to Soviet comrades ... in helping the Chinese revolution." He further stated that: "the interests of communism and the Three Principles of the People are the same" (Yang, 2008, pp. 125–127).

With the aid and establishment provided by the Soviet Union and with the Whampoa Military Academy as the foundation, the NRA of the KMT, in alliance with the CCP, gradually came into being. Soviet advisors became the de facto leaders of nearly all the military departments within the KMT. This significantly bolstered the actual power and influence of the CCP within the KMT (Shen et al., 2016a, pp. 27–31).

10.2.2 *The First Full-Scale Armed Uprising by the CCP and the Breakup with the KMT*

Thanks to the supportive environment fostered by China's endogenous institutional genes, the Comintern was remarkably successful in dismantling the remaining constitutional order in China. While supporting the KMT and CCP in the south and preparing for war, the Soviet Union backed General Feng Yuxiang in the north, offering substantial military aid to engineer a coup and topple the Beijing-based government of the Republic of China, also known as the Beiyang government. After enduring a series of blows, from Sun Yat-sen's "Second Revolution" to Yuan Shikai's ascension to the throne, this military coup ended a republic that had ruled since the fall of the Empire. Consequently, China not only lost any remnants of its constitutional order but was also plunged into a full-blown civil war. Subsequently, Zhang Zuolin's Northeast Army defeated Feng, seized control of Beijing, and established a military regime. In this context, in July 1926, the NRA, a collaborative force of the KMT and the CCP, launched the Northern Expedition.

The Northern Expedition was designed and facilitated by the Soviet Red Army, beginning with an operational plan put forward by Soviet military advisor Galen (the alias of V. K. Blyukher). Galen and his staff assumed overall command, with Soviet military advisors integrated into nearly all divisions to ensure implementation. Apart from supporting the KMT-CCP NRA, the Soviet Union maintained substantial military aid to Feng Yuxiang's Guominjun (Nationalist Army) as it targeted Beijing from the northwest. With the Soviet command and substantial military aid, the NRA made such impressive advances that Stalin and the Comintern misjudged the situation and prematurely concluded that the time was ripe for the CCP to seize power in China. By the end of the year, the Comintern Executive Committee issued a directive to the CCP calling to strive for the establishment of a "people's democratic dictatorship ... of the proletariat." Upon receiving this mandate, the CCP declared in early 1927 that "the Chinese national revolution now has a solid foundation, and it is time for the proletariat to seize leadership." Under Comintern directives, the CCP escalated preparations to instigate riots in several major cities in an attempt to seize power, including plans to take control of Shanghai (Shen, 2009, pp. 27–31).

At the outset of the Northern Expedition, the CCP already held a third of the seats on the KMT's Executive Supervisory Committee and 77 percent of leadership positions on the Central Committee of the KMT. Almost all political commissars across the various units of the NRA, along with party representatives of all divisions and a majority at the regimental level in the First Army commanded by Chiang Kai-shek, were CCP members. Moreover, the CCP controlled 2,000 armed worker pickets and 6,000 peasant self-defense units in Guangdong, leading approximately 100,000 workers and 600,000 members of peasant associations (Shen, 2009, pp. 27–31). As the Northern Expedition made swift progress, the CCP extended its leadership within the army, established trade unions and peasant associations, and effectively assumed control in numerous locations. However, before the CCP's secret plan to seize power could be implemented, numerous conflicts had already erupted between the KMT and the CCP across various regions, which dramatically escalated calls within the KMT to purge the CCP (Chen, 1981, p. 61).

As the CCP accelerated its efforts for an uprising, tensions flared between the KMT and the CCP, especially in Shanghai. In February, the CCP Central Committee initiated a general strike in Shanghai. On March 21, it instigated an armed insurrection involving 800,000 participants in the city. By the end of March, the CCP issued a manifesto entitled "A Call to the Working Class of China on the Shanghai Street Battles."[18]

The exposure in early April of the Comintern's plans to stage a coup in Beijing and orchestrate a CCP takeover from the KMT served as the final straw that turned the KMT into a staunch enemy of the Communists. Foreign embassies, primarily those of the signatories to the 1901 Boxer Protocol, along with the Beijing government, received intelligence suggesting that Soviet Russia was instructing the CCP to incite a riot with the intent to seize power in Beijing. Responding to this, the foreign diplomatic corps issued a search warrant to the Beijing Police Department, leading to an abrupt raid on the Soviet Embassy on April 6. This extensive search yielded a significant amount of evidence, resulting in the arrest of 22 Russians and 36 KMT-CCP members, including Li Dazhao, who were hiding in the embassy. This evidence, amounting to seven truckloads of documents, detailed the Comintern's support for the KMT and the CCP, intelligence gathering activities, the construction of armed forces, and the instigation of revolutions and uprisings (Twitchett and Loewe, 1986, part 1, chapter 11). Those Soviet secret files clearly documented the Comintern's plan to utilize the KMT to seize power for the CCP. A secret telegram from Moscow to Borodin was also discovered, indicating the objective was to use the Northern Expedition to distract imperialist nations and that the NRA was to therefore be prevented from unifying China (Zhang and Peking Police Compilation Commission, 1928).

Chiang Kai-shek was furious upon learning of these exposed secrets (Chen, 1981, p. 54). On April 12, he launched a coup in Shanghai, openly instigating a comprehensive anti-communist and anti-Soviet campaign (in KMT official language, this coup is called a "Qingdang" [Purge]). Stalin likened the comprehensive defeat suffered by the CCP and the Comintern to the setback experienced by the Bolsheviks in July 1917, predicting that the revolution could soon "return to the streets" (Lenin and Stalin, 1950, p. 281). Guided by this misjudgment, Stalin and the Comintern dispatched Galen to instruct the CCP to launch the Nanchang Uprising on August 1.[19] On August 7, the Comintern dispatched Vissarion Lominadze to Hankou to preside over an emergency meeting of the CCP's Provisional Central Committee, known as the August 7th Meeting, at which Chen Duxiu was replaced as leader of the CCP by Qu Qiubai. Qu had joined the RCP in May 1921 and had previously held important positions in the Comintern and the RCP. Mao Zedong, Zhou Enlai, and Zhang Guotao were appointed alternate members of the Central Committee which marked Mao's first promotion to the central leadership.

The August 7th Meeting also decided to immediately launch a series of armed uprisings across various regions, with the RCP serving as the decision-maker and provider of military and financial assistance. From August 1927 to February 1928, in the name of Stalin and the RCP's Politburo, over ten resolutions and telegrams were issued to direct the CCP's uprisings.[20]

During a period of three months beginning in September, the CCP, under the guidance and support of the Soviet Union, orchestrated uprisings in parts of Hubei, Hunan, and Guangdong. The intent was to seize political power swiftly via a comprehensive uprising. The first Soviet-style regime was established during the Guangzhou Uprising towards the end of 1927. Another Soviet regime was subsequently set up in Changsha (Shen et al., 2016a, p. 41). While these attempts swiftly collapsed, their historical significance is clear: they represented the initial steps towards the establishment of a central Soviet regime by the CCP.

By March and April of 1928, under the leadership of Bukharin, the Comintern and the Soviet Army collaboratively developed a plan to establish multiple dispersed guerrilla bases in the rural areas of southern China. The Soviet Union provided both military and financial aid to support this endeavor.[21] The Comintern believed that the comprehensive uprising they led for the CCP could quickly achieve victory.

To prepare for the seizure and consolidation of power, the Comintern, led by Bukharin, urgently convened the 6th Congress of the CCP in Moscow.[22] During the congress, Bukharin made a report on behalf of the Comintern, while Qu Qiubai and Zhou Enlai presented important reports on the party's military and political affairs. The preparations for the seizure of power were either directly based on the RCP's model or modified based on the translation of its documents. Among them, the Resolution on Organizational Issues Concerning Soviet Political Power made comprehensive and detailed provisions for establishing Leninist Soviet power in China, including deciding its name, the relationship between the party and political power, and the organization and operation of the regime.[23]

10.3 SECRET SOCIETIES: THE INSTITUTIONAL GENE FOR BUILDING THE PARTY AND ITS ARMY

A communist totalitarian party is a tightly organized, violent, secret group based on Leninist ideology. One of the reasons the

Comintern was able to swiftly see results in its party-building efforts in China was the training it provided to the Chinese revolutionaries in the 1920s. Over 2,000 members of the CCP (including the Youth League), as well as a large number of KMT members, received systematic training in the Soviet Union. This training primarily took place at Oriental University, established by the Comintern, which was later renamed Moscow Sun Yat-sen University in 1925. Bo Gu, a leading figure in the CCP, praised the program for its effectiveness in rapidly transforming the CCP into a "completely Bolshevized" entity within just a few years. Most senior leaders of the CCP, with a few exceptions like Mao Zedong, received training in the Soviet Union (Shen et al., 2016a, p. 36).

However, in societies that are incompatible with a secretive Leninist party structure, for example, in advanced democracies, training party leaders alone would not be sufficient to bring about significant change. Thus, while the systematic and large-scale training provided by the Comintern was vital for the establishment and development of the CCP, it was not the most decisive factor. Instead, the presence of compatible institutional genes within a society, which can accommodate and foster the growth of a Leninist party, proved to be the determining factor.

A Leninist party is characterized by its top-down absolute rule and consists of professional revolutionaries. Prior to seizing power, the party functions as an organization that clandestinely plans and orchestrates armed takeovers. Once in power, it uses a highly secretive, top-down approach to make decisions, implementing policies and constructing institutions to control society. Even though the Bolshevik's protocols were crafted by Lenin, their core attributes largely emerged from Russia's inherent institutional genes and one of those was secret political organizations, as discussed in Chapter 8.

Similarly, the imperial system in China historically did not allow for the existence of organized, independent social forces that were open and separated from the court. Any groups perceived as threatening to government power were strictly prohibited. Throughout history, the only large-scale organizations that could transcend regional boundaries and survive independently of the court were secret societies. Parallel to the institutional genes of secret terrorist organizations in Tsarist Russia, China has carried the institutional genes of secret societies since ancient times. These include societies like the White Lotus, which emerged during the Song dynasty, and the extensive development of groups such as the Hong Fraternity, the Brotherhood Society, and the Red Spear Society since the Qing dynasty.

On the other hand, openly competitive political parties only briefly emerged among a small group of social elites in the early twentieth century. Most people in China, especially those who joined the CCP, were oblivious to the concept of open party competition. This provided an excellent social foundation for the establishment of a Leninist party. Moreover, these institutional genes laid the spiritual and organizational groundwork for all other Chinese revolutionary groups, like the Tongmenghui-KMT and the ultimately unsuccessful Chinese Revolutionary Party, as discussed in Chapter 9.

10.3.1 *Comintern Instructions and the Starting Point*

Indeed, the Comintern explicitly instructed the CCP to fully utilize China's long-standing secret societies as its social foundation in the early days of the CCP's establishment. Early CCP documents pointed out that "secret societies such as the Brotherhood Society (*Gelaohui*) were originally organizations of the oppressed class ... they have a very strict organization ... we should recruit the masses who have traditionally been under the guidance of old-style secret societies" (quoted in Shao, 2010, p. 186).

In 1925 and 1926, CCP leader Li Dazhao noted that "the Brotherhood Society and Red Spear Society were originally organizations for the self-defense of farmers," calling on intellectuals to "hurry up and join the Red Spear Society" in order to achieve "the goal of overthrowing the local tyrants." He explicitly instructed that joining the Red Spear Society was in line with Leninism (Li, 1984, pp. 564–569).

CCP leaders such as Chen Duxiu and Qu Qiubai also instructed that the secret societies be integrated into the CCP's peasant movement. The 3rd Plenary Session of the 4th Central Committee of the CCP passed the Resolution on the Red Spear Society Movement, asserting that the Red Spear Society be "an important force in breaking down the warlords in the national revolution." It proposed a secret alliance with the Red Spear Society (Shao, 2010, pp. 166–171).

A Comintern report documented that the peasant movement in China was flourishing, and the peasant associations were developing rapidly because "secret societies have joined the peasant associations."[24] Among the large number of documents discovered in the Soviet embassy by Zhang Zuolin's police in 1927, a significant portion was related to the Comintern's interest in organizations such as the Red Spear Society (Zhang and Peking Police Compilation Commission, 1928).

As both the KMT and CCP had close ties to the secret societies, and given that integration with the secret societies was a policy of the Comintern, CCP members were allowed to openly and vigorously develop alliances with secret societies during the first KMT-CCP cooperation. Through this channel, the CCP achieved considerable growth in peasant associations and the armed forces.

In the early stages of party-building, as the majority of CCP members were from rural areas, gang-style initiation rituals were adopted in many CCP branches. These included ceremonies such as drinking chicken blood, beheading chickens, and burning incense as part of the oath-taking for joining the CCP. The oath proclaimed that betrayers would be punished by "merciless knifing and shooting." Some regions also issued deadly disciplinary rules, stipulating that "those who violate discipline shall be killed" and "those who leak secrets shall be killed" (Shao, 2010, pp. 304–307).

Mao Zedong recognized the potential of secret societies such as the Triad Society, the Brotherhood Society, and the Green Gang. He estimated that these organizations collectively encompassed around 20 million individuals, many of whom were vagrants. Mao believed that "if guided properly, [they] could turn into a revolutionary force" (Mao, 1952). He also suggested that peasant associations could supersede secret societies, arguing that "after the secret societies join the peasant associations, their members could openly and legally air their grievances and there [no longer would be] any need for various secret societies" (Mao, 1949).

Between 1925 and 1926, in his role as the head of the National Peasant Movement Training Institute under the KMT's Central Peasant Department, Mao organized specific courses discussing how to attract secret society members to the peasant movement. This strategy of recruiting many secret society members to join the peasant associations proved to be a significant driving force for the early development of these associations (Schram, 1966; Chesneaux, 1972, p. 13). Mao once noted in 1927 that most of the revolutionary army were vagrants (Schram, 1966).

Since the KMT launched a coup and openly opposed the CCP, the most critical aspects for the CCP's development, and even survival, was the establishment of its armed forces and revolutionary bases. This could not have been achieved without relying on China's long-standing secret societies and clandestine armed forces to build military power and develop peripheral organizations. Under the guidance of the Comintern and the Soviet Red Army, the CCP's attempts to establish Soviet power through urban uprisings were repeatedly unsuccessful. Even though Bukharin had formulated plans to establish several bases in rural South China,[25] this was a mission impossible for Bolshevik intellectuals, whether Russian or Chinese.

10.3.2 *The First Chinese Soviet Regime and the Red Army*

The Bolshevik Party did not emerge purely from the ideas of the Russian intelligentsia but rather it developed from the institutional genes of Russian secret political organizations. Similarly, the CCP, despite being sowed and nurtured by the Comintern, had to rely on more than just abstract strategic plans from the Bolsheviks when faced with practical challenges. The Bolsheviks were unable to design specific tactics for the CCP. After a series of failures, the CCP eventually managed to establish its first stable Central Soviet regime. However, this was not through independent growth but by co-opting the territory and military forces of a secret society. The base in the Jinggang Mountains area was initially established by Yuan Wencai and Wang Zuo, leaders of the Hong Fraternity (Hongmen), and was subsequently integrated into the CCP. The establishment of the CCP's second Central Soviet regime in Yan'an also heavily relied on the power and influence of secret societies such as the Brotherhood Society.

Yuan and Wang had controlled most of the Jinggang Mountains area with the Hong Fraternity troops since 1925 and, one year later, Yuan was persuaded to join the CCP (Shao, 2010, p. 187). In 1927, Mao Zedong, Zhu De, Chen Yi, Tan Zhenlin, and others each led rebel forces to the Jinggang Mountains. There they merged with the forces of Yuan and Wang, transforming the Jinggang Mountains base into the first stronghold of the CCP. Mao assigned He Changgong as the political commissar for Wang's forces (Shao, 2010, pp. 247–251). Yuan became the Chief of Staff for the Fourth Front Army, the strongest branch of the Red Army at that time (Wang, 2012). Tan Zhenlin later recalled that without Yuan and Wang, it would have been impossible to establish the Jinggang Mountains base. It was from this base that the Chinese Soviet Republic, with Ruijin as its capital, was established in 1931 (to be discussed in Chapter 11). The CCP bases established on the foundations of the Hong Fraternity and the peasant rebel army consisted of over 80 percent of cadres originating from the peasantry.[26] These cadres later formed the backbone of the CCP's development. Their interests and influence determined much of the fundamental characteristics of the CCP and its army.

The establishment of the Jinggang Mountains base serves as a prime example of how the CCP effectively utilized secret societies to build military power and establish bases. However, it is crucial to note that this was not an exception but rather a representation of the general development pattern of the CCP. Chen Duxiu, a former CCP leader who was later expelled from the party and criticized as a Trotskyist, wrote in 1930, "The so-called Red Army was mostly composed of the proletariat class of vagrants (bandits and deserters)." He further noted that, "He Long's Second Army, Brother He's old forces are purely bandits ... this Red Army has nothing to do with the party or peasant organizations" (Shao, 2010, p. 315).

In fact, He Long, prior to joining the CCP, was a leader of the Brotherhood Society. After the failure of the Nanchang Uprising, he returned to his hometown, and by leveraging his connections with the Brotherhood Society and other secret societies, he consolidated the forces of the Brotherhood Society, thereby establishing what later became known as the Second Red Army (Shao, 2010, pp. 261–269). Records indicate that He Long subsequently spent considerable effort addressing the challenges posed by the armed gangs within his army (Shao, 2010, p. 307). Similarly, Zhu De had once been one of the key leaders of the Brotherhood Society (Smedley, 1956, p. 88), and Liu Bocheng was also a member of the Brotherhood (Mitani, 2002, pp. 19–20).

10.3.3 Yan'an: The Second Chinese Soviet Regime

The role of secret societies was equally significant in the establishment of the CCP's second Central Soviet regime. After abandoning their base in the Jinggang Mountains, the CCP took Yan'an as the capital of their northern Shaanxi base, in 1937, following the Long March. Much like the Jinggang Mountains base, the northern Shaanxi base was also established by leveraging the power of the Brotherhood Society.[27] In 1928, Liu Zhidan, a local CCP leader, was introduced to the Brotherhood Society by its local leader, Ma Xiwu. After joining the secret society, Liu was granted the title of "Master of Wisdom," which made him the second highest ranking local leader. Subsequently, Ma Xiwu and six other Brotherhood Society leaders joined the CCP and more than twenty Brotherhood Society leaders became officers of the Red Army, at the regimental level or above. The commander of the 27th Red Army, He Jinye, was also a member of the Brotherhood before joining the Red Army (Shao, 2010, p. 379).

In recognition of Ma Xiwu's contributions to the CCP, he was appointed Chairman of the Soviet government of Shaanxi-Gansu-Ningxia in 1936 and even became the Vice-President of the Supreme People's Court in the early 1950s. It was the pervasive and far-reaching influence of the Brotherhood Society in the Shaanxi, Gansu, and Ningxia regions that facilitated the CCP to establish bases there by leveraging the strength of the secret society. Chen Yun once recalled that "the Brotherhood was ubiquitous in Shaanxi, Gansu, Ningxia, and Suiyuan provinces in the northwest" and that "nine out of ten people in Heshui area and Huan County were Brotherhood members ... and in Heshui and Baoan areas, even children and women had joined the Brotherhood."[28]

After the Central Red Army arrived at the Shaanxi-Gansu-Ningxia base, it immediately used the pretext of resisting Japan to further exploit the Brotherhood Society to strengthen the Red Army. In the autumn of 1936, Mao Zedong, the Chairman of the Chinese Soviet Central Government, issued a "Declaration to the Brotherhood Society." The CCP Central Committee stated in the Directive on Winning over the Brotherhood that "the broad masses in secret societies across China sympathize with and support the Soviet regime, and fight for its victory" (Shao, 2010, pp. 390–391). The CCP even convened a Brotherhood Society National Congress and appointed many leaders of the Brotherhood as its commanders. The development of the armed forces in many of the Soviet areas was fueled by members of the Brotherhood, who held their own secret meetings within the Red Army units for a period of time. Some of them flaunted their privileges in the Soviet areas extravagantly. Brotherhood members in Zhidan County said, "Brothers can get opium from the Soviet government" (Shao, 2010, pp. 381–387).

10.3.4 Totalitarian Rule over the Secret Societies within the Party and Its Army

The CCP was built, both politically and militarily, by leveraging the institutional structures of the secret societies. Yet, such reliance on organizations like the Hong Fraternity, the Brotherhood Society, and the Red Spear Society also presented significant challenges. Given the totalitarian nature of the party, maintaining absolute control was imperative. To ensure unwavering control over the party and its military, party leaders were compelled to eliminate all dissident forces stemming from the secret societies, particularly those that had not fully submitted to totalitarian rule.

From the early stages of the CCP, the Comintern directed that the party should harness the strength of these secret societies during its growth. However, as the party gained momentum, it was crucial to establish firm control over these societies. The Resolution on the Organization of Soviet Political Power, which was adopted at the 6th CCP Congress held in Moscow in 1928, made specific provisions concerning the so-called "bandit problem" within the Red Army. It suggested forming "alliances with bandit-like groups or similar organizations" before an armed insurrection. It recommended a dual strategy: first, it was necessary to "covertly establish the core of political power, seize the masses from secret societies like the Red Spear Society" and "isolate their leaders." Second, following the insurrection, it was required to "disarm them and suppress them harshly ... treating their leaders as counterrevolutionaries ... who should be completely annihilated."[29]

Implementation of this strategy was articulated in the Resolution of the Gutian Congress held by the Fourth Red Army in 1929, which eventually facilitated the CCP's complete control over its armed forces. At that time, the Fourth Red Army was the CCP's most critical military force and many of its officers later rose to the highest ranks of the CCP's military leadership. The principles established at the Congress solidified the fundamental system: the army was under the control of the party leadership through the party, not directly under the generals. The resolution also imposed numerous restrictions on secret society members and addressed what it referred to as "the problem with local thugs" (Mitani, 2002, p. 21).

This resolution was swiftly put into action and the principle was applied across the entire Central Soviet base area, resulting in devastating consequences. Tens of thousands of CCP cadres, Red Army officers, and soldiers lost their lives in the ensuing internal struggle (a topic to be discussed in the next section). Yuan Wencai and Wang Zuo, the founders of the Jinggang Mountains base, were labeled as bandits and traitors during the purge and were subsequently executed (Shao, 2010, pp. 308–312; Mitani, 2002, p. 21).

10.4 REIGN OF TERROR AND THE EMERGENCE OF A TOTALITARIAN LEADER

Any totalitarian system is preceded by a totalitarian political party. The operational mechanism of this party dictates the functioning of the society under its control. Extreme centralization of power and total control over the populace leaves no room for any option other than obedience or power ascendancy. Inevitably, this leads to severe power struggles, resulting in the simultaneous existence of personality cults and reigns of terror (also see Chapter 8).

When the Comintern helped establish and develop the CCP, the basic system and mechanisms of the Bolshevik Party that it had systematically developed were passed onto the CCP through its directives and deep involvement in decisions and operations. Once this basic system was established, many of the system's details and mechanisms evolved autonomously.

When a highly centralized totalitarian system that controls everything and permits no space for competition or political diversity is established, everyone's fate rests in the hands of the top leader. Leninist "democratic centralism" necessitates that individuals and organizations in subordinate positions must obey the orders of their superiors or face harsh penalties. Anyone attempting to challenge the leader or the power center must be ruthlessly eliminated. When a system compels people to choose between obedience and commanding obedience, it draws its members into power struggles. This results in an extraordinarily brutal struggle for control and leadership. It was true of both the Jacobins and the Bolsheviks. The newly established CCP, despite its initial struggles for survival, was no exception.

10.4.1 Initial Formation of Totalitarian Institutional Genes

From participating in the inaugural National Congress of the CCP, funded by the Comintern, to joining the KMT under Comintern directives, Mao gradually rose through the ranks to become a mid- and upper-level cadre of the CCP, bolstered by the recognition and support of the Comintern. Following significant setbacks for the Comintern and CCP in 1927, Mao consolidated the Fourth Red Army and established the Jinggang Mountains base, thus commanding the party's most formidable regional forces of that time. In 1930, the CCP instituted the first Central Soviet Area in the Jinggang Mountains, further enhancing Mao's standing within the Comintern. Consequently, the totalitarian machinery of the Red Regime soon began to take shape, reminiscent of the Jacobin and Bolshevik regimes, including the orchestration of the Red Terror and the emergence of an absolute leader.

The genesis of the Red Terror within the CCP emerged from seemingly minor differences of opinion on strategic and tactical matters, which might appear as minor or even random incidents to outsiders. However, the nature of these incidents was inherently totalitarian, as such dynamics can only occur and escalate in a totalitarian organization. As the incumbent Secretary of the General Front Committee of the Central Soviet Area, Mao saw these differences as a challenge to his authority. As a result, he initiated a purge within the party and military of the Central Soviet Area under the pretext of eliminating the KMT's Anti-Bolshevik (AB) League known as the Anti-AB League campaign.[30]

In the early stages of the purge, the Comintern received reports alleging that 100,000 AB-Leaguers had infiltrated the ranks of 300,000 party members, while Mao Zedong, Zhu De, and Peng Dehuai had purged 4,000 men from their armies.[31] The CCP and Red Army cadres accused of being part of the AB League were subjected to brutal torture.[32] The CCP's official records document the appalling methods of torture employed: "beating hands with thunderbolts, burning bodies with incense, burning the vagina and cutting breasts with knives."[33] A Comintern document of the time recorded that:

> Mao accused the Secretary of the provincial committee (Li Wenlin) of having connections with the AB League and proposed his dismissal. Mao appeared isolated during the vote, ... Mao then began to accuse the entire provincial committee. Some of the Party Committee members were later rescued by the 20th Corps. In response, Mao ordered ... the disarmament of the 20th Corps.[34]

After its generals were purged, the 20th Corps launched an anti-Mao rebellion, which was ultimately annihilated and thereafter disbanded from the Red Army.

Mao's capacity to conduct such a sweeping purge, even while the CCP was still in its formative stages and focused on survival and establishing its power bases, was in part determined by the inherent nature of the CCP and Red Army. The party and army, which had their roots in secret societies and rebel peasant groups, carried the institutional genes of brutal secret societies. This made it exceedingly easy to provoke mass responses through incitement to violence.

Equally significant was the authority granted to Mao by the Comintern, legitimizing his use of violence to eliminate opponents. In the early 1930s, Mao first demonstrated his leadership over the Fourth Red Army and the Central Soviet Area through the establishment of the Jinggang Mountains base. Nonetheless, as a branch of the Comintern, the CCP was bound to carry out orders from the Comintern and Mao was not yet the leader of the CCP Central Committee. However, the continued support of the Comintern, even as Mao purged the ABs from the party and the army, emboldened him to initiate the Rectification Movement in the years to come.

At the CCP's 6th National Congress in 1928, Mao was elected to the Central Committee for the first time. The Comintern also designated Mao as one of the leaders of the Central Soviet Area, declaring in their document, "The mandated Central Bureau of the Central Soviet Area comprises nine people: Xiang Ying, Ren Bishi, Qu Qiubai, Wang Jiaxiang, Cai Hesen, Mao Zedong, Zhu De, Gu Zuolin and Li Wenli." As the Comintern did not consider Mao Zedong or the others qualified enough to serve as a secretary, they suggested "having Zhou Enlai, or Xiang Zhongfa, or Zhang Guotao enter the Central Bureau as the secretary."[35]

While not yet the supreme leader of the CCP, Mao, with the Comintern's endorsement, self-declared himself the symbol of the Red Army and the party. He contended that he was the central authority within the Central Base Area and was the Comintern's hand in China (Gao, 2000, p. 119). The Comintern was well aware of the existing dynamics. Its representative reported the conflict incited by Mao's power consolidation within the party and the army such that:

> Mao Zedong has demoted Zhu De to merely executing his commands, stripping him of virtually all his executive powers ... Mao and Peng Dehuai have significant disagreements ... though they have not yet openly confronted each other ... the seasoned political commanders privately harbor resentment towards Mao, and most local party organizations are in opposition to Mao ... The delegation holds Mao wholly responsible ... the situation is critically serious. I am herein forwarding a report from Zhou Enlai on the matter.[36] I suggest that Zhou Enlai immediately escalate the matter to the Politburo for resolution.[37]

The Comintern, fearing that Mao's purge in the name of Anti-AB could severely damage the newly established CCP, asked the CCP Central Committee to send a delegation to the Central Soviet Area to mediate. However, in light of Mao's de facto and official power in the Central Soviet Area, neither the Comintern nor the Central delegation sought to challenge Mao's authority. Instead, they emphasized the need for unity against the enemy, which effectively amounted to endorsing Mao (Gao, 2000, pp. 37–39). Zhou Enlai, in the name of the CCP Central Committee, explicitly validated that in the Central Soviet Area, "the fight against the AB League is absolutely correct and essential."[38]

The Anti-AB League movement set a precedent for the violent purging of political opponents and rule through terror within the CCP. Since then, purges within the party and the army have been a continuous occurrence, even during the desperate days of the Long March. The Yan'an Rectification Movement in later years, followed by the Anti-Rightist Campaign and ultimately the Cultural Revolution, were all continuations of this tactic.

General Xiao Ke, who had first-hand experience of these events, commented in the early 1980s: "Our Party had undergone numerous purges: the fight against the AB League, the Reorganization Clique, the Third Party, the Social Democratic Party during the Agrarian Revolutionary War; the Rescue Campaign during the War of Resistance against Japan; the exaggerated Anti-Rightist Campaign and the CR's campaign against capitalist roaders post-National Liberation; all share striking similarities."[39] Recalling the terror of the Anti-AB League, he said, "The movement wrongfully executed leading cadres, leaving the Red Army in a very difficult situation. The Second Corps had previously grown to 20,000, but only 4,000 or so remained by the time it merged with the Sixth Corps" (Xiao, 1997, p. 214).

Official CCP documents acknowledge that the Anti-AB League campaign killed 70,000 CCP members and Red Army soldiers (Hu, 1991, p. 307). Many high-ranking CCP cadres were killed during the Anti-AB League campaign, 21 of the most prominent ones being listed in the *Zhongguo dabaike quanshu* (*Encyclopaedia of China*; Editorial Board of China Encyclopedia, 1993). In 1983, authorities in Jiangxi province posthumously recognized 238,844 victims of the campaign as martyrs (Li, 2009).

Since the Anti-AB League campaign, an atmosphere of terror has been created within the CCP. A contemporary report by the CCP Jiangsu Provincial Committee portrayed the campaign as creating an environment where "everyone felt insecure." Deng Xiaoping conceded in the same year that the campaign had "instigated a climate of terror that made comrades afraid to express their ideas."[40] The move from suppressing dissent to inciting widespread terror required the involvement of many people and the active implementation of ruthless measures. This transformation would not have been possible without the institutional genes of secret societies inherited by the CCP and those of the Bolsheviks instilled by the Comintern. As was observed in the secret societies and among the Russian Bolsheviks, the creation of a climate of terror within the party was a prerequisite for producing an unshakeable leader.

The type of purging campaign seen in the Anti-AB League in the Central Soviet Area was enacted in other Communist bases. Notably, the arrest of the CCP leaders in the Shaanxi–Gansu base area on the eve of the Red Army's incursion into that area had the most significant historical impact (Gao, 2000, pp. 244–245). Nie Hongjun, then Chairman of the CCP's Northwest Military Commission, recounted receiving "a letter from the Shaan-Gan-Jin Provincial Committee" in September 1935. This letter disclosed that the Commission's officials arrested in the purge "have confessed that many senior leaders, including Liu Zhidan and Gao Gang, are rightist counterrevolutionaries, and that ... Liu and Gao should be arrested immediately." Nie recounted that, "Liu Zhidan was arrested as soon as he returned to the base ... followed by the arrests of Gao Gang, Xi Zhongxun [Xi Jinping's father], Liu Jingfan, and others from the front line." In addition, more than 200 individuals were executed (Nie, 2005, pp. 17–21, 41–47).

Xi Zhongxun later recalled being detained in a prison where "pits had been dug for burials," adding, "we were in danger of being buried alive at any moment" (Xi, 1979). Mao Zedong eventually released Liu, Gao, and other senior leaders. Gao became Mao's main follower until his suicide in 1954 during an internal power struggle. A year later, the highly respected Liu died mysteriously on the front lines of a minor battle, the only high-ranking leader in CCP history to die under such unusual circumstances. Thereafter, Mao replaced Liu as the authoritative leader in the revolutionary base of

Shaan–Gan–Ning, initially established by Liu (Chang and Halliday, 2006, pp. 144–147; Gao, 2000, pp. 243–248).

Operating the machinery of a totalitarian party, Mao pioneered the strategy of using mass movements to purge opponents, even years before Stalin's Great Purge. Mao's methods not only preceded Stalin's but were also distinct in nature. While Stalin relied on formal institutions such as the secret police to instill terror, Mao utilized the informal system of mass movements to create a more pervasive sense of terror under the guise of eliminating hostile forces. Hence, instigating mass movements to induce a Red Terror became a fundamental strategy for Mao to establish his personal authority and control over the entire party. This was a strategy he repeated roughly every decade.

The most impactful of these movements were the Yan'an Rectification in the early 1940s, the Anti-Rightist Campaign in the 1950s, and the CR, which spanned the 1960s and 1970s. The Red Terror compelled the entire nation, including all party cadres, to submit unconditionally to authority – a form of submission that was passed down through generations. This unwavering obedience under the shadow of terror gave rise to a supreme leader and the absolute power that this leader held. From these beginnings, a rudimentary totalitarian system was synthesized in China's Central Soviet Area. It was based on the institutional genes of its past and those imported from Soviet Russia. Once this system took root, it began to spawn its own institutional genes.

10.4.2 The Comintern and the Supreme Leadership of the CCP

Establishing the supreme leadership of a totalitarian party is a necessary condition for the party to exist and operate independently. The Comintern could support the establishment of the CCP but it could not directly produce a capable party leader on its own. Therefore, both the Comintern and Mao, who held the most substantial de facto power within the CCP, shared similar motives in establishing leadership for the CCP.

By the late 1930s, despite having already established his de facto authority within the CCP and the Red Army, Mao was not yet the official leader of the CCP Central Committee, and the CCP was still a branch of the Comintern. In 1937, to legitimize his de facto power, Mao sent his long-time confidant Wang Jiaxiang to Moscow to seek the Comintern's support.[41]

Reportedly, on the eve of Wang's return to China after serving as the representative to the Comintern in Moscow for more than one year, the General Secretary of the Comintern, Georgi Dimitrov, told Wang that, "Mao's leadership will be supported by the Comintern and Wang Ming should no longer serve in a leadership role."[42] In August 1938, Wang returned to Yan'an carrying this historical milestone message. Mao immediately convened a meeting of the Central Committee and had Wang convey the directive from the Comintern to the Politburo (Gao, 2000, pp. 169–173).

Several weeks later, at the end of September, Wang delivered Dimitrov's message at the 6th Plenary Session of the 6th Central Committee of the CCP in Yan'an. This confirmation established Mao's leadership across the party. Subsequently, as the supreme leader, Mao delivered an extensive report for two to three consecutive days. All CCP leaders, including the previous top leader Wang Ming, who had been appointed by the Comintern, expressed their support and praised Mao as a leader (Gao, 2000, pp. 173–177). At the conclusion of the plenum, the expanded 6th Central Committee sent a telegram to Stalin and Dimitrov stating, "Comrades Stalin and Dimitrov, your directives are entirely correct … under your leadership and assistance, and the correct leadership of our party's Central Committee … a historic transition has been achieved."[43] Mao later stated that, "the 6th Plenum determined the fate of China" and "without the directive from the Comintern, it would have been difficult for the 6th Plenum to resolve the issues" (Mao, 1996, vol. 3, p. 425).[44]

Since the establishment of the CCP, the party leaders' legitimacy and power were all derived from the Comintern as they all had been appointed by the Comintern. The Comintern frequently replaced them, much as the CCP Central Committee frequently replaced local party officials. Mao Zedong was not any exception either before 1927, when, as a mid- and upper-level cadre of the CCP, his position in both the CCP and the KMT was determined by the Comintern. However, what made Mao special since 1938 was that he was the only CCP leader recognized by the Comintern on the basis of his de facto power,[45] a power he had established through the creation of the Jinggang Mountains and northern Shaanxi bases and his ruthless purge under the guise of the Anti-AB League campaign.

Although Mao became the supreme leader of the CCP after the 6th Plenum, there were still differing opinions within the CCP and factional leaders who had competing power with Mao. Moreover, Wang Ming had closer ties with Stalin and the Comintern. In any totalitarian party, the leader must possess absolute authority and the party must be completely subservient to him. Furthermore, internal party factions must be eliminated.

The party needs a leader with absolute authority and the individual serving as the leader requires this absolute authority even more so. Therefore, totalitarianism inevitably produces absolute authority, which cannot be achieved without simultaneously creating myths and terror on a mass scale within society. Lenin pioneered totalitarianism and absolute authority. After Lenin's death, Stalin established absolute authority by instigating even more extreme terror within the party after he won the power struggle (as discussed in Chapter 8). Now it was Mao's turn in China.

While Mao had managed to establish absolute authority in certain parts of the party and the army through the Anti-AB League campaign, his authority was not yet fully consolidated throughout the entire party. But now, armed with the endorsement as the top leader of the CCP from the Comintern, Mao was ready to take the next step.

The Yan'an Rectification, which commenced in 1941 and spanned over two years, marked a critical juncture in establishing Mao as the totalitarian leader of the entire party. It was only after this campaign that the CCP acknowledged Mao as its true supreme leader. With a supreme absolute leader, the CCP transformed itself from a branch of the Comintern into an independent, communist totalitarian party.

The power and legitimacy of the CCP's upper echelons came from the Comintern, and Mao was no exception. However, in order to establish his absolute authority, Mao had to purge those Comintern-aligned individuals who did not entirely submit to his rule. As Bukharin and his allies were purged by Stalin, Wang Ming's patrons in Moscow were also removed, paving the way for Mao to purge Wang. The purge began by eroding Wang's power and severing Wang's ties with the Comintern. At an enlarged Politburo meeting in September 1941, under the pretext of criticizing Bukharin, Mao initiated the dissolution of the group of Comintern-aligned "internationalists" spearheaded by Wang Ming, which included high-ranking CCP leaders such as Bo Gu, Zhang Wentian, and Wang Jiaxiang. Once Wang Ming was divested of power, the leading "internationalists" in the party had no choice but to surrender to Mao (Gao, 2000, pp. 261–295).

Complementing the creation of terror, the creation of myths is another crucial element in establishing absolute authority. In this regard, Mao took a leaf out of Stalin's book. After taking control of the party through purges, Stalin personally fabricated miracles by rewriting the history of the CPSU, authoring the *History of the Communist Party of the Soviet Union (Bolsheviks): Short Course* (Stalin, 1975). This book was propagated by Central Committee resolutions and Comintern directives, which systematically mandated that all CPSU branches and all foreign Communist parties study and disseminate it.

During his tenure as the CCP representative to the Comintern, Ren Bishi, a close aide of Mao's, not only helped convince Stalin of Wang Ming's serious mistakes but also promptly relayed Stalin's purges to Mao. Moreover, he swiftly delivered the newly published *Short Course* to the CCP, instructing an immediate full translation and organizing party-wide study sessions (Gao, 2000, pp. 187–188).

Upon receiving those instructions, Mao promptly declared the rectification campaign with studying the *Short Course* as the core.[46] This move achieved two ends. Not only did he gain Stalin's support but Mao was also able to use the same tactics as Stalin, namely fabricating miracles by rewriting the history of the CCP, to establish his legitimacy and absolute authority. In 1942, Mao penned *Historical Issues*, on the basis of which the *Resolution on Certain Issues in the History of Our Party* was passed at the 7th Plenary Session of CCP's 6th Congress in 1945.

The Yan'an Rectification, a mass movement designed to create a Red Terror, holds particular importance in the establishment of totalitarianism with Chinese characteristics, as it served as a model applied and re-applied many times in the following decades. During the Cultural Revolution, Wang Ming aptly described it as a rehearsal for the Cultural Revolution (Wang, 2004). The first major step in launching this mass movement was Mao's comprehensive report delivered at the Yan'an Central Party School in February 1942. Mao then encouraged prominent writers such as Xiao Jun, Ding Ling, and Wang Shiwei to actively participate in the Rectification, using them to counteract what he called the dogmatic internationalists. Lured by him, these writers criticized the bureaucratism of the CCP and inequality in Yan'an, eliciting an enthusiastic response from both inside and outside the party, including senior CCP cadres. Subsequently, criticism of the CCP flooded in (Gao, 2000, pp. 299–332). However, this "liberalization" lasted only a few weeks before the direction of the movement took a sharp turn. Under Mao's leadership, the CCP Central Propaganda Department issued the historical document known as the April 3rd Decision (Li, 1986, p. 486), requiring the party's leading organs at all levels to lead the rectification and each individual to reflect on his/her entire history.[47]

In addition to the Anti-AB-League style approach that Mao invented on his own, the CCP also systematically learned from the Soviet Union about purging. A key person in this regard is Kang Sheng. He had been the head of CCP's Special Operations Section (the CCP's

"Cheka") from 1932 and became the deputy head of the CCP's delegation to the Comintern in 1933. He received systematic training from the KGB (Committee for State Security; the Main Directorate of State Security, then known as GUGB) and directly participated in purging the so-called Trotskyists among the CCP members in the Soviet Union, which earned him a position as an alternate member of the Executive Committee of the Comintern in 1935. Upon his return to Yan'an in 1939, Mao appointed him to lead the CCP's intelligence and political security agency (Gao, 2000, pp. 226–228).

The mass terror campaign began in mid-April 1942 at a Politburo meeting, where Kang Sheng identified a wall poster of the Central Youth Committee as a tool of the KMT's secret service. Mao explicitly stated at the meeting that the rectification should, "Implement censorship, in the process of which identify counterrevolutionaries and eliminate them." Subsequently, Kang Sheng declared Wang Shiwei as a Trotskyist and a spy. The Central Political Research Department then exposed the anti-party group led by Wang Shiwei. In this context, at the end of November, Mao formally announced that "the rectification ... should pay attention to the struggle against spies" (Gao, 2000, pp. 411–417). Later, Wang Shiwei was executed, only to be posthumously rehabilitated by the CCP in 1991.

As with the Anti-AB League and Stalin's purges, torture was widely used in the rectification. Through interrogations, the so-called Zhang Keqin Case was fabricated, "revealing" a vast list of spies. As a result, virtually all revolutionary youths who had defected to Yan'an from KMT-controlled areas were suspected of being spies, marking the beginning of the brutal purge phase of the Rectification (Shi, 1992, pp. 195–197). To conceal its brutal nature, the CCP referred to the detention of the revolutionary youth as "saving" them, naming this spy-catching campaign the Rescue Movement. Thousands were arrested in April 1943 alone. A single prison, known as the "Social Department" (the CCP's KGB-like organization), housed some 3,000 people while the vast majority of those under scrutiny were confined within their respective units (a term used by the CCP to refer to schools or institutions). Thousands died, including many who committed suicide under brutal torture (Chang and Halliday, 2006, pp. 21–22). Bo Yibo, vice premier of the PRC and Bo Xilai's father, recalled uncovering a place in Yan'an where hundreds of "rescued" people were detained and forced to admit they were spies, many of whom showed signs of mental instability (Bo, 1996, p. 362).

Just as the Jacobins and Bolsheviks each made their unique contributions to creating the Red Terror, the CCP's notable invention was the mass movement, a more accurate term for which would be the mass terror movement. During these movements, work units became prison cells and colleagues turned into jailers. The terror created in this manner surpasses that of physical incarceration and even execution. As the purpose of creating terror is to ensure that the majority obeys orders, imprisonment and execution alone are not good enough because these approaches only directly affect a handful of people. In contrast, a mass movement invented by the CCP could create terror that easily threatens everyone. A person conducting interrogations today could be the one interrogated tomorrow. No one is safe in this system.

Mao proudly declared that "100 percent" of the people in the party and the army were rectified by him (Li, 1988, pp. 349–350). Among that 100 percent, the most important were the senior cadres of the CCP. Included in this group were the so-called "dogmatists" led by Wang Ming, Bo Gu, and Zhang Wentian who were purged from the leadership. The so-called "empiricists" who were led by Zhou Enlai and included Chen Yi and Peng Dehuai were first stripped of their power in the party and the army. Then, in the process of being "rectified," while developing fear and awe of Mao, they found themselves being grateful to him for his forgiveness which allowed them to survive the serious mistakes they had admitted to. The totalitarian machine they themselves participated in leading and implementing, by persecuting them, prompted them to admire and worship Mao and to become Mao's apostles. Senior officials like Zhou, Chen, Peng, and others solemnly admitted and reviewed the serious mistakes they had committed, thanking Mao for his guidance and tolerance (Gao, 2000, pp. 615–625).

One of the purposes of the Rectification was to make Zhou Enlai, a former boss of Mao, completely submit. To accomplish this, the General Learning Committee was set up in July 1943, with Mao serving as the director and Liu Shaoqi and Kang Sheng as deputy directors. Officially, the task of this committee was to criticize the so-called empiricist faction allegedly led by Zhou Enlai and Peng Dehuai. Right at the start of the criticism, Zhou declared, "Comrade Mao Zedong's direction is the direction of the CCP! Comrade Mao Zedong's route is the route of China's Bolsheviks!" But this was to no avail. Under sustained pressure, Zhou ultimately made self-criticisms for five consecutive days during the rectification study meetings, reviewing his own mistakes at several key historical phases. The movement lasted for three months. Zhou finally stated: "I truly and wholeheartedly believe in Mao Zedong's leadership" (Central Literature Research Office of the CCP, 1998).

Establishing the personality cult of the leader is a prerequisite for any totalitarian party and creating such a cult is inseparable from terror. The personality cult of Stalin in the Soviet Union arose from the Great Purge (see Chapter 8). In a similar vein, a wave of glorification of Mao was set in motion by all senior CCP cadres during the Rectification Movement, in which, according to Mao, everyone was rectified. Not only Zhou Enlai but also CCP elders such as Wu Yuzhang and Xu Teli, along with senior generals Zhu De, Peng Dehuai, and Chen Yi, fervently praised their leader. Moreover, there was even sound support from former heads of the CCP, Wang Ming and Bo Gu, who had been appointed by the Comintern. In the autumn of 1942, Deng Tuo, the editor of the CCP's leading newspaper, the *Jinchaji Daily*,[48] published an editorial coining the term "Maoism." Fearing it might arouse Stalin's resentment, Mao personally suppressed the term "Maoism." However, in July 1943, at the peak of the Red Terror, Wang Jiaxiang, who was undergoing rectification as a representative of the "erroneous line," invented the term "Mao Zedong Thought." It was publicly promoted by Liu Shaoqi in the same month. In 1945, at the 7th National Congress of the CCP, Liu formally proposed that the theoretical foundation of the CCP was Mao Zedong Thought (Gao, 2000, pp. 606–614).

The CCP had thus established a leader with absolute authority, a group of makers of the absolute leader led by Liu Shaoqi and Ren Bishi, senior cadres defending the absolute leader led by Zhou Enlai, and a large number of mid- and lower-level cadres and party members who blindly obeyed the absolute leader. Furthermore, with the outbreak of the Second World War, Stalin stopped talking about the world proletarian revolution and disbanded the Comintern to allay the suspicions of the American and British allies about the Soviet Union. As a result, the CCP was transformed from a branch of the Comintern into a largely independent, communist totalitarian party with its own absolute leader.[49]

NOTES

1. Xu Xingzhi, "The Worker-Peasant Movement during the Founding Period of the Party," (党成立时期的工农运动) in Wang (2008).
2. Subsequent historical developments revealed the transitory and revocable nature of Lenin's promise to China in 1918, much like his pledges to Russia's electorate ten months prior. Indeed, the fact is that the Soviet Union did not fully cede Port Arthur (Dalian) until the early 1950s, which had been under Russian control since the Tsarist era.
3. The First Research Department of the Party History Research Office of the Central Committee of the CCP (1997a, vol. 1, pp. 41–42).
4. The First Research Department of the Party History Research Office of the Central Committee of the CCP (1997a, vol. 1, pp. 31–35).
5. Museum of the Chinese Revolution, Hunan Provincial Museum (1980a, p. 23).
6. The First Research Department of the Party History Research Office of the Central Committee of the CCP (1997b, vol. 2, pp. 171–188).
7. The Manifesto of the Chinese Communist Party and the First Resolution of the Chinese Communist Party are included in CASS-Institute of Modern History ([1980a], vol. 1). These documents were back-translated from the CPSU Central Committee Archives, as the original Chinese texts had been lost.

8. Institute of Marxism Leninism and Institute of Modern History, CASS (1989, pp. 1–9).
9. Reference Room of the Department of Communist Party History, Renmin University of China (1979, pp. 149–191).
10. Maring's report to the Executive Committee of the Comintern (Malin xiang gongchanguoji zhixingweiyuanhuide baogao), July 11, 1922, in Modern History Research Office of CASS (1980b, p. 12).
11. Central Committee Archives (1989a, vol. 1, pp. 47–55).
12. Central Committee Archives (1989a, vol. 1, pp. 62–72).
13. Central Committee Archives (1989a, vol. 1, p. 93).
14. The First Research Department of the Party History Research Office of the Central Committee of the CCP (1997a, vol. 1, p. 161).
15. The First Research Department of the Party History Research Office of the Central Committee of the CCP (1997a, vol. 1, pp. 86–87).
16. However, CCP leaders had strong disagreements with the Comintern in concrete implementations and expressed their views accordingly (Tang, 2013, chapter 5), leading the Comintern to issue an order requiring the CCP to obey Maring's instructions (Order of the Comintern to the CCP Central Committee, in Institute of Marxism Leninism and Institute of Modern History, CASS (1989).
17. The First Research Department of the Party History Research Office of the Central Committee of the CCP (1997a, vol. 1, pp. 103, 109, 126, 134, 144, 165).
18. Central Committee Archives (1989b, vol. 3, pp. 24, 32).
19. The First Research Department of the Party History Research Office of the Central Committee of the CCP (2002a, vol. 7, p. 83).
20. The First Research Department of the Party History Research Office of the Central Committee of the CCP (2002a, vol. 7, pp. 5–6).
21. The First Research Department of the Party History Research Office of the Central Committee of the CCP (2002a, vol. 7, p. 10).
22. The First Research Department of the Party History Research Office of the Central Committee of the CCP (2002a, vol. 7, pp. 10–12).
23. Central Committee Archives (1989c, vol. 4, pp. 295–482).
24. The First Research Department of the Party History Research Office of the Central Committee of the Communist Party of China (1997c, vol. 3, pp. 253–254).
25. The First Research Department of the Party History Research Office of the Central Committee of the CCP (2002a, vol.7, p. 10).

26. *Dangde ganbu tongjibiao* (Statistical Tables of Party Cadres), in Jiangxi Provincial Archives, Party History Teaching and Research Office of the Party School of the Jiangxi Provincial Committee of the CCP (1982, p. 662).
27. For more details, see Esherick (2022), particularly chapter 3, "Bandits and Bolsheviks."
28. Chen Yun, "Collected Works of Chen Yun (*Chen yun wenji*)," quoted in Shao (2010, p. 380).
29. Central Committee Archives (1989c, vol. 4, p. 399).
30. Literature Research Office of the Central Committee of the CCP (1993, pp. 314–319).
31. The First Research Department of the Party History Research Office of the Central Committee of the CCP (2002b, vol. 10, p. 84).
32. The First Research Department of the Party History Research Office of the Central Committee of the CCP (2002b, vol. 10, pp. 74–84).
33. Provincial Executive Committee Emergency Circular No. 9, December 15, 1930, from Gao (2000, p. 117).
34. The First Research Department of the Party History Research Office of the Central Committee of the CCP (2002b, vol. 10, p. 62).
35. The First Research Department of the Party History Research Office of the Central Committee of the CCP (2002b, vol. 10, p. 63).
36. In the original texts, senior CCP leaders, including Zhou Enlai, appear under their Russian names. For clarity, Russian names in these quotations are replaced with the Chinese originals.
37. The First Research Department of the Party History Research Office of the Central Committee of the CCP (2002b, vol. 10, pp. 62–63).
38. Central Literature Research Office of the CCP (1989, p. 212).
39. Party History Research Office of the Museum of the Chinese Revolution (1983, p. 410).
40. From *Qijun gongzuo baogao* (*Report on the Work of the Seventh Army*), 1931, quoted in Gao (2000, pp. 37–38).
41. Gao (2000, pp. 168–171). As General Secretary of the CCP Central Committee, Hu Yaobang admitted in his eulogy to Wang Jiaxiang that it was "the Central Committee that sent" Wang to the Soviet Union "to inform the leaders of the Comintern about the situation of the Chinese revolution and to provide his personal views on the leadership of the CCP" (Hu Yaobang, *Commemorating Comrade Wang Jiaxiang* [*Shenqiede jinian Wang Jiaxiang tongzhi*], quoted in Gao (2000, p. 168).

42. The First Research Department of the Party History Research Office of the Central Committee of the CCP (2012a, vol. 18, p. 15). For more discussion on the historical context of the events in question, see Gao (2000, pp. 168–171), He (2005), and Yang (2005).
43. The First Research Department of the Party History Research Office of the Central Committee of the CCP (2012a, vol. 18, p. 94).
44. Mao (1996, vol. 3, p. 425).
45. In terms of determining leadership within the CCP, the significance of Dimitrov's message concerning Mao for the Comintern was substantial. However, no written record of Dimitrov's comments has been found among declassified documents. Furthermore, there is no other documentation from either Dimitrov or the Comintern providing circumstantial or supporting evidence for this conversation. This lack of documentation is contrary to the operational norms of the Comintern, an organization that placed considerable emphasis on record-keeping and whose declassified documents reveal details covering the broadest to the most minute aspects. Therefore, both participants involved in the events of that time, including A. S. Titov, and historians have expressed skepticism concerning Dimitrov's purported comments. Some even question the existence of such a message (Kampen, 2003, pp. 93–96; Gao, 2000, pp. 170–171). Nonetheless, the 6th Plenum cabled Stalin and the Comintern, which accepted Mao's leadership of the CCP and continued to do so in its subsequent serious disagreements with Mao.
46. Gao (2000, p. 282; The First Research Department of the Party History Research Office of the Central Committee of the CCP (2012b, vol. 21, pp. 127–151).
47. Central Committee Archives (1991, vol. 13, pp. 364–366).
48. This was the predecessor of the *People's Daily*, where Deng Tuo subsequently assumed the role of editor-in-chief. In 1966, he became one of the first "anti-party elements" to be targeted during the Cultural Revolution.
49. After the dissolution of the Comintern, Stalin and Dimitrov maintained their engagement with the CCP on significant matters. Simultaneously, the CCP continued to rely on Soviet political and military assistance across a range of areas. The primary change, compared to the previous state of affairs, was that the CPSU no longer exercised direct control over the leadership and party line of the CCP.

11 Building a Totalitarian Regime

From the Chinese Soviet to the People's Republic

At the core of any totalitarian regime lies a totalitarian political party, the nature of which defines the regime's character. From the establishment of the Chinese Soviet Republic by the CCP in 1931 to the formation of the People's Republic later on, the fundamental character of these regimes has remained consistently totalitarian. However, although the Comintern founded the CCP based on CPSU principles, as discussed in Chapters 8 and 10, the unique institutional genes of China and the external environment that the CCP faced resulted in certain differences between the two Communist parties. These differences led the CCP to adopt tactics that slightly diverge from those of the CPSU, with the totalitarian nature of the party constant. Regrettably, from the 1940s to the present, many individuals both within and outside China have been deceived by these tactics, leading them to misunderstand the true nature of the CCP and to falsely believe that it is not a genuine Communist Party.

A factor that profoundly influenced the Russian Bolshevik strategy was its intimate relationship with the constitutional movement of Russian populist socialism. Prior to the establishment of the Bolsheviks, most of Russia's intelligentsia believed that the goal of political parties and revolution was to establish a constitutional government and that constitutionalism was their basis of legitimacy, despite their advocacy against private property rights. Among the various factions of radical intelligentsia, the Bolsheviks, fundamentally opposed to constitutionalism, emerged from an environment striving for constitutional governance. Lenin had to persuade his followers of the rationale against constitutionalism and the Bolsheviks had to make great efforts to conceal the essence of their opposition to constitutionalism, disguising their agendas and actions that violated it.

Later, after the Bolsheviks bloodily suppressed their opponents and seized political power, it was still necessary to create a Soviet charter in the guise of a constitution that violated the principles of constitutionalism. This was the first article of the Russian Soviet Constitution of 1918 drafted by Lenin, the *Declaration of Rights of the Working and Exploited People*. Since then, all totalitarian regimes followed this disguised approach in law-making, including the Fascists and the Nazis.

In contrast, the CCP has almost no connection with constitutionalism. Among the major founding members of the CCP, none had ever participated in the struggle for constitutionalism. They had almost no connection with the constitutional reform at the end of the Qing dynasty or the Republican Revolution. Even the few early CCP members who had participated in the Republican Revolution did so with the aim of "saving the country" through constitutionalism, rather than taking constitutionalism as a goal. After the Comintern reorganized the KMT, the latter implemented the principles of totalitarianism: One Doctrine, One Party, One Leader. It demanded that "everyone in the country abides by the doctrine of our party" (Sun, 2011, p. 282), striving to unify the thought of the entire population with the Three Principles of the People and aiming to monopolize national power. The KMT central government declared, "Our Party rules the country by the Party, and all officials under the Party and government must join the Party,"[1] with paramount power to be held by the party's leader. And Sun had said years earlier that the KMT is a revolutionary party, not a political party (see Chapter 9). He also asserted that the premier had the final say on the resolutions of the party's Central Executive Committee.

With China's long-standing institutional genes of a hierarchical imperial system and secret societies, it was relatively easy to introduce the similar institutional genes of a totalitarian party into the country. From the inception of the CCP, the Comintern implemented Leninist principles of high centralization, obedience, and iron discipline throughout the party. It also instituted a one-party dictatorship in the newly established Chinese Soviet regime. But in order to fully seize power and establish a Soviet regime in China under the full control of the party, the Comintern directed the CCP to build a united front and attract as many people as possible, including those dedicated to liberal, constitutional democracy. Under this guiding principle, the CCP not only promised to abide by the principles of constitutionalism but even presented itself in a distorted way as actively promoting constitutionalism, winning widespread support at home and abroad. However, as soon as the party seized national power, all such undertakings were scrapped.

11.1 THE ESTABLISHMENT OF THE CHINESE SOVIET REPUBLIC

The institutional genes of the Chinese imperial system, which was more autocratic and centralized than Tsarist Russia, led to a lack of independent political forces and a foundation for establishing independent political parties in China. Thus, the parties that emerged in post-Qing China, including the early CCP, the early KMT, the China Democratic League (CDL), and others, were all predominantly composed of intellectuals. During the Anti-Japanese United Front and the War of Liberation, the CCP, under the guidance of the Comintern, adopted a strategy similar to that of the Bolsheviks before the October Revolution, that is to say, using constitutionalism as a main unification instrument and using the promotion of direct democracy and nationalism as a tool to counter the KMT and win support from intellectuals and democratic parties. This approach misled many Western intellectuals and governments into believing that the CCP was not a true communist party, fundamentally impacting US policy towards China.

As previously mentioned, after representatives of the Comintern entered China in early 1920, *La Jeunesse*, presided over by Chen Duxiu, had dramatically shifted from advocating the value of science and democracy to promoting class struggle, violent revolution, and proletarian dictatorship. A decade later, in 1931, under the guidance of the Comintern, the CCP established the Chinese Soviet regime, officially proclaiming "all power to the Soviets," directly applying the slogan designed by Lenin for the October Revolution.

Bulletin No. 1 of the Central Executive Committee of the Chinese Soviet Republic, signed by Mao Zedong and others declared, "From today onwards, within the territory of China, there is ... the Chinese Soviet Republic ... its banner is ... to establish a Soviet government throughout China."[2] Article One of the Outline Constitution of the Chinese Soviet Republic adopted at the Second All-China Congress of Soviets in 1934 stipulated that the task of this constitution "is to guarantee the power of the worker-peasant democratic dictatorship in the Soviet areas and to achieve its victory throughout China. The purpose of this dictatorship is ... to transform it into the dictatorship of the proletariat." Article Two stated, "The Chinese Soviet power ... is the democratic dictatorship of workers and peasants." Article Six declared, "The Chinese Soviet power ... aims to achieve nationalization of land." It stipulated that the organizational form of the state is the democratic centralist system of worker-peasant-soldier representative assemblies; it designated the All-China Central Executive Committee of the Soviets as the highest organ of power.

The essence of this constitution came from the 1924 Constitution of the Soviet Union. It is particularly worth noting that democratic centralism is the basic principle of the totalitarian party invented by Lenin. Russia's Soviets were not originally established by the Bolsheviks, with many non-Bolshevik members within the Soviets. Therefore, it was impossible for the constitution of the Soviet Union to impose democratic centralism on the Soviet administration in early years. But the Chinese Soviet was completely established by the CCP and there was no distinction between the party and the Soviet regime from the beginning. Moreover, the Chinese people generally lacked an understanding of the essence of democracy. Even intellectuals who did not support communism were not sensitive to or concerned about the implications when "democracy" was replaced with "democratic centralism." Therefore, from the first constitution, the party principles became the regime's principles, which have continued to this day. After the Long March, when the central authority of the Chinese Soviet moved from Ruijin to Yan'an, the official name of the regime was changed to the Chinese Soviet People's Republic.

On December 12, 1936, Zhang Xueliang, the General of the Northeast Army who had close ties with the CCP, staged the Xi'an Incident, arresting Chiang Kai-shek and requesting that he stop suppressing the Communists in favor of a united front against Japan (K. Yang, 2006). In order to ease Japanese pressure on the Soviet Union, Stalin, through the Comintern, required that the CCP cooperate with the KMT.[3] Under this pressure, an agreement for a united resistance against Japan was reached between the KMT and the CCP in September 1937. According to the agreement, the CCP and its regime were recognized by the KMT government. The CCP regime henceforth was renamed the Government of the Shaanxi-Gansu-Ningxia Border Region, a special administrative region of the ROC. The Red Army of the CCP was reorganized as the 18th Army (also known as the Eighth Route Army) and the New Fourth Army of the National Revolutionary Army.

After gaining official recognition, the CCP was once again able to openly establish a united front. Temporarily downplaying its objectives of land revolution and the establishment of a proletarian dictatorship, the CCP began its campaigns against the KMT dictatorship in a covert manner by advocating constitutionalism. This was paired with strategies aimed at attracting all possible forces to strengthen itself and the revolutionary base areas.

Publicly, CCP leaders expressed opposition to the KMT's one-party dictatorship, telling media both within and outside China that the CCP is not a true Communist Party and has always sought constitutional democracy. This propaganda strategy employed by the CCP during this period not only led to substantial development of the party but also garnered support from the American public and government. This set the stage for its manipulation of US–China policy up to this present day.

Mao Zedong said, "Now some people who have always opposed constitutionalism are also talking about it.... They push one-party dictatorship in the guise of constitutionalism, like serving up wine while selling vinegar ... They talk about constitutionalism while denying the people any freedom ... We must ... strive for democracy and freedom, and must establish a new democratic constitutional government."[4] Liu Shaoqi stated in the same year, "It is a malicious rumor that the CCP wants to seize power and establish a one-party dictatorship. The CCP opposes the one-party dictatorship of the KMT."[5] Talking to American reporters in 1944, Mao said, "We do not seek to achieve the communist social and political system of Soviet Russia ... We neither demand nor plan for proletarian dictatorship ... We do not advocate a collectivism that would discourage individual creativity ... We believe in and practice democracy, adopting the 'three-thirds system' and limiting the possibility of any one-party dictatorship."[6] The CDL leader, Huang Yanpei, recorded that in a conversation with Chinese democrats, Mao once said, "We have found a new way, ... democracy ... Only by letting the people supervise the government will the government dare not slack off. Only when everyone takes responsibility will the government outlive its leadership" (Huang, 1945, p. 65).

The "three-thirds system," as dubbed by Mao Zedong, was a covertly designed electoral system that ensured CCP rule. Many individuals, both Chinese and foreigners, were misled by this system due to its democratic appearance. This system was implemented in the Shaanxi–Gansu–Ningxia and Shanxi–Hebei–Chahar border areas starting from 1939. Its central stipulation was that one-third of the elected representatives should come from the CCP, another third from the CCP-aligned left wing, and the remaining third from the centrists. The elected government was obligated to adhere to the principle of Leninist democratic centralism (Zhang, 1994, pp. 334–335). These tactics bear a striking resemblance to Lenin's control of Soviet elections prior to the October Revolution. Moreover, similar methods have been used by the CCP to manipulate elections in Hong

Kong after the territory's sovereignty reverted to China. Because China's institutional genes lacks a tradition and culture of constitutionalism, it was common for people to mistake the politics of the revolutionary base as a nascent form of constitutional democracy. This in itself was one of the main contexts for the mass exodus of young intellectuals to Yan'an at the time (see Chapter 10).

The CCP's emphasis on constitutional propaganda was primarily aimed at counteracting the KMT and any attempts to establish constitutional rule in China. In 1931 after the Northern Expedition, the KMT promulgated the Provisional Constitution of the ROC. The provisions specified that the KMT would rule the country (known as the party-state) during the period of political tutelage and once half of the provinces in the country had implemented public elections, a constitutional convention would be convened to establish a constitution and end the period of political tutelage. In 1943, the KMT central government announced that a constitutional convention would be held one year after the end of the War of Resistance Against Japan to implement constitutional governance. The CCP immediately prioritized strategies preventing the implementation of constitutional governance. Just as Lenin used the slogan "All Power to the Soviets" to counter Russia's Constituent Assembly, the CCP Central Committee immediately issued instructions stating that the KMT's discussions on constitutional governance were intended to "deceive the people" and proposed the convening of a congress of people's representatives in the liberated areas: "The Central Committee has decided that our party should participate in such constitutional activities in order to attract as many democratic individuals as possible to our side" (Central Committee Archives, 1992, vol. 14, p. 178).

The CCP's proactive propaganda on constitutionalism was aimed not only at domestic audiences but also at the US government. Among the most successful propaganda efforts was Mao's speech at the CCP's 7th Congress, "On Coalition Government." The US government interpreted Mao's speech as a genuine intention and it shifted its policy from unconditionally supporting the Nationalist government to advocating for a democratic coalition government that included all parties. Meanwhile, the CCP was secretly mobilizing its troops. In early August 1945, before the end of the Second World War, Mao ordered the armed forces of the CCP to seize power throughout the country. However, Stalin, for strategic reasons related to the secret Yalta agreement on the postwar order among the United States, Britain, and the Soviet Union, urged Mao to enter into peace talks with the Nationalist government. Mao, accompanied by Zhou Enlai and the US ambassador to China, Patrick Hurley, agreed to negotiate with the KMT government in Chongqing at the end of August (Yang, 2005, pp. 184–187).

The US government took Mao's proposal for a coalition government at face value and mistakenly made it the cornerstone of its policy towards China. It limited its support for the KMT, hoping to avoid a civil war in China and to establish a democratic system of multi-party cooperation. The new ambassador, General George C. Marshall, exerted significant pressure and influence on both the KMT and the CCP, promoting a political consultative conference involving multiple parties and attempting to pave the way for constitutional rule in China (Hsü, 1970, pp. 632–634). History has shown that this was a fundamental misjudgment of Chinese history and politics, as well as of the Soviet Union, the Leninist parties, and the CCP. The profound consequences of this misjudgment are still evident today.

On the surface, the Chongqing peace talks appeared to have borne fruit in terms of constitutional development. The KMT, the CCP, and other democratic parties began to hold political consultation meetings to debate the specifics of the constitution. However, twenty years later, during the Cultural Revolution, Zhou Enlai revealed in his criticism of Liu Shaoqi in 1967 that the CCP's engagement in constitutional arrangements with the KMT was merely a ruse. He exposed the true purpose of the CCP's participation in the constitution and political consultation meetings, saying, "After the old CPPCC [Chinese People's Political Consultative Conference] meeting, I returned to Yan'an and reported to Chairman Mao....

Chairman Mao said that this peace was to stall for time, to help us build up our strength and train our army. We ... should strengthen the agrarian revolution and prepare for war" (Lee, 1993, p. 127).

On the surface, the KMT and the CCP each put forward their principles for constitution-making at the CPPCC meetings. The KMT proposed indirect democracy and centralization of power, while the CCP, in disagreement, pushed for a more radical proposal of direct democracy and federalism.

Specifically, the KMT proposed that the National Assembly, elected by the people, should exercise the right to vote, the right to impeach, the right to popular initiative (allowing citizens to propose new laws or amendments to existing laws or the constitution), and the right to referendum (allowing citizens to approve or reject laws or policies that have already been passed). The central government would consist of five constitutional bodies: the Executive Yuan, Legislative Yuan, Judicial Yuan, Examination Yuan, and Control Yuan. The localities would be ruled by the central government and the president would possess semi-independent and centralized powers.

In contrast, the CCP and the Democratic League demanded a form of direct democracy similar to that of Switzerland, with all voters exercising the four powers directly. They sought a relationship between the Executive and Legislative branches akin to a parliamentary system, so as to limit the powers of the president as much as possible. They also insisted on a federal system with decentralized local authority.

After four rounds of discussions, the KMT made concessions on all of these issues and on January 25, 1946, all parties agreed on a draft constitution (Lee, 1993, pp. 247–250), which is essentially the constitution implemented in Taiwan today.

Zhou Enlai, the chief representative of the CCP at the political consultative conference, said in a report to Marshall on January 31:

> We believe that the form of democracy China should adopt should emulate that of the United States. The conditions necessary for the adoption of socialism in China are currently not present.

While the Chinese Communists theoretically regard socialism as our ultimate goal, we do not intend to implement it in the near future, nor do we believe it is possible to do so. When we say we will follow the path of the United States, we are referring to achieving American-style democracy and science ... Hopefully, this can establish an independent, free, and prosperous China.

At the time, not only CCP cadres, the majority of China's democratic parties, and many intellectuals but even the US government represented by the ambassador to China, Stuart Stanton, had unwavering faith in the declarations of the top CCP leadership (Lee, 1993, pp. 284–286).

To the public, the CCP Central Committee issued a directive on February 1, stating that, "China has henceforth entered a new stage of peaceful democratic construction ... the party will cease its direct command of the army." However, at the CCP Central Committee meeting ten days later, Mao and Liu said just the opposite. They firmly opposed the idea of nationalizing the army (Yang, 2005, pp. 208–209).

Later, on November 30, 1947, Mao reported to Stalin the CCP's plan, stating, "by the final victory of the Chinese revolution, following the models of the USSR and Yugoslavia, all political parties other than the CCP should disappear from the political stage."[7]

When the United States decided not to support the KMT government, the Soviet Red Army took a series of actions to strengthen the CCP army. From early March to mid-April 1946, the Soviets abruptly withdrew their troops en masse from several cities in Northeast China, handing over strategic locations and arms (including captured Japanese armaments) to the CCP forces. This directly led to the outbreak of civil war across the Northeast (Yang, 2005, pp. 209–214).

Nevertheless, the KMT government still tried to convene a constitutional assembly in November. The CCP claimed that the KMT's provision violated the Political Consultative Conference's resolution that a coalition government should be established before the assembly and was therefore illegal. On November 15, the National Constituent Assembly was formally convened. Representatives from the KMT and three other parties held 90 percent of the total seats, while the CCP and Democratic League representatives, who held 10 percent of the total seats, boycotted the meeting. On December 25, 1946, the Assembly passed the "Constitution of the Republic of China." However, the Nationalist government cited the civil war as the reason for postponing the enactment of this constitution, which was not fully implemented in Taiwan until 1987. On the other hand, the Chinese Communist Party not only completely disavowed the constitution it had participated in formulating on the grounds that the KMT had illegally convened the National Congress but also took this as an opportunity to formally declare all-out war with the KMT (Lee, 1993, pp. 417–438).

General Marshall, who considered it his duty to mediate the civil war, announced the cessation of aid to the Nationalist government just as the Assembly convened. Nevertheless, when he was recalled to the United States a few weeks later, he commented, "The Assembly has indeed passed a democratic constitution, which is in line with the principles set by the Political Consultative Conference in all major aspects and includes all the key points demanded by the CCP, yet it is most unfortunate that the CCP deemed it inappropriate to participate in the Assembly" (quoted in Lee, 1993, p. 433).

But General Marshall might not have known that the situation was much worse than he thought as the CCP also fully utilized the opportunity to debate constitutional matters for propaganda purposes and to prepare for the seizure of power. Such a strategy was learned from the Bolsheviks, who used the parliament as a propaganda tool during the years of constitutional reform in Tsarist Russia (see Chapter 8). One important strategy the CCP's use of constitutionalism as a tool for united front politics was to promote provincial (i.e., liberated area) constitutions. In 1945, while discussing the draft constitution at the 9th Political Consultative Conference, Wu Yuzhang, on behalf of the CCP, proposed learning from the parliamentary systems of the advanced democratic countries like Britain and the United States to limit central power. He thought China should adopt bottom-up universal suffrage with provinces as autonomous units, with provincial governors elected by the people, provincial autonomy, and provincial constitutions. The military would not serve any one individual or factions (Lee, 1993, pp. 235–236). By promoting autonomy for the provinces, the CCP not only attempted to affirm the legitimacy of the liberated areas but also to claim that it was truly democratic. The propaganda was so successful that the CDL not only echoed it but also enthusiastically propagated it vigorously (Lee, 1993, pp. 239–240).

The CCP advanced a form of disguised "constitutionalism," assuring one-party leadership in each liberated area. In April 1946, the Principles of the Constitution of the Shaanxi–Gansu–Ningxia Border Area were passed. This new constitution not only lacked any references to a proletarian dictatorship but also emphasized that the upper chamber of the assembly, known as the Congress of People's Representatives, would wield power. Representatives at all assembly levels would be selected through direct popular vote and these representatives would elect government officials. Both the government and the representatives were held accountable to each other and to the electorate.

Other liberated areas adopted constitutions mirroring these principles, such as the Common Program of Governance for the Democratic Administrations of the Northeast Provinces and Cities, the Program of Governance for the People's Administration of North China, and the Program of Governance for the Autonomous Administration of Inner Mongolia.

Interestingly, all these new constitutions of the liberated areas bore no relation to the Leninist constitution, nor did they exhibit any links to the constitution of the Chinese Soviet. Specifically, all the crucial terms such as proletarian dictatorship, socialism, and deprivation of private property were conspicuously absent.

The actions of the CCP impressed Chinese people and observers around the world, leading them to believe that, aside from its name, the party was no longer communist. It appeared that the liberated areas were moving towards universal suffrage and judicial independence, at least according to their constitutions (Yang et al., 1987). Actually, this entirely misleading characterization of the CCP had already been conveyed to an American journalist two years earlier, in 1944, when Mao declared to Harrison Forman, "You've seen it ... we are no longer the so-called Communist Party in the Soviet sense ... The name of our political party ... is not important ... What is important are the contents and practices, not the name!" (Forman, 1988, p. 200).

However, regardless of the CCP's rhetoric, the liberated areas remained under totalitarian control, albeit disguised. Once the party succeeded in seizing power, it demonstrated through its actions that its constitutionalism advocacy was merely a united front strategy for seizing power. Three years later, on September 29, 1949, on the eve of formally establishing the People's Republic of China, the CCP officially replaced all the "constitutions" recently established in each liberated area. It achieved this by passing the Common Program of the Chinese People's Political Consultative Conference, which served as a de facto interim constitution.

The fundamental principles of this Common Program reverted to those of the Chinese Soviet Constitution, created in the early 1930s under the guidance of the Comintern. Among other provisions, it stated, "the people's democratic dictatorship should be led by the working class" (Article 1) and "democratic centralism should be implemented at all levels of government agencies ... people's governments at all levels must be subordinate to the Central People's Government" (Article 15). All of these principles fundamentally contradicted the constitutional principles that the CCP had proposed during the previous Political Consultative Conference debates on the constitution.

The first constitution of the PRC, adopted in 1954, further affirmed that the country was led by the Chinese Communist Party, effectively establishing a one-party system. At this juncture, the

CCP mirrored what Lenin and the Bolsheviks had achieved in Russia between 1917 and 1918, establishing a totalitarian regime on the Chinese mainland. From that point onward, the institutional genes of totalitarianism continued to evolve and deepen within China.

11.2 MOBILIZATION AND DOMINATION: LAND REFORM AND THE SUPPRESSION OF COUNTERREVOLUTIONARIES

Unprecedented centralization of power and resources is a prerequisite for any totalitarian regime. Achieving this requires forcibly depriving the majority of their basic rights, a move that is bound to encounter significant resistance. As such, unprecedented levels of violence and terror must be employed to counter this resistance and establish a totalitarian system. However, violence on such a scale necessitates the unleashing of frenzied mobs across society and totalitarianism can only emerge in places where this phenomenon can occur. This was the case in Münster during the Middle Ages, Paris during the French Revolution (Chapter 6), Russia during the Bolshevik Revolution (Chapter 8), and even more so in China during the Communist Revolution. Chapter 10 discusses the internal violence of totalitarian parties. Similarly, a totalitarian party's process of controlling society relies on initiating a brutally violent revolution throughout society, as this is a necessary condition for societal control. Given the conditions fostered by China's institutional genes, the earliest and most widespread violent movement launched by the CCP was land reform.

One of the CCP's revolutionary goals was to establish a system in which the party could control all property rights, including land rights. Soon after establishing the Chinese Soviet, its constitution stipulated that it aimed to "nationalize the land" (Article 16 of the Outline Constitution of the Chinese Soviet Republic). This goal, clearly contrary to the basic interests of the peasants, was completely incompatible with the peasants' incentives. Totalitarian regimes depend on mass movements for large-scale social and military mobilization. Without massive peasant mobilization, there would have been no Communist revolution or Communist rule. Indeed, in the second year after its establishment, the CCP declared at its Second Congress that, "China's 300 million peasants are the most crucial component of the revolutionary movement ... when a large number of poor peasants can unite with workers, the success of the Chinese revolution is guaranteed" (Shi et al., 1985, p. 103).

To mobilize the peasants, the Comintern-CCP resorted to using Leninist deception tactics, crafting a temporary slogan for equal land division, which was in line with the peasants' interests. Historically, land redistribution had been used as a tactic to mobilize many peasant revolts throughout Chinese history, most notably during the Taiping Rebellion, which both Sun Yat-sen and Mao Zedong admired. However, in the communist totalitarian revolution, land reform was used as a stimulus for the peasant movement rather than to establish an egalitarian system of private land ownership. This differentiated the CCP's revolution from traditional peasant uprisings in China. Shortly after the formation of the CCP and the reorganization of the KMT, the Comintern urged both parties to launch a peasant movement. It encouraged the CCP to utilize traditional secret organizations like the Red Spear Society to spur the movement while prompting both parties to ignite peasant revolutions through land reform.

The CCP proclaimed that the Chinese peasant movement led by Mao was, in fact, first carried out by the KMT but initiated and guided by the Comintern, which discussed the issue of launching peasant workshops with Sun Yat-sen and Liao Zhongkai in 1924.[8] Under the Comintern's auspices, the newly reorganized Kuomintang established the Peasant Movement Committee, with Mao Zedong and Song Ziwen serving as members. Backed by Wang Jingwei, Mao Zedong assumed the role of acting Minister of the Central Propaganda Department of the KMT and took control of the Peasant Movement Institute. This was the first time that Mao played an important role in the Chinese Communist revolution.[9]

Mao's seminal work, *A Report on an Investigation of the Peasant Movement in Hunan*, composed while he headed the Peasant

Movement Institute, gave an enthusiastic account of spontaneous violent tendencies within the peasant movement. In this work, Mao explored and summarized ways to harness these spontaneous violent tendencies to mobilize the masses, inciting larger-scale violent movements. He systematically legitimized violence, contending that it was necessary for initiating mass movements and revolutions. This work subsequently became the CCP's first theory on using violence and served as the fundamental guiding principle for decades of revolutionary movements launched by the CCP. Forty years later, during the CR, Kang Sheng and Jiang Qing, quoting passages from this text that incited violence, successfully turned the CR into a widespread killing spree at Red Guard mass rallies.

Soon, the theory of violence was given a chance to come into full play. After Chiang Kai-shek staged an anti-Soviet and anti-Communist coup on April 12, 1927, the Comintern organized an emergency meeting known as the "August 7th Conference." At that meeting, Mao famously stated, "Political power grows out of the barrel of a gun." The conference also declared, "China has entered a period of agrarian revolution."[10] The Central Committee went on to map out plans for the Autumn Harvest Uprising under the slogan, "Uprising, killing all the landlords and oppressing gentries."[11] The specific instructions issued by the Central Committee were to "exercise Red Terror as far as possible" (cited in Zhao, 1983, p. 87).

Guided by violent revolution and Red Terror principles, the CCP established its earliest revolutionary bases, the Luhaifeng and Jinggang Mountain Soviets, and immediately launched land reform there, mobilizing poor peasants and expanding military and financial resources.

A directive issued by the Central People's Commission for Land stipulated that, "we must deepen the land reform ... not only all the land but also all the property of the landlord class should be confiscated and distributed to the poor, ... only in this way can the poor workers and peasants ... fight enthusiastically ... this is the most effective way to consolidate Soviet power ..."[12] The Soviet Land Law promulgated by the Chinese Revolutionary Military Committee under the chairmanship of Mao Zedong in 1930 clearly stipulated that "immediately after the overthrow of the power of the landlords by a riot, all private or collective ... fields, mountains, forests, ponds and houses must be confiscated and returned to the Soviet government."[13]

Within three months of the establishment of the CCP's first regime, 1,686 "landlords, gentries, and counterrevolutionaries" were killed in Haifeng County alone and some 10,000 people from Haifeng and Lufeng counties fled to Shantou and Hong Kong.[14] Senior CCP leaders later admitted that the brutal land reform coupled with the Anti-AB purges (see Chapter 10) and the war had reduced "the population of the old base areas by nearly 20 percent." It was also admitted that in the massively depopulated Soviet bases, "the CCPs killed even more [Communists] than the KMT did. Many good cadres were killed by our forces" (Qiu, 2011, p. 139).

Land reform proved effective in mobilizing the masses to join the Red Army. In the Central Soviet Area, which had a population of only 2 million, the Red Army expanded by 110,000 from 1933 to 1934 alone (Chen, 1998, p. 279). However, this "red expansion" and the relentless violence associated with it exhausted both the human and material resources of the Soviet area. This forced the CCP regime to rely heavily on looting the local wealthy and properties in other regions as its primary source of revenue.[15] Fearful of being robbed, people in surrounding areas made every effort to avoid trading with the Central Soviet Area, causing its economy to wither and leaving it in a state of self-imposed isolation. This unsustainable pattern of plunder led to a severe economic disaster in the Central Soviet Area.

Historians believe that all these factors ultimately threatened the survival of the Red Army in the Jinggang Mountains, forcing the CCP to abandon the Central Soviet Area and begin the Long March (Song, 2019, pp. 178–198). In fact, the confiscation of landlords' property and the so-called "looting the rich" were very similar to the traditional peasant revolts and banditry of Imperial China. The reason the CCP could carry out such large-scale violence in the so-called Soviet areas was that those areas, such as the Jinggang Mountains base, were mostly ruled by bandits, for example, the Brotherhood (see Chapter 10), and the associated institutional genes were already deeply rooted there.

As the Second World War approached, Stalin instructed the CCP to set aside land reform and instead collaborate with the KMT in resisting Japan. This strategic move aimed to keep Japan in check and prevent any attack on the Soviet Union. Following the Xi'an Incident and the transformation of the CCP Soviet regime into a regional administration under the national government, the CCP transitioned from violent land reform to milder policies. Additionally, the CCP officially recognized private land rights by law.[16] These steps helped the CCP to mask its true intentions, thereby consolidating its base and gaining wide-ranging support both domestically and internationally.

However, as the war against Japan neared its end, the CCP resumed land reform as a means to expand its armed forces and seize power. Land reform aimed to mobilize poor peasants to forcibly dispossess all landowners and wealthy peasants of their land, which was then equally distributed among poor peasants. The slogan was, "Land to the tiller" (Bo, 1996, pp. 416–417). As the purpose was mobilization, the CCP intentionally refrained from providing legal or policy definitions for landlords or peasants subject to dispossession. Instead, these definitions were left to be decided by the peasants participating in the movements. In addition to incitement, the party also regulated an approximate percentage, such as 5 or 10 percent, as landlords and rich peasants. This proportion was stipulated from above.

As most of the poor peasants lacked the motivation to engage in large-scale violence, full mobilization of the masses, which relied on inciting "class hatred" and violence, was necessary to reach the targets set by their superiors (Zhi Xiaomin, see Song, 2019, p. 235). Once poor peasants were sufficiently mobilized to seize land and property for themselves, their interests aligned with those of the

CCP regime (Qin Hui, see Song, 2019, p. 552). This alignment meant that protecting the liberated areas was equivalent to protecting their newly acquired land, thereby providing a strong incentive for them to enlist in the army and support the front.

Mao Zedong instructed the Northeast Liberated area that, "Our party must provide the people of the Northeast with tangible material benefits so that the masses will support us and oppose the KMT's attack" (Mao, 1960, pp. 1124–1125). By material interests, he was referring to land. Liu Shaoqi said, "When land reform is carried out thoroughly and the masses are well mobilized, the power is infinite.... Implementing land reform is the most essential part of striving for victory in the patriotic war of self-defense" (Liu, 1981, Vol.1, pp. 394–395). The land reform was indeed a magic formula for expanding the People's Liberation Army's (PLA) power and a primary source of the PLA soldiers' morale during the "Liberation War" (and also in the later Korean War). In the Jin-Hebei-Lu-Yu border area alone, for instance, as a result of land reform, "240,000 labor reformed peasants joined the army ... and the number of guerrillas and militias increased to over one million. Millions of militia workers joined the army, supported the front line and engaged in enormous war services" (Bo, 1996, pp. 416–417).

This round of land reform was not only much larger in scale than the one in the Chinese Soviet region a decade earlier but also significantly bloodier, both in design and reality. Unlike the Bolsheviks in the Soviet Union, who primarily relied on the Cheka to instigate terror, the CCP mainly used mass movements, such as land reform, to incite violence and terror. Just like the Cheka in Russia, the terror created from land reform was a general tool, targeting not only enemies but also party members and cadres.

The Directive on the Land Issue, drafted by Liu Shaoqi and other top leaders (known as the May 4 Directive), was issued by the CCP Central Committee, triggering a violent phase of land reform. Following this, Liu directed the party press to incite class hatred among the masses through various propaganda means.[17] He called for land reform to be tied to party rectification, mobilizing the masses and launching intense struggles.[18] Rectifying the party meant motivating party cadres and members to use violence proactively and brutally, or risk finding themselves in trouble.

The CCP condoned horrific torture by "the masses" and used struggle sessions to stoke "popular anger." Executions occurred without trial, further inciting hatred and violence. Anyone accused of being a landlord, a local tyrant, a gentry, or a counterrevolutionary could be brutally tortured or even killed due to "popular anger." Even CCP cadres with dissenting views were purged in this manner.

Taking Shanxi's land reform as an example, cadres in the Jinsui region initiated an exceptionally violent campaign after being criticized by Liu Shaoqi for not being thorough enough in implementing the land reform. According to official CCP records, 2,074 people died during the land reform in Xing County. Of these, 1,152 were killed, 859 committed suicide, and 63 died from freezing or of starvation. Two-thirds of those killed were classified as "landlords and rich peasants" and one-third were poor peasants. In the violent party rectification that accompanied the land reform, 357 CCP cadres died in the Jinsui region, including 7 at the county level and 33 at the district level (Song, 2019, pp. 262–264).

To mobilize the masses to join the army and lend their full support to the "War of Liberation," violent land reform was launched in nearly all of the "liberated areas." The level of violence was strongly correlated with the need to mobilize military support. During the three years of land reform, mainland China economically, and sometimes physically, wiped out the so-called landlord and gentry classes. However, since the vast majority of the killings occurred during mass movements, there are hardly any statistical figures available. Historians can only estimate the death toll caused by land reform through demographic statistics. Song's estimate places the death toll at 4.7 million.[19]

Inciting class hatred to mobilize the masses, utilizing the mobilized masses to create pervasive terror and then suppressing the masses through their participation in terror actions – this is a method repeatedly employed by totalitarian parties to seize power and establish a totalitarian regime. The party then uses this terror to centralize power, establish absolute authority, and compel obedience from everyone. The Bolsheviks relied on inciting class hatred among soldiers, workers, and citizens to initiate a violent revolution. The CCP, in the rural liberated areas, whipped up class hatred among the poor peasants to launch a violent revolution, thus establishing the first totalitarian regime in the countryside.

Applying similar approaches to cities, the CCP launched the Campaign to Suppress Counterrevolutionaries (*Zhenfan yundong*) a few months after seizing national power by force. It was the first nationwide mass movement centered in the cities to establish and consolidate a totalitarian system. The 1950 Instructions on the Suppression of Counterrevolutionaries was the first step in promoting a comprehensive campaign to create terror. Similar to the Hunan Peasant Movement, Anti-AB League campaign, Yan'an Rectification Movement, and Land Reform movement, the key part of launching this movement was to incite violence. Mao instructed that the suppression "is not so much about killing a few counterrevolutionaries, but more about mobilizing the masses" (Yang, 2009, pp. 234–236). More specifically, Mao said, "Some tyrants must be killed first, otherwise the masses will not dare to rise" (see Mao, 1989, vol. 2, p. 138).

Although it was necessary to create internal terror to establish the absolute authority of a totalitarian system, the CCP tried to hide this campaign of terror from the outside world because the regime had not yet been consolidated. To provide a cover, this large-scale suppression campaign was launched the day after Chinese troops were sent into North Korea. On October 10, 1950, Mao Zedong himself presided over the adoption of the historically significant "Double Ten Directives" on the suppression of counterrevolutionaries. Liu Shaoqi further explained, "When the gongs and drums of the War to Resist US Aggression and Aid Korea resound so loudly, those of land reform and the suppression of counterrevolutionaries are not heard as much, making it easier to implement them" (Yang, 2009, pp. 234–236). Mao Zedong told the Minister of Public Security that it was a "once-in-a-millennium" opportunity to carry out large-scale killings, "Don't waste this opportunity; the chance to suppress may only come this once, and it won't come again ... You must make good use of this capital" (Yang, 2009, pp. 234–236).

In order to rapidly create an atmosphere of terror, Mao instructed that 1 to 1.5 per thousand of the local population should be killed in areas that were particularly hostile to the CCP, while 0.5 per thousand should be killed in ordinary areas. Additionally, he directly issued concrete instructions to various regions. He demanded that Shanghai "arrest more than 10,000, kill 3,000 ... and after the arrests, the first batch should be killed within half a month, and then a batch should be sentenced every few days. Only then will the masses believe that we will kill and they will actively help us." He further instructed that "more should be killed in Nanjing" and demanded the central and southern regions to "kill several batches on a large scale ... kill eight or nine thousand people in Guangdong this year."

Mao was very excited about Beijing's plan to kill another 1,500 people after 150 people were killed there, saying, "killing counter-revolutionaries is more uplifting than having a downpour after a drought, say the people." He hoped that other large and medium-sized cities "could kill several batches of counterrevolutionaries."

Subsequently, Shanghai arrested 8,359 people on April 27 alone. Three days later, 285 people were executed and then a batch was executed every few days, resulting in nearly 2,000 people being killed within half a year (Yang, 2009, pp. 189–203). More than half a million people were killed nationwide in the first few months of the campaign alone. The death toll was higher than the sum of the casualties on both sides in the three largest battles of the Civil War (Yin, 2014).

A few years later, Mao proudly explained why mass killings had been necessary for the campaign against counterrevolutionaries, saying, "It was necessary to suppress counterrevolutionaries and kill a million people ... when the rightists attacked in 1957, we turned against them, and our opponents have not risen for years now ... Out of more than six hundred million people, we wiped out a million-plus in the campaign against counterrevolutionaries ... it should be hailed" (Li, 1988, p. 302).

Creating terror through violence and ruling by terror is not just a characteristic of the CCP or Mao personally. The essential institutional components used to create violence and terror are part of the institutional genes of totalitarian regimes. Every totalitarian communist regime in world history, from the seizure of power to nationalization and total control, has invariably relied on violence and terror. These tools are necessary to confront the total resistance of the dispossessed, suppress challengers to power, and silence dissenters.

11.3 EMERGENCE OF REGIONALLY ADMINISTERED TOTALITARIANISM DURING THE REVOLUTIONARY ERA

The regionally administered characteristics of the Chinese Soviet regime prior to 1950 had a profound impact on the evolution of Chinese totalitarian institutions. From the start, Chinese Soviet areas were established and operated with a significant degree of autonomy in various rural regions. Except for highly centralized decision-making on ideology, party lines, strategic policies, and top personnel appointments, each local Soviet regime for its survival was responsible for its administration, finance, and military affairs within its jurisdiction.

Above all, the specifics of where and how to establish the Soviet regime were unpredictable and entirely dependent on the outcomes of uprisings. Thus, the initial instructions from the Comintern regarding uprisings were to instigate full-scale rebellions wherever possible and establish Soviet regimes. In practice, Chinese Soviet regimes established through uprisings were scattered in remote areas where the KMT military presence was weak and hard to reach. This resulted in these Soviet regimes being isolated from each other in terms of communication, finance, military, and commerce.

Furthermore, at that time, the CCP was under the direction of the Comintern in all matters and did not have a substantial central leadership, leaving the Chinese Soviet areas largely to their own devices.

The first Chinese Soviet regime was the Hailufeng authority established by Peng Pai and Ye Ting. Later, Mao Zedong and Zhu De established the second Chinese Soviet regime in the Jinggang Mountains area previously controlled by the Brotherhood, which became the central seat of the Chinese Soviet Republic due to its successful expansion. The Shaanxi–Gansu border area authority established by Liu Zhidan, Gao Gang, and Xi Zhongxun was the third significant Chinese Soviet regime. In addition, there were many smaller Chinese Soviet regimes in different areas.

All of these Chinese Soviet areas were relatively independent in administration, finance, and military affairs, with their leaders enjoying substantial autonomy. Each Soviet area had its own laws, regulations, banks, and even its own banknotes. The Soviet governments of western Fujian, Hunan Province, the Hubei–Henan–Anhui region, and the Hunan–Jiangxi region all had their own organic laws, which set the system and determined their rules of governance (Zhang, 1994).

During the Anti-Japanese War, these quasi-federal CCP bases further solidified. As the CCP participated in the 1945 Political Consultative Conference to discuss constitution-making, it proposed that each province independently draft its own constitution, an effort to strengthen its influence scattered across various regions. Consequently, the CCP instructed all large liberated areas, such as the Shaanxi–Gansu–Ningxia Border Area, the Northeast United Front Liberated Area, and the Inner Mongolia Autonomous Area, to establish their area-specific constitutions and parliaments, and they held elections in their respective jurisdictions in 1946 (Zhang, 1994, pp. 583–594).

By doing so, the CCP not only challenged the KMT and its constitution-making efforts but also solidified the illusion that it was not a communist party. This tactic further strengthened public support for the CCP both domestically and internationally. Additionally, it further embedded the power of local factions within the CCP, laying a deeper foundation for subsequent institutional evolution in China.

It is interesting to note that a formal Chinese Soviet Federation did indeed exist in the history of the CCP. After the CCP abandoned the Central Soviet Area and embarked on the Long March, Zhang Guotao, the leader of the Fourth Front Red Army, established the Northwest Federal Government of the Soviet Republic of China in Beichuan County, Sichuan Province, in May 1935 (Lu, 2011; Zheng, 1989).

Zhang Guotao argued that, "the Chinese Soviet Central Government can no longer exercise its functions ... the Northwest Federal Government that we are organizing as per the needs will remain as a part of it when the Chinese Soviet Central Government is able to perform its duties" (Zhang, 1991, p. 213). Following this, the Central Red Army (the First Front Red Army) and Zhang's Fourth Front Red Army joined forces in Sichuan. The strength of the Fourth Front Red Army was seven to eight times greater than that of the Central Red Army.

According to Zhang's recollections, he and Mao had disagreements on strategic issues. Mao then led a small portion of the troops and senior cadres to leave the main force of the Red Army. To restore the leadership structure of the CCP and the main force of the Red Army, Zhang convened a meeting of the vast majority of senior CCP cadres who had marched with the two armies, including Zhu De, Liu Bocheng, Xu Xiangqian, and Ren Bishi, to establish the Provisional Central Committee.[20]

However, the Comintern ultimately chose to support Mao in this power struggle (Wang, 2006, pp. 585–589; Zhang, 1991, pp. 294–308, 420, 432). The Comintern and CCP Central Committee dissolved the Northwest Federal Government and there was no official federation thereafter.

Nevertheless, the various Chinese Soviet areas, which had always operated in a quasi-federal manner, were not affected by the change of name and the operation of this system continued until the early 1950s. For instance, there was no unified system in the CCP-controlled areas until 1951 in terms of banking, currency, and finance but rather, each liberated area decided for itself. Since its establishment, the four Chinese Soviet areas such as the Haifeng–Lufeng region and the Jinggang Mountains each established their own banks, issued currency within their jurisdictions, and resolved their own financial issues. The currency issued by the Chinese Soviet National Bank established in 1932 had a larger circulation range but was still only limited to the Soviet areas located in southwestern Jiangxi and western Fujian. Other Chinese Soviet areas, such as the northern Fujian, eastern Jiangxi, Fujian–Zhejiang–Jiangxi, Hubei–Henan–Anhui, northwestern Anhui, and Hunan–Jiangxi regions, all established their own Soviet banks, issuing currency to circulate within their own areas. After the Central Soviet Area moved to the Shaanxi–Gansu–Ningxia region, a northwest branch of the Soviet National Bank was established in 1935 and issued currency. Moreover, in practice, there was no national bank or common currency across all Chinese Soviet areas (Xu, 2008, pp. 27–33). At the end of the Anti-Japanese War, the CCP had established seven major base areas composed of nineteen smaller bases in fifteen provinces across the country. Each of these major base areas had its own independent bank, issued currency that circulated within its own area, and handled its own financial matters (Xu, 2008, pp. 42–50).

The liberated areas during the War of Liberation and their banking and monetary systems all inherited this quasi-federal operation. However, the large-scale war, which brought together troops from various liberated areas, posed a significant challenge to the disintegrated financial system. For instance, in the Huaihai Campaign, CCP troops from everywhere used the currencies of the six liberated areas. In response, the CCP had to set a fixed exchange rate between the currencies and establish a unified national bank in order to eventually issue a unified currency (Xu, 2008, pp. 67–68) and a nationally unified finance system.

In June 1948, the CCP established its first Central Ministry of Finance and in December, it merged several banks in the liberated areas of the north to form the People's Bank of China (PBOC), issuing Renminbi (RMB) and banning foreign currency from circulation. The first liberated areas to unify their domestic currencies, in the form of the RMB, were those of northeast China and Mongolia in early 1951 (Xu, 2008, pp. 75–83). The RMB became the single currency across the southern provinces only later when Communist control was stabilized.

One of the fundamental features of the CCP's totalitarian regime before 1950 was that each liberated region enjoyed administrative and financial autonomy within its jurisdiction under highly centralized control over politics, ideology, and military strategy. That system was neither designed by the Comintern nor the CCP but evolved during the CCP's struggles for its survival and expansion based on pre-existing institutional genes. Under the imperial *junxian* system, local authorities at all levels, from the provinces to the counties, had relatively complete governmental functions. Local governments were fully responsible for administration and operations within their jurisdictions. The central government controlled the appointment of officials and the revenue targets. On the premise of ensuring officials' loyalty to the central government and meeting tax obligations, local governments, except for in matters involving the regular army, were left to manage local issues independently.

Beginning in the Song dynasty, local governments were prohibited from intervening in the affairs of the regular army in an effort to prevent local powers from challenging the emperor and to avert the emergence of a feudal aristocracy. However, as the Qing dynasty neared its end, the imperial army proved incapable of suppressing the Taiping Rebellion, leaving the Qing Empire on the brink of collapse.

In a desperate move, the imperial court encouraged local authorities to develop their own military power to counter the rebels. As a result, forces like the Xiang Army, the Huai Army, and later the Beiyang Army, emerged, their strength surpassing that of the empire's old regular army. From that point on, these local armies became the primary military forces of the empire.

This alteration of the institutional genes of the *junxian* system played a significant role in the eventual collapse of the Chinese Empire and was inherited by successive Chinese regimes.

During the 1911 Revolution, the Chinese Empire, having lost central control, was forced to rely on provincial forces, including the powerful Beiyang Army, to combat revolutionary forces. This was the institutional background that made it possible for provinces to declare independence from the empire. As a result, when the Republic of China was established in 1912, it did not have a unified national army. The independent and powerful military forces in each region became the de facto power in the political struggles. Under this system, following the "Second Revolution" launched by the KMT, the country descended into a chaotic warlord era.[21]

Even after the Northern Expedition, the KMT's central army was unable to fully control the country. Under such circumstances, the CCP's local forces relied on the development of local secret societies, peasant associations, and local armed forces to seize power from the local governments and establish local Soviet regimes. The few successful local forces grew and collectively formed the backbone of the CCP power. However, these relatively independent forces also challenged the central authority, something intolerable for a totalitarian party. To establish united and absolute leadership, Mao labeled the CCP's major local forces as "mountaintops" and criticized the so-called "mountaintop-ism" as sectarianism during the Yan'an Rectification Movement. Mao chose the term "mountaintop" because the establishment of Soviet areas in the Jinggang Mountains and Shaanxi–Gansu–Ningxia regions bore similarities to the hilltop bastions of China's "heroes of the Greenwood" (the Chinese version of Robin Hood).

The inherent characteristic of the CCP regime, which consisted of a multitude of local "mountaintops" or autonomous regions, was a significant obstacle to centralization. However, given the CCP's primary objective at the time – to marshal all possible resources to seize national power – recognizing these autonomous "mountaintops" and maintaining their existing power structures provided a compelling incentive to senior cadres and was therefore seen as a strategic choice.

Moreover, Mao Zedong's primary concern was not the local powers but rather his rivals within the party's central leadership. The fragmented power structure meant that establishing authority within the party without the support of the various "mountaintops" was difficult. In this regard, Mao was in a stronger position than those appointed by Moscow, as he was more attuned to the realities on the ground and more adept at navigating the complexities of the local power dynamics. That is, Mao needed to utilize the collective power of various "mountaintops" to weaken his rivals at the center.

At the 7th National Congress of the CCP, Mao declared "mountaintop-ism" to be a feature of the Chinese revolution that must be officially recognized. He stated that the elimination of "mountaintop-ism" was a future task.[22] Gao Gang later reflected on Mao's strategy of appeasing the "mountaintops" at the 7th National Congress, saying, "Chairman Mao ... deliberately suppressed the advancement of personnel from the First Army Corps of the Jinggang Mountains, who were directly related to him, and he promoted personnel from other army corps and regions" (Yang, 2009, part 1, p. 371). Consequently, in the 7th Central Committee of the CCP, nearly 77 percent of the members represented various "mountaintops," while only a little more than 23 percent were from the central authorities (Wang and Wang, 2015). It was with the backing of these various power bases that Mao was able to officially assume the position of the supreme leader of the CCP.

At the onset of the newly established PRC, the CCP's fundamental political, economic, and military forces were distributed across six major administrative regions. Each region had a Central Bureau of the CCP. Most of the top CCP leaders were also regional leaders with their own power bases in the regions they governed. These included Liu Shaoqi, Bo Yibo, and Nie Rongzhen of the North China Bureau, Gao Gang of the Northeast Bureau, Chen Yi and Rao Shushi of the East China Bureau, Lin Biao, Luo Ronghuan, Deng Zihui, and Ye Jianying of the South Central Bureau, Peng Dehuai and Xi Zhongxun of the Northwest Bureau, and Liu Bocheng, Deng Xiaoping, and He Long of the Southwest Bureau. Indeed, these regional leaders either hailed from these areas, had spent more than a decade working there, or possessed considerable prestige underpinned by actual power in the region they administered (like Gao Gang) (Yang, 2009, part 1, pp. 370–371). As a result, each had genuine authority tied to the areas under their respective jurisdiction instead of depending solely on power delegated from the Central Committee.

Indeed, the CCP's fragmented power structure was, in some ways, an institutional legacy from a collapsing empire, that is, the local armies of the late Qing dynasty, and its successor, the warlord era of the ROC. However, within the typical imperial *junxian* system, local officials' power at all levels had to be granted through appointments from the imperial court and they could not possess their own local forces. The imperial court had to maintain a monopoly on power to prevent the emergence of an aristocracy or local power blocs. Mao and the CCP leadership were acutely conscious of the logic and power structure inherent in this institutional gene.

What is more crucial is that the CCP, as a totalitarian party, had always strived to establish a Soviet system since its inception. The new China not only sought complete Sovietization but also relied on comprehensive assistance from the Soviet Union. And a Soviet-style totalitarian system necessitated absolute and high-level centralization.

It was therefore imperative to change the power structure of the CCP regime and eliminate all the real regional powers for the sake of full Sovietization and the consolidation of power, even though these local powers were also abiding by totalitarian rule. The first step in this process was to move the top leaders, who held real regional power, to central leadership positions, effectively stripping them of their local power bases.

In early 1953, coinciding with the commencement of the first Five-Year Plan, several regional leaders including Gao Gang, Rao Shushi, Deng Zihui, Deng Xiaoping, and Xi Zhongxun were simultaneously transferred to Beijing to assume various central party-state positions. Among them, Gao was appointed as the Vice-Chairman of the State and put in charge of the State Planning Commission. This commission was responsible for nearly all industries in China and Gao oversaw thirteen departments, reflecting the significance of this position. This change in leadership roles marked a key step in the CCP's path to centralizing its power and aligning with the Soviet model.

The intense power struggle that occurred during the centralization of power reflected the deeply rooted local powers within the CCP. This struggle formed the foundation for later institutional changes. The Northeast Bureau, under Gao Gang's leadership (unlike the multiple-leader format of other regional Bureaus), was China's most robust economic region at that time. Gao was also a critical figure in the founding and development of the Northwest Bureau and he played a significant role in supporting both the Liberation War and the Korean War. Therefore, he was well known to and trusted by Mao and also received support from most of the top military figures. All of these factors arguably positioned Gao as the party's most potent regional leader. His transfer to the central authority was a significant move in the process of centralizing power, reflecting Mao's strategy to dilute local powers while simultaneously strengthening central control.

According to Gao's secretary, Mao relocated the five regional leaders to Beijing with the aim of diminishing their local powers and controlling the "vassal princes." Simultaneously, he sought to restrain the influence of Liu Shaoqi and Zhou Enlai by forming a triumvirate with them and other regional leaders, effectively redistributing power and establishing a new balance within the central party leadership (Zhao, 2008, p. 76). In multiple private conversations with Mao, Gao learned that Mao was significantly dissatisfied with the work of the central government. Believing himself to fully understand Mao and to hold substantial power, Gao took the initiative to form an alliance with another "warlord," Rao Shushi, and instigated a power struggle against Liu, Zhou, and Bo Yibo (Zhao, 2008).

However, Gao and Rao lost that power struggle and were labeled as being counterrevolutionary, which further accelerated the centralization of power. By mid-1954, the central government had completely dissolved the six major administrative regions, whose powers were handed over to the central government, and general administration was transferred to provincial and municipal governments (Yang, 2009, part 1, p. 374). From then on, military and political powers were highly concentrated at the central level and the party-state system in China became highly consistent with that of the Soviet Union, laying the foundation for the further establishment of a thoroughly Soviet-type totalitarian system.

11.4 SOVIETIZATION: BUILDING A FULL-FLEDGED CLASSICAL TOTALITARIAN SYSTEM

The slogan, "Today's Soviet Union is tomorrow's China" (*People's Daily*, October 15, 1951), which was most prevalent in the 1950s, underscores the significance of complete Sovietization. In fact, after seizing power, the CCP's most crucial task in establishing a comprehensive totalitarian regime was to transplant the Soviet totalitarian system in all respects. The intent was to create a centralized and tightly controlled political structure, mirroring the Soviet Union's highly centralized and state-controlled economic and political systems.

Before the CCP took over national power, in July 1949, Liu Shaoqi wrote to Stalin, proposing to fully emulate the Soviet Union's national organization, economic planning and management, culture and education, and party organization, while also soliciting Soviet assistance in all these areas.[23] The Soviet Union promptly and systematically responded, providing assistance that directly facilitated and expedited China's complete adoption of the Soviet system. The institutional elements transplanted during this process are not only deeply embedded in China's system but have also evolved into integral components of its institutional genes, to the extent that many people, including experts, erroneously believe that they developed independently within China.

The drafting of the PRC Constitution was among the most symbolic parts of the process of complete Sovietization. Initially, the

CCP Central Committee planned to temporarily hold off on drafting a constitution and instead use the Common Program of the CPPCC. However, from 1952 onwards, Stalin put pressure on Liu Shaoqi and others who were visiting the Soviet Union for assistance, insisting that the CCP must pass a constitution as soon as possible (Central Literature Research Office of the CCP, 1996). The reason for this insistence was that a formal constitution would help the Soviet-led socialist camp, including the newly established PRC, to refute critiques from Western countries directed at the socialist nations. After extensive negotiations, the CCP Central Committee agreed to draft a constitution with the assistance of Soviet experts.

In 1954, the first constitution of the PRC, reviewed by Stalin himself, was adopted (Zhang, 2014). This constitution was fundamentally a revised version of the Soviet Constitution. One of the most significant differences from its Soviet counterpart was that this constitution acknowledged the land rights of peasants and the property rights of entrepreneurs. This was due to strategic considerations. The CCP had just come to power, largely by forming a united front with peasants and the national bourgeoisie. Whether for the consolidation of power or economic reasons, the CCP was not yet in a position to openly and immediately strip away these rights. However, right after passing this constitution, the CCP publicly announced that it was transitional, hinting at future changes in line with the Soviet model.

Indeed, total party control of society's assets is the foundation of a totalitarian system. A few months after the enactment of the 1954 Constitution, the CCP launched nationwide campaigns for agricultural collectivization and the transformation of industry and commerce, effectively revoking all the provisions of the constitution that protected private property rights. This was strikingly similar to Lenin's betrayal of his own constitutional promises when the Soviet Union was first established (see Chapter 8).

In the countryside, CCP cells, established in every village following the land reform, directed the collectivization of local holdings into agricultural cooperatives. By directly heading these cooperatives, the party effectively took complete control of the land and the peasants. Meanwhile, in the cities, a massive drive for "joint state–private ownership" was launched, aiming to comprehensively transform private businesses and reshape the capitalist bourgeoisie. The first significant move was taken in 1952 with the name of the Five Anti Campaign, which avoided ownership issues at that time. The campaign targeted capitalists under the pretext of fighting against bribery, tax evasion, fraud in labor and materials, theft of state property, and espionage targeting state economic information.

Much like the land reform movement, the Five Anti Campaign applied high pressure on capitalists through a mass movement, creating a climate of fear. The movement caused difficulties for private enterprises and even led to the death of many capitalists, including by suicide. Ultimately, it coerced the so-called national capitalists – domestic entrepreneurs who were originally a central focus of the CCP's united front – into "willingly donating" their assets to the government "with fanfare." By 1956, virtually all private enterprises in China had been nationalized (Yang, 2009, pp. 455–505).

Thus, the CCP's goal, as clearly defined in its party charter when it was first established – to "eliminate the private ownership of capitalists, to confiscate machines, land ... and other means of production and return them to social ownership" – was accomplished. A Soviet-type system of property rights was achieved in a distinctively Chinese way, with the party controlling all means of production. This laid the foundation for the establishment of a complete totalitarian system.

Apart from control of property rights throughout society by the party-state, a thorough transplantation of a Soviet-type totalitarian system also required formalizing party control in all areas. Besides the economy, crucial domains that needed to be controlled included domestic security and the legal system, the propaganda system, the education system, and the United Front system. On the economic front, the most vital tasks entailed establishing a central planning system, setting up mechanisms for bureaucratic resource allocations, and implementing macro- and micro-management strategies.

In terms of the security and judicial system, as early as 1927, following the model of the Bolshevik's Cheka, the CCP established a Special Operations Section responsible for intelligence and political defense work. After establishing the Chinese Soviet regime, the CCP set up a rudimentary Soviet-style judicial system. Upon the founding of the PRC, the CCP formally established a comprehensive national system of public security, prosecution, and justice under the party's unified leadership.

Legislation in China was entirely controlled by the party through the People's Congress, which was under party control. However, due to the unrelenting waves of political campaigns, legislative work in China was largely paralyzed until the end of the Cultural Revolution. With neither civil nor criminal law in place, the PRC truly was a lawless state (Mao even described himself as a lawless leader during the Cultural Revolution). The only official laws applied at a significant scale were the Provisions for Punishing Counterrevolutionaries.[24]

The CCP often refers to its judicial and law-enforcement system as a "sword," signifying its role in consolidating power. At the founding of the PRC, the internal security force was essentially an offshoot of the regular army and the first Minister of Public Security was the highly decorated general Luo Ruiqing.

Propaganda is another fundamental instrument of totalitarianism. The CCP refers to propaganda as the "pen," placing it alongside the "gun" and the "sword" as the foundational elements of power and control. Indeed, under the guidance of the Comintern, the CCP's activities began with propaganda.

A totalitarian system implies that the party not only directly engages in propaganda but also controls all discourse, press, and performing arts throughout society. Additionally, the party controls culture, arts, media, and the social sciences, turning them into tools for propaganda. Drawing on the CPSU's comprehensive control over propaganda, the CCP, upon its establishment, formally instituted a system governed by the party's Central Propaganda Department, exerting control over all media, culture, literature, art, and social science institutions.

Government bodies like the Ministry of Culture, the Central Broadcasting Bureau, and the Division of Philosophy and research institutions in the social sciences, among others, all fell under the party's absolute control. All previously non-government cultural, arts, media, and social science organizations that were willing and able to survive were henceforth placed under the management of the respective party-state departments. All ministries and their subordinate institutions were required to set up party committees or branches, led by party-appointed secretaries, to carry out the commands of the Central Propaganda Department. This allowed the CCP to maintain control over culture, art, and media, particularly their content.

However, Soviet universities had been formed through a cultural revolution (a concept coined by Lenin) and a series of transformations after 1917. The CPSU controlled Soviet universities both organizationally and ideologically, establishing a totalitarian education system. From ideology to specific subject content, from teaching methods to research methods, most professors in China were out of step with Soviet-style higher education. The restructuring of faculties thus fundamentally weakened the existing system of universities and provided the basic institutional conditions for the introduction of a fully Sovietized system of higher education and Soviet experts into Chinese universities.

The first step in Sovietizing China's education system took place in higher education. Upon establishing the Ministry of Education in 1952, the CCP immediately launched a program to restructure faculties in line with the Soviet model.

Modern higher education in China had originated from the West. Most universities were established during the Beiyang period, and leading professors at the best universities, research institutes, as well as the Academia Sinica (the predecessor of the Chinese

Academy of Sciences [CAS]) were primarily trained in the West. These institutions represented the most Westernized and liberalized facets of China.

Although the Tsarist Russian higher education had also originated from the West, Soviet universities were forged through a Leninist cultural revolution and a series of transformations after 1917 (see Chapter 8). The CPSU maintained organizational and ideological control over Soviet universities, thereby establishing a totalitarian education system. From ideology to specific subject content and from teaching methods to research methods, most professors in China were at odds with Soviet-style higher education.

In order to fundamentally weaken the existing university system, the CCP embarked on a restructuring of faculties, laying the basic institutional groundwork for the introduction of a fully Sovietized system of higher education. This restructuring also facilitated the entry of Soviet experts into Chinese universities.

Following this restructuring, universities lost their autonomy and fell under the direct control of the Ministry of Education. All departments within public universities were entirely reorganized according to the plans set forth by the Ministry and all private universities were dissolved or taken over by the Ministry.

This drastic transformation fundamentally altered the structure of top universities. They transitioned from Western-style institutions to replicas of the Soviet system, a change that marked a significant departure from their former status. Three-quarters of science and engineering professors nationwide were transferred from their original institutions and the total number of universities in the country dropped from 211 to 183 (Li, 2003).

Specific universities underwent radical changes. Tsinghua University and Zhejiang University, for example, transitioned from multidisciplinary universities to engineering schools. Their existing faculties of arts, sciences, law, and agriculture were abolished and professors from these disciplines were transferred to other universities or the CAS.

Across all universities, there were significant cuts in the humanities, arts, and social sciences. Many leading professors in these fields were removed from teaching positions and placed in the CAS, where teaching responsibilities were non-existent. Soviet experts were introduced into the CAS and top universities to guide the restructuring process, thereby fundamentally transforming China's higher education and research systems.

Compared to other fully Sovietized areas, the United Front Work Department (UFWD) of the CCP had distinctively Chinese characteristics. The concept of the United Front was a strategic invention of the Bolsheviks that was exported to China. After the Comintern established the CCP, it instructed CCP members to join the KMT and form a united front with the KMT in order to strengthen their political and military influence. Since then, the United Front work has been a core strategy of the CCP and the UFWD has been one of its central organs.

However, in the Soviet Union, once anti-Bolshevik forces were domestically eliminated, the United Front became irrelevant to internal governance. Therefore, after Stalin dissolved the Comintern, although the CPSU still adhered to the principle of the United Front in the context of the world revolution, the Soviet Union no longer maintained a United Front organization domestically.

In contrast to the situation in the Soviet Union, the UFWD has been one of the most influential bodies of the CCP since its establishment in 1938. The UFWD has not only managed the United Front work but has also overseen a significant portion of intelligence activities. Even though the name of the UFWD has changed over time, it has consistently been led by the top leaders of the CCP, such as Zhou Enlai and Liu Shaoqi.

Independent democratic parties, including pro-CCP factions of the KMT, were once targets of the United Front work before 1949. After the establishment of the PRC, particularly after 1957, all of these parties essentially became subsidiaries of the UFWD, with their budgets allocated by the UFWD. Moreover, the role of the UFWD has since been expanded to include control over religious institutions, as well as all churches and temples nationwide. Additionally, the UFWD is responsible for intelligence and united front work related to various regions and groups such as Taiwan, Hong Kong, Macau, Tibet, Xinjiang, the business community (capitalists), intellectuals, and overseas Chinese, among others.

The central planning system that China established, such as the Chinese State Planning Commission and the State Statistics Bureau, mirrored the model of the USSR in everything from name and organizational structure to operations. The newly created People's Bank of China followed a similar pattern. It served dual roles as China's central bank and the country's sole commercial bank,[25] thereby monopolizing the commercial banking sector. Much as in the Soviet Union, the bank was directly under the State Council and lacked independence in all respects. All private banks were either shut down or nationalized and incorporated into the PBOC. With state-owned banks and the comprehensive nationalization (collectivization) of the economy, China's economic system was fully aligned with that of the Soviet Union. This effectively realized Lenin's vision, which he had articulated years before the October Revolution in his book *State and Revolution*, of a nation with one enterprise and one bank, that is, a nation where the party-state is the sole holder of property rights.

One of the most important elements in the institutional genes of any system is the set of beliefs, rules, and specific execution techniques formed in that system. It might have been feasible to establish a preliminary totalitarian system in the relatively small and rudimentary Chinese Soviet areas through ideology, propaganda, and organized violence. However, without the necessary skills and knowledge, it would have been challenging to establish a modern totalitarian system throughout China. At the time of its founding, China was one of the world's poorest countries and few people had received a higher education. Those who had were trained in Western or traditional Chinese education systems. Even if they were politically subservient to the CCP, they would have found it challenging to directly serve in a centrally planned economy. As such, China lacked the human and material foundation necessary to establish a comprehensive modern totalitarian system, including a centrally planned economy.

The pressing challenge in establishing a complete modern totalitarian system was to train a large number of cadres as quickly as possible to accept the entire set of beliefs and rules and to master the specific totalitarian execution techniques, skills, and know-how. The comprehensive assistance that the Soviet Union provided to China met this need just in time, playing a crucial role in establishing a totalitarian system in the country. The Soviet Union dispatched a considerable number of experts and advisors to China for guidance, training, and education. This was most concentrated in central departments, such as those related to the centrally planned economy, the CAS and top universities, and key Soviet aid projects.

From 1949 to 1960, the Soviet Union sent 18,000 advisors and experts to China, with most of them arriving during the First Five-Year Plan period (Shen et al., 2016a, p. 214). Between 1954 and 1957, the Soviet Union provided China with 4,261 teaching syllabi (Shen et al., 2016a, pp. 214–216). The number of people China sent to the Soviet Union for study and training was several times this figure. Moreover, Russian was primarily the only foreign language taught in Chinese middle schools and universities at the time and the teaching materials for universities all came from the Soviet Union.

Training personnel on a large scale is essential for full Sovietization. Renmin University of China (RUC) was the most representative in this aspect. As the faculty restructuring devastated all of China's top universities in the humanities and social sciences, Renmin University, originating from North China University in the liberated area of North China, virtually overnight became the most important university and research base in the social sciences in China. This was achieved through teaching provided directly by a large number of Soviet experts. Within a few years, nearly 100 Soviet experts joined RUC, including 10 in law and 35 in economics (in political economy, statistics, industrial economics, agricultural economics, and trade economics (see Wu et al., 2013).

With the help of the Soviet experts, RUC trained a large number of specialists to implement a classic totalitarian system. It established a Soviet-style teaching system in China and provided teaching materials for all universities by translating and simplifying Soviet teaching materials. Experts trained by this system were placed in key positions for central planning, the judicial system, government agencies, and other universities. Taking important positions in the Soviet-style system, they became essential for the totalitarian system to be able to function fully. RUC thus became the most important base for talent, policy, and scholarship in China.

The Soviet-style judicial and economic system established during that period, as well as the system of teaching and research, has since become deeply embedded in China's judicial, economic, and teaching systems and become part of the PRC's institutional genes. Today, even after decades of reform and opening-up, China's political, judicial, and economic systems are still based on the foundation laid down at that time. The faculties of law and economics in most universities and the Chinese Academy of Social Sciences are still partly under the shadow of the system set up by the Soviet Union.

Institutions are established and evolve through their operation, rather than being created from classroom instruction. The Soviet Union not only aided China in formulating its First Five-Year Plan but also provided comprehensive guidance in executing the entire plan. Soviet assistance came in the form of systematic manpower, equipment, project management, and technology, touching upon every aspect of the central plan from design to execution.

In 1951, the Soviets provided China with a proposal for the formulation of the First Five-Year Plan, based on the principles of the Soviet Central Plan. According to correspondence between Liu Shaoqi, the CCP Central Committee, the CPSU, and the Soviets' chief economic advisors, China's First Five-Year Plan was not only jointly formulated by China and the Soviet Union but also had to be sent to the CPSU's Central Committee for the record (see Chen 2020, p. 85).

China, the world's most populous country at the time, established a Soviet-style communist totalitarian regime and became a member of the socialist group led by the Soviet Union. This was a great achievement of the CPSU in the world communist revolution. Strengthening China's communist totalitarian system was in the common interests of both the CCP and the CPSU. Indeed, the Soviet Union had already massively aided China before the First Five-Year Plan. Between 1950 and 1952, Soviet aid constituted over 70 percent of all newly invested fixed assets in China, with the majority centered on heavy industry, which is fundamentally important to the economy. Beyond financial and material aid, Soviet experts also helped in plant location selection, design and technical document provision, and in providing guidance on installation and operations, among other aspects. The Soviets mobilized a force of over 30,000 individuals dedicated to assisting China. From 1950 to 1953, the Soviet Union donated a total of 120,000 books to 300 Chinese institutions and provided 2,928 sets of scientific and technical documents. Furthermore, 1,210 Soviet experts were dispatched to China to provide assistance, while the number of Chinese students and technical personnel sent to the Soviet Union for learning and training was several times this figure (Shen, 2016a, pp. 182–185). Many of those who studied in the Soviet Union became pillars of the PRC, including Jiang Zemin, who later became general secretary of the CCP, and Li Peng, who became premier of China.

With significant assistance from the USSR, by the mid-1950s, China established a comprehensive Soviet-style modern industrial system. Of all the newly established basic and defense industrial capacity, 70–80 percent, or even 100 percent, was built with Soviet assistance. Most notable among these were the 156 key projects built with Soviet aid and the other 992 large-scale construction projects partially aided by the Soviet Union. The total amount of Soviet aid to China during these years was equal to 7 percent of the Soviet Union's national income in 1959. Between 1950 and 1959, the Soviet Union unconditionally provided 31,440 sets of complete scientific technical documents, 12,410 sets of machinery and equipment design sketches, and 11,404 sets of complete technical documents to China (Shen et al., 2016a, pp. 214–216). This new industrial system served as the material foundation for the Soviet-type totalitarian system in China, which was implemented by the newly trained Sovietized bureaucrats and technicians. As a result, China not only recovered from the extreme poverty brought about by war and revolution but also fundamentally came to resemble the Soviet Union, albeit it remained much poorer than the USSR. However, the development of totalitarianism in China did not converge with the Soviet trajectory, as the institutional genes of totalitarianism have continued to evolve within China.

NOTES

1. Editorial Department of Modern History Materials, Institute of Modern History, CASS (1989, p. 136).
2. Research Office of Party History of the Jiangxi Provincial CCP (2011, vol. 6, pp. 46–129).
3. The First Research Department of the Party History Research Office of the Central Committee of the CCP (2002c, vol. 17, pp. 317–372).
4. 《新民主主义的宪政》 (New Democratic Constitutionalism), February 20, 1940, in Mao (1975).
5. *Lun kangRi minzhu zhengquan* (*On the Anti-Japanese Democratic Regime*), 1940, in Liu (1981, pp. 172–177).
6. *Beijing Manji* (Report from Beijing), originally published by Xinhua Press in, 1988, and reproduced in Forman (1988, pp. 198–200).
7. "Kuznetsov Report to Stalin: Mao Zedong Cables about the Situation in China (December 10, 1947)." See Shen (2015, vol. 1).
8. The First Research Department of the Party History Research Office of the Central Committee of the CCP (1997a, vol. 1, pp. 515–517).
9. Literature Research Office of the Central Committee of the CCP (1993, part 1, pp. 153–154).
10. Central Literature Research Office of the CCP (2011, vol. 4, p. 387).
11. Central Literature Research Office of the CCP (2011, vol. 4, p. 545).
12. Research Office of Party History of the Jiangxi Provincial CCP (2011, p. 553).
13. Research Office of Party History of the Jiangxi Provincial CCP (2011, p. 15).

14. Guangdong Provincial Committee of the Communist Party of China Party History Research Committee et al. (1989b, p. 58).
15. Research Office of Party History of the Jiangxi Provincial CCP (2011, pp. 19, 377).
16. 陕甘宁边区地权条例 (Land Rights Regulations in the Shaanxi–Gansu–Ningxia Border Region), in Zhang (2021, vol. 2).
17. Central Literature Research Office of the CCP (1996, p. 45).
18. Central Literature Research Office of the CCP (1996, pp. 84–85).
19. Song Yongyi (2019, p. 17), and Xie Youtian (2010, p. 268), put the number at over 5 million.
20. Zhang claimed that 3,000 senior cadres were present at the conference where he was elected as the Provisional Central Secretary (Zhang, 1991, pp. 272–273). Even the official CCP history, which is always pro-Mao and anti-Zhang, admits that the majority of the most important senior CCP officials attended the meeting to form the Provisional Central Committee, although it states that Zhang left the Central Committee unilaterally and only a few dozen people were present at the meeting to establish Zhang's Provisional Central Committee (Wang, 2006, p. 526).
21. Following the end of the Qing empire, most political, economic, and military power in China was held by local governments. On this basis, Liang Qichao and Chen Jiongming proposed a system of federated provincial autonomy and tried to introduce a federal structure.
22. 第七届中央委员会选举方针 (Election Guidelines for the 7th Central Committee), in Mao (1996).
23. Liu Shaoqi, *Gei Liangong (bu) Zhongyang Sidalin de xin* (*Letter to Stalin of the CPSU (Bolshevik) Central Committee*), in Chen (2020).
24. Before the adoption of the constitution in 1954, China passed only this ordinance as well as laws related to land reform, labor, elections, and marriage. All of these were replicas of the laws from the previous Chinese Soviet era (Potter, 2014, p. 13). No further legislation was introduced from 1954 until the Cultural Revolution ended in 1976.
25. In the early 1950s, all state-owned banks were merged into the PBOC. The CCP also had established the Agricultural Bank of China but it, too, was merged into the PBOC in 1957. Thereafter, China's banking system became similar to that of the Soviet Union – the whole country had only one bank until the post-Mao reforms.

12 Regionally Administered Totalitarianism

Regionally administered totalitarianism (RADT) embodies a form of communist totalitarianism infused with Chinese characteristics. It not only indigenizes the communist totalitarian system in China but also greatly enhances its adaptability. RADT enabled the Chinese Communist Party to reform its economy without altering the foundational principles of the communist totalitarian system, culminating in more than three decades of rapid economic growth. This adaptability enabled communist totalitarianism in China to withstand significant internal and external shocks, ultimately transforming China into a superpower. Chapters 12 and 13 delve into how the CCP transitioned its institutions from a classic communist regime into RADT and how RADT contributed to China's ascent to superpower status.

The institutional genes of the Chinese Empire not only provided the basis for communist totalitarianism to take root in China but also facilitated the conditions for this system to mutate within the country. After establishing a fully Sovietized system in China, the CCP did not continue developing along the Soviet trajectory. Instead, it dismantled the Soviet-style central planning and instituted totalitarianism with Chinese characteristics, RADT, which has been maintained up to the present day.

Throughout the process of the transformation of Chinese institutions into RADT, the fundamental nature of the totalitarian party and the totalitarian system remained unchanged. What evolved was the governance structure within this totalitarian system. In such a system, political power holds sway over all other powers and dictates the allocation of all resources. Consequently, the struggle for political power, as the ultimate asset, becomes extraordinarily vicious. The quest for ultimate power steered China's totalitarian system's evolution, leading it to absorb the institutional genes of Imperial China. While it might appear that Mao was personally responsible for these changes, it was in fact the institutional genes of the indigenous Chinese systems ... apart from the imported mechanism of communist totalitarianism ... that played the most substantial role in enabling Mao to instigate this transformation.

12.1 TOTALITARIAN RULE BY INSTILLING FEAR: THE ANTI-RIGHTIST MOVEMENT

The all-encompassing control a totalitarian party exerts over society hinges on the mobilization of the masses to conduct violent suppression against their adversaries and instill terror. Once terror has been established, it is imprinted onto the institutional genes, becoming a legacy to be passed down from generation to generation. To rally the masses, a totalitarian party must exercise comprehensive control over ideology and rigorously suppress individual free speech, especially that of intellectuals. The Anti-Rightist Movement (ARM), as Communist China's inaugural large-scale ideological control initiative, served not only to consolidate totalitarianism but also to pave the way for the systemic evolution of Chinese totalitarianism.

12.1.1 *The Anti-Hu Feng Campaign and Khrushchev's Secret Speech*

In the early years of the PRC, the CCP executed its first comprehensive purge of intellectuals, almost concurrently with its Campaign to Suppress Counterrevolutionaries, known as the Anti-Hu Feng Campaign.[1] This campaign, analogous to the Russian Cultural Revolution launched by the Bolsheviks after the October Revolution, was broader and more ruthless than its Russian counterpart. Official statistics show that more than 1.3 million intellectuals, a quarter of China's total by then, were scrutinized during the Anti-Hu Feng Campaign, unmasking 3,800 "counterrevolutionaries." Eyewitnesses state that "the masses were mobilized for the campaign like a violent storm ... all means were used to extort confessions." Virtually all intellectuals "no longer dared to reveal any dissent" (Zhu, 2005, pp. 220–221). From then on, the majority of intellectuals, burdened by fear, suppressed their grievances and refrained from expressing themselves.

While the Anti-Hu Feng Campaign was primarily targeted at intellectuals within the CCP, the so-called "democratic parties" that represented intellectuals were also rapidly losing political power and subsequently became primary targets of the CCP's purges during the same period. These "democratic parties" refer to the political entities that collaborated with the CCP in the 1940s to oppose the KMT's one-party dictatorship. This alliance remained in place until just before the establishment of the PRC.

In September 1949, the CCP convened the inaugural meeting of the CPPCC, portraying it as the parliament of the new China. This gathering appeared to uphold the multiparty system that the CCP had promised a few years prior. However, the Common Program passed during this conference, which effectively acted as a constitution, completely overturned the CCP's recent commitments to constitutionalism.

Under such circumstances, to placate the democratic parties, the CCP arranged for their leaders to occupy various significant roles, such as Vice-President of the State, Vice-Chairman of the CPPCC, head of the Government Affairs Council (GAC), and ministers. Furthermore, the Common Program stipulated that these democratic parties would coexist with the CCP, provided they accepted the CCP's leadership. The China Democratic League, the largest of these democratic parties, attempted to comfort its members with the phrase "long-term coexistence, mutual supervision." This phrase was later co-opted by the CCP's 8th National Congress as its own policy.

However, just four years after its adoption, the CCP abandoned the Common Program. Since the enactment of the PRC Constitution, which is modeled after the Soviet type of constitution, the Standing Committee of the NPC – which is entirely controlled by the CCP – has officially become the highest organ of power, with a unified parliamentary and executive structure. In contrast, the multiparty CPPCC transformed from a legislative body to a so-called advisory body in an official capacity.

Simultaneously, the CCP also abolished the Central Government Council and the GAC, both of which were platforms where the democratic parties had significant presence and roles. The GAC was restructured into the State Council, which was monopolized by the CCP. Furthermore, the number of democratic party members serving as government ministers declined significantly, reducing these parties to largely nominal entities.

The Communist Party has been an international organization and a world phenomenon since its birth and so have the Stalinist purges since the 1930s. Communist Party members and people in the Soviet Union, China, and Central and Eastern Europe harbored deep discontent towards the persecution and suppression brought about by these purges in the regime. Against this backdrop, in February 1956, Khrushchev delivered a secret speech at the 20th Congress of the CPSU, in which he sharply criticized Stalin's brutal persecution of individuals both inside and outside the CPSU and his cult of personality. This secret report, once exposed by the Western media, shook the entire Soviet-led socialist camp, including China.

As a response to Khrushchev's secret speech and the challenges within the socialist camp to the cult of personality, Mao personally arranged for the *People's Daily* editorial, "On the Historical Experience of the Dictatorship of the Proletariat." In it he emphasized that the dictatorship of the proletariat was the best system and that Stalin's record was mostly one of achievements with some minor errors. Yet, overall, the CCP still maintained that it would follow the CPSU's leadership, including the principles of the 20th Congress.

12.1.2 One Hundred Flowers versus Luring the Snake Out of the Hole

In late April 1956, Mao underscored the party's intention for long-term coexistence with and mutual supervision of the democratic parties. He stated that this strategy was exploration of a development path that differed from that of the Soviet Union (Mao, 1976). Following this, he proposed allowing "a hundred flowers to bloom" in the arts and "a hundred schools of thought to contend" in academia. These policies appeared to be a stark contradiction to the Campaign to Suppress Counterrevolutionaries and the Anti-Hu Feng Campaign.

A few months later, at the 8th Congress of the CCP, these notions were not only formalized but were also further extended to protect citizens' freedoms. Following the precedent set by the CPSU's 20th Congress, which opposed the cult of personality, the 8th Congress stressed the rejection of "personality cults" and the "supremacy of any individual over the party." In the new constitution of the CCP, passed at its 8th Congress, the phrase "Mao Zedong Thought is ... the guiding theory" was removed.

However, for both the CPSU and CCP, declaring opposition to the personality cult was a policy change aimed at sustaining the communist totalitarian system. It is the power structure inherent in totalitarian rule, not merely policy or personal preference, that ensures the party leader invariably supersedes the party itself. The fight for supreme power within the party is always intense and brutal. In these power struggles, individuals who are adept at manipulating the totalitarian machinery and fostering personality cults are the ones who emerge victorious. Furthermore, the nature of totalitarianism dictates that suppression is a primary means of governance.

After Khrushchev's secret report, the public in Poland and Hungary, deeply discontented with totalitarianism, launched large-scale anti-Soviet and anti-communist movements. Two months after the 8th Congress of the CCP, Soviet tanks rolled into Hungary to suppress the "rebellion."

Shortly after the incidents in Poland and Hungary, Mao convened the 2nd Plenary Session of the 8th CCP Central Committee and proposed a rectification-type campaign to prevent similar upheavals in China. Mao said, "I ... propose a rectification ... mobilize all students to criticize [liberal intellectuals] ... professors are afraid of the proletarian democracy" (Li, 2008). CCP cadres familiar with the

Yan'an Rectification understood Mao's intentions, but any intellectual who had not been to Yan'an in those days had no comprehension of how ruthless a rectification could be.

In January 1957, Mao further elaborated to the secretaries of the provincial party committees across the country that the CCP's removal of power from the democratic parties in China resulted in them "not causing trouble during the unrest in Poland and Hungary." More specifically, he attributed this to their "lack of [political] capital." Thus, to thoroughly subdue intellectuals and democratic parties, it was necessary to "strip them of their political capital" to ensure that "political capital ... is not in their hands, but in ours. We must strip their political capital ... until it is completely stripped."

Moreover, Mao further clarified his strategy of "luring the snake out of the hole," targeting the democratic parties and intellectuals.[2] In his words, "For democrats, we need to set them up against each other ... let them be exposed, we will attack them afterwards, not beforehand" (Mao, 1977, vol. 5, pp. 330–362). After these preparations, at the end of April 1957, Mao convened a talk with the leaders of the democratic parties. He encouraged them to assist the CCP with the rectification: "speak out everything, and do not withhold; the speaker is not guilty, and the listener takes the warning." On May 1, the *People's Daily* published the Central Committee's Instructions on the Rectification Campaign, calling on non-CCP members to "speak out," assisting the CCP and the government in the rectification movement. It was historically known as the Speak Your Mind Campaign (*Daming dafang*). Three days later, Mao issued an instruction in the name of the Central Committee, explicitly instructing all CCP organizations to encourage non-party members to criticize the CCP and help with its rectification efforts (Mao, 1992a, vol. 6, p. 455).

Intellectuals and numerous others had amassed profound grievances during the Suppression of Counterrevolutionaries Campaign, the Anti-Hu Feng Campaign, and the sweeping imposition of a Sovietized totalitarian model across all sectors. Encouraged by the Speak Your Mind Campaign and rectification initiated by the CCP, and oblivious of the CCP's true intentions, prominent figures from the democratic parties publicly demanded the CCP to honor its commitments to establish a multiparty coalition government, replacing the existing CCP monopoly.

Big-character posters criticizing the party emerged on the campuses of Peking University and Renmin University. A large number of intellectuals publicly criticized the CCP's constitutional and administrative flaws. Students started forming independent associations and workers began calling for strikes. The criticism of the CCP caused public outrage, and many campuses showed signs of the CCP losing control (Mao, 1992a, vol. 6, pp. 238–240). At that time, many renowned professors were members of the CDL. On June 6, six professors affiliated with the CDL proposed that they would intervene to alleviate the students' agitation. The leaders of the CDL consulted Zhou Enlai on this proposal on the same day but were immediately rejected and had to abandon their efforts (Ye, 1999, pp. 100–101).

12.1.3 The Anti-Rightist Movement's Great Purge

Two days after Zhou Enlai's refusal of the CDL leading members' offer, Mao issued a secret directive to the CCP, formally initiating the Anti-Rightist Movement led by Deng Xiaoping. Mao said,

> This is a major battle (the battlefield is both within and outside the party). Without winning this battle, socialism cannot be established. There is a danger of a Hungarian Incident. Now we are taking the initiative to rectify the situation, bringing the possible Hungarian Incident out in the open, allowing it to play out in every office, every school ... there are reactionaries in the society, ... chaos will happen one day.

The strategy he arranged was: "Hold symposiums of university professors ... Let the rightists spit out all their toxins ... Let the reactionary professors, lecturers, teaching assistants and students speak freely and expose all their toxins" (Mao, 1977, vol. 5, pp. 431–433). The offers made by the six CDL professors to assuage campus unrest were construed as attempts to seize the CCP's dominance over universities (Zhu, 2005, p. 129).

On July 1, the *People's Daily* published an editorial authored by Mao stating that: "Some say it was a conspiracy; we say it was an open conspiracy as the enemy had been told in advance. Demons can only be destroyed by releasing them from their cages, and poisonous grass can only be weeded if it grows above the ground." The editorial charged that:

> the role played by the CDL in the Hundred Schools of Thought and the rectification was particularly pernicious. It is organized and planned, with a program and a line, ... it is anti-communist and anti-socialist. The Peasants and Workers Democratic Party is exactly the same [in anti-communism] ... Throughout the spring, dark clouds churned in the sky, the source of which was the Zhang-Luo Alliance (the heads of the CDL Zhang Bojun and Luo Longji) ... These people not only have voices, but also actions. They are guilty, and the [CCP's] policy that the speaker is not guilty does not apply to them. (Mao, 1977, vol. 5, pp. 434–439)

From then on, virtually all democratic party leaders became the "snakes" "lured out of the hole," labeled as "rightists" by the CCP, and purged. Every democratic party lost its independence. Those who expressed views slightly diverging from the party line in schools, governmental agencies, and businesses were quickly, within a matter of months, branded as rightists. This included many of China's most prominent scientists, writers, scholars, and even CCP cadres, such as Zhu Rongji, who later became Premier during the post-Mao reform era. Rightists were sent to prisons, labor camps, and other re-education venues, with some being dismissed from public service (all academic positions were in this category). Rightists with particularly high social status, such as the leaders of the democratic parties and esteemed professors, were, despite being spared labor reform, still stripped of their publishing and teaching rights, and some were even subjected to de facto house arrest.

According to the CCP's Central Committee Document No. 55 of 1978, a total of 550,000 intellectuals were purged as rightists during the ARM, which accounted for 5.7 percent of the national cadres (a category that included teachers and researchers, as all schools and research institutions were nationalized) at the time (Hu, Z., 2013). However, many historians estimate that the actual number of people who were categorized as various types of rightists and purged was between 2.01 million and 3.17 million. The purged rightists ranged in age from primary school students to centenarian imams and monks (Shen, 2017, pp. 7–12).

It is worth noting that by the standards of developed countries, China had fewer than 240,000 engineers in 1956, and even fewer intellectuals in business, finance, science, and the humanities (Orleans, 1961, pp. 68–69, 74–75). By China's standards of the time, the total number of intellectuals including primary school teachers and others with college or higher levels of education (excluding students) was about 5.5 million (Li, 2008). However, the ARM cast a wider net, targeting high school and university students as well as educated cadres in factories and the military. Notably impacted students included Lin Zhao, a Peking University student who was brutally tortured in prison and eventually executed during the Cultural Revolution, and Lin Xiling, a student from Renmin University who was imprisoned until after the Cultural Revolution when she was released and sought refuge in France.

One of the leading goals of the ARM was to completely eradicate the concept of the rule of law. Despite the lack of a tradition of rule of law within China's institutional genes, the number of intellectuals advocating for this principle had been increasing since the late nineteenth century, including many who equated the Soviet judicial system with the rule of law. In the ARM, all advocates of the rule of law, encompassing law professors, judicial workers, party cadres, and other intellectuals, including advocates of a Soviet-style judicial system, were labeled rightists and purged.

In 1958, in the heat of the Anti-Rightist Movement, the CCP Central Committee denounced the entire party group in the Ministry of Justice as an anti-party group opposing the dictatorship of the proletariat and subsequently disbanded it. A substantial number of judges and lawyers were purged, even without expressing any distinct viewpoints (Xiong, 2003). Further deepening the impact of the purge on legal education and practice, all law schools were ordered to reduce enrolments, and universities ceased offering mandatory courses on constitutional law. The legislative process was also brought to a standstill, leaving China with essentially no functional laws beyond the constitution and marriage law for an extended period. It was not until the post-Mao era of reform that new legal frameworks, such as the Criminal Law and Civil Law, were drafted and passed.

The ARM was an extension of the Yan'an Rectification. If the Yan'an Rectification had been about transforming the CCP from an appendage of the Comintern into a fully independent totalitarian party, the ARM went a step further by cementing the ideological underpinnings of totalitarianism throughout China. The ARM's wide-reaching purge not only stifled dissent among intellectuals and party cadres but it also instilled a culture of anticipatory obedience, with people learning to predict and align themselves with the party leader's intentions.

After the ARM, Liu Shaoqi proclaimed that party members ought to become "compliant tools" or "screws" (Liu, 1958). From that point onwards, students were educated to be either critical of or, at the very least, oblivious to individual rights and interests, basic civil liberties, constitutional principles, and the principles of checks and balances of power. The "role models" held up by the party have typically been individuals who devoted themselves to serving the needs of the party and its top leadership. The ARM's purge not only led to individuals ceasing to express divergent political views but more devastatingly, many intellectuals even started aiding the CCP in indoctrinating the younger generations. As a result, China rapidly transformed into a fully-fledged totalitarian state.

12.2 THE GREAT LEAP FORWARD: THE FIRST WAVE OF ESTABLISHING RADT

The ARM reinforced the inextricable relationship between the totalitarian system and its ideology and laid the foundation for introducing the personality cult throughout the country. These actions not only strengthened the totalitarian roots in China but also laid the groundwork for transforming the system from classic communist totalitarianism into regionally administered totalitarianism (RADT). The first step of this transformation was the campaign known as the Great Leap Forward. The chaos and disasters caused by the GLF have been well documented. Yet, the deeper significance of the GLF, that is, its role in transforming China's institutions, has not been sufficiently studied in the literature. In fact, from the very beginning, the GLF was a push for institutional changes, motivated as much by the desire to accelerate economic growth as by the desire to demonstrate the superiority of a distinctly Chinese system.

12.2.1 *Growth versus Power*

Promoting rapid economic growth is a common feature of communist totalitarian regimes all over the world as it is the basis for the legitimacy of such regimes. Communist ideology asserts that superior systems grow faster. Achieving rapid economic growth that catches up with, and surpasses, developed capitalist nations is key to validating the superiority of socialism, which is characterized by a one-party rule, thus legitimizing such a totalitarian dictatorship. Central planning was formulated, from the Soviet Union to China, on the principle of maximizing economic growth at any cost, including lives. Moreover, both the CPSU and the CCP viewed economic power as the key to ensuring the survival of their respective regimes. The well-known saying of Lenin and Stalin, "those who fall behind get beaten,"[3] has been passed on to the CCP as a cornerstone of its ideology for generations.

The pace of development was also relevant to the power struggle between the CCP and the CPSU for the leadership of the world communist movement. Following the Marxist principle regarding institutional superiority, a more superior totalitarian regime should also grow faster than others. If China's system were superior to that of the Soviet Union, China should have developed at a faster pace, enabling the CCP to supplant the CPSU as the leader of the world communist movement. Indeed, as early as 1956, Mao had begun discussing reforms to the system, which were copied wholesale from the Soviet Union. He stressed that:

> on the premise of consolidating the unified central leadership, the powers of the local governments should be expanded a bit, giving them more autonomy ... It is much better to have both central and local initiatives than to have only one. We can't, like the Soviet Union, concentrate everything in the center, stifling localities and leaving them without any maneuverability. (Mao, 1976)

In November 1957, not long after claiming to bury capitalism by rapid growth, Khrushchev proposed, at the Communist and Workers' Party Conference in Moscow, the goal of the Soviet Union to overtake the United States in fifteen years.[4] At the same conference, Mao announced that the East wind of socialism would overwhelm the West wind of capitalism, setting a goal for China to catch up with Britain in fifteen years (Mao, 1992a, vol. 6, pp. 625–647). Upon returning from Moscow, Mao promptly launched the GLF.

Although economic growth is very important for totalitarian systems, power and the ruling structure that ensure it are always of primary importance. The GLF was no exception. In addition to speeding up development, the initiative of the GLF aimed at refining the CCP's governance structures, strengthening the leader's power, and creating the capacity to overtake leadership from Moscow in the global communist movement.

Institutional changes are inseparable from existing institutional genes. Under the influence of China's institutional genes, before the full-scale centralization in 1950, the CCP had developed a federal-like governance structure of a totalitarian system with multiple local power bases called "liberated areas." Local forces have always been a significant part of the power base of the CCP since the establishment of the Chinese Soviet (see Chapter 11), constituting the greatest difference between the CCP regime and the Soviet Union in institutional structure. Under the so-called "Large Area System," each large area enjoyed substantial autonomy in the newly founded PRC. Later, the CCP centralized power on a massive scale, abandoning the Large Area System and weakening local authority. This was accepted by most of the party's top local leaders, both from a historical perspective – in terms of building a new imperial dynasty – and in light of comprehensive Sovietization. However, in the implementation of Sovietization, the central ministries took all the resources and power from local governments, leading to discontent among local officials and affecting their motivation.

Furthermore, the excess concentration of power in central ministries and the substantial diminution of local authority rendered the supreme leader vulnerable to the influence of these central ministries. The more resources these ministries controlled, and the stronger they became, the greater their capacity to counterbalance the supreme leader's power. Conversely, when local power was weak, transferring extensive authority to the local level would diminish the power of the central ministries, enhancing the supreme leader's political influence.

12.2.2 *A Fusion of Marx and Qin Shi Huang*

Mao's specific idea about reforming the Soviet totalitarian system can be traced back to the institutional genes of the Chinese imperial system. In promoting the GLF, Mao proclaimed himself, in a speech at the 1958 Beidaihe Conference, as a fusion of Marx and Qin Shi Huang. Here, "Marx" represented imported communist totalitarianism while "Qin Shi Huang" referred to the Chinese imperial system, particularly its *junxian* system established in the Qin dynasty (see Chapter 4). Mao subsequently repeated this statement several times in two decades, reflecting the importance to him of this self-depiction. During the CR, he made it even clearer that China had always lived under the Qin system up to the present ("Qin still exists"; Wang, 1988, p. 470). The way of ruling the vast empire under the *junxian* system was to delegate most of the administrative power to centrally appointed local bureaucrats, whereas the emperor had the final say on major political, military (except for during a few periods), and personnel matters, backed by his monopolistic power on sovereignty and land title (ultimate control rights) (see Chapter 4).

Since China's existing totalitarian system was essentially co-established with the CPSU, and most CCP cadres and pro-communist intellectuals were trained in classic communist totalitarianism, a purging of Soviet-style governance thinking was necessary. Thus, the GLF began with an ideological attack on all viewpoints that did not align with Mao's doctrine. This marked the prelude of the GLF and involved critiquing the ideology and governance structures of a Soviet-type totalitarian system, which paved the way for the establishment of totalitarianism with Chinese characteristics. This critique further weakened the already fragile checks and balances within the party and intensified the supreme leader's political power, guaranteeing his absolute control over both the Central Committee's members and the ideological direction.

12.2.3 Initiating the GLF

On the surface, the GLF appeared to be a mass movement driven by competing local authorities. However, its essence was the dismantling of the Soviet-type centrally planned system and its replacement with a regionally decentralized totalitarian system. This new governance structure required the delegation of substantial authority to the local level, particularly in terms of executive and managerial powers as well as control over local resources. As a result of this change, the power of the central ministries was significantly diluted. Moreover, during the GLF, an entirely new grassroots system, the People's Commune, distinct from any Soviet enterprise, was created.

Mao initiated the GLF shortly after his return from Moscow in January 1958. He convened a Central Committee meeting, in which Zhou Enlai was criticized by Mao for his conservatism.[5] Two months later, at the Central Committee Work Conference, Mao systematically criticized the operating mechanisms of the Soviet system and the party leaders who followed these mechanisms. He said that the rules and regulations of the Soviet Union were deadly and criticized those who questioned the GLF. His tone in criticizing Zhou's conservatism became even more severe, asserting that Zhou was "only 50 meters away from being a rightist." At the same time, Mao's cult of personality was elevated to new heights. At the same meeting, the head of the Shanghai CCP said, "We should believe in the Chairman to the extent of superstition and obey him to the extent of blind obedience."[6]

The 2nd Session of the CCP's 8th Congress in May 1958 was a pivotal turning point for the GLF. The premier and vice-premiers of the State Council in charge of the economy, Zhou Enlai, Chen Yun, Li Xiannian, and Bo Yibo, were all forced to self-criticize during that meeting to clear the way for the full launch of the GLF. Immediately afterwards, the Central Committee set up several working groups directly under the Politburo and Secretariat. These groups effectively took over the tasks of the State Council, thereby sidelining the Soviet-style central planning bureaucracy of the Planning Commission and various ministries under the State Council (Xin, 2006, pp. 138–141). These structural and personnel changes profoundly influenced both the GLF and the subsequent Cultural Revolution, marking the beginning of a reconfiguration of China's totalitarian system.

The dissolution of central planning and the decentralization of power were the first institutional changes during the GLF. The totalitarian system, which was originally managed through top-down central planning coordinated by the State Planning Commission, was replaced by a system dominated by regional management and regional competition. One key aspect of this decentralization was the devolution of corporate jurisdiction, which began immediately after the 2nd Session of the CCP's 8th Congress. A few months later, by the end of 1958, the industrial output of enterprises directly under central government control only accounted for 13.8 percent of the country's total industrial output. By 1959, 88 percent of central government-managed enterprises had been devolved to different local authorities (Wu, 2010, pp. 38–41). Local party-state authorities were empowered to adjust industrial and agricultural production targets, manage construction and investment, regulate the use of materials, and allocate a certain percentage of surplus products. Overall, this effort made each local economy more "self-contained," which was another feature distinguishing it from the Soviet model.

12.2.4 Regional Experimentation and Regional Competition: Mechanisms for Creating the People's Communes

The totalitarian party exerts control over every aspect of society, drawing all elements within the scope of the party-state bureaucracy. As such, the totalitarian party-state bureaucracy is the most extensive and comprehensive form of bureaucracy human society has ever seen. All bureaucracies rely on a top-down chain of command. Due to the asymmetry of power and resource allocations along this chain, as well as the information asymmetry between different levels, all bureaucracies grapple with significant incentive problems. The longer the command chain, the more pronounced these problems become.

In the locally administered totalitarian system that evolved under the CCP, a high degree of political, ideological, and personnel centralization was maintained while other powers and resources were decentralized, thereby fostering competition among regions (as was the case in the liberated areas or large administrative regions). This regional competition motivated CCP bureaucrats to proactively take initiatives like land reform, civil war, and other campaigns, and to meet or exceed central government goals. In this way, the CCP regime largely mitigated the severe incentive problems typically encountered within any large-scale bureaucracy.

The full-scale Sovietization process in the 1950s replaced the tradition of federal-like totalitarianism with a top-down chain of command encompassing all specific operations. However, the capabilities of central planners are inherently limited, and incentive issues are inherently severe, making it difficult to fulfill the overarching but abstract directives of the supreme leader through centralized command orders.

With the advent of the GLF, the dismantling of the top-down command chain characteristic of the Soviet-style central plan led to the revival of local governments as competitive units. As had been the case in CCP history, the supreme leader could stimulate regional competition, expecting local leaders to devise their own solutions in response to his calls. In addition, the superiors could also disseminate more successful solutions from one region to others, creating a scenario reminiscent of regional experiments.

For the sake of simplicity, we will refer to the competition among regions to fulfill the leader's directives as "regional competition" from here on. Concurrently, the proactive efforts by these regions to find their own methods of realizing the leader's directives will be referred to as "regional experiments."

The large-scale decentralization of power and the devolution of resources laid the foundation for economic growth in the Chinese way. The competition for economic growth among provinces, cities, and counties led to an average annual growth of 39.5 percent in fixed asset investments from 1958 to 1960. The number of employees in state-owned enterprises increased by 84.9 percent and 143.5 percent in 1958–1959 and 1959–1960, respectively, and the urban population across the country rose by over 30 percent (Wu, 2010, p. 42).

However, China at that time was primarily an agricultural economy. Therefore, investment was heavily reliant on the surplus generated by agriculture, while labor input into industry was dependent on labor transferred from agriculture. As such, agricultural development was the determining factor not only for industrialization but for the entire economy. In order to secure resources for industrialization, the Soviet Union created government-controlled collective farms during the first five-year plan, enabling the government to squeeze as much funding and manpower out of the farms as possible, leading to the infamous Great Famine (see Chapter 8).

The CCP wanted to take an even more ambitious path in collectivizing agriculture than the Soviet Union. During the GLF, a new system called People's Communes was created through a process of regional experimentation and regional competition. The new system was named "Commune" after the Paris Commune, which, according to Marxist-Leninist ideology, came closer to communism than the Soviet collective farms. Indeed, as early as 1932, the Chinese Soviet Central Government annnounced in its official newspaper that "the Chinese proletariat and peasantry, having inherited the heroic spirit of both the Paris Commune and the worker struggles of the Soviet Union, ... have established the first Soviet Republic in the East. They will continue to strive to complete the Chinese revolution and fight for the realization of the Paris Commune" (Central Archives, 2016, p. 238).

Since 1954, the CCP had been promoting the collectivization of agriculture, drawing on the model of the Soviet collective farms as a means to erode the private land rights of peasants that the constitution claimed to protect. These collectives had steadily expanded in scale ever since. However, Mao was keen on transitioning to communism more rapidly than the Soviet Union. He sought to establish a grassroots system in China that was more closely aligned with communist ideals. Shortly after returning from Moscow in early 1958, Mao discussed the idea of creating communes and integrating political and communal functions in the rural areas. He had these discussions with Chen Boda, his secretary and the CCP's leading propagandist, as well as with Liu Shaoqi, the president of the PRC (Li, 1988,

p. 8). Following his directives, the Politburo officially issued a call in March of that year, encouraging local party-state entities to try out the new system.

Encouraging local governments to compete in pioneering new institutional reform experiments, such as communes, sets the CCP operations apart from those of the CPSU. This approach allows the CCP to operate more adaptively because local trials can help the party learn about local conditions and design concrete policies. Furthermore, fostering regional competition to create a model that could be replicated nationwide may, under certain conditions, better address incentive issues than relying solely on bureaucratic orders.

Shortly after the Central Committee issued its call for creating communes, the first People's Commune was established in Chayashan town, Henan Province, named Chayashan Satellite People's Commune. The commune was named "Satellite" to draw a parallel with the first human-made satellite launched by the Soviet Union just six months prior – representing institutional innovation, the other representing technological innovation. Henan Province immediately promoted this experiment on a large scale. Between April and August, more than 99 percent of rural households in the province were incorporated into more than 1,300 newly founded People's Communes.

In August, Mao visited the People's Commune near Chayashan and expressed his praise: "People's Communes are good." The following month, *Hongqi* (*Red Flag*), the leading magazine run by the Propaganda Department of CCP Central Committee, published the Preliminary Charter for the Chayashan Satellite People's Commune. This charter, revised by Mao, became the official model for People's Communes nationwide. It stipulated that private ownership was to be replaced by so-called collective ownership in the sense that all means of production belonged to the commune and would be distributed to its members following a system of wages and rations.

To speed up the establishment of the commune system nationwide, the CCP Central Committee organized 300,000 people from across the country to visit Chayashan between July and September, aiming to promote its experiment. In October, the Central Committee issued the Resolution on the Nationwide Establishment of People's Communes in the Rural Areas, encouraging local governments to compete and experiment with various methods for organizing People's Communes, including different modes of production and collective living (Xin, 2006, pp. 149–153).

By design, the CCP's commune system was intended to be distinctively different from the collective farms of the Soviet Union, which were party-controlled agricultural collectives. Unlike the Soviet collective farms, a People's Commune was intended to function as a small, comprehensive basic unit or cell within a totalitarian society. The goal was for each commune to be an economically self-sufficient grassroots unit, following a utopian communist model.

In July 1958, Chen Boda publicly unveiled Mao's comprehensive strategy for reconfiguring Chinese society, proclaiming that industry, agriculture, commerce, culture, education, and the militia "should gradually and sequentially … be consolidated into large communes, which will become the fundamental units of Chinese society." From their inception, each commune established dozens, even hundreds, of industrial enterprises, termed "commune and brigade enterprises," which laid the groundwork for the township and village enterprises of the later post-Mao reform period. Following some substantial setbacks and contentious debates, the CCP, at its 1959 Lushan Conference, officially characterized the People's Commune as an organization that was "larger and more public (yida ergong 一大二公)," meaning it had "integrated political and social functions" and facilitated a "five-in-one" integration of industry, agriculture, commerce, culture-and-education, and the militia (Li, 1988, p. 90).

The key mechanism that drove millions of party-state cadres to participate fervently in the GLF movement was interregional competition. During that period, the substance of this competition was political, centered around the implementation of Mao's party line, with the promised performance of the local economy serving as an essential part of demonstrating loyalty and implementation. Penalties for falling short in this competition were extremely severe and promotions often defied the norm. As the competition intensified, the behavior of party and government officials quickly escalated to a frenzy.

The extremely high-powered incentives ingrained in the multi-level regional competition propelled Henan to become the first province to establish a People's Commune and to universalize the People's Commune system. In early 1958, Pan Fusheng, the First Secretary of the Hunan CCP Committee, faced criticism for his hesitation about the GLF. His agricultural development plan was denounced as a "program for developing capitalism" and he was branded a right-leaning opportunist. In addition, 200,000 local cadres who followed Pan were labeled "Pan Fusheng Jr.s," creating a climate of fear in the province.

At the same time, the Central Committee lauded the provincial governor, Wu Zhipu, who actively backed and boldly boasted about the GLF, as a model for the nation. It also promoted a group of "leftists," represented by the Secretary of the Xinyang Party Committee, Lu Xianwen, to lead the GLF in Henan (Xin, 2006, pp. 143–144). The ruthless penalties against "rightist" cadres and the rapid promotion of "leftists" turned Henan Province into the GLF's vanguard. Following the CCP Central Committee's promotion and instructions, other provinces quickly began to compete with each other to replicate Henan's model.

12.2.5 The Great Famine: Regional Competition and Catastrophe

A fundamental incentive mechanism that drove the GLF was regional competition. For regional competition to provide effective incentives, it must meet two conditions. First, its competition objectives must be single-item indicators. Second, there must be proper institutional arrangements to ensure the credibility of the data of the single-item indicators used as competition objectives. Only when both of these two conditions are satisfied can effective competition between regions be organized, which rewards the winners and punishes the losers. Regarding the economy, the GLF proposed single-item guiding principles for both agriculture and industry: "The key link of agriculture is grain and the key link of industry is steel." Thus, the GLF met the first condition.

However, the GLF violated the second basic condition. It not only eliminated the market, thereby destroying a primary source of information, but it also destroyed the remaining system of checks and balances and undermined information verifications within the bureaucratic system, creating conditions conducive to fabrication and exaggeration. For pushing forward Mao's party line, while relatively honest cadres were excoriated, those who misrepresented and exaggerated their performance ascended swiftly. These distorted incentives, amplified by the powerful mechanism of regional competition, turned the GLF into a boastful race and a disaster-making machine.

Since its establishment, the newly created People's Communes, an institutional innovation, had to showcase their superior performance in terms of per-unit-area grain yields. Indeed, the Chayashan Satellite People's Commune claimed a wheat yield of 3,800 *jin* (one *jin* equals half a kilogram) per *mu* (one *mu* roughly equals one-sixth of an acre) – a figure eight to nine times the typical yield of that time (Xin, 2006, pp. 149–153). Following the model commune, in the race to establish People's Communes, regions also competed to fabricate per-unit yields. As regions vied to broadcast inflated figures in the media, yields escalated to astonishing heights. On June 16, the *China Youth Daily* published an article by the renowned scientist Qian Xuesen, providing scientific justification for the extraordinarily high yields publicized daily in the media. He argued that a slight improvement in the efficiency of photosynthesis could result in yields "more than twenty times the two thousand-plus *jin* per year!" Armed with such "scientific evidence," regions became bolder in their falsifications. The *People's Daily* reported on July 23 that the wheat yield of the Heping Agricultural Cooperative in Xiping County, Henan Province, was 7,320 *jin* per *mu*, and on September 18, it reported a mid-season rice yield of 130,434.14 *jin* per *mu* from the Huanjiang Red Flag People's Commune in Guangxi Province.

It was Stalin, who invented the principle of prioritizing heavy industry, particularly the steel industry, to speed up the economic growth of a socialist economy and to subsidize industry with agriculture. However, Mao took it to an even more extreme level. The notion of focusing on grain in agriculture aimed at extracting as many resources as possible from agriculture to develop industry. The higher the per-unit yield claimed by a local government, the more resources that could be extracted from its agricultural sector. However, with the government forcibly removing excessive quantities of grain from the countryside based on ridiculously exaggerated figures, the basic life of rural people was severely threatened. To survive, some peasants, and even grassroots CCP party-state cadres, found ways to secretly hoard food and seeds. In response to this passive resistance, the CCP launched a large-scale "anti-concealment" campaign.

Reserving basic quantities of food and seeds was a matter of life and death for peasants and thus the anti-concealment campaign directly conflicted with the fundamental interests of all peasants. The campaign was able to proceed due to the omnipresent party organization and the newly established grassroots totalitarian units – the People's Communes. Communes controlled all property rights, resources, and decision-making over all political and economic activities in the countryside, even basic family and personal activities. By forcing all peasants to dine in public canteens, communes eliminated individual family kitchens, making it difficult for them to privately store food.

Henan Province as the first to establish and popularize People's Communes was also the first to promote the anti-concealment campaign, once again serving as a model for the nation. The CCP provincial committee first put pressure on the party leaders of cities and counties within the province, requiring them to self-report the quantity of grain procured in their respective jurisdictions. This so-called grain procurement was mandatory, conflated with the levying of agricultural taxes. Since the early 1950s, the government had monopolized the purchase and sale of grain through the implementation of a policy of "unified purchase and sale" and the market had been almost completely eliminated since the GLF. The government's mass, compulsory grain procurement at officially set prices amounted to imposing a massive and irresistible tax-in-kind. At a provincial party committee meeting, the party secretary stated, "We have to work hard to do well in grain procurement ... brutally fighting against and ruthlessly attacking any ... hesitation, or concealment" (quoted in Xin, 2006, p. 180). Furthermore, regions that self-reported high procurement figures were used to pressure those that reported lower numbers, creating competition between regions and forcing them to constantly inflate their self-reported figures.

This pressure was then passed down through the hierarchy to the grassroots level. The Chayashan People's Commune held struggle meetings similar to those during the land reform to combat landlords, where they harshly criticized and even tortured some brigade cadres who protected peasants' interests, forcing them to disclose information about hidden grain. It created an atmosphere of fear, threatening all other grassroots cadres and peasants to voluntarily surrender their hidden grain. And it was announced that those who took the initiative to reveal the hidden grain could keep half of what was recovered and would be recognized as paragons of the anti-concealment campaign. Under such a strong incentive mechanism, many people confessed, resulting in numerous false reports of concealed production. Those false concealment figures were then reported through the party bureaucracy at all levels as achievements of the anti-concealment campaign, leading the central government to believe that the concealment problem was extremely serious, thus further fueling the campaign (Xin, 2006, pp. 180–183).

The policies of the GLF were more absurd than those of Stalin so that even the CPSU sharply criticized the CCP, fueling a split among the two leading communist entities. However, from a social science perspective or a standpoint of rational reasoning, how could

Mao, who came from a rural background, be so "duped" about grain yields? Why would Mao, who was well aware of incentive problems, attack honest subordinates while encouraging those who falsified their achievements? The key to addressing these issues is that as the supreme leader of the CCP, Mao's primary concern was not with the yields (whether grain or steel) or the economy per se but rather with power and his political campaigns. Those who fabricated achievements were the primary proponents of the campaign that would have been curtailed by honesty. So, even though it was known that fictitious performance would distort information, the most zealous and insincere "revolutionary trailblazers" were rewarded for promoting the campaign. This mechanism has been repeated throughout the CCP's history, including during the anti-AB campaign in the Jinggang Mountains and the Yan'an Rectification (see Chapter 10), as well as the nationwide Land Reform movement (see Chapter 11).

Mao's way of handling the famine further confirms his priority. A major crisis occurred in the first year of the GLF because of the massive exaggeration of grain production and the massive drive against the concealment of production throughout the country. In the spring of 1959, the State Council reported famines in fifteen provinces, affecting an estimated 25.17 million people (Xin, 2006, p. 185). On receiving that report, Mao wrote to Zhou demanding that the report be "dispatched by plane to the first secretaries of the provincial committees in each of the fifteen provinces, asking them to quickly address the situation to save 25.17 million people from a temporary (two-month) emergency ... The document should be titled The Major Issue of 25.17 Million People without Food in 15 Provinces" (Mao, 1993, vol. 8, p. 209).

Faced with severe economic challenges and humanitarian disasters, Mao convened an expanded meeting of the CCP Politburo, known as the Lushan Conference, in July 1959. The original intention of the meeting was to find solutions. However, when several high-ranking leaders, including then Defense Minister Peng Dehuai, who had been loyal to Mao since the Jinggang Mountain era, revealed the severity of the famine caused by the GLF, Mao perceived this as a challenge to his authority. In response, he launched the Anti-Rightist Opportunist Movement, branding all those who spoke out about the famine as anti-party factions. Rather than striving to rectify the disaster caused by the GLF, the meeting transformed adherence to its policies into a so-called party line struggle. High-level CCP leaders who sought to address the issues were purged as anti-party cliques and other leading cadres who attempted to rectify the problems were labeled as rightwing opportunists and punished (Xin, 2006, pp. 185–211; Li, 1988, pp. 29–401). Subsequently, Mao's personality cult reached new heights, driven by the efforts of new Defense Minister Lin Biao, Kang Sheng, Chen Boda, and others.

In a totalitarian system, the powers and resources of the entire society are concentrated in the hands of a very few top leaders, who are obligated to submit to the supreme leader. This power structure dictates that power struggles at the top are not only vicious but also frequent. Even slight differences in strategy or technical issues often evolve into power struggles. The brutal struggles lead to the ruthless suppression of genuine information, making the system not only prone to errors but also difficult to correct when errors occur, leading to disasters. The Anti-Rightist purge during and after the Lushan Conference magnified the chaos caused by the GLF and the People's Communes, leading to an unprecedented famine that claimed the lives of approximately 40 million people over three years.[7]

Located in the Xinyang region of Henan Province, the trailblazing People's Commune at Chayashan was one of the worst affected regions in China. According to the recollections of the Deputy Secretary of the CCP Committee in Suiping County, a founder of the Commune,

> From the winter of 1959 to the spring of 1960 alone, over a million people starved to death in the Xinyang region ... In the birthplace

of the People's Commune – the Chayashan People's Commune of 40,000 residents, nearly 4,000 starved to death in three months, accounting for 10 percent of the total population, with some brigades reaching as high as 30 percent ... Over 2 million people died from starvation in Henan Province (more accurately, 2.93 million). (Quoted from Xin, 2006, p. 217)

The famine caused by the GLF brought China's economy to the brink of collapse. In 1961, the 9th Plenary Session of the CCP's 8th Congress was forced to supplement the GLF policy with a new strategy of "adjustment, consolidation, enrichment, and improvement." This new policy aimed to consolidate the achievements of the GLF, the essence of which was the RADT institution, including the People's Communes.

Nonetheless, rescuing the Chinese economy from the great famine was an inescapable issue. To address this challenge, in 1962 the CCP convened an unprecedentedly large conference. Known historically as the 7,000 Cadres Conference, this expanded Central Committee meeting included all leading cadres at the county level and above throughout the country. At the meeting, Mao acknowledged that problems had arisen during the implementation of the GLF and announced that he would step back from daily government and party work to focus solely on strategic issues. The daily tasks would be presided over by state Chairman Liu Shaoqi and Party General Secretary Deng Xiaoping.

Interestingly, during the CR, Liu, Deng, and almost all of the 7,000 CCP cadres who attended this meeting were purged. Many scholars have identified this meeting as a key event that played a significant role in igniting the CR. This interpretation certainly has merit but a more fundamental factor underlying these events lies in the nature of the communist totalitarian institution. First, Mao himself, his power, and the power structure of the system were products of this institution. Second, the motivation for the CR went beyond power struggles; it was directly related to consolidating and improving the newly created RADT institution. Moreover, the CR was both launched and carried out based on the existing RADT system, albeit a preliminary version.

12.3 THE CULTURAL REVOLUTION: CONSOLIDATING RADT

Following four years of recuperation after the GLF, Mao initiated the "unprecedented Proletarian Cultural Revolution" (referred to as the "Cultural Revolution" or the "Great Proletarian Cultural Revolution"). The CR entrenched the RADT institutional genes, which is the institutional foundation of the post-Mao reform and have thus dictated the trajectory of China's development in the present. Its evolution would influence China's future and thus the world at large.

The CR was a nationwide mass movement instigated by the supreme leader and enthusiastically participated in by party cadres, party members, and the general masses across the country. The movement commenced with the objective of dismantling the party-state system, only to then rebuild it. In this regard, the CR was a unique political movement in the history of civilization. The catastrophe provoked by the CR turned many CCP cadres and ordinary citizens into dissenters, inciting them to seek change. However, at the same time, the totalitarian system and ideology, reinforced by the CR, also made many individuals more dedicated to communist totalitarianism. China's reform and opening-up began at the end of the CR and perpetuated RADT and, paradoxically, for a time, inspired hopes for a fundamental change in the communist totalitarian system.

Although the CR began in the context of anti-Soviet revisionism, the ideology that predominated during the CR was largely derived from Soviet Russia and the French Revolution. In fact, the world's first movement known as a "Cultural Revolution" was an ideological movement initiated by Lenin and Trotsky in the early 1920s in the Soviet Union. However, China's CR extended beyond the realm of ideology. Following the GLF, the CR further dismantled the Soviet-style system by consolidating and refining the RADT system in all respects, making it a crucial part of China's institutional genes.

The RADT system newly established by the GLF, although primitive, became the institutional foundation for the CR. By weakening all the central authorities of the party-state except the supreme leader and delegating greater administrative and economic autonomy to local party-state agencies, the RADT system allowed the supreme leader to better control political, personnel, and other strategic matters, enabling him to focus more on capturing and holding power. It also paved the road for furthering the personality cult of the supreme leader. Moreover, under the RADT regime, the bulk of the Chinese economy primarily consisted of numerous self-contained local economies. This ensured that the country and its economy did not collapse on the magnitude of the GLF during the CR when all central planning agencies were paralyzed and markets were banned.

Unlike all other campaigns by the CCP, which were measures to consolidate the party-state apparatus, the CR was a "revolution" aimed at dismantling the party-state bureaucracy, at least in its initial stage. Moreover, it was led by the Cultural Revolution Group (CRG), personally created by Mao, rather than the formal CCP apparatus, the Politburo, or the Central Committee.

To encourage the Red Guards and the Revolutionary Rebels to demolish the party-state machine, the most frequently cited Mao quote propagated by the CRG was, "Revolution is an insurrection, a violent action by one class to overthrow another." With the participation of fervent masses, the CRG initiated a wildly violent campaign that purged and eliminated those alleged to be disloyal to the leader, simultaneously elevating the cult of personality to an unparalleled level. Mao was proclaimed the "Great Savior" and the "Red Sun." The party's ideology degenerated into loyalty to Mao, his guidelines, and the dogma explaining those guidelines.

Mass violence, stemming from frenzied personal idolization, systematically dismantled the party-state bureaucracies, eroded the authority of central departments, and significantly bolstered Mao's personal power. This established a precedent for an unprecedented large-scale decentralization of administrative and economic authority, leading to its institutionalization. The extreme devolution of administrative power, conversely, further reinforced the political power of the supreme leader to the other extreme.

The RADT system established through the GLF and the CR was formally recognized in the amended constitution of the CCP adopted at the party's 10th Congress in 1973 and the amended constitution of the PRC adopted in 1975. In this system, political, ideological, and personnel powers are highly concentrated in the hands of the top leader, while most of the administrative power and economic resources are delegated to subnational levels. Such a governance structure ensures that no individual or organization within the central party-state machinery possesses the power and resources to enable any check on the top leader.

This has undermined the central institutions to the point where they retain little practical operational function. The leader can command society by issuing ideas and slogans that bypass the need for technical detailing by central agencies and are instead directly interpreted and executed by local grassroots.

In 1975, when the new constitution was passed, only 12 percent of national fiscal revenue was derived from the central-controlled enterprises. Furthermore, the self-sufficient local party-state institutions were all under the control of "revolutionaries" who professed "infinite loyalty to the leader."

12.3.1 Regional Competition and Regional Experimentation under a Fanatic Personality Cult

From an institutional evolutionary perspective, the GLF and the CR represent two successive phases in transforming China's totalitarian regime from a classic one into RADT. Both movements relied on the entire population's fanatical participation, which ended in catastrope for the population. The question to be addressed is, what kind of force drove an entire population to engage in actions leading to their own detriment? What were their motivations? This question is particularly acute regarding the CR, as it was more predominantly a top-down "revolution" provoked by the cult of personality, with the masses everywhere engaged in smashing the "old" system. New power structures and institutions were then created through regional experimentation and propagated by regional competition.

To address this issue, it is crucial to first examine a peculiar phenomenon: the elevation of Mao's personality cult to new heights after the devastation caused by the GLF. This phenomenon is itself a byproduct of totalitarianism. Within such a system, the supreme leader, by controlling the party, dominates all aspects of power and resources in society, deciding the fate, including life and death, of everyone, including those at the top. Therefore, seizing control of the party and becoming the supreme leader is a life-or-death struggle.

In a totalitarian regime, the more disasters a leader incurs, the more the leader needs to guard his power by all means and with all his strength. Additionally, a disaster presents an ideal opportunity for political opportunists to ardently support the leader by promoting a cult of personality and attacking any political rivals. This dynamic results in a paradoxical situation where the leader's power and cult of personality can grow even amidst widespread societal upheaval and disaster.

Indeed, following the GLF, all the top leaders, notably Liu Shaoqi, Lin Biao, Zhou Enlai, Kang Sheng, and Chen Boda, collectively elevated the cult of Mao's personality to unprecedented heights. Alongside endorsing Mao's initiatives, they vigorously promoted class struggle and proletarian dictatorship, while opposing what they termed "Soviet revisionism." Their focus at that time revolved around "preventing the emergence of revisionism and peaceful evolution," "cultivating successors to the cause of communism," and "vigorously implementing the class line." The leaders aimed to maintain the revolutionary fervor and communist ideology in the wake of the societal disruptions caused by the GLF.

As a specific measure, in 1963, Mao proposed launching the Four Cleanups campaign, aiming to clean up politics, the economy, organizations, and ideology everywhere in order to "prevent the emergence of revisionism and peaceful evolution." In retrospect, this campaign was a precursor to the CR.

Liu Shaoqi and his wife Wang Guangmei took the initiative to promote and implement this by introducing the concept of dispatching work groups to the People's Communes and enterprises to engage in class struggle. The work groups, composed of members dispatched from party-state organs and universities, focused on targeting so-called class enemies and searching for evidence of their sabotage. Consequently, any sabotage discovered was deemed to be the root cause of the disasters and troubles that occurred in the People's Communes.

The methodology that Liu and Wang invented in this campaign was popularized throughout the party with Mao's strong support. This modus operandi carried over into the CR. In the early stages of the CR, when Liu was responsible for leadership, he again dispatched work groups to universities and high schools to incite class struggle and suppress "reactionary" teachers and students.

Meanwhile, Defense Minister Lin Biao transformed the People's Liberation Army into a propaganda machine that amplified the cult of personality in innovative ways. Lin touted Mao Zedong Thought as the pinnacle of contemporary Marxism-Leninism and widely distributed *The Little Red Book* (officially titled *Quotations from Chairman Mao*), initially within the military and later to the general population. Subsequently, Mao and the CCP urged the entire nation to emulate the PLA, the core of which was to promote Mao's personality cult just as the PLA had done.

Years of indoctrination escalated the ideologies of class struggle and anti-revisionism to unprecedented levels within the party, the military, and the populace. Loyalty to the leader was heightened to a state of religious zealotry, resulting in harsh punishment for anyone deemed insufficiently loyal. This pervasive fanaticism laid the social groundwork for the initiation of the CR.

12.3.2 *The Privileged Class and the Red Guard Movement*

The initial aim of the CR was to dismantle the system imported from the Soviet Union, that is to say, the CCP's own party-state bureaucracy. For "smashing the old world," it was essential to establish pioneering organizations to spearhead the CR and to mobilize the masses. The Red Guards, a product of the totalitarian system, fulfilled this role. The Red Guards' worship of their leader, use of violence, and much of their attire bore a striking resemblance to the Nazi Stormtroopers.

The emergence of the Red Guards was primarily underpinned by the privileged class within the totalitarian system, the party's system for cultivating successors to the communist cause, and the class line doctrine. Despite the CCP's official assertion that the "succession issue" was a key lesson learned from the CPSU aimed at preventing the emergence of revisionism in China, in reality, it fundamentally revolved around the distribution of power among generations of elites. This issue bore close ties to the institutional genes inherited from China's imperial system.

In the imperial tradition, descendants of meritorious generals who played pivotal roles in the change of dynasty could inherit a portion of their ancestors' privileges. This was not only an incentive to encourage generals to topple the old and to contribute to the new dynasty but it also formed an integral part of the power structure of the new dynasty.

Most senior members of the CCP viewed the establishment of a "revolutionary regime" as similar to the founding of a new dynasty, with the new titles being purely nominal. To them, "Marxism-Leninism" was seen as comparable to the names given to the rebellions that led to a change in dynasty, such as the Society of

God Worshippers or the White Lotus. Additionally, the strict organizational discipline of a totalitarian party strongly echoes the secret societies (see Chapter 10), in which hierarchy and privilege were the norm.

A majority of senior CCP officials, especially those with military backgrounds, inherently subscribed to the principle of inherited privilege, encapsulated in the saying, "the father conquers, the son rules." After Mao raised the issue of succession, many senior CCP officials passed on this concept of traditionally inherited privilege to their children, albeit cloaked in the language of Marxism-Leninism. In fact, when the CCP criticized the CPSU for neglecting the issue of succession in the 1960s, it was underscoring the differences in the institutional genes between China and Russia.

As the CCP's criticism of the CPSU reached its peak in 1964, Mao formally introduced the issue of cultivating successors at a Central Committee Work Conference as a preventive measure against the emergence of revisionism in China. Subsequently, the party's Organization Department, in tandem with other agencies, arranged for the systematic cultivation of successors for leadership positions across all party-state institutions (Xu, 2014). The Organization Department functioned in a manner similar to the bureaucratic nomination system in Imperial China.

Beyond formal bureaucratic arrangements, Mao was more invested in the power consciousness and class consciousness among the offspring of senior cadres, as they were the ones poised to inherit the party's core powers. Moreover, Mao held the belief that real power was secured through struggle, not bureaucratic appointments.

In 1964, Mao, through a conversation with his niece Wang Hairong, conveyed a message urging the offspring of senior cadres to rebel. He said, "We are very concerned about our cadres' children … what's there to fear, … go back and take the lead in rebellion … the student you mentioned may accomplish more than you [as] he dares to defy the school's system."[8] Mao further advised his nephew, Mao

Yuanxin, to study the "five conditions for a successor," the first of them being Marxism-Leninism, and said,

> The basic idea of Marxism–Leninism is to revolutionize ... The revolutionary task is not completed, and it is not certain who will win.... We still have the bourgeoisie in power.... Studying Marxism–Leninism is to study class struggle, which is everywhere, even in your college ... Class struggle is your main course ... everyone, from cadres to students, in your college, should go to the countryside for the Four Cleanups.[9]

With Mao's guidance or tacit consent, the transcripts of these conversations were secretly circulated among the offspring of senior cadres on the eve of the CR and became one of the important factors in stimulating the offspring to become vanguards and lead the destruction of the offspring CCP order.

Another pivotal message that stirred the power consciousness of the offspring of senior cadres in the early stages of the CR was delivered by Lin Biao at an enlarged Politburo meeting on May 18, 1966. He clarified that the central issue of the CR was political power. He stated that, "With political power, ... you have everything. Without it, you lose everything.... We must always be mindful of political power.... [political power] is a tool for one class to oppress another.... political power is the power to suppress." He also declared that, "Every word of Chairman Mao's is the truth; one sentence of his surpasses ten thousand of ours ... His words are the guidelines for our actions. Whoever opposes him will be condemned by the entire party and the entire country."[10]

In that revolutionary era, dominated by Mao Zedong Thought, this speech was a confidential document reserved only for the upper echelons. The Red Guards, mainly composed of the offspring of senior cadres, were the sole group privileged enough to access this unvarnished theory of power. They understood that the party's revolution was fundamentally about the pursuit of political power. This revelation led the Red Guards to intertwine their fanatic personal worship of Mao with their pursuit of power and suppression of class enemies. Consequently, they persecuted students, teachers, and anyone deemed to have reactionary class origins, both on and off campuses, all under the guise of revolution and for the ultimate objective of seizing power.

The CR was initiated as a mass movement, prompting students to dismantle the party-state apparatus within the school system and target official propaganda agencies perceived to oppose Mao's ideology. Eventually, the wider masses were galvanized to destabilize the basic order of society. Therefore, instigating this mass movement was a key step. The earliest precursors of the CR were the self-organized Red Guard groups, formed spontaneously and covertly by the offspring of senior cadres from Tsinghua High School, Peking University High School, and other elite high schools in Beijing.[11] Much like the inception of the People's Communes, the Red Guard groups were created by the masses in response to the call of the supreme leader. With a pledge to defend Chairman Mao with their lives through rebellion, the Red Guards declared, "Whoever opposes Chairman Mao shall be brought down."

However, no totalitarian system permits the existence of organizations independent of the totalitarian party. This is particularly true for the Red Guards, who openly advocated rebellion against the party-state apparatus. Drawing their experiences from the Anti-Rightist and Four Cleanups campaigns, the CR work groups sent to the schools by Liu Shaoqi and Deng Xiaoping identified the Red Guards as rightist-style counterrevolutionary organizations and suppressed them accordingly. In contrast to Liu and Deng, Mao staunchly supported the Red Guards and welcomed millions of them in a series of rallies on Tiananmen Square. This led to a nationwide rush to establish Red Guard organizations in schools, effectively paralyzing the country's education system.

When the top leaders were divided, the personality cult not only determined whom the masses would follow but also enabled the supreme leader to leverage the cult to achieve his ambitions. As the personality cult reached a feverish climax, Mao, along with figures like Kang Sheng and Jiang Qing, incited the Red Guards to "take up arms (yao wu)" and employ "violent action" against the reactionary classes. Such incitement transformed many Red Guards into vicious thugs who acted with extreme brutality.

The fanatic brutality of the Red Guards in their quest to eliminate class enemies had its roots in decades of communist education. This education criticized humanism as a bourgeois ideology and instilled in people the belief that individuals are defined solely by their class. It held that class enemies were not to be considered human and that revolution was about eradicating the enemy through violence. In schools, students and teachers from bourgeois and reactionary families were labeled class enemies. The Red Guards from various schools in Beijing competed in their violence against these perceived enemies and the levels of violence and terror escalated dramatically. During the "Red August" of 1966, the Beijing Red Guards ushered in a period of "Red Terror" under the slogan "Long live the Red Terror." From August 25 to September 2 alone, the Red Guards killed 1,550 people in Beijing (Y. Wang, 2004, p. 740). The first victims were high school principals, teachers, and students. From then on, the CR became a nationwide movement of violence and terror. Importantly for China and the world today, many of the most prominent political figures in twenty-first-century China were once Red Guards.

While the Red Guard movement was disrupting order in schools and society, Mao, at the 11th Plenary Session of the 8th CCP Central Committee in August 1966, accused Liu Shaoqi and Deng Xiaoping of following a reactionary bourgeois line during their leadership of the CR. As a result, all bureaucrats under the leadership of Liu and Deng were labeled "capitalist roaders" and leaders of party-state organizations at all levels generally became the targets of the revolution. As the Red Guards were predominantly made up of senior cadres' offspring, they were deemed "conservatives" and opposed to the CR when their parents became targets. Some core members of the Red Guards were suppressed and even imprisoned for opposing the CR. However, this did not shake their conviction and determination to hold party-state power. They saw themselves as "masters of the Tianxia (world, empire, or nation)," having been groomed for power since childhood. A quote from a Beijing Red Guard in early 1967 illustrates this sentiment: "Don't be so arrogant, you son of a bitch, ... In 20 years, the Tianxia will belong to us, the offspring of cadres, so you stand aside!" The "son of a bitch" being cursed at here refers to fellow students from intellectual or bourgeois families. The once popular Red Guard couplet, "a hero's son is a legend; a reactionary's son is a bastard," expressed the same belief that social status is determined by birth (Yang, 2016, chapter 7).

It is worth noting that the journeys of the majority of the most important political figures in China today began with or are intimately related to what is discussed above. Shortly after the end of the CR, in the early 1980s at the dawn of the reform era, the party's Central Organization Department established a special agency to systematically select and cultivate the offspring of senior cadres. CCP elders, including Chen Yun, Bo Yibo, and Wang Zhen, directly involved themselves in nurturing these individuals (Yan, 2017). Many of those chosen later became leading figures in the party-state apparatus, including Xi Jinping, Wang Qishan, Li Yuanchao, and Bo Xilai, while many others ascended to roles as ministers and generals.

Guided by their consciousness of power and the philosophy of class struggle, the Red Guards not only indiscriminately degraded the "enemy" or "inferior" classes but also carried out a Red Terror, which they believed to be an essential part of power and class struggles. Their persecution of large numbers of students, teachers, and citizens provoked widespread and intense resistance.

Tragically, almost all of those resisting had also been brainwashed under the totalitarian regime and were also worshippers of Mao. In addition to resisting the persecution by the Red Guards, some radical resistors also opposed the work groups sent by Liu

Shaoqi, the class line, and the party-state bureaucracy. These rebels formed the so-called Revolutionary Rebel Faction (or Rebel Faction for short).

Some rebels saw the CR as a class struggle between ordinary people and the privileged class, consisting of high-ranking officials and their offspring. Faced with the CCP's class line and systematic persecution inflicted by the Red Guards, a few intellectuals began to fundamentally question the class line and the socialist system that had given rise to a bureaucratic or privileged class. By "bureaucratic or privileged class," they meant the party-state bureaucrats (also known as "capitalist roaders") and their offspring, who believed they were born to rule. However, such discussions were absolutely intolerable to the totalitarian system and were swiftly and brutally suppressed.[12]

One of the most notable rebel groups was led by Kuai Dafu, a student at Tsinghua University at the time. The members of this group were labeled as counterrevolutionaries by Liu Shaoqi's wife, Wang Guangmei. In an effort to leverage rebel groups like this one against Liu Shaoqi, during the 11th Plenary Session of the 8th Central Committee, Zhou Enlai and the CRG led over 100 Central Committee members to Tsinghua University to redress the injustices suffered by the Rebel Faction at Tsinghua on behalf of Mao and the Central Committee. The evidence Zhou presented at the 11th Plenary Session of Liu's persecution of the rebels was crucial in bringing down Liu, as it proved that Liu's party line had suppressed the masses. From then on, the rebel faction thrived nationwide, becoming the main force in overthrowing the "capitalist roaders" and dismantling the party-state system.

12.3.3 Seizing Power and Catastrophe

Guided and supported by Mao, Zhou Enlai, and the CRG, the Rebel Factions effectively incapacitated nearly all leaders of central party-state agencies, including those within the judicial and security systems, branding them as capitalist roaders. This caused paralysis in the leadership and operations across all levels and sectors of the party-state bureaucracy, resulting in what Mao referred to as "complete chaos," a state he delightfully described as "excellent." Amid this chaos, spurring the rebels to seize power from the capitalist roaders emerged as a major turning point in the CR.

It was only at this juncture that the Rebel Factions fully grasped the core premise of Lin Biao's 1966 speech, affirming that the essence of the CR lay in seizing power. However, in this power-seizing movement, factions that publicly declared their infinite loyalty to Mao were immersed in brutal power struggles, driven primarily by the pursuit and preservation of their own interests. As various military districts and commands of the PLA, along with the local militias usually controlled by them, began siding with different factions in the fight for local dominance, the country descended into a state of unmanageable chaos. Many regions plunged into localized civil wars and amidst this pandemonium, Mao began to lose his grip on the situation.

At a theoretical level, the CCP made it abundantly clear that the seizure of power was the primary objective of the CR. This was explicitly stated in the key historical documents that initiated the CR, such as the "May 16 Notification" and the "Sixteen Articles," which highlighted the purpose of the CR was to wrest power from the hands of the so-called capitalist roaders. However, the practical implications of this objective, and how it would be implemented, remained nebulous. Similar to the establishment and promotion of People's Communes and the Red Guard movement, the practical mechanics of seizing power were not crafted by Mao or the CRG but emerged from a process of experimental adaptation and nationwide emulation spurred by regional competition.

On January 8, 1967, a workers' Rebel Faction in Shanghai, led by Wang Hongwen, with Mao's and the CRG's support, seized control from the CCP Shanghai Municipal Committee and Shanghai Municipal Government, placing the municipality under the jurisdiction of the Shanghai Revolutionary Committee. Once the *People's*

12.3 THE CULTURAL REVOLUTION: CONSOLIDATING RADT 583

Daily and *Red Flag* magazine published reports of Mao's backing of the Shanghai rebels' seizure of municipal power, Rebel Factions across the country initiated their own power-seizing movements and raced to assume control over party-state institutions at every level. Within a month, the provinces of Shanxi, Guizhou, Heilongjiang, and Shandong sequentially fell to the Revolutionary Committees established by these Rebel Factions. Across the country, party-state agencies, enterprises, and People's Communes all became targets of power seizures.

While launching a mass movement and creating chaos was relatively straightforward, leveraging the same mass movement to re-establish order and end the power-seizing movement proved to be a significantly tougher task. The widespread power seizures affected everyone's interests and the various Rebel Factions, all claiming loyalty to Mao, represented a diverse array of interests. When it came to seizing power, these interests inevitably clashed, sometimes quite violently. Groups competing for control would often strategically label their adversaries as conservatives or as disloyal. Ultimately, only those rebels who managed to secure the joint backing of the CRG and the PLA could successfully seize power. However, members of the CRG and the PLA generals did not always see eye to eye. Adding to the complexity, many party-state bureaucrats criticized as "capitalist roaders" remained active, seeking support from Mao, the CRG, Zhou Enlai, and the military to help them retain power. The factions rallying to protect these individuals also declared themselves loyal to Mao.

The chaos escalated further when Rebel Factions emerged within the Foreign Ministry and even within the headquarters, commands, and military districts of the PLA, asserting their authority over diplomatic and military affairs. This development directly threatened Mao's strategy of relying on the PLA to maintain stability.

The power-seizing movement across the country deteriorated into violent, armed conflicts. With military backing, some cities experienced civil wars involving thousands, even tens of thousands, of militiamen, some of whom were equipped with heavy weaponry. The official term for these local civil wars was *Wudou* (Violent Struggle). Official statistics suggest that the *Wudou* resulted in over 230,000 deaths and injured more than 7 million people nationwide (Yang, 2013). Based on incomplete official local publications, Walder (2019) documents monthly death counts at the provincial and national levels during this period, providing valuable detailed information.

As the power-seizing campaign spiraled out of control, the CRG and Lin Biao sent in "PLA Mao Zedong Thought Propaganda Teams" (Military Propaganda Teams) to all party-state institutions, schools, and universities. Eventually, through military intervention, the Rebel Factions that were backed by the CRG and Lin Biao took control, and established Revolutionary Committees across the nation. Subsequently, they surrendered their power to the reestablished CCP committees, dissolving their "rebel" organizations that had served as their power base during the power-seizing phase.

Simultaneously, while reestablishing control over the country, the CCP launched nationwide campaigns with the intent to disband all non-compliant organizations by purging any individuals who disobeyed, were seen as suspicious, or were dissidents. The roles and fates of the Red Guards and the Rebels during the CR bore striking similarities to those of the secret societies during the early days of the CCP (as discussed in Chapter 10). The most extensive of these campaigns was the so-called "One-Strike, Three-Antis." These campaigns, in their nature and function, also resembled the Suppression of Counterrevolutionaries campaign, which had been initiated shortly after the founding of the People's Republic of China (PRC) in 1950 (as explored in Chapter 11).

According to official records, these campaigns unearthed over 1.84 million counterrevolutionaries, with more than 280,000 arrested (Wang, 1988, p. 337). Independent studies estimate that the number of people who died of persecution during the "One-Strike,

Three-Antis" campaign alone was in the tens or hundreds of thousands (Ding, 2014).

12.4 THE DEEP-ROOTED RADT SYSTEM AND THE SHATTERING OF IDEALS

By supplanting most central bureaucratic functions with local party-state bureaucratic mechanisms, the CCP transformed China's institutional framework from classic communist totalitarianism into a regionally administered totalitarianism. This transformation was achieved by demolishing the central bureaucracy through the GLF and the CR, particularly the latter. At the peak of the CR's power-seizing campaign, all central ministries, with the exception of the Ministry of Defense, were incapacitated. Several ministries, including those responsible for metallurgy, coal, machinery, and commerce, were officially disbanded. The management of nearly all centrally controlled enterprises was transferred to subnational levels, thereby elevating the power of local party-state authorities to an unprecedented degree.

The total number of state-owned enterprises directly under the central government fell from 10,533 in 1965 to 142 in 1970, that is, more than 98 percent of the nation's central SOEs were transferred to local governments (Qian and Xu, 1993). Taking the proportion of local revenue to total national revenue as a measure of decentralization, it is noted that it was less than 20 percent in 1958 when the Soviet-style system peaked and it reached nearly 79 percent in 1961 when decentralization under the GLF was at its height. At the end of the readjustment policy led by Liu and Deng in 1966, that proportion had dropped to nearly 65 percent. However, by 1975, after the RADT system was consolidated and strengthened during the CR, it rose to over 88 percent (Xu, 2011).

The complete paralysis of the central ministries resulted in the CR descending into chaos far greater than that witnessed during the GLF. Despite the total breakdown of the central ministries, the CR did not lead to an economic disaster on the scale of the GLF, which allowed the CR to endure for a decade. This can be attributed to the fact that by the onset of the CR, the RADT system had already been put in place and most regions had formed their own self-contained economies. Therefore, the functions of the central machinery were no longer as crucial as they once were. This observation can also be interpreted as evidence of the impossibility of instantaneously transforming China's classic totalitarian institution to a RADT system, even when Mao did not care about the human cost of such a change, as he showed in the GLF and the CR.

Mao's utopian idea of turning communes into self-contained economic units was proven impractical by the disaster of the GLF. Yet, he never abandoned his vision. In the CR, the second phase of the push towards a RADT system, the focus shifted from communes to counties. The goal was to achieve self-sufficiency through the establishment of the so-called "Five Small Industries" – which referred to small-scale enterprises in coal mining, steel, cement, machinery, and fertilizer. This strategic move greatly fortified the institutional genes of the RADT system and its far-reaching impact can still be observed today.

This policy, initiated in 1970, not only spurred the establishment of state-owned small and medium-sized enterprises at the provincial, municipal, and county levels but also promoted substantial development of Commune-Brigade Enterprises (CBEs) within the People's Communes, pushing local economies towards self-sufficiency. By the end of the CR, the national economy had essentially morphed into a network of numerous self-sufficient local economies. Most cities and hundreds of counties had established industrial systems spanning all sectors, including energy, metals, building materials, construction, machinery, and chemicals, thereby becoming largely self-reliant subnational regions. This specific economic structure later formed a critical component of the institutional foundation for China's economic reforms. In particular, the Township-Village Enterprises (TVEs), which played a pivotal role in the reform, were the direct descendants of the CBEs.

However, the underlying purpose of devolution was ultimately to centralize power further, enabling the supreme leader to concentrate on the most pivotal aspects of governance. The purge of Liu Shaoqi, Deng Xiaoping, and the party-state bureaucrats loyal to them, together with the significant weakening of the central bureaucracy, led to even greater centralization of power in politics, personnel, and ideology in the hands of the central organs directly under the supreme leader's control. Furthermore, by completely eliminating the meager checks and balances within the party, the cult of personality surrounding the supreme leader was greatly magnified and the leader's direct control over the army, police, and ideological apparatus was further solidified.

For the same reason, the significant autonomy granted to local authorities in administration and resource allocations was not only conditional upon a high degree of political control by the center but was in itself an element supporting the centralization of political power.

Regarding operations, the system adopted a two-pronged approach. On the one hand, in terms of economic operations, administration, and resource allocations, it largely depended on the local authorities taking initiatives. On the other hand, loyalty to the Leader and maintaining a high degree of alignment with the central authorities was a prerequisite for becoming local party-state cadres.

The central authorities tightly controlled personnel and ideological matters, sternly penalizing cadres who demonstrated disloyalty or failed to align with the center and rewarding the loyal ones. In the post-Mao reform, this RADT system of grasping ultimate control (political and personnel powers), while delegating executive authority (administrative and operational powers), proved to be more flexible and adaptive than classic totalitarian regimes in terms of operations and incentive provision.

A personality cult surrounding the supreme leader is an essential element of a totalitarian regime. However, the sustainability of such a personality cult, as well as the communist totalitarian ideology itself, is often questionable. Mao sought to harness the power of his personality cult to ignite "great chaos" and "shatter the old world," subsequently employing the same force to achieve "ultimate rule of the land." But in the end, the uncontrollable chaos and even the civil wars that ensued forced Mao to restore order through military rule.

At the 9th Congress of the CCP in 1969, when the grand achievements of the CR were celebrated, the true winner of the CR was the PLA led by Lin Biao. Military officers constituted 52.4 percent of the Politburo members and 49 percent of the full and alternate members of the Central Committee. The vast majority of subnational agencies and central ministries were directly or indirectly under the control of PLA officers. The key point is that the CR had purged most of Lin Biao's rivals in the military as well as many senior generals who had never been subordinate to him.

Thus, Mao grew alarmed at the military's expansive control over most party-state institutions. After the 9th Congress, Mao vehemently criticized Lin and his followers, using their dissenting views about re-establishing the state chairmanship as a pretext. The conflict between Mao and Lin rapidly intensified. In a shocking turn of events, Lin was killed on September 13, 1971, in a mysterious plane crash in Mongolia while allegedly trying to flee to the Soviet Union.

The "Lin Biao Incident" marked a pivotal point in the history of the PRC, as it was the first significant blow to Mao's personality cult, paving the way for the post-Mao reforms. Operating under the pretense of cleansing the party of Lin Biao's anti-party group, the CCP arrested and purged numerous high-ranking military officials, including the Chief of the General Staff and the Commanders of the Air Force and Navy. This was followed by a nationwide campaign known as "Criticizing Lin and Confucius," which bizarrely labeled Lin as a Confucianist. This campaign served a dual purpose: not only did it help to obscure Lin's substantial role in shaping Mao's personality cult but it also prominently enforced a draconian, Legalistic principle of severe punishment and harsh laws (as discussed in Chapter 5).

Within the party, it was well known that Lin had assisted Mao in purging many of his adversaries within the party and the army,

12.4 DEEP-ROOTED RADT AND THE SHATTERING OF IDEALS 589

a pattern that started during the Jinggang Mountains era and continued through the recent purges of Peng Dehuai, Liu Shaoqi, and Deng Xiaoping. Since taking charge of the day-to-day operations of the Military Commission in 1959, Lin had politically reshaped the army in line with Mao's directives, turning the PLA into a machine for promoting Mao's personality cult. This set the stage for the CR.

Lin's critical role in the creation of Mao's personality cult and in driving the CR elevated him to the top echelons of the party leadership, second only to Mao. At the 9th Congress of the CCP, he was formally designated as Mao's successor. However, Lin's abrupt downfall and the subsequent campaign to criticize Lin and Confucius shattered any semblance of coherence in the continuous political persecution since the onset of the CR. Doubts began to emerge about the legitimacy of the CR and Mao's judgment. If Lin was indeed opposed to Mao and the party, why had Mao, who was always regarded as wise and infallible, selected Lin as his successor in the first place?

After purging most of the party cadres in the early phase of the CR and another substantial group following the Lin Biao Incident, Mao found himself in a precarious situation on all fronts. Seizing the moment, Deng Xiaoping re-pledged his loyalty to Mao, earning himself a return to the political scene. Along with Zhou Enlai, Deng championed the Four Modernizations, emphasizing economic recovery, which garnered widespread support from the CCP and the general public. However, Mao perceived this as an attempt to undermine the CR.

Following Zhou Enlai's funeral, Deng was quickly expelled again and a campaign to criticize him was initiated. After the Lin Biao Incident had already caused people to question their faith, the criticism of Deng led to an even deeper skepticism towards the CR, particularly among ousted CCP officials and persecuted intellectuals. Despite Zhou Enlai being a key player in both the development of the personality cult and the CR, his efforts to protect – at least apparently – cadres loyal to Mao during the CR and to promote the Four Modernizations painted him and Deng as heroes resisting the CR and standard-bearers of dissenting views.

The relentless and widespread persecution, further complicated by the arbitrary criticism of Lin and Deng, gave rise to many dissidents, ranging from the upper ranks of the CCP to ordinary citizens. These individuals opposed the CR and the ceaseless class struggle and advocated for a return to order and economic recovery, thereby laying the groundwork for the end of the CR. However, under the oppressive suppression of the totalitarian regime, no one dared show any disrespect towards Mao. Instead, these dissidents focused their anger on Mao's closest associates, such as Madame Mao, Jiang Qing, and her followers, dubbing them the Gang of Four.

This resentment culminated in action. For the first time since the CCP took power, spontaneous mass political protests erupted on April 5, 1976. In what was framed as mourning for Zhou, hundreds of thousands of people spontaneously protested against the Gang of Four and the CR in Tiananmen Square. Similar events unfolded in Shanghai and other cities around the same time.

Despite the violent suppression of all protests, opposition to the Gang of Four and the CR spread ever wider. Against this backdrop, just four weeks after Mao's death, a coup d'état was staged by the upper echelons of the CCP, leading to the arrest of all members of the so-called Gang of Four. The catastrophic CR finally came to an end amid nationwide celebrations.

In the early years following Mao's death, the CCP publicly condemned the CR and acknowledged the tragedy it had wrought in an effort to regain its legitimacy. According to statistics provided by the CCP Central Committee, the CR resulted in the deaths of more than 1 million people and left over 10 million injured or disabled.[13] Of the 800 million people in the country, more than 113 million were purged.[14] Every intellectual or cadre family had at least one victim of persecution. On average, one in every seven people was persecuted during the CR. This was more brutal than the Great Purges of the Stalinist era.[15] However, much like the post-Stalin CPSU, the CCP had no intention of relinquishing its totalitarian rule. Instead, the enduring, intergenerational terror engendered

12.4 DEEP-ROOTED RADT AND THE SHATTERING OF IDEALS

by the CR became a part of the institutional genes that proved beneficial to its governance.

In this chapter, we have dedicated a considerable portion to Mao, as both the GLF and the CR bore his strong personal imprint. However, the essence of the transformation to RADT transcended the individual characteristics of the Leader and was instead a result of the combined efforts of both the Leader and the masses to fortify totalitarianism with Chinese characteristics. The Leader is an essential component of a totalitarian system, encapsulating both ideology and a cult of personality. The Leader propagates ideology, while followers extol the cult of personality. The masses, in turn, adhere to the Leader's ideology and participate in the glorification of the Leader.

By "masses," we refer to atomized, isolated individuals, a collective that is largely unaware of its own interests, in line with the conceptualization by Arendt (1973). The totalitarian system annihilates individual beliefs and personal will by robbing every individual of their property and political rights, while also denying them the right to expression and association. The system employs compulsion and persuasion to make individuals accept party indoctrination, fostering in them an unconditional loyalty to the supreme leader, an intense hatred for enemies, and a readiness to utilize violence. The ascent of a supreme leader to a position of paramount importance can only be accomplished by inciting an ardent cult of personality amongst the masses. Essentially, it is the masses who create the supreme leaders and, in turn, it is these leaders who generate mass movements. They form an inseparable pair in this dynamic.

The GLF and the CR reinforced the power of the Leader and the party to the extreme. Within the RADT system that formed through these movements, the authorities that devolved to local party-state agencies were only the minor ones, confined to local administrative and local resources. The intention of this decentralization was to empower the Leader and the party center to consolidate their grasp of primary power, thereby reducing more party members and cadres to the status of the "masses."

The party and the Leader were the core elements of the Leninist totalitarian system, the institutional genes that had been implanted. On the other hand, the mechanism of decentralizing minor powers to the local level was in part inherited from the *junxian* system of Imperial China, serving as the indigenous institutional genes.

To conclude this chapter, it is important to emphasize the dissidents who emerged from the CR, as they set the stage for the post-Mao reforms. However, the vast majority of these dissidents were opposed only to the extreme personality cult and endless class struggle. Their primary desire was for an economic recovery and the restoration of order. A subset of "liberal" dissidents hoped to foster a market economy while keeping the basic system of the PRC intact. On the other hand, some "conservative" dissidents aspired to return to the Soviet system of the 1950s.

Moreover, most dissidents were still living in a state of fear, which is a fundamental characteristic of the institutional genes under totalitarianism. Those brave enough to question the totalitarian system represented an exceptionally small fraction and expressing or communicating their views often entailed considerable risk. As of January 2025, this situation largely persists, if not is worse, indicating that communist totalitarianism, having been wielded by the CCP for over seventy years, has become deeply embedded in China's institutional genes.

NOTES

1. Hu Feng, formerly a member of the Japanese Communist Party, was a renowned pro-CCP left-wing writer and intellectual leader. In 1955, at the commencement of a nationwide purge of intellectuals, Hu was arrested by the CCP on accusations of opposing Mao Zedong's directives on arts and literature. Hu was eventually released in 1979 and posthumously exonerated by the CCP in 1988.
2. Ding Shu's work, *Yangmou: "Fanyou" qianhou* (*Open Conspiracy: The Complete Story of the "Anti-Rightist" Campaign*) (Ding, 1993), offers a systematic compilation of documents and facts pertaining to the Anti-Rightist Campaign and the "luring-out-the-snakes" strategy.

3. Stalin said: "One of the features of the history of old Russia is that she has suffered constant blows ... because of her backwardness ... We are 50 or 100 years behind the advanced countries. We must close this gap within ten years. Either we do this or they crush us" (Stalin, 1931, p. 356).
4. In 1956, Khrushchev (1959) claimed that the socialist system would overtake the Western world and eventually bury it.
5. *Zai Nanning huiyi shang de jianghua* (Speech at the Nanning Conference), in Mao (1966a).
6. *Chengdu huiyi* (The Chengdu Conference), in Mao (1966b); Xin (2006, p. 138); Mao (1992b, vol. 7, pp. 108–125).
7. Yang Jisheng estimates that 36 million people died during the Great Leap Forward (Yang, 2008). In contrast, Liao Gailong, a CCP official historian, cites official statistics and estimates the number of deaths to be around 40 million (Liao, 2000).
8. 6月24日与王海容的谈话 (A Talk with Wang Hairong on June 24), in Mao (1968b).
9. 8月与毛远新的谈话 (A Talk with Mao Yuanxin in August) in Mao (1968).
10. *Zai zhongyang zhengzhiju kuoda huiyi shangde jianghua* (*Speech at the Enlarged Meeting of the Politburo*), May 18, 1966. *Zhongwen makesizhuyi wenku* (Chinese Library of Marxism): Lin Biao.
11. In English, the term "Red Guards" is also used to refer to the militia units established by the CCP in its early years, named after the Bolshevik paramilitary units of the October Revolution.
12. A significant number of these individuals were influenced, both directly and indirectly, by a banned book, *The New Class*, by Milovan Djilas. Among them, the most notable was Yu Luoke, who was tragically executed in the late stages of the CR.
13. *Jiangguo yilai lici zhengzhi yundong shishi* (*Facts about the Political Campaigns since the Founding of the PRC*), May 1984, edited by *Dangshi yanjiushi* (Party History Research Office of the CCP Central Committee) et al., cited in Yang (2013).
14. Statistics: Ye Jianying, Enlarged Meeting of the Politburo Following the 1st Plenary Session of the 12th Central Committee, cited in Yang (2013).
15. According to human rights organizations, more than 1.3 million people were persecuted during the purges in the Soviet Union; an average of 1 in 129 people out of a population of 168 million.

13 The Post-Mao Reform and Its Cessation

The Rise and Fall of Regionally Decentralized Authoritarianism

With total control over resources, all communist totalitarian economies have experienced a period of rapid growth in the early stages of catching up, propelled by extremely high investments. However, none of these economies managed to complete the catching-up process. Before they could evolve into developed economies, their growth rates rapidly declined to levels below those of the advanced capitalist economies. According to Marxist historical materialism, sustained slow growth under a communist totalitarian system is evidence that such a system is inferior to a capitalist system. This not only undermined the Communist Party's legitimacy to rule but also weakened the Soviet and Eastern bloc's capacity to confront developed capitalist countries. Consequently, economic reform became a necessary measure to save the communist totalitarian system. However, the principle of eliminating private ownership, inherent in classical communist totalitarianism, hampered the Soviet and Eastern European economies' ability to undertake effective reforms, ultimately leading to the collapse of the Soviet and Eastern bloc system.

In contrast, post-Mao China embarked on economic reforms to salvage the communist totalitarian system driven by different impetus: a profound crisis that had accumulated through the Great Leap Forward and the Cultural Revolution, leaving China as one of the world's poorest economies. Yet, under the governance of regionally administered totalitarianism, the CCP succeeded remarkably in cultivating a vast private economy, albeit unintentionally, while adhering to the principles of communist totalitarianism. This led to almost four decades of rapid economic growth in China. Consequently, not only was the communist totalitarian system salvaged but a new superpower was also created. At the same time, the contemporary system of communist China perplexes many observers. The primary source of this confusion lies in the fact that people often overlook that the CCP's reform, from its inception to this day, has been aimed at rescuing and expanding the communist totalitarian system.

To understand the mechanism of China's reform, and more importantly, the CCP's purpose in launching it, one must recognize a basic historical fact: the beginning of China's reform was the end of the CR. The goal of the reform was to save the totalitarian regime. And the institutional foundation of the reform was the RADT system inherited from the CR. The key point is that this RADT system has enabled the CCP to achieve something that classical communist totalitarian regimes could not.

Any reform within a totalitarian system requires a vast force to push it through. The resistance to and the introspection about the catastrophic CR instigated a tremendous impetus for reform. The GLF and the CR, which killed tens of millions of people and persecuted more than 100 million, not only shook Mao's image but also undermined the ideology and the legitimacy of the CCP in the eyes of the general public, prompting the CCP to focus on the economy by abandoning the class-struggle line. But those with vested interests in the totalitarian system always tried to protect the system and its institutional genes in various ways. Deployment began at the beginning of the reform to block the creation of new, pro-democracy institutional genes during the reform and to ensure that the reform would not deviate from the totalitarian system. Even before the reform took off, Deng Xiaoping proclaimed four totalitarian cardinal principles that had to be upheld, the core of which was the perpetuation of the dictatorship of the proletariat and the total control of the CCP. Later, Deng made it clear that China's reform was a reenactment of Lenin's New Economic Policy, implying, like Lenin had said, that it was an expediency for preserving the regime. Alongside economic development, the violent repression of dissidents spanned the decades of reform. The terror that developed during the early campaigns against counterrevolutionaries and rightists in China, and later during the GLF and CR movements, not only still grips society but has also evolved further with the support of the internet and digital technology.

13.1 REFORMS FOR THE SURVIVAL OF TOTALITARIANISM

> Without reform and opening-up, ... we inevitably navigate towards a dead end.
>
> —Deng Xiaoping (1993, p. 370)

The quote by Deng Xiaoping, made in the wake of the dissolution of the Soviet Union, has a particular resonance. It reflects the consensus of the CCP's highest ranks during a time of global political upheaval. The fall of the communist regimes across the Eastern bloc left the CCP as the world's sole significant communist totalitarian regime. Consequently, there was a sense of desperation within the party to preserve its rule.

Indeed, for any communist regime, economic reform in itself constitutes an ideological shift, as it inevitably deviates from the principles of total control and central planning, hallmarks of totalitarian regimes. Moreover, from the perspective of the CCP, what is termed "reform" aligns closely with what it labeled as "revisionism" in the CPSU.

However, in the aftermath of the GLF and the CR, the CCP was faced with an urgent challenge: to restore its credibility and persuade the public to continue submitting to the party and its totalitarian rule. This was a particularly pressing issue following Mao's death and the incarceration of his followers, the so-called Gang of Four. Yet, so long as ideology and politics continued to follow the CR's radical lines, no meaningful reform could take place.

It is in this context that the common perception that China underwent only economic reform, neglecting political reform, is incorrect. While this perception holds some truth for the post-1989 period, it overlooks significant transformations that occurred following the end of the CR. The basic fact is that China's reforms from 1977 onwards began with political restructuring.

However, it is crucial to stress that the political reforms undertaken by the Chinese Communist Party were propelled by its need to restore and consolidate the legitimacy of its rule, rather than to denounce its totalitarian communist regime. The brutal suppression of the pro-democracy movement in 1989 provides evidence of this point. This nuanced understanding is essential for anyone seeking to fully grasp the nature and scope of China's reform process as well as the underlying characteristics of China's contemporary political system.

In October 1976, a few weeks after Mao's death, a coup d'état was staged by CCP Chairman Hua Guofeng, Defense Minister Ye Jianying, and others. They arrested Jiang Qing and other members of the Gang of Four, an event that was met with broad support and helped stabilize the political climate. However, influential figures within the party, including Deng Xiaoping, were left in a state of uncertainty after the purge. Most leaders of the party-state departments of that time, including ideology and the media, had come to power either by seizing power or were installed by the PLA during the CR.

Hu Yaobang, who assumed the leadership of the CCP's Central Party School in March 1977 and subsequently took charge of the party's Organization Department, played a crucial role in advocating for reforms. These included revising the party's ideology and political power structures, particularly those related to personnel control. In response to Hua Guofeng's rigid adherence to "whatever" Mao had instructed, Hu sparked a debate on the "criterion of truth." This philosophical debate, seemingly focused on Marxist principles, actually served to trigger a comprehensive questioning of Mao's political line and initiate a conversation about dismantling the personality cult surrounding Mao. Thus, it laid the groundwork for the abandonment of Mao's class struggle policies at the 3rd Plenary Session of the CCP's 11th Central Committee. This meeting marked a significant shift in the party's priorities towards economic reconstruction and it redefined the party line, solidifying Deng Xiaoping's leadership.

However, contrary to the CCP's subsequent official narrative, this session was not a landmark event in launching reforms. In fact, the conference did not discuss reform in any substantial sense. More critically, it explicitly prohibited altering the collective ownership structure of the People's Communes, reflecting an enduring commitment to some key tenets of Mao's ideology.

China's reform agenda in the early 1980s was pioneered by the so-called "Deng-Hu-Zhao" troika, referring to the party's first generation of reformist leaders. Despite the apparent guise of collective leadership, the troika did not truly embody this notion. Deng Xiaoping was nominally the chairman of the Central Military Commission but in practice, he was the supreme leader of the party, government, and military. The fact that the person who wields military power is the supreme leader highlights the characteristics of a totalitarian system.

Hu Yaobang served as the party's general secretary, focusing primarily on political and personnel reforms. Zhao Ziyang, in his capacity as premier, was at the forefront of economic reform. However, both Hu and Zhao had to yield to Deng and other elder party statesmen in practice. Throughout the 1980s, until their eventual displacement by Deng, both Hu and Zhao played critical roles in driving political, ideological, personnel, and economic reforms.

This period marked the only time in the history of the PRC that the CCP attempted some level of political reform, albeit limited. Some reformists have documented this phase as the Hu–Zhao Reformation (Hu, 2012), in recognition of the significant impact that these two figures had on China's reform process.

The first significant initiative undertaken by Hu was a massive rehabilitation campaign, which laid the personnel foundation for the reform to be subsequently launched and partially alleviated the legitimacy crisis of the totalitarian regime created by the CR. What set Hu apart in CCP history is that he advocated for the vindication not only of the CCP top-level victims of the CR, including Liu Shaoqi and Bo Yibo but also for a very large number of people purged in various campaigns throughout the decades of CCP history. As the largest rehabilitation campaign in the history of the CCP, it vindicated nearly 550,000 "rightists," 1.25 million "right-leaning opportunists," 450,000 "KMT rebels," and more than 20 million so-called "landlords, rich peasants, counterrevolutionaries, bad elements, and rightists" (Hu, 2012).[1]

By the end of 1982, more than 3 million unjust cases had been vindicated across the country, involving 100 million people (Yang, 2010, p. 126). On the other hand, Hu pushed to cleanse the ranks of those who had seized or risen to power during the CR, a process that involved all levels of the party-state organs. After the rehabilitation, by 1977 over 55 percent of the Central Committee members of the previous congress had been replaced (Yang, 2010, p. 127). This not only paved the way for the reform during the following decade but also weakened the terror that the CCP had instilled in society since the Suppression of Counterrevolutionaries and Anti-Rightist campaigns of the 1950s, shaking the foundation of totalitarianism and laying the groundwork for "liberalization."

Dissidents who emerged in the late years of the CR played substantial roles in pushing for liberalization during the post-Mao reform. While the party's top leaders were debating Mao's spiritual legacy, big-character posters appeared on the streets of Beijing and other cities in late 1978. These posters criticized Mao and even communist totalitarianism in general. These soon evolved into spontaneous civil rallies, associations, and publications that openly criticized Mao and demanded human rights protections and political reform. Crowds traveled to Beijing from across the country to demonstrate for redress, an end to persecution, human rights, and democracy.

The phenomenon was unprecedented since the Anti-Rightist Campaign of the 1950s. Facing this severe challenge to CCP rule, all factions of the CCP's top echelon felt threatened. In March 1979, Deng responded firmly by laying down the Four Cardinal Principles, which were to become the bottom line for any operation in China. The summary of these principles is that the socialist road, the dictatorship of the proletariat, the party's leadership, and Marxism-Leninism and Mao Zedong Thought are inviolable, unassailable, and unshakeable (Deng, 1994). Subsequently, the authorities arrested and harshly sentenced the main authors of the big-character posters who had challenged the totalitarian regime. In the following year, the CCP had the NPC amend the constitution to outlaw big-character posters (Yang, 2010, pp. 107–114). The Four Cardinal Principles, proclaimed by Deng on the eve of the reform, have since become the basic principles of the reform. They unambiguously signal that the reform was never solely for economic purposes but aimed to salvage, uphold, and consolidate the totalitarian system.

The institutional genes of the CCP exhibit greater resilience in safeguarding the totalitarian system compared to their Soviet and Eastern European counterparts. In 1956, Khrushchev and his followers tried to defend the CPSU and restore the reputation of totalitarianism by blaming Stalin personally for the various crimes of the Soviet system. To a certain extent, Gorbachev's reform, known as *Perestroika*, decades later was a continuation. In contrast, Deng supported by his allies made a starkly different decision to sustain CCP rule. Given that Mao's followers constituted the majority within the CCP, how to terminate Mao's line to save the CCP was a significant challenge. From November 1979 to June 1981, more than 4,000 senior CCP cadres participated in drafting the "Resolution on Certain Issues in the History of our Party Since the Founding of the State," presided over by Deng and Hu (Yang, 2010, pp. 114–117).

Arguably, the heated debates in the top echelons of the CCP during these months-long meetings were unprecedented, but also the last such debates in CCP history. Many former top CCP leaders denounced the injustices created by Mao over the decades, attributing the CCP's problems to Mao, and suggested separating the party from Mao and abolishing the reference to Mao Zedong Thought. For a moment, there was a chance for some sort of substantive political reform at the top of the CCP, similar to the changes in the CPSU in the mid-1950s or even in the mid-1980s. However, Deng decisively

13.1 REFORMS FOR THE SURVIVAL OF TOTALITARIANISM

suppressed this debate, stating that to negate Mao Zedong Thought was to deny the party's history and shake the legitimacy of the regime (Zhang, 2015, p. 106). Deng prevailed in this matter because he represented the will and interests of a sizable share of the party's leading figures who were more conservative than he was, such as Hua Guofeng and Chen Yun. If one has to use the terms "reformist" and "conservative" to define a person, Deng was clearly a conservative, politically. In fact, the "reform" that most party members desired was to end class struggle and quickly restore China to the pre-GLF Maoist era. The major forces within the CCP determined that the role of the few political leaders, such as Hu Yaobang and Zhao Ziyang, who attempted a broader reform, was limited to their impact at the early stage of the reform. Thereafter, they were either annihilated or neutralized by the traditional totalitarian forces within the party.

Similar to the internal political debates within the CCP and the limited ideological and political personnel reforms after the CR, China's economic reform also aimed at preserving totalitarian rule. The first economic reform that took effect in China was the rural land reform, not the reform of state-owned enterprises (SOEs), which concerned the CCP the most. However, the rural land reform was not intentionally designed or initiated by Deng or any CCP leader rather, it was a spontaneous effort by peasants in the poorest regions when they were given a chance to escape the poverty. The role of the so-called reformists was to set aside, or disguise, the socialist principles and partially tolerate the peasants' spontaneous and daring departure from "collectivism."

In 1978, while the CCP's top echelons were focusing on ideological debates such as the "criterion of truth," and the power struggle between Deng and Hua was in full swing, the poverty-stricken peasants of Xiaogang Village in Fengyang County, Anhui Province, improvised a "reform," which was actually a way of surviving, later to be known as the land-contracting system. To save themselves from starvation or begging, they risked imprisonment by contracting the collectively owned land to individual households, transforming collective farming into individual farming. It was a high-stakes gamble because the land, "collectively owned" by them by law, could not, in practice, be disposed of by the collective. Not long before this, allotting land for private use had been condemned and punished with imprisonment in China. However, this venture took place just as the reform was about to begin and it received political protection from Wan Li, the then Anhui Party Secretary, who shielded them so as to avoid famine in an area of extreme poverty. Zhao Ziyang, then Sichuan Provincial Party Secretary, promoted similar agricultural reforms in Sichuan. The land-contracting system, a spontaneous grassroots experiment, proved to provide peasants with strong incentives, leading to a rapid increase in agricultural output in those areas.

After the spontaneously emerged land-contracting system was successfully initiated, it quickly spread throughout Anhui and Sichuan provinces. In 1980, Zhao and Wan, the leaders of these provinces, were respectively appointed as premier and vice-premier, responsible for promoting such a contracting system nationwide. With the full implementation of the land-contracting system, in 1984 the CCP formally abandoned the People's Commune system nationwide, ending its two-decade-long communist totalitarian experiment. This marked the first breakthrough in China's economic reform (Xu, 2011). The success of the rural reform not only increased agricultural output but also released large amounts of labor for industry and other sectors. The resulting boom of the township and village enterprises (TVEs) a few years later led to a rapid increase in industrial output. The successful development of agriculture and industry in rural China lifted hundreds of millions of people out of the absolute poverty created by the People's Commune system.

The next major breakthrough in China's reforms was the establishment of the Special Economic Zones (SEZs) to attract foreign investment and boost exports. This reform emerged not out of a desire for global engagement per se, but rather as a policy response to extreme poverty and political pressure. Since the 1950s, a significant number of people had fled mainland China for Hong Kong, then a British colony, to escape political persecution and poverty. The exodus peaked in the late 1970s when 100,000 people attempted to flee to Hong Kong and in 1979 alone over 30,000 succeeded, placing enormous pressure on the party committee of neighboring Guangdong Province. Xi Zhongxun, then Provincial Party Secretary, received a proposal from his subordinates to lease part of the land in what is now Shenzhen to Hong Kong entrepreneurs. The aim was to attract Hong Kong capital to stimulate local economic development and mitigate the problem of exodus. In April 1979, Xi proposed at the party's Central Work Conference to pilot this approach, with support from Hua Guofeng and Deng Xiaoping (Yang, 2010, pp. 188–192; Wu, 2015). However, some party top leaders, such as Chen Yun, branded this as a "national betrayal" and a restoration of semi-colonialism (Zhao, 2009). As a political compromise, Deng proposed limiting it to small-scale local experiments and coined the term "Special Economic Zone," meaning it generally would not be applicable across China. After the initial success of the first four SEZs, their number and scale continued to increase beginning in 1984, becoming a nationwide phenomenon. This reform turned China from a country with almost no foreign investment or exports into the world's largest exporter and one of the largest recipients of foreign investment.

As discussed earlier, regional experimentation and competition played important roles in both the GLF and the CR. Inheriting the same institution but arguably for different goals, these mechanisms were deployed again during the reform and at times they played even more significant roles. The two most crucial reforms in the initial stage of China's economic reform – land-contracting and the SEZ reforms – are good examples. Both were local "experiments," initiated and implemented at the local level. The role of the central authorities was to either arouse or call for local experimentation without design. Success at the local level was then replicated through regional competition (Xu, 2011). This important mechanism is based on and executed by the RADT system. It will be analyzed further in the second half of this chapter.

13.1.1 Totalitarian Principles: The Red Line That Reform Cannot Cross

The Four Cardinal Principles, declared by Deng before economic reform had even commenced,[2] define the nature and scope of the reforms. The Principles represented a consensus among CCP's upper echelons across all factions that the reforms were intended to serve the survival and development of the totalitarian regime. Any person or action that violated the Principles was to be prohibited or suppressed.

Just a few years into the reform, Deng further clarified that China's reform was Lenin's "New Economic Policy." He stated that adhering to the Four Cardinal Principles was to prevent anyone from "correcting" Marxism-Leninism or "correcting" socialism, stressing that the CCP's "belief and ideal is to promote communism." He foresaw that "opening-up would be risky and would bring in some of the decadence of capitalism," but he claimed, "our socialist policies and state apparatus are strong enough to overcome such things" (Deng, 1993, vol. 3, pp. 136–140). Regarding the upholding of communist principles, the evidence clearly shows that there is no fundamental difference between Deng and current leader Xi Jinping. Thus, Xi's apparent change of course in China's post-Mao reform since 2013 represents much more than merely his personal choice.

Both the "reformists," represented by Deng, and the "conservatives," represented by Chen Yun, asserted that reform was necessary for the sake of socialism, that is to say, for the survival of the totalitarian regime. The debates were centered around how to reinterpret Marxist dogma and determine which reform path had socialist legitimacy. In the early years of reform, Chinese economists struggled to reconcile Marxist dogma with China's new economic policy, often by interpreting or misinterpreting Marxist principles. Intraparty debates over economic reform were similar to the factional disputes within the Catholic Church during the Reformation when Catholic reformers had to reinterpret doctrine to justify their reforms in response to the Protestant movement. Those outside the Church, especially those unfamiliar with Christianity, often found it challenging to understand the true implications of the doctrinal debates within the Church. A similar logic led to many wishful misunderstandings about China's reforms over the decades, thus leading people to get China wrong (Friedberg, 2022).

Meanwhile, since the Anti-Rightist Campaign, Chinese economists trained in Western countries had been either purged from academic institutions or marginalized. Those economists who played significant roles within academia and the government were usually Soviet-style Marxists who had been trained in the Soviet Union or indoctrinated with Soviet-style teachings in China. Almost all influential economists were long-standing CCP members, or even senior cadres, or those associated with them.

Deng Xiaoping, much like Lenin in his era, clung to the principles of totalitarianism while searching for practical ways to sustain the system. Having studied in France and the Soviet Union in his youth and having visited the United States and Japan on the eve of the reform, Deng had a profound understanding of China's backwardness and its implications for the survival of the communist regime. Moreover, he was keen to establish a track record in economic development to consolidate his power. Supported by enthusiastic and capable reformists, such as Hu Yaobang, Zhao Ziyang, and Wan Li, Deng Xiaoping gained the upper hand in the political power struggle due to the great success of the land-contracting system and the establishment of the SEZs. They sought to resolve the problems with the state sector by promoting market exchange and contracting management without altering state ownership. But taboos inherited by the regime, and the Four Cardinal Principles declared by Deng, restricted the reforms to purely economic aspects.

Chen Yun, by contrast, was like Trotsky in his day, adhering to fundamentalist Marxism and ignoring practicality. He adhered to the dogma of a Stalinist political economy that maintains that a socialist economy must follow the law of planning and proportionality, which includes Soviet-style public ownership, allocation of products by plan, and opposition to a commodity economy based on market exchange (Chen, 1986, p. 278).

In response to imminent economic challenges and after striking a balance between Deng and Chen, Hu Yaobang and Zhao Ziyang secured adoption of the CCP's first comprehensive document on reform at the party's 3rd Plenary Session of the 12th Central Committee. The document emphasized, in Marxist terms, that China's socialist economy was a planned commodity economy based on public ownership and it must implement plans through the law of value. Chen praised the document for emphasizing the principles of public ownership and the planned economy, saying, "We are the Communist Party, which advocates socialism," and adding that a socialist economy must "primarily be a planned economy, with market adjustments as a supplementary element" (Chen, 1986, p. 304). This was a major breakthrough in the eyes of the Deng-Hu-Zhao faction that legitimized the introduction of market mechanisms as Marxist terms in the document, such as "commodity economy" and "law of value".

In practice, at that time, the market was only partially legal. Many forms of trading, such as cross-region trading, were banned. Both market prices and government-set planned prices coexisted in the market. This so-called dual-track system was not only a pricing mechanism but also a distinguishing feature of the economy. It existed where planned and market economies operated simultaneously in all aspects of the economy, with state ownership predominating. The dual-track system created countless opportunities for collusion between officials and businesses, leading to widespread corruption. Meanwhile, it created a fissure in a society where the party-state controlled all resources, allowing for the growth of non-state firms, particularly the TVEs. This led to one of the greatest achievements of China's early economic reform, as during a time when private enterprises had no legal status, 83 to 86 percent of de facto private enterprises registered as TVEs for protection (Zhang, 1996, p. 112). This development was entirely spontaneous and outside the CCP's reform plan. In fact, on the one hand, Deng admitted that he had "completely failed to anticipate" the "surprising rise" the TVEs (Deng, 1993, vol. 3, p. 238). On the other hand, at a time when controlling inflation was critical, he demanded that local party-state cadres vouch for their party membership to suppress the TVEs (Yang, 2010, p. 312).

All enterprises in China in the early 1980s were state-owned, including some collective enterprises, which were state-controlled under another name. Economist János Kornai has observed that in all economic reform efforts in the Soviet Union and Central Eastern Europe, whenever state-owned enterprises became insolvent, the government would bail them out to prevent bankruptcy. Anticipating a bailout, SOEs would irresponsibly over-borrow for investment, which would ultimately lead to debt distress for both the SOEs and the economy as a whole. This phenomenon is known as the "soft budget constraint" syndrome. No reform upholding state ownership could remedy this problem, which was one of the institutional reasons for the complete failure of the economic reforms in the Soviet Union and Central Eastern Europe (Kornai, 1992).

Given the unassailable position of state ownership, SOE reform in China during the 1980s was obligated to imitate the land-contracting system by contracting enterprises to managers.[3] This approach aimed to escape the issue of state ownership but it ultimately failed. Although it provided incentives for managers when SOEs were profitable, the SOEs would still be rescued by the party-state when incurring losses. The failure to address the SBC issue left SOE reform stymied and the situation continued to deteriorate (Xu, 2011). Eventually, the SBCs of the SOEs and the dual-track system caused severe inflation. While the party restricted the scope of reform with the intention of sustaining the totalitarian system, the resulting economic problems ended up seriously threatening the system's survival.

13.1.2 *From the Four Cardinal Principles to Tiananmen*

A necessary condition for the post-Mao reform to be pushed forward quickly was the enthusiastic initiatives taken by intellectuals, including CCP cadres. Their enthusiasm was inseparably linked to their awakening by the catastrophic CR and their desire to prevent such a disaster from repeating, which went far beyond mere economic needs. This profound mindset was openly expressed in a spirit of humanism. Many of them questioned the communist ideology and the inhumane totalitarian system, eliciting significant responses in society. However, these trends were perceived as threats to CCP rule and were anticipated and prepared for by the party's upper echelons, led by Deng Xiaoping.

As the Chinese reform began by following the steps of the communist Eastern bloc, the CCP closely watched the sequence of events in Eastern Europe's communist regimes, in a manner similar to the situation in 1956 (see Section 12.1). They insisted that it was necessary to deal sternly with dissenters to prevent phenomena akin to Poland's Solidarity movement while implementing "reform." At a Central Committee Work Conference in late 1980, Deng reiterated the Four Cardinal Principles and stressed, "Any attempt to weaken ... and oppose the leadership of the party ... must be fought ... as necessary" (Deng, 1995, vol. 2, pp. 358–359). In 1981, before economic reform had taken shape, the party and military media in China launched a campaign to criticize the film script of *Unrequited Love*, perceiving it as a challenge to the CCP by promoting humanitarianism. Deng supported the criticism and reiterated that "the core of upholding the Four Cardinal Principles is to adhere to the leadership of the party" (Deng, 1995, vol. 2, p. 391). Eventually, Hu Yaobang had to defuse the situation by downplaying the criticisms against the screenplay (Yang, 2010, pp. 203–209). However, this incident was only the prelude to a series of suppressive actions by the CCP.

To ensure the CCP's total control over ideology, Deng Xiaoping officially launched the Anti-Spiritual Pollution Campaign at the 2nd Plenary Session of the 12th CCP Central Committee in October 1983. He claimed that the "essence of spiritual pollution ... is the spread of distrust towards socialism, the communist cause, and the leadership of the Communist Party." The CCP's Central Discipline

Commission, party media, and the so-called "conservatives" immediately embarked on a nationwide campaign that severely challenged the already difficult economic reform process. Hu Yaobang and Zhao Ziyang resisted this challenge, and, arguing on the grounds of economic reform, they persuaded Deng to halt the campaign, thereby preserving the incipient economic reform. Shortly before his death, Hu stated, "Because Ziyang and I resisted, other Secretariat members were not in favor of [the campaign against 'spiritual pollution'], and ... this Cultural Revolution-like campaign lasted only 28 days.... But ... [the conservatives] wouldn't let it go and turned their fire on bourgeois liberalization instead" (Yang, 2010, pp. 227–233).

Although Hu and Zhao promoted economic reform for the benefit of the CCP, their relaxation of control for the sake of reform was perceived by the CCP leadership as a challenge to totalitarian rule. Deng's two campaigns to consolidate the totalitarian system received widespread support among the party's senior ranks. The CCP leadership could not tolerate any emergent institutional genes that might challenge the totalitarian system under the guise of reform.

Under numerous constraints, economic reform hardly made headway in the early 1980s, except in the rural areas. Facing the thorny problem of the survival of totalitarianism, Deng proposed political system reform in 1986 based on adherence to the Four Cardinal Principles (Zhao, 2009, pp. 273–274). "Without political reform, economic reform is difficult to implement," said Deng (Deng, 1993, vol. 3, p. 177). Regardless of the true intention behind the call for so-called political reform, it sparked a hugely enthusiastic reaction across society, with many hoping to break the shackles of totalitarianism through it. From 1986 to early 1989, debates about political reform unfolded, unintentionally making that period a golden age or the most liberal period of Communist rule in China.

College students were among the most passionate in pushing for political reform. In early December 1986, students from the University of Science and Technology of China, discontented with the fraudulent election of representatives to the Hefei Municipal

People's Congress, rallied on campus. The vice-chancellor, physicist Fang Lizhi, stated at the rally, "Democracy is not granted from top to bottom, but is strived for from bottom to top." Subsequently, students took to the streets to demand voting rights, igniting a nationwide student movement. University campuses across twenty-eight cities witnessed the rise of big-character posters and marches demanding political reform and democracy. Deng Xiaoping, whose stance represented that of most of the party's top leaders, ordered Hu Yaobang, Zhao Ziyang, and others to deal resolutely with the protesting students. However, Hu refused a crackdown, hoping to resolve the issue through communication and dialogue. On the other hand, the president of the Central Party School, General Wang Zhen, publicly declared, "You have three million university students; I have three million PLA soldiers. I am going to behead a bunch of them." The secretary of the Tianjin CCP Committee, Li Ruihuan, asserted, "The leadership of the CCP was traded for the lives of tens of thousands of revolutionary martyrs. Whoever wants our leadership must pay an equal price!" (Yang, 2010, pp. 268–270).

With Hu's refusal to execute the order, Deng summoned Hu, Zhao, and other Politburo Standing Committee members on December 30, blaming the student movement on Hu. He equated anti-bourgeois liberalization and adherence to the Four Cardinal Principles with the Anti-Rightist Movement. Hu was forced to resign. A few days later, Deng appointed a five-person group, led by Zhao, to govern the party and government (Zhao, 2009, pp. 193–194). They immediately launched the Anti-Bourgeois Liberalization Campaign, publicly expelling people like Fang Lizhi and launching criticism against many intellectuals both within and outside the party. Students in China, under suppression, were temporarily unable to express resistance. Chinese students and visiting scholars from more than 100 universities in the United States launched a public-letter initiative, published in Chinese language media in the United States, with over 2,000 signatures, opposing the Anti-Bourgeois Liberalization Campaign and calling for the rehabilitation of Hu, Fang, and others.[4]

Deng's political campaign resulted in an immediate impact on the reform. A few months later, Zhao reported to Deng that some people, under the guise of Anti-Bourgeois Liberalization, were opposing economic reform and the reform could be severely damaged. Deng, worried about the impediment to economic reform, instructed, "failing to reform will also encourage bourgeois liberalization." That allowed Zhao to suspend the campaign in the name of economic reform (Yang, 2010, pp. 303–304).

The path to reform in China was fraught with obstacles, particularly with SOE reform being mired in difficulty. The party's monopoly on power and resources transformed the dual-track system into a mechanism that allowed power to profit in the market, fostering corruption at an unprecedented level. Moreover, the SBCs linked to state ownership led to serious inflation. Political persecution escalated and these factors together ignited widespread societal dissatisfaction.

Numerous renowned intellectuals called for political reform and spoke out against the persecution of dissidents. In the first quarter of 1989, several intellectual groups, including members of the Chinese Academy of Sciences, issued open letters demanding the release of political prisoners. A survey conducted in April at five universities in Beijing, including Peking University and Tsinghua University, found that over 50 percent of students favored a multi-party system, with nearly 22 percent opposing socialism.

The party's upper echelons broadly agreed that urgent suppression was necessary. Even Hu Yaobang's follower, Politburo Standing Committee member Hu Qili, warned in March, "The current situation mirrors that of 1957; if we do not suppress now, we will be forced into an Anti-Rightist Movement." Almost simultaneously, Hu Jintao, then the secretary of the Tibet Autonomous Region and a leader groomed within Hu Yaobang's Youth League system, led a military crackdown against Tibetans in Lhasa (Yang, 2010, pp. 316–319). Deng was impressed by his resolute action and thus later personally designated Hu Jintao as the successor to Jiang Zemin.

On April 15, 1989, Hu Yaobang's sudden death sent shockwaves throughout China. Many in the public associated his unexpected passing with the persecution he had endured for defending the people's freedom of speech. Consequently, the student and intellectual communities, which had suffered gravely from the recent suppression, reacted vehemently to Hu's sudden demise.

As the official funeral was being held in the Great Hall of the People, over 50,000 students and other citizens overcame official obstructions to hold spontaneous memorials in Tiananmen Square. They sought to redress the injustices against Hu and called for democracy and freedom. Large-scale demonstrations also took place in other cities, posing a formidable challenge to the government.

However, Deng Xiaoping labeled these student actions as anti-party and anti-socialist, characterizing them as "turmoil." He ordered the *People's Daily* to publish an editorial on April 26, declaring that the unrest was against the leadership of the party and should be suppressed. Far from quelling the protests, this move incited a massive demonstration of 100,000 students in Beijing. They broke through police blockades, marched several miles to Tiananmen Square, and occupied the area, demanding a dialogue with the government. Their demands included the retraction of the April 26 editorial and assurances that students participating in the demonstrations would not face persecution (Yang, 2010, pp. 319–337).

Beginning from the end of April, Zhao Ziyang made attempts to persuade Deng Xiaoping to retract the controversial editorial in an effort to quell the burgeoning student movement. He openly asserted that the students were not opposing the party and its fundamental system. However, his views and strategy were rejected by Deng and most of the party's top leadership.

Feeling hopeless and backed into a corner, the students escalated their protests by embarking on a hunger strike in Tiananmen Square, with thousands taking part. This coincided with a historic visit by Mikhail Gorbachev to Beijing, the first time a Soviet leader had visited the Chinese capital in over three decades. The timing meant that the eyes of the world were fixed on Tiananmen Square, amplifying the impact of the students' actions.

Shortly after Gorbachev's departure, Deng convened an emergency meeting at his home, attended by five top civilian leaders and eight PLA generals. Notably absent were General Secretary Zhao Ziyang and Politburo Standing Committee member Hu Qili. Deng expressed his belief that the unrest stemmed from an alternative center of command within the party that opposed his views. He ordered the mobilization of troops from a dozen divisions to enforce martial law in Beijing. Veteran party leader Chen Yun firmly supported Deng's decision, declaring that failing to act would risk allowing the socialism achieved through the sacrifices of 20 million revolutionary martyrs to transform into capitalism.

On the evening of the same day, Zhao went to Tiananmen Square to appeal to the students, urging them to evacuate the square as soon as possible. The students on the square insisted that the government respond to their demands, which were widely supported by intellectuals, citizens, and many cadres of the party-state central agencies. They also gained widespread support from Hong Kong and overseas Chinese. The Chairman of the NPC, Wan Li, who was on a trip abroad, made a statement in Canada to protect the students. Upon his return, his plane was forced to land in Shanghai for "medical treatment". Eight generals, including Zhang Aiping and Xiao Ke, who had not attended the meeting at Deng's home, co-signed a letter to Deng and the Central Military Commission, requesting that the military not enter the city. The commander of the 38th Group Army refused to execute the order and was sentenced by a military court. The 100,000 martial law troops summoned from all over the country were intercepted by millions of Beijing citizens and their orders could not be executed for over ten days (Yang, 2010, pp. 339–388).

The CCP has been known to crush any organized dissidents, regardless of their intention, a pattern repeated countless times since the party's inception. In the early hours of June 4, hundreds of thousands of soldiers, acting on orders and backed by tanks, armored vehicles, and live ammunition, seized control of Tiananmen Square. This bloodshed event became known as the June 4th or Tiananmen Square Massacre. Officials whose stances were similar to those of Hu and Zhao, including Zhao himself, were sequentially deprived of all official posts. Jiang Zemin, instrumental in suppressing the "turmoil" in Shanghai, was urgently appointed general secretary to replace Zhao. Many reformists and senior CCP officers aligned with Hu and Zhao fled overseas, while many dissidents were arrested, exiled, or put under house arrest, with some, including Zhao, remaining in that state until their deaths. Democratic countries, such as the United States and the members of the then European Economic Commission, imposed severe sanctions on China, marking the end of the post-Mao honeymoon between the United States and China.

13.2 ECONOMIC REFORM: URGENT REACTION TO THE COLLAPSE OF THE USSR

The Tiananmen Square Massacre had a profound impact on both China and the world (Beja, 2011). This landmark event was a critical aspect of China's post-Mao reform, which began by emulating the path of the Soviet Union and Eastern Europe, encountering similar challenges. Deng's Four Cardinal Principles not only formed a consensus among the CCP's top echelons in the reform era but also continued the anti-peaceful evolution principles of Mao's era, principles upheld by the Soviet and Eastern European Communist parties until their demise. Within the CCP, most disagreements between so-called reformists and conservatives focused on how to more effectively safeguard the totalitarian system. The Tiananmen Massacre bore a striking resemblance to the Prague Spring of 1968; however, while the latter event saw Soviet tanks suppress Czech citizens, in Tiananmen it was the PLA troops that suppressed their fellow Chinese citizens.

The two landmark events, the Tiananmen Massacre and the Prague Spring, have been interpreted drastically differently by the majority of Chinese and their counterparts in the Eastern bloc.

The Tiananmen Massacre was justified by the CCP and most "reformists" and accepted by the population as a means to provide social stability, allowing China to concentrate on growth. In contrast, the Prague Spring was viewed as one of the critical factors that led to the downfall of communist totalitarian rule in the Eastern bloc. Such a stark difference attests to the power of totalitarian institutional genes in China to sustain the regime, particularly during times of crisis in the communist totalitarian world and the collapse of the Eastern bloc. This divergence warrants further analysis and reflection.

Merely five months after the June 4 Incident, the fall of the Berlin Wall signaled the domino-like fall of the East European totalitarian states, culminating in the dissolution of the Soviet Union. The once dominant Communist Bloc was reduced to China and a few peripheral countries, such as North Korea and Cuba. This was a significant blow to the CCP, which had followed the Eastern bloc's lead, attempting to salvage the totalitarian regime through economic reform.[5] The ousting of Hu and Zhao, the Tiananmen Massacre, and the collapse of the Eastern bloc empowered the hard-liners within the CCP, represented by Chen Yun. Jiang Zemin, who assumed power amidst this crisis, to adhere strictly to this hard line. The accommodative practices adopted for economic reform during the Hu and Zhao era were now criticized from a rigid, fundamentalist Marxist standpoint, and banned as acts of bourgeois liberalization. This shift invited a sharp economic decline that directly endangered the economic and social stability of the totalitarian system itself.

Under the triple blows of international sanctions, regressive reforms, and the collapse of the Eastern bloc, many TVEs failed. The economy shrank, public sentiment became unstable, and Deng's status as paramount leader was shaken. Faced with domestic and international crises since 1989, along with the devastating threat to totalitarianism posed by the collapse of the Soviet Union, Deng took decisive action to save the CCP regime. In early 1992, he visited several parts of southern China to reinvigorate economic reform and refocus the CCP on economic reconstruction.

To add grandeur to Deng's efforts, the CCP borrowed the imperial vocabulary used for emperors' inspection tours, glorifying his inspections as the "Southern Tour." In the face of a newly disintegrated Soviet Union and a China that was repressed (though propagandized as having attained political stability), Deng identified the failure in economic reform as the most pressing threat to the CCP's survival. He stated that the Soviet Union's biggest mistake was "not putting economic construction at the center, not concentrating forces to carry out economic construction." Confronted with severe challenges from the sanctions following the Tiananmen Massacre and the disintegration of the Soviet Union, Deng proposed the diplomatic strategy called "concealing our strengths and biding our time" (Yang, 2010, pp. 431–433).

Feeling a sense of urgency, Deng asserted that the bourgeois-liberalized upheaval was a rightist attempt to "bury socialism"; whereas, by rejecting market reform, the leftists would lead to the same outcome. He went further by threatening Jiang and other top party leaders, vowing to bring down anyone who refused to implement reform (Deng, 1993, vol. 3, pp. 371–375). Deng contended that the Tiananmen Massacre had provided China with decades of stability and this had allowed the CCP an opportunity to shift the focus of the party's Four Cardinal Principles from political repression to economic reform. Jiang thereafter was closely aligned with Deng's position. Due to gross misunderstandings of communist totalitarianism both within China and globally, Deng's justification of repression combined with reform, as well as his deceptive strategy, succeeded in strengthening the regime while concealing the CCP's true intentions. This veil remained intact until Xi Jinping recently exposed it.

The determination to pursue reform prevailed once again in China. However, having the determination to reform the economy and actually being able to solve economic problems are two distinct matters. Communist leaders, from Khrushchev to Gorbachev, recognized the severity of economic issues and issued numerous orders, particularly since the 1970s, in hopes of addressing these problems

13.2 URGENT REACTION TO THE COLLAPSE OF THE USSR 617

through reform. Yet their economic reforms, aimed at rescuing the totalitarian system, were constrained by the system itself, leading to comprehensive failure.

The biggest differences between China and the Eastern bloc regimes lay in the RADT system, which emerged from the GLF and the CR, and an awakening both inside and outside the CCP due to the disaster of the CR. The former aspect led to local experimentation and regional competition that prevailed in China during the reform. The latter gave rise to social forces at the beginning of the reform that sought to break free from the constraints of the totalitarian system, including allowing the establishment of private enterprises.

However, the development of private enterprises implied capitalism, contravening the Four Cardinal Principles and challenging the foundations of totalitarianism. It was these social forces that Deng aimed to target through the Principles. This created a deep contradiction between the reform's goal and practice, a contradiction that has been overwhelming since the inception of the reform.

There is no evidence that a communist totalitarian regime can save itself by launching reforms. However, China experienced short-term success with reform. The efficacy of using reform to preserve the communist regime in the short run hinges on whether it can alleviate the various constraints hindering economic development, particularly those pertaining to private property and enterprises.

While Deng was preoccupied with combating spiritual pollution and bourgeois liberalization and with deploying troops to suppress students in Beijing, the newly established SEZ in Shenzhen and spontaneously emerging private businesses in areas like Wenzhou began to grow. These entities overcame substantial challenges and risks inherited from the system. Their progress was inseparable from the entrepreneurs' diligence and the risks taken by local party-state authorities motivated by self-interest.[6] Ironically, the incentives for local party-state authorities to actively participate in reform, along with their capacity, resources, and administrative powers, were facilitated by the very system they were trying to reform, the RADT system. This irony not only revealed the inherent contradiction but also intrinsically set the limit of the reform. Meanwhile, Deng's Four Cardinal Principles served as the explicit declaration of this limit.

Within the SEZs, where special policies were allowed for private business, it was less challenging to develop the private sector. Dealing with the huge challenge, outside of the SEZs, many local authorities, exemplified by those in Wenzhou, clandestinely facilitated the development of private enterprises in their regions. They crafted protections for private firms, even though they were not legal. Even after the Tiananmen Massacre, under the enormous pressure of the anti-bourgeois liberalization movement, these regions covertly supported the growth of private and foreign enterprises. Ironically, it was these developments that provided Deng with an opportunity to witness and support Shenzhen's rapid growth during his Southern Tour, furnishing the call for economic reform with specific implementation rather than mere rhetoric. But Deng never recognized Wenzhou's achievements in the private sector due to the intrinsic capitalistic nature of that development.

13.3 TOWARDS REGIONALLY DECENTRALIZED AUTHORITARIANISM

While both China and the Eastern bloc countries initiated economic reforms in an attempt to salvage their totalitarian systems, the strategies they adopted were different and so were the outcomes. Soviet and Eastern European reforms, which were unable to touch upon the issue of ownership, failed to reverse the economic decline and eventually led to the collapse of the totalitarian system. In contrast, China, which initially had closely followed the Eastern bloc after the CR, managed to reverse the economic downturn through its reforms, aiding the survival of its regime. The "miracle" here lies in China's relaxation of ownership restrictions, including partially opening up to capital from developed countries and regions and allowing the development of private enterprises in China. However, even partial relaxation of restrictions on private ownership contradicted the ideology of communist totalitarianism and, in effect, at the cost of relinquishing some of the party-state's power and monopolies.

In contrast to the Eastern bloc regimes, the CCP's approach was twofold: on the one hand, it suppressed citizens' demands for human rights more severely and brutally; on the other hand, it unintentionally allowed the development of a private economy and pragmatically relaxed restrictions on property rights, something the Eastern bloc did not do. The former strategy ensured that sufficient fear was instilled to suppress dissenting voices, while the latter facilitated economic growth.

Though at first glance this combination may seem like a perfect strategy to ensure the survival of CCP rule, it presents a self-contradictory approach from both the institutional and ideological perspectives. Developing private enterprises to save communist totalitarianism is an unsustainable paradox in the long run. Eventually, either the communist totalitarian regime will be loosened and shaken as an outcome of such a strategy or the private sector will be crushed. Yet, the CCP's propaganda machine spun this apparent inconsistency as "socialism with Chinese characteristics," falsely crediting Deng with inventing market socialism.[7] It praised him for his strategic foresight and pragmatism, lauding him as the chief architect of reform.

In fact, the CCP consciously prepared to exert control over the private sector. Any discussion of privatization was strictly forbidden and private enterprises were not even permitted to be labeled as "private"; instead, they were labeled as *minqi*, people's enterprises.[8] The term *minqi*, officially used to this day, was an attempt to blur the line between private and collective enterprises to provide ideological cover for the former to develop. Contrary to the CCP propaganda and popular belief, the rapid growth of China's private economy was neither a strategic design by Deng nor a calculated move by the CCP. Rather, the emergence of this "miracle" – a term that contradicts communist principles – was closely tied to the party's urgent need for economic revitalization following the catastrophe of the CR. It was also intrinsically linked to the mechanisms stemming from the RADT system, which enabled the totalitarian regime in China to exhibit a greater degree of flexibility and adaptability.

Like any totalitarian system, RADT operates under a strictly top-down party-state bureaucratic structure, governing appointments, supervision, and execution. However, a unique feature of this regime is the control local party-state authorities exert over their self-contained local economies, from the provincial to the county level. This control has established a foundation for regional experimentation and competition. For more than three decades after 1979 – excluding the period from 1989 to 1992 – the CCP adhered to Deng's Four Cardinal Principles and his declaration that "development is the absolute priority." This approach was taken as the party's fundamental strategy, with a primary focus on fostering economic growth as a means to sustain the regime. Accordingly, the career advancement of party-state officials at all subnational levels depends on the growth rates of the areas under their jurisdictions relative to other areas. This mechanism, known as yardstick competition, provides high-powered incentives for local officials (Qian and Xu, 1993; Maskin, Qian, and Xu, 2000; Li and Zhou, 2005). Driven by this mechanism, many local governments took the initiative to find ways to facilitate local economic development, even experimenting with risky ways to disguise and protect local private enterprises (Xu, 2011).

Prior to the mid-1990s, the CCP's reform policies were focused mainly on the state sector and they explicitly prohibited private enterprises from employing more than eight people, a restriction derived from Marx's *Capital*. This constraint posed serious obstacles to reform, turning the state sector into not only a hindrance to economic growth but also a threat to stability. Meanwhile, the massive expansion of TVEs, which were legally recognized as collective enterprises but mixed with many private firms, became the driving force of the economy. Under the yardstick competition principle, in areas like Wenzhou where collective ownership was less developed, local governments permitted private enterprises to disguise themselves as

TVEs, fostering growth in the private sector and stimulating local economic development. Witnessing that such "experiments" spurred economic growth and the career advancement of local leaders, many local governments followed suit, facilitating the disguised development of private enterprises in their regions. Despite the absence of legal recognition, the de facto private economy thrived and became the main driving force for the economy (Huang, 2008).

In the first two decades of reform, China's SOE reform floundered, much like the Soviet and European economic reforms on the eve of the collapse. Heavy loss-making was widespread among SOEs after a series of ineffective reforms, and many cities faced a fiscal crisis due to losses incurred by their local SOEs. In response to these challenges, some municipalities de facto privatized state assets under the banner of *"gaizhi,"* an official term for the restructuring of SOEs. This maneuver allowed local governments to address financial troubles, mirroring the local shielding of private businesses. With China grappling with precarious economic circumstances and SOE indebtedness causing widespread concern, both local and central governments were desperate for solutions. Driven by this urgency, Premier Zhu Rongji and Jiang Zemin endorsed these locally initiated "experiments" of SOE privatization nationwide, again under the guise of *gaizhi*.

Significantly, the policy of "grasping the large and letting go of the small" (*zhuada fangxiao*) was officially introduced at the 15th CCP Congress in 1997. Under this policy, local party-states' de facto ownership of their SOEs became their de jure rights, empowering local authorities to privatize local SOEs, particularly those of small and medium size. Nevertheless, privatization as an ideological taboo remained unaltered and it had to be framed as *gaizhi*. The CCP's focus was on *zhuada* (grasping the large), with *fangxiao* (letting go of the small) considered merely as a temporary crisis management measure. However, in reality, it was only the *fangxiao* that yielded substantial results. Under the impetus of yardstick competition, local governments privatized vast quantities of local state assets within a few years. From 1997 to 2005, the scale of state assets sold under the guise of *gaizhi* in China surpassed any privatization process ever seen globally (Xu, 2011).

As the rapid growth of de novo private firms and privatization gained momentum, by the time China was on the brink of joining the WTO, the majority of its economy had transitioned to private ownership. This transformation in property rights structure alleviated the economic strain created by the state-owned enterprises' SBC issue, effectively enhancing China's financial and fiscal foundations and paving the way for subsequent rapid growth.

The widespread presence of private enterprises in China had evolved into a fait accompli and their vital role in the economy had become undeniable. This reality prompted the CCP to modify its regulations and corresponding laws to confer legal status on private businesses. In a significant shift, the CCP constitution formally acknowledged the social status of entrepreneurs in 2002. Two years later, in 2004, the state constitution officially recognized private property rights. These landmark amendments to the party and state constitutions were part of a broader legislative overhaul focusing on property rights protection and contract enforcement. Of particular note was the establishment of civil codes, a first under communist rule.

In addition to the burgeoning private sector, the urgent need to lure foreign investment and cultivate the securities market were two other vital catalysts leading the CCP to recognize private enterprises and endeavor to establish civil codes. When the central government gave a green light to the formation of SEZs in places like Shenzhen in the early 1980s to attract foreign investment, it quickly faced challenges due to China's fundamental lack of civil codes and legal protections for foreign investments. The push to develop financial markets since the late 1980s stumbled upon similar substantial obstacles. Being a platform for trading property rights, the growth of the securities market is inherently tied to the legal safeguarding of private property rights and the guarantee of contract enforcement.

The formal recognition of private property rights, together with the establishment of civil codes to enforce them, was not only an unprecedented move under CCP rule but also unparalleled in other communist countries. Thus, this marked a de facto institutional evolution toward a more lenient authoritarian regime, allowing limited growth of private property rights and fostering a degree of ideological and social pluralism.

However, it is crucial to note that the CCP never intended to replace communist totalitarianism with capitalist authoritarianism, even though debates on the concept of authoritarianism did indeed emerge during the mid-to-late 1980s. Confronted with the complexities of SOE reform, the failures of the reforms in the Eastern bloc, and Gorbachev's sweeping political-economic changes, Deng and Zhao broached the topic of political reform in 1986. Although their intent was confined to administrative reform, it sparked heated debates within and outside the CCP between factions advocating for democracy and those endorsing "new authoritarianism," a view that found favor with Deng and Zhao.[9]

Constrained by the Four Cardinal Principles, proponents of democracy did not dare to challenge the one-party totalitarian rule or propose a multiparty system. Instead, they explored more conservative possibilities, such as allowing factions within the party and conducting intraparty elections. Deng was open to examining authoritarianism as a means to maintain CCP rule but he never signaled a willingness to relinquish totalitarianism or to ease the party's core control. These debates came to an abrupt end with the 1989 crackdown and any further discussion on the subject became taboo.

Despite the de facto shift toward a somewhat more relaxed authoritarian system, the CCP never relinquished its ultimate control over power, striving to maintain a totalitarian regime. The party retained unchallenged authority over the legislature, the judiciary, all branches of government, the armed forces, and the police. Additionally, it monopolized the economy's vital sectors, the so-called commanding heights in the words of Lenin and Deng, including finance, land, energy, and key industries.

The CCP's continued efforts to control every facet of society were still far-reaching, implementing mandatory censorship in all fields. The kinds of political and ideological debates that existed in the 1980s were no longer tolerated. Even purely academic discussions were strictly confined within the bounds of the Four Cardinal Principles, while relatively pluralistic discourse was mainly limited to technical fields.

The suppression of dissent was routine, with arrests and house arrests of political dissidents becoming commonplace. Notably, Liu Xiaobo, who was imprisoned for advocating constitutional rule, became the only Nobel laureate to die in prison without receiving his prize (Link and Wu, 2023). The CCP also cracked down on various religious groups and beliefs, suppressing Falun Gong practitioners and communities in all provinces, including Tibet and Xinjiang, without regard to ethnicity or region.

Nonetheless, reform and opening-up led to a massive influx of foreign capital, a surge in private enterprises, and rapid establishment and expansion of markets. Most economic activities in China turned into market-based (or semi-market based), private-enterprise activities. The vast majority of the national workforce was employed in the private sector, including NGOs. For a period of time, the absence of party cells in most private businesses and NGOs meant that the party did not have direct control over most organizations in China, an unprecedented challenge since the establishment of the totalitarian regime.

This limited pluralism in the economic field simultaneously fostered limited pluralism in other areas, such as education, media, and civil society. Economics, law, political science, sociology, and other social sciences and humanities, which are closely connected with business and the economy, developed significantly amidst careful self-censorship. Many of these disciplines were developed virtually from scratch, as they had been banned generations earlier. Ideas once criticized as bourgeois became mainstream in universities and academic circles.

The period also saw the emergence of private universities and business schools that attracted senior professors from prestigious

13.3 TOWARDS REGIONALLY DECENTRALIZED AUTHORITARIANISM 625

overseas institutions with competitive salaries. These institutions provided high-quality teaching and research independent of the CCP's education system. The party's direct control over content in academia and higher education also shrank for a time, with its focus shifting to personnel decisions and the censorship system. Meanwhile, commercial media independent of the CCP's propaganda system thrived, transitioning from mere commercial news providers to mainstream media outlets covering a wide range of fields.

In the wake of the significant growth of private enterprises, NGOs emerged and developed rapidly. The proliferation of NGOs in society allowed Chinese citizens to organize openly and voluntarily to safeguard their interests or to aid others for the first time since the founding of the PRC, albeit with self-censorship so as not to offend the CCP, as they were all monitored by the party. Such organizations were found, for a while, in various fields, including education, scientific research, and even in the sphere of promoting township and village elections. Increasingly, many overseas NGOs entered China as well, serving the Chinese and collaborating with Chinese NGOs. The population not only began to experience some characteristics of civil society but the term "civil society" also became widespread for a time.

However, regardless of how careful the NGOs had been in imposing self-censorship, the very existence of NGOs was a fundamental challenge to the totalitarian rule over society. Through the Ministry of Civil Affairs, the United Front Work Department, the Ministry of Public Security, and other departments, the CCP maintained close scrutiny and control over the operation and development of NGOs to prevent the formation of a civil society truly independent of the CCP. It mandated that all NGOs, and their activities and donations, must be non-political. At the 5th Plenary Session of the 16th CCP's Central Committee in 2005, it reiterated the policy to "strengthen the supervision of NGOs."

The CCP mandated that all NGOs must register with the Ministry of Civil Affairs. This ministry combined non-state bodies with some peripheral official agencies, such as those responsible for social welfare and religion, and labeled them as "social organizations," or *shehui zuzhi*. Part of the motivation for doing this was because the name NGO sent a signal of independence from party-state control. As of 2017, there were 762,000 registered social organizations nationwide, with recorded social donations amounting to 152.6 billion RMB (Zhu, 2020). The vast majority of these social organizations were NGOs and most of the donations came from private enterprises. In fact, there was a much larger number of unregistered but functioning community-based spontaneous organizations, such as homeowners' associations.

Control over NGOs has been significantly further tightened since 2017. This led to a substantial decrease in donations and a significant slowdown in the growth of NGOs (Zhu, 2020). Under these strict restrictions, most NGOs operating outside the realm of charity either transitioned into solely charitable operations or ceased activities altogether, with many being disbanded. The CCP intentionally confined NGOs to charitable roles, turning them into social welfare auxiliaries of the Ministry of Civil Affairs. These restrictions were aimed at downgrading the NGOs' roles in defending citizens' interests and weakening most NGOs' functions in representing citizens' pursuits. In short, the limited pluralism that emerged during the reform period was for a time conditionally tolerated as a last resort to save the totalitarian system through economic development. Simultaneously, the CCP has always been highly vigilant against pluralism in areas such as property rights, private enterprises, NGOs, ideologies, and so on, ensuring that all of these areas remain under its control. The party has taken steps to contain pluralism, preventing it from ever threatening its monopolistic total power.

13.4 SUCCESSION IN TOTALITARIAN PARTIES

From the CCP's standpoint, being able to maintain its total control over society determines its survival. Xi Jinping's numerous repetitions of Mao's famous phrase, "the party leads everything," is a warning to the party and society in the context that the CCP was loosening its grip on society. But the more imminent challenging issue facing the totalitarian party's sustaining of power is its succession, which is created by the nature of the regime.

A totalitarian party controls all aspects of society, including all resources. Its supreme leader, or the Leader, relies on his personality cult and violence to control the party and society. However, a personality cult is not something that can be easily passed from one leader to another to facilitate succession. Given the complete eradication of checks and balances both within and outside the party, the Leader possesses absolute power. In the history of the CCP, only Mao Zedong and Deng Xiaoping have been recognized as such Leaders. Mao aspired to be worshipped enduringly so that his spirit would forever rule China and influence the world. Deng Xiaoping, a longtime close follower of Mao (each step of his rise in the CCP was facilitated by Mao's promotion), was perceived as saving the CCP through reform and opening-up. At the same time, he maintained Mao's spiritual status and established a different type of personality cult for himself, one that set him apart as a unique figure within the party's history.

Personality cults are a joint product of the system and of a leader's personal characteristics. From Lenin–Stalin to Mao–Deng, the personality cult was constructed by the totalitarian party's inner circle at the pinnacle of power, using myths and terror. On the one hand, this group acquired power by following the leader; on the other hand, the charismatic leader controlled the party and society through them. The leader's power is inextricably linked to theirs, and vice versa. For a party that controls everything, it is not difficult to pass on nominal rulership from one generation to the next. However, it is challenging to bequeath a personality cult by decree and by granting power to a chosen successor. Therefore, all totalitarian states suffer from succession crises upon the death of a leader who rules with a personality cult. Deng designated Jiang Zemin and Hu Jintao as his successors after the purge of Hu Yaobang and Zhao Ziyang.

Deng's well-established personality cult cemented their legitimacy and they continued the Deng line after he was gone. However, a succession crisis can only temporarily be averted in this way.

Aware of the challenge posed by the succession crisis, Deng tried to preserve the party by establishing a system of collective leadership, along with a mechanism for limiting the tenure of leaders based on age, by leveraging his personality cult and paramount leadership position. However, in a totalitarian system without checks and balances of power, the implementation of any mechanistic rule must rely on the paramount leader's self-restraint. The latter condition was violated by Deng himself as he did not exert self-constraint after his nominal retirement (Zhao, 2009).

Fundamentally, both limited tenure and collective leadership are incompatible with totalitarian rule and therefore unsustainable. A totalitarian party is stable only if it has established a personality cult around its leader. When this type of party is controlled by several oligarchs under the guise of collective leadership, internal power struggles always destabilize it. This is because, although the power of any top leader is nominally assigned by the totalitarian party, real power is acquired through power struggles. This was true for Stalin, Mao, Deng, and their followers. Without checks on power, the internal power struggle becomes never-ending and ruthless. At the very top, anyone who gains control can dominate the party and society, even controlling the life and death of everyone. In a life-and-death struggle for power, the more power the top leader holds, the greater his incentive and capability to dismantle the so-called collective leadership and tenure system to seize even more power.

With the personality cult and absolute power that he enjoyed both within and outside the party, the limited tenure and collective leadership systems under Deng's rule were merely decorative (Zhao, 2009). In reality, the top leadership positions of Jiang and Hu were only nominal for an extended period. When it came to major decisions, Jiang had to defer to Deng and Hu had to defer to Jiang. Their de facto powers were more focused on implementation, so they never had a chance to establish a personality cult of their own. Thus, on the surface, it appeared as though the party was practicing limited tenure and collective leadership. However, the power struggle inherent in the regime eroded the relative stability of the system that the CCP had re-established in the post-Mao era.

Xi Jinping, who does not have a direct connection to Deng's power but was cultivated and promoted within the CCP system due to his father's position in the party, ascended to power by forming alliances with various political forces. Upon reaching the top, he quickly and openly abolished the decorative collective leadership system, using the Bo Xilai-Zhou Yongkang affair as a cover. Then, imitating Mao's Yan'an Rectification and Four Cleanups campaigns, he launched an anti-corruption initiative to purge all those whom he perceived as political rivals, including many who had supported him in his rise to power.

According to an official source, in Xi's first term, that is, between 2012 and 2017, hundreds of thousands of party-state bureaucrats were purged, including one at the state level, six at the vice-state level, two central military commissioners, and several dozen ministerial-rank cadres. A total of 440 cadres at the vice-provincial and vice-army-corps-commander military level or above were placed under investigation, including 43 at or above the level of alternate members of the 18th Central Committee and 9 members of the Central Commission for Discipline Inspection. More than 8,900 cadres at prefecture-and-bureau levels, 63,000 at county-and-division levels, and 278,000 other grassroots cadres were investigated.[10]

In addition to purging political rivals, Xi and his followers repeatedly attempted to establish his personality cult through propaganda and by intimidating leading cadres at all levels. In a totalitarian party with no checks on power, it is easy to dismantle collective leadership and limited tenure. However, establishing a new leadership with a personality cult is another matter. Lacking achievements and relying only on terror, intimidation, and empty-worded propaganda, charisma cannot be demonstrated even within the small circle at the top of power. For several years, efforts by Xi and his aides to create a personality cult for him have proved ineffective and often counterproductive. Every clumsy attempt to mimic the Cultural Revolution has been met with strong backlash both inside and outside the party. A totalitarian regime incapable of building a personality cult will become a degenerating regime. Similar to the Soviet Union during the Brezhnev era, the party-state bureaucrats in such a system are generally alienated, afraid to raise issues and to solve problems, thus further destabilizing the degenerating totalitarian system.

13.5 THE EVOLUTION OF OPPOSING INSTITUTIONAL GENES DURING THE REFORM PROCESS

> The party exercises leadership in everything, in every area of endeavor and every corner of the country.
>
> —Mao Zedong (1968);[11] Xi Jinping (2012, in Lin, H. et al., 2022)

"The party exercises leadership over everything" reflects the most fundamental part of the institutional genes of communist totalitarianism. These institutional genes manifest as a trinity structure (see Chapter 1, Figure 1.1). Its core component is the party bureaucracy, which rules the whole society with no separation between the party and all branches of the government, including the legislature and judiciary. Supporting this core component are the base and control components. As the base component, complete state ownership of the means of production serves as the property rights and jurisprudential foundation for the party-state.[12] The control component ensures that the party controls the entire society, including the bureaucracy's personnel and ideology.

Although the fundamental institutional nature of the RADT system is no different from the classic communist totalitarian system, its governing mechanism is different. Concretely, regional decentralization is the key difference. In the RADT regime, within each of the core components of the trinity structure of the totalitarian institutional genes, there are similar administrative functions at each regional level of the structure, from the central to every local level. This self-contained structure, complemented by decentralized resources, enables the superiors to control their subordinates primarily through their control over personnel, party line, and ideology, instead of issuing concrete, quantified orders directly, like their counterparts in the Soviet Union.

13.5.1 The Evolving RADT/RDA Institutional Genes

In the early stages of the reform, as China's system unintentionally and gradually evolved towards relatively looser authoritarianism, each component underwent some changes, although the basic structure of the institutional genes remained intact. The most significant change was in the base component, where private enterprises became the main pillar of the national economy albeit still being controlled by the party-state. Even without looking at the political and legal aspects, the state ownership of land, banking, and upstream sectors ensured that the party-state at all levels could maintain control over the economic commanding heights, thus controlling the economy and obtaining ample resources to support the operation of the party-state bureaucracy. That is, this part of the institutional genes of communist totalitarianism was not fundamentally shaken, although on the surface the change was significant.

As for the core component, there was a time when hundreds of millions of people working in non-SOEs and NGOs were without party organizations and the party-state could not directly exert control over such social organizations. However, the one-party system's bureaucracy still controlled the entire society through its complete monopoly of the armed forces and the judicial system.

In terms of the control component, for a while the party could no longer directly control most personnel of non-SOEs or NGOs through appointment and promotion, let alone the ideology within those entities. During that period, newly emerged non-state media were not entirely under the party's direct control, although they were subject to the party's strict censorship requirements. Nevertheless, in addition to maintaining direct control over the personnel and the main body of the ideology of the party-state bureaucracy, the judiciary, and the armed forces, the party-state retained many other means, such as the police, the secret police, and censorship, to ensure its control over society.

13.5.2 Emerging New Institutional Genes

Along with the development of private enterprises, private property rights have become widespread in Chinese society. Most of China's employment is in the private sector, 96 percent of urban households live in owner-occupied housing, and real estate accounts for 59 percent of urban household assets (Chowdhury, 2022). Although entrepreneurs and real estate owners do not own the property rights to the land they use, they do own the property rights to the enterprises and houses. Awareness of property rights and the importance of protecting one's rights have been initially formed in the minds of many Chinese.

Many private companies and property owners have sought to protect their rights and seek social influence, leading to a boom in chambers of commerce, charities, media, and private schools. When the government infringes upon the rights and interests of the public, an increasing number of property owners, entrepreneurs, and farmers, backed by lawyers and public opinion, defend their basic rights based on newly enacted civil codes. In intellectual and business circles, the appeal of the rule of law and constitutionalism is on the rise.

Although political repression has increased since 1989, with most people choosing not to involve themselves in politics, and with the arrest of dissident figures like Liu Xiaobo making constitutional governance a forbidden topic of discussion, the substantive changes are significant. A large number of non-SOEs and NGOs have started to claim their rights under the law and pluralism has been rapidly developing. New institutional genes have arisen and grown in various ways, reflecting a shift in societal values and expectations that may have far-reaching implications for China's governance and social fabric.

Had private property rights been extended to the land, banking, and upstream sectors so that their resources were no longer monopolized by the party, the base component of the totalitarian institutional genes would have been shaken. If the majority of businesses and organizations had been allowed to become independent, citizen-run entities, so that most Chinese were no longer directly controlled by the party, the core component of the totalitarian institutional genes would have changed. Had most of the personnel and ideological matters been removed from party control, the control component of totalitarian institutional genes would have been substantially weakened. Had all these changes been allowed to evolve naturally, new institutional genes would have flourished, driving China away from totalitarianism or even from one-party-rule authoritarianism. Such a transformation would potentially have set the country on a path towards constitutional democracy.

Modernization theory, once popular in academia and Western political circles, posits that the growth of the middle class and economic development will eventually lead to constitutional democracy. The evolution of China's totalitarian system towards an authoritarian regime at one point seemed to validate that theory. However, the development and survival of any new institutional genes inevitably face resistance from the old ones, driven by the vested interests of the old regime. Thus, establishing a constitutional democracy is never an automatic outcome of economic development; instead, it depends on the strength of the new institutional genes supporting such a system and on their ability to overcome the old institutional genes' resistance to change. The power of the old institutional genes and their capacity to protect the old regime are often deeply rooted and should not be overlooked. This is particularly true in a totalitarian regime.

13.5.3 Endeavors to Control and Contain Emerging New Institutional Genes

Given the fundamental purpose of the CCP's economic reform has always been to preserve totalitarianism, the party has consistently been highly vigilant against anything that might undermine its system. It has never allowed new institutional genes conducive to an evolution towards the rule of law and constitutionalism to develop, always prioritizing prevention of what they call "peaceful evolution" and "color revolutions" over economic concerns. The principles upheld by Deng Xiaoping both before and after the Tiananmen Massacre, as well as during his Southern Tour, remain unchanged. Nor was there any alteration in Jiang Zemin's principles before and after Deng's Southern Tour. All the changes or seemingly contradictory measures and the presence of the so-called reformists or conservatives within the CCP were merely different strategies adopted to ensure the same goal: the survival of totalitarianism.

As previously mentioned, China's large-scale privatization occurred under the CCP policy of *zhuada fangxiao*, implemented in response to the failure of SOE reform. However, the emphasis of this policy was on developing large-scale SOEs, not on privatization. For this purpose, the CCP specifically established the State-owned Assets Supervision and Administration Commission. Representing the interests of state-owned assets, SASAC has always been a staunch force resisting the privatization of SOEs, working to consolidate and enhance the status of SOEs. Since private enterprises have been allowed to develop, the Commission has spared no effort in emphasizing the fundamental principle that state assets are the foundation of CCP rule. This statement became an important component of Xi Jinping's ideology.

While the surge in the private sector has saved the communist regime by revitalizing the Chinese economy and keeping it on track for rapid economic growth, CCP vigilance has increased dramatically. Apart from worrying that the private sector would overtake the state sector in the economy, the party leaders were particularly concerned about the lack of a party presence in the non-SOEs and NGOs, which were springing up like mushrooms after a spring rain, and where the majority of entrepreneurs were not party members. The fact that businesses and organizations employing hundreds of millions of people across the country were not under the direct control of the party constituted a challenge the CCP had never encountered since taking power.

The continuous recruitment of new members and establishment of new party branches, which Lenin referred to as "party-building," are the lifeblood of a Leninist party. Faced with the decline of party-building and the party's "loss of control" over the private sector and the dilemma between the critical role of the private sector in saving the CCP regime and the fundamental anticapitalist principle of the communist regime, Jiang Zemin proposed the Three Represents theory.[13] This theory legitimized the recruitment of entrepreneurs into the CCP and their participation in the NPC and the CPPCC, helping to reassert the party's control over the burgeoning private sector.

As a reward to those entrepreneurs who joined the party, they were granted preferential treatment in many areas, such as policy, protection, access to land, financing, and other matters. Under this strategy, founders and executives of almost all the largest non-SOEs in China acquiesced to CCP control by demonstrating their loyalty to the party. This "ransom" approach once played a significant role in reversing the decline of party-building in the private sector, ensuring the CCP maintained its influence in a rapidly growing private sector.

However, as the number and importance of private businesses continued to soar, the ever-increasing "ransom" cost made this approach unsustainable. Moreover, as party-member entrepreneurs began to exert their influence within the party and the party-state apparatus, questions arose about who was truly controlling whom. Furthermore, this approach proved ineffective in controlling the pluralism that had developed on many fronts, such as in media, academia, and civil society. One of the key issues was the growing discussions, voices, and actions related to the rule of law and constitutionalism. During the Hu Jintao era (2002–2012), the CCP was already becoming alert to these developments.

An example of such alertness is a stark warning issued by the Chinese Academy of Social Sciences (CASS), a subordinate of the

CCP's Propaganda Department, in its Global Security Report in 2006, about the danger that "color revolutions" could pose to the CCP regime. The report argued that the democratic electoral system with a separation of powers was the basic condition for the occurrence of a color revolution (Li and Wang, 2006).

Such warnings were swiftly translated into official actions. At the 2nd Session of the 11th NPC, Wu Bangguo, the chairman of the Standing Committee, proposed five "no-go" measures. These prohibitions effectively banned discussions on multiparty systems, ideological pluralism, separation of powers, bicameralism, federalism, and privatization within the party and the broader public sphere. A few years later, these prohibitions were embraced by Xi Jinping as part of his broader political philosophy, officially referred to as "Xi Jinping Thought."

With the strengthening of party-state power, the old institutional genes have been revitalized. After the global financial crisis of 2008, the CCP's confidence surged, dramatically strengthening its control in every sphere. From 2012 onwards, these old institutional genes struck back with renewed ferocity, eventually suppressing growth of new system genes in all areas.

13.5.4 *Reverse the Course: Reinstate Totalitarian Control*

Transforming from a communist totalitarian regime towards an authoritarian regime was never intentional; in fact, the CCP was deeply worried when it realized this evolutionary trend. Over the years, frustration and vigilance towards "bourgeois liberalization" had accumulated among the upper echelons of the CCP and they found a representative in Xi Jinping. Shortly after becoming general secretary of the CCP in late 2012, Xi mimicked Deng Xiaoping's Southern Tour by visiting Shenzhen. Like Deng twenty years earlier, Xi's main concern was to prevent China from experiencing a collapse similar to that of the Soviet Union.

However, the difference between Xi and Deng lies in the timing, and their perceptions, diagnoses, and strategies. In Deng's time, China

13.5 THE EVOLUTION OF OPPOSING INSTITUTIONAL GENES 637

was in the wake of the Tiananmen crackdown and was desperately poor. Deng believed that the CCP had adequately controlled society through force and terror and that the failure of economic reform or collapse of the economy posed the greatest threat to the party's fate. To address this, he strived to repair relationships with the United States and other developed countries.

By the time Xi took power, China had become the second-largest economy in the world, driven by the private sector and exports to the advanced economies. Xi believed that China's economy was incredibly strong and would soon surpass the United States to become the largest in the world. However, he was concerned about the prevailing influence of private businesses and NGOs in society. Unlike post-Tiananmen-Massacre Deng, who focused on economic considerations, Xi saw ideological heresy and disloyalty within the party and the military as the critical factors that had led to the Soviet Union's fall.

With deep concerns about the direction in which China had been evolving, Xi claimed that the Soviet Union collapsed because there was "not a single real man" among its leaders and called for the CCP to return to traditional Leninism (Buckley, 2013). A few months later, Xi made a speech stating, "The collapse of a regime often starts in the realm of ideology ... regime can change overnight ... Once the ideological front is breached, other defenses will be hard to hold. We must firmly grasp the leadership of ideological work ... or we will commit irreversible historical mistakes."[14] Xi emphasized that China's reform "must not make subversive mistakes on fundamental issues, and once they occur, they are irretrievable and irreparable" (Xi, 2013b).

Over a year later, Xi specifically pointed out, "Western countries plotting color revolutions often start from attacking the political system, particularly the party systems, of their targeted countries" (Xi, 2022). The official CCP interpretation of Xi's thoughts stated that the Soviet Union's collapse was a "subversive mistake" in which the country was sacrificed for the sake of the economy.

From 2013 onwards, step by step and surely, the CCP reversed the evolving trend of the past decades, fully reinstating its totalitarian control in all sectors of mainland China. This reversal was a daunting task, as it ran against China's main growth engine, the private sector, hurt employment, and destabilized the economy. The reason it was possible to accomplish this under Xi's leadership is that he represents a force in the party and society at large and he controls the RADT machine. This institutional foundation in China has never been shaken.

The CCP thus systematically suppressed private enterprises and NGOs and clamped down on ideological pluralism in media, education, and academia. By 2022, new textbooks guided by CCP ideology were rolled out across all social science areas and new journals were published to fully supplant their Western counterparts. Even academic conferences in purely technical fields like econometrics were turned into fronts for propagating Xi's thinking.

Mao's famous statement during the CR, *"The party exercises leadership in everything, in every area of endeavor and every corner of the country,"* is now at the core of Xi's ideology, forming the basis of the CCP's constitution. More importantly, it has once again become China's reality. The communist totalitarian institutional genes, now evolved with Chinese characteristics, have prevailed across the board. They have crushed the already limited pluralism that had only recently developed to the point where it could only survive underground, wrenching China back into a totalitarian system.

13.5.5 Reversing the Course: From "One Country, Two Systems" to Totalitarian Rule

The great reversal goes beyond reinstating totalitarian rule within mainland China. In 2020, the CCP directly legislated for the control of Hong Kong, effectively abolishing the "one country, two systems" policy. Courts and the police force in Hong Kong must now follow the commands of the CCP. Dissidents have been arrested, demonstrations have been banned, tough censorship has been imposed, media outlets have been forced to close, and NGOs have been dissolved. This is the first time in the history of Hong Kong that totalitarian rule is in the process of being established.

As a former British colony, Hong Kong enjoyed the rule of law, secure private property rights, and a highly developed civil society.[15] These were the institutional foundations that made Hong Kong a world-leading international financial center. In addition to the unique role it played in the greater Chinese economy, particularly in international trade and finance, Hong Kong also made indispensable contributions to China in areas such as corporate management, institutions, capital, and technology during the first three decades of reform. In 1984, the United Kingdom and China signed the Sino-British Joint Declaration, accepting Deng Xiaoping's promise of "one country, two systems." Under the premise that the CCP would guarantee Hong Kong's capitalist system, including an independent judiciary and police force, for fifty years, the United Kingdom returned sovereignty over Hong Kong to China in 1997.

Many anticipated that, given Hong Kong's immense influence on mainland China, China would become like Hong Kong after fifty years. Deng himself had made similar comments. Associated with the policy of attracting investments from Hong Kong, since the post-Mao reform Hong Kong investors, corporations, NGOs, and media outlets have entered and impacted mainland China considerably. Many of China's regulations, particularly those concerning the financial market and regulatory systems, were deeply influenced by or even directly based on Hong Kong's regulations.

However, since the party's primary concern is sustaining the totalitarian system, it has carefully designed a firewall to prevent "harmful" elements such as an independent judiciary, NGOs, and publications and speeches covering a broad range of facts and ideas from impacting the mainland. Activities by Hong Kong NGOs in the mainland have been heavily restricted. Most Hong Kong publications on the humanities and politics are deemed illegal and journalists and booksellers from Hong Kong are frequently detained in China. As a result, Hong Kong's institutional genes have not had much chance to take root in the mainland.

Moreover, since taking over Hong Kong, the CCP has attempted to change the region's institutions and its institutional genes. Beijing has constantly sought to control elections at all levels in Hong Kong through various methods and has endeavored to alter Hong Kong's basic laws. These actions have triggered several large-scale protests, including the Occupy Central movement in 2014. From 2013 to 2015, several Hong Kong booksellers were kidnapped by mainland police within Hong Kong or lured into traps on the mainland because of what they had published, causing widespread fear among Hong Kong citizens.

In early 2019, the Hong Kong government introduced the Fugitive Offenders Bill, allowing mainland China to demand the arrest of suspects in Hong Kong for extradition to the mainland. Fearing losing their freedom and judicial independence, people in Hong Kong spontaneously organized the globally shocking anti-extradition bill protests. Several mass demonstrations involving millions of people were held in the following months. Many believed that Beijing would handle the situation rationally as Hong Kong was China's only international financial center.

However, the CCP not only required the Hong Kong police force to suppress the protests violently but also issued and imposed the Hong Kong National Security Law in 2020, granting Beijing the power to directly control the Hong Kong government and even to dismiss Hong Kong judges. The British government objected, citing a violation of the 1984 Joint Declaration, while the Chinese dismissed it, arguing that the Declaration was an irrelevant historical document. With direct rule from Beijing, Hong Kong steadily adopted the mainland system, most often involuntarily. Many legislators, journalists, media personnel, and dissidents were arrested, and many media and NGOs (including student associations) were forced to shut down or disband. The foundation of Hong Kong as an international

13.6 TOTALITARIAN INSTITUTIONAL CONSTRAINTS ON ECONOMIC GROWTH

financial center was fundamentally shaken. Since then, the institutional genes of Hong Kong have been moving towards those of China.

The collapse of the Eastern bloc totalitarian regimes was caused by political and economic factors, chronic slow growth, and failure in international competition. The question now arises: Can China continue to reform, sustain its high economic growth, and simultaneously retain its totalitarian system? This question is as critical for the future of China as it is for the world. With nearly four times the population of the United States and more than three times that of the EU, the answer has far-reaching global implications.

The Soviet Union, under its totalitarian regime, also experienced rapid growth for three decades following the Second World War. However, once the Soviet Union's per capita GDP reached a third of that of the United States, growth slowed markedly and the nation lost its ability to catch up with the advanced capitalist countries. The failure of the Soviet economic reforms, which strictly forbade private enterprise, became a crucial factor in the downfall of the totalitarian system. The very nature of totalitarianism eventually suffocated the Soviet regime. Can China, which permits limited development of private business, fundamentally differentiate itself from the Soviet Union at that time?

Since the first Industrial Revolution, some backward countries have caught up with the advanced countries mainly by learning from and imitating their practices and technologies (Gerschenkron, 1962). According to this logic, the wider the per capita GDP gap, the more opportunities there are for latecomers to catch up, provided that institutional conditions are comparable (Acemoglu et al., 2006, pp. 37–74).

In the early stages of reform, China, as one of the world's poorest nations, allowed the development of private ownership and emulated the advanced nations, opening the door for over three decades of rapid economic growth. Per capita GDP grew from roughly one-sixteenth that of the United States (and one-sixth that of the Soviet Union) at the onset of reform (Maddison, 2003) to about one-fourth that of the United States by the 2020s (IMF, 2022b). This gap is equivalent to that between Japan and the United States in the late 1960s (Maddison, 2003).

Had China's system allowed and protected the comprehensive development of private enterprises, as Japan did in those days, China might have continued its rapid development, with a possibility of approaching the Japanese level of per capita GDP. However, the Chinese system, transplanted from the Soviet Union and similar in nature, intrinsically limits how far its reform can go. The CCP's intention is to preserve the totalitarian system, and it is unwilling to tolerate further growth of the private sector, even if that growth is vital to the economy. The very survival of the totalitarian system takes precedence over economic considerations, a stance that has profound implications for China's future economic trajectory.

13.6.1 Change of Incentive Mechanisms within the party-state Bureaucracy

Why would China, which relies on the private sector for growth, want to curb private enterprises? To understand the rationale, it is necessary to know the mechanism by which private firms arise under the RADT system. In a totalitarian system, the society is governed in every respect by the party-state bureaucracy. Within the hierarchy of the largest bureaucratic machine in human history, serious problems with incentives exist. Tackling these problems is of paramount importance and must be addressed by any totalitarian regime undergoing reform. The Soviet Union relied on the bureaucracy to design comprehensive top-down targets and assessments to motivate party apparatchiks, yet the ineffectiveness of this approach resulted in a vicious cycle.

Unlike the Soviet system, China's RADT, which is based on the local party-state's control over local administration and resources, can unleash interregional yardstick competition to tackle the incentive problem. Furthermore, the catastrophes of the GLF and CR, along with the resulting extreme poverty, made the CCP more desperate for economic development as a basis for the legitimacy of its rule. When economic development was seen as the key to salvaging totalitarianism and it became the primary indicator for determining career advancement, regional yardstick competition incited considerable motivation among local officials, propelling economic development. Under such high-powered incentives, some officials risked sheltering private enterprises to promote local economic growth, and regional competition drove others to follow suit. The extremely fast growth of the private sector under these unique conditions saved the Chinese economy and the CCP regime at the turn of the twentieth and twenty-first centuries (Xu, 2011).

Yet, after three decades of rapid growth, when China became the world's second-largest economy, and given that its ultimate goal of economic reform has been to salvage the totalitarian system, the CCP's greatest concerns inevitably shifted to preventing peaceful evolution or a color revolution when feeling safe or even powerful economically. Moreover, the incentives of the party-state bureaucracy have shifted as well. The loyalty of party-state bureaucrats at all levels has taken on greater importance and become more critical. Since the first decade of the twenty-first century, the CCP has gradually downplayed, if not abandoned altogether, regional yardstick competition, the incentive mechanism that led to the "China miracle." Instead, it has introduced a series of evaluation targets, including party loyalty, social stability, and environmental protection, among others, in addition to economic development. The intrinsic problem with regional yardstick competition is that it only works when there is a single competing objective. When local officials are evaluated by multiple targets, regional competition is no longer effective (Xu, 2019). This change in incentive mechanisms turned the incentive problem faced by China's party-state bureaucracy back to the similar but grave problems once faced by Eastern bloc totalitarian systems.

As a result, since the 2010s local officials at all levels have gradually lost their drive for economic development, not to mention the devastating impact of the anti-corruption campaign since 2013.

13.6.2 The Fate of the Private Sector

If private enterprises, relatively independent of party-state bureaucracy in business decisions and operations, had continued to grow significantly and become the true mainstay of the economy, the bureaucratic incentive problem would not have significantly impacted China's economy. However, the CCP has always feared that the ever-enlarging private sector would eventually shake up the foundations of totalitarian rule and it has always kept a tight rein on private enterprises. As early as private enterprises first gained legal status, the phenomenon of *guojin mintui* ("the state sector advances, the private sector retreats") was already in place. At that time, this phenomenon was driven not only by the discrimination of private enterprises by both party-state authorities at all levels and SOEs (especially state-owned banks) out of their own interests but also by the central authority's policy of "grasping the large" that systematically excluded private enterprises from the commanding heights of the economy. In fact, the "grasping the large" policy was simply a new expression of "occupying the commanding heights of the economy" in the Lenin–Deng New Economic Policy. When some private enterprises grew into the world's largest multinational corporations with a significant impact both domestically and internationally, the CCP became even more concerned about the challenge they posed. To alleviate the party's concerns, the founding entrepreneurs of several large private firms publicly declared that their "property and their lives belong to the party" (Liang, 2012).

What has happened to China's e-commerce companies since 2020 testifies to the CCP's priority: controlling big private businesses at the expense of the economy. This priority is fully consistent with the Lenin–Deng prescription for occupying the "commanding heights of the economy." E-commerce, being at the core of the new economy,

13.6 TOTALITARIAN CONSTRAINTS ON ECONOMIC GROWTH 645

was completely dominated by private entrepreneurs due to the CCP's failure to predict its importance during its emergence.

When e-commerce entities like Amazon and Google first emerged in the United States, nobody could have predicted the scale and impact of this new economy. The CCP could neither predict nor strategically place state-owned enterprises to occupy these future commanding heights in advance. Coincidentally, the emergence of e-commerce occurred at a time when private enterprises in China were just beginning to have an opportunity to develop quickly. At that time, the party-state authority considered the emerging e-commerce as an inconsequential downstream and service-oriented industry, so the development of private enterprises in these areas was not restricted. Private enterprises like Alibaba and Tencent[16] took this opportunity to grow very rapidly, quickly building a huge new economy in China, capturing its commanding heights, and becoming some of the biggest e-commerce corporations in the world.

Entrepreneurs who understand the demands and pressures of the CCP regime voluntarily submit to the party's leadership and proactively serve the party, and many have even established party cells within their firms. However, this is far from sufficient. From the CCP's perspective, a particularly pressing issue is that e-commerce has created commanding heights in the new economy, which are completely in the hands of private entrepreneurs. The party's first step towards total control over these sectors has been to contain the largest non-state firms in this sector.

Among the commanding heights of the new economy, the foremost area is e-finance, as it has deeply eroded the traditional finance sector, which was firmly controlled by the party-state. Following the international trend of e-finance, companies like Ant Finance-Alibaba and Tencent developed e-finance services in China. These services overcame many drawbacks of the state-monopolized banking sector, transforming some retail financial services into a rapidly expanding part of the new economy. While the CCP still maintains a firm grip on the national financial sector, it is concerned that non-state-owned e-commerce could encroach on, and even undermine, the traditional commanding heights of finance.

In order to control and weaken non-state-owned e-commerce enterprises, from 2020 onwards, regulatory authorities such as the Cyber Administration of China (CAC), the State Administration for Market Regulation (SAMR), and the Securities Regulatory Commission have collaborated with state media to launch a comprehensive campaign to promote rectification against private companies in the e-commerce sector.[17]

On November 20, 2021, SAMR filed cases against almost all the big non-state-owned e-commerce platforms in China, including Alibaba, Tencent, Meituan, Didi, JD.com, Baidu, and Tiktok.[18] In early 2022, the CAC issued a document claiming that they handled 166 million online violations nationwide in 2021. Two incidents in the campaign shook the global financial world. One is the CCP's calling-off of what would have been the largest IPO (initial public offering) in world history by Ant Group; the other is the harsh penalties imposed on Didi Global shortly after its IPO on the New York Stock Exchange.

The systematic punishment and massive smear campaign against private e-commerce companies have shaken investor confidence, leading to significant losses in both growth and global competitiveness for China. In 2017, Alibaba and Tencent were in the same bracket as Amazon by capitalization, with the total Chinese e-commerce sector once approaching the value of its US counterpart. However, by 2022, the market value of e-commerce in China was lagging far behind that in the United States, with the combined market value of Alibaba and Tencent amounting to only half that of Amazon and the total market value of all Chinese e-commerce companies together dropping to less than that of Apple alone (Data source: Wind, July 29, 2022).

13.6.3 Major Constraints on China's Economy Imposed by Communist Totalitarianism

The issues discussed in the preceding subsection primarily concern the private sector. However, communist totalitarianism is fundamentally a system aimed at eradicating private property. Therefore, it should come as no surprise if the CCP begins to curb and ultimately eradicate private firms entirely. The crux of the matter is that, even when issues related to the private sector are completely set aside, the constraints that the regime imposes on Chinese society render the country's economy unsustainable.

The first of such constraints is the fundamental system of state ownership, including the total state ownership of the land, as a basic principle shared by all communist totalitarian regimes. From day one of its reform, the CCP emphasized state assets as the foundation of its rule (for thorough discussions on the fundamental importance of state ownership, see Chapters 8 and 11). Although the private sector was later unintentionally permitted to develop, the party stressed completely controlling the economy's commanding heights by SOEs, such as finance, banking, energy, mining, and upstream sectors. But SOEs are bound to create SBC problems (Kornai, 1992). The collapse of the Eastern bloc's totalitarian economies was directly related to inefficiencies and deteriorating debts caused by such problems. China was no exception. Although massive privatization of medium and small SOEs eased the state sector's problems for a time, the policy of "grasping the large" has brought back serious SBC problems among large SOEs and local governments. This has resulted in a rapid and sustained increase in China's economic leverage since 2008, with an irrepressible trend towards deterioration over the past decade. By 2023, China's total debt-to-GDP ratio had exceeded 286 percent (Cho, 2024).

The danger that debt may pose to financial stability is not only related to the leverage ratio but also to the nature of the debt, as a large proportion of debts, including local government debts, are collateralized mortgage loans. Long-term bonds, common in market economies, can support higher leverage. Collateralized mortgage loans, however, are pro-cyclical and pro-crisis, as they create a vicious cycle when an economy is in a downturn since the collateral value drops automatically. China's deep trouble is caused by its RADT institution. As the central authority worried about moral hazard issues caused by local authorities' SBCs, they forbade local governments from issuing bonds. At the same time, all land in China is state-owned and the local government is the only landlord in its jurisdiction.[19] Thus, instead, local governments borrow mortgage loans from state-owned banks using land as collateral. As a result, much of China's public debt consists of bank loans secured by land, which will inevitably cause leverage to skyrocket if the real estate market bubble bursts. But under the SBC, anticipating bailouts by the central authorities in the event of insolvency, local authorities and SOEs do not factor in these kinds of risks in their borrowing decisions.

The driving force behind local authorities' extensive borrowing is rooted in the RADT system. In this system, they are the landlords of all the land within their jurisdictions and they also bear responsibility for local public finance, including infrastructure. Since 1998, most local authorities have relied on the sale or lease of land for a substantial portion of their revenue. Driven by yardstick competition and fiscal pressures, local governments, acting as monopolistic land suppliers, have catalyzed fast development in the real estate market and unprecedented growth in land prices (Xu, 2011). Approximately 30 percent of China's GDP is derived from real estate and related sectors (Chowdhury, 2022). China's property market value soared to 62.6 trillion USD in 2020 (Ren, 2021), more than four times China's GDP. SBCs have encouraged local governments to accrue massive debt without the fear of bankruptcy. After more than a decade of accumulation, 40–50 percent of the country's bank loans are tied to land and real estate mortgages. The debt burden of real estate developers approached 84.6 percent of GDP by 2020 (Chowdhury, 2022). In 2022, the colossal real estate bubble showed signs of an imminent burst. If real estate prices plummet and the value of the vast amount of land-backed assets collapses, it could lead many banks and the entire financial system to insolvency. This scenario raises a significant risk of igniting a financial and fiscal crisis.

The second major factor that impedes the sustainability of China's growth is its chronically low domestic demand. Again, this is a common feature of communist totalitarian economies and stems from the totalitarian control over every facet of society. With the state controlling most resources, the government continues to allocate an overwhelming amount of resources to investment and maintaining the bureaucracy. This leaves the total household disposable income as a small share of the economy, thus suppressing household demand. China's domestic demand, measured by its ratio to GDP, ranks among the world's lowest. In the first two or three decades of reform, the lack of domestic demand did not hinder China's economic growth, as the rapid increase in China's exports compensated for it. However, once China became the world's largest exporter and second-largest economy, relying solely on global demand for China's exports to support its growth became unsustainable. This made domestic demand a necessary condition for maintaining China's economic growth. China's residents' disposable income as a percentage of GDP has long been less than 40 percent, far lower than the 60 percent level found in most countries. In fact, the pressure of insufficient domestic demand on China's economic growth rate began to appear as early as 2008, but it was overshadowed by the global financial crisis. The extraordinarily large fiscal stimulus package at that time created a short-lived high growth rate, creating an illusion that led to further neglect of the domestic demand issue.

Another significant factor accounting for sluggish domestic demand in China is the vast population living in poverty. According to a survey cited in 2019 by Premier Li Keqiang, 964 million of China's 1.4 billion people live in households with a per capita monthly disposable income of less than 2,000 RMB (300 USD), and this includes 547 million with a monthly income of less than 1,000 RMB, that is, below the absolute poverty line of 5 USD per person per day (Cheng and Hu, 2022). The majority of this large impoverished population is officially defined as peasants with rural *hukou* (household registration).

Under China's *hukou* system, those officially categorized as "peasants" have been trapped at the bottom of China's social class (akin to a caste system) for generations under CCP rule. Deprived of land titles (as detailed in Chapters 11 and 12), these individuals lack the means to capitalize on the land they collectively "own," nor can they share in the benefits of their land's significant appreciation. Whether they are employed in agriculture or other sectors, these so-called peasants, who move to the cities for work, are permanently referred to as migrant workers. They are not entitled to public health care or other social benefits, their children are not allowed to attend public schools in the cities, and in larger urban areas, they are not permitted to purchase housing. Furthermore, their descendants continue to be classified as peasants. Thus, it is impossible to effectively increase China's domestic demand without addressing the institutional causes of extreme poverty on such a large scale.

The third factor affecting China's long-term growth is its population decline. The CCP's one-child policy, initiated in 1979 and enforced stringently throughout the post-reform period, has led to a steady reduction in China's population. This policy is inseparable from the reforms, reflecting the party's belief that China's large population was a burden on the economy. However, it was the totalitarian party-state, with its complete control over individual and family life, that made this policy implementable. Through the heavy use of punitive measures and coercion, countless women were forced to undergo sterilization or abort their unborn children. Hundreds of millions of families were forced to raise no more than one child over several generations, resulting in disastrous consequences.

Finally, in 2022, China officially admitted to its population decline (Li et al., 2023). Demographers predict that by 2025, the elderly will make up over 20 percent of the total Chinese population and the share of working-age people will decrease steadily. This reduction will impact both domestic demand and labor supply, increasing the burden on families and society at large (Mao et al., 2020). One immediate consequence is a decline in housing demand, which is fueling the burst of the real estate market bubble. Furthermore, with hundreds of millions of people living in extreme poverty and possessing only moderate levels of labor productivity, the combination of hindered growth and an aging population will exacerbate the impact on the impoverished, leading to significant social problems.

The fourth constraint imposed on China's growth by its institutions is inefficiency, encompassing constraints on labor productivity and technological progress. Chinese party-state authorities have heavily invested in science and technology, hoping to sustain economic growth by boosting Total Factor Productivity (TFP) through technological innovation mirroring the strategy used by the Soviet Union during its last two decades. However, TFP is not just about technological progress. For China, the most crucial elements of TFP are institutional, managerial, and allocational factors.

With respect to the "pure efficiency" issue, the most significant challenge affecting China's long-run growth is its low labor productivity. China's manufacturing labor productivity is only about a tenth of that of the United States. Dictated by its low labor productivity and other institutional burdens, China's labor costs per manufacturing unit have been higher than those in many developed countries (CBNRI, 2016). Therefore, improving labor productivity and reducing unit labor costs are prerequisites for sustaining China's growth. However, given China's very low labor productivity, the urgent need for accomplishing these goals practically and cost-effectively lies in improving general human capital, easing the excessive costs incurred from institutional obstacles, and improving general technology, rather than overly focusing on frontier technology.

One of the most prominent challenges in China's human capital development is the inferior education available to hundreds of millions of poor peasants. As a result, China has the lowest high school enrolment rate among all middle-income countries in the world (Hell and Rozelle, 2021). Moreover, the institutional costs for doing business are high, including various taxes and fees imposed on companies by all levels of government, as well as extremely high land prices. In addition, the survival and employment of these second-class citizens in the city are faced with significant additional costs, both direct and indirect, caused by this system. Without addressing these issues, labor productivity cannot be improved and economic growth cannot be sustained by relying solely on investing in technology and attempting breakthroughs in a few cutting-edge tech areas.

Lastly, when it comes to frontier science and technology and their contributions to TFP, historical cross-country evidence from the past century indicates that disruptive inventions applicable to economic development have seldom originated from communist totalitarian regimes, including China (Kornai, 2013; Xu, 2017). The underlying reason is that the majority of breakthroughs in disruptive technology have been the result of independent, free scientists, engineers, and entrepreneurs, stemming from unrestricted exploration and market-driven selection. Such innovations neither spring from overarching national strategies nor can they be orchestrated by the state. In a totalitarian system, assets, research, and higher education are all state-owned, with primary decisions largely tethered to blueprints set by party-state bureaucrats. Additionally, the inescapable SBC problem of SOEs dictates that in the face of the high uncertainty of disruptive innovation, state institutions cannot weed out insolvent projects in the same timely manner as the market, relying instead mainly on bureaucratic selection, that is to say, plans. The few exceptions can be found in national key projects that have clearly delineated imitation objectives. By marshalling national resources and crafting plans rooted in imitation, often incurring exorbitant costs, remarkable progress can be realized. China's nuclear missile satellite project from the 1960s serves as a notable example.

However, even when marshalling national resources, SOEs struggle to compete in uncertain frontiers that cannot be anticipated and planned for. The lag of the Soviet Union in the past and China's current shortfall in cutting-edge sectors like semiconductors and biomedicine serve as glaring examples (Qian and Xu, 1998; Guo et al.,

2021). To quickly bridge the gaps with leading nations in fields like semiconductors and biomedicine, the Chinese government attempted to emulate the market by setting up numerous state-owned venture capital institutions. However, inherent SBCs hindered these institutions from truly mimicking the market's survival-of-the-fittest selection mechanism.

The plight of China's chip industry is a case in point. In the decade-long process of China's national efforts to develop chips, not only has it been difficult to close the substantial technological gap but hundreds of billions of RMB in fraudulent cases have emerged. In late July 2022, the Central Commission for Discipline Inspection announced a high-profile investigation into five senior officials responsible for the chip industry, including the Minister for Industry and Information Technology (*Caixin*, July 28, 2022). The "Big Funds" implicated in the case had a capital scale of several hundred billion RMB, which was just one of many major scandals in China's semiconductor industry.

Another significant factor influencing China's science and technology development is its international relations. Since the post-Mao reform, virtually all pivotal, cutting-edge technologies that have left a mark on China's economy have been sourced from the developed nations. The majority of China's leading scientists and engineers received their training in these advanced countries. All of China's scientific and technological advancements have built upon the achievements of the developed countries, often in collaboration with them. However, the CCP's challenges to the international order have severely strained China's global relations, thus jeopardizing its access to science and technology from these developed nations and making its technological progress unsustainable.

13.7 SUMMARY

While the CCP's underlying totalitarian principles and motivations for initiating reforms align with those of the CPSU, the specific operations of their reforms differ. In China's RADT system, much of the administrative power and resources influencing local economies and societies are delegated to local party-state agencies, rather than centralized in national party-state authorities. Such institutional configurations paved the way for the post-Mao reform policies. As a result, the Chinese system, in its efforts to preserve the communist regime, gradually transitioned towards a more lenient authoritarian model, which was somewhat open to limited pluralism. This shift led to a relaxation in controls over ideology, ownership, and NGOs, fostering the emergence of new institutional genes like private property rights, entrepreneurial communities, civil society organizations, and a broader diversity in ideas and associations.

However, the fate of these emergent institutional genes, akin to saplings sprouting from rock, hinged on their resilience against a hostile backdrop. Their evolutionary direction and development were significantly shaped and restricted by the prevailing system. The CCP never tolerated any independent organization, including religious groups, especially those hinting at political inclinations. As the new institutional genes took root, the call for constitutional rule and law, borne out of self-preservation, grew louder. It was echoed by a wider segment of the population, encompassing those within and outside the party as well as voices from Hong Kong. This so-called "peaceful evolution" was flagged by Deng at the onset of the reforms and has remained under the CCP's vigilant scrutiny. To halt this drift, the CCP ceased its gradual transition towards a more liberal authoritarian system, prioritizing the prevention of this evolution and potential "color revolutions" even if it meant economic compromises. Under Xi's leadership, the party took a definitive stance, striving to revert to a totalitarian system while pro-actively suppressing these emerging pro-constitutionalist institutional genes.

Measured by per capita GDP relative to that in United States, China's current development level still lags behind the Soviet Union of the early 1970s. This positions China to have a significant "backwardness advantage" following Gerschenkron's argument, meaning that it is easier to catch up. Even more beneficial for China is its vast private sector and its ties with advanced nations, both cultivated during the post-Mao reform era.

Excluding institutional factors, the majority of economists and Wall Street analysts once believed that, based on growth models or by comparing China's trajectory with that of Japan and Taiwan, China's rapid growth would continue. Thus, they predicted China's future by extrapolating its past growth. A popular expectation was that China's per capita GDP would eventually match that of Japan or Taiwan, or roughly 80 percent of the US level. With such an illusion, the Soviet Union was out of the picture as in its peak years it was only 35 percent of the US level.

However, China has been firmly controlled by the CCP, whose objective for reform has always been to sustain its power. Whenever the party perceives the ongoing evolving trajectory as a potential threat to its dominance, a reversion to tighter control is inevitable, even when such a trajectory is a result of the party's previous reform policies. Such institutional back-pedaling, which includes bolstering the state sector, restraining the private sector, and harming foreign investments, pushes China's institutions backward towards the pre-reform era. As a result, much like the Soviet Union in the mid-1970s, China's era of high-speed growth has ended. The nation is now witnessing not only a declining growth rate but also escalating financial and fiscal vulnerabilities.

NOTES

1. The party's determination to affirm the legitimacy and rationality of its initial campaigns was evident in the terminology – "correction," "redress," and "de-labeling" – used to describe various categories of rehabilitation for the myriad infractions committed.
2. When Deng announced the Four Cardinal Principles, he was not yet aware of the reform initiatives taking place in Xiaogang Village, Fengyang County. At that time, there had been no discussions or plans for such reforms. It was only a month later that the proposal from the Guangdong Provincial Party Committee, advocating for the establishment of an SEZ, emerged.

656 THE POST-MAO REFORM AND ITS CESSATION

3. The principle was stated in 《中共中央关于经济体制改革的决定 [*The Decision of the CCP Central Committee on the Reform of the Economic System*]》, which was approved by the 3rd Plenum of the 12th Central Committee of the CCP in 1984.
4. Original draft of the open letter.
5. Soon after the CR ended, the CCP sent delegations to learn from the reform practices in Eastern European countries and invited economists from those countries to visit China and present their experiences of reform. The most influential among them, for China's economic reforms, was the Hungarian economist János Kornai.
6. Liang Xiang, the inaugural mayor and municipal party secretary of Shenzhen, ardently championed the development of the SEZ. He played a pivotal role in attracting and safeguarding Hong Kong's capital but he was criticized within the party and consequently removed from his position. Following the June 4 crackdown, he was detained due to his affiliations with Hu Yaobang and Zhao Ziyang. Several of the CCP's prominent reformists expressed their discontent about his treatment (for a detailed account, see *Asiaweek*, no. 9, 2008).
7. This concept was invented by Oskar Lange and formed the cornerstone of the reforms in the Eastern bloc, which were subsequently adopted by China.
8. To avoid contradicting its anti-private-ownership principle, during the early days of the reform, the CCP allowed for "enterprises run by individual citizens," a classification that also encompasses collective enterprises under public ownership. Instead of being voluntary associations among individual holders of private property rights, these collective enterprises were controlled by local-level party organizations.
9. Yang (2010, chapters 5 and 8). Nathan and Link (2001) provide more documentation on the crackdown and the background.
10. Website of the Supervision Division of the Central Commission for Discipline Inspection. Cited from, "Anti-corruption Efforts since the 18th National Congress of the Communist Party of China (中共十八大后的反腐)," Wikipedia: https://zh.wikipedia.org/wiki/%E4%B8%AD%E5%85%B1%E5%8D%81%E5%85%AB%E5%A4%A7%E5%90%8E%E7%9A%84%E5%8F%8D%E8%85%90%E8%B4%A5.
11. Mao, "在扩大的中央工作会议上的讲话" [Speech at the Expanded Central Work Conference], January 30, 1962 (Mao, 1968b, p. 22).

12. Although today the bulk of the Chinese economy is run by the private sector, all the land, almost all the banks, and all the commanding heights sectors of the economy have always been completely state-owned.
13. This theory was stoutly resisted within the party (by Deng Liqun, among others) and Jiang was accused of violating Marxist principles.
14. Xi (2013a). Three weeks after the speech by Xi (2013a), an important article was published in the *People's Daily* with a title similar to that of Xi (2013b) (*People's Daily*, 2013).
15. Declassified documents from the United Kingdom reveal that, during the 1950s, the colonial administration endeavored to implement a democratic system in Hong Kong. However, these plans were curtailed when Beijing issued threats of forcibly reclaiming Hong Kong should the British conduct elections there. Consequently, the authorities were compelled to suspend their democratic plans for the territory. Only in the final decade of British rule were grassroots elections introduced (Jacobs, 2014).
16. The term "private" is deliberately employed here to denote these listed companies, highlighting their features of being founded based on private property, as opposed to state assets.
17. Like the historical campaigns and suppressions targeting counterrevolutionaries, the major private-sector e-commerce entities were simultaneously subjected to punitive measures, although ostensibly for different reasons.
18. Liu, J. et al., (2021).
19. The "collectives" that nominally own agricultural land possess merely the right to utilize and manage it solely in relation to agricultural activities. The ultimate rights of control are in the hands of the party-state because once the land undergoes a transition towards non-agricultural utilization, ownership reverts to the state.

14 Conclusion

> In the last sixty or eighty years in every country eminent citizens have become alarmed about the rising tide of totalitarianism. They wanted to preserve freedom and Western civilisation and to organise an ideological and political movement to stop the progress on the road to serfdom. All these endeavours failed utterly ...
>
> —Ludwig von Mises, "Observations on Professor Hayek's Plan" (Mises, [1946] 2009, p. 1)

14.1 THE GREAT CHALLENGE: UNDERSTANDING TOTALITARIANISM

Over seven decades ago, when Mises made his observations, the world had already seen the defeat of Nazi-Fascist totalitarianism. Thus, his references were primarily directed towards communist totalitarianism, the only enduring form of totalitarianism. As outlined in Chapter 6, the origins of communist totalitarianism can be traced back to the Middle Ages. In fact, Nazi-Fascist totalitarianism was, in many ways, an imitation of its communist counterpart. From a historical vantage point, the primary institution of totalitarianism has been communist. Emphasizing "totalitarianism" over "communism" is an attempt to uncover and recognize the inherent coercive nature of communism. This is crucial because the profound misunderstandings associated with communism serve as foundational elements in the creation and perpetuation of totalitarian regimes.

Shortly after Mises made these remarks, the rapidly expanding communist totalitarian system took control of a third of the earth's population. His assertion that "all these efforts have been a complete failure" became evident. The modern totalitarian regime, underpinned by a totalitarian party, arose from the most extensive and fanatical secular religious movement in history. Totalitarianism categorically differs from traditional autocracy in ideology, operating mechanisms, and institutional origins. From the First World War and the October Revolution to the Second World War, the Cold War, and today's emerging "New Cold War," communist totalitarian regimes have exhibited a willingness and capacity to expand rapidly wherever they could at the cost of many lives. These are the direct consequences of the unique mechanisms inherent in totalitarianism. A thorough understanding of the ideology and mechanisms of communist totalitarianism is essential to meet its challenges. Unfortunately, both academic and policy circles have paid far too limited attention to this grave matter, which affects the lives of a significant portion of the world's population. In the limited literature, most research on totalitarianism is confined to philosophy, historical records, or idiosyncratic issues. Comprehensive research on the basic mechanisms of communist totalitarianism is sorely lacking. The challenges posed by the lack of a deep understanding are particularly acute in the face of the urgent situation of the rapid expansion and threat of a communist totalitarian China.

The totalitarian system of the Eastern bloc collapsed at the end of the 1980s before its nature was fully understood. This lack of understanding is accompanied by a widespread misconception that communist totalitarianism is extinct in the world and that the CCP is not a totalitarian party. As a result, interest in further research into the poorly understood communist totalitarianism has declined. It is common to confuse the system under the CCP as authoritarian, likening it to the pre-1990s regimes in Taiwan and South Korea. Therefore, many scholars and politicians mistakenly believe that like the historical trajectory in Taiwan and South Korea, China will progress towards liberal democracy along with its rapid economic growth. This book aspires to offer a systematic empirical analysis of China's communist totalitarian regime, as well as its institutional origins, with significant analysis on Russia. The concept of institutional genes, introduced in this book, serves as the theoretical framework for this empirical analysis. The systematic nature of this analysis sets it apart from previous academic studies on China, socialism, communism, and totalitarianism.

14.2 SUMMARY OF INSTITUTIONAL GENES AND INSTITUTIONAL EVOLUTION

This book introduces the concept of institutional genes, intending to provide a framework for analyzing institutional evolution. Based on empirical observations of institutional evolution, it draws inspiration from the ideas of many scholars. Scholars such as Hume, Smith, Mises, Hayek, Popper, and North have all emphasized that institutions emerge and evolve from the mass of spontaneous interactions among individuals and groups within society. Furthermore, institutions are structured and some of the structural components bear more significance than others. Those foundational and recurrent components in institutional evolution are what I designate as institutional genes. The incentive-compatibility nature of institutional genes dictates that the individuals who play a role in the institutional evolution recreate those basic institutional components under new names in new situations out of their self-interest. That is why those components are repetitive and foundational. The term "incentive-compatibility" originates from mechanism design theory but its essence was explored by Adam Smith and Friedrich Hayek long before the birth of that theory. Smith argued that in the grand chessboard of human society, every individual adheres to their "principle of motion" (motion in this context corresponds to action or behavior in contemporary economics), whereas the legislator envisages rules to regulate everyone with another set of principles. It is only when "those two principles coincide and act in the same direction, [that] the game of human society will go ... harmoniously" (Smith, 2011, part 6, chapter 2). The mechanism that enables these two principles to coincide and act in unison, as Smith articulated, is precisely the mechanism of incentive-compatibility. Of course, Smith's discussion focuses on naturally occurring coincidences. While Smith's discussion centers on naturally occurring alignments, mechanism design theory, in contrast, examines the behavior of individuals in society and, based on those observations, identifies or designs mechanisms that align with their incentives.

Smith's theory centers on a harmonious society governed by the rule of law. This book extends this theory to autocratic systems where violence is widely practiced. When a system is based on violence, everyone's principle of motion is forcibly altered due to tyranny. I refer to this as the tyrannical incentive-compatibility condition (see Chapter 2). Excessive brutality that violates this condition can destabilize and undermine the system. For an autocratic regime to endure, the rulers must ensure they adhere to this tyrannical incentive-compatibility condition. In addition to coercive force, this also encompasses controlling public opinion, brainwashing, and cultivating ideologies and societal norms that serve to endorse and validate the tyranny. Once entrenched, these ideologies and norms perpetuate themselves, influencing individual beliefs and guiding their incentives. Therefore, in any system, everyone follows their own principle of motion. Those principles are conditioned and influenced by the system in which people live and have lived, by historically formed social norms (which include culture, and beliefs, and so on), and they are based on the institutional genes.

The incentive-compatibility character of institutional genes includes both perfect rationality, which is the premise of game theory and mechanism design theory, and bounded rationality. The latter is prevalent in rules, in social consensus, and in social norms, that have evolved over time. Individuals who breach those rules or norms violate the incentive-compatibility condition of the society in which they live and, as a result, they tend to isolate themselves or even be punished. Hayek argued that the human capacity for collecting information and reasoning is extremely limited. To mitigate the heavy burden of information collection and rational reasoning, social behaviors performed by most individuals are grounded in compliance with long-standing and incentive-compatible rules, rather than relying solely on their rational reasoning. Hayek thus described man as a creature that follows rules (Hayek, 1973, chapters 1, 2, 4). Recent developments in contract theory and law and economics, both theoretically and empirically, further affirm Hayek's argument. Hart and Moore demonstrate that in devising contracts, people intentionally use social rules or norms that must be adhered to as contractual provisions (Hart and Moore, 2008). That is because the contract is always incomplete in practice, due to bounded rationality in designing contracts (Hart and Moore, 2008; Frydlinger and Hart, 2022). Bolton and Brooks (2022) demonstrate that court enforcement of contracts is often based on compliance with social norms due to the insolvable difficulties of relying on an entirely rational approach to enforcement in reality.

The relationship between the concept of "institutional genes," introduced in this book, and the notions of "institutional evolution" or "change" prevalent in the literature is of paramount importance. The framework of institutional genes, primarily employed for positive analysis, can also be normative when directed towards policy recommendations; its relationship with institutional change can be articulated in the following manner:

- Any stable institutional evolution or change, including reforms or revolutions, that is effectively realized within a society is considered to be based on the evolution or mutation of that society's institutional genes.
- The evolution or mutations of institutional genes arise as a result of interactions among various interest groups, especially as they navigate new circumstances or address emerging crises.
- Initiatives or campaigns aimed at reforms or revolutions that neglect the characteristics or evolution of institutional genes or that fail to stimulate the requisite mutations of these genes will likely miss their intended objectives. In simpler terms, any institutional change that reformers or revolutionaries hope to effectuate successfully must be fundamentally rooted in institutional genes. Notable examples include the British Glorious Revolution and the establishment of constitutional democracy in the

United States, both of which can be attributed to such foundational genes. Often, mutations in institutional genes are prompted by potent external factors, as seen in the totalitarian systems established in Russia and China.

14.3 AN EMPIRICAL ANALYSIS OF TOTALITARIAN REGIMES

> Communism had an insane plan: to remake the "old breed of man," ancient Adam. And it really worked ... Seventy-plus years in the Marxist-Leninist laboratory gave rise to a new man: Homo sovieticus.... People who've come out of socialism are both like and unlike the rest of humanity ... We're full of hatred and superstitions. All of us come from the land of the gulag and harrowing war, collectivisation, dekulakization ...
>
> —Svetlana Alexievich (2016, p. 9)

The Chinese are also *Homo sovieticus*, created in the same Marxist-Leninist laboratory, as studied in this book. However, Marx predicted that the communist revolution could only occur in developed capitalist countries like Germany. In reality, no developed capitalist country has established communist totalitarianism. The question is, why, contrary to Marx's basic principle and prediction, was this laboratory able to establish itself in a pre-capitalist Russia and then in an even more "backward" China and why has it been so enduring and powerful in China? Understanding the origins and evolution of totalitarianism in China extends beyond mere scholarly endeavor. It touches on pressing contemporary issues that span the global economy, international relations, geopolitics, and the delicate balance between war and peace on the international stage. This book delves into the aforementioned question. Its main points can be summarized as follows:

1) Essential parts of the institutional genes of Tsarist Russia and Imperial China served as the institutional origins of the Leninist party and the communist totalitarian regimes. Built upon these institutional genes, the totalitarian regimes in both nations were "created" through violent revolutions led by the party (see Chapters 4, 5, and 9–11 on China; Chapters 8 and 9 on Soviet Russia; and Chapter 6 on the origins of totalitarianism).

2) When communist totalitarian ideology and systems (including systematic incitement and the use of terror as a threat) are effectively governing, their mobilization capacity is extremely powerful.
3) Totalitarian parties' superior mobilizing capacity stems from strategically exploiting the short-term interests of the vast majority of the population, including party members and cadres. They segment long-term goals that fundamentally infringe upon popular interests into multiple short-term, incentive-compatible phases. These phases are then implemented sequentially in a piecemeal manner (refer to Chapters 8, and 10–12 for empirical evidence). This strategy resembles constructing a vast, centralized, multistage Ponzi scheme, where each stage operates as its own distinct Ponzi scheme, furnishing exceptionally compelling incentives for the participants. By capitalizing on people's short-term behaviors, subsequent Ponzi schemes are established and sustained. In addition to this feature, unlike traditional Ponzi schemes, which hinge exclusively on financial incentives, communist totalitarian Ponzi schemes also harness the tools of incitement and violence. These provide additional mechanisms to bolster short-term incentives alongside the allure of promotions and rewards. Moreover, incitement and violence often surpass the power of money in stimulating irrational group behavior.
4) The inherent nature of communist totalitarian ideology and regimes necessitates continuous expansion, both internally and externally. This nature also dictates the brutal character of its expanding power. To safeguard democracy in the world, it is imperative to resolutely contain this expansion. However, achieving this requires a deep understanding of the system's true essence. Discussing the avoidance of the so-called Thucydides Trap (Allison, 2017) by equating the forces of emerging totalitarian regimes with those of other regimes not only misconstrues the nature of the Chinese totalitarian regime but also gravely misdirect the policy responses to its challenges.
5) The first communist totalitarian regime, the Soviet Union, and its Eastern bloc, collapsed by themselves. Such self-termination is contingent upon its degeneration, including the totalitarian party's losing control of society and the abandonment of the totalitarian ideology by society universally, even by a substantial portion of the party apparatus. During the degeneration process, the totalitarian system may transition into relatively lax authoritarian rule or it might suddenly collapse.

6) The decline or collapse of a totalitarian regime is a necessary precursor for a shift towards constitutional democracy but it does not ensure such a transformation. A robust constitutional democracy is anchored in the right institutional genes, which necessitate the right conditions and adequate time to develop and flourish. Complicating this transition, totalitarian regimes, in their bid for survival, invariably strive to suppress or obliterate these emerging institutional genes at every opportunity. This makes a post-totalitarian transition to democracy even more challenging.

The conceptual framework introduced in this book, encompassing institutional genes and incentive-compatible institutional evolution, is heavily influenced by mechanism design theory and various branches of the social sciences, including political economy, political science, and jurisprudence. Evidence of institutional genes, as well as their emergence and evolution, is elucidated through historical narratives.

I am a political economist and an institutional economist with a passion for history but I am neither a historian, political scientist, or a legal scholar. Given this, I fully anticipate critiques of this book from experts in these fields. Even within political economy or institutional economics, I expect many will find points of contention with the arguments presented here. However, if this book brings more attention to the topic of communist totalitarianism or sparks debates about the methodology of institutional genes or institutional evolution in general, I will consider it a success from a purely academic point of view.

As for the broad and exploratory nature of this book, I can only offer a humble explanation: the topics discussed necessitate such a wide-ranging journey. Without venturing beyond the traditional boundaries set by academia in terms of disciplinary fields, historical periods, and geographical regions, it would be impossible to comprehensively address the origins and evolution of institutions.

It is particularly worth remarking that transcending the traditional disciplinary boundaries of the social sciences is essential when analyzing communist totalitarian regimes and their institutional origins. In such regimes, political power dictates resource allocations, while the economy reciprocally wields profound influence on political power, offering both foundation and function. Concurrently, the regime dominates the entirety of society, ensuring that economic and non-economic social organizations are indivisible from the party's authority. Furthermore, the party directly controls the legislative and judicial systems, leveraging the law to regulate both the economy and society.

The historical narratives in this book serve as evidence for the empirical analysis of institutional genes, including their origins, evolution, and mutations. The narratives largely draw upon accounts considered authoritative within historical circles, as the primary aim of this book is not to unveil new historical materials or evidence. In terms of CCP history, the works of Gao Hua, Shen Zhihua, Yang Kuisong, and others have been extensively cited. For insights into the Cultural Revolution and the early stages of reform, references are made to works by Yang Jisheng and his contemporaries. On Soviet Russia, this book leans significantly on the works of scholars like Richard Pipes.

However, due to the unique perspective of this book, certain essential pieces of evidence are not available in secondary sources, requiring the sourcing of primary evidence. For example, certain key pieces of evidence pertaining to the origins and evolution of the CCP are cited directly from declassified official documents of the Comintern, the CPSU, and the CCP. This includes writings by Mao Zedong, Zhang Guotao, Chen Duxiu, and others, encompassing material not officially released within the PRC. Similarly, documents of the *Narodnaya Volya* are cited as evidence of the Bolshevik institutional genes.

14.4 LITERATURE OVERVIEW

An enormous body of literature directly concerns or is relevant to the topics addressed in this book. Due to considerations of space, only a small portion that is most relevant to this book is briefly discussed here.

14.4.1 China Studies

In studies on China, its history, political economy, and institutions, there is a significant lack of literature analyzing communist totalitarianism. This book fills this gap in the literature. The final chapters of *China: A New History* by Fairbank and Goldman (2006) offer a brief discussion on the CCP totalitarian regime, including some historical material and background that is complementary to this book. However, that book does not discuss the central question explored here, that is to say, the institutional origins, mechanisms, and evolution of communist totalitarian rule in China. It is also worth noting that Fairbank's early work, such as *The United States and China*, which has had a profound influence in academia and US policy circles since its publication in 1948, lacks basic understanding of the substance of the CCP's totalitarianism on the one hand, while misinterpreting the authoritarian KMT as totalitarian on the other (Fairbank, 1948). For instance, that book erroneously takes the so-called New Democracy invented by the CCP in the 1940s as its united front strategy (see Chapter 11) at face value while criticizing the KMT as a fascist totalitarian party. In the "Roots of Totalitarianism" section of the book, instead of discussing the totalitarian CCP created by the Comintern, the author is devoted to the so-called anti-Marxist Confucian totalitarianism of the KMT.

Esteemed scholars like MacFarquhar and Schoenhals (2008), Andrew Walder (2017), and Frank Dikötter (2010, 2017) have delved extensively into CCP rule, especially during the Great Leap Forward and the Cultural Revolution. Their well-documented findings and insights complement the relevant sections of this book. However, this book analyzes institutional evolution before, during, and as a result of the GLF and CR, events that are critical to the transition from classic Soviet-style totalitarianism to the RADT system. This perspective distinguishes this book from the existing literature. Moreover, the resulting RADT institution served as the institutional bedrock for the reform and opening-up phase and continues to be the institutional foundation of the Xi Jinping-era political economy.

Several notable scholars, including Susan Shirk (1993), Jean Oi (1999), Bruce J. Dickson (2003), Barry Naughton (2018), Minxin Pei (2006), David Shambaugh (2008), Kjeld Erik Brodsgaard (2016), and Xueguang Zhou (2022), have extensively analyzed the social, economic, and political institutions and their operations in post-Mao China. Yasheng Huang (2023) specifically delves into China's enduring tradition of autocracy and its implications for contemporary China. The insights from these works greatly complement the corresponding chapters in this book.

However, the analysis in this book distinguishes itself from the existing literature by emphasizing the origins and evolution of totalitarianism through the prism of institutional genes. For instance, in contrast to Huang (2023), the imperial examination system is analyzed in Chapter 5 as a pivotal institutional gene that not only sustained the imperial order but also contributed to the emergence and persistence of the communist totalitarian regime in modern China. The emphasis here is on the origins and evolution of institutional genes and their impact. By doing so, this work offers coherent narratives for seemingly disparate historical events.

The content of this book, in many aspects, is broadly related to the ongoing debate on the "great divergence" between China and the West (Pomeranz, 2000; Rosenthal and Wong, 2011), although discussions on this issue are brief as it is not the priority subject of this book. In the mainstream of that literature, the debate has focused on economic history. Hui (2005) and Zhao (2015) have extended this debate to the state systems, that is, the formation of a grand unified empire in China versus the multinational competition in Europe. Their discussions deal with the competition among states, the military, and other aspects but rarely discuss the role of fundamental institutional elements (property rights, human rights, and political decision-making power). In contrast to that literature, in addition to methodological differences, this book argues on the basis of evidence from archaeological discoveries that China and the West have been fundamentally different since prehistory. That is, from the outset of civilization, China has fundamentally differed from ancient Greece and Rome in terms of its institutional genes. These foundational differences influenced the evolutionary paths of both China and the West, transitioning from basic disparities in prehistoric times to the more pronounced divergence in later eras. This so-called "Great Divergence" manifested in every aspect, from the economic and state systems to economic development and military structures and power. In the life sciences, without a foundation in genetics there is no way to understand evolution or competition. Similarly, this book posits that the evolution of institutional genes provides a basis for understanding institutional evolution, the divergence, and the consequent economic divergence.

Compared to the China studies literature, the main novelties related to modern China in this book can be summarized as follows.

1) The institutional genes of the Chinese imperial system (including the institutional gene for rebel secret societies) clashed directly with those required for constitutionalism, yet closely resembled those needed for totalitarianism (see Chapters 3–5, and 9).
2) It was this condition that made it possible for the Comintern missionaries to implant communist totalitarian institutional genes in China. The direct involvement and support from the Comintern were essential in establishing a totalitarian system in China. The Comintern not only provided organizational, financial, and military assistance to undermine the faltering constitutional regime (the Whampoa Military Academy and the Northern Expedition) but, more significantly, it supplied some of the institutional genes that were lacking in China for the establishment of a communist totalitarian system (see Chapter 10).
3) After more than twenty years of cultivation by the Comintern, the CCP eventually developed its own totalitarian institutional genes and leaders, became an independent totalitarian party, and armed its way to power, establishing a complete Soviet-type totalitarian system in China (see Chapters 10 and 11).
4) Subsequently, through the GLF and the CR, and at the cost of tens of millions of lives, the CCP transformed its institutions into totalitarianism

with Chinese characteristics, i.e., RADT (regionally administered totalitarianism) (see Chapter 12).
5) Deng Xiaoping, who was trained by the CPSU and the Comintern, and who was promoted and valued by Mao Zedong, made a significant contribution to rescuing the totalitarian system in China after the CR and again after the collapse of the Eastern bloc totalitarian camp. Raising the banner of the Four Cardinal Principles, he initiated the reform, which he proclaimed to be a Leninist New Economic Policy, to save totalitarianism through economic development, while ruthlessly suppressing any threats to totalitarian rule.
6) A more important factor behind China's reform than Deng Xiaoping, the individual, was the RADT system, which proved to be more adaptable than the Soviet-style totalitarian system. It was this system that enabled private ownership and allowed the economy to flourish under totalitarian control, temporarily preserving China's totalitarian system (see Chapter 13). Without truly understanding what the CCP stood for, the international community, including Wall Street, for a time admired the totalitarianism with Chinese characteristics and its economic performance. The once booming private ownership was accompanied by a relaxation of social control. This shift led to an evolution towards a comparatively more relaxed authoritarian rule and generated institutional genes conducive to constitutional democracy.
7) However, the CCP has never relaxed its vigilance against the "hostile" developments that it refers to as "peaceful evolution" or "color revolutions." Xi Jinping, both a product and representative of China's totalitarian institutional genes, has decisively acted to prevent peaceful evolution by countering all "threats" to totalitarian rule, even if they come at the economy's expense (see Chapter 13). In conclusion, it is the deeply rooted institutional genes of totalitarianism in China that have enabled Xi to re-establish a staunch totalitarian stance, even after four decades of economic reform, just as societal forces that might have championed constitutionalism were gaining traction.

14.4.2 *Methodology and Institutions*

In terms of methodology, the work most closely aligned with this book is that of Douglass North. The concept of institutional genes introduced in this book seeks to unpack the black box of path-dependency theory regarding institutional evolution. Underlying the notion of institutional genes is the concept of incentive-compatible institutional change. This has been heavily influenced or inspired by mechanism design theory, credited to Hurwicz, Maskin, and Myerson (see Chapter 2). I recognize property rights as one of the fundamental institutional elements (see Chapter 3), a perspective influenced by property rights theory as advanced by Coase and Hart.

Several works by Acemoglu and Robinson relate to this book in terms of both methodology and content. Their 2009 book (Acemoglu and Robinson, 2009) derives conditions for the emergence of dictatorship and democracy by analyzing the choices of individuals and social groups within a perfectly rational game-theoretical framework. A significant principle they propose posits that the relationship between the state and society determines the choice of institutions. The state refers to the regime, while society encompasses various structures of civil autonomy. When the government is overly strong and society is too weak, autocracy arises. Acemoglu and Robinson (2019) rationalizes these core views using historical narratives, while their 2012 book focuses on autocracy. However, this body of work does not address totalitarianism, which is distinctively different from traditional autocratic systems. Modern totalitarianism arose from the most extensive and fervently secular religious movements in human history. The bounded rationality of humans played a pivotal role in the birth and operation of totalitarianism. The concept of institutional genes proposed in this book aims to establish a cohesive framework for analyzing both perfectly rational and bounded rational behaviors.

Mises (1988) and Hayek (2007) were pioneers in analyzing totalitarianism from a political economy perspective and they remain today the most profound in this regard. Their analyses focus on abstract reasoning, including the origins of totalitarianism in the Middle Ages, but they overlook the specific mechanisms by which the Bolsheviks emerged and operated. Arendt (1973), one of the renowned early works on totalitarianism, particularly emphasizes the aspects of organization, propaganda, and the operation of contemporary totalitarian parties, as well as the totalitarian system after such parties seize power. She provides a comprehensive analysis of the common features of communist totalitarian parties and Nazi totalitarian parties, along with the origins of Nazism. However, she does not delve deeply into the origins of the Bolsheviks. In contrast, this book investigates the origin, evolution, and operating mechanisms of the Bolsheviks, the world's first totalitarian party, and delves more deeply into those in China. Moreover, the methodology of this book, rooted in the framework of institutional genes, distinguishes it from the analytical approaches of earlier works.

Karl Popper analyzes the philosophical origins of totalitarianism. It is important to note that the version of totalitarianism to which Popper refers encompasses a vast array of ideas and philosophies present in human civilization since antiquity. This is far broader in scope than the communist totalitarianism that is defined and analyzed in this book. Popper's concept of totalitarianism includes ideas that propose comprehensive blueprints for regimes or societies, utopian visions, and collectivist ideologies that stand in opposition to individualism. Specifically, in *The Open Society and Its Enemies*, Popper analyzes how totalitarian thinking originated with Plato, was developed by Hegel, and eventually culminated in Marx's work.

Rather than concentrating solely on pure ideas or philosophy, this book zeroes in on communist totalitarianism as a significant social phenomenon. It emphasizes the basic institutional elements that profoundly influence the formation of the masses, the birth of movements, and the ignition of revolutions. As such, this book adopts the descriptive and operational definition of totalitarianism provided by Friedrich and Brzezinski (1956). Communist totalitarian movements are violent secular religious campaigns. Marx's paramount contribution to this movement is his messianic apocalyptic prophecy, which includes the promise of a new world of absolute equality, the incitement of class struggle, and the blueprint for a violent takeover and governance through a proletarian dictatorship.

Notably, within the Bolshevik Party, only a select few intellectuals genuinely grasped Marxist theory. Nonetheless, they were mandated to comply with their superiors and forbidden from voicing their personal interpretations of Marxism if they contradicted the directives of their leaders. In truth, the philosophies of Plato and Hegel, as discussed by Popper, hold little significance in the context of communist totalitarianism. The CCP leadership and elite had even fewer individuals acquainted with the intricacies of Marx, let alone Plato and Hegel. In the first half of the twentieth century, only a smattering of scholars in China were familiar with Plato and Hegel and almost none had ties to the communist revolution.

Barrington Moore (1966) is among the earliest works that compares and analyzes Soviet and Chinese totalitarianism. In some respects, this book can be viewed as a continuation of that endeavor. Moore, by focusing on the traditional agrarian organization and feudal traditions of various societies, elucidates the divergent evolutionary trajectories in modern world history: explaining why Russia and China veered towards communist revolution while Germany shifted towards fascism. He argues that a unifying feature of totalitarianism is the exploitation or mobilization of peasants. While Communists "mobilized" the peasants from the ground up, the Fascists, being a reactionary political alliance between the feudal aristocracy and the upper bourgeoisie, "mobilized" the peasants through a top-down approach. However, Moore fails to acknowledge the influence of Orthodoxy and clandestine political organizations in Tsarist Russia on the Bolshevik Party. He also neglects the fact that the CCP had been a branch of the Comintern for more than two decades and the deep-seated ties between the CCP, its military, and the age-old secret societies of China, not to mention the enduring institutional imprints of the imperial system. Distinct from Moore's approach, this book, grounded in historical evidence, highlights the roles of Tsarism and the Chinese imperial system – both markedly distinct from feudalism – in shaping the institutional underpinnings of the totalitarian regimes that subsequently evolved in these regions.

Karl Wittfogel's (1957) examination of the Chinese absolutist imperial system remains one of the most in-depth and extensive in the scholarly literature. Drawing from Montesquieu and Marx, Wittfogel places the Tsarist Russian system alongside China's as emblematic of oriental despotism, labeling them as totalitarian. He perceives communist totalitarianism as merely an extension of the ancient "totalitarian systems" found in China and Russia. However, he overlooks important institutional and ideological distinctions between these absolutist imperial systems and communist totalitarianism. Furthermore, he misses crucial aspects of communist totalitarianism in China and Soviet Russia, such as the nature of the totalitarian party, their governance structures, and their origins. Similarly, while Francis Fukuyama (2011) characterizes the Chinese imperial system as totalitarian, he abstains from delving into China's communist totalitarianism in his work. Wittfogel posits that hydraulic societies underpin Oriental despotic systems, a perspective rooted in Marx's historical materialism and the idea of the Asiatic mode of production. In contrast, this book investigates how Marxist ideology, merged with institutional genes from China and Russia to spawn the secular religious movement of communist totalitarianism, leading to the establishment of the communist totalitarian party-state institution and institutional genes.

This book, while not primarily centered on it, has notable connections to modernization theory (for example, Lipset, 1959) which posits that economic development inevitably leads to democracy. Communist totalitarianism emerges from extensive and fervent secular religious movements that take shape during the modernization process. Such movements endow totalitarianism with a distinctly demagogic and inflammatory nature, granting it substantial mobilizing strength and the capacity to curtail individual freedoms. Interestingly, these systems often display robust economic growth until they reach the middle-income level. Yet, economic advancements therein, and even the presence of nominal "private property rights," do not lead to democratization. This perspective significantly challenges the tenets of modernization theory. When viewed through the prism of institutional genes, it seems that modernization theory either neglects the essential prerequisites for private property rights and economic growth to spur constitutional democracy or it prematurely assumes that these prerequisites are invariably met.

These essential prerequisites can be summarized as follows:

1) Property owners must be sufficiently protected so that they are not only aware that property rights are their inherent rights but also that they possess the will and capability to defend them. This entails:
   - A statutory framework that systematically protects private property rights.
   - An independent judicial system that enforces these rights.
   - Fundamental protection of human rights for all, with particular attention to property owners. Without such safeguards, even if private property rights are legally recognized, the mere control of the owners by the ruler's denying their human rights can coerce the owners into complying with the ruler's wishes.
2) For democratic constitutional systems to evolve in a bottom-up process, property owners must possess political decision-making power, at the very least, at the community and grassroots levels. The ability of property owners to influence collective decisions beyond individual private property rights is pivotal. Only when they hold substantial collective decision-making power at the community level can the institutional genes of democratic constitutionalism take root. This empowers them to unify communities under the banner of constitutionally protected rights of association, facilitating collective decisions on a grander scale.

14.5 THE TRANSFORMATION PATH IN TAIWAN: AN INSTITUTIONAL GENE ANALYSIS

Finally, using Taiwan as a case study, we employ the analytical framework of institutional genes to dissect the differing institutional evolutions between Taiwan and the PRC (mainland China). The focus is on the connection between Taiwan's institutional genes and its institutional transformation.

Contrasting starkly with the totalitarian nature of the PRC, Taiwan underwent a peaceful transition from the KMT's one-party authoritarian regime to a multiparty democratic constitutional system from the late 1980s to the early twenty-first century. Presently, Taiwan thrives as an affluent, advanced economy with a well-established constitutional democracy. In terms of democracy, freedom, and per capita GDP (adjusted for purchasing power), it ranks at the pinnacle in Asia, even outstripping Japan (EIU, 2022; Tyrrell and Kim, 2022; IMF, 2022a).

Did Taiwan and mainland China ever share the same institutional genes? If they did, a challenging question arises: Why was Taiwan able to undergo a successful institutional transformation, while mainland China remained ensnared in the totalitarian system inherited from Imperial China and the Soviet Union? Can the analytical framework of institutional genes explain Taiwan's institutional transformation? What insights can Taiwan's successful institutional transformation provide for the future development of mainland China?

Several prevalent explanations from the literature on Taiwan's institutional transformation are delineated below. The first explanation, grounded in modernization theory, posits that the creation of a constitutional government in Taiwan stemmed from its economic development. Economic development in Taiwan was indeed marked by the significant rise of a middle class with private property rights, which became an institutional gene supporting constitutional transformation. However, it is important to note that, in contrast to Taiwan, whilst mainland China has engendered a substantial private sector and a sizable middle-income class during its economic reform, these businesses and individuals are denied the right to act freely in numerous domains. Consequently, business owners operate in perpetual uncertainty and are aware that ultimate control lies beyond their grasp. It is seriously misleading to assert in general terms that economic development will lead to democratic constitutionalism without distinguishing the actual mechanisms of ownership, considering the human rights of individuals in economic development, or identifying how the economy develops. The illusory expectation that China might transition to democracy as part of the economic development process was once largely misguided by such assertions that overlooked human rights issues.

The second popular explanation underscores the personal roles played by successive KMT heads Chiang Ching-kuo and Lee Teng-hui, asserting that their personal stance, vision, and charisma served as a pivotal factor. Although such an interpretation partially reflects the reality, it neglects other foundational and significant historical elements. Terminating authoritarian rule in Taiwan and establishing a constitutional and democratic system was a protracted and fraught process spanning many stages. Each significant stride in this process was not a proactive strategy orchestrated by the politically powerful but rather it emerged as a result of a gradual process, wherein leaders either acclimatized to or were compelled to capitulate to intense social pressure. Chiang suppressed several peaceful movements advocating for democracy before the mid-1980s. It was not until the later stages of his life when the change transpired. Starting from the late 1980s, and particularly from the 1990s onwards, the KMT leaders elected to conform to social trends in the face of substantial pressure. Throughout this process, they endeavored to surmount the resistance from the conservative faction of the KMT that defended the authoritarian rule, thus asserting themselves as respected political leaders. History demonstrates that significant social pressure was critical for overcoming the conservative forces within the KMT. Even if Chiang and Lee championed constitutional reform owing to personal beliefs and proficiently mastered the political tactics necessary to advance democratic reform, in the absence of this intense societal pressure, the vested interest groups of the KMT would have had sufficient power to depose them. Moreover, the forces that exerted such potent pressure towards democratic constitutional reform in Taiwan are the result of the evolutionary reinforcement of Taiwan's institutional genes for constitutional democracy.

The third opinion attributes Taiwan's successful institutional transformation to Confucianism or Neo-Confucianism. From a philosophical perspective, the academic community holds differing views concerning the relationship between Confucianism and constitutional democracy. Samuel Huntington perceives the two as conflicting values, while Yu Ying-shih sees them as complementary (Huntington, 1996, p. 238; Yü, 2016, chapter 13). We will not delve into Confucian philosophy here but rather provide an empirical overview of the extent of Confucianism's popularity in Taiwan and its influence on Taiwan's institutional transformation. Before Taiwan became a Japanese colony, Confucianism was far less prevalent there than it was in mainland China. Taking the imperial examinations for the *jinshi* (Presented Scholar) degree as an example, a mere 29 individuals from Taiwan were awarded the *jinshi* degree under Chinese imperial rule, compared with 1,373 in Fujian Province during the same period (and 26,813 nationwide; data from Zhu, 1963). Thus, Taiwan accounted for only 2 percent of those from Fujian and 0.11 percent of the total nationwide, despite Taiwan representing 19 percent of the population of Fujian and 0.73 percent of China's population in 1880 (Cao, 2001, vol. 5, pp, 694, 704). That is, it was many times below the national average.

After Taiwan became a Japanese colony in 1895, the standardized Japanese education system implemented since the Taishō period (1912–1926) had a profound impact on Taiwan's ideology. In contrast, the Confucian component of standard Japanese education was limited to the level of literacy. Confucianism did not really become a major part of Taiwan's education and ideology on a large scale until after the Second World War, when it was brought in by the Nationalist government. Moreover, the individuals who played the most significant roles in Taiwan's democratic constitutional transformation (for example, the core members of the Democratic Progressive Party [DPP]) were primarily native Taiwanese who were not deeply influenced by Confucianism. For example, Lee Teng-hui, the KMT chairman, received a comprehensive Japanese education in his early years

14.5 THE TRANSFORMATION PATH IN TAIWAN 679

and later became a devout Christian. Among the Chinese intellectuals and KMT members who arrived in Taiwan after 1945 and were deeply influenced by Confucianism, some supported constitutional democracy in principle and others were against constitutionalist reform. An indisputable fact is that the majority of KMT conservatives during Taiwan's institutional transformation were Confucian adherents, often citing the Confucian classics in their opposition to democratic constitutionalism.

A notable fact is that Taiwan's institutional genes markedly differed from those of the mainland when the Nationalist government took over Taiwan after the Second World War. First, the institutional genes of the Chinese imperial system had only superficial roots in Taiwan. It was not until the Qing dynasty that Taiwan officially became a prefecture of the empire. Prior to this, during the Ming dynasty's reign, after General Zheng Chenggong's conquest of the island in 1662, control over Taiwan was largely symbolic without effective administration. The first regime to rule the whole island of Taiwan was established by the Dutch in 1624. Qing rule in Taiwan was rudimentary, both in terms of ideology and the formal institutions of imperial control. "The sky is high, and the emperor is far away"; the provisions for Chinese imperial control were never profoundly incorporated into the Taiwanese mindset. The limited influence of the imperial examination system and Confucianism during Qing rule in Taiwan underscores the minimal impact of these imperial institutions. As a result, Taiwan became a sanctuary for covert rebel groups escaping from Guangdong and Fujian. One of the most significant armed revolts in the Qing dynasty's history was sparked by a faction of the Heaven and Earth Society in Taiwan during Emperor Qianlong's reign, which then extended to the mainland.

Second, when the KMT and the CCP in mainland China were embracing Bolshevism in the 1920s, Taiwan was deeply influenced by the Japanese constitutional reforms, further differentiating its institutional genes from those in the mainland. In the late nineteenth century, Japan was the primary channel for introducing democratic constitutional thinking to both mainland China and Taiwan but such ideas were embraced much more in Taiwan. Under the Treaty of Shimonoseki between China and Japan, Taiwan was ceded to Japan in 1895 and has since taken a different path of development from that of the mainland. Perhaps the most important of these was the change that took place in Taiwan during the Taishō period (1912–1926) in Japan. Influenced by the European democratic movements of the time, the Japanese elite promoted democratic constitutionalism in both Japan and its colonies, allowing the institutional genes of democratic constitutionalism to gain an initial boost in Taiwan. In 1914, Japanese constitutional reformers and the Taiwanese elite formed the Taiwan Dōkakai (Taiwan Assimilation Society), advocating for equal treatment for Taiwanese and Japanese nationals and hoping that Taiwan would be incorporated into the Japanese constitutional system and have the right to elect representatives to the Japanese Diet. Taiwan's first political party, the New People's Society, was subsequently established and a petition campaign was launched to demand an elected parliament for Taiwan. From then on, the spontaneous, bottom-up demand for democratic autonomy has become part of Taiwan's institutional genes.

As part of the Taishō Democracy policy, from 1919 onwards, Japan implemented the so-called "Extension of Home Rule Policy," treating Taiwan as an extension of Japan, with the aim of establishing a system of local administration, law, and schooling in Taiwan identical to that of Japan. Although only partially executed, it incorporated elements of Taishō-Democracy-era democratic constitutionalism into Taiwan's institutional genes, including bottom-up demands for grassroots autonomy and pressure for democracy. Under pressure from Taiwanese society, in 1935, the Japanese government decided that half of Taiwan's prefectural (county), city, town, and village deputies would be elected by popular vote and this was fully implemented twice, in 1935 and in 1939 (Rubinstein, 2007, pp. 220–234). Entering the Shōwa era, Japan's domestic politics changed. From the 1930s, militarist groupings in the army seized political power in Japan through assassinations and coup attempts. In the 1940s, Japan's militarist government suppressed civil society and democratic demands both in Japan and in its colonies.

However, the institutional genes of constitutionalism that had formed in Taiwanese society in the 1920s were not completely eradicated by the suppression of militarism and resurfaced as soon as they had the opportunity to do so. Since being taken over by the ROC in 1945, there has been popular sentiment in Taiwan to restore local autonomy. Thus, in 1946, general elections for representatives of villages, towns, and cities were held in Taiwan. These were more driven by the demand of Taiwanese society than by the KMT. Evidently, a general election in Taiwan took place before the ROC Constitution was passed and no such comprehensive general election took place in any KMT-controlled province on the mainland. These representatives then indirectly elected county-level delegates, who, in turn, selected thirty senators. From 1950 onwards, administrative heads at the county level and below, as well as provincial and municipally directly governed council members and grassroots representatives, were directly elected by citizens. This means that from 1950 onwards, local governors at and below the county and city level, members of provincial and municipal councils, and deputies at the community level were directly elected by citizens.

Taiwan's democratization process was severely hindered by the February 28 Incident of 1947, during which the ROC government killed more than 30,000 Taiwanese (Fulda, 2019, p. 124). Subsequently, the government implemented martial law. The following year, the "Temporary Provisions Effective during the Period of Communist Rebellion" (hereinafter referred to as "Temporary Provisions") were enacted, superseding the constitution. However, the expansion of local autonomy did not entirely cease. Moreover, despite the ban on forming political parties and the restrictions of elections to local grassroots levels, the relatively stable and limited grassroots elections over several decades allowed the institutional genes of constitutionalism to continue evolving in Taiwan. The

February 28 Incident and the subsequent repression intensified the conflict between the KMT as foreign rulers and the Taiwanese citizens, further fostering democratic consciousness and amplifying the local demand for autonomy in Taiwan.

Third, in stark contrast to the CCP's continuous efforts to prevent "peaceful evolution" during its reforms, the significant development of the private economy, under thorough protection of private ownership in Taiwan, has become an integral part of the institutional genes of constitutionalism. The widespread recognition and relative security of private property rights shape the general motivation and capacity of the population to safeguard their interests. Aiming to eradicate the social roots of the Communist Party, the ROC government executed extensive land reforms in Taiwan, starting from the early 1950s. Under the ROC constitution, these reforms empowered Taiwanese farmers to own their land. Consequently, private enterprises began to thrive, shifting the state-centric economy of the 1950s towards one dominated by the private sector. Under the KMT's one-party rule, the so-called "state assets" were, in essence, KMT resources. Even though the KMT ardently worked to uphold one-party authoritarianism, it diverged significantly from communist totalitarianism that sought to abolish private property. To foster economic growth, the KMT championed the expansion of private enterprises. In 1953, over three-quarters of loans issued by banks (predominantly state-owned) were issued to SOEs, with less than a quarter provided to private enterprises. With the steady development of the private sector, by 1979 the proportion of bank loans issued to private enterprises had risen to 77 percent (Kuo and Ranis, 1981, p. 59). In 1986, on the eve of the lifting of bans on political parties and the press in Taiwan, the share of SOEs in GDP had fallen to just 17 percent.

Private property rights is the economic foundation for the development of independent associations, political parties, and the media. In the 1970s, Taiwan saw a surge in independent media and NGOs opposing the KMT's one-party rule through active participation in local elections. However, a turning point emerged at the close of 1978. After the United States declared its recognition of the People's Republic of China and terminated official diplomatic ties with the Republic of China, Chiang Ching-kuo announced a halt to all elections, leveraging powers vested by the Temporary Provisions. This decision ignited fervent opposition. The government's response was a violent crackdown, leading to the Kaohsiung Incident in late 1979. Yet, the KMT does not embody a totalitarian ethos. Consequently, it cannot openly oppose the basic principles of constitutional democracy or fundamentally undermine its institutional genes. Thus, this suppression of demands for associational freedom and press freedom paradoxically bolstered appeals for reinstating elections and ending the prohibition on political parties and media. This shift piled immense pressure onto the KMT, accelerating the emergence of oppositional political factions.

Having developed over several decades, by the 1980s the institutional genes of constitutionalism in Taiwan were strong enough not only to render the authoritarian violent rule ineffective but also to spark stronger resistance. Ultimately, the KMT government was forced to lift its bans on political parties and the press in 1987, heralding the end of authoritarian rule.

In addition to internal pressures, strong external pressures and influences also made significant contributions. Foremost among these were pressures and influences from the United States on the KMT and the Chiang family. Those pressures intensified after Taiwanese agents assassinated the author of a biography of Chiang Ching-Kuo in the United States in 1984. It weakened the hardline conservatives in the KMT and forced Chiang Hsiao-wu, son of Chiang Ching-kuo and the then head of Taiwan's secret service, to leave Taiwan and henceforth withdraw from politics. As a direct result, the influence the Chiang family had on Taiwan's politics declined after the death of Chiang Ching-kuo in 1988, enabling Lee Teng-hui to resist conservative forces within the KMT and keep pace with public sentiment.

The other major external shock to Taiwan was the democratic transition in South Korea following the 1980 Gwangju Massacre, which was marked by violent upheavals. This was especially relevant as South Korea shared many similar circumstances with Taiwan. In late June 1987, under pressure from both domestic society and the United States, South Korean presidential candidate Roh Tae-woo, the one responsible for the Massacre a few years earlier, declared a democratization manifesto. This manifesto promised to end military rule, ensure freedom of speech, and amend the constitution based on constitutional principles. Facing similar internal and external pressures, just two weeks after Roh's announcement of the democratic manifesto, Chiang announced the lifting of martial law in Taiwan, as well as the cessation of bans on political parties and the press.

Finally, while the maturation of institutional genes supporting constitutional democracy in Taiwan and the escalation of external pressures rendered the demise of authoritarianism in Taiwan nearly inevitable, both Chiang Ching-Kuo and Lee Teng-hui played undeniable roles in easing Taiwan's peaceful transition from authoritarian governance to constitutional democracy. However, in many ways, the actions of these two figures – especially their respective behaviors – can also be interpreted as outcomes of the prevailing institutional genes within Taiwan. Chiang, as an authoritarian leader, maintained a repressive stance up until the late 1980s amidst rising demands for democratic constitutionalism. Yet, he progressively relaxed his control in deference to public opinion and largely sidestepped events akin to the Gwangju Uprising in South Korea in May 1980. His astute decision to appoint Lee Teng-hui as his vice-president in early 1984 and, later, his wise concession to popular sentiment in 1987 by lifting bans on political parties and the media, further underscore his responsive leadership.

Shortly after the bans on political parties and the media were lifted, several political parties, including the DPP, sprang to life, ardently advocating for a democratic government to protect their rights. Yet, entrenched conservative elements within the KMT clung to the aspiration of preserving the one-party authoritarian regime, staunchly opposing any reforms that might erode their dominance.

Demands for constitutional democracy and clamors for reform, driven by opposition parties, students, and a plethora of social groups, reached an unprecedented crescendo. In March 1990, on the eve of the National Assembly's presidential elections, university students in Taipei initiated the Wild Lily Movement. They outlined four core demands: the dissolution of the antiquated National Assembly, which had been elected on the mainland in 1947; the convening of a national affairs conference; the annulment of the Temporary Provisions and the reinstatement of the constitutional order; and the charting of a roadmap for democratic reform. Thousands congregated in the city's main square advocating for their cause, while the DPP rallied tens of thousands in solidarity. Amid this groundswell of public sentiment, the freshly re-elected President Lee Teng-hui engaged with numerous protest leaders at the Presidential Palace, committing to actualizing their four demands. He concurred that the students could form an inter-school entity to monitor the national affairs conference and the progression of democratic reforms, assuring them of their enduring right to stage further demonstrations (Lin, M., 1990, p. 141).

After being elected as the eighth President of the ROC by the National Assembly, Lee harnessed the impassioned student protests and the accompanying social movement, transforming them from a challenge into a powerful catalyst for democratic reform. In tune with public sentiment, within two years he fulfilled the four demands he had pledged to the movement. The annulment of the Temporary Provisions and the dissolution of the National Assembly not only had an immediate and profound influence on society but also laid the groundwork for the subsequent establishment of a robust constitutional system in Taiwan.

The primary obstacle to establishing a constitutional system in Taiwan originated from among the social elite, many of whom were influential KMT members who had retreated from the mainland to Taiwan. These individuals represented the traditional power bloc within the KMT and controlled vast resources across various sectors in Taiwan. The establishment of a constitutional system is incentive-incompatible with their interests. It is unlikely that the ruling party in an authoritarian system would voluntarily relinquish power, automatically abandoning one-party rule and transforming the authoritarian system into a constitutional system of multiparty competition with checks and balances.

Responding to strong societal pressure for local grassroots autonomy, Taiwan introduced grassroots local elections as early as the 1940s. Initially, these elections seemed not to pose a direct threat to KMT dominance. However, as these local elections gained momentum and substance, they began to challenge the KMT's authoritarian rule. Local KMT officials, a product of these elections, often held views distinct from those of many KMT dignitaries from the mainland. They were more inclined towards expanding the scope and scale of elections, as well as pushing for constitutional reforms. This divergence in views created a rift within the KMT. Lee Teng-hui capitalized on this internal divide, promoting reforms within the KMT. He empowered KMT officials who had emerged from local elections, thereby intensifying the divisions within the party. Consequently, the social changes brought about by the early local elections and the changes within the KMT became the driving force behind electoral reform at the provincial and municipal levels, as well as in the National Assembly and the Legislative Yuan.

The foundations laid by local elections, land reform, privatization, civil society organizations, social movements, and several other early reforms set the stage for transformation to constitutional democracy, marked by the opposition party's maiden victory in the 2000 presidential elections. Since that pivotal moment, both the KMT and the DPP have experienced victories and losses in presidential and legislative elections. The evolution and maturity of constitutional democracy in Taiwan have guaranteed its freedom, stability, and continuous economic growth. Under this democratic framework, Taiwan transitioned from a middle-income economy at the end of its authoritarian era to one of the world's most advanced economies. By 2022, its per capita GDP by purchasing power parity surpassed

Australia, Canada, the United Kingdom, all large EU countries, and it was three times more than that of mainland China (IMF, 2022a).

In the following I provide a brief summary of Taiwan's institutional transformation from the perspective of institutional genes.

1) *Divergent Institutional Genes from the Beginning*: Before becoming a Japanese colony in 1895, Taiwan's institutional genes were already different from those of mainland China, owing to the relatively short duration of Chinese imperial rule over Taiwan. The Japanese colonial period further differentiated Taiwan's institutional genes from those of China.
2) *Emergence of Institutional Genes of Constitutionalism*: The institutional genes that Taiwan inherited were already starkly different from those of the mainland when the KMT took over after the Second World War. The Taishō Democracy period under Japanese rule endowed Taiwan with democratic-leaning institutional genes. In contrast, the mainland gravitated towards communist totalitarianism, heavily influenced by the Soviet Union, whilst Taiwan remained largely untouched by such influences.
3) *KMT versus Institutional Genes of Constitutionalism*: Unlike the CCP, the KMT exhibited a duality. On the one hand, the party's real power lay with conservative forces rooted deeply in the Chinese imperial tradition. On the other hand, a faction, primarily made up of intellectuals, championed constitutional democracy. This internal dichotomy was mirrored in the party's overarching goal, which leaned towards constitutionalism, epitomized by the ROC Constitution. While conservative elements attempted to suppress democratic inclinations, they could not completely eradicate the inherent institutional genes supportive of constitutionalism. Because the KMT anchored the legitimacy of its rule in constitutionalism, any deviations from this path necessitated justifications. This contrasts sharply with communist ideology, which regards constitutionalism as its foremost adversary (following the lines of Marx, Lenin, Mao) and seeks to eliminate any trace of it.
4) *External Influence*: The United States played a pivotal role in nurturing the growth of pro-democracy institutional genes in Taiwan and in reinforcing their prominence within the region.

The implications of Taiwan's transformation to constitutional democracy for China can be outlined as follows:

1) *Enlightenment*: The seeds of constitutional democracy had been sown in Taiwan well before its institutional transition. Key components include an appreciation for individual freedoms and rights, a consciousness of a democratic constitutional framework, and active civil society engagement. The awareness and education of both the elite and the general populace form a vital part of the genetic makeup for constitutionalism.
2) *Private Property Rights and Civil Society as a Foundation*: The long-term development of private property rights and civil society, which includes community and grassroots autonomy, combined with the fortification of social forces safeguarding property rights and civil liberties, laid the foundation for Taiwan's institutional transition.
3) *Decay or Fall of Totalitarianism as a Precursor*: The collapse or substantial decline of a totalitarian regime is a prerequisite for nurturing constitutional institutional genes and for spawning societal demands for such governance. Taiwan was never subjected to totalitarian rule. The KMT, while authoritative, was not totalitarian; it did not monopolize every facet of society nor did it eradicate every avenue for the growth and survival of constitutional institutional genes.

14.6 INSTITUTIONAL TRANSFORMATION OF THE COMMUNIST BLOC AND THE ROLE OF INSTITUTIONAL GENES[1]

The communist totalitarian bloc led by the CPSU, primarily the former FSU-EE countries, once aspired to conquer the world but it collapsed peacefully three decades ago. Since 1991, the Soviet Union, and since 1989, the CEE countries of the Communist Bloc have ended their totalitarian communist systems and moved towards market economies and constitutional systems based on private ownership. Since the implantation of the totalitarian communist system in China from the Soviet Union, the foreign totalitarian institutional genes have hybridized with China's traditional institutional genes. This hybridization has gradually evolved into the institutional genes of the totalitarian communist system with distinct Chinese characteristics.

14.6 COMMUNIST BLOC AND THE ROLE OF INSTITUTIONAL GENES

What drove the collapse of the communist totalitarian regimes in the FSU-EE? What lessons can we learn from these collapses? And how can these lessons help us understand the future of China's communist totalitarian system?

It is well documented that the collapse of the totalitarian system of the FSU-EE Bloc was closely linked to the failure of its economic reforms (Zhuravskaya et al., 2024). However, economic failure was not the sole factor. Instead, this collapse was also caused by a combination of highly complementary political and economic factors, as well as institutional genes inherited from each country's history. These factors are summarized as follows.

First, on the political front, since the 1980s, there was an emerging social consensus among some social elites and leadership within the FSU-EE Bloc to loosen or even abandon totalitarian control.[2] This shift was related both to the long and widespread popular resistance to totalitarian rule and to the awakening of humanity as the economic situation continued to deteriorate. The long-term resistance to totalitarian rule and the awakening of humanity were tied to the institutional genes of these countries. The worsening economic situation and the long-term failure of the economic reforms stemmed from the severe incentive problems created by the communist totalitarian system. These economic failures intensified the disillusionment, antipathy, disgust, and resistance to the communist totalitarian system. In turn, political dissatisfaction with the communist totalitarian system further worsened the incentive problems.

Totalitarian systems are built and sustained by violence. However, violence cannot sustain economic growth. Essentially, all the countries of the Communist Bloc achieved high growth rates for a period through massive centralized resource mobilization. In the early 1960s, Khrushchev confidently vowed at the United Nations that the superior socialist system, with its rapid growth, would bury capitalism. However, no communist totalitarian economy has ever achieved economic development (measured by GDP per capita) above the middle-income level. Instead, all Communist Bloc countries experienced a rapid decline in economic growth after reaching the middle-income level and even the most advanced Communist Bloc members achieved significantly lower levels of economic development compared to the advanced capitalist countries.

One of the fundamental factors hindering the economic development of a communist totalitarian system is its economic and institutional foundation, namely, state ownership. State-owned enterprises are the core assets of the Communist Party. Whether in manufacturing or finance, SOEs functioning as party and government agencies were only responsible for managing state assets. Since the government will never let an insolvent SOE go bankrupt and will surely bail it out, SOE executives, aware of this situation, generally take on large amounts of debt to expand and strengthen the SOEs without worrying about the risks associated with borrowing. This common phenomenon under a communist totalitarian system is called the soft budget constraint syndrome (Kornai, 1980).

The SBCs severely distort the incentives of SOEs, leading them to prioritize expansion by investment over efficiency. Inefficient SOEs expand by accumulating high debt to gain scale advantages, compensating for their innovation disadvantages. This results in deteriorating efficiency, operating losses, and economic stagnation throughout the entire economic system. In response to these pressures, the FSU-EE countries embarked on economic reforms, beginning in the late 1960s. Since the aim of the reforms was to preserve the communist totalitarian system while reversing the economic decline, these reforms were premised on retaining state ownership and striving to improve the planned economies and management. Even the most radical Hungarian reforms were limited to so-called market socialism, that is to say, replacing centralized planning with market competition without changing the dominance of state ownership in the economy. In summary, the failure of economic reforms in the FSU-EE countries was because these reforms did not address state ownership. State ownership always creates the problem of SBCs, which inevitably lead to the failure of reforms (Kornai, 1992). The inability to change the constraints of state ownership stems from the ideological and institutional incompatibility of communist totalitarian regimes with private ownership.

Prolonged economic stagnation posed enormous difficulties and challenges for the FSU-EE countries. Social discontent was rampant, with large-scale strikes and demonstrations in many countries and regions. In 1982, after his promotion from head of the KGB to leader of the USSR, Andropov openly stated that the greatest threat to the security of the USSR came from poverty and the resulting riots or strikes, rather than from imperialism and dissidents (Medvedev, 2017, p. 39). This clearly demonstrated the anxiety among the top echelons of the FSU-EE communist parties due to the failure of economic reforms.

When Mikhail Gorbachev came to power in 1985, there was a general consensus among the top leadership of the Soviet Communist Party that the main cause of the prolonged economic stagnation was a general loss of enthusiasm and motivation in Soviet society, coupled with widespread rebellious sentiment. The Soviet Central Committee referred to those negative factors as a "mechanism of deceleration" resisting the Soviet system and believed the Soviet Union was on the brink of crisis. Consequently, they believed that to move forward, it was necessary to launch reforms addressing a range of political, economic, and ideological issues simultaneously (Yakovlev, 1989, in Aganbergyan, 1989). Under this guiding principle, Gorbachev promoted Perestroika, meaning comprehensive restructuring or reforms, to address all of these problems holistically. The 27th Congress of the Communist Party of the Soviet Union (CPSU) proposed reforming the economic mechanisms and introducing democratization to reverse the stagnation of the past decade. Perestroika and democratization became the main slogans of the Communist Party. Additionally, the Soviet Communist Party gradually liberalized freedom of speech and allowed dissident physicist and Nobel laureate Andrei Sakharov to return to Moscow (Lowenhardt et al., 1992, pp. 74–75).

Gorbachev's economic reforms were toothless. The 12th Five-Year Plan under Gorbachev's presidency focused on machinery manufacturing and technological improvements (Medvedev, 2017, p. 38). Specific reforms aimed to address issues of over-centralization and bureaucracy. During subsequent inspections, Gorbachev emphasized that the central government should not intervene in the day-to-day operations of basic economic institutions and that enterprises should be left to fend for themselves. He also suggested, in principle, that most problems should be resolved locally and that the best management methods should align with both industrial and regional principles (Medvedev, 2017, pp. 43–45). At the same time, he pushed for the legalization of individually owned enterprises under the guise of reform but avoided mentioning the concepts of privatization and private property rights.

To gain political legitimacy, Gorbachev referred to his reforms as the second wave of the Leninist New Economic Policies (Aganbergyan, 1989, p. 9), which appeared similar to Deng Xiaoping's 1982 articulation of the nature of China's economic reforms. However, in essence, Gorbachev was more concerned with political democratization, which eventually violated Leninist principles. In terms of economic reform, his efforts failed to make any substantial progress because he did not and could not address the incentive problems of economic issues within the party-state bureaucracy.

Not only in the Soviet Union but in all Eastern bloc countries, economic reforms were ineffective and their economies were deteriorating. They faced urgent challenges to their financial, fiscal, economic, and social stability. This led more elites in these countries to fundamentally question the reformability of the communist totalitarian system (Hewett, 1990a). Even those primarily concerned with the economy recognized that fundamentally changing the communist totalitarian system was unavoidable. The root of the problem was state ownership but communist regimes were not allowed to abandon it. Many social elites in the FSU-EE Communist Bloc, including economists, intellectuals, and even high-ranking Communist Party figures, began to focus on human rights issues, freedom, and democracy, rather than limiting themselves to economic issues. They gradually converged on a consensus to abandon totalitarian control in all aspects (Zubok, 2021).

In 1990, after the collapse of all the CEE communist totalitarian regimes, the Soviet economy slumped to a level deemed dangerous by the Soviet leadership. Under multiple political and economic pressure, Gorbachev tentatively accepted the "500-Day Reform Program" drafted by Stanislav Shatalin and Grigory Yavlinsky that summer. This comprehensive reform proposal garnered support from reformers both within and outside the CPSU, especially from Gorbachev's political rival Boris Yeltsin. However, Gorbachev eventually abandoned it due to strong opposition from conservative factions in the CPSU. With the abandonment of this reform program, the Soviet leadership began to focus on managing the increasingly divisive political situation, leaving economic reforms off the agenda (Zubok, 2021, pp. 131–216; Taubman, 2017, chapters 14–15).

The discussion of this unimplemented "500-Day Reform Program" is important here because it fully reflects the reform ideas of the CPSU and the Soviet social elite at that time. Fundamentally different from any reform plan or idea of the Chinese Communist Party, this plan was a comprehensive scheme to abandon totalitarianism. Building on the political reforms already underway in the Soviet Union (see below), the plan proposed returning sovereignty to the republics, stipulating that the new Soviet government would be limited to serving the republics without interfering in their internal affairs.[3] Economically, the plan called for the establishment of a market economy within two years, with prices determined primarily by market supply and demand and the full privatization of most enterprises. The ruble was to become a freely convertible currency and the economy as a whole was to be transformed from bureaucratic and military-oriented to consumer-oriented. The plan also stipulated that the republics would independently determine the method and pace of introduction of the market but that the USSR had to maintain a unified market with uniform tariffs and no economic borders between the republics. The "500-Day Reform Program" included rapid privatization and measures to strengthen fiscal discipline to control inflation, aiming to create conditions for a fully open market (Hewett, 1990b).

The "500-Day Reform Program" was not an isolated incident. Five years before the plan was proposed, at the beginning of Gorbachev's rise to power, Yakovlev had already submitted a comprehensive reform program with similar ideas. He noted that the Soviet Union's "problems are not just economic, but fundamentally political." With regard to political reform, he emphasized democracy, human rights, transparency, and the independence of the judiciary. He asserted that "the judiciary must be truly independent of all other powers." Notable reform suggestions included the institutional reform of the Communist Party, transforming it into a Communist Union with two factions or even two parties with a joint Politburo as the supreme ruling body and the direct election of the national president. The directly elected president would also serve as the chairman of the joint Politburo and Parliament (Yakovlev, 1999, pp. 205–212).

It is particularly noteworthy that the mere failure of economic reforms or economic stagnation is not sufficient to drive the social elites of communist societies to form a consensus to abandon totalitarianism because the elites' interests are nested in the system and rely on totalitarian political power. The Communist leadership, as the ruling group of the totalitarian regime, is the largest vested interest group holding power. Without other factors, the rational choice for the rulers and ruling groups during economic stagnation would be to maintain power at all costs. To preserve their power, totalitarian rulers would use violence to suppress dissent and eliminate any potential resistance in its infancy.

Therefore, the formation of a social consensus among social elites and within the Communist leadership to relax control or even abandon totalitarianism in a totalitarian society largely depends on factors beyond the economy. One such factor is the importance and prevalence of humanity and humanitarianism as intrinsic values in society. Indeed, the upper echelons of the Communist Party of the Soviet Union, as well as those in Poland, Czechoslovakia, Hungary, and other countries, showed tendencies to relax totalitarian control long before the economy had collapsed. The institutional genes inherited from their histories were crucial in this aspect. Additionally, the Eastern bloc region had close interconnections historically. A shock to one country often triggered chain reactions in many other countries in the region.

Despite the fact that the countries of the Central and Eastern European bloc were established under communist totalitarian rule by the violence of the Soviet Red Army, the different institutional genes that the countries inherited from history have resulted in varying degrees of acceptance of or resistance to communist totalitarianism in each country. This influenced not only the stability of totalitarian rule in these countries but also the direction of institutional transformation after the collapse of totalitarianism. Some countries historically progressed further and earlier in the pursuit of human rights, freedom, and democracy. Without exception, all of these countries, such as Poland, Czechoslovakia, and the Baltic States, had long possessed certain institutional genes in favor of democratic constitutionalism. These countries not only led the way in rejecting communist totalitarianism but also relatively smoothly established constitutional democracies, becoming economically developed nations. In contrast, countries with a history of highly autocratic systems often ended up with authoritarian regimes disguised as democracies after the collapse of totalitarianism. Under such authoritarian regimes, economic development has also been difficult. Most of the former Soviet Union countries, except the Baltic States, fall into this category.

Poland, Czechoslovakia, Hungary, the Baltic States, and Germany, for example, had experienced elected monarchs and some form of parliament since the Middle Ages. In these countries, a sense of preference for constitutionalism and national independence had long existed in society. These institutional genes made it difficult to establish communist totalitarianism in the absence of external violence. The violent revolutions waged by the Comintern in Hungary and Germany both failed and development in other Central and Eastern European countries was also slow. Although Poland did not experience a complete modern democratic constitutional system in its history, it had a long tradition of parliamentary systems dating back to the Middle Ages, nurturing a rudimentary constitutional consciousness. Poland had established a national parliament, known as the Sejm, since the fifteenth century, one of the oldest national parliaments in Europe. The subsequent Polish–Lithuanian Commonwealth, which lasted for over two centuries, had monarchs elected by the nobility and national parliament members elected from various regions, with local governance relying on local parliaments (Jędruch, 1998). Although not a modern democratic system, the social consensus formed by this elite parliamentary system became the foundation for resisting totalitarian rule. Under the influence of this social consensus, even radical Marxists, such as Rosa Luxemburg, a Polish-born leader of the Second International (the global proletarian revolutionary organization founded by Engels), firmly opposed Leninism and Bolshevik totalitarianism.

In Poland, although the Polish United Workers' Party (PUWP), the communist party in Poland, gained a majority of votes and came to power, it was never able to establish a solid totalitarian regime due to the constraints of Poland's inherited institutional genes. Throughout the history of the communist regime, none of the PUWP's leaders were staunch totalitarian rulers. Their general weakness was itself an important factor in fueling the forces of resistance to the totalitarian system in Polish society. The institutional genes unfavorable to totalitarianism that Poland inherited from its history include the enormous influence of the Catholic Church, the tradition of civil organizations among the Polish populace, and the tradition of protecting private land ownership by farmers.

Intimidated by the powerful influence of Catholicism in Poland, the PUWP never managed to take over or suppress the Church since the establishment of its totalitarian regime, making Poland the only communist totalitarian state to allow the existence of a Church independent of communist rule, entirely out of the PUWP's control. Catholicism had been the state religion of Poland since the tenth century, and the vast majority of Poles were devout Catholics when the communist regime was established. To avoid inciting resistance from Catholic believers, the PUWP had no choice but to allow the Catholic Church, which maintained close ties with the Vatican, to continue operating in Poland. This allowed the Catholic Church to become a part of Polish society that the PUWP could not control, increasing its influence over time.

While the PUWP did not dare to follow Soviet control of the Russian Orthodox Church by relying on both carrots and sticks, it still tried to compete with the Church for influence in order to maintain its rule in Poland. However, it lost this competition. In 1960, two years after the PUWP suppressed the Poznań uprising (discussed below), the government decided to grandly celebrate the millennium of Polish Christianity to win public favor, trying to influence the majority of Poles, who were Catholic. On July 22, 1966, PUWP leaders presided over the official celebration of the millennium of Polish Christianity, with the participation of the PUWP military. On the same day, the Polish Cardinal led another large-scale celebration (Davies, 2005).

The Catholic world provided significant support to Polish Catholics and the Polish Catholic Church. In 1967, the Vatican appointed the distinguished Polish priest Karol Wojtyła as a cardinal. In 1978, he was elected by the Vatican to be the Pope of the Catholic Church as Pope John Paul II. This further connected the Polish Catholic Church to the global Catholic world. Facing this overwhelming influence, the PUWP had no choice but to continue adopting a conformist strategy on Catholicism.

The year after Pope John Paul II ascended to the papacy, the PUWP invited him to return to Poland where he co-hosted a grand commemoration of the 900th anniversary of the death of Poland's Patron

Saint Stanislaus, a martyr killed by the crown. This elevated the influence of the Church in Poland to new heights. The establishment of the Independent Self-Governing Trade Union "Solidarity" (Solidarność) by Polish workers two years later was closely related to this growing influence.

Pope John Paul II's significant impact on Polish society was directly linked to Poland's institutional genes. First, the historical importance of Catholicism in Poland prevented the PUWP from banning or fully controlling the Church, allowing it to survive and expand, and allowing the Pope to exert substantial influence over the Polish populace. Second, what set Pope John Paul II apart from other Popes was his direct challenge to totalitarian rule. His philosophy and courage to directly challenge totalitarian rule were shaped by the environment that nurtured him, rooted in Poland's institutional genes and the social consensus in Polish society that pursued human rights, constitutionalism, and resistance to totalitarianism.

Another institutional gene in Poland is the long-standing tradition of labor unions and worker movements. The large-scale worker movements in Poland not only deeply influenced the country but also acted as a catalyst for the collapse of the entire CEE Communist Bloc. In 1956, four months after Khrushchev's secret report, a general strike of 100,000 workers broke out in Poznań. This was the first large-scale spontaneous workers' movement in the whole communist world. The strike was temporarily quelled by tanks and military police. However, there had been sporadic spontaneous workers' movements throughout Poland since then. The 1970s saw a resurgence of the labor movement in many parts of the country, producing many labor movement leaders. In 1980, the dismissal of labor movement leaders from the Gdańsk shipyard (then the Lenin Shipyard) triggered a general strike on a scale never seen before. Workers from hundreds of factories across Poland joined the strike in support of the Gdańsk workers. The nationwide strike forced the government to concede to many of the workers' demands, leading to the famous Gdańsk Agreement (Gdańsk Social Accord) (Persky, 1981). This

14.6 COMMUNIST BLOC AND THE ROLE OF INSTITUTIONAL GENES 699

agreement not only recognized independent trade unions but also paved the way for freedom of association. Legalized unions and social organizations continually staged strikes and demonstrations, including nationwide strikes, to defend human rights. This made it difficult for the PUWP to maintain totalitarian control over the population (Ekiert and Kubik, 2001).

Immediately after the signing of the Gdansk Agreement, Polish workers established Solidarity (Independent Self-Governing Trade Union). This was the first national independent workers' organization in the Communist Bloc. Subsequently, Poland saw a surge in civil organizations, strikes, and demonstrations (Persky, 1981). The Polish government then suppressed the Solidarity movement and imprisoned its leader, Lech Wałęsa. However, in 1983, Pope John Paul II visited Poland again and insisted on meeting the imprisoned Wałęsa. He publicly encouraged people to continue their fight for human rights and stated that martial law must end. Everywhere the Pope went, people were enthusiastic and openly expressed their grievances with the communist regime. A month after the Pope left Poland, martial law ended (Ekiert and Kubik, 2001).

The establishment of Solidarity and the government's concession to end martial law under public pressure was the first time in the communist world that a government resolved a conflict through peaceful means due to civilian pressure. This highlighted the weakening of totalitarian rule and marked the first step toward the peaceful dissolution of the FSU-EE communist regimes a few years later.

The series of events in Poland had a profound and broad impact on the entire Communist Bloc. Since the Poznań strike in 1956, each instance of Polish resistance against communist totalitarianism triggered a domino effect within the bloc. After the suppression of the Poznań workers' movement, the moderate PUWP leader Władysław Gomułka took office, attempting to introduce reforms and pacify the Poles. This immediately sparked a nationwide revolution in Hungary, demanding the withdrawal of Soviet troops and calling for freedom and constitutional governance. Although the Hungarian revolution was brutally crushed by Soviet forces and the Warsaw Pact, the deterrent effect of the suppression was only temporary and localized.

Parallel to Poland, Czechoslovakia served as another catalytic force in bringing down Eastern bloc communist totalitarianism. As one of the birthplaces of the Reformation, Czechoslovakia was a republic with a relatively well-developed parliamentary democracy before the Second World War. The country's institutional genes made establishing a totalitarian regime particularly difficult. At the 1945 Yalta Conference, Stalin promised Roosevelt and Churchill that the people of Central and Eastern Europe would be allowed to determine their governing systems through popular voting. However, to ensure they could gain ruling power in the Soviet-occupied countries, the Communist parties supported by the Soviet Union relied on violence, coercion, and distortion of votes or referendums to gain sufficient votes in most of those countries (Plokhy, 2010; Nohlen and Stöver, 2010). Reflecting the social sentiments of the time, the Communist Party of Czechoslovakia (KSC) was unable to establish a communist totalitarian regime as it failed to secure enough seats until the KSC staged a coup in 1948 (Korbel, 1959).

In 1967, under the relatively relaxed control of the Communist Bloc, some writers in Czechoslovakia began systematically criticizing the Communist Party, demanding literary independence from party control (Williams, 1997, p. 55). Like dissenters in any totalitarian regime, they were purged. However, there was sympathy for these dissidents in Czech society, even within the Communist Party. Influenced by this social consensus, the KSC leader who purged these writers was soon forced to step down and Alexander Dubček became the party leader. While claiming to uphold Communist Party leadership, he simultaneously relaxed totalitarian controls, limited the power of the secret police, advocated for freedom of speech, and even considered moving towards a multiparty system. In 1968, the KSC introduced a political program called "socialism with a human face," initiating the reforms known as the Prague Spring (Williams, 1997).

"Socialism with a human face" was an attempt to infuse communist totalitarianism with a degree of humanity. However, ideologically and institutionally, humanity directly conflicts with totalitarianism. Even if the intent of the reforms was to consolidate totalitarian rule, emphasizing humanity fundamentally undermines such a regime. Recognizing the threat that the KSC's reforms posed to the entire Communist Bloc, the Warsaw Pact, the military alliance of the bloc led by Brezhnev, sent troops to suppress the Prague Spring. However, the spirit represented by "socialism with a human face" was not extinguished by military suppression; instead, it spread widely across the Communist Bloc, influencing leaders like Gorbachev and some others within the FSU-EE Communist parties.

Marxism, the ideology of communist totalitarianism, asserts that human society consists only of classes, with no humanity separate from class. In a class society, there is only the dictatorship of the ruling class over the ruled; socialism must be the dictatorship of the proletariat. This theory has been highly effective in inciting revolution and violence (see Chapters 6, 8, 10, and 11). With this ideology, the Communists eliminated humanity and humanitarianism, which enabled Lenin to create a violent totalitarian system based on the institutional genes inherited from Tsarist Russia. It was this ideology that enabled Stalin, Mao, and other communists to perfect the communist totalitarian system and to use this machine to persecute large numbers of their political enemies and challengers both inside and outside the party. The continuous purges within the communist parties created immense fear among party members. This forced some communists to re-examine the consequences of a dictatorship of the proletariat that utterly denies humanity, driven by concerns for their own safety.

The introspection on humanity within the Communist Bloc began with the Soviet Union's de-Stalinization in 1956. Khrushchev's secret report at the 20th Congress of the CPSU started this process. Out of the self-interest of the majority of the CPSU leadership and party members, Khrushchev attempted to reduce the fear that had permeated the Communist Bloc during Stalin's era (Jones, 2006). However, using violence to instill fear both within and outside the party is a necessary component of totalitarian rule and maintaining fear is a pillar of communist totalitarianism.

Khrushchev's de-Stalinization had barely begun when it triggered Polish uprisings and Hungarian revolutions that shook the totalitarian regimes. To prevent a domino effect within the Communist Bloc and to maintain totalitarian rule, Khrushchev responded to the events in Poland and Hungary with Stalinist-style violent repression, abruptly halting the nascent introspection on humanity. His successor, Brezhnev, fully restored Stalinism and the suppression of the Prague Spring was part of this restoration. However, repression is one thing, eradicating humanity is another. During the revolutionary period, the Communist Party relied on inciting class hatred. Nevertheless, inciting class consciousness after the establishment of a totalitarian system inevitably created instability (as seen in China's Cultural Revolution, see Chapter 12).

In the absence of class consciousness, even the most twisted ideology struggles to find convincing reasons to eradicate humanity. Therefore, no other autocratic regime, apart from Marxist-Leninist ones, has attempted to completely eradicate humanity. Even during the most brutal periods of Tsarist and imperial Chinese rule, there was still some space for humanity. In any society, the extent to which people identify with humanity is a significant part of the social consensus and is part of society's institutional genes. Thus, the fundamentally anti-humanity nature of Marxist-Leninist ideology will inevitably clash with the pre-existing humanity in any society. De-Stalinization and the Prague Spring's call for "socialism with a human face" were the initial steps taken by communist leaders toward reclaiming humanity.

In 1985, Mikhail Gorbachev, influenced by the spirit of the Prague Spring, became the supreme leader of the CPSU. Upon taking office, he promoted socialist democracy and relaxed totalitarian control on several fronts. While attending the funeral of his predecessor,

Chernenko, Gorbachev openly repudiated Brezhnevism in front of the leaders of the Eastern European Communist parties, fundamentally rejecting the juridical basis for Soviet intervention in East Germany, Hungary, and Czechoslovakia. He emphasized that the CPSU valued equality among the allies and respected their sovereignty and independence (Taubman, 2017, p. 363). These principles he emphasized later ensured that the people of those countries could choose to abandon totalitarianism without fear of Soviet intervention.

Although Gorbachev genuinely believed in socialism-communism and was committed to preserving the Soviet Union, he also believed that socialism must have a human face and that the plight of the communist camp was brought on by a lack of humanity. The core of Gorbachev's "new thinking" was that the CPSU could rule without the use of violence. Such perceptions, represented by Gorbachev and Dubček, fundamentally contradicted the basic ideology of communist totalitarianism and effectively undermined the totalitarian rule of the Communist Bloc. When the countries of Central and Eastern Europe realized that their actions against totalitarian rule would no longer be met with violent repression by Soviet and Warsaw Pact troops, movements opposing totalitarianism quickly spread, putting an end to totalitarian rule that had abandoned its violent oppression.

Gorbachev's comprehensive reforms primarily focused on political system reform. Shortly after taking office, he promoted the ideology of socialist democracy, advocating for new political thinking, democratization, and socialist pluralism, and encouraging the formation of informal associations (Aganbergyan, 1989). Socialist democracy had been included in the Stalin Constitution as early as 1936 and was a typical anti-democratic propaganda term. However, Gorbachev's version of socialist democracy was genuine; it seriously loosened totalitarian control and continued the de-Stalinization process. This ultimately pushed the totalitarian regime towards its demise.

The conservative faction within the CPSU, both ideologically driven and vested-interest-driven, persisted in its repression of dissidents at home and abroad, including the suppression of the Prague Spring. To them, the concept of socialist democracy could only be used as a deceptive propaganda slogan and it was prohibited in any serious discussions. Andropov, Chernenko's predecessor, who was followed by Gorbachev, had clearly warned about the dangers of socialist democracy (Zubok, 2021, p. 42).

The current of promoting socialist democracy within the CPSU had its origins in the brief period of de-Stalinization under Khrushchev. Although de-Stalinization was quickly reversed at the institutional level, the liberalization movement continued to simmer beneath the surface. One of the strategies was to deliberately leverage the so-called writings of the young Marx (philosophical articles written by Marx before he became involved in the communist movement and when he was not yet a Marxist) as the theoretical foundation for advocating humanity. Since the 1960s, Soviet intellectuals had introduced these writings from the West. They sought to find an orthodox Marxist path to a socialist democracy that embraced humanity. Some of them, including Gorbachev and his key aide Medvedev, viewed the advocacy of socialist democracy and individual freedoms as part of Marxist-Leninist and socialist ideology, without realizing that this fundamentally contradicted Marxist-Leninist communist totalitarianism.

In his 1987 book, *Perestroika: New Thinking for Our Country and the World* (Gorbachev, 1988), Gorbachev systematically outlined his ideas for implementing democratic socialism. His Perestroika intended to launch fundamental political reforms by allowing freedom of assembly and freedom of speech and publication. He emphasized that democratization was the central task of the CPSU, stating that Glasnost meant openness and transparency, allowing people to know everything and giving them the right to learn the truth about past events in the Soviet Union. To ideologically support the shift towards humane socialism and democratic socialism, Gorbachev urged Politburo members and Soviet leaders to read and discuss the writings of the young Marx on humanity and humanitarianism

(Zubok, 2021, pp. 32–35). He genuinely believed that reform or socialist economic modernization had to rely on socialist democracy, otherwise, the people would feel alienated and become lazy, like slaves (Zubok, 2021, p. 34).

In addition, there was also a group within the CPSU that no longer believed in communist ideology. Represented by Gorbachev's key aide, Yakovlev, they strategically used certain writings of Marx and Lenin to promote democracy and freedom with the purpose of undermining communist totalitarianism (Taubman, 2017; Medvedev, 2017; Yakovlev, 1999). Meanwhile, many of the leading figures in Russia and the Baltic States who promoted independence movements, including Boris Yeltsin, never used Marxist-Leninist rhetoric as a cover (Medvedev, 2017).

The constitutional amendments and parliamentary elections carried out between 1988 and 1989 were the most significant political system reforms in the USSR. According to the planned reform, new Congresses of People's Deputies of the Soviet Union would be created at all levels through universal suffrage in the republics of the USSR and the elected chairmen of the Congresses would simultaneously be the first secretaries of the Communist Party of the republic. With this institutional reform, Gorbachev tried to form an alliance between the Communist Party Secretariat and Parliament to counteract the traditional bureaucratic system formed by the central ministries of the Soviet Union (Lowenhardt et al., 1992, pp. 76–77). In pushing for this reform, Gorbachev demanded that party members vote and express their opinions based on their conscience and that in return the CPSU would not use party discipline to punish members for their voting choices (Taubman, 2017, chapter 12). This effectively abandoned the basic principles of a Leninist party.

Gorbachev later summarized that the purpose of this reform was to peacefully end the Communist Party's one-party rule. He stated that the goal was to transfer power from the Communist Party to the Soviets through free elections, forcing the party to "voluntarily relinquish its dictatorship." Gorbachev described his mission as "cutting off" the Kremlin conservatives and replacing them with new external forces (Taubman, 2017, pp. 558–559). Whether or not posterity believes Gorbachev's retrospective statements, and regardless of his original intentions, the indisputable fact is that this reform of the political system transformed the Soviets into parliaments of the people. By enabling the election of deputies and presidents of Soviet republics, this reform fundamentally undermined the foundations of totalitarianism.

Although Gorbachev tried hard to preserve the Soviet Union, the efforts to dissolve it went hand in hand with those dismantling the Communist Party's political monopoly almost simultaneously within the country. After the republics elected their parliaments and leaders, the calls for sovereignty and independence grew louder in Russia, the Baltic States, and other republics. The newly elected parliaments and leaders, in their legitimate capacities, demanded a multiparty system and sought independence from the Soviet Union. Russian leader Yeltsin openly called for a multiparty system as early as 1988 (Zubok, 2021, p. 39). Lithuanian leaders also called for a multiparty system while seeking independence. Although Gorbachev publicly accepted their demands for a multiparty system, he still tried to prevent the dissolution of the Soviet Union (Zubok, 2021, p. 104).

While Russia and the Baltic States were struggling for independence from the Soviet Union, Poland, Hungary, and Czechoslovakia were the first countries in history to peacefully rid themselves of totalitarian regimes by ending communist rule. After two major strikes in Poland in 1988, the PUWP was forced to negotiate with the Solidarity movement in early 1989. The negotiations resulted in recognition of Solidarity's legal status and an agreement to hold national parliamentary elections on June 4. Solidarity won the national elections, replacing the PUWP to form the Polish cabinet. Solidarity leader Lech Wałęsa was elected president of Poland in 1990. The leaders of the PUWP, who had served as prime ministers and presidents of Poland, resigned in August 1989 and early 1990, respectively (de Nevers, 2003, chapter 3). After more than three decades of resistance and repression, the communist totalitarian system collapsed peacefully in Poland.

Similar to the events in Poland, Hungary's political situation quickly followed suit. At the end of 1988, the Hungarian parliament introduced a package of democratic reforms, lifting press and party bans and allowing the establishment of independent trade unions. On National Day in March 1989, large-scale demonstrations demanded negotiations between the Communist Party and non-communist political forces. These negotiations began in April and resulted in a constitutional reform agreement by September. In October, the Hungarian parliament announced that multiparty elections and the direct election of the president would be held in 1990. The Communist Party was defeated in the elections and stepped down from power, bringing an end to the totalitarian communist rule in Hungary (de Nevers, 2003, chapter 4).

The domino effect of the fall of communist totalitarianism spread quickly in CEE countries. Between 1988 and 1989, numerous demonstrations erupted across Czechoslovakia to commemorate the Prague Spring of twenty years earlier and to mourn its victims. The indecisive repression by anti-riot police led to even larger demonstrations and a nationwide general strike. Under such pressure, the KSC announced at the end of November 1989 that it would relinquish one-party rule. Multiparty elections held in December produced a new parliament and president (de Nevers, 2003, chapter 5). Since then, the moderate "Velvet Revolution" has peacefully transformed Czechoslovakia from a communist regime to a constitutional democracy.

When Poland, Hungary, and Czechoslovakia peacefully ended communist rule, they were still members of the Warsaw Pact, the world's largest military alliance capable of suppressing challenges to communist regimes. At that time, the Soviet Union still had tens of thousands of troops stationed in Poland and hundreds of thousands in other CEE countries. The fate of the CPSU was closely tied to the fate of the CEE Communist Bloc. However, the Soviet Union decided not to use military force to suppress Poland, Hungary, Czechoslovakia, and East Germany. The Communist leaders in these countries, facing pressure from demonstrations and strikes, also chose not to use their own military forces to suppress the protests, which made it possible for these nations to avoid repeating past tragedies.

Totalitarian regimes begin with violence and end with the cessation of violence. Ending violent repression of dissent is a necessary condition for ending totalitarian rule. The question is, what conditions lead totalitarian rulers to stop using violence?

Totalitarian rulers typically do not refrain from using violence to protect their power when their rule is threatened. However, Gorbachev honored his promise, made when he first took office, to respect the sovereignty of other Communist Bloc countries and did not resort to violence even when the survival of the Communist Bloc was seriously challenged. This decision was influenced by changes in the balance of social forces and social consensus, including changes in the social consensus among some top communist leaders. The connections between these changes in social consensus and institutional genes will be explained later.

On the one hand, the forces advocating for freedom in Poland, Hungary, and Czechoslovakia had grown stronger after decades of repression and setbacks. Nationwide organizations and trade unions and the nationwide demonstrations and strikes they organized made the cost of repression prohibitively high. On the other hand, some members of the Soviet Bloc's upper echelons, including Gorbachev and his aides, as well as the leaders of the Polish, Hungarian, and Czechoslovak Communist Parties, underwent a cognitive or ideological change. They abandoned or relaxed their belief in the dictatorship of the proletariat, believing that socialist democracy, or negotiation and compromise, should be the way to address the challenges they faced. Gorbachev hoped that each of the CEE countries would produce their own version of Perestroika. He was relieved and even pleased when Poland, Hungary, Czechoslovakia, and East Germany each ended communist rule in their own way (Taubman, 2017, chapter 13; Gorbachev, 1995, chapters 31–33).[4]

In contrast, the so-called "reformists" of the CCP, represented by Deng Xiaoping, differed greatly in their perceptions and objectives from the Communist Party leaders of the FSU-EE Bloc who pushed for reforms in the 1980s, represented by Gorbachev. The CCP viewed talk of democracy merely as a tool to maintain the party's power. Deng Xiaoping regarded Gorbachev as an "idiot" for genuinely implementing political democratization, as doing so would inevitably lead to loss of power. At the same time, Deng believed that economic reform was necessary to maintain and strengthen power, which required maintaining firm control (Vogel, 2011, pp. 423–424).

In fact, the difference between the CCP and the FSU-EE communist parties in adhering to totalitarianism had been evident shortly after Stalin's death. Soon after Khrushchev's secret report on behalf of the CPSU in 1956, the CCP publicly opposed de-Stalinization in various forms, with Deng playing a crucial role and earning Mao's high praise (Vogel, 2011, chapter 12). To prevent an anti-communist trend similar to that in Poland and Hungary from occurring in China, Mao quickly launched the Anti-Rightist Campaign to comprehensively purge intellectuals, with Deng being one of the top leaders and the main executor of this campaign (Vogel, 2011, chapter 12).

Although de-Stalinization was brief in official terms, from the perspective of fundamentalist communists, it opened a Pandora's box of humanitarianism within the totalitarian regimes. Its impact on the FSU-EE countries was profound and long-lasting. Gorbachev and many of his top aides, such as Yakovlev, were deeply influenced by de-Stalinization (Taubman, 2005, chapter 11). De-Stalinization allowed and induced the recognition of human rights within Soviet and Eastern European societies to flourish, fostering doubt and even resistance against the fundamental values and practices of communist totalitarianism. This trend, labeled "revisionism" by the CCP, continued to grow even during Brezhnev's return to Stalinism. Dubček's "socialism with a human face" in 1968 and Gorbachev's promotion of democratic socialism starting in 1986, which intentionally relaxed totalitarian control, were both consequences of this "revisionist" trend.

In contrast to the de-Stalinization trend in the FSU-EE Bloc, shortly after Mao's death, Deng Xiaoping in 1979 ordered the arrest of dissidents calling for "political modernization," that is to say, political liberalization, and declared the Four Cardinal (Totalitarian) Principles as the untouchable red lines for China's reforms. In the early 1980s, Deng and other CCP elders thoroughly suppressed any attempted de-Maoization efforts within the CCP, preventing de-Maoization from ever starting in China. Moreover, during the 1980s, Deng initiated two anti-bourgeois liberalization campaigns and removed Hu Yaobang from his position as the General Secretary of the CCP for failing to suppress bourgeois liberalization vigorously. In 1989, Deng personally mobilized tanks and hundreds of thousands of troops to crush the peaceful demonstrations in Beijing and placed Zhao Ziyang under house arrest (Vogel, 2011, chapter 13).

After Poland, Hungary, and Czechoslovakia ended totalitarian rule by universal suffrage, the CPSU also decided to end its one-party rule in August 1991. Responding to these serious threats, Deng Xiaoping convened an emergency meeting with General Secretary of the CCP Jiang Zemin, who had recently returned from Moscow, military leader Yang Shangkun, Premier Li Peng, and other top CCP leaders. He emphasized that regardless of what happened in the Soviet Union, the CCP must maintain its unchallengeable leadership and not be influenced by external events (Vogel, 2011, p. 657). Deng assessed that the collapse of the CPSU was due to the failure of Soviet economic reforms. In this emergency, he went on a southern tour a few months later and pushed for economic reforms with all his might to keep the CCP in power. The success of these economic reforms, driven by the development of a private economy under China's RADT governance structure and the integration of trade and investment with developed countries, not only preserved the CCP's power but also allowed China to replace the Soviet Union as a totalitarian superpower (Vogel, 2011, chapter 13).

However, the decade-old issue of the reformability of the socialist economy now applied to China. Like the Soviet Union in the 1980s, soon after China became a middle-income country, its economic growth rate continued to decline sharply, entering a period of stagnation beginning in 2019. Starting in 2023, China faced increasing risks of financial and fiscal crises. Similar to the stagnation in the FSU-EE countries during the 1980s, the CCP has found itself at a loss. Nevertheless, economic stagnation or even crises do not necessarily mean that China will undergo an institutional transition similar to that of the FSU-EE countries.

The collapse of the Eastern bloc totalitarian regimes was not only due to the failure of economic reforms but also political changes. The reforms in those countries in the 1980s were comprehensive attempts to transform the totalitarian system into democratic socialism (or socialism with a human face) in the face of severe socioeconomic challenges. An economy under socialist ownership could not improve efficiency through reforms and the utopia of democratic socialism was unachievable. However, the Soviet and Eastern European Communist parties genuinely hoped to present a more humanized face towards that utopia. They took a big step towards democratization by loosening the totalitarian grip on all fronts. This essentially shook up totalitarian rule. Under tremendous social pressure and with the desire for a human face, the communist leaders of the Soviet Union, Poland, Hungary, and Czechoslovakia all stepped down peacefully following democratic procedures, one after the other.

In contrast, the CCP's economic reforms, unlike those in the Soviet Union and Eastern Europe, are of a different nature – a new-age Leninist New Economic Policy designed solely to salvage the communist totalitarian system, always on alert for any threat to totalitarian rule, including from entrepreneurs (see Chapter 13). When totalitarian rulers are determined to cling to power at any cost, they will not relax their grip on totalitarian control even in the face of economic collapse. Additionally, the CCP's strategy of implementing economic reforms to preserve power and the institutional genes of the governance structure inherited from its history are different from those of the Soviet Union.

Despite being revisionist in terms of leaning towards humanitarianism, the Soviet and Eastern European Communists firmly believed in socialism, particularly socialist ownership. Their economic reforms adhered to state ownership, which led to SBCs. Economic reforms that maintained this ownership structure were doomed to fail. In contrast, under the slogans of socialism and Marxism-Leninism, the CCP allowed for significant changes in the ownership structure of the Chinese economy, permitting private enterprises to become the mainstay of the economy, which led to China's economic growth. Kornai in the 1990s described the CCP as a party akin to a Christian church that does not believe in Jesus.[5]

However, a caveat is necessary here. As previously mentioned, the development of the private economy in China was not a result of a deliberate policy of the CCP but rather the outcome of two institutional genes at work: the RADT governance structure and some market economy elements inherited from history. As the private sector saved the Chinese communist regime, its legitimacy was recognized in 2004 (see Chapter 13).

Nevertheless, fearing that the further growth of the private sector could become the foundation for peaceful evolution or a color revolution, thus undermining its power, the CCP has maintained strict totalitarian control over private enterprises and entrepreneurs. Particularly since 2019, the CCP has tightened its control and cracked down on private firms, including all the largest e-commerce companies. Combined with other factors, this ultimately halted China's growth, leading to more serious economic stagnation and even risks of severe financial or economic crises in China. In stark contrast to China's economic woes, about half of the FSU-EE countries transitioned to democratic constitutional systems and became developed economies through free private ownership and market economies.

It is worth noting that the constitutional reforms promoted by Gorbachev and the Soviet elite played a crucial historical role in peacefully ending totalitarian rule. This also provided the Central and Eastern European countries with the opportunity to choose their own systems, helping them to end their totalitarian regimes. However, most former Soviet states lacked the institutional genes necessary to establish a democratic constitutional system. Concretely, the lack of universal private ownership, the lack of civil society based on private ownership, and the lack of a social structure evolving from the bottom up based on civil society make it difficult for these countries to form a social basis for checks and balances on power. Under these conditions, establishing the institutions of electoral and parliamentary systems could formally end totalitarian rule but this was not sufficient to establish a democratic constitutional system. Thus, the transition of many former Soviet states, particularly Russia and Belarus, to authoritarian regimes was neither accidental nor solely the result of individual leaders such as Putin. To some extent, the drastic collapse of the Soviet Union in 1991 followed by the changes to authoritarian rule in Russia and Belarus resemble the 1917 February Revolution and its consequences (see Chapter 8). Indeed, Yakovlev, one of Gorbachev's main aides involved in planning the political reforms, later lamented that the lessons of the Russian 1917 February Revolution had not been learned (Yakovlev, 1999, p. 107).

The genuine belief in socialist democracy or socialism with a human face by some FSU-EE communist leaders or elites was a key factor behind the collapse of totalitarianism there. This belief sharply contrasts with that of the CCP leaders and elites, who launched reforms to safeguard their power and thus always resolutely defended totalitarian rule at any cost. Although the CCP was derived from or cultivated by the CPSU and its fundamental communist totalitarian ideology was imported from the Soviet Union, the difference regarding humanity and humanitarianism, which is not part of communist ideology, is related to the institutional genes and social consensus on humanity across the regions. Specifically, it is related to whether historically one had experienced or been influenced by the Enlightenment.

Mankind's systematic recognition of human rights and humanity began with the Enlightenment and the social consensus on human rights formed the ideological foundation of modern democratic constitutionalism. Most FSU-EE countries had gone through the Enlightenment or had been influenced by it, thus shaping the related social consensus and institutional genes. China, however, never experienced the Enlightenment and was largely unaffected by it. During the Enlightenment period, China remained in a state of self-imposed isolation. Only a few Chinese intellectuals in the late nineteenth century had a superficial understanding of the Enlightenment.

Contrary to the social consensus required for democratic constitutionalism, the ideological basis for the establishment of a totalitarian system was class struggle against humanity. Marxist-Leninist theories of class and class struggle are tools for systematically eradicating people's recognition of human rights and humanity. The Communist Party relied on class struggle to replace humanity in order to mobilize the masses to establish a communist totalitarian regime. After establishing a totalitarian regime, ensuring that people do not form a social consensus about humanity is crucial for maintaining totalitarian rule of repression. However, traditional Marxist-Leninist theory did not provide a framework for this. On the contrary, Marxist theory asserts that socialism is a classless society. When class theory no longer applied to a classless socialist society, it rendered all Marxist-Leninist theories opposing humanity obsolete. In 1936, when Stalin declared that the Soviet Union had established socialism, he also announced that classes were eliminated in the Soviet Union. Stalin's justification for the Great Purge was to eliminate the 5th Column, or spies from the West. But that could only be a short-lived excuse. In the long run, without a theory of class and class struggle, the presence or absence of institutional genes about human nature in the original society became important in guiding the people's social behavior.

In the FSU-EE countries, including Russia, which is the furthest in that region from the center of the Enlightenment and arguably among the weakest in receiving its influence, the social elite had been influenced by the Enlightenment since the eighteenth century. The institutional genes that evolved from the Enlightenment contained a certain longing or social consensus for humanity, human rights, and freedom. A recognition of humanity and human rights, even in their most primitive form, fundamentally conflicts with totalitarian rule. The widespread recognition of humanity and human rights in the FSU-EE societies enabled the push for de-Stalinization after Stalin's death and triggered the revolutions in Poland and Hungary. It also fostered the advocacy of socialism with a human face and democratic socialism in the 1960s and 1980s.

The anti-totalitarian uprisings in Poland and Hungary in 1956 and the Prague Spring in 1968, were all violently suppressed by the military. However, violence could not extinguish the pursuit of human rights and freedom. By the 1980s, the consensus on de-Stalinization had gradually spread within society, including among some Communist Party upper echelons in the FSU-EE Bloc. Gorbachev and many around him had long been influenced by de-Stalinization and the Prague Spring. His friends included Czech comrades who had participated in the Prague Spring (Zubok, 2021, pp. 32–35). One of his main aides was Soviet theorist Georgy Shakhnazarov,[6] who worked in Prague during the Prague Spring, was deeply influenced by the idea of "socialism with a human face," and systematically advocated for "socialist democracy" by publishing related works (Taubman, 2017).

At least partly driven by their awareness of human rights and humanity, the communist parties of the Soviet Union, Poland, Hungary, and Czechoslovakia gradually loosened their grip in the name of political democratization, to varying degrees. They ceased using party discipline against political opponents, abandoned severe purges such as exile and imprisonment, and limited violent repression of demonstrators. In turn, the relaxation of totalitarian rule, while gaining social support, created or consolidated a social consensus for popular political participation.[7] Social participation generated continuous pressure for further democratization.

In addition to the relaxation of control, in the final years before the collapse of totalitarian rule there were open discussions among the upper echelons of the communist parties in the Soviet Union, Poland, Hungary, and Czechoslovakia about establishing a multiparty system or creating institutionalized factions within the communist parties. These developments clearly demonstrate that the transition from relaxing totalitarian control to ending it in the FSU-EE countries was the result of both social pressure and an enlightened social consciousness.

In stark contrast to the Soviet and Eastern European experience, China did not undergo the Enlightenment in its history. Consequently, people in China hold very rudimentary or primitive views on humanity or are influenced by Confucianism, completely lacking the concept of human rights. From the perspective of the Enlightenment and a social consensus and from the standpoint of humanity and humanitarianism, China's institutional genes differ significantly from those of the Soviet Union and Eastern Europe.[8] These differences in institutional genes have led the CCP not only to firmly resist the de-Stalinization initiated by the CPSU but also to use the opportunity of resisting de-Stalinization to further tighten its totalitarian control in a more extreme direction.

During the Khrushchev era, the CCP labeled the CPSU's de-Stalinization and revival of humanity as revisionism, insisting that class struggle continues throughout the socialist phase. It subsequently launched the Anti-Rightist Movement and the Cultural Revolution. These campaigns in China further entrenched class consciousness, justified the use of violence, and eradicated the already weak awareness of humanity from Chinese mind. No sooner had humanity begun to recover after Mao than Deng decisively and resolutely blocked de-Maoization efforts within the CCP, declared the Four Cardinal Principles to uphold Mao Zedong Thought, and suppressed the peaceful pro-democracy demonstrations in 1989. For more than thirty years since then, the CCP has continuously imprisoned and suppressed anyone demanding respect for human rights and political freedom.

14.6 COMMUNIST BLOC AND THE ROLE OF INSTITUTIONAL GENES

At the same time, the CCP has deliberately distorted the meanings of humanity and human rights in various ways and waged an extensive information war against democratic systems and the institutional transformation of the Soviet Union and Eastern Europe. This strategy has contributed to the prevalence of widespread materialism in Chinese society and deepened a cynical or distrustful attitude towards human rights and humanity among the populace. Ironically, when a society is solely concerned with materialism, it becomes difficult for that society to evolve towards a democratic constitutional system, thereby hindering its further economic development. Even in the face of serious economic problems, such a society's institutional framework remains resistant to change.

Let us conclude this section by briefly outlining a few other major differences between the institutional transitions in the FSU-EE Communist Bloc (before 1989) and the efforts of the CCP to prevent such a transition. One significant difference worth noting is the institutional arrangement for successors within the party.

Within the CCP, there are two competing groups for power succession, the so-called "princelings faction" and the "Youth League faction" in the literature on the Chinese Communist Party. In fact, these two groups are not political factions in the usual sense but rather reflect the origins of their power or their different social strata. The princelings faction refers to a power group composed of the descendants of high-ranking party officials,[9] whereas the Youth League faction refers to a power group originating from the Communist Youth League.

In contrast, the succession system in the FSU-EE communist parties was fully institutionalized, moving from the Komsomol (Communist Youth League) to the Communist Party, with no phenomenon akin to the Chinese princelings. After Stalin, Soviet leaders such as Khrushchev, Brezhnev, Andropov, Chernenko, Gorbachev, and Yeltsin all came from blue-collar families, received higher educations, and were gradually selected and promoted within the system from the Komsomol to the upper echelons of the Communist Party (Lowenhardt et al., 1992, p. 73). Understanding this difference between the Chinese and Soviet totalitarian regimes helps explain the emergence of figures like Xi Jinping (also Bo Xilai and Wang Qishan) in China and Khrushchev–Gorbachev in the Soviet Union.

The Communist Youth League system within the CCP was transplanted from the Soviet system. As a branch of the Comintern, the CCP duplicated the Komsomol system under the name of the Communist Youth League (originally called the Chinese Socialist Youth League) from its inception. Deng Xiaoping and Hu Yaobang both started their communist careers as members of the Youth League. The princelings in the CCP, however, are a product of the CCP's opposition to de-Stalinization, known as a successor cultivation system established during the Sino-Soviet split. This system was set up by Mao with strong support from the upper echelons to prevent de-Stalinization (or de-Maoization) in the future in China. It was to a considerable extent inherited from the Chinese imperial system and the institutional arrangements for power succession in Chinese secret societies and was highly incentive-compatible with high-ranking CCP cadres and their descendants.

Driven by the motivation to hold power, this successor cultivation system played a crucial role in the launch of the CR. The core members of the so-called Red Guards, who later became known as the princelings, were significantly empowered during the CR, which further strengthened this system. After the CR, the CCP further bolstered it (see Chapters 12 and 13). Xi Jinping, Bo Xilai, Wang Qishan, as well as Jiang Zemin and Li Peng, are all princelings. Hu Jintao, Wen Jiabao, and Li Keqiang belong to the Youth League faction. Many with princeling backgrounds have a strong sense of entitlement to power, seeing themselves as the rightful inheritors of totalitarian power, which, in turn, generates a stronger motivation to maintain the totalitarian system.

The second major difference lies in the influence of the military within the power structure of the Communist Party. In the Soviet Union, the military did not have the ability to significantly influence major decisions at the highest levels of the Communist

14.6 COMMUNIST BLOC AND THE ROLE OF INSTITUTIONAL GENES 719

Party. The CPSU heavily relied on the secret police, the KGB, in the power struggles. This arrangement allowed Gorbachev to resist military pressure to use force both domestically and internationally. In contrast, the Chairman of the Central Military Commission in the CCP, a position that controls the military, has held a decisive role in the party's power structure since Mao Zedong (from the Anti-AB League purge to the Cultural Revolution) (see Chapters 10 to 12).

Mao's famous quote, "Political power grows out of the barrel of a gun" not only applied to the CCP's seizure of power but also to its internal power struggles and, more importantly, to safeguarding the CCP's totalitarian regime. This is evidenced by the actions of CCP leaders. In May 1989, Zhao Ziyang, the General Secretary of the CCP, met with Gorbachev during the student demonstrations in Tiananmen Square. He mentioned that the Chinese were watching the democratization reforms in Soviet Union enthusiastically.[10] He also stated that the Communist Party must grant democratic rights to the masses under a one-party system; failing that, the problem of multipartyism will become inevitable (Gorbachev, 1995, pp. 489–491). However, Deng Xiaoping, leveraging his established power base within the CCP's military, personally mobilized hundreds of thousands of troops to suppress the peaceful demonstrations, rendering the hopes for political reform mentioned by Zhao futile. More than thirty years later, Xi Jinping's first move after taking office was to consolidate military power under the guise of an anti-corruption campaign. He then relied on military power to reassert tight control, pulling China back towards totalitarianism.

Finally, let me briefly summarize the comparison between the institutional transitions in the FSU-EE countries and China's forty years of economic reforms:

1) Communist totalitarian systems are fundamentally unreformable, making economic reforms destined to fail, leading to economic stagnation. Recognizing the irreformability of the system was a primary motivation for the FSU-EE countries to abandon totalitarianism. China,

having experienced relatively successful reforms in driving a desperately poor economy to become a middle-income country, is now on a path similar to the Soviet Union in the late 1970s, i.e., stagnation.
2) Totalitarian rulers can always use violence to maintain their power and rule. The peaceful abandonment of totalitarianism in the Soviet Union and Eastern Europe was not solely due to economic stagnation. Significant social pressure and a societal awareness of human rights and humanity were also decisive factors. Such social pressures and awareness are highly complementary to each other and are related to its institutional genes.
3) China's weak societal awareness of humanity and human rights, the institutional characteristics of military intervention in politics, and the princeling succession system, make the peaceful abandonment of totalitarianism in China more difficult.
4) For a transition from a totalitarian system to another system, the collapse of totalitarianism must occur first. However, transitioning to democratic constitutionalism requires the presence of relevant institutional genes in society, which include widespread private property rights, a civil society, and a social consensus on human rights, property rights, and the rule of law and constitutionalism.

14.7 CONCLUDING REMARKS ON THE CONCEPT OF INSTITUTIONAL GENES

In this book, the trajectories of the evolution of institutional genes are shaped by institutional constraints, random mutations arising from shifts in ideology and preferences, and external forces or shocks. Consequently, institutions evolve based on a mix of regularities and random factors, meaning they are neither wholly random nor completely deterministic. While we cannot predict specific details, we can identify key determining factors, making the general directions of change somewhat predictable.

Much as in the life sciences, where our comprehension of evolution of the species is directional and probabilistic rather than deterministic, institutional evolution, when analyzed through the lens of institutional genes, also exhibits a directional and probabilistic character. In the realm of the life sciences, the stochastic nature of evolution primarily arises from the randomness of genetic

14.7 CONCLUDING REMARKS ON INSTITUTIONAL GENES

mutations. Likewise, in the social sciences, the mutation of institutional genes is stochastic. A unique distinction, however, emerges: humans perpetually use their understanding of society to influence it directly. Such human intervention can consequently induce mutations in the institutional genes. In this context, the line differentiating the researcher from the subject of study becomes blurred. Moreover, the ways in which human actions sway these institutional genes, combined with the ensuing consequences, are dictated by a myriad of random factors.

As a result, those who trigger these institutional gene mutations, be it Qin Shi Huang, Mao, or anyone else, might remain oblivious to or dismissive of the long-term implications of their actions. Emperor Qin Shi Huang's comprehensive eradication of the nobility induced mutations in institutional genes, laying the foundation for the *junxian* system. Emperor Wu of Han's exclusive promotion of Confucianism resulted in mutations which became the institutional genes of Confucianism and the imperial examination system. The Comintern's role in founding the CCP led to mutations which set China on a path to totalitarianism, and Mao Zedong's instigation of the GLF and the CR prompted mutations that culminated in totalitarianism with Chinese characteristics, that is, RADT.

By comparison, efforts like the 1898 Hundred Days' Reform and the 1901 Gengzi Reform, both of which aimed to establish a constitutional monarchy, as well as the 1911 Xinhai Revolution which sought to institute a republic, did not incite a notable evolution of institutional genes favorable to constitutionalism in China. Similarly, neither the Russian 1905 Constitutional Revolution, which resulted in a constitutional monarchy, nor the Russian February Revolution of 1917 that set up a de facto republic, managed to catalyze a significant progression of institutional genes supportive of constitutionalism in Russia.

Yet, when viewed from the perspective of institutional genes, these ostensibly random, major historical phenomena are not wholly arbitrary. Amidst a multitude of incidental events, the pivotal factor determining the success or failure of a policy, reform, or revolution lies in the incentive-compatibility or-incompatibility of each institutional change. This compatibility, in turn, is profoundly influenced by its relationship with the existing institutional genes. As such, historical events that seem random are not entirely devoid of patterns. Instead, they are probabilistic outcomes influenced by specific stochastic regularities.

Lastly, I want to underscore that while this book primarily centers on China, the concept of institutional genes is a general one. Beyond understanding China, my aspiration is for this concept to be further developed and applied across various contexts. This would enable us to systematically uncover patterns of institutional evolution, deepen our analysis of the path-dependence phenomenon in institutional changes, and strengthen our ability to comprehend the trajectories of institutional evolution across past, present, and future timelines.

NOTES

1. To conserve space, this section does not aim to analyze the institutional genes of each involved country but rather to briefly discuss how the concept of institutional genes can be applied to understand the institutional transformation of the FSU-EE countries. For the same reason, the discussion of institutional transitions in the FSU-EE countries is limited to the Soviet Union, Poland, Hungary, and Czechoslovakia, not covering East Germany, the Berlin Wall, other CEE countries, and the various republics of the former Soviet Union.
2. Relaxing totalitarian political control may lead to the eventual collapse of a totalitarian system. The reason for this is that violence and terror are necessary to maintain totalitarian rule.
3. The independence movements of the Soviet republics, especially the separatist movements in Russia, Ukraine, and the Baltic States, were among the main driving forces for the dissolution of the Soviet Union. The issue of nationalism was inherited from the Tsarist Empire. The early Soviet Union attempted to mitigate this issue through ideology and propaganda, interpreting ethnic or nationalistic issues as derived from class struggle, while using the armed forces and the KGB to suppress nationalism. In the early 1980s, Andropov and the KGB viewed

the rising nationalism in Russia and Ukraine as a major threat to the Soviet Union and attempted to push for radical constitutional reforms aimed at altogether eliminating nationalism from the totalitarian Soviet Union (Zubok, 2021, pp. 51–53). In contrast, China, where Han Chinese make up more than 90 percent of the population, faced relatively weaker pressures from ethnic problems. As the subject is too detailed to consider here, this section will not delve into the subject of national independence movements.

4. Viewing the independence movements of the Baltic States as a threat to the survival of the Soviet Union, and under pressure from conservative forces within the CPSU, Gorbachev did not prevent Soviet generals from deploying troops to suppress these movements. However, he strenuously argued that he was not personally responsible for the bloodshed in Lithuania (Gorbachev, 1995, chapter 41; Taubman, 2017, chapter 16).

5. Source: private conversation with the author.

6. As an aide to Gorbachev, he played a significant role in the partial withdrawal of Soviet troops from Czechoslovakia in 1987 and their complete withdrawal from Central and Eastern Europe in 1989 (Savranskaya, 2010, Documents 10 and 93). He was also instrumental in the transfer of party power to Parliament (Montgomery, 2001).

7. By the end of 1989, Soviet public opinion polls found that 80 percent of respondents supported Gorbachev's political reforms (Brown, 2022).

8. The profound differences between China and Russia can be exemplified by the works of their most prominent scholars on their respective intellectual histories. For instance, Plekhanov's monumental work *History of Russian Social Thought*, first published in 1925, illustrates the deep and inseparable influence of the Enlightenment on Russian intellectual history (Plekhanov, 1967). In contrast, the Enlightenment and the Western influence are entirely absent in Liang Qichao's *History of Chinese Scholarship in the Last Three Hundred Years*《中国近三百年学术史》, published in 1926 (Liang Qichao, [1926] 2010). Contemporary scholar Ge Zhaoguang's *An Intellectual History of China* provides a comprehensive account of the extremely shallow influence of Western thought on China (Ge, 2001).

9. The term "princelings" (or "second-generation Reds") more accurately reflects their social strata and interests. This group does not have a unified political stance. Similar to the term "sans-culottes" during

the French Revolution, the term "princelings" lacks a clear definition in social scientific terms but is widely used in Chinese popular discourse and media and is thus an important social phenomenon.

10. When Gorbachev's motorcade passed through the streets of Beijing that were filled with demonstrators, countless protesters chanted slogans, hailing Gorbachev as a leader of democratic reform (Taubman, 2017).

References

Acemoglu, D. and Robinson, J. (2009) *Economic Origins of Dictatorship and Democracy*, Cambridge: Cambridge University Press.
Acemoglu, D. and Robinson, J. (2012) *Why Nations Fail: The Origins of Power, Prosperity and Poverty*, New York: Crown Publishing.
Acemoglu, D. and Robinson, J. (2019) *The Narrow Corridor*, London: Penguin Books.
Acemoglu, D., Aghion, P., and Zilibotti, F. (2006) "Distance to Frontier, Selection, and Economic Growth," *Journal of the European Economic Association*, vol. 4, no. 1, pp. 37–74.
Acta Patriarchatus Constantinopolitani, II, 188–192; cf. *Russkaya Istoricheskaya Biblioteka*, VI, Appendix 40, cols. 265–276.
Aganbergyan, A. (1989) *Perestroika 1989*, New York: Charles Scribner's Sons.
Alef, G. (1967) "Reflections on the Boyar Duma in the Reign of Ivan III," *Slavonic and East European Review*, vol. 45, no. 104, pp. 76–123.
Alexievich, S. (2016) *Secondhand Time: The Last of the Soviets*, New York: Random House.
Allison, G. (2017) "The Thucydides Trap," *Foreign Policy*, June 9, 2017.
Anderson, P. (2013) *Lineages of the Absolutist State*, London: Verso Books.
Andrew, C. and Mitrokhin, V. (2000) *The Mitrokhin Archive: The KGB in Europe and the West*, New York: Penguin.
Archaeological Committee (1880) *Russkaya Istoricheskaya Biblioteka, VI, 577*, St. Petersburg: St. Petersburg Press.
Arendt, H. (1973) *The Origins of Totalitarianism*, San Diego, CA: Harcourt, Brace, Jovanovich.
Aristotle (1988) *The Politics*, Cambridge: Cambridge University Press.
Babeuf, G. ([1795] 2010) *Le Manifeste des Plébéiens*, Paris: Fayard Mille et une nuits édition.
Bacon, F. ([1625] 1999), *The Essays or Counsels Civil and Moral*, Oxford: Oxford University Press.
Bai, Y. (2005) 《先秦两汉铁器的考古学研究》 (*Archaelogical Study of Ironware in the Pre-Qin Period and Han Dynasty*), Beijing: Science Press.

Bao, H. (1983) 《包惠僧回忆录》 (*Memoirs of Bao Huiseng*), Beijing: People's Publishing House.

Baron, H. B. (1995) *Plekhanov in Russian History and Soviet Historiography*, Pittsburgh, PA: University of Pittsburgh Press.

Baumgartner, F. J. (1995) *France in the Sixteenth Century*, New York: Palgrave Macmillan.

Beja, J. (2011) *The Impact of China's 1989 Tiananmen Massacre*, New York: Routledge.

Bentham, J. ([1795] 1914) *Theory of Legislation*, London: H. Milford, Oxford University Press.

Bentham, J. (1843) *Works*, vol. 1, Edinburgh: W. Tait; London: Simpkin, Marshall.

Bergman, J. (1983) *Vera Zasulich: A Biography*, Stanford, CA: Stanford University Press.

Berlin, I. (2013) *Three Critics of the Enlightenment: Vico, Hamann, Herder*, Princeton, NJ: Princeton University Press.

Bo, Y. (1996) 《七十年奋斗与思考》 (*Seventy Years of Struggle and Reflection*), Part 1, Beijing: CCP History Publishing House.

Bolton, P. and Brooks, R. (2022) "Incomplete Contracts, Writings and the Duty to Perform in Good Faith and Best Efforts Clauses," Working Paper, Imperial College London.

Borsanyi, G. (1993) *The Life of a Communist Revolutionary, Bela Kun*, New York: Columbia University Press.

Brodsgaard, E. (2016) *Critical Readings on the Communist Party of China*, Copenhagen: Brill.

Broue, P. (2006) *The German Revolution: 1917–1923*, Chicago, IL: Haymarket Books.

Browder, R. P. and Kerensky, A. F. (1961) *The Russian Provisional Government, 1917: Documents*, 3 vols., vol. 1, Stanford, CA: Stanford University Press.

Brown, A. (2022) "The End of Communist Rule in Europe: A Comparative Perspective on the Fragility and Robustness of Regimes," in R. N. Lebow (eds), *Robustness and Fragility of Political Orders: Leader Assessments, Responses, and Consequences*, Cambridge: Cambridge University Press; pp. 141–175.

Buckley, C. (2013) "Vows of Change in China Belie Private Warning," *The New York Times*, February 14.

Busky, D. F. (2002) *Communism in History and Theory*, Westport, CT: Praeger Publishers.

Cai, S. (1987) 《中国近代会党史研究》 (*Study of the History of Chinese Secret Societies in the Modern Era*), Beijing: Zhonghua Books.

Cao, S. (2001) 《中国人口史（第5卷）》 (*History of the Chinese Population*), vol. 5, Shanghai: Fudan University Press.

Carr, E. H. (1985) *The Bolshevik Revolution: 1917–1923*, 3 vols., vol. 1, New York: W. W. Norton and Co.

CASS-Institute of Modern History (Chinese Academy of Social Sciences) (1980a) 《"一大"前后：中共第一次代表大会前后资料选编》(*Before and After the First Congress: Selected Materials from Before and After the First Congress of the CCP*), 3 vols., Beijing: People's Publishing House.

CASS-Institute of Modern History (1980b) 《马林在中国的有关资料》(*Materials related to Maring in China*), Beijing: People's Publishing House.

CBNRI (2016) "中国制造业单位劳动力成本直逼美国 (China's Manufacturing Unit Labor Costs Closing in on the U.S.)," March 22. Yicai Research Institute [online]. Available at: www.cbnri.org/news/5226806.html.

Central Archives (2016) 《红色中华》(*Red China*), no. 14, Complete Edition, vol. 1, Nanchang: Jiangxi People's Publishing House.

Central Committee Archives (1989a) 《中共中央文件选集（第1卷）》(*Selected Documents of the CCP Central Committee*), vol. 1, Beijing: CCP Central Party School Press.

Central Committee Archives (1989b) 《中共中央文件选集（第3卷）》(*Selected Documents of the CCP Central Committee*), vol. 3, Beijing: CCP Central Party School Press.

Central Committee Archives (1989c) 《中共中央文件选集（第4卷）》(*Selected Documents of the CCP Central Committee*), vol. 4, Beijing: CCP Central Party School Press.

Central Committee Archives (1991) 《中共中央文件选集（第13卷）》(*Selected Documents of the CCP Central Committee*), vol. 13, Beijing: CCP Central Party School Press.

Central Committee Archives (1992) 《中共中央文件选集（第14卷）》(*Selected Documents of the CCP Central Committee*), vol. 14, Beijing: CCP Central Party School Press.

Central Literature Research Office of the CCP (1989) 《周恩来年谱》(*Zhou Enlai Chronicles*), Beijing: Central Literature Publishing House.

Central Literature Research Office of the CCP (1996) 《刘少奇年谱》(*Liu Shaoqi Chronicles*), 2 vols., Beijing: Central Literature Publishing House.

Central Literature Research Office of the CCP (1998) 《周恩来传》(*Biography of Zhou Enlai*), Beijing: Central Literature Publishing House.

Central Literature Research Office of the CCP (2011) 《建党以来重要文献选编（1921–1949）》(*Selected Important Documents Since the Founding of the Party [1921–1949]*), vol. 4, Beijing: Central Literature Publishing House.

Chai, R. (2007) 《中国古代物权法研究》(*Study of Property Rights in Ancient China*), Beijing: China Prosecutorial Publishing House.

Chang, H. (2016) 《梁启超与中国思想的过度》 (*Liang Ch'i-chao and Intellectual Transition in China*), Beijing: Central Compilation-Translation Press.

Chang, J. and Halliday, J. (2006) 《毛澤東：鮮為人知的故事》 (*Mao: The Little Known Story*), Hong Kong: Open Press. (All the references cited from Chang and Halliday are from this Chinese version.)

Chang, K. C. (1983) *Art, Myth, and Ritual: The Path to Political Authority in Ancient China*, Cambridge, MA: Harvard University Press.

Chang, K. C. (1987) *The Archaeology of Ancient China*, 4th ed., New Haven, CT: Yale University Press.

Chapman, H. O. (1928) *The Chinese Revolution*, London: Constable.

Chen, E. M. (1975) "The Dialectic of *Chih* (Reason) and *Tao* (Nature) in the Han Fei-tzu," *Journal of Chinese Philosophy*, vol. 3, no. 1, pp. 1–21.

Chen, G. (1981) 《苦笑錄》 (*Bitter Laughter*), Hong Kong: Asian Centre of the Chinese University of Hong Kong.

Chen, J. (2024) "State Formation and Bureaucratization: Evidence from Pre-Imperial China," *Journal of Economic History*, vol. 84, no. 3, pp. 690–726.

Chen, X. (ed.) (2020) 《奠基》 (*Laying the Foundation*), Beijing: Tiandi Publishing House.

Chen, Y. (1986) 《陈云文选（1956–1985）》 (*Selected Writings of Chen Yun, 1956–1985*), Beijing: People's Publishing House.

Chen, Y. (1998) 《中国共产革命七十年》 (*Seventy Years of the Chinese Communist Revolution*), Taiwan: Linking Publishing Co.

Cheng, J. and Hu, Z. (2022) 《中国居民收入分配年度报告（2021）》 (*On China Household Distribution [2021]*). Beijing: Social Sciences Literature Publishing House.

Chesneaux, J. (1972) *Popular Movements and Secret Societies in China*, Stanford, CA: Stanford University Press.

Chiang, K. (2016) "July 1943," in 《抗日戰爭時期之蔣介石先生：事略稿本》 (*Chiang Kai-shek during the Second Sino-Japanese War: A Biographical Manuscript*), Taipei: Academia Historica Office.

Cho, M. (2024) "China's Debt-to-GDP Ratio Rises to Fresh Record of 286.1%," Bloomberg, January 16, 2024.

Chowdhury, S. (2022) *China Economic Update: Between Shocks and Stimulus*, Geneva: World Bank.

Coase, R. (1960). "The Problem of Social Cost." *Journal of Law and Economics*, vol. 3, no. 1, pp. 1–44.

Coase, R. (1992) "The Institutional Structure of Production," *American Economic Review*, vol. 82, no. 4, pp. 713–719.

Compilation and Translation Bureau of the CCP Central Committee (ed.) (1983) "人民党纲领 (Program of the People's Party)," in 《俄国民粹派文选》 (*Selected Narodnik Writings*), Beijing: People's Publishing House.

Courtois, S., Werth, N., Panné J.-L., Paczkowski, A., Bartošek, K., Margolin, J.-L., and Kramer, K. (eds.), (trans. J. Murphy) (1999) *The Black Book of Communism: Crimes, Terror, Repression*, Cambridge, MA: Harvard University Press.

Cronk, N. (2009) *The Cambridge Companion to Voltaire*, Cambridge: Cambridge University Press.

Curtiss, J. S. (1957) *The Russian Revolutions of 1917*, Washington DC: Van Nostrand Reinhold.

Daniel-Rops, H. (1964) *History of the Church of Christ*, New York: Dutton.

Davies, N. (2005) *God's Playground: The Origins to 1795*, New York: Columbia University Press.

de Nevers, R. (2003) *Comrades No More: The Seeds of Change in Eastern Europe*, Cambridge, MA: The MIT Press.

Deng, X. (1993) 《邓小平文选》 (*Selected Writings of Deng Xiaoping*), vol. 3, Beijing: People's Publishing House.

Deng, X. (1994) "坚持四项基本原则 (Uphold the Four Cardinal Principles)," in 《邓小平文集》 (*Selected Writings of Deng Xiaoping*), vol. 2, Beijing: People's Publishing House.

Deng, X. (1995) 《邓小平文选》 (*Selected Writings of Deng Xiaoping*), vol. 2, Beijing: People's Publishing House.

Dewatripont, M. and Maskin, E. (1995) "Credit and Efficiency in Centralised and Decentralised Economies," *Review of Economic Studies*, vol. 62, no. 4, pp. 541–555.

Dickson, B. (2003) *Red Capitalists in China*, Cambridge: Cambridge University Press.

Dikötter, F. (2010) *Mao's Great Famine: The History of China's Most Devastating Catastrophe, 1958–62*, London: Bloomsbury Press.

Dikötter, F. (2017) *The Cultural Revolution: A People's History, 1962–1976*, London: Bloomsbury Press.

Ding, S. (1993) 《陽謀:「反右」前后》 (*Open Conspiracy: The Complete Story of the "Anti-Rightist" Campaign*), Hong Kong: The Nineties Magazine Publishing.

Ding, S. (2014) "1970年一打三反运动纪实 (A Record of the 1970 One Strike, Three Anti Campaign," 爱思想 [online]. Available at: www.aisixiang.com/data/73854.html.

Doyle, W. (1989) *The Oxford History of the French Revolution*, London: Oxford University Press.

Drake, F. (1990) 《徐繼宇及其應瀛環志略》 (*China Charts the World: Hsu Chi-yu and His Geography of 1848*), Taipei: Wen Chin Publishing Co.

Du, Y. (1988) 《通典》 (*Comprehensive Statutes*), Beijing: Zhonghua Books.

Duan, Y. (2009) 《中山先生的世界觀》 (*Mr. Sun Yat-sen's Worldview*), Taipei: Xiuwei Press.

Durant, W. (1933) *The Story of Philosophy*, 2nd ed., London: Simon & Schuster.

Durant, W. and Durant, A. (1961) *The Age of Reason Begins: The Story of Civilization*, New York: MJF Books.

Durant, W. and Durant, A. (1967) *Rousseau and Revolution, The Story of Civilization*, New York: MJF Books.

Economic Intelligence Unit (EIU) (2022) "EIU Democracy Index, 2021: The China Challenge," Economist Intelligence Unit [online]. Available at: www.eiu.com/.

Editorial Board of China Encyclopedia (1993) 《中国大百科书》 (*Encyclopaedia of China*), Beijing: China Encyclopedia Publishing House.

Editorial Department of Modern History Materials, Institute of Modern History, CASS (1989) "中国国民党第一届中央委员会会议记录 (Minutes of the First Central Committee Meeting of the Chinese Nationalist Party)," 《近代史资料》 (*Modern History Materials*), no. 76.

Ekiert, G. and Kubik, J. (2001) *Rebellious Civil Society: Popular Protest and Democratic Consolidation in Poland, 1989–1993*, Ann Arbor, MI: The University of Michigan Press.

Ellicott, C. J. and Plumptre, E. H. (1910) "III. The Church in Jerusalem. I. Christian Communism," in *The Acts of the Apostles*, London: Cassell.

Engels, F. (1844) "Letter to the Editor on Communism in France," *The New Moral World*, Third Series, No. 32, February 3 [online]. Available at: www.marxists.org/archive/marx/works/1844/01/28.htm.

Engels, F., (1895) *A Contribution to the History of Primitive Christianity*, Mountain View, CA: Socialist Labor Party of America [online]. Available at: www.slp.org/pdf/marx/prim_christ_engels.pdf.

Engels, F. (1926) "Precursors: Peasant Uprisings, 1476–1517," in *The Peasant War in Germany* [online]. Available at: www.marxists.org/archive/marx/works/1850/peasant-war-germany/index.htm.

Engels, F. (2010) *Anti-Dühring*, Whitefish, MT: Kessinger Publishing.

Engerman, D. C. (2000) "Modernization from the Other Shore: American Observers and the Costs of Soviet Economic Development," *American Historical Review*, vol. 105, no. 2, pp. 383–416.

Esherick, J. (2022) *Accidental Holy Land: The Communist Revolution in Northwest China*, Berkeley, CA: University of California Press.

Fairbank, J. (1948) *The United States and China*, Cambridge, MA: Harvard University Press.

Fairbank, J. K. (1985) 《剑桥中国晚清史》 (*Cambridge History of China, Volumes 10–11: Late Qing*) Parts 1&2, Beijing: China Social Sciences Press.

Fairbank, J. K. (1992) *China: A New History*, Cambridge, MA: Belknap Press of Harvard University Press.

Fairbank, J. K. (2013) 《中国：传统与变革》 (*China: Tradition and Transformation*), Changchun: Jilin Publishing Group.

Fairbank, J. K. and Feuerwerker, A. (1994) 《剑桥中华民国史》 (*Cambridge History of China, Vols. 12–13: The Republic of China*), Parts I & II, Beijing: China Social Sciences Press.

Fairbank, J. and Goldman, M. (2006) *China: A New History, Second Enlarged Edition*, Cambridge, MA: Belknap Press of Harvard University Press.

Feng, Y. (1985) 《中国哲学史新编》 (*A New History of Chinese Philosophy*), vol. 3, Beijing: Renmin University Press.

Figes, O. (2017) *A People's Tragedy*, London: Bodley Head.

Finley, M. I. (1981) *Economy and Society in Ancient Greece*, Shaw, B. D. and Saller, R. (eds.), London: Vintage/Ebury.

Forman, H. (1988) 《北行漫记》 (*Report from Red China*), Beijing: Xinhua Press.

Friedberg, A. L. (2022) *Getting China Wrong*, Cambridge: Polity Books.

Friedman, M. (1962) *Capitalism and Freedom*, Chicago, IL: University of Chicago Press.

Friedrich, C. and Brzezinski, Z. (1956) *Totalitarian Dictatorship and Autocracy*, Cambridge, MA: Harvard University Press.

Frydlinger, D. and Hart, O. D. (2022) "Overcoming Contractual Incompleteness: The Role of Guiding Principles," Working Paper, Harvard University.

Fu, Z. (1996) *China's Legalists: The Earliest Totalitarians and Their Art of Ruling*, Armonk, NY: M. E. Sharpe.

Fukuyama, F. (2011) *The Origins of Political Order*, New York: Farrar, Straus and Giroux.

Fulda, A. (2019) *The Struggle for Democracy in Mainland China, Taiwan and Hong Kong: Sharp Power and Its Discontents*, New York: Routledge.

Gao, F. (2012) 《清末立宪史》 (*History of Late-Qing Constitutionalism*), Beijing: Sino-Culture Press.

Gao, H. (2000) 《紅太陽是怎樣升起的》 (*How the Red Sun Rose*), Hong Kong: The Chinese University of Hong Kong Press.

Garnsey, P. (2009) "Chapter 7 – Property as a Legal Right," in *Thinking about Property*, Cambridge: Cambridge University Press.

Ge, Z. (2001) 《中国思想史》 (*An Intellectual History of China*), Shanghai: Fudan University Press.

Ge, Z. (2018) *What Is China? Territory, Ethnicity, Culture, and History*, Cambridge, MA: Harvard University Press.

Gellately, R. (2007) *Lenin, Stalin, and Hitler: The Age of Social Catastrophe*, New York: Alfred A. Knopf.

Gerschenkron, A. (1962) *Economic Backwardness in Historical Perspective: A Book of Essays*, Cambridge, MA: The Belknap Press of Harvard University Press.

Getzler, I. (1967) "The Mensheviks," *Problems of Communism*, vol. 16, no. 6, pp. 15–29.

Gill, G. (2010) *The Origins of the Stalinist Political System*, London: Cambridge University Press.

Glotz, G. (2013) *Ancient Greece at Work: An Economic History of Greece from the Homeric Period to the Roman Conquest*, Whitefish, MT: Literary Licensing.

Goodnow, F. (1924) "Monarchy or Republic?," in *Papers Relating to the Foreign Relations of the United States, 2015*, U.S. Department of State, pp. 53–58.

Gorbachev, M. (1988) *Perestroika: New Thinking for Our Country and the World*, New York: Harper & Row.

Gorbachev, M. (1995) *Memoirs*, New York: Doubleday.

Gorky, M. (1918) "January 9, 1905, and January 5, 1918," *Novaia Zhizn*, no. 6, p. 1.

Greer, D. (1935) *The Incidence of the Terror During the French Revolution: A Statistical Interpretation*, Cambridge, MA: Harvard University Press.

Grief, A. (2006) *Institutions and the Path to the Modern Economy*, New York: Cambridge University Press.

Gu, D. and Zhu, S. (2003) 《春秋史》 (*History of the Spring and Autumn Period*), Shanghai: Shanghai People's Publishing House.

Guan, X. (2017) 《科举停废与近代中国社会》 (*The Removal of the Imperial Examination System and Chinese Society in Modern Times*), Beijing: Social Sciences Academic Press.

Guangdong Provincial Committee of the Communist Party, Party History Material Collection Committee (ed.) (1989b) 《东江革命根据地史》 (*History of the Dong River Revolutionary Base Area*), Beijing: History of the CCP Press.

Guo, D., Huang, H., Jiang, K., and Xu, C. (2021) "Disruptive Innovation and R&D Ownership Structures," *Public Choice*, vol. 187, no. 1, pp. 143–163.

Guo, P. (2017) 《中国科举制度通史, 明代卷》 (*General History of the Imperial Examination System of China: Ming Dynasty*), Shanghai: Shanghai People's Publishing House.

Guo, S. (1982) 《郭嵩焘日记》 (*The Diary of Guo Songtao*), Changsha: Hunan People's Publishing House.

Guo, T. (1979) 《近代中國史綱》 (*Outline of Modern Chinese History*), Hong Kong: The Chinese University of Hong Kong Press.

Guthrie, D. (1992) "Early Problems," in *The Apostles*, Grand Rapids, MI: Zondervan.

Haar, B (1992) *The White Lotus Teachings in Chinese Religious History*, Leiden: E. J. Brill.

Haar, B (1998) *Ritual and Mythology of the Chinese Triads*, Leiden: E. J. Brill.

Halsall, P. (1997) "Maximilien Robespierre: Justification of the Use of Terror," in *Internet Modern History Sourcebook*, History Department of Fordham University [online]. Available at: https://sourcebooks.fordham.edu/mod/robespierre-terror.asp.

Hart, O. (1995) *Firms, Contracts, and Financial Structure*, New York: Oxford University Press.

Hart, O. (2017) "Incompete Contracts and Control," *American Economic Review*, vol. 107, no.7, pp. 1731–1752.

Hart, O. D. and Moore, J. (2008) "Contracts as Reference Points," *Quarterly Journal of Economics*, vol. 123, no. 1, pp. 1–48.

Hayek, F. (1973) *Law, Legislation and Liberty, Volume 1: Rules and Order*, Chicago, IL: University of Chicago Press.

Hayek, F. (2007) *The Road to Serfdom*, Chicago, IL: University of Chicago Press.

He, F. (2005) 《黨史：從遵義會議到延安整風》(*Notes on the History of the Party: From the Zunyi Meeting to the Yan'an Rectification*), Hong Kong: Liwen Publishing.

Hecker, J. F. (1927) *Religion under the Soviets*, New York: Vanguard Press.

Hecker, J. F. (1933) *Religion and Communism: A Study of Religion and Atheism in Soviet Russia*, London: Chapman and Hall.

Hegel, G. F. (1991) *Elements of the Philosophy of Rights*, Cambridge: Cambridge University Press.

Hell, N. and Rozelle, S. (2021) *Invisible China: How the Urban-Rural Divide Threatens China's Rise*, Chicago, IL: University of Chicago Press.

Hewett, E. (1990a) "Is Soviet Socialism Reformable?" *SAIS Review of International Affairs*, vol. 10, no. 2, pp. 75–87.

Hewett, E. (1990b) "The New Soviet Plan," *Foreign Affairs*, vol. 69, no. 5, pp. 146–167.

Hinsley, F. H. (1986) *Sovereignty*, Cambridge: Cambridge University Press.

Hirayama, S. (2017) 《中国秘密社会史》(*A History of Chinese Secret Societies*), Beijing: Commercial Press.

Hobson, J. A. (1902) *Imperialism: A Study*, New York: James Pott & Co.

Honoré, T. (2002) *Ulpian: Pioneer of Human Rights*, London: Oxford University Press.

Hou, J. (2005) 《中國經濟史》(*An Economic History of China*), vol. 2, Taipei: Linking Publishing Co.

Hou, W. (1954) "中国封建社会土地所有制形式的问题 (Problems with the Form of Land Ownership in Chinese Feudal Society)," 《历史研究》 (Historical Research).

Hsu, C.Y. (2001) 《中國近代史》 (The Rise of Modern China), Hong Kong: The Chinese University of Hong Kong Press.

Hsü, I. C. Y. (1970) The Rise of Modern China, New York: Oxford University Press.

Hu, J. (2012) 《胡赵新政启示录》 (Hu Zhao New Policy), Hong Kong: New Century Media & Consulting Co. Ltd.

Hu, P. and Li, S. (2017) 《中国科举制度通史,清代卷（上册）》 (General History of the Imperial Examination System of China, Qing Dynasty vol. 1), Shanghai: Shanghai People's Publishing House.

Hu, S. (1991) 《中国共产党历史》 (History of the Chinese Communist Party), Beijing: CCP History Publishing House.

Hu, Z. (2013) "回忆'摘帽办': 解决55万人的问题 (Recalling the 'Hat Removal Office': Resolving the Problem of the 550,000 People)," China Newsweek, no. 3.

Huang, R. (1996) China: A Macro History, 2nd ed., New York: Routledge.

Huang, Y. (1945) 《延安归来》 (Return from Yan'an), Chongqing: Guoxun Bookstore.

Huang, Y. (2008) Capitalism with Chinese Characteristics: Entrepreneurship and the State, Cambridge: Cambridge University Press.

Huang, Y. (2023) The Rise and Fall of the EAST: How Exams, Autocracy, Stability, and Technology Brought China Success, and Why They Might Lead to Its Decline, New Haven, CT: Yale University Press.

Hui, V. (2005) War and State Formation in Ancient China and Early Modern Europe, New York: Cambridge University Press.

Hume, D. ([1739] 1978) A Treatise of Human Nature, London: Oxford University Press.

Huntington, S. P. (1996) The Clash of Civilisations and the Remaking of World Order, New York: Simon & Schuster.

Hurwicz, L. (2008) "But Who Will Guard the Guardians?," American Economic Review, vol. 98, no. 3, pp. 586–603.

International Monetary Fund (IMF) (2019) World Economic Outlook, Global Manufacturing Downturn, Rising Trade Barriers [online]. Available at: www.imf.org/en/Publications/WEO/Issues/2019/10/01/world-economic-outlook-october-2019.

Institut marksizma-leninizma (Moscow, Russia) (1956) Reminiscences of Marx and Engels. Moscow: Foreign Languages Publishing House.

Institute of Marxism Leninism and Institute of Modern History, CASS (1989) 《马林与第一次国共合作》 (*Maring and the First KMT-CCP Alliance*), Beijing: Guangming Daily Publishing House.

IMF (2022a) *World Economic Outlook Database, April 2022* [online]. Available at: www.imf.org/en/Publications/WEO/weo-database/2022/April.

IMF (2022b) *World Economic Outlook Report: Countering the Cost-Of-Living Crisis* [online]. Available at: www.imf.org/en/Publications/WEO/Issues/2022/10/11/world-economic-outlook-october-2022.

Ishikawa, Y. (2006) 《中国共产党成立史》 (*The Formation of the Chinese Communist Party*), Beijing: China Social Science Press.

Israel, J. (2015) *Revolutionary Ideas*, Princeton, NJ: Princeton University Press.

Israel, J. (2020) *The Enlightenment That Failed*, New York: Oxford University Press.

Jacobs, A. (2014) "Hong Kong Democracy Standoff, Circa 1960," *New York Times*, October 27, 2014.

Jędruch, J. (1998) *Constitutions, Elections, and Legislatures of Poland, 1493–1977: A Guide to Their History*. New York: EJJ Books.

Jiangxi Provincial Archives, Party History Teaching and Research Office of the Party School of the Jiangxi Provincial Committee of the CCP (1982) 《中央革命根据地史料选编》 (*Selected Historical Materials on the Central Government Revolutionary Base Areas Part 1*), Nanchang: Jiangxi People's Publishing House.

Jones, P. (2006). *The Dilemmas of De-Stalinization: Negotiating Cultural and Social Change in the Khrushchev Era*, New York: Routledge.

Ju, Z. (1954) "中華革命黨時代的回憶 (Memories of the Chinese Revolutionary Party Era)," 《革命文獻》 (*Revolutionary Literature*), Taipei, no. 5.

Kampen, T. (2003) *Mao Zedong, Zhou Enlai and the Evolution of the Chinese Communist Leadership*, Copenhagen: Nordic Institute of Asian Studies.

Kautsky, K. (1897) *Communism in Central Europe in the Time of the Reformation* (trans. J. L. & E. G. Mulliken), London: Fisher & Unwin.

Kautsky, K. (1919) *The Dictatorship of the Proletariat*, Manchester: National Labour Press.

Kautsky, K. (1920) *Terrorism and Communism: A Contribution to the Natural History of Revolution*, London: George Allen & Unwin.

Kautsky, K. (1946) "Is Soviet Russia a Socialist State?," in *Social Democracy versus Communism*, New York: Rand School Press.

Khrushchev, N. (1959) *Let Us Live in Peace and Friendship*, Moscow: Foreign Languages Publishing House.

Khrushchev, N. (2005) *Memoirs of Nikita Khrushchev*, vol. 1, University Park, PA: Pennsylvania State University Press.

Klever, W. (1990) "Hume Contra Spinoza?" *Hume Studies*, vol. 16, no. 2, pp. 89–105.
Kliuchevskii, V. O. (1960) *A History of Russia*, vol. 2, New York: Russell & Russell.
Korbel, J. (1959) *The Communist Subversion of Czechoslovakia, 1938–1948: The Failure of Co-existence*, Princeton, NJ: Princeton University Press.
Kornai, J. (1980) *Economics of Shortage*, Amsterdam: North-Holland Publishing.
Kornai, J. (1992) *The Socialist System*, Oxford: Oxford University Press.
Kornai, J. (2013) *Dynamism, Rivalry, and the Surplus Economy*, Oxford: Oxford University Press.
Kornai, J., Maskin, E., and Roland, G. (2003) "Understanding the Soft Budget Constraint," *Journal of Economic Literature*, vol. 41, no. 4, pp. 1095–1136.
Kroncke, J. J. (2012) "An Early Tragedy of Comparative Constitutionalism: Frank Goodnow and the Chinese Republic," *Pacific Rim Law & Policy Journal*, vol. 21, no. 3 [online]. Available at: https://digitalcommons.law.uw.edu/cgi/viewcontent.cgi?article=1593&context=wilj.
Kropotkin, P. (1915) *Ideals and Realities in Russian Literature*, New York: Alfred A. Knopf.
Kuo, S. and Ranis, G. (1981) *The Taiwan Success Story: Rapid Growth with Improved Distribution in the Republic of China, 1952–1979*, New York: Routledge.
Kurdyukov I. F. et al. (eds) (1959) 《苏中关系（1917–1957）文件汇编》(*Soviet-Chinese Relations (1917–1957) Compendium of Documents*), Moscow: Vost Lit.
Landry-Deron, I. ([1735] 2002) *La preuve par la Chine: la description de J.-B. Du Halde, jésuite, 1735*, Paris: Editions de l'Ecole des hautes études en sciences sociales.
Le Blanc, P. (2015) *Lenin and the Revolutionary Party*, Chicago, IL: Haymarket Books.
Lee, B. (1993) 《政治協商會議與國共談判》(*The Political Consultative Conference and the KMT-CCP Negotiations*). Taipei: Lifework Press.
Leggett, G. (1987) *The Cheka: Lenin's Political Police*, London: Oxford University Press.
Lenin, V. I. (1965) "The Constituent Assembly Elections and the Dictatorship of the Proletariat," in *Collected Works*, vol. 30, Moscow: Progress Publishers.
Lenin, V. I. (1972a) "Draft Resolution on Freedom of the Press," in *Collected Works*, vol. 26, Moscow: Progress Publishers.
Lenin, V. I. (1972b) "Decree on the Arrest of the Leaders of the Civil War Against the Revolution," in *Collected Works*, vol. 28, Moscow: Progress Publishers.
Lenin, V. I. (1972c) "Theses on the Constituent Assembly," in *Collected Works*, vol. 26, Moscow: Progress Publishers.
Lenin, V. I. (1972d) "The Socialist Fatherland Is in Danger!," in *Collected Works*, vol. 27, Moscow: Progress Publishers.

Lenin, V. (2017) 《列宁全集（第33卷）》 (*Collected Works of Lenin*), vol. 33, Beijing: People's Publishing House.

Lenin, V. I. (2021) *The State and Revolution*, New York: Dover Publications.

Lenin, V. and Stalin, J. (1950) 《列宁斯大林论中国》 (*Lenin and Stalin on China*), Yan'an: Liberation Publishing House.

Leroy-Beaulieu, A. (1896) *The Empire of the Tsars and the Russians, Part III: The Religion*, vol. 3, New York: G. P. Putnam.

Li, C. et al. (2023) "专家解读：如何看待中国人口出现负增长 (Expert Interpretation: How to Explain the Negative Growth of China's Population)," *China News*, January 18, 2023. Available at: http://finance.people.com.cn/n1/2023/0118/c1004-32609112.html.

Li, D. (1979) "布尔什维克主义的胜利 (The Victory of Bolshevism)," in Party History Department of the PLA Political Academy (ed.) 《中共党史参考资料》 (*CCP History Reference Materials*), vol. 1. Beijing: Party History Department of the PLA Political Academy.

Li, D. (1984) 《李大钊文集》 (*Collected Works of Li Dazhao*), Beijing: People's Publishing House.

Li, G. (2003) "大学的终结 (The End of the University)," *China Reform*, no. 8, pp. 36–37.

Li, I. and Zhou, I. (2005) "Political Turnover and Economic Performance: The Incentive Role of Personnel Control in China," *Journal of Public Economics*, vol. 89, no. 9–10, pp. 1743–1762.

Li, R. (1988) 《庐山会议实录》 (*Records of the Lushan Conference*), Beijing: Spring and Autumn Publishing House; Changsha: Hunan Education Publishing House.

Li, R. (2008) "毛泽东与反右派斗争 (Mao Zedong and the Anti-Rightist Struggle)," 《炎黄春秋》 (*Spring and Autumn Annals*), no. 7, pp. 26–31.

Li, S. (1999) 《中国儒教史（上卷）》 (*History of Confucianism in China*), vol. 1, Shanghai: Shanghai People's Publishing House.

Li, S. (2000) 《中国儒教史（下卷）》 (*History of Confucianism in China*), vol. 2, Shanghai: Shanghai People's Publishing House.

Li, S. and Wang, Y. (eds.) (2006) 《2006年全球政治与安全报告》 (*Annual Report on International Politics and Security 2006*), Beijing: Social Sciences Literature Press.

Li, W. (1986) 《回忆与研究》 (*Recollections and Research*), Beijing: CCP History Information Press.

Li, W. (2009) "从共产国际档案中看反'AB团'斗争 (Comintern Archives on the Struggle Against the AB League)," 《炎黄春秋》 (*Spring and Autumn Annals*), no. 7.

Liang, Q. (1899) "自由书·豪杰之公脑 (Freedom Writings: The Heroic Public Brain)," 《清议报》 (*The Qingyi Gazette*), December 3, 1899.

Liang, Q. (1989) "论中国成文法编制沿革得失 (On the Evolution of Codified Law in China)," in 《饮冰室合集, 文集（第16卷）》 (*Ice-Drinker Studio Compilation, Collected Works*), vol. 16, Beijing: Zhonghua Books.

Liang, Q. (2006) 《论中国学术思想变迁之大势》 (*On the Main Developments during Chinese Academic Thought*), Shanghai: Shanghai Ancient Books Publishing House.

Liang, Q. ([1926] 2010) 《中国近三百年学术史》 (*History of Chinese Scholarship during the Last Three Hundred Years*), Beijing: Zhongguo Huabao Press.

Liang, W. (2012) "绝不放弃商从政 (Never Abandon Commerce-Follows-Politics)." *Xinhuanet*, November 12 [online]. Available at: www.xinhuanet.com/politics/2012-11/12/c_123943690.htm.

Liao, G. (2000) "毛泽东号召'进京赶考'回眸 (Looking Back on Mao Zedong's Call to 'Go to the Capital for the Examinations')," 《炎黄春秋》 (*Spring and Autumn Annals*), no. 3, pp. 28–32.

Liberman, S. I. (1945) *Building Lenin's Russia*, Chicago, IL: University of Chicago Press.

Lin, B. (1966) 《在中央政治局扩大会议上的讲话》 (*Speech at the Enlarged Session of the Politburo*), May 18, 1966. Chinese Marxist Library. Available at: www.marxists.org/chinese/linbiao/mia-chineselinbiao-19660518.htm

Lin, G. (ed.) (1990) 《中国封建土地制度史（第1卷的统计）》 (*History of the Feudal Land System in China, vol. 1 Statistics*), Beijing: China Social Sciences Press.

Lin, H. et al., (2022) "党政军民学, 东西南北中, 党是领导一切的 (The party exercises leadership in everything, in every area of endeavor and every corner of the country)," *People's Daily*, February 14, 2022.

Lin, M. (1990) 《憤怒的野百合：三一六中正堂學生靜坐紀實》 (*The Angry Wild Lily: A Documentary Account of the March 16 Student Sit-in at Chiang Kai-Shek Memorial Hall*), Taipei: Avanguard Books.

Link, P. and Wu, D. (2023) *I Have No Enemies: The Life and Legacy of Liu Xiaobo*, New York: Columbia University Press.

Linton, M. (2004) *The Terror in the French Revolution*, Surrey: Kingston University.

Linton, M. (2006) "Robespierre and the Terror," *History Today*, vol. 56, no. 8, pp. 23–29.

Linz, J. J. (2000) *Totalitarian and Authoritarian Regimes*, Boulder, CO: Lynne Rienner Publishers.

Lipset, S. M. (1959) "Some Social Requisites of Democracy: Economic Development and Political Legitimacy," *The American Political Science Review*, vol. 53, no. 1, pp. 69–105.

Literature Research Office of the Central Committee of the CCP (ed.) (1993) 《毛泽东年谱》 (*Chronicles of Mao Zedong*), vol. 1, Beijing: Central Literature Publishing House.

Liu, J. et al. (2021), "反垄断监管重锤, 涉腾讯阿里滴滴等43起案件 (Heavy Blow From Antitrust Regulators, Involving 43 Cases Including Tencent, Alibaba, Didi, etc.)," 《第一财经》 (*The First Finance*), November 20, 2021.

Liu, S. (1958) "同北京日报社编辑的谈话 (A Talk with the Editors of the Beijing Daily)," June 30 [online]. Available at: www.marxists.org/chinese/liushaoqi/1967/112.htm.

Liu, S. (1981) 《刘少奇选集》 (*Selected Works of Liu Shaoqi*), Beijing: People's Publishing House.

Locke, J. (1988) *Two Treatises of Government*, Cambridge: Cambridge University Press.

Long, A. A. (1997) "Stoic Philosophers on Persons, Property-Ownership and Community," *Bulletin of the Institute of Classical Studies. Supplement*, no. 68, pp. 13–31.

Lopata, B. B. (1973) "Property Theory in Hobbes," *Political Theory*, vol. 1, no. 2, pp. 203–218.

Lowenhardt, J., Ozinga, J., and Ree, E. (1992) *The Rise and Fall of the Soviet Politburo*, New York: St. Martin's Press.

Lu, Q. (2011) "土地革命战争后期的川康革命根据地 (The Chuan-Kang Border Region Revolutionary Base Area in the Late Period of the Land Revolution War)," *Bridge of Century*, no. 12.

Lu, Z. and Su, R. (eds.) (2005) 《析論中國歷史：治亂因果篇（上冊）》 (*Analyzing Chinese History: Causes and Consequences of Order and Chaos, Book I*), 2nd edn, Hong Kong: Cypress Publishing.

Luxemburg, R. (2006) "Leninism or Marxism," in *Reform or Revolution*, New York: Dover.

MacFarquhar, R. and Schoenhals, M. (2008) *Mao's Last Revolution*, Cambridge, MA: Belknap Press of Harvard University Press.

Maddison, A. (2003) *World Economy: Historical Statistics*, Paris: OECD Publishing.

Maier, H. (ed.) (2004) *Totalitarianism and Political Religions*, New York: Routledge.

Maine, H. S. (1861) *Ancient Law: Its Connection with the Early History of Society, and Its Relation to Modern Ideas*, London: John Murray.

Mao, G., Lu, F., Fan, X., and Wu, D. (2020) "China's Aging Population: The Present Situation and Prospects," in Poot, J. and Roskruge, M. (eds.), *Population Change and Impacts in Asia and the Pacific*, New York: Springer Publishing, pp. 269–287.

Mao, T.-T. (1965) *Reform Our Study*, Beijing: Foreign Languages Press.

Mao, Z. (1949) 《湖南农民运动考察报告》 (*Report on an Investigation of the Peasant Movement in Hunan*), Yan'an: Liberation Publishing House.

Mao, Z. (1952) 《中国社会各阶级的分析》 (*Analysis of Classes in Chinese Society*), Beijing: People's Publishing House.

Mao, Z. (1960) 《毛泽东选集》 (*Selected Works of Mao Zedong*), vol. 4, Beijing: People's Publishing House.

Mao, Z. (1966a) 《毛泽东选集》 (*Selected Works of Mao Zedong*), Beijing: People's Publishing House.

Mao, Z. (1966b) 《毛泽东思想万岁》 (*Long Live Mao Zedong Thought, vol. 1958–1960*), Unknown: Unknown publisher.

Mao, Z. (1968a) "在八大二次会议上的讲话（摘要）(Speech at the Second Meeting of the Eighth CCP Congress [summary])," in 《毛泽东思想万岁》 (*Long Live Mao Zedong Thought*), Wuhan: Chinese Library of Marxism.

Mao, Z. (1968b) 《毛泽东思想万岁》 (*Long Live Mao Zedong Thought*), Wuhan: Chinese Library of Marxism.

Mao, Z. (1975) 《新民主主义的宪政》 (*New Democratic Constitutionalism*), Beijing: People's Publishing House.

Mao, Z. (1976) 《论十大关系》 (*On the Ten Major Relationships*), Beijing: People's Publishing House.

Mao, Z. (1977) 《毛泽东选集》 (*Selected Works of Mao Zedong*), vol. 5, Beijing: People's Publishing House.

Mao, Z. (1989) 《建国以来毛泽东文稿》 (*Manuscripts of Mao Zedong Since the Founding of the State*), vol. 2, Beijing: Central Literature Publishing House.

Mao, Z. (1992a) 《建国以来毛泽东文稿》 (*Manuscripts of Mao Zedong Since the Founding of the State*), vol. 6, Beijing: Central Literature Publishing House.

Mao, Z. (1992b) 《建国以来毛泽东文稿》 (*Manuscripts of Mao Zedong Since the Founding of the State*), vol. 7, Beijing: Central Literature Publishing House.

Mao, Z. (1993) 《建国以来毛泽东文稿》 (*Manuscripts of Mao Zedong Since the Founding of the State*), vol. 8, Beijing: Central Literature Publishing House.

Mao, Z. (1996) 《毛泽东文集》 (*Collected Works of Mao Zedong*), vol. 3, Beijing: People's Publishing House.

Maréchal, S. (1796) "The Manifesto of Equals" (trans. M. Abidor) [online]. Available at: www.marxists.org/history/france/revolution/conspiracy-equals/1796/manifesto.htm.

Marx, K. (1938) *Critique of the Gotha Program*. New York: International Publishers.

Marx, K. (1964) *Class Struggles in France*. New York: International Publishers.

Marx, K. and Engels, F. (1972) 《马克斯恩格斯全集, 第25卷》 *(Collected Works of Marx and Engels)*, vol. 25 [Chinese translation], Beijing: People's Publishing House.

Marx, K. and Engels, F. (1973) 《马克思恩格斯全集, 第28卷》 *(Collected Works of Marx and Engels)*, vol. 28, Beijing: People's Publishing House.

Marx, K. and Engels, F. (1975) 《马克思恩格斯全集, 第45卷》 *(Collected Works of Marx and Engels)*, vol. 45, Beijing: People's Publishing House.

Marx, K. and Engels, F. (1975) *Collected Works of Marx and Engels*, vol. 40, Moscow: Progress Publishers.

Marx, K. and Engels, F. (1993) *Capital*, reissued edn, New York: Penguin Classics.

Marx, K. and Engels, F. ([1848] 1998) *The Communist Manifesto*, London: The Merlin Press.

Marx, K. and Engels, F. (2001) 《马克斯恩格斯全集, 第5卷》 *(Collected Works of Marx and Engels)*, vol. 5 [Chinese translation], Beijing: People's Publishing House.

Marx, K. and Engels, F. (2010) *Collected Works of Marx and Engels*, vol. 22, London: Lawrence Wishart.

Marx, K. and Engels, F. (2012) 《马克斯恩格斯选集, 第三版 第3卷》 *Selected Works of Marx and Engels*, vol. 3, 3rd edn, [Chinese translation], Beijing: People's Publishing House.

Maskin, E. S. (2008) "Mechanism Design: How to Implement Social Goals," *American Economic Review*, vol. 98, no. 3, pp. 586–603.

Maskin, E., Qian, Y., and Xu, C. (2000) "Incentives, Information, and Organizational Form," *The Review of Economic Studies*, vol. 67, no. 2, pp. 359–378.

Maskin, E. S. and Tirole, J. (2001) "Markov Perfect Equilibrium: I. Observable Actions," *Journal of Economic Theory*, vol. 100, no. 2, pp. 191–219.

Matheron, A. (2020) *Politics, Ontology and Knowledge in Spinoza: Essays by Alexandre Matheron*, Edinburgh: Edinburgh University Press.

Mathews, C. (2009) *Modern Satanism: Anatomy of a Radical Subculture*, Westport, CT: Greenwood Publishing.

Mathias, P. and Pollard, S. (eds.) (1989) *The Cambridge Economic History of Europe: VIII. The Industrial Economies: The Development of Economic and Social Policies*, Cambridge: Cambridge University Press.

Mayer, N. (1993) "Lenin and the Concept of the Professional Revolutionary," *History of Political Thought*, vol. 14, no. 2, pp. 249–263.

McManners, J. (1998) *Church and Society in 18th Century France*, vol. 1, London: Oxford University Press.

McMeekin, S. (2017) *The Russian Revolution: A New History*, London: Profile Books.

Medvedev, R. (2017) 《苏联的最后一年》 *(The Last Year of the USSR)*, Beijing: Social Sciences Academic Press.

Merrill, T. W. and Smith, H. E. (2001) "What Happened to Property in Law and Economics?," *The Yale Law Journal*, vol. 111, no. 2, pp. 357–398.

Meslier, J. (2009) *Testament: Memoir of the Thoughts and Sentiments of Jean Meslier* (trans. M. Shreve), Amherst, NY: Prometheus Books.

Metzger, M. (ed.) (1989) *NRSV (The Holy Bible: New Revised Standard Version)*, Washington, DC: National Council of the Churches of Christ [online]. Available at: www.biblegateway.com.

Meyer, A. G. (1957) *Leninism*, Boston, MA: Harvard University Press.

Miklosich, F. and Müller, J. (eds.) (1860) *Acta Patriarchatus Constantinopolitani, MCCCXV-MCCCCII*, Vindobonae, C. Gerold.

von Mises, L. (1981) "Christianity and Socialism," in *Socialism*, New Haven, CT: Yale University Press.

von Mises, L. (1988) *Socialism: An Economic and Sociological Analysis*, 6th edn., Indianapolis, IN: Liberty Classics.

von Mises, L. (2009) "Observations on Professor Hayek's Plan," *Libertarian Papers*, vol. 1, no. 2, pp. 1–3.

Mitani, T. (2002) 《秘密结社与中国革命》 (*Secret Associations and the Chinese Revolution*), Beijing: China Social Sciences Press.

Miyazaki, I. (1980) 《中國史》 (*A History of China*) (trans. T. Qiu), Taipei: Huashi Publishing House.

Modern History Research Office of CASS (1980b) 《马林在中国的有关资料》 (*Materials Relating to Marin in China*), Beijing: People's Publishing House.

Montefiore, S. (2017) *The Romanovs*, New York: Vintage.

Montero, R. A. (2017) *All Things in Common: The Economic Practices of the Early Christians*, Eugene, OR: Wipf and Stock Publishers.

Montgomery, I. (2001) "Georgy Shakhnazarov: Obituary," *The Guardian*, May 28, 2001.

Moore, B. (1966) *Social Origins of Dictatorship and Democracy: Lord and Peasant in the Making of the Modern World*, Boston, MA: Beacon Press.

Moss, W. G. (2010) *A History Of Russia, Volume II: Since 1855*, London: Oxford University Press.

Murray, H. (1834) *An Encyclopaedia of Geography*, London: Longman.

Museum of the Chinese Revolution of the Hunan Provincial Museum (1980a) 《新民学会资料》 (*Xinmin Society's Documents*), Beijing: People's Publishing House.

Mussolini, B. (2015) *The Doctrine of Fascism*, London: Free Thought Books.

Myerson, R. (2008) "Perspectives on Mechanism Design in Economic Theory," *American Economic Review*, vol. 98, no. 3, pp. 586–603.

Nagao, A. (2019) 《有贺长雄论学集》 (*Collected Eessays of Nagao Ariga*), Beijing: Commercial Press.

Nathan, A. J. and P. Link (2001) *The Tiananmen Papers*, New York: PublicAffairs.

Naughton, B. (2018) *The Chinese Economy: Adaptation and Growth*, Cambridge, MA: The MIT Press.

Nie, H. (2005) 《聂洪钧回忆与文稿》 (*Nie Hongjun Recollections and Manuscripts*), Beijing: CCP History Publishing House.

Nohlen, D. and Stöver, P. (2010) *Elections in Europe: A Data Handbook*, Baden-Baden, Germany: Nomos Publishing.

North, D. (1990) *Institutions, Institutional Change and Economic Performance*, New York: Cambridge University Press.

North, D. (1991) "Institutions," *Journal of Economic Perspectives*, vol. 5, no. 1, pp. 97–112.

Obolensky, D. (1970) *The Relations between Byzantium and Russia (Eleventh to Fifteenth Century)*, Moscow: Nauka Publishing House [online]. Available at: http://archaeology.kiev.ua/pub/obolensky.htm.

Offord, D. (1986) *The Russian Revolutionary Movement in the 1880s*, London: Cambridge University Press.

Oi, J. (1999) *Rural China Takes Off: Institutional Foundations of Economic Reform*, Berkeley, CA: University of California Press.

Onfray, M. (2006) "Jean Meslier and 'The Gentle Inclination of Nature'" (trans. M. Mandell), *New Politics*, vol. 10, no. 4 [online]. Available at: https://newpol.org/issue_post/jean-meslier-and-gentle-inclination-nature/.

Orleans, L. (1961) *Professional Manpower and Education in Communist China*, Washington, DC: National Science Foundation.

Orwell, G. (2013) *1984*, Boston, MA: Mariner Books Classics.

Ostrowski, D. (1998) *Muscovy and the Mongols: Cross-Cultural Influences on the Steppe Frontier, 1304–1598*, Cambridge: Cambridge University Press.

Parry, N. (2006) *Terrorism*, New York: Dover Publications.

Party History Research Office of the Museum of the Chinese Revolution (1983) 《党史研究资料》 (*Party History Research Materials*), vol. 4, Chengdu: Sichuan People's Publishing House.

Peffer, N. (1958) *The Far East: A Modern History*, Ann Arbor, MI: The University of Michigan Press.

Pei, M. (2006) *China's Trapped Transition: The Limits of Developmental Autocracy*, Cambridge, MA: Harvard University Press.

Peirson, N. (2000) "Increasing Returns, Path Dependence, and the Study of Politics," *The American Political Science Review*, vol. 94, no. 2, pp. 251–267.

People's Daily (2013) "在意识形态领域领导干部要敢于亮剑 (In the Field of Ideology, Leading Cadres Should Dare to Show the Sword)," September 2 [online]. Available at: http://theory.people.com.cn/n/2013/0902/c40531-22771397.html.

Persky, S. (1981) *At the Lenin Shipyard: Poland and the Rise of the Solidarity Trade Union*, Vancouver, BC: New Star Books.

Phillips, W. A. (1911) "Babeuf, François Noel," in *Encyclopædia Britannica*, vol. 3, 11th ed., Cambridge: Cambridge University Press.

Pines, Y. (trans. and ed.) (2017) *The Book of Lord Shang: Apologetics of State Power in Early China*, New York: Columbia University Press.

Pipes, N. (2000) *Property and Freedom*, London: Vintage.

Pipes, R. (1991) *The Russian Revolution*, New York: Vintage.

Pipes, R. (1995a) *Russia under the Bolshevik Regime*, New York: Vintage.

Pipes, R. (1995b) *Russia under the Old Regime*, London: Penguin.

Pistor, K. (2019) *The Code of Capital: How the Law Creates Wealth and Inequality*, Princeton, NJ: Princeton University Press.

Plekhanov, G. (1967) *History of Russian Social Thought*, New York: H. Fertig.

Plokhy, S. M. (2010) *Yalta: The Price of Peace*, New York: Viking.

Pomeranz, K. (2000) *The Great Divergence: China, Europe, and the Making of the Modern World Economy*, Princeton, NJ: Princeton University Press.

Popper, K. (1945) *The Open Society and Its Enemies*, New York: Routledge.

Potter, P. (2014) *China's Legal System*, Cambridge: Polity Books.

Pu, J. (2003) 《中国古代法制丛钞》 (*Collected Writings on Legal Institutions of Ancient China*), Beijing: Guangming Daily Press [online]. Available at: https://cn.govopendata.com/renminribao/1954/10/3/3/.

Pusey, J. R. (2008) 《中国与达尔文》 (*China and Charles Darwin*) [Chinese trans.], Nanjing: Jiangsu People's Publishing House.

Qian, M. (2010) 《国史大纲》 (*A General History of China*), Beijing: Commercial Press.

Qian, Y. and Xu, C. (1993) "Why China's Economic Reforms Differ: The M-Form Hierarchy and Entry/Expansion of the Non-State Sector," *Economics of Transition*, vol. 1, no. 2, pp. 135–170.

Qian, Y. and Xu, C. (1998) "Innovation and Bureaucracy under Soft and Hard Budget Constraints," *Review of Economic Studies*, vol. 65, no. 1, pp. 151–164.

Qin, B. and Tan, S. (2002) 《中国秘密社会》 (*Chinese Secret Societies*), 7 vols., Fuzhou: Fujian People's Publishing House.

Qing Dynasty Record Bureau [清历朝实录馆] (ed.) (1986) [清实录 Qing Shilu] (*Qing Dynasty Records*) vol. 50, [德宗实录 Dezong Shilu] (*Emperor Dezong's Records*), vol. 562, Beijing: Zhonghua Books.

Qiu, H. (2011) 《邱會作回憶錄》 (*Memoirs of Qiu Huizuo*), Hong Kong: New Century Press.

Reference Room of the Department of Communist Party History, Renmin University of China (1979) 《共产主义小组和党的"一大"资料汇编》 (*Compendium* of Materials on Communist Groups and the First National Congress), Beijing: Renmin University of China, Department of Party History, Reference Room.

Ren, J. (1999) "Introduction" in S. Li (ed.) 《中国儒教史》 (History of Confucianism in China), Shanghai: Shanghai People's Publishing House.

Ren, Z. (2021) 《中国住房市值报告》 (China Housing Market Value Report: 2021), Zeping Macro [online]. Available at: https://finance.sina.cn/zl/2021-10-28/zl-iktzscyy2178849.d.html?vt=4&cid=79615&node_id=79615.

Research Office of Party History of the Jiangxi Provincial CCP (2011) 《中央革命根据地历史资料文库》 (The Central Revolutionary Base Area Historical Data Library), vol. 6, Nanchang: Jiangxi People's Publishing House.

Riasanovsky, N. V. and Steinberg, M. D. (2011) A History of Russia, Oxford: Oxford University Press.

Riley, P. (1986) The General Will Before Rousseau: The Transformation of the Divine into the Civic, Princeton, NJ: Princeton University Press.

Rong, Z. (1947) "明太祖的《孟子节文》 (Ming Taizu's Excerpts from Mencius)," 《读书与出版》 (Reading and Publishing), vol. 2, no. 4.

Rose, R. B. (1978) Gracchus Babeuf: The First Revolutionary Communist, Stanford, CA: Stanford University Press.

Rosenthal, J.-L. and Wong, R. B. (2011) Before and Beyond Divergence: The Politics of Economic Change in China and Europe, Cambridge, MA: Harvard University Press.

Rossabi, M. (1994) "The Reign of Khubilai Khan," in H. Frabje and D. Twitchett, The Cambridge History of China, vol. 6, Cambridge: Cambridge University Press, pp. 414–489.

Rousseau, J. J. (1923) The Social Contract and Discourses by Jean-Jacques Rousseau (trans. G. D. H. Cole), London and Toronto: J. M. Dent and Sons.

Rousseau, J. J. (1997) Discourse on the Origin and the Foundations of Inequality Among Men, Cambridge: Cambridge University Press.

Rowley, D. G. (2017) Millenarian Bolshevism 1900–1920: Empiriomonism, God-Building, Proletarian Culture, New York: Routledge.

Rubenstein, J. (2011) Leon Trotsky: A Revolutionary's Life, New Haven, CT: Yale University Press.

Rubinstein, M. (2007) Taiwan: A New History (Expanded Edition), New York: Routledge.

Rummel, R. J. (1990) Lethal Politics: Soviet Genocide and Mass Murder Since 1917, New York: Routledge.

Russell, B. ([1946] 1957) The History of Western Philosophy, New Delhi: Popular Book Services.

Savranskaya, S. (2010) *Masterpieces of History: The Peaceful End of the Cold War in Europe, 1989*, Budapest and New York: Central European University Press.

Schapiro, L. (1987) *The Origin of the Communist Autocracy: Political Opposition in the Soviet State, First Phase, 1917–1922*, New York: Palgrave Macmillan.

Schram, S. R. (1966) "Mao Tse-tung and Secret Societies," *China Quarterly*, no. 27, pp. 1–13.

Schwarcz, V. (1992) *Time for Telling Truth is Runing Out: Conversations with Zhang Shenfu*, New Haven, CT: Yale University Press.

Schwartz, B. (2010) 《寻求富强：严复与西方》 (*In Search of Wealth and Power: Yen Fu and the West*), [Chinese trans.] Nanjing: Jiangsu People's Publishing House.

Sebestyen, V. (2017) *Lenin the Dictator*, London: Weidenfeld & Nicolson.

Shafarevich, I. (1980) *The Socialist Phenomenon*, New York: Harper & Row.

Shambaugh, D. (2008) *China's Communist Party: Atrophy and Adaptation*, Berkeley, CA: University of California Press.

Shang, X. (2013) "有贺长雄与民初制宪活动几件史事辨析 (A Few Historical Facts Concerning Ariko Nagao and Constitution-making Activities in the Early Republican Era)," *Modern Chinese History Studies*, no. 2, pp. 129–137.

Shanin, T. (ed.) (1983) *Late Marx and the Russian Road: Marx and the "Peripheries of Capitalism,"* New York: Monthly Review Press.

Shao, Y. (2007) "朱元璋删《孟子》 (Zhu Yuanzhang Deletions in *Mencius*)," 《文汇读书周报》 (*Wenhui Weekend Book Review*), Shanghai, June 29, 2007.

Shao, Y. (2010) 《秘密社会与中国革命》 (*Secret Societies and the Chinese Revolution*), Beijing: Commercial Press.

Shao, Y. et al. (1993) 《中国帮会史》 (*The History of Chinese Secret Societies*), Shanghai: Shanghai People's Publishing House.

Shen, Y. (2017) 《新編五七右派列傳》 (*New Series of Biographies of the May 7 Rightists*), Hong Kong: May 7 Scholarly Publishing.

Shen, Z. (1994). 《新经济政策与苏联农业社会化道路》 (*The New Economic Policy and the Soviet Road to Socialization of Agriculture*), Beijing: China Social Sciences Press.

Shen, Z. (ed.) (2009). "苏维埃政权和立宪会议 (The Soviet Regime and the Constituent Assembly)" in Z. Shen (ed.) 《一个大国的崛起与崩溃》 (*The Rise and Fall of a Great Power*), Beijing: Social Sciences Academic Press.

Shen, Z. (ed.) (2015) 《俄罗斯解密档案选编》 (*Selected Declassified Russian Archives*), vol. 1, Shanghai: Oriental Publishing Center.

Shen, Z., et al. (eds.) (2016a) 《中苏关系史纲》 (*Outline History of Sino-Soviet Relations*), vol. 1, 3rd ed., Beijing: Social Sciences Academic Press.

Shen, Z., et al. (eds.) (2016b) 《中苏关系史纲》 (*Outline History of Sino-Soviet Relations*), vol. 2, 3rd ed., Beijing: Social Sciences Academic Press.

Shennan, J. H. (1998) *The Parlement of Paris*, Stroud: The History Press.

Shi, G. et al. (1985) 《二大和三大：中国共产党第二、三次代表大会资料选编》 (*Selected Archives of the CCP Second and Third National Party Congresses*), Beijing: China Social Sciences Press.

Shi, Z. (1992) 《峰与谷》 (*Peaks and Valleys*), Beijing: Hongqi Publishing House.

Shirk, S. (1993) *The Political Logic of Economic Reform in China*, Oakland, CA: University of California Press.

Shusterman, N. (2013) *The French Revolution: Faith, Desire, and Politics*, New York: Routledge.

Sima, Q. (2010) [annot. Z Q. Han], 《史记 (*Shi ji*)》 (*Record of the Grand Historian*), Han Zhaoqi annot., vol. 1, Beijing: Zhonghua Books.

Slezkine, Y. (2017) *The House of Government: A Saga of the Russian Revolution*, Princeton, NJ: Princeton University Press.

Smedley, A. (1956) *The Great Road: The Life and Times of Chu Teh*, London: Monthly Review Press.

Smirnov, N. N. (1997) "Constituent Assembly," in E. Acton et al. (eds.), *Critical Companion to the Russian Revolution 1914–1921*, Bloomington, IN: Indiana University Press.

Smith, A. [[1777] 2011] *The Theory of Moral Sentiments*, 6th edn, Gutenberg Project [online]. Available at: www.gutenberg.org/ebooks/67363.

Smith, D. M. (1983) *Mussolini: A Biography*, New York: Vintage.

Snow, E. (1979) 《西行漫记》 (*Wanderings in the West: Red Star Over China*) (trans. L. Dong), Shanghai: Joint Publishing House.

Soboul, A. (1972) *The Sans-Culottes*, Princeton, NJ: Princeton University Press.

Soboul, A. (1975) *The French Revolution 1787–1799*, New York: Vintage.

Soboul, A. (1983) "巴贝夫、巴贝夫主义和为平等而密谋 (Babeuf, Babeufism and the Conspiracy for Equality)" (trans. L. Chen and M. Gu), in 《论巴贝夫主义》 (*On Babeufism*), Beijing: Commercial Press [online]. Available at: www.marxists.org/chinese/reference-books/mia-chinese-babeuf-1975.htm.

Song, Y. (ed.) (2019) 《重审毛泽东的土地改革》 (*Revisiting Mao Zedong's Land Reform*), Part 1, Hong Kong: Pastoral Bookstore.

Spitzer, A. B. (1957) *The Revolutionary Theories of Louis Auguste Blanqui*, New York: Columbia University Press.

Stalin, J. (1931) *Problems of Leninism*, 1947 edn, Moscow: Foreign Languages Publishing House.

Stalin, J. (1945) *Problems Of Leninism*, Moscow: Foreign Languages Publishing House.

Stalin, J. (1954a) "The Tasks of the Industrial Managers," in *Collected Works of Joseph Stalin*, vol. 6, Moscow: Foreign Languages Publishing House, pp. 75–77.

Stalin, J. (1954b) "The Political Tasks of the University of the Peoples of the East," in *Collected Works of Joseph Stalin*, vol. 7, Moscow: Foreign Languages Publishing House, pp. 135–154.

Stalin, J. (trans. The Compilation Bureau of the CCP Central Committee) (1975), *History of the All-Union Communist Party (Bolsheviks): Short Course*, Beijing: People's Publishing House.

Stalin, J. (2016) 《斯大林的全集附卷》 (*Complete Works of Stalin, Accompanying Volumes*), vol. 1 [online]. Available at: www.marxists.org/chinese/pdf/russian_communists/stalin/nf1-10.pdf.

Straumann, B. (2016) *Crisis and Constitutionalism: Roman Political Thought from the Fall of the Republic to the Age of Revolution*, Oxford: Oxford University Press.

Sun, Y. (1981) 《孙中山全集》 (*Collected Works of Sun Yat-sen*), 11 vols, Beijing: Zhonghua Books.

Sun, Y. (2011) 《孙中山全集》 (*Collected Works of Sun Yat-sen*), vol. 8, 2011 edn, Beijing: People's Publishing House.

Suny, R. G. (2010) *The Soviet Experiment: Russia, the USSR, and the Successor States*, London: Oxford University Press.

Talmon, J. L. (1952) *The Origins of Totalitarian Democracy*, London: Secker & Warburg.

Tamura, E. H. (1997) *China: Understanding Its Past*, vol. 1, Honolulu, HI: University of Hawai'i Press.

Tang, B. (2013) 《陈独秀全传》 (*Complete Biography of Chen Duxiu*), Beijing: Social Sciences Academic Press.

Tao, C. ([1928] 2020) 《教會源流考》 (commentary by M. Zhou) (*Study of the Origins and Development of Secret Societies in China*), Amazon Kindle Edition.

Tatsuhito, T. (2015) 《难忘的会谈：记王岐山与福山、青木的会见》 (An Unforgettable Meeting: On Wang Qishan Meeting with Francis Fukuyama and Masahiko Aoki) [online], Available at: https://goldenrunnner.blogspot.com/2015/05/blog-post_78.html.

Taubman, W. (2005) *Khrushchev: The Man & His Era*, London: Simon & Schuster.

Taubman, W. (2017) *Gorbachev: His Life and Times*, London: Simon & Schuster.

The First Research Department of the Party History Research Office of the Central Committee of the CCP (trans.) (1997a) 《共产国际、联共（布）与中国国民革命运动》 (*Comintern, CPSU (Bolshevik) and the Chinese National Revolutionary Movement*), vol. 1, Beijing: Beijing Library Press.

The First Research Department of the Party History Research Office of the Central Committee of the CCP (trans.) (1997b) 《共产国际, 联共（布）与中国国民革命运动》 (*Comintern, CPSU (Bolshevik) and the Chinese National Revolutionary Movement*), vol. 2, Beijing: Beijing Library Press.

The First Research Department of the Party History Research Office of the Central Committee of the CCP (trans.) (1997c) 《共产国际, 联共（布）与中国国民革命运动》 (*Comintern, CPSU (Bolshevik) and the Chinese National Revolutionary Movement*), vol. 3, part 1, Beijing: Beijing Library Press.

The First Research Department of the Party History Research Office of the Central Committee of the CCP (trans.) (2002a) 《联共（布），共产国际与苏维埃运动》 (*The CPSU (Bolshevik), the Comintern and the Chinese Soviet Movement*), vol. 7, Beijing: Central Literature Publishing House.

The First Research Department of the Party History Research Office of the Central Committee of the CCP (trans.) (2002b) 《联共（布），共产国际与苏维埃运动》 (*The CPSU (Bolshevik), the Comintern and the Chinese Soviet Movement*), vol. 10, Beijing: Central Literature Publishing House.

The First Research Department of the Party History Research Office of the Central Committee of the CCP (trans.) (2002c) 《联共（布），共产国际与苏维埃运动》 (*The CPSU (Bolshevik), the Comintern and the Chinese Soviet Movement*), vol. 17, Beijing: CCP History Publishing House.

The First Research Department of the Party History Research Office of the Central Committee of the CCP (trans.) (2012a) 《联共（布), 共产国际与抗日战争时期的中国共产党》 (*The CPSU (Bolsheviks), the Comintern and the Chinese Communist Party during the Anti-Japanese War*), vol. 18, Beijing: CCP History Publishing House.

The First Research Department of the Party History Research Office of the Central Committee of the CCP (trans.) (2012b) 《联共（布), 共产国际与抗日战争时期的中国共产党》 (*The CPSU (Bolsheviks), the Comintern and the Chinese Communist Party during the Anti-Japanese War*), vol. 21, Beijing: CCP History Publishing House.

The General Office of the CCP Central Committee (2013) 中办发〔2013〕9号《关于当前意识形态领域情况的通报》 (CCPCC General Office Doc. No. 9 [2013]: Notice on the Current Situation in the Ideological Sphere), in 《明镜月报》 (*Mirror Monthly*), August 20, 2013, and *The New York Times*, August 20, 2013.

Tian, X. (1999) 《万军》 (*Wanjun [Anhui Army]*), Taiyuan: Shanxi People's Publishing House.

de Tocqueville, A. (1856) *The Old Regime and the Revolution* (trans. J. Bonner), New York: Harper & Brothers.

de Tocqueville, A. (2001) *The Old Regime and the Revolution, Vol. II: Notes on the French Revolution and Napoleon*, eds. F. Furet and F. Mélonio, Chicago, IL: University of Chicago Press.

Toutain, J. (1930) *The Economic Life of the Ancient World*. New York: A.A. Knopf.

Trotsky, L. (1972) *The Young Lenin*, New York: Doubleday.

Trotsky, L. (1975) *The Challenge of the Left Opposition (1923–1925)*, New York: Pathfinder Press.

Twitchett, D. and Loewe, M. (1986) *Cambridge History of China*, vol. 1, Cambridge: Cambridge University Press.

Tyrrell, P. and Kim, A (2022) *2022 Index of Economic Freedom: Economic Freedom Declining Worldwide*, The Heritage Foundation [online]. Available at: www.heritage.org/sites/default/files/2022-02/FS229.pdf.

Vernadsky, G. (1939) "Feudalism in Russia," *Speculum*, vol. 14, no. 3, pp. 300–323.

Vile, M. J. C. (1967) *Constitutionalism and the Separation of Powers*, 2nd edn, Carmel, IN: Liberty Fund.

Vogel, E. (2011) *Deng Xiaoping and the Transformation of China*, Cambridge, MA: Harvard University Press.

Voltaire (2009) *Letters Concerning the English Nation*, ed. N. Cronk, Oxford: Oxford University Press.

Wade, I. O. (1933) "The Manuscripts of Jean Meslier's Testament and Voltaire's Printed Extrait," *Modern Philology*, vol. 30, no. 4, pp. 381–398.

Walder, A. (2017) *China Under Mao: A Revolution Derailed*, Cambridge, MA: Harvard University Press.

Walder, A. (2019) *Agents of Disorder: Inside China's Cultural Revolution*, Cambridge, MA: Harvard University Press.

Wang, B. (1963) 《民法總則》 (*General Principles of Civil Law*), Taipei: Cheng Chung Book Company.

Wang, F. (2018) *The China Order: Centralia, World Empire, and the Nature of Chinese Power*, Albany, NY: State University of New York Press.

Wang, L. (2008) 《中共創始人訪談》 (*Interviews with the Founders of the CCP*), Hong Kong: Mirror Publishing House.

Wang, M. (2004) 《中共五十年》 (*Fifty Years of the CCP*), Beijing: Oriental Publishing House.

Wang, N. (1988) 《大动乱的年代》 (*An Age of Great Upheaval*), Zhengzhou: Henan People's Publishing House.

Wang, P. (2012) "袁文才" (*Yuan Wencai*), *Communist Web* [online]. Available at: https://fuwu.12371.cn/2012/06/12/ARTI1339473240471204.shtml.

Wang, Q. and Wang, Q. (2015) "七大前后毛泽东如何破除山头主义 (How Mao Zedong Eradicated the Mountain Stronghold Mentality Before and After the 7th Congress)," 《党的文献》 (*Party Literature*), no. 4, pp. 122–124.

Wang, S. (1976) 《严复传》 (*Biography of Yan Fu*), Shanghai: Shanghai People's Publishing House.

Wang, S. (1982) 《论严复与严译名著》 (*On Yan Fu and Yan's Major Translations*), Beijing: Commercial Press.

Wang, S. (2006) 《长征》 (*The Long March*), Beijing: People's Literature Publishing House.

Wang, T. and Gao, S. (2017) 《明史：多重性格的时代》 (*History of the Ming: An Age of Multiple Characteristics*), Beijing: CITIC Press.

Wang, Y. (1978) "难忘的记忆 (Indelible Memories)," 《人民日报》 (*People's Daily*), July 30, 1978.

Wang, Y. (2004) 《文革受难者》 (*Victims of the Cultural Revolution*), Hong Kong: Open Magazine Press.

Wang, Z. (2010) 《进化主义在中国的兴起》 (*The Rise of Evolutionism in China*), Beijing: China Renmin University Press.

Watson, A. (1992) 《民法法系的演变及形成》 (*The Evolution and Characteristics of the Civil Law System*), Beijing: China University of Political Science and Law Press.

Weber, M. (1978) *Economy and Society*, Berkeley, CA: University of California Press.

Weber, M., Baehr, P., and Wells, G. C. (eds.) (2002) *The Protestant Ethic and the "Spirit" of Capitalism and Other Writings*, London: Penguin Books.

Williams, K. (1997) *The Prague Spring and its Aftermath: Czechoslovak Politics, 1968–1970*, Cambridge: Cambridge University Press.

Witte, S. (2016) *The Memoirs of Count Witte* (trans. S. Harcave), New York: Routledge.

Wittfogel, K. A. (1957) *Oriental Despotism. A Comparative Study of Total Power*, New Haven, CT: Yale University Press.

Wu, B. (2011) 《我们不搞多党轮流执政和联邦制不搞私有化》 (*We Will Not Employ a System of Multiple Parties Holding Office in Rotation, Use a Federal System, or Carry Out Privatization*), 新华网 Xinhuanet, March 10, 2011. Available at: www.chinacourt.org/article/detail/2011/03/id/443624.shtml.

Wu, H. (1984) "论皇权 (On Imperial Authority)," in 《吴晗史学论著选集，第2卷》 (*Selected History Essays of Wu Han*), vol. 2, Beijing: People's Publishing House.

Wu, H. et al. (2013) "苏联专家与中国人民大学学科地位的形成 (Soviet Experts and the Development of Academic Status at the Renmin University of China)," *Journal of Renmin University of China*, no. 6 [online]. Available at: http://xuebao.ruc.edu.cn/CN/Y2013/V27/I6/143.

Wu, J. (2010) 《当代中国经济改革教程》 (*A Course on Contemporary Chinese Economic Reform*), Shanghai: Far Eastern Publishing House.

Wu, N. (2015) "亲历经济特区的决策过程 (Personal Account of the Special Economic Zone Decision-making Process)," 《炎黄春秋》 (*Spring and Autumn Annals*), no. 5, pp. 6–11.

Xi, J. (2013a) "网传习近平8•19讲话全文：言论方面要敢抓敢管敢于亮剑 (The Full Text of Xi Jinping's Speech on August 19 Circulated Online: We Must Dare to Take Control, Manage, and Draw Our Swords When Dealing with Public Speech)," *China Digital Times* [online]. Available at: https://chinadigitaltimes.net/chinese/321001.html.

Xi, J. (2013b) "习近平在亚太经合组织工商领导人峰会上的演讲(全文) (Xi Jinping's speech [full text] at the APEC leaders' summit)," Xinhua, October 8, 2013. Available at: www.gov.cn/govweb/ldhd/2013-10/08/content_2501676.htm.

Xi, J. (2022) "在中共统战工作会议上的讲话 (Speech at the CCP United Front Work Conference)," May 18, 2015. 《习近平关于社会主义政治建设论述摘编》 (Compilation of Xi Jinping's Discourses on the Construction of Socialist Politics). Beijing: Central Literature Publishing House.

Xi, Z. (1979) *People's Daily*, October 16, 1979.

Xiao, G. (2003) "清末新政时期的立宪论证及其现代启示 (The Constitutionalist Controversy of the Late Qing New Policies Period and Its Modern Implications)," Conference on Constitutionalism in Modern and Contemporary China, Sydney, Australia, January 16–18, 2003.

Xiao, K. (1997) 《萧克回忆录》 (*Memoirs of Xiao Ke*), Beijing: People's Liberation Army Press.

Xiao, T. and Tan, X. (2007) "孙中山为何视同门会为革命党而非政党 (Why Sun Yat-sen Regarded the Tongmenghui as a Revolutionary Party Rather than a Political Party)," *Journal of Central South University*, vol. 13, no. 1. pp. 62–66.

Xie, Y. (2010) 《鄉村社會的毀滅》 (*The Destruction of Rural Society*), New York: Mirror Publishing House.

Xin, Z. (2006) 《紅太陽的殞落：千秋功罪毛澤東》 (*The Fall of the Red Sun: A Thousand Successes and Crimes of Mao Zedong*), Hong Kong: Shuzuofang Press.

Xiong, X. (2003) "1959年司法部被撤销的真相 (The Truth Behind the Abolition of the Ministry of Justice in 1959)," 《炎黄春秋》 (*Spring and Autumn Annals*), no. 12, pp. 30–32.

Xu, C. (2011) "The Fundamental Institutions of China's Reforms and Development," *Journal of Economic Literature*, vol. 49, no. 4, pp. 1076–1151.

Xu, C. (2017) "Capitalism and Socialism: A Review of Kornai's Dynamism, Rivalry, and the Surplus Economy," *Journal of Economic Literature*, vol. 55, no. 1, pp. 191–208.

Xu, C. (2019) "The Pitfalls of a Centralized Bureaucracy," *Acta Oeconomica*, vol. 69, no. 1, pp. 1–69.

Xu, L. and Wang, L. (2015) 《民主的历史》 (*The History of Democracy*), Beijing: Law Press.

Xu, S. (2008) 《中国革命根据地货币史纲》 (*Outline History of Currency in the Chinese Revolutionary Base Areas*), Beijing: China Financial Publishing House.

Xu, T. (2014) "六十年代的接班人计划 (Succession Planning in the 1960s)," *China Newsweek*, no. 33.

Yakovlev, A. (1989) "The Political Philosophy of Perestroika," in A. Aganbergyan (ed.), *Perestroika 1989*, New York: Charles Scribner's Sons.

Yakovlev, A. (1999) 《一杯苦酒：俄罗斯的布尔什维主义和改革运动》 (*A Bittersweet Tale: Russia's Bolshevism and Reform Movements*), Beijing: China Social Sciences Academic Press.

Yan, F. (1986) 《严复集》 (*Selected Works of Yan Fu*), vol. 4, Beijing: Zhonghua Books.

Yan, Z. (2017) 《進出中組部》 (*In and Out of the Central Organisation Department*), Hong Kong: Mirror Publishing House.

Yang, J. (2008) 《墓碑：中國六十年代大饑荒紀實》 (*Tombstone: A Chronicle of the Great Famine in China in the 1960s*), Hong Kong: Cosmos Books.

Yang, J. (2010) 《中國改革年代的政治鬥爭》 (*Political Struggles in China's Reform Era*), Hong Kong: Cosmos Books.

Yang, J. (2013) 《道路·理论·制度：我对文化大革命的思考》 (*Path · Theory · System: My Thoughts on the Cultural Revolution*), 《记忆》 (*Remembrance*), no. 104, pp. 1–23.

Yang, J. (2016) 《天地翻覆–中國文化大革命史》 (*Heaven and Earth Turned Upside Down – A History of the Chinese Cultural Revolution*), Hong Kong: Cosmos Books.

Yang, K. (1997) 《戰國史》 (*History of the Warring States*), Taipei: Commercial Press.

Yang, K. (2005) 《毛泽东与莫斯科的恩恩怨怨》 (*Mao Zedong's Grievances Against Moscow*), 3rd edn, Nanchang: Jiangxi People's Publishing House.

Yang, K. (2006) 《西安事变新探》 (*A New Inquiry into the Xi'an Incident*), Nanjing: Jiangsu People's Publishing House.

Yang, K. (2008) 《国民党的"联共"与"反共"》 (*The Kuomintang's Alliance with and Opposition to the Communists*), Beijing: Social Sciences Academic Press.

Yang, K. (2009) 《中华人民共和国建国史研究》 (*Studies on the History of the Establishment of the People's Republic of China*), Nanchang: Jiangxi People's Publishing House.

Yang, K. (2010) 《孔子与保罗：天道与圣言的相遇》 (*Confucius and Paul: The Way of Heaven Meets the Word of God*), Shanghai: East China Normal University Press.

Yang, N. (2004) 《元代白莲教研究》 (*On the White Lotus Sect in the Yuan Dynasty*), Shanghai: Shanghai Guji Press.

Yang, T. (2017) "倒孙风潮与蒋介石暗杀陶成长实践 (The Campaign to Bring Down Sun Yat-sen and Chiang Kai-shek's Assassination of Tao Chengzhang)," 《近代史研究》 (*Modern Chinese History Studies*), no. 2, pp. 127–137.

Yang, Y. et al. (1987) 《陕甘宁边区法制史稿》 (*Draft History of the Legal System in the Shaanxi-Ganjing-Ningxia Border Region*), Beijing: Law Press.

Yao, H. (2009) "历史性的转折 (A Historic Turning)," in Z. Shen (ed.), 《一个大国的崛起与崩溃, 上册》 (*The Rise and Fall of a Great Power*, vol. 1), Beijing: Social Sciences Academic Press.

Ye, D. (1999) 《虽九死其犹未悔》 (*No Regrets, Even unto Death*), Beijing: October Literature and Art Publishing House.

Yin, S. (2014) "毛泽东与第三次全国公安会议 (Mao Zedong and the Third National Public Security Conference)," 《炎黄春秋》 (*Spring and Autumn Annals*), no. 5. Available at: www.difangwenge.org/forum.php?mod=viewthread&tid=20630.

Yu, J. (2003) 《近代中国民法学中的私权理论》 (*Private Rights Theory in Modern Chinese Civil Jurisprudence*), Beijing: Peking University Press.

Yu, Y. (1991) 《猶記風吹水上鱗：錢穆與現代中國學術》 (*Recalling Breezes Across Rippling Water: Qian Mu and Modern Chinese Learning*), Taipei: Sanmin Books.

Yu, Y. (2005) 《试说科举在中国史上的功能与意义》 (*Exploring the Function and Significance of the Imperial Examination System in Chinese History*), 21st Century, Hong Kong [online]. Available at: www.cuhk.edu.hk/ics/21c/media/online/0505036.pdf.

Yü, Y. (2016) *Chinese History and Culture, Volume 2: Seventeenth Century Through Twentieth Century*, New York: Columbia University Press.

Yuan, W. (2001) "A Valuable Beginning of Social Change in China in the 20th Century – My Views on the New Policies of the Late Qing Dynasty," *21st Century*, no. 63 (February).

Zhang, B. (2015) 《跟随邓小平四十年》 (*Forty Years of Following Deng Xiaoping*), Beijing: CCP Literature Press.

Zhang, C. (2016) 《唐律，高丽律比较研究：以法典及其适用为中心》 (*A Comparative Study of the Tang and Goryeo Codes: Centering on the Code and Its Applications*), Beijing: Law Press.

Zhang, G. (1991) 《我的回忆》 (*My Recollections*), Beijing: Oriental Publishing House.

Zhang, J. et al. eds. (1984) 《李大钊生平史料编年》 (*Chronology of Li Dazhao's Life*), Shanghai: Shanghai People's Publishing House.

Zhang, M. (2014) "1954年宪法是怎么来的 (How Did the 1954 Constitution Came To Be?)," 《炎黄春秋》 (*Spring and Autumn Annals*), no. 10, pp. 28–33.

Zhang, P. (2007) 《立宪派与辛亥革命》 (*The Constitutionalists and the Xinhai Revolution*), Changchun: Jilin Publishing House.

Zhang, P. (2008) 《中国民主政治的困境》 (*The Dilemma of Chinese Democracy*), Changchun: Jilin Publishing House.

Zhang, S. (2004) 《中国近代民法法典化研究》 (Research on the Codification of Modern *Chinese Civil Law*), Beijing: China University of Political Science and Law Press.

Zhang, T. (1974) 《明史：卷70, 选举二》 (*History of the Ming Dynasty, vol. 70, Selection and Appointment of Officials*), collated edition, Beijing: Zhonghua Books.

Zhang, X. (1994) 《革命根据地法制史》 (*History of the Legal System in the Revolutionary Base Areas*), Beijing: Law Press.

Zhang, X. (2021) 《革命根据地法律文献》 (*Selected Legal Documents from the Revolutionary Base Areas*), vol. 3, Beijing: China Renmin University Press.

Zhang, X. (ed.) (1996) 《中国私营经济年鉴, 1996》 (*China's Private Economy Yearbook 1996*), Beijing: China Industry and Commerce United Press.

Zhang, Z. and Peking Police Compilation Commission (eds.) (1928) 《苏联阴谋问政汇编》 (*A Compilation of Soviet Political Conspiracy Inquiries*), Unknown: Wenhai Publishing House.

Zhao, D. (2015) *The Confucian-Legalist State: A New Theory of Chinese History*, London: Oxford University Press.

Zhao, G. (2005) 《永佃制研究》 (*Study of Permanent Land-leasing*), Beijing: China Agriculture Press.

Zhao, J. (2008) 《高岗在北京》 (*Gao Gang in Beijing*), Hong Kong: Strong Wind Press.

Zhao, X. (ed.) (1983) 《中国革命根据地经济史》 (*Economic History of the Chinese Revolutionary Base Areas) [1927–1937]*), Guangzhou: Guangdong People's Publishing House.

Zhao, Z. (2009) *Prisoner of the State: The Secret Journal of Zhao Ziyang*, New York: Simon & Schuster.

Zheng, J. (1989) "'西北联邦政府' 成立日期考证 A Study to Determine the Date of Establishment of the 'Northwest Federal Government,'" *CCP History Studies*, no. 1, p. 33.

Zhong, S. (1993) 《走向世界》 (*Heading Out Towards the World*), Beijing: Zhonghua Books.

Zhou, X. (2022) *The Logic of Governance in China: An Organizational Approach*, Cambridge: Cambridge University Press.

Zhou, Z. and Li, X. (2009) 《中国行政区划通史：总论, 先秦卷》 (*General History of Chinese Administrative Divisions: Overview and Pre-Qin Dynasty*), Shanghai: Fudan University Press.

Zhu, B. (ed.) (1963) 《明清进士提名碑录索引》 (*Indexed Roster of Jinshi Graduates in Ming and Qing Dynasty*), Shanghai: Ancient Books Publishing House.

Zhu, J. (2020) 《公民社会与中国公益： 四十年公益转型研究报告》 (*Civil Society and Public Welfare in China: A Study on the Transformation of Public Welfare Across Four Decades*), Beijing, Working Paper.

Zhu, Z. (2005) 《报人浦熙修》 (*The Journalist Pu Xixiu*), Wuhan: Hubei People's Publishing House.

Zhuravskaya, E., Guriev, S., and Markevich, A. (2024) "New Russian Economic History," *Journal of Economic Literature*, vol. 62, no. 1, pp. 47–114.

Zou, L. (2011) 《中国国民党史稿》 (*A Draft History of the Chinese Kuomintang*), vol. 1. Beijing: Dongfang Press.

Zubok, V. (2021) *Collapse: The Fall of the Soviet Union*, New Haven, CT: Yale University Press.

Zuo, Y. (2013) "从帝制祸首到中共秘密党员：晚年杨度的华丽转身, (From the Scourge of the Imperial System to a Secret Member of the Chinese Communist Party: The Magnificent Transformation of Yang Du in His Later Years)," 《党史博览》 (*Party History Exposition*), no. 2, pp. 44–47.

Index

500-Day Reform Program, the, of the USSR, 693–694
1905 revolution, the, of Russia, 12, 71, 160
7,000 Cadres Conference, the, of the CCP, 569

absolute monarchy, the, 54, 258
admonishers (*jiang guan*), 157
admonishment system, the (*jian-guan zhi* 谏官制), 157
agricultural reform, the, of China, 602
Alexander I, 279, 292, 310
Alexander II, 294, 297–298, 301–302
Alexander III, 298, 302
All-Russian Constituent Assembly, the, 320, 354
Anabaptists, the, 209–213, 240, 439
Andropov, Yuri, 691, 704, 717, 722
Anti-Bolshevik (AB) League Movement, the, 482–486, 489, 519, 567, 719
Anti-Bourgeois Liberalization Campaign, the, 610, 710
anti-concealment campaign, the, 565
Anti-Hu Feng Campaign, the, 544–545, 547
Anti-Japanese United Front, the, 501
Anti-Rightist Movement (ARM), the, 28, 35, 485, 487, 491–492, 515, 544–553, 568, 599, 605, 610–611, 709, 716
Anti-Spiritual Pollution Campaign, the, 608–609
April 3rd Decision, the, of the CCP, 491
April 26 editorial, the, of the *People's Daily*, 612
Aquinas, Thomas, 284
Ariga, Nagao, 429–430
aristocracy, 23, 79, 93, 114, 117, 130–134, 136–137, 140, 160, 165, 179, 186, 189, 216, 218, 221–223, 231, 239, 244, 277, 279, 525, 528, 673
  hereditary, 113
  landed, 68, 115, 126, 130, 141, 182

authoritarianism
  authoritarian regime, 3, 13, 54, 69, 623, 633, 636, 676, 684, 695, 713
  authoritarian rule, 9, 664, 670, 677, 683, 686, 713
  evolution toward, 49, 88, 238, 623, 631, 633
  of KMT, 682, 684
  regionally decentralized authoritarianism (RDA), xvii, 17, 41, 49, 618–626, 631, 633
  vs. constitutionalism, 49
  vs. totalitarianism, 49

Babeuf, Gracchus, 16, 203–205, 213–215, 217, 221, 225, 232–237, 241–243, 245, 249, 254–255, 257, 259, 384
Babeuvism, 217, 234
backwardness advantage, 654
Baihu tongyi (白虎通义), 183
Bao Huiseng, 459, 462
Barmby, John, 203, 233, 257, 259
Bastille, the, 227, 230
Beijing, 107, 305, 409, 419, 424, 452, 457, 469–470, 520, 528–529, 578–580, 599, 611–613, 617, 640, 657, 710, 724
Bentham, Jeremy, 65, 67, 105
Berlin, 347, 352, 384
Bible, the, 257
Blanqui, Auguste, 213–215, 323
Bo Gu, 473, 490, 493–494
Bo Xilai, 493, 580, 629, 718
Bo Yibo, 493, 527, 529, 557, 580, 598
Bodin, Jean, 109, 219–220, 250
Bolsheviks, the, 12, 18, 25, 27–31, 34–35, 56–57, 160, 214, 229, 232, 234, 236, 245, 256, 261, 264–265, 287–289, 291, 294–297, 299, 303, 306–309, 311–313, 316–321, 323–330, 335–337, 340, 344–346, 348–369, 371–372, 374, 377–378, 385–387,

Bolsheviks, the (cont.)
389–391, 429, 434, 450, 453–455,
462, 464, 471, 476, 482, 486, 490,
493–494, 497, 499–502, 509, 512,
517, 519, 536, 544, 671–672
Boxer Rebellion, the, 107, 409, 442
Boyar Duma, the, of Russia, 275–277
Brezhnev, Leonid, 630, 701–702, 709, 717
Brzezinski, Zbigniew, 1
Bukharin, Nikolai, 2, 65, 328, 331, 333, 335,
372, 379–380, 385, 387, 389, 472,
476, 490
Byzantine, 153, 160, 169, 266, 270–273, 275,
281, 283, 286–287

Cai Hesen, 405, 408, 456, 484
Cai Yuanpei, 441, 444
Calvin, John, 252, 282
Campaign to Suppress
 Counterrevolutionaries, the
 (Zhenfan yundong), 519–521
capitalist roaders, 485, 579, 581–583
Catherine the Great, 286, 300, 339
Catholic Church, the, 258
Censorate, the (yushi tai 御史台), 159
Central Commission for Discipline
 Inspection, of the CCP (CCDI), 653
Central Committee meeting, of the CCP,
508, 557, 569
Central Executive Committee (CEC), 362,
363, 373, 500, 502
Central Government Council,
 of China, 546
Central Leading Groups, of the CCP
 (lingdao xiaozu), 155
Central People's Commission for Land, 514
Central Youth Committee, of the CCP, 492
Chancellor, 133, 139–140, 142–143,
154–159, 179
Chancellorship, the, 78, 154, 159–160
Changsha, 472
Charles I, 222
Chayashan, 561–562, 564, 566, 568
checks and balances, 37, 54, 132, 155–156,
158, 216, 263, 274, 281, 309, 326,
338–340, 371, 393, 398, 414, 424,
426, 440, 552, 556, 564, 587,
627–628, 686, 713
Cheka, the, 289, 368–369, 372–373,
375–376, 378, 492, 517, 533

Chen Boda, 560, 562, 568, 573
Chen Duxiu, 25, 405, 407, 454–458, 461–462,
465, 471, 475, 477, 501, 666
Chen Yi, 477, 493–494, 527
Chen Yun, 479, 497, 557, 580, 601, 603, 605,
613, 615
Chernyshevsky, Nikolay, 288, 293, 295,
298, 319–320, 322–324
Chiang Ching-kuo, 467, 677, 683–684
Chiang Kai-shek, 444–445, 464, 466–468,
470–471, 503, 514
China Democratic League (CDL), 501, 510,
545, 549–550
Chinese Academy of Sciences (CAS),
535–536, 538, 611
Chinese Academy of Social Sciences (CASS),
539, 635
Chinese imperial system, the, 3, 7, 9–10,
18, 23, 25, 27, 56–57, 80, 83, 94,
105, 116–117, 119, 122–127, 129,
133–134, 137, 149, 152, 154–156,
159–160, 164, 167, 178, 181, 190,
262, 267, 280, 290, 392–393,
400–401, 409, 434, 453, 501,
555–556, 669, 718, 721
Chinese People's Political Consultative
 Conference (CPPCC), 506–507, 511,
531, 545
Chinese Revolutionary Party (CRP), 428, 429
Chinese Soviet Republic, 33, 449, 477, 499,
502, 512, 522
 Central Soviet Area, 482–484, 486–487,
 515, 523–524
 eastern Jiangxi Soviet area, 524
 Fujian–Zhejiang–Jiangxi Soviet area, 524
 Hailufeng Soviet area, 522, 524
 Hubei–Henan–Anhui Soviet area,
 522, 524
 Hunan–Jiangxi Soviet area, 522, 524
 Jinggang Mountains Soviet area,
 477–478, 481–483, 489, 514, 516,
 522, 524, 526–527, 567, 589
 Luhaifeng Soviet area, 514
 Northern Fujian Soviet area, 524
 Northwestern Anhui Soviet area, 524
 Shaanxi–Gansu–Ningxia Soviet area,
 479, 503–504, 510, 522, 524, 526
 Shanxi–Hebei–Chahar border area, 504
 Southwestern Jiangxi Soviet area, 524
 Western Fujian Soviet area, 524

Chongqing, 506
Christianity, 29–30, 32, 57, 82, 102–104, 136,
    164, 166–168, 171–172, 177–178, 181,
    184, 202–204, 206, 208–209, 214,
    217, 224–225, 233, 242–246, 248,
    253, 255, 259, 271, 273, 281–283,
    288–290, 294, 384, 388, 394, 407,
    437–440, 450, 453, 605, 697
  Bible, 29–30, 102, 104, 167–169, 171, 177,
    184, 190, 202, 206, 209, 214, 245,
    248, 271, 282–284, 289, 335, 437–438
  Catholic Church, 169–170, 223–224,
    242, 244, 282–284, 287, 329, 384,
    388, 604, 696–697
  Church, the, 29, 31, 79, 82, 136, 148,
    164, 166–167, 169–173, 209,
    216–217, 224–225, 233, 242–246,
    252, 273, 282, 284–287, 296, 329,
    388, 399, 453, 605, 696–698
  clerics, 221, 282–283
  Eastern Orthodoxy, 270, 273, 300
  Old Testament, the, 31, 102, 104, 130,
    212, 248
  Orthodox Church, the, 28, 30, 103,
    169, 261, 266, 270–272, 274, 281,
    283–287, 292, 314, 316, 329–330,
    359, 450, 697
  priests, 217, 229, 234, 271, 284, 286
  Protestant Church, the, 170
  Protestant movement, the, 605
  Reformation, the, 29, 102–103, 109,
    167–168, 170, 172, 177, 206–207,
    209–210, 216–217, 224, 241–242,
    244, 254, 261, 281–282, 285, 301,
    315, 360, 394, 604, 700
  Russian Orthodoxy, 6, 30, 281–282, 284,
    287–288, 291, 336, 450
Chunyu Yue, 139, 179
civil law, 104, 106–107, 109, 153
civil society, 9, 51, 54, 101, 303, 415,
    624–625, 635, 639, 654, 681, 686,
    688, 713, 720
clan, 129–130, 141–142, 186, 193, 280,
    434, 436
clan-based rule, 142
class hatred, 349, 516–518, 702
class struggle, xv, 6, 39, 41, 214, 294, 408,
    501, 573–574, 577, 580–581, 590,
    592, 595, 597, 601, 672, 714, 716, 722
Coase, Ronald, 3, 671
  Coase theorem, the, 97

color revolutions, the, 634, 636–637, 643,
    654, 670, 712
Commune-Brigade Enterprise (CBE), 586
communism, 13, 29, 38, 202–203, 205, 378,
    450, 468, 550, 560, 573, 604, 658, 703
  Christian communism or utopianism or
    utopian communism, 206–211, 217,
    240–241, 254, 294, 440
  coercive/forced communism vs.
    voluntary communism, 207–210,
    212, 214, 254, 658
  communist revolution, 31, 210, 214,
    233, 243, 254–255, 264, 294,
    303, 323, 325, 369, 376, 383–385,
    387–388, 390, 405, 439, 449, 455,
    457–459, 464, 502, 540, 663, 673
  communist totalitarianism, xvi, 1–2, 7–8,
    18, 24, 30, 32, 38, 88, 202, 213–216,
    225, 234–235, 251–255, 261–264, 281,
    299, 303, 315–317, 326, 383, 385, 392,
    395, 404, 445, 450–451, 543–544, 553,
    555–556, 570, 585, 592, 594, 599, 616,
    619, 623, 630–631, 646, 658–659, 663,
    665, 667, 671–675, 682, 687, 695–696,
    699–705, 707, 709
  concept of, 203
  origins of or ideology of, 29, 202–203,
    206, 233–234, 237, 383
  and proletarian dictatorship or
    socialism, 370, 390
  secular communism or secular religion
    or secular messianism, 6, 29, 204,
    213–214, 217, 225, 232–233, 238,
    240–241, 243, 245, 249, 254, 360, 383
  and totalitarianism, 38, 234, 241, 294,
    658, 660, 663
Communist and Workers' Party
  Conference, 554
Communist Party
  Chinese Communist Party (CCP), 5–10,
    17–20, 25, 27–28, 33–35, 37, 39, 41–51,
    53, 55, 57–58, 81, 151, 155, 180, 255,
    265, 299, 332, 372, 376, 388–391, 405,
    407, 420, 427, 429, 434, 437, 442, 447,
    449–451, 454–457, 459–537, 539–563,
    565–566, 568–572, 574–577, 579–582,
    584–585, 588–590, 592–602, 604–606,
    608–610, 613–617, 619–627, 629,
    633–640, 642–647, 650, 653–656, 659,
    666–667, 669–670, 673, 679, 682, 687,
    709–713, 716–719, 721

Communist Party (cont.)
    Comintern or International Communist Party, 7, 9, 13, 31–33, 48, 206–210, 265, 335, 385–390, 392, 407, 429, 434, 436, 449–451, 453–476, 480–492, 494–503, 511, 513–514, 521–523, 525, 533, 536, 546, 552, 666–667, 669–670, 673, 696, 718, 721
    Leninist principles of, 325, 328, 386, 500
    of nations other than Soviet Union and China or abstract, 376, 385, 387, 696, 700, 706
    Soviet Communist Party (CPSU) or Bolsheviks or Russian Communist Party (RCP), 328, 330–331, 334, 377, 456–457, 465–467, 471–472
    totalitarian nature of, 6, 232, 327, 329, 480, 499, 690–691, 713–714
Communist Party of Czechoslovakia (KSC), 700, 701, 707
Condorcet, Marquis de, 230, 240
Confucian scholars, book-burning and live burials of, 140, 178–179
Confucianism (*Rujia*), 78, 83, 105–106, 128–129, 137, 139–140, 163–166, 168–171, 173–193, 195–196, 198–200, 287, 400, 438, 446, 678–679, 716, 721
    Confucian classics, 140, 165, 177, 179, 182, 184, 190, 192–193, 196–197, 679
    Confucian scholars, 184
    Confucian teachings, 181–184
    Neo-Confucianist teachings, 195
    Three Principles and Five Virtues, 184, 192–193
Confucius, 168, 180, 190, 193, 400, 404, 588–589
Conspiracy of the Equals, the, 213, 234–235, 237
Constantine the Great, 82–83
Constantine XI, 272
Constantinople, 272, 281, 283
Constitution, of the CCP, 463, 622
Constitution, of the PRC, 33, 46, 49, 530, 545
Constitution, of the ROC, 9, 53, 509, 681, 682, 687
Constitution, of the US, 16, 64, 96, 371

Constitutional Democratic Party, the, of Russia, 310–313, 338, 341, 343, 366
constitutional monarchy, 447
constitutional reform, 14, 19, 50, 74, 85, 106, 160, 215–216, 220, 226, 263–264, 274, 280, 302, 304, 308–309, 316, 337, 339, 358, 404, 407–408, 410, 412–413, 415–416, 419, 421, 445, 500, 509, 677, 707
constitutionalism, xvi, 3, 7, 9–12, 14, 16–19, 24, 26–27, 43, 49–50, 53–54, 59, 62, 64, 68, 81, 84–85, 88, 92–93, 99, 101, 105–106, 108, 111, 120, 124, 134, 136, 156–157, 159–160, 216, 220, 233, 236, 238, 240, 243, 247–248, 251, 260, 263–264, 277–278, 281, 285, 290–293, 299–302, 304, 306, 308–310, 312–313, 320, 329, 337–338, 340, 344–345, 370, 392, 394–398, 400, 402–409, 411–416, 424, 427, 429, 431–433, 441, 445, 449, 452, 499–501, 503–505, 509–511, 541, 545, 632, 634–635, 669–670, 675–676, 679–684, 687–688, 695, 698, 714, 720–721
Council of People's Commissars (CPC), 357, 360, 363, 364, 366, 372, 373
counterrevolutionaries, 373, 486, 492, 515, 518–519, 529, 533, 544, 581, 599
coup d'état, 234, 264, 279, 300, 321, 327, 339, 365, 590, 597
criminal law, 103, 106, 119, 150, 152–153, 413, 533, 552
Cultural Revolution (CR), the, of China, 7, 14, 21, 28, 37–39, 41, 45–47, 51, 55, 72, 155, 180, 214, 332, 334, 376, 390, 485, 487, 491, 498, 506, 514, 533, 542, 551, 556–557, 569–571, 575, 577–578, 580–581, 594–595, 601, 609, 630, 666–667, 702, 716, 718–719
Cultural Revolution, the, of Soviet Union, 377, 534–535, 544, 570
Cultural Revolution Group (CRG), 571, 581, 582, 583, 584
Czechoslovakia, 387, 695, 700, 703, 706–708, 710–711, 715–716

Darwin, Charles, 406
Das Kapital, 29, 257

Daxue yanyi (*Expanded Interpretation of the Great Learning*), 195
Declaration of the Rights of Man and of the Citizen, the, of France, 96, 101, 227–228, 232, 234, 238
de-Maoization, 710, 716, 718
Democratic Progressive Party (DPP), 678, 684, 685, 686
Deng Xiaoping, 39, 42, 45, 379, 381, 485, 528, 549, 569, 578–579, 587, 589, 595–598, 603, 605, 608, 610, 612, 627, 634, 636, 639, 670, 692, 709–710, 718–719
Deng Zihui, 527–528
Descartes, René, 242–243, 245
de-Stalinization, 53, 701–704, 709–710, 715–716, 718
dictatorship, of the proletariat, 57, 259
Diderot, Denis, 300
Dimitrov, Georgi, 389, 488
Ding Ling, 491
disintegration, 56, 123, 147–148, 150, 165, 189, 216, 616
Dong Zhongshu, 140–141, 182
dual-track system, the, 606–607, 611
Dubček, Alexander, 700, 703, 709

Eastern bloc, the, 39, 51, 204, 594, 596, 608, 614–615, 617–619, 623, 641, 643, 647, 659, 664, 670, 692, 700, 711
education system, 173–174, 532, 534–535, 537, 578, 625
egalitarianism, 203, 206
Eighth Route Army, the. See Red Army, of the CCP
elections, 9, 12, 48, 53, 226, 230, 250, 264, 295, 299, 302, 308, 310, 312–313, 320, 333–334, 337, 341–342, 344, 346–347, 354, 358, 362, 365–366, 368–369, 401, 409, 413, 415–417, 423, 428–429, 504–505, 522, 542, 609, 623, 625, 640, 657, 681–683, 685–686, 694, 705–707
electorate, 311, 510
Emperor/Empress/King, of Imperial China
Emperor Chengzu/Yongle of Ming, 195
Emperor decree, 164
Emperor Gao Zu of Han, 181
Emperor Guangxu of Qing, 263, 401–402, 409, 412
Emperor Jing of Tang, 181

Emperor Qianlong of Qing, 679
Emperor Renzong of Yuan, 195
Emperor Shenzong of Song, 191–192
Emperor Shi Zong of Ming, 275
Emperor Taizong of Tang, 188
Emperor Taizu of Song, 190
Emperor Taizu/Hongwu of Ming, 154, 159, 198
Emperor Wang Mang of Xin, 192
Emperor Wen of Sui, 152, 186
Emperor Wen of Tang, 181
Emperor Wudi of Han, 122, 182, 721
Emperor Xiaowen of Northern Wei, 147, 392
Emperor Xuanzong of Tang, 188
Emperor Yang of Sui, 186
Emperor Yongzheng of Qing, 155
Emperor Zhongzong of Tang, 158
emperorship, 142, 192
Empress Dowager Cixi of Qing, 409
Empress Wu Zetian of Tang, 158, 188
King Wen of Zhou, 168
King Wu of Zhou, 168
Qin Shi Huang, 37, 122, 124, 128, 134, 139–140, 145, 165, 178–180, 198, 274–275, 555–556, 721
Engels, Friedrich, 29, 203, 205–206, 210, 214, 231, 233–234, 245, 252, 288, 296, 384, 390, 696
England, 16, 64, 96, 110, 168, 170, 215, 218–219, 221, 226, 233, 244, 246, 250, 282, 291, 344, 399
Enlightenment, the, 168, 172, 220, 224–225, 230, 237–245, 247, 278–279, 285, 300–301, 394, 688, 713–714, 716
"equal-fields" system (*juntian* 均田), 116
Erasmus, Desiderius, 167, 282, 284
Estates-General, the, 226
European Union (EU), 11, 141, 641, 687

faith, 79, 82–83, 89, 175–176, 199, 203, 207, 209–210, 214, 217, 225, 240, 242, 248, 261, 271, 273, 287–288, 292, 296, 360, 508, 589
Falun Gong, 624
Fang Lizhi, 610
February Revolution, the, of Russia, 263–264, 344–345, 349, 385, 408, 713, 721
February 28 Incident, the, of Taiwan, 681
federation, 136, 142, 145, 367, 523

Feng Youlan, 185, 199
Feng Yuxiang, 469
Fengyang, 601
feudal system (fengjian(封建)), 89, 93, 123, 126, 130, 134–135, 137–142, 144–146, 148, 178, 218, 268, 275
first estate, the, of France, 221
Five Anti Campaign, the, of China, 532
Five-Year Plan, the, of China, 528, 538–540
Five-Year Plan, the, of Soviet Union, 379, 381–382, 560, 692
Former Soviet Union and Eastern European Countries (FSU-EE), 6, 11, 40, 42, 45, 688–719, 722
Four Cardinal Principles, the, of Deng Xiaoping, 42, 45, 57, 599–600, 604–605, 607–610, 614, 616–618, 620, 623–624, 655, 670, 716
Four Cleanups, the, of the CCP, 51, 574, 577–578, 629
Fourth Front Army, the, of the CCP. see Red Army
Fourth Red Army, the, of the CCP. see Red Army
France, 112, 162, 203, 208, 213, 215–220, 222–226, 228, 230–231, 233, 238, 242–243, 246, 248–249, 255, 257–258, 260–261, 282, 291–292, 336, 339, 346, 356, 387, 411, 605
Frederick II, 244
freedom, 2, 51, 64–65, 79, 104, 170, 177, 198, 243, 246, 249, 251, 279, 300–302, 326, 332, 336, 349–350, 363, 383, 414, 428, 504, 612, 640, 658, 676, 683–684, 686, 691, 693, 695, 699–700, 704–705, 708, 715–716
French Revolution, the, 12, 16, 96, 102, 111, 121, 203–204, 210, 213–215, 217, 219, 221–222, 225, 227, 229–232, 237–244, 247–248, 254, 258, 264, 279, 290, 292, 301, 313, 315, 326–327, 360, 369, 512, 570, 724
Friedrich, Carl, 1
Friends of the Constitution Association (FCA), 419, 420, 421, 422
Fronde rebellion, the, of France, 222

Galen (alias of V. K. Blyukher), 469
Gang of Four, the, of China, 590, 596–597
Gao Gang, 486, 522, 527–529

Gdańsk Agreement, the, 698
Gengzi Reform, the, of China, 73, 721
German Peasants' War, 210–211, 439
Germany, 29, 66, 112, 211, 255, 282, 291, 319, 336, 351, 368, 384–385, 387, 411, 449–450, 452, 466, 663, 673, 695, 703, 708
Girondins, the, of France, 228, 230
Glorious Revolution, the, 16, 62, 64, 68, 71, 86, 96, 110–111, 168, 170, 172, 222, 226, 237–238, 243–244, 260, 338, 344, 662
God, 29–30, 32, 84, 110, 163, 170–173, 177, 203, 219, 245, 273, 286–289, 292, 302, 435, 437–439
Golden Horde, the, 267–272, 274, 435
Gomułka, Władysław, 376, 699
Gong Zizhen, 185
Goodnow, Frank, 429–432
Gorbachev, Mikhail, 53, 600, 612–613, 616, 623, 691–694, 701–706, 708–709, 712, 715, 717, 719, 723–724
governance structure, 19, 39, 60, 108, 113, 124, 130, 146, 151–152, 219, 410, 543, 554–556, 572, 674, 710, 712
Government Affairs Council (GAC), 545–546
Grace Decree (Tui-en Ling 推恩令), of Han dynasty, 182
Grand Duke Michael Alexandrovich, 342
Grand Prince of Muscovy, 268–269, 272
Grand Prince of Vladimir, 268
grasping the large and letting go of the small (zhuada fangxiao), of the CCP, 621, 634
Great Famine, the, of PRC, 563–570
Great Famine, the, of Soviet Union, 381, 560
Great Leap Forward (GLF), the, of PRC, 7, 14, 17, 21, 37–39, 55, 57, 122, 152, 155, 553–557, 559–560, 562–564, 566–573, 585–586, 591, 593–596, 601, 603, 617, 643, 667, 669, 721
Great Purge, the, of Soviet Union, 51, 328, 332–334, 375, 387, 389, 487, 494, 714
Greece, 67, 91, 93–94, 96, 100, 104, 109, 111, 113–114, 123, 669
Gross Domestic Product (GDP), 10, 11, 41, 642, 647–649, 654, 655, 676, 682, 686, 689

Gu Zuolin, 484
Guangfuhui (Restoration Society), 441–442, 444, 448
Guangzhou, 416, 443, 461, 466–467, 472
Guchkov, Alexander, 343
guojin mintui, ("the state sector advances, the private sector retreats"), 644
Gwangju Massacre, the, of S. Korea, 683
Gwangju Uprising, the, of S. Korea, 684

Hall of Government Affairs, the/*Zhengshi tang*, 156–157
Han Empire, 145, 149, 179–183
Hart, Oliver, 5, 662, 671
Hayek, Friedrich, 4–5, 55, 59, 67, 87–88, 90, 94, 96, 205, 658, 660–662
He Changgong, 477
He Jinye, 478
He Long, 478, 528
hereditary aristocracy, 56
Herzen, Alexander, 293–295, 319–320
Hobbes, Thomas, 110
Holy Roman Empire, 126, 136, 141, 210–211
Hong Fraternity, the, 448
Hong Kong, 443, 505, 515, 537, 603, 613, 638–640, 654
Hong Xiuquan, 32, 437–438, 440–441
household empire, of China, 142
Hu Jintao, 611, 627, 635, 718
Hu Qili, 611, 613
Hu Shih, 403, 407, 455–456, 458
Hu Yaobang, 45, 55, 335, 372, 497, 597–598, 601, 605–606, 608–612, 627, 656, 710, 718
Hua Guofeng, 597, 601, 603
Huang Xing, 426, 428, 441
Huang Yanpei, 504
Huaxinghui (Chinese Revival Society), 441
hukou system, of China, 649–650
human rights, 4–5, 8, 16, 60, 63–65, 69, 79–81, 96, 100, 108–109, 113–114, 119, 172, 205, 220–221, 227–228, 230, 232, 237–239, 243, 248, 301, 317, 371, 408, 599, 619, 668, 675, 677, 693–695, 698–699, 709, 714–717, 720
humanitarianism, 8, 579, 608, 694, 701, 704, 709, 712–713, 716

humanity, 203, 207, 260, 289, 323, 663, 689, 694, 701–704, 713–717, 720
Hume, David, 61, 65, 660
Hunan New People's Society, 458
Hundred Days' Reform, the/ Wuxu Reform, 14, 25–26, 73, 108, 174, 185, 191, 280, 398–403, 408, 410, 721
Hundred Schools of Thought, 547, 550
Hungarian revolution, the, of 1956, 35, 699, 702
Hungary, 267, 376, 387, 547–548, 695, 699, 702–703, 706–711, 715–716
Huxley, Thomas, 404–405, 447

Imperial China, 12, 18, 22, 33, 68, 99, 107, 112–113, 174, 186, 262, 270, 277, 394, 515, 544, 576, 592, 663, 676
imperial court, the, of China, 23–24, 26, 39, 117–118, 125, 139, 144, 147, 151–152, 157, 173–176, 186–187, 189, 277, 287, 395, 397, 401–402, 412, 415–416, 421, 525, 528
imperial *junxian* system, the, of China, 22–23, 37, 77–78, 115, 116, 124–128, 131–132, 134, 137, 139, 143, 145, 147, 151, 178–179, 181, 186, 525–526, 528, 556, 592, 721
junxian bureaucracy, 124, 127, 146–147, 149–150
imperial rule, 23–24, 26, 28, 57, 78, 118, 127, 129, 134, 136, 140, 142, 150, 160, 164, 168–169, 171, 177, 181–182, 189, 192, 199, 262, 263, 301–302, 329, 402, 415, 422, 424, 427, 440, 451, 678, 687
imperial system, the, 263, 673–674, 679
incentive mechanism, 28, 43, 86–87, 390, 563, 566, 643
incentive-compatibility, 19, 26, 36, 68–76, 78, 83, 87, 98, 660–661, 722
Incentive-incompatibility, 36
independent scholarship, 171, 173
Industrial Revolution, the, 86, 394
institutional change, xvi, 4, 9, 17, 19, 26, 37, 52–53, 56, 70, 72–78, 81–82, 85–90, 131, 137, 529, 553, 555, 557, 662, 671, 722
institutional divergence, 9–10

764 INDEX

institutional genes
  of absolutism, 219
  of autocracy, 84
  of Bolsheviks or of Communist Party or of totalitarian party, 30–31, 319–320, 325, 329, 336, 429, 439, 592, 666
  of Chinese communist system or of totalitarian China or of RADT, 7, 18, 21, 23–27, 32, 35, 37, 39–40, 42, 487, 499, 570, 586, 615, 638, 688, 712
  of Chinese imperial system or of traditional China, 7, 18–19, 23–27, 31–37, 78, 123–141, 143–166, 190, 267, 392, 398, 400, 403, 415, 424, 429–434, 451, 463, 468, 500, 512, 555, 575, 679, 688
  of Christianity or Church, 82, 102, 166–171, 206, 329
  concept of, 3–4, 52, 59, 76–77, 660–665, 720
  of constitutionalism, 9, 41–54, 108, 318, 338, 403, 415, 417, 424, 432, 654, 665, 674–688, 702, 712–720
  of Eastern European countries (FSU-CEE), 688–720
  evolution of and institutional change, 4, 75–77, 81–84, 91–93, 434, 668–670, 721
  of feudalism or feudal system, 137–139, 144–148, 181, 185
  identification of or characteristics of, 76–79
  of *junxian* system, 23, 526, 592
  of *keju* system, 163–165, 177, 190, 199, 721
  and legal system, 104, 132
  and mechanism design or incentive-compatibility, 19, 77–79, 84–89, 297, 473, 595, 661, 665
  mutation of or emerging of new, 609, 632–634, 654, 662, 665
  and path dependence, 85–89, 670
  and political power, 141
  and property rights, 5, 84, 91–93, 101–104, 110, 114, 127, 135, 182
  of Russian imperial system or of Russian Empire, 7, 27, 122, 261, 265, 270–271, 273–274, 293, 297, 299, 313, 315–316, 336–337, 339, 358–359, 363, 369, 372, 395, 450, 473, 701
  of Russian Orthodoxy, 78, 270–274
  of Russian secret terrorist organizations, 234, 270–274, 290–299, 474, 476
  of secret society system, 440, 445, 474, 476, 483, 486
  and social consensus or ideology, 79, 101, 112, 215, 537, 702, 708, 713–714
  of Soviet Union, 8, 31, 53, 701–706
  of Taiwan, 8, 52, 675–688
  of totalitarianism, or of communism, or of communist totalitarianism, 7, 30–31, 37, 160–161, 202–204, 232, 253, 315, 382, 390, 450, 482–483, 512, 521, 630–632, 669–670, 674
institutional transformation, 8–9, 42, 52–53, 71, 88, 675–676, 678–679, 687, 695, 717, 722
institutional transition, 137, 688, 711, 717, 719
intelligentsia, the, of Russia, 16, 263, 288, 290–291, 293–298, 302, 309, 394–395, 476, 499
Ivan I, 272
Ivan III, 269, 272, 274–275, 280
Ivan IV, 269, 275–276

Jacobins, the, 16, 215, 228–230, 232–234, 240, 242, 247, 264, 298, 323, 327, 389, 482, 493
James II, 338
Japan, xix, 9, 11, 13–14, 25, 70, 86, 88, 107, 153, 262, 304–305, 395, 397–399, 401–402, 410, 412, 414, 433, 448–450, 452, 457–458, 479, 503, 516, 605, 642, 655, 676, 679–680
Jiang Qing, 514, 579, 590, 597
Jiang Zemin, 540, 611, 614–615, 621, 627, 634–635, 710, 718
Joffe, Adolf/ Yue Fei, 465
Joint State Political Directorate (OGPU), 378
judicial system, 60, 103, 135, 428, 533, 539, 551, 631, 666, 675
July Days Coup, the, of Russia, 351–352
June 4th Massacre, the (Tiananmen Square Massacre), 614–615
Justinian Code, the, of Byzantine Empire, 152
Justinian I, 273

Kaihuang Code, the, of Chinese Empire, 152
Kamenev, Lev, 332–333, 354, 466
Kang Sheng, 491–492, 494, 514, 568, 573, 579

Kang Youwei, 180, 185, 191, 199, 280, 398, 400–401, 404, 407, 421, 446
Kaohsiung Incident, the, of Taiwan, 683
Kautsky, Karl, 29, 206, 209–210, 231, 326–327, 374, 390
Kazakhstan, 381
keju (科举), the imperial examination system of China, 124, 128, 149–150, 163–165, 170–179, 183, 185–192, 194–199, 401, 410, 440
   baguwen (八股文), 197–198
   gongshi (贡士), 197
   Grand Academy, the (taixue 太学), 173, 182–183, 186–187, 191
   Hanlin, 196
   Hanlin Academy, the, 196
   Imperial University, the (guozi jian 国子监), 173, 186–187, 196
   jinshi degree, 187, 194, 196, 678
   jinshi examination, 187, 191, 678
   jinshi section, 187
   juren degree, 197
   keju examination, 128, 174–176, 191, 195
   metropolitan examination, 197–198
   palace examination, 150, 166, 188, 194, 197
   provincial examination, 194, 197, 437
   xiucai degree, 197
   xiucai section, 187
   Zhuangyuan, 197
Kerensky, Alexander, 304, 343, 346, 348, 351–354, 362, 367
KGB (Committee for State Security), the, 334, 372, 375, 492, 691, 719, 722
Khrushchev, Nikita, 35, 53, 333, 546–547, 554, 593, 600, 616, 689, 698, 701–702, 704, 709, 716–717
Khrushchev's secret speech, 544–546
Kiev, 266, 271, 274
Kievan Rus', 265–270, 272, 274, 284
KMT (Kuomintang), 9, 53, 265, 332, 388, 420, 422, 425–455, 463–476, 482, 489, 492, 500–509, 513, 515–517, 522, 526, 536, 545, 549, 667, 676–688
KMT-CCP cooperation, 475
   Chongqing peace talks, 506
Kornai, János, xv, 3, 90, 607, 656, 712
Kornilov Affair, the, 351–353

Kropotkin, Peter, 288, 295
Kuai Dafu, 581

Lafayette, Marquis de, 227
Land and Freedom Society, the, 295, 322
land control system, of Imperial China, 23, 114, 124, 127
Land Reform movement, the, of China, 28, 35, 72, 513–519, 567
Lange, Oskar, 55, 59, 87, 90, 656
Lee Teng-hui, 677–678, 683–686
Legalism (Fajia), of China, 105, 132–133, 181
legalist, 178
legalist, 161
legitimacy, 2, 31, 34–35, 41, 45, 54, 61–62, 78–80, 129, 146, 164, 167, 169, 172, 176, 179, 181, 189–190, 194, 199, 226, 271–272, 283, 331, 344, 361, 364–365, 381, 437, 440, 447, 488, 490–491, 499, 510, 553, 589–590, 594–595, 597–598, 601, 604, 628, 643, 655, 687, 692, 712
Lenin, Vladimir, 16, 28, 31, 48, 81, 90, 95, 122, 204–205, 214, 225, 234, 256, 265, 288, 296–299, 303, 312, 318, 322–334, 340, 345–355, 357–359, 361–367, 369, 371–372, 374, 376–379, 381, 384–388, 391, 442, 453, 462, 464–465, 473, 489, 495, 499, 502, 504–505, 512, 531, 534, 537, 553, 570, 595, 604–605, 623, 627, 635, 644, 687, 698, 701, 705
Leninism, 2, 30–33, 46, 57, 84, 202, 204, 249, 294, 323, 331, 333, 335–336, 388, 447, 455, 458–459, 464, 474, 496, 574–577, 600, 604, 637, 696, 712
Li Da, 456
Li Dazhao, 25, 405, 408, 454–458, 467, 471, 474
Li Hongzhang, 304, 397, 399–400, 410, 437
Li Keqiang, 649, 718
Li Kui, 133–134
Li Peng, 540, 710, 718
Li Ruihuan, 610
Li Si, 134, 139–140, 179
Li Wenlin, 483–484
Li Xiannian, 557
Li Yuanchao, 580

Liang Qichao, 25, 106, 180, 199–200, 395, 400–401, 403–404, 406–407, 413, 418–419, 432–433, 446, 542, 723
Liao Ping, 185, 199
Liao Zhongkai, 25, 467, 513
Liberation War, the, of China, 517, 529
Lin Biao, 390, 527, 568, 573–574, 577, 582, 584, 588–589, 593
Lin Biao Incident, the, 588–589
Liu Bingzhong, 195
Liu Fenglu, 185
Liu Shaoqi, 2, 30, 65, 335, 372, 494–495, 504, 506, 517–519, 527, 529–531, 536, 539, 552, 560, 569, 573–574, 578–579, 581, 587, 589, 598
Liu Xiaobo, 50, 624, 632
Liu Xin, 180, 183, 185, 192, 446
Liu Zhidan, 478, 486, 522
Locke, John, 4, 15–16, 64–65, 90, 94, 96, 101, 111, 120, 172, 205, 237–238, 242, 244, 247–248, 395, 431
London Communist Propaganda Society, the, 203
Long March, the, 478, 485, 503, 515, 523
looting the rich, by the CCP, 515
Louis XIV, 218, 223, 245
Louis XVI, 226–228, 247, 339
Lu Xun, 176, 456
Luo Longji, 550
Luo Lun, 419
luring the snake out of the hole, of Mao, 548
Lushan Conference, 562, 567–568
Luther, Martin, 167–168, 252, 282, 284
Luxemburg, Rosa, 326, 390, 696
Lvov, Georgy, 343, 351

Ma Xiwu, 478–479
Mably, Abbé de, 237, 239, 241
Magna Carta, the, 168, 219, 338
Main Directorate of State Security (GUGB), of USSR, 492
Manchu, 18, 155, 159–160, 198, 406, 423, 438, 441, 444
Mao Yuanxin, 577, 593
Mao Zedong, 31–33, 46, 48, 51, 62, 128, 155, 180, 204, 381, 405, 408, 437, 458, 461, 467, 471, 473, 475, 477, 479, 482, 484, 486, 489, 494–495, 502, 504, 513, 515, 517, 519–520, 522, 527, 547, 574, 577, 584, 600–601, 627, 630, 666, 670, 716, 719, 721

Maring/Sneevliet, Henk, 460–461, 465
Marshall, George, 506–507, 509
Marx, Karl, 5, 16, 27, 29, 37, 67, 95–96, 102, 111, 113, 122, 129, 202–205, 210, 213–214, 225, 231, 233–234, 236, 239, 245, 253–255, 288–289, 294, 296, 303, 355, 360, 368–370, 374, 384–385, 389–390, 405–406, 408, 459, 555, 620, 663, 672–674, 687, 704–705
Marxism, 2, 29–33, 46, 57, 84, 112, 202–204, 209, 214, 249, 253, 255–257, 288–289, 291, 295–297, 303, 322–323, 384, 404–405, 408, 447, 450, 453, 455, 458–459, 496, 574–577, 593, 600, 604–605, 673, 701, 712
  dictatorship of the proletariat, the, 2, 7, 42, 202, 205, 214, 236–237, 254–255, 290, 312, 318, 326–328, 335, 345, 348, 355, 360–361, 368–372, 374, 376, 379, 389–390, 455, 458–460, 501–504, 546, 552, 573, 595, 600, 672, 701, 708
Maskin, Eric, 90, 671
mass movement, 454, 491, 493, 519, 532, 556, 570, 578, 583
masses, the, 32, 72, 140, 206, 217, 225, 229, 236, 249, 253, 255, 322, 324, 341, 349–351, 365, 464, 474, 480, 514–520, 544, 573, 575, 578, 581, 591, 672, 714, 719
May 4 Directive, 517
mechanism design, xv–xvi, 3, 59, 68–69, 73, 75–76, 87, 660–661, 665, 671
Meiji Restoration, the, 11–12, 70, 89, 108, 397–398, 402–403, 412
Mencius, 180, 193, 196
Menxia sheng (Chancellery), of Chinese Empire, 143
Meslier, Jean, 225, 237, 239, 241, 243–245, 247, 249, 254, 259
Middle Ages, 126, 136, 205, 218, 221, 242, 316, 384, 439–440, 512, 658, 671, 695
Mikoyan, Anastas, 334
Milyukov, Pavel, 343
Ministry of Personnel, the, of Chinese Empire, 143, 151, 187
Mises, Ludwig von, 5, 75, 206, 658, 660, 671
monarchy
  absolute monarchy, 10, 110, 148, 215–216, 218–220, 222, 224, 226–227, 230–231, 239, 249–250, 252, 276, 280, 286, 291, 305, 339

constitutional monarchy, 9, 12, 25–26, 81, 216, 226–228, 238, 263, 292–293, 299, 301, 306, 310–312, 337–338, 340, 344, 347, 393–395, 400–403, 405, 408–409, 412–413, 417, 419, 433, 451, 721
feudal monarchy, 102, 123, 166, 220
Mongol Empire, the, 266–270, 435
Mongols, 18, 154, 160, 195, 266–270, 273–274, 286, 305
Montesquieu, 114, 121, 129, 228, 237–238, 243, 246–248, 250, 252, 259, 270, 395, 405, 674
Morelly, Étienne-Gabriel, 237, 239, 241
Moscow, 268–269, 272, 281, 285, 342–343, 350, 355, 368, 384–387, 459–460, 465–466, 471–472, 480, 488, 490, 527, 554, 557, 560, 691, 710
Moscow Oriental University, 473
Münster, 211–212, 315, 360, 370, 439–440, 512
Müntzer, Thomas, 210–211, 257, 439
Muscovy, 266, 268–270, 272

Nanjing, 421, 423, 438, 520
Napoleon, Bonaparte, 12, 227, 232, 339
Narodnaya Volya, the/ People's Will, the, 28–29, 297–298, 321–323, 336, 389, 666
National Assembly, the, of China (Zizheng Yuan), 413, 417
National Peasant Movement Training Institute, of China, 476
National People's Congress, the, of China (NPC), 545, 635–636
National Revolutionary Army (NRA), the, of China, 468–469, 503
Nationalist government, the, of China, 506, 509, 678–679
Nazism, 406, 672
Nechayev, Sergey, 323–324
Neiman-Nikolsky, Vladimir, 460–461
neo-authoritarianism, or new authoritarianism, 15, 623
Netherlands, 212, 282, 299
New Cold War, 659
New Economic Policy (NEP), of Lenin, 256, 332, 595, 604, 644, 670, 711
New Fourth Army, the. See Red Army, of the CCP

New People's Society, the, of Taiwan, 680
Newton, Isaac, 242, 244
Nicholas I, 292–293
Nicholas II, 122, 304–305, 308, 311, 329, 339–340, 342, 374
Nie Hongjun, 486
nobility, 23, 26, 56, 113, 115, 125–126, 130–131, 133–134, 136, 138–139, 141, 146–148, 150, 161, 165, 186–187, 189, 216, 218–223, 226, 228, 232, 252, 268–270, 274–277, 279–280, 294, 300–301, 309–310, 374, 696, 721
non-government organization (NGO), 41, 48, 626
North, Douglass, 3, 60, 67, 85–86, 90, 99, 660, 670
North Caucasus, 381
Northeast Army, 469, 503
Northern Wei dynasty, 116, 147, 392
Northwest Federal Government of the Soviet Republic of China, the, 523
Novgorod, 266

October Revolution, the, 2, 12, 33, 57, 72, 81, 202, 262, 264, 295–297, 315, 320, 325, 334, 345, 358–359, 361, 364–365, 381, 385, 390, 449, 454, 501–502, 504, 537, 544, 593, 659
Oprichnina, 276
Ottoman Empire, the, 88–89, 113
overlords, 117, 147, 268

Pan Fusheng, 563
papal directive, 164
Paris, 121, 222–223, 230–231, 233, 257–258, 512
party-state agencies/party-state bureaucracy, 17, 19, 155, 558, 571, 575, 581–583, 591, 631–632, 642–644, 654, 692
peaceful evolution, 42, 43, 573, 574, 634, 643, 654, 670, 682, 712
peasant mobilization, 512
Peasant Movement Committee, the, of China, 513
peasant uprising, of China, 24, 295, 513
Peking University, 456, 549, 551, 578, 611
Peng Dehuai, 335, 380, 482, 484, 493–494, 527, 567, 589

768 INDEX

Peng Pai, 522
People's Bank of China (PBOC), 525, 537, 542
People's Commissariat for Internal Affairs, the (NKVD), of the USSR, 332, 334, 375
People's Commune, the, of China, 38, 214, 557, 560–566, 568–569, 574, 578, 582–583, 586, 598, 602
People's Liberation Army, the (PLA), of China, 517, 574, 582–584, 588–589, 597, 610, 613–614
People's Republic of China (PRC), 10, 33, 45, 493, 511, 527, 530–531, 533, 536, 539–540, 544–545, 555, 560, 572, 584, 588, 592, 598, 600, 625, 666, 675–676, 683
Perestroika, 53, 600, 691, 704, 708
personality cult, 38, 329–332, 334, 450, 481, 494, 547, 553, 571–573, 587–589, 592, 597, 627–629
personnel system, 149, 163, 165
Peter the Great, 271, 273, 275–277, 279–280, 286, 300
Petersburg, 306, 366, 391
Petition to the Throne, the (*Gongche shangshu*), of China, 401–402
Petrograd, 331, 342–343, 347–348, 350–356, 365–368, 391
Poland, 267, 287, 387, 547–548, 695–700, 702, 706–711, 715–716
Polish United Workers' Party (PUWP), 376, 696–699, 706
Politburo, of the Central Committee, of the CCP, 51, 492, 557, 561, 567, 571, 577, 588
    Standing Committee, 610–611, 613
Politburo, of the Central Committee, of the RCP, 333, 465, 472, 490, 694, 704
political power
    centralization of, 67, 153, 281, 587
    centralized, 66, 530
    of the Chinese Empire or the Russian Empire, 108, 114–115, 125, 142, 165, 270, 272, 281
    under constitutional rule, 71, 425
    decentralization of, 141, 557, 559
    decentralized, 66, 135
    dispersed, 79, 84, 136, 145
    and human rights, 4, 66, 79
    monopolization of, 115
    monopolized, 6, 31, 79, 84
    and property rights, 4, 63, 65–67, 79, 84–85, 100, 108, 116, 134–136, 141, 153, 205, 214, 666
    seizure of, 234–235, 354, 472, 500, 672, 680
    structure of, 5, 43, 60, 66, 79, 84, 108, 597
    of the totalitarian leader, 37, 62, 556, 572, 577
    in a totalitarian system, xvii, 68, 71, 254, 366, 390, 472, 480, 530, 543, 572, 577–578, 587, 605, 666, 694, 719
Pope John Paul II, 697–699
Popper, Karl, 67, 259, 660, 672–673
post-Mao era, 8, 39, 552, 629
power struggles, 145, 175, 331, 361, 375, 379, 402, 481, 547, 568–569, 582, 628, 719
Poznań strike, the, of Poland, 699
Prague, 715
Prague Spring, the, 614–615, 700–702, 704, 707, 715
princelings faction, the, of China, 717
Princess Sophia Palaiologina, 272
private law, 93, 103–104, 106–109, 118, 153
privatization, 47, 117, 208, 621–622, 634, 647, 686, 693
    Gaizhi, of China, 621
property rights, 60, 63–73, 79, 84, 87–88, 94–95, 119, 207, 268, 306, 419, 531, 619, 626, 630, 668, 671
    abolition or deprivation of, 254, 320, 344, 359, 371, 377–378, 380, 382–383
    as a bundle of rights, 5, 94–99
    centralization of, 67, 153
    centralized, 66, 92
    and constitutionalism, 415–417, 441, 531, 682, 688, 720
    as control rights, 5, 94–99
    decentralization of, 141
    decentralized, 66
    dispersed, 71, 79, 91, 93, 99, 136, 300
    as human rights or inseparable from human rights, 4, 65–66, 96, 102, 108–109, 111, 114, 119, 237, 239, 248, 394, 415, 441, 720
    monopolized, 6, 79, 84, 92

private, 16, 41, 43, 49, 54, 62, 66, 79, 88, 91–93, 96–97, 99–106, 108–111, 113, 116, 119–120, 135, 153, 205, 232–233, 235, 248–249, 278, 300, 385, 415, 531, 622–623, 632, 639, 654, 656, 674–676, 682, 688, 692, 720
and sovereignty, 10, 108–119, 251–252, 275, 278
state control over, 19, 512, 532, 537, 565
structure of, 5, 31, 67, 71, 79, 84–85, 88, 91–92, 141, 209
in a totalitarian system, 71
Provincial Advisory Councils, of China (*Ziyi Ju*), 412–415, 417, 419
Prussia, 244
Pu Dianjun, 419–420
public law, 93, 103–105, 107, 109, 119, 153

Qin Empire, 62, 125, 133, 136, 139, 149, 168, 179, 392
Qin Ji (Annals of Qin), 140
Qing dynasty, 53, 71, 107–108, 119, 151, 154–155, 160, 173, 176, 197–199, 393, 396, 407, 409–410, 413, 415, 421, 426, 435, 444, 474, 500, 525, 528, 679
Qing Empire, the, 10–11, 25, 107, 304, 409–410, 419, 421, 436–437, 440, 445, 525
Qu Qiubai, 471–472, 475, 484

Railway Protection Movement, the (RPM), of China, 419–420, 422
Rasputin, Grigori, 342
Red Army, of the CCP, 81, 477–485, 488, 503, 515, 523
Red Guard movement, the, of China, 579, 582
Red Guards, the, 38, 369, 514, 571, 575, 577–581, 584, 718
Red Regime, the, 482
Red Terror, the, 7, 368–370, 373–376, 387, 389, 482, 487, 491, 493–494, 514, 579–580
reform and opening-up, of China, 45, 119, 202, 379, 539, 570, 624, 627
regional competition, of China, 38, 40, 43–44, 558–564, 573, 582, 603, 617, 643
regional experiment, of China, 38, 559–560, 573, 603, 620

regionally administered totalitarianism (RADT) or totalitarianism with Chinese characteristics, 8, 14, 16–27, 37–42, 44, 123, 152, 543, 630, 638, 642, 653, 667, 670, 710, 712
and classic totalitarianism, 39, 41, 123, 543, 620, 630, 667
feature of, 17
and the Great Leap Forward or the Cultural Revolution, 17, 152, 553–575, 585–592, 667, 670
institutional genes of, 37–42
and the post-Mao reform, 595, 604, 617, 620, 630, 642, 648, 653, 670, 710
and regional competition/experiment, 40–44, 558–572, 642
and regionally decentralized authoritarianism (RDA), 17, 41, 49, 618–626
Reign of Terror, the, 29, 229, 251, 370, 374
Ren Bishi, 484, 490, 495, 523
Renaissance, the, 168, 285, 300–301, 394
Renmin University of China (RUC), 538–539
Renminbi (RMB), 525, 626, 649, 653
reorganization of the KMT, the, 463, 465, 467, 513
A Report on an Investigation of the Peasant Movement in Hunan, 513
Republican Revolution, the, of 1911/Xinhai Revolution, the, 14, 73, 81, 263, 409, 413, 419, 421–422, 428, 443, 721
republicanism, 13, 160, 230, 432
Resolution of the Gutian Congress, of the CCP, 480
revisionism, 573–576, 596, 709, 716
Revolutionary Committee, the, of China, 214, 350, 355–356, 363–364, 582, 584
Revolutionary Rebel Faction (Rebel Faction), the, of China, 429, 581–584
rightists, the, of China, 180, 521, 549–552, 596, 599
Rites of the Zhou, 184, 438
Robespierre, Maximilien, 214–215, 220, 225, 229–230, 232, 234, 237, 243, 247, 374
Roh Tae-woo, 684
Roman Empire, 30, 82–83, 102–104, 109, 123, 135, 164, 167–169, 178, 181, 184, 209, 273, 283, 285, 384
Roman law, 96, 103–105, 120, 135, 153, 273–274

Roman Republic, 103–105, 109, 123, 135–136
Rousseau, Jean-Jacques, 16, 111–112, 121, 204, 220, 224–225, 228, 234, 237–239, 243–244, 247–252, 257, 260, 298, 395, 431
royal household, 142
Ruijin, 477, 503
rule by law, 106
rule of law, the, 43, 51, 65, 89, 91–93, 97–98, 103, 105, 172, 402, 431, 551, 632, 634–635, 639, 661, 720
Rurik, 266
Rus' system, 275
Russell, Bertrand, 251, 456
Russian Communist Party (RCP), 328, 330, 331, 334, 335, 377, 378, 386, 456, 457, 465–467, 471, 472
Russian Social Democratic Labor Party, the, 28, 296, 318–319, 321, 336

Sangang Wuchang, 184, 192
sans-culottes, the, of France, 230–231, 258, 723
Sarai, 267, 269
Second Red Army, the, of the CCP, 478
Second World War, 5, 15, 33, 53, 388–389, 495, 506, 516, 641, 659, 679, 687, 700
secret society, the, of China, 420, 429, 442, 444, 476–480
  Big Swords Society, 442
  Brotherhood Society, the, 32, 420, 441–442, 474–480
  Green Gang, 32, 475
  Heaven and Earth Society, 32, 436, 679
  Hong Fraternity, 442–444, 451, 474, 477, 480
  Red Spear Society, 474–475, 480, 513
  Society of God Worshippers, 435, 576
  Triad Society, 438, 441–442, 475
  White Lotus, 32, 434–435, 442, 474, 576
secular religion, the, 29, 204, 225, 360, 383
secular religious movements, 671–672, 674
separation of Church and state, 167–168, 170–171
separation of powers, the, 110, 112, 219, 227, 238, 247–248, 414, 636
serfdom, 88, 117, 274, 276, 278, 292, 294–295, 307, 658
SEZ, the, of China, 603, 617, 656
Shaanxi–Gansu–Ningxia, 542

Shakhnazarov, Georgy, 715
Shang Yang, 115, 134, 147
Shang Yang's reform, 134
Shanghai, 457, 460–461, 469–471, 520, 557, 582, 590, 613–614
Shangshu sheng (Department of State), of Chinese Empire, 143
Shao Yichen, 185
Shatalin, Stanislav, 693
Shen Dingyi, 466
Shi ji (史记)(*Record of the Grand Historian*), 140
Short Course, The History of the Communist Party of the Soviet Union (Bolsheviks), 31, 335, 490
Siberia, 267, 301, 337, 380–381
Sieyès, 227
Sima Guang, 183–184, 200
Sima Qian, 140
Shi jizhu (*Collected Commentaries on the Four Books*), 195
Smith, Adam, 61, 89, 99, 120, 214, 243, 256, 660–661
special economic zone (SEZ), of China, 602, 603, 605, 617, 618, 622, 655, 656
social consensus, 5–6, 8, 31, 60–62, 69, 78–80, 84–85, 99–101, 117, 661, 689, 694, 696, 698, 700, 702, 708, 713–716, 720
Social Darwinism, 403–408, 447, 452, 459
social elite, 53, 69, 80, 137–138, 165, 176, 255, 338, 341, 425, 474, 685, 689, 692–694, 715
socialist democracy or socialism with a human face, 713
  Russian Communist Party (RCP), 328, 330, 331, 334, 335, 377, 378, 386, 456, 457, 465–467, 471, 472
soft budget constraint (SBC), 88, 607, 611, 622, 647–648, 652–653, 690, 712
Solidarity movement, the, of Poland, 608
Son of Heaven, the, 131, 141, 168, 171, 173, 175, 181, 184, 194
Song dynasty, 23, 98, 116–118, 124, 128, 145, 150, 154, 158–159, 165, 179, 190–192, 194–195, 197, 199, 392, 434, 451, 474, 525
Song Jiaoren, 427–428, 445
Song Ziwen, 513
South Korea, 11, 71, 86, 659, 683–684

INDEX 771

Soviet Red Army, the, 3, 334, 369, 387, 466, 469, 476, 508, 695
Sovietization, 16, 528, 530, 538, 555, 559
Special Economic Zone (SEZ), of China, 603, 617, 656
Spencer, Herbert, 404, 406
Spinoza, Baruch, 65, 90, 247
Stalin, Joseph, 30, 33, 51, 204, 225, 275, 289, 328, 330–335, 346, 357, 359, 372, 375–376, 379–381, 387–388, 389, 391, 465, 469, 471, 487–490, 492, 494–495, 498, 503, 506, 508, 516, 530–531, 536, 541–542, 546, 553, 565–566, 593, 600, 627–628, 700–703, 709, 714–715, 717
State Admnistration for Market Regulation (SAMR), 546
State-owned Assets Supervision and Administration Commission (SASAC), 47, 634
State Council, of China, 151, 310, 537, 546, 557, 567
State Duma Election Law, 308
state ownership, 7, 19, 42, 55, 65, 88, 95, 99, 119, 124, 376, 378–379, 439, 605–607, 611, 630–631, 647, 690, 692, 712
State Planning Commission, of China, 529, 537–558
State Planning Committee (Gosplan), of USSR, 378
State Political Directorate, the, of Soviet secret police (GPU), 332
state power, 113, 173, 389, 580, 636
state religion, 30, 82–83, 102, 164, 166–168, 171, 178, 180–181, 184, 193, 209, 271, 281–284, 384, 697
state-owned enterprises (SOEs), 44, 47, 559, 585, 601, 607, 611, 621–623, 634, 644–645, 647–648, 652, 682, 690
Stürmer, Boris, 341
Sui dynasty, 116, 128, 147–153, 165, 179, 186–187
Sun Yat-sen, 25–26, 28, 32, 81, 264, 388, 400, 420–421, 423, 426–428, 437, 441–442, 444, 448, 463–466, 468–469, 473, 513
Sun-Joffe Manifesto, the, 465

Taishō period, 678, 680
Taiwan, xix, 8, 11, 52, 71, 86, 160, 507, 509, 537, 655, 659, 675–688

Tan Zhenlin, 477
Tang Code, the, 107, 152–153
Tang dynasty, 116, 154–156, 158, 188–189, 194, 453
Tao Chengzhang, 441–442, 444, 448
theory (theories) of social evolution, or social evolutionary theory, the, 231, 403–408, 447
Third Estate, the, of France, 221, 226–227
Three Represents Theory, the, of the CCP, 49, 635
Tkachev, Pyotr, 323–324
Tocqueville, Alexis de, 245
Tongmenghui (United League), of China, 420–424, 428, 434, 441–445, 448, 451, 474
total factor productivity (TFP), 651, 652
totalitarian ideology, the, 2, 204, 215–217, 253, 345, 383, 389, 405, 587, 664, 713
totalitarian regime, the, xv–xvi, 1–3, 5–8, 12–13, 18–19, 27, 33–34, 39, 42, 52, 54, 57, 64, 66, 68, 71, 88, 119, 202–205, 209, 211, 213, 217, 226, 229, 233, 240–242, 255, 259, 261–262, 264, 291, 293, 299, 306, 312–317, 327, 330, 336, 355, 358, 360, 363, 369–370, 374–378, 382, 389, 440, 499–500, 512, 519, 521, 525, 530, 540, 553–554, 572, 580, 587, 590, 595–596, 598, 600, 604, 615, 617, 619–620, 623–624, 630, 633, 636, 641–642, 647, 652, 658–659, 663–668, 673, 688–689, 691–694, 696–697, 700, 702–703, 706, 711, 713–714, 718–719
totalitarianism
  China shares features with, 122–125, 148, 180
  collapse of, 688, 693–695, 699–700, 703, 707, 713, 720
  communist totalitarianism, xvi, 1–2, 7–8, 18, 30, 38, 88, 202, 213–216, 225, 234–235, 251–255, 262, 264, 281, 299, 303, 315–317, 326, 359, 383, 385, 392, 395, 404, 445, 450–451, 543–544, 553, 555–556, 570, 585, 592, 594, 599, 616, 619, 623, 630–631, 646, 658–659, 663, 665, 667, 672, 674, 682, 687, 695–696, 699–705, 707, 709
  definition of, 1, 659, 672

totalitarianism (cont.)
  discontent with or resistance to, 547, 695–696, 698–701, 704–706
  evolution of or history of, 4, 663
  expansion of or rise of, 13–14, 674
  ideology of, 214–215, 218, 220, 225–226, 229–230, 234–235, 251–256, 701–705, 709
  in China, 24–28, 31–37, 392, 404, 445, 449, 451
  misunderstanding of, 3, 6, 616, 658–659, 667, 670
  operation or mechanism of totalitarianism or totalitarian system, 370, 383, 389, 489, 512, 547, 552, 573, 592, 641, 659, 671–672, 709
  origin of, 4, 27–31, 202, 216–218, 220–221, 226, 229–230, 234–235, 253–256, 663, 672
  Russian creation of, 315–318, 326, 328, 395
  Russian origin of, 261–265, 279–282, 292, 299, 303, 450
township and village enterprises (TVEs), 562, 586, 602, 606–607, 615, 620–621
Trotsky, Leon, 2, 307, 325, 328, 331–333, 335, 337, 345, 350, 352–354, 356–357, 359, 363–364, 369, 372, 379, 386, 465–466, 570, 605
Tsarism, 169, 274, 276, 278, 337, 451, 673
Tsarist imperial system, the, 10, 276, 309, 314, 316, 336, 338–339, 358–359
Tsarist Russia, 7, 12, 27–28, 30, 32, 103, 122, 261–262, 265, 270, 272, 274, 277, 291, 299, 304, 316, 339–340, 369, 394–395, 413, 434, 450–451, 455, 474, 501, 509, 535, 663, 673–674, 701
Tsinghua University, 535, 581, 611
Tver, 268
tyranny, 36, 113, 179, 369–370, 661

Ukraine, 381, 722
Ulpian, Domitian, 109, 111
unification, 152, 186, 268–269, 272, 401, 501
Union of Liberation, the, of Russia, 306, 308
Union of Railway Workers (URW), 362

Union of Soviet Socialist Republics (USSR), 84, 375, 508, 537, 540, 541, 614–617, 691, 693, 705
Union of Unions, the, of Russia, 307–308
United Front system, 532
United Front Work Department (UFWD), of China, 536
United Nobility, the, of Russia, 341

vassals, 127, 130–131, 145–147, 149, 182, 267, 286
Versailles, 223
Vilensky-Sibiryakov, Vladimir, 457
Voitinsky, Grigori, 456–458, 460
Voltaire, M.de, 141, 224, 237–240, 243–247, 250, 260, 300

Wałęsa, Lech, 699, 706
Wan Li, 602, 605, 613
Wang Anshi, 190–192, 201, 392
Wang Guangmei, 574, 581
Wang Hairong, 576, 593
Wang Jiaxiang, 484, 488, 490, 494
Wang Jingwei, 25, 468, 513
Wang Ming, 488–491, 493–494
Wang Qishan, 51, 580, 718
Wang Shiwei, 491–492
Wang Tao, 400, 404, 446
Wang Zhen, 580, 610
Wang Zuo, 477, 481
War of Liberation, the, of China, 501, 518, 524
War of Resistance against Japan, the, of China, 485, 505
War to Resist US Aggression and Aid Korea, the, of China, 517, 519, 529
Warring States period, of China, 18, 106, 131–134, 136–137, 147, 161, 181
Warsaw, xix, 700–701, 703, 707
Wei Yuan, 185, 396
Wen Jiabao, 718
Western Wei, 147
Whampoa Military Academy, the, of China, 467–468, 669
Wild Lily Movement, the, of Taiwan, 685
Witte, Sergei, 304, 308, 310, 339
World Trade Organization (WTO), 44, 644
Wu Yuzhang, 420, 494, 509
Wudou (Violent Struggle), 584
Wuhan, 421, 430, 462

Xi Jinping, 44, 46, 51, 58, 155, 486, 580, 616, 626, 630, 634, 636, 670, 718–719
Xi Zhongxun, 486, 522, 527–528, 603
Xi'an Incident, the, of China, 81, 503, 516
Xiang Ying, 484
Xiang Zhongfa, 484
Xiao Jun, 491
Xiao Ke, 485, 613
Xiao Xiang, 419
Xingzhonghui (Revive China Society), 441, 443–444

Yakovlev, Alexander, 694, 705, 709, 713
Yan Fu, 122, 399–400, 403–407, 431–432
Yan'an, 477–478, 488, 492, 503, 505–506, 548
Yan'an Central Party School, of the CCP, 491
Yan'an Rectification, of the CCP, 33, 335, 389, 485, 487, 489, 491, 519, 552, 567, 629
Yang Du, 431–432
Yang Shangkun, 710
Yang Xiuqing, 438, 440
Yavlinsky, Grigory, 693
Ye Jianying, 527, 593, 597
Ye Ting, 522
Yeltsin, Boris, 53, 693, 705–706, 717
Yijing, 168, 195
Youth League faction, the, of China, 717–718

Yuan Shikai, 107, 405, 410, 422–423, 426–433, 445, 447, 452, 469
Yuan Wencai, 477, 481

Zhang Aiping, 613
Zhang Bojun, 550
Zhang Guotao, 454, 456–459, 462, 465, 471, 484, 523, 666
Zhang Juzheng, 392
Zhang Shengfu, 456
Zhang Tailei, 459, 465–466
Zhang Wentian, 490, 493
Zhang Xueliang, 503
Zhao Ziyang, 2, 55, 335, 372, 598, 601–602, 605–606, 609–610, 612–613, 627, 656, 710, 719
Zheng Guanying, 400, 404
Zhenguan zhengyao (*The Essentials of Governance of Emperor Taizong's Reign*), 195
Zhongshu sheng (Palace Secretariat), of Chinese Empire, 143, 154
Zhou dynasty, the, 168, 178, 193
Zhou Enlai, 456, 471–472, 484, 493–495, 506–507, 529, 536, 549, 557, 573, 581, 583, 589
Zhou li, 184–185
Zhu De, 448, 456, 477–478, 482, 484, 494, 522–523
Zhu Rongji, 550, 621
Zhu Xi, 176, 192–195, 197
Zinoviev, Grigory, 330–333, 352, 354, 372, 385–387, 389, 466
Zizhi tongjian (*Comprehensive Mirror in Aid of Governance*), 195, 200